24

01. OC:

09.

29

28

Ireland and the Jacobite cause, 1685-1766

A fatal attachment

Éamonn Ó Ciardha

FOUR COURTS PRESS

Set in 10.5 on 12.5 point Adobe Garamond for
FOUR COURTS PRESS LTD
Fumbally Lane, Dublin 8, Ireland
e-mail: info@four-courts-press.ie
http:www.four-courts-press.ie
and in North America
FOUR COURTS PRESS
c/o ISBS, 5824 N.E. Hassalo Street, Portland, OR 97213.

A catalogue record for this title
is available from the British Library.

ISBN 1–85182–534–7

Printed and bound in Great Britain by
MPG Books, Bodmin, Cornwall

I GCUIMHNE AR MO CHAIRDE

AIDAN CONNOLLY

EIBHLÍN NÍ CHNÁIMHSÍ

Illustrations

Buíochas

Tá mé buíoch leis na daoine a chabhraigh liom ar bhealaí éagsúla nuair a bhí an leabhar seo á scríobh agam. Ag an tús, stiúraigh Breandán Bradshaw mo thaighde agus bhí sé fial flaithiúil lena chuid cabhrach agus a chuid ama. Chuir cuid mhór scoláirí eile leis an obair seo, léigh siad dréachtaí agus thug siad míreanna, leabhair, altanna agus comhairle dom ó am go chéile. Ar ndóigh má tá aon mheancóg ann, mise amháin atá ciontach. Léigh Kevin Whelan an dréacht, cúpla uair, phléigh sé an t-ábhar liom agus is minic a d'éist sé le mo chuid smaointe faoin seacaibíteachas. Is minic a labhair mé faoin ochtú aois déag le James Kelly agus is annamh nár fhoghlaim mé rud éigin uaidh. Tá tionchar Bhreandáin Uí Buachalla ar an tráchtas seo le feiceáil sna fo-nótaí agus sa liosta léitheoireachta. Theagasc sé Gaeilge dom don bhun chéim agus bhí sé féin i gcónaí toilteanach a mhion eolas faoin ábhar a roinnt liom. Léigh Marc Caball, Vincent Morley agus Éamonn Ó hÓgáin tríd an dréacht deireanach agus cheartaigh siad meancóga sa Ghaeilge agus sna haistriúcháin. Má bhíonn a thuilleadh fágtha níl locht ar bith orthu. Bhí an-tionchar ag James McGuire ar mo thaighde ó thosaigh mé ag obair ar iar-chéim staire agus chuidigh sé go mór liom nuair a bhí an taighde idir lámha agam. Tá mé i bhfiacha fosta le Jane Ohlmeyer, Oisín Ó Siochrú, John Morrill, Eveline Cruickshanks, Peter MacDonagh, Micheál Ó Siochrú, Allan Macinnes, Andrew McKillop, Jim Smyth, Breandán Mac Suibhne, Jennifer Molidor agus Hilary Radner as an ábhar a léamh dom agus mé ag iarraidh é a chríochnú. D'fhoghlaim mé cuid mhór faoin seacaibíteachas agus faoin stair i gcoitinne i gcaidreamh le mo chairde is mo chomh-scoláirí, ina measc Breandán Mac Suibhne, Micheál Ó Siochrú, Eoghan Ó Mórdha, Vincent Morley, Marc Caball, Éamonn Ó hÓgáin, Colm Ó Baoill, Billy Kelly, Ivar McGrath, John McCafferty, John Bergin, Doron Zimmerman agus Natalie Genet-Rouffiac.

Lena chois, thug mo chairde agus mo chomh-scoláirí tacaíocht, spreagadh agus comhluadar dom in Éirinn agus i mBaile Átha Cliath, i gCambridge, i Londain, in Obar Dheathain i gColáiste Mhichíl, Ollscoil Thoronto agus sa Roinn Léinn Éireannach, Ollscoil Notre Dame, ina measc Roel Sterckx, Raymond Delahunt, Caoimhín Ó Faoláin, Aíne Ní Chearnaigh is a clann, Fiona agus James Henderson, Marian Wiercigroch, Arash Mohthashmi-

Maali, Sarah Wright, David Farr, Pádraig McQuaid, Séamas McQuaid agus David Beattie.

Tá mé faoi chomaoin ag foirne na leabharlanna a bhfuair mé cuidiú agus cineáltas i gcónaí iontu; Leabharlann Náisiúnta na hÉireann, Leabharlann Choláiste na Trionóide, Acadamh Ríoga na hÉireann, Leabharlann an Bhardais (Sr. an Phiarsaigh), Cartlann Náisiúnta na hÉireann, British Library, Cambridge University Library, Bodleian Library, Oxford, Lambeth Palace Library, Public Record Office, Kew Gardens, Hesburgh Library, University of Notre Dame. Lena chois ba mhaith liom mo bhíochas a ghabháil leis na daoine a chuidigh go mór liom leis na léaráidí a chur le chéile; Matthew Stout a tharraing na learscáileanna, Richard Oram a chur an clárleabhar le chéile, Jane Fenlon (Dúchas); Eachtair Mac Domhnaill; John, Samantha Leslie agus Ultan Bannon (Caisleán Leslie); Desmond Fitzgerald (Caisleán an Ghleanna); Mary Clare Morley (Clochar an Choill Mhóir); Michael Kenny (Iarsmalann Náisiúnta na hÉireann); Joanna Finnegan (Leabharlann Náisíunta na hÉireann); Edwina Mullvaney (Cartlann Náisíunta na hÉireann); Christopher Foley (Lane Fineart Gallery Londain); Richard Sharp (Ollscoil Oxford); Isabelle L'hoir agus Jan Pierrick (Réunion des Musées, Nationaux, Paris); Kenneth Ferguson (Irish Sword); Severine de Bréteuil (Château de Breteuil); Jane Cunningham (Courthauld Institute); Anna Skeppard (Tate Gallery); Matt Bailey (National Portrait Gallery, London); Charlotte Ames, David P. Williams, Jane Devine agus Chris Clarke (Ollscoil Notre Dame).

I wish to express my gratitude to the following sources from which I received the funding and resources to enable me to undertake and complete this research: the British Academy, the Robert Gardiner Memorial Scholarship, the Prince Consort and Thirlwall fund, Clare Hall, St Michael's College, University of Toronto and the Keough Institute of Irish Studies, University of Notre Dame. Finally, I greatly appreciated the continued generosity, support and wit of my own family, particularly my parents Tommy and Sheila, my brothers Roger and Brendan, my sisters Anne and Patricia, my brothers-in-law Brian and Tom and my nephews Paul and Rory. I owe the greatest debt to Lis Henderson for her unfailing support and encouragement.

Contents

Abbreviations

Add. Mss.	Additional Manuscripts
A. N. (A.A).	Archives Nationales (Archives Anciennes)
A. N. (M.G.).	Archives Nationales (Ministère de la Guerre)
A. N. (A.E.).	Archives Nationales (Archives Etrangères)
Anal. Hib.	*Analecta Hibernica* (Dublin, 1930–)
Archiv. Hib.	*Archivium Hibernicum: or Irish historical records* (Maynooth, 1912–)
B. L.	British Library
B. N.	Bibliothèque Nationale
Bodl.	Bodleian Library Oxford
Cambs. Hib.	Cambridge, Bradshaw Collection
C.I.	*Carson's Intelligencer*
C.	*The Censor*
Coll. Hib.	*Collectanea Hibernica: sources for Irish history* (Dublin, 1958–)
Dalton's Dub. Imp. N.	*Dalton's Dublin Impartial Newsletter*
Dub. Daily P.	*Dublin Daily Post*
Dick. Fly. P.	*Dickson's Flying Post*
Dick. I.	*Dickson's Intelligencer*
Dick. P.	*Dickson's Postman*
Dub. J.	*Dublin Journal*
Dub. Cour.	*Dublin Courant*
Dub. Evening P.	*Dublin Evening Post*
Dub. Gaz.	*Dublin Gazette*
Dub. Imp. N.	*Dublin Impartial Newsletter*
D.H.R.	*Dublin Historical Record*
Dub. N.	*Dublin Newsletter*
Dub. P.	*Dublin Postman*
Dub. Week. J.	*Dublin Weekly Journal*
E.C.I.	*Eighteenth-Century Ireland: Journal of the Eighteenth Century Ireland Society* (Dublin, 1986–)

Éigse.	*Éigse: a journal of Irish studies* (Dublin, 1939–)
Fau. Dub. J.	*Faulkner's Dublin Journal*
Fau. Post.	*Faulkner's Postboy*
Fl. P.	*Flying Post*
F.	*Freeholder*
Flower, *Cat. Ir. mss.*	*Catalogue of Irish manuscripts in the British Museum*
in B.L.	*[British Library]*, 3 vols (London, 1926-53): i, *ed.*
	Standish Hayes O'Grady, ii *and* iii, *ed.* by Robin
	Flower, completed by Myles Dillon.
Galway. His.	*Galway Historical and Archaeological Society Journal*
Arc. Soc. Jnr.	(Galway, 1900–)
Hist Irel.	*History Ireland* (Dublin, 1993–)
H.J.	*Historical Journal* (Cambridge, 1958–)
Hume's Cour	*Hume's Courant*
Hume's Dub. Cour.	*Hume's Dublin Courant*
Hume's P.	*Hume's Postman*
Harding's Dub.	
Imp. N.	*Harding's Dublin Impartial Newsletter*
Harding's Imp. N.	*Harding's Impartial Newsletter*
Harding's Week.	
Imp. N.	*Harding's Weekly Impartial Newsletter*
H.M.C.	Historical Manuscripts Commission
I.E.R.	*Irish Ecclesiastical Record* (Dublin, 1864–)
I.I.	*Impartial Intelligencer*
I.O.	*Impartial Occurrences*
Ir. Booklover	*Irish Booklover* (Dublin, 1909–1957)
Ir. Ec. and Social His.	*Irish Economic and Social history* (Dublin, 1974–)
I.H.S.	*Irish Historical Studies: the joint journal of the Irish*
	Historical Society and the Ulster Society for Irish
	Historical Studies (Dublin, 1938–)
Ir. Monthly	*Irish Monthly* (Dublin, 1879–1954)
Ir. Sword.	*Irish Sword: the journal of the Military History*
	Society of Ireland (Dublin, 1949–)
J.C.H.A.S.	*Journal of the Cork Historical and Archaeological*
	Society (Cork, 1892–)
J.K.A.H.S.	*Journal of the Kerry Archaeological and Historical*
	Society Journal (Tralee, 1968–)
Lloyd's N.	*Lloyd's Newsletter*
L.A.J.	*Journal of the County Louth Archaeological Society*
	(Dundalk, 1904–)
mf. p.	microfilm (positive)
N.A.	National Archives, Bishop Street, Dublin

Nelson's Dub. Cour	*Nelson's Dublin Courant*
Need. Dub .Cour.	*Needham's Dublin Courant*
Need. P.	*Needham's Postman*
N.H.I.	*A New History of Ireland,* ed. Moody, T.W. , Williams, T.D., Beckett, J.C., Martin, F.X. (Dublin, 1968–)
N.L.I.	National Library of Ireland
N.L.S.	National Library of Scotland
N.L.W.	National Library of Wales
N. Munster Antiq. Jn.	*North Munster Antiquarian Journal* (Limerick, 1936–)
O'Grady, *Cat.Ir. mss. in B.L.*	*Catalogue of Irish manuscripts in the British Museum* [British Library], 3 vols (London, 1926–53): i, ed. Stanish Hayes O'Grady, ii and iii, ed. Robin Flower, completed by Myles Dillon.
Proc. Ir. Cat. His. Comm.	*Proceedings of the Irish Catholic Historical Committee* (Dublin, 1955–)
P.R.O.	Public Record Office (London)
P.R.O.I	Public Record Office Ireland (now National Archives)
P.R.O.N.I.	Public Record Office of Northern Ireland
Pue's O.	*Pue's Occurrences*
R. A.	Royal Archive, Windsor Castle, (Stuart papers, unless otherwise stated)
Reilly's Dub. N.	*Reilly's Dublin Newsletter*
Report. Nov.	*Reportorium Novum (Dublin, 1955—)*
R.I.A.	Royal Irish Academy
R.I.A., Proc.	*R.I.A., Proc.: Proceedings of the Royal Irish Academy* (Dublin, 1836–)
R.S.A.I. Jnr.	*Journal of the Royal Society of the Antiquaries of Ireland* (Dublin, 1892–)
S.A.	*Seanchas Ardmhacha: journal of the Armagh Diocesan Society* (Armagh, 1954–)
S. P.	State Papers, Public Record Office, London
St James's Eve. P.	*St James's Evening Post*
Stud. Hib.	*Studia Hibernica* (Dublin, 1961–)
T.C.D.	Trinity College Dublin
Toulman's Dub. P.	*Toulman's Dublin Post*
Toulman's P.	*Toulman's Post*
U.C.C.	University College Cork
U.C.D.	University College Dublin
U.C.G.	University College Galway
U.L.	University Library (Cambridge)
Walsh's Mer.	*Walsh's Mercury*

Walsh's Cas. Cour	*Walsh's Castle Courant*
Walsh's Dub. P.	*Walsh's Dublin Postboy*
Walsh's Dub. Week	*Walsh's Dublin Weekly Impartial Newsletter*
Imp. N.	*Impartial Newsletter*
Weekly Post.	*Weekly Post*
Whalley's N.	*Whalley's Newsletter*

Genealogical table of the Houses of Stuart and Hanover Kings and Queens of England, Scotland and Ireland

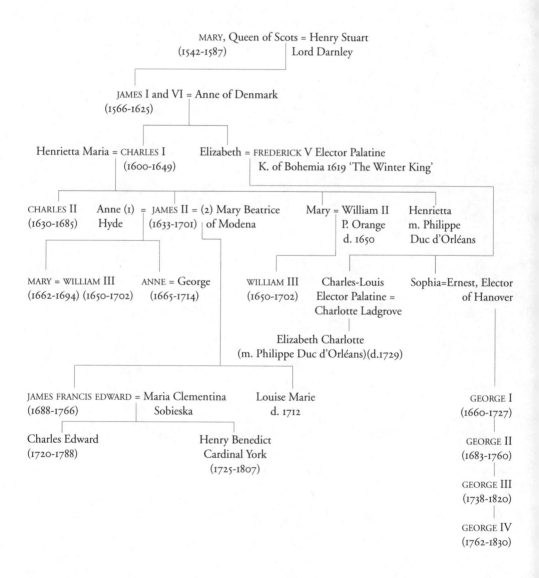

MARY, Queen of Scots = Henry Stuart
(1542-1587) | Lord Darnley

JAMES I and VI = Anne of Denmark
(1566-1625)

Henrietta Maria = CHARLES I
(1600-1649)

Elizabeth = FREDERICK V Elector Palatine
K. of Bohemia 1619 'The Winter King'

CHARLES II (1630-1685)

Anne (1) Hyde = JAMES II = (2) Mary Beatrice
(1633-1701) of Modena

Mary = William II
P. Orange
d. 1650

Henrietta
m. Philippe
Duc d'Orléans

MARY = WILLIAM III
(1662-1694) (1650-1702)

ANNE = George
(1665-1714)

WILLIAM III
(1650-1702)

Charles-Louis
Elector Palatine =
Charlotte Ladgrove

Sophia=Ernest, Elector
of Hanover

Elizabeth Charlotte
(m. Philippe Duc d'Orléans)(d.1729)

JAMES FRANCIS EDWARD = Maria Clementina
(1688-1766) Sobieska

Louise Marie
d. 1712

GEORGE I
(1660-1727)

Charles Edward
(1720-1788)

Henry Benedict
Cardinal York
(1725-1807)

GEORGE II
(1683-1760)

GEORGE III
(1738-1820)

GEORGE IV
(1762-1830)

Ireland

Rathlin Island

Aran Island
Killygarvan
Derry   DERRY   ANTRIM
Raphoe   Strabane
DONEGAL   Newtownsterwart   Randalstown
Killybegs   Lough   TYRONE   Lough   Carrickfergus
            Derg   Neagh   Belfast
                  Castlecaulfield   Lisburn
            Enniskillen   Dromore   Charlemont   Dromore
            Sligo   FERMANAGH   Armagh   Loughgall   DOWN
Killala   ARMAGH   Downpatrick
      SLIGO   LEITRIM   Monaghan Fews Newry
Foxford   Castleblayney   Creggan Omeath
MAYO   Carrick-on-   Carrickmacross Inniskeen Carrickfergus
Castlebar   Shannon   CAVAN   MONAGHAN   Dundalk
      Clonalis   Belanagare   Kilbride   LOUTH
Inishbofin   Longford   Granard   Donore Drogheda
         LONGFORD   MEATH Julianstown
      ROSCOMMON   Mullingar Hill of Tara Duleek Rush
Iar-Chonnacht Tuam   Athlone WESTMEATH Kilcock Drumcondra
      GALWAY   Moate Celbridge Dublin
Moycullen   Rathcoffey DUBLIN
Galway   Clonfert OFFALY Yeomanstown Bray
      Aughrim   Birr   KILDARE
Aran Islands   Maryborough WICKLOW
      CLARE   LAOIS   Glendalough
Milltown Malbay   Timahoe   Wicklow
      Ennis
   Cratloe   Thurles   CARLOW Gorey
Kilrush   Kilkenny
   Limerick TIPPERARY Ferns
Ardagh   Bennetsbridge
   LIMERICK Cashel KILKENNY
Ardfert Charleville Tipperary Kilcash WEXFORD
Tralee Kilmallock Clonmel Carrick on Suir
Smerwick Castleisland Doneraile Clonmel Wexford
Dingle   R. Blackwater Waterford Duncannon
Ventry Kanturk WATERFORD Passage
Aghadoe KERRY Mallow Lismore
   CORK Aghern Dungarvan
Valencia Island Iveragh Ballyvourney Blarney Youghal
Portmagee Kilgarvan   N
Ballinskelligs Kenmare Macroom R. Lee Cork Little Island
   Glengarrif   Midleton
Beare   Kinsale   Nohaval
      Charles' Fort   Land over 300m OD
Bantry Bay Castlehaven
Skibbereen Ross Carbery   0   50 miles
Crookhaven   0   80 km
Clear Island

Preface

Quotations from edited collections of Irish Jacobite poetry[1] have been used throughout this book, as opposed to original manuscripts. One can rely on the edited work of Tadhg Ó Donnchadha, Risteard Ó Foghludha, Énrí Ó Muirgheasa, Pádraig Ua Duinnín, Seán de Rís, Tomás Ó Fiaich, Breandán Ó Buachalla, J.L. Campbell and Colm Ó Baoill as the quality of their editions of eighteenth-century political poetry has not been called into question.[2]

The original Irish poems and songs are the bedrock sources upon which this study is based. They have been fully cited as edited, in text or footnote wherever possible. For brevity's sake (and because I am a historian and not an Irish-language scholar or translator of verse), I have chosen not to provide line by line translations of the poetry and song. Instead, my translations have been paraphrased and are incorporated into the textual analysis that precedes the verse cited in the text and footnotes. These, in so far as possible, convey the true meaning of the original Irish. I have, in some cases, changed the tense and person to accommodate indirect speech in the text. An ellipse (…) denote abbreviations in the poetry extracts. Cross-referencing relates to particular page numbers or footnote reference. All birth and death dates come from the *Dictionary of National Biography*, the *Dictionnaire de Biographie Française* and the database of the forthcoming *Dictionary of Irish Biography*.

To avoid confusion, the abbreviation B.Á.C. (Baile Átha Cliath) has been used in the bibliography when Dublin is given as the place of publication in collections of edited Irish poetry and books published in that language. Dún Éideann is similarly used in the case of Edinburgh for editions of Scots-Gaelic literature. The abbreviation (eag.) 'eagraithe' (edited) has been used for all collections of Irish and Scots-Gaelic poetry.

For clarity's sake, James Francis Edward Stuart, son of James II and Mary Beatrice d'Este of Modena (otherwise 'The Old Pretender') is referred to as

---

1 Irish literature, in this case, refers to material written in the Irish language. Literature in English by Irish-born authors will be referred to as Irish literature in English.   2 Indeed, Mícheál Mac Craith has recently stated that reprints of Pádraig Ua Duinnín and Risteard Ó Foghluadha's editions of eighteenth-century poetry are well overdue, editions that should provide the contextualisation and commentary lacking in the originals; Mac Craith, 'Review of *Aisling Ghéar*', p. 171.

James III or the Stuart king/claimant. He was recognised as king by the pope and occasionally by the kings of France, Spain, Sweden, the tsar and tsarina of Russia, as well as by his Scottish Episcopalian and English non-juring Protestant subjects. More importantly, his loyal Irish subjects at home and abroad upon whom this study is based recognised him as such.[3] His eldest son Charles Edward Stuart is invariably the Stuart prince or Charles III.

The word 'Tory' ('tóraidhe', robber, highwayman and persecuted person) emerged in the English language in the 1640s and evolved through the Popish Plot and Exclusion Crisis as a nickname for those who supported the high-church and Jacobite succession. During the Jacobite war, it was used synonymously with 'rapparee' to describe robbers and those rapparees (from ropaire [robber], 'rapaire' [rapier, half-pike]) or Jacobite irregulars who often supported James II. Throughout the first half of the eighteenth century, it denoted both Irish highwaymen and robbers, and the high-church political interest which evolved from the 1680s. To avoid confusion I will use 'rapparee' wherever possible, 'Tory' when referring to the political interest and 'tory' while referring to the robbers.[4]

Ireland and Britain used the old (Julian) calendar until 1752 which put their date ten days behind continental Europe in the seventeenth century and eleven days in the eighteenth century. Due to the international nature of this study, all dates have been left as they are in the particular domestic or continental source cited.

---

3 James III was 'undoubtedly the *de jure* king of Great Britain and Ireland (or England, Scotland and Ireland as the Jacobites did not accept the union of the crowns in 1707) … the real Pretender was sitting on the throne of England'; Irwin, 'review of Fagan (ed.), *Ireland and the Stuart papers*', p. 477.
4 For definitions of the word 'tory' and 'rapparee, see Welch, *Oxford companion to Irish literature*, pp 490, 566.

Introduction

I

Until the early 1990s, there was no article or review, much less a monograph, on post 1691 Irish Jacobitism (Irish support for the exiled house of Stuart), the ideology which principally sustained Irish Catholic nationalist identity between the Glorious and the French Revolutions. In the absence of such a survey, a chronological format has been adopted in this book.[1] The thematic approach of Paul Monod's study of English Jacobitism in the eighteenth century often loses sight of the political context and the all-important European dimension, both absolutely vital to its Irish counterpart. Jacobitism was a complex ideology, which evolved over the course of one hundred years. Breandán Ó Buachalla and Howard Erskine-Hill, the two leading authorities on Jacobite poetry in these islands, have both emphasised that the poetry, one of the major sources for the study of this multi-faceted and ever-evolving ideology, does not lend itself to a straightforward thematic analysis. A poem, pamphlet, sermon or memoir cannot be detached from its proper political context in the 1690s and lumped together with material from the 1760s simply because they have similar themes. Such an analysis can give the source a timelessness, which detracts from its explicit political relevance at any given time.[2] This book provides a chronological study of Irish Jacobitism over its main six phases (1684-1703, 1703-16, 1716-26, 1726-39, 1739-49, and 1752-66). It also charts the evolution of aspects of the

1 Just before the final completion of the thesis upon which this study is based, Breandán Ó Buachalla's monumental work *Aisling Ghéar: na Stíobhartaigh agus an tAos Léinn 1603-1788* was published. This is an extensive study of Irish support for the house of Stuart between the succession of James VI and I to the throne of England in 1603 and the death of his great-great-grandson Charles Edward in 1788. A seminal work, it is the single most authoritative study of political literature in Irish in the seventeenth and eighteenth centuries. I attended Professor Ó Buachalla's lectures as an undergraduate and benefited from his scholarship on Irish Jacobitism and literature. I have therefore inevitably been influenced by his duly acknowledged opinions. I had researched and read the edited corpus of Irish Jacobite poetry referenced in the bibliography as part of my doctoral research and drawn my own conclusions before the appearance of Ó Buachalla's book. Although there has been a number of recent reviews there has been a deafening silence from Irish historians; See Titley, *Saol*, Feabhra 1998, p. 4; Mac Craith, 'Review of *Aisling Ghéar*'. 2 Ó Buachalla, 'review of O'Riordan, *The Gaelic mind*', p. 150; Erskine-Hill, *Poetry of Opposition and Revolution*, pp 10-13.

Jacobite phenomenon. These include Catholic and Protestant Jacobitism, recruitment for the foreign service as a manifestation of Irish Jacobitism, Irish Jacobite poetry and literature and the Irish diaspora. In my conclusion these themes are drawn together within this chronological framework.

One reason for the absence of any serious study of Irish Jacobitism derives from the association between royalism and defeat, confiscation and persecution and the emergence of republicanism as the ascendant political ideology within Irish nationalism in the late eighteenth and nineteenth centuries. The Irish state, established in 1922, found no place in its national pantheon for the absolutist Stuart king who deserted the country in its hour of need. The 1990 tercentenary celebrations of the Battle of the Boyne and the second Siege of Limerick brought little acclaim to James II: the perennially popular Patrick Sarsfield, earl of Lucan stole the limelight.[3] The heroes of the Irish nationalist tradition disdained the Stuarts. Sarsfield wished to exchange kings and fight again. A century later in the 1790s, Theobald Wolfe Tone scoffed at the suggestion of a 'Henrician' restoration. James Connolly dismissed James II as 'the most worthless representative of a worthless race that ever sat on a throne'.[4]

Connolly's judgement of the Stuart king and his scorn for Ireland's Jacobite and royalist past cannot be dismissed as the bias of a socialist republican. John O'Daly, a pioneer editor of Jacobite poems and songs, reached the same conclusion, regarding James II as 'the most dastardly poltroon that ever set foot on Irish ground'. O'Daly underplayed the significance of Ireland's Jacobite literary past. He asserted that 'it would be wrong to consider these songs purely Jacobite (in the Scotch sense) for the Irish cared less for a king than for a deliverer of that land which they loved with an intensity beautifully shown in the ballads'. James Hardiman, another prolific editor of Jacobite verse, suggested that the Irish supported the Jacobite cause 'more out of principle than allegiance, with perhaps a vain hope of regaining their estates, than from any particular attachment to himself or his ungrateful race'. Accusing 'the pusillanimous king' (James) of betraying them 'on the very verge of victory', he concluded that during the rebellions of 1715 and 1745, the Irish moved 'neither tongue, pen or sword ... in their favour'.[5] Such views ignore the religious dimension to Irish

---

3 Sarsfield's most recent biography has reaffirmed his place in Irish nationalist hagiography; Wauchope, *Sarsfield.* Liam Irwin has proffered a less sympathetic view; Irwin, 'Sarsfield: man and myth', pp 108-26. **4** 'Henrician' restoration, in this case, refers to the proposal made to Tone by the French Directory in the 1790s to place 'Henry IX', Cardinal York, brother of the deceased 'Charles III' (Bonnie Prince Charlie) on an Irish throne; Moody, MacDowell and Woods (eds.) *Writings of Wolfe Tone,* ii, p 157; also ibid., p. 160. There are many other examples of disrespect for the Jacobite tradition in Irish politics and literature; ibid., p. 83; Connolly, *Labour,* pp 9-10; Curtayne, *Sarsfield,* p. 74. Ó Buachalla, *Aisling Ghéar,* pp 650, 652. **5** O'Daly (ed.), *Poets and poetry,* p. 31. Hardiman (ed.), *Irish minstrelsy,* ii, p. 7. Leerssen has provided a context for Hardiman's work; Leerssen, *Remembrance and imagination,* pp 176-8. See also O' Daly (ed.), *Reliques of Irish Jacobite poetry,* p. iv. This distaste for Jacobitism and 'Charley-over-the-waterism' pervaded Irish literature; Breatnach, 'The end of a tradition', p. 147; Knott (ed.), *Poems of Tadhg Dall,* i, p. lxiii; O'Conor, *Military history,* p. 115.

Jacobitism. James II was king by divine right, the pope continued to recognise his claim to the three kingdoms, and he attracted the loyalty of many Irish Catholics because of his influence over the Catholic Church. The Stuarts retained the exclusive right to nominate bishops to the Irish sees, a privilege which they jealously guarded, vigorously defended and judiciously exercised until James III's death in 1766. The political outlook of many of those he nominated is a strong counter to facile claims that the Stuarts were irrelevant to the bulk of Irish Catholics.[6]

The context in which O'Daly and Hardiman wrote should also be borne in mind.[7] By the mid-nineteenth century, the 'dejacobitisation' of the Irish political tradition, initiated by Cornelius Nary, continued by Charles O'Conor of Belanagare, Arthur O'Leary and the United Irishmen Miles Byrne, Charles Teeling and Mícheál Óg Ó Longáin, had achieved its purpose.[8] Despite occasional royalist posturings by Daniel O'Connell, there was no equivalent in the Irish literary or political experience to the contemporary 'Balmoralisation' of the British royal family or of the Scottish Jacobite romantic history concocted by Sir Walter Scott and Lady Carolina Nairne.[9]

English historians have also either underplayed or dismissed the Irish Jacobite threat. Robert Dunlop suggested that there was not the slightest danger from Irish Jacobitism.[10] Lord Macaulay claimed that the fallen dynasty meant absolutely nothing to the Irish who regarded the 'foreign sovereign of his native land with the feeling with which a Jew regarded Caesar'.[11] Irish historians have suggested that apathy rather than hostility characterised Irish attitudes towards the Stuarts. W.E.H. Lecky concluded that no great enthusiasm existed among Catholics in the eighteenth century for a return of the Stuarts, and that the surviving gentry did not wish to risk their estates again.[12] The Catholic apologist Canon W.P. Burke, in his eagerness to show the injustices of the penal laws against Catholics in the eighteenth century, minimised Irish Jacobitism, citing Richard Cox and Jonathan Swift, both with motives for deliberately underplaying Jacobitism. Fr Daniel McCarthy had gone further. He suggested that 'when the Catholic heir of their favourite monarch [James II] attempted in 1715 and 1745 to recover his lost dominions, not a single Catholic raised an arm to maintain his pretensions'. He also pointed out that there was no attempt

6 Giblin, 'Stuart nomination of bishops', pp 35-47.   **7** Leerssen, *Remembrance and imagination*, pp 176-8.   **8** Fagan, *The second city*, p. 148; Ward and Ward (ed.), *Letters of Charles O'Conor*, p. 29 and no. 94; Charles O'Conor, *The case of the Roman Catholics of Ireland*, pp 43-4; Teeling, *History of the rebellion of 1798*, pp 103-5; *Memoirs of Miles Byrne*, p. 7; O'Reilly, *The Irish abroad*, p. 33. Kelly, 'A wild Capuchin of Cork'; Mitchel, *History of Ireland*, pp 41-3, 47. See Conclusion.   **9** There are other examples of O'Connell's royalism; MacDonagh, *O'Connell*, pp 441, 453, 462; Leerssen, *Remembrance and imagination*, pp 77, 79. Indeed Thomas Davis, Ireland's national bard, disinfected his cult of the Irish Brigades from any references to Jacobitism.   **10** Dunlop, 'Ireland in the eighteenth century', pp 479-84.   **11** Macaulay, *History of England*, iii, p. 1472; Hayes, 'Ireland and Jacobitism', pp 101-6.   **12** Lecky, *Ireland*, i, p. 413. O'Donoghue's M.A. thesis provides a useful historiographical overview of Jacobite historiography, see O'Donoghue, 'Jacobite threat', introduction.

by 'Ormonde, lately lord lieutenant, then a chief rebel, [to] corrupt or even dare to tempt the fidelity of his own Catholic tenantry'. Another of Burke's contemporaries, Reginald Walsh, stated that Catholics had been reduced to such an extremity that the government had not the slightest reason to apprehend disturbance and dismissed the penal laws as a mere pretext for satisfying its hatred of the ancient faith.[13]

Richard Hayes, historian of the Irish diaspora, echoed James Connolly, disparaging the Battle of the Boyne as a struggle for kingship between two foreign princes.[14] Stressing the absence of loyalty and devotion to James II and his descendants among Irish Catholics in the eighteenth century, Hayes castigated the native nobility and their followers for deserting their country after the end of the Jacobite wars. In more recent years, Irish Jacobitism has been the victim of its most authoritative historian J.G. Simms. His classic 1969 monograph *Jacobite Ireland* concluded with the resounding defeat of the Irish Jacobite nation in 1691. Marcus Beresford's picture of Irish Catholic quiescence after the Treaty of Limerick reflects a well-established historiographical practice. Although he conceded that the political situation in Ireland in 1691 and 'for many years afterwards' remained 'potentially explosive', Beresford claimed that 'a combination of time and penal laws stifled temporarily the political ambitions of Catholics'. Catholics of the succeeding generations had become 'politically apathetic'.[15] The reasons advanced for this 'collapse of Catholic political will' include the crushing finality of the Williamite victory, the fact that 'the greater proportion of the wealth of the country lay in the hands of a small minority', and the 'erosion of the natural leaders of the Irish Catholic political nation'.[16] David Dickson's *New foundations* followed suit. He treated the decapitation of St Ruth at the Battle of Aughrim in 1691 as a metaphor for the definitive truncation of Jacobite Ireland.[17] Thomas Bartlett refers to the destruction of the Jacobite cause at the Boyne and Aughrim eight times in the first forty pages of his *Fall and rise of the Irish nation*. David Hayton also stated that 'the Jacobite War and its aftermath and the exile of the so-called Wild Geese had resulted in the destruction of the Catholic gentry; 'without their natural leaders it was unthinkable that the common people could rebel'.[18]

13 Burke, *Irish priest*, p. 111. [Renehan] (ed.), *Collections on Irish church history*, p. 88. Walsh; 'Glimpses of Ireland', p. 260. In more recent times Moody suggested that 'the Old English and the Old Irish shared a common ruin, fighting on the side of one English king [James II] against another rival English king [William III]; Moody, 'Irish history and Irish mythology', in Brady (ed.), *Interpreting Irish history*, pp 72, 76. Accusations of Jacobite fellow-travelling were made against Swift and Cox see pp 171, 215-17.   14 Hayes, 'Ireland and Jacobitism', p. 101.   15 Beresford, 'Ireland', pp 3-4. These views have been reiterated by Connolly and Bartlett; Connolly, *Religion*, pp 244-6; Bartlett, *Fall and rise*, preface, pp 2, 9-10, 17, 24, 31, 34-5, 38.   16 Beresford, 'Ireland', pp 3-4. See also Kelly, 'A light to the blind', p. 431.   17 Simms, *Jacobite Ireland*; Dickson, *New foundations*, p. 32; Ó Buachalla, review of Cruickshanks and Black, p. 189.   18 Bartlett, *Fall and rise*, pp 2, 9-10, 17, 24, 31, 34-5 38; Hayton, 'Walpole and Ireland', p. 96.

Despite this impressive and longstanding historiographical consensus, the arguments on which it is based are not entirely persuasive. When Sarsfield led the Irish Jacobite army from Limerick in 1691, neither he nor his Protestant or Catholic contemporaries and their successors believed that exile would terminate their involvement in Irish political affairs. The greatest proportion of land and wealth had indeed passed into the hands of the Protestant minority. Yet, Cullen on the Catholic middle-classes, Power on the suspect political loyalties of Protestant converts, Whelan on the 'underground gentry', Leighton on the Catholic *ancien régime* and Fenning and Fagan on the Catholic church, all suggest that the political shipwreck and ideological bankruptcy of the Catholic political interest in the eighteenth century have been exaggerated.[19]

While Irish historians and political commentators between Nicholas Plunkett and James Connolly preoccupied themselves with the deflation of Irish Jacobitism and the Stuart king, their consensus was disputed by the stridently nationalist author Brian O'Higgins. He introduced these themes to a popular readership in the *Wolfe Tone Annual* in the 1950s. His articles reiterated the conventional view. On the one hand, he argued that James II and William of Orange 'faced each other across the Boyne as antagonists for the crown of England'. He believed that 'they had no interest in Ireland or its freedom, except in so far as it might be useful as a granary, a breeder of soldiers, a strategic outpost and a source of revenue'. On the other, he refuted the aspersions cast on the Jacobite general Patrick Sarsfield, questioned the tendency of historians to dismiss the penal laws, and explained Irish inactivity in 1744/5 with reference to the great famine of 1740/1 which claimed the lives of over 400,000 people.[20] He censured those who 'despised the people of Ireland who lived through the terrible penal days because they endured so much without rising out against their oppressors because of their slavish loyalty to the mean and worthless Stuarts'.

O'Higgins's notion that their view of Séarlas Óg (Charles Edward Stuart) as the Gaelic son of a Gaelic king was as separatist as any republican might desire is overstated. Nevertheless, his trenchant belief that the songs and ballads represented more than 'old Hidden Ireland rubbish' or the 'product of the mind of a defeated people' is vital to understanding the place of Irish Jacobitism in the eighteenth century.[21] His contention that those Catholics who stood by King George in 1745 were a minority phalanx of 'castle slaves' is supported in the correspondence from Ireland to the Stuart court relating to the spurned approach

19 Cullen, 'Catholic social classes under the penal laws', pp 57-84; idem, 'Catholics under the penal laws', pp 23-37; Power, 'Converts'; Fenning, *Undoing of the friars*; idem, *Irish Dominican province*; Fagan, *Dublin's turbulent priest*; idem, *An Irish bishop*; Leighton, *Catholicism*; Whelan, *Tree of liberty*, pp 3-56. See also Bartlett, *Fall and rise*, p. 49; Ó Buachalla, *Aisling Ghéar*, pp 221, 315.   **20** Higgins, 'Ireland', pp 20-21, 30, 70, 74-5, 106; Dickson, *Arctic Ireland*.   **21** Higgins, 'Ireland', pp 20-1, 30, 70, 74-5, 106. For a biographical note, see Connolly (ed.), *Oxford companion*, p. 321. Jacobite poetry has remained a popular choice on the Irish language syllabus for the Leaving Certificate, 'Árd-teastas' and university courses; see, for example, Ó Foghludha (eag.) *Míl na hÉigse*; Ó Conaire (eag.) *Éigse*.

to George II in 1727.[22] The collapse of this approach also underlined the gulf
between Stuart royalists and those who sought an accommodation with the
Hanoverian regime in this period and in the later 1750s and 1760s.[23]

In recent years, English and Scottish Jacobite history has experienced a resurgence but Irish Jacobitism still languishes outside the mainstream of an
eighteenth-century Irish history still dominated by ascendancy history, the
United Irishmen and the Catholic Church.[24] As recently as 1988, Breandán Ó
Buachalla drew attention to the neglect by Irish historians of the Jacobite question despite its growing centrality in English and Scottish historical circles.[25]
More recently, calls have resounded in Irish historiographical circles for an
appraisal of Jacobitism using a variety of different sources. Marianne Elliott
questioned Seán Connolly's explanation of the enactment and enforcement of
the penal laws in his well-received *Religion, law and power: the making of
Protestant Ireland* (1992). She suggests that penal legislation against Catholics
was retained long after the storm had passed, not because of state-sponsored
sectarianism but due to the Jacobite threat, an argument already familiar to
historians of eighteenth-century Britain. She concludes that the age-old issue
of whether Catholic Ireland posed a serious Jacobite threat would not be
resolved until further research has exhaustively explored Irish-language, and
continental, as well as British and Irish sources.[26] Toby Barnard concurs. In his
authoritative overview of eighteenth-century Irish historiography, he maps
the recent inroads on the *terra incognita* of Irish history between 1659-1760.[27]
Barnard notes Connolly's general discomfort in dealing with Irish Catholic
political consciousness. He also questions his contradictory thesis on the penal
laws; his insistence that 'Protestants had genuine reasons for fearing their
Catholic neighbours, who had risen twice and kept dangerous links and doctrines' and his discountenance of any serious threat after 1715.[28] Of Bartlett's *Fall
and rise of the Irish nation*, Barnard points out that although he has stretched
the parameters of eighteenth-century Ireland to breaking-point the book is
heavily weighted towards the last decades of the eighteenth century. Little time

22 pp 241-3.   **23** pp 358-66.   **24** Ó Buachalla, 'Seacaibíteachas', pp 31-64. See fn. 1.   **25** Ó Buachalla,
review of Cruickshanks and Black, pp 186-90; Ó Buachalla, *Aisling Ghéar*. See also Mac Craith, 'Filíocht
Sheacaibíteach', pp 57-75; Morley, *An crann os coill*; idem, 'Idé-eolaíocht an tSeacaibíteachais', pp 14-24.
26 Elliott, 'Irishry down to the roots'. See also O'Donoghue, 'Jacobite threat', p. 30. Irish Jacobitism
after 1714 has recently been described as 'terra incognita'; Smyth, *Men of no property*, p. 41. James Kelly
has stated that 'Jacobite activity, overwhelmingly if not exclusively Catholic, remains little studied'; Kelly,
'The glorious and immortal memory', p. 32.   **27** Barnard, 'Old Ireland', p. 910; Froude, *English in
Ireland*, i, p. 657; O'Brien, *Parliament, politics and people,* introduction, p. 7; Bartlett, *Fall and rise*, p. 30.
28 Barnard, 'Old Ireland', pp 916, 919. David Hayton raises the same paradox in a review of Whelan
and Power (ed.), *Endurance and emergence*, p. 449. In another review Barnard expressed the view that
Connolly's book focused 'on the worlds and values of the Castle and College Green'; Barnard, 'review of
Connolly', p. 321. Patrick Fagan has recently claimed that there has been an excessive concentration on
the Protestant minority at the expense of the Catholic majority whose history has not been adequately
explored; Fagan (ed.), *Stuart papers*, i, p. 5.

or energy is expended on collective or individual mentalities, ideas or ideologies and, like Connolly's book, the bulk of the population gets little more than a walk-on part on the historical stage.[29]

Bartlett and Connolly have arrived at similar conclusions in relation to the penal laws. These so-called 'popery laws' or 'penal laws' had been on the statute-books since the reign of Queen Elizabeth and were periodically imposed with different levels of intensity throughout the seventeenth and eighteenth centuries.[30] No single topic has generated such controversy in seventeenth and eighteenth-century Irish history or spawned such diverse interpretations. Maureen Wall suggests that the penal laws 'operated to exclude the Catholic majority from all positions of importance in the country … in the same way as the colour bar has operated to ensure white ascendancy in African countries in recent times'.[31] Connolly has questioned the validity of this comparison: 'From this point of view the most appropriate modern parallel would not be the apartheid system so frequently cited but rather the policies which successive Irish governments have adopted towards the Irish language'.[32]

This tendency to underplay the psychological effects of the penal laws has been underlined by Buttimer and Elliott.[33] More recently Ó Buachalla has also questioned recent dismissals of Wall's comparison between the penal laws and the apartheid regime in South Africa. He points out that this would be similar to saying to a black man in South Africa that the apartheid regime was not so bad or to telling a Derry Catholic that he was not being persecuted under the Stormont administration.[34]

---

29 Barnard, 'Old Ireland', pp 910-12. Bartlett displays little sensitivity towards its linguistic diversity of this so-called Irish 'nation'. Indeed one could read this book and be totally oblivious to the fact that the majority of his Irish Catholic 'nation' was Irish-speaking. Ignoring Irish-language sources serves to further prejudice the centrality of Jacobitism as its primary political ideology.   **30** Connolly (ed.), *Oxford companion*, pp 438-9; Bartlett, *Fall and rise*, pp 1-81.   **31** Wall, *The penal laws*, p. 9.   **32** Connolly, 'Religion and history', p. 79; Bartlett also uses this analogy; Bartlett, *Fall and rise*, p. 28. Even if the penal laws were not regularly and rigidly imposed, a view that is not borne out in diverse historical sources from the period, this comparison defies belief. English speakers were not banned from voting or taking their seats in Dáil Éireann. They were not executed, harassed, branded, banished from the country or threatened with castration. If one is to make far-fetched comparisons to modern history and society it might be more appropriate to compare the penal laws against Catholics in the period after the 'Forty-five' and the laws against homosexuals in Ireland in the 1980s. Although the laws were not being imposed they were still on the statute books, causing great offence to otherwise law-abiding people who were considered second-class citizens in their own land. Connolly and Bartlett's revisionist interpretations of the penal laws are a classic case of the overreaction against the excessive persecution mentality of the nineteenth and early twentieth-century Catholic apologists being taken to extreme. They underline the need for a serious re-appraisal of the penal laws.   **33** Buttimer remarked that 'while she [Maureen Wall] may have questioned the practical implementation of the rules, the issue of the spirit of the laws still remain'; Buttimer, 'An Irish text on the war of Jenkins's ear', p. 83. Elliott states that 'the tendency to play down the penal laws- though accurate in terms of actual enforcement – can perhaps go too far. For the atmosphere they created was as important as their actual impact', Elliott, 'Irishery'.   **34** Ó Buachalla, *Aisling Ghéar*, p. 594. Other historians have expressed similar views regarding the oppressive nature of the penal laws; Burke, *Irish priests*, p. 287; Cullen, 'Catholic social classes under the penal laws', p. 75;

If people believed they were subject to discrimination, they were being persecuted and it is immaterial whether the legislation is being imposed or not. Irrespective of the views of Irish historians, the penal laws were inexorably linked to the Jacobite cause in the minds of Irish Catholics. They rejoiced at the Jacobite succession, lauded the imminent eclipse of the Protestant religion, the restoration of their ancient rights and the Catholicisation of the army and judiciary. The Williamite government copper-fastened this association by punishing Catholic priests for rapparee attacks and committing reprisals against their flocks. Fears of a possible Jacobite invasion in the 1690s also directed government attention against the Catholic clergy and both prompted and justified the imposition of the laws. In the early eighteenth century, the hardships caused by penal legislation against Irish Catholics preoccupied their clergy, literati and other political commentators. Attempts to prevent pilgrims from visiting holy wells, the enforcement of the laws against unregistered priests and bishops in the period before Ormonde's abortive invasion in 1719, and the correspondence of Irish clergymen to Rome and the Stuart court, all suggest that they affected every strata of Irish society. Cryptic correspondence showed the dangers of communication with Europe, the verses of the Irish poets, the correspondence of Irish clergy to Rome and the sermons of William Smith uncover something of the persecution mentality of their contemporaries. The accusations of recruitment witnesses and apostate clergy indicate the dangers facing the Catholic aristocracy and gentry. Pronouncements against the penal code often appear in recruitment depositions, while unregistered Catholic priests and friars were often associated with the trade. Many of these saw flight to the continent and a speedy return with James III as the only visible means of delivery from the penal yoke. Those who communicate with Rome and the Stuart and French courts continually dwell on the burden of the penal laws. Even when Jacobitism languished between 1722 and 1739, Irish Catholics at home and abroad still deemed them to be an intolerable burden. The hopes for a Stuart restoration and the rehabilitation of the Catholic church in contemporary Irish poetry were borne out by the onset of the 'Fifteen' and the 'Forty-five', and in the recurring invasions scares throughout the Jacobite period. The often harsh reaction of the government warns against denying that the penal laws were a real burden on Catholics. Irish clergymen still exercised caution when communicating with Rome between the 'Forty-five' and the end of the Jacobite period. Priests and bishops were arrested on suspicion of Jacobite activity. Many poets still wished for an alleviation of the penal yoke and the exiles retained their persecution mentality until the end of the Jacobite period.

Elliott, 'Irishery'; Fenning, *The undoing of the friars*, pp 34-5; idem, *Dominican province*, pp 187-8; Smyth, *Men of no property*, p. 12; Murphy, *Killaloe*, pp 27, 33; Corish, *Catholic community*, p. 106; Leighton, *Catholicism*, p. 8; McLaughlin, 'A crisis for the Irish in Bordeaux', pp 127-47; Kelly, 'The impact of the penal laws', pp 145-50, 174.

Hugh Fenning best sums up the accepted attitude towards the penal laws in his survey of the Irish Dominican province in the eighteenth century:

> It is however precisely between 1707 and 1708 that one finds the first evidence of what was to become a general policy regarding the regular clergy, the policy of ignoring their presence save when there was fear of a revolution in favour of the Stuarts or when an individual cleric brought himself to unfavourable notice of the authorities.[35]

The successive Jacobite invasion scares between 1692 and 1760 and the isolated incidences of persecution of individual clergy ensured that the penal code remained a grievance amongst Catholics throughout the century. There is no agreed orthodoxy among Irish historians. Much work remains to be done on the mechanics of penal legislation, the influence of the Catholic powers of Europe on English and Irish government policy and the psychological effects of the penal laws on Irish Catholics. However, the continued invasion scares and the psychological burden of the penal laws as manifested in Irish poetry, Jacobite prose and Roman correspondence are all important. The main contention here is that contemporary Catholic views of the penal yoke must take precedence over the opinions of latter-day historians. The Jacobite threat was used to justify the maintenance of the penal code while the Irish poets, priests and Jacobite supporters of the Stuart king saw his restoration in terms of its alleviation.[36] A systematic examination of Irish Jacobitism, the ideology that prompted the imposition and intermittent enforcement of penal legislation against Catholics between 1690 and 1760, should be considered an important plank in any re-examination of the penal code.[37]

The role of the standing army in Irish politics is related to the question of the penal laws. The idea of leaderless, disarmed, 'poor, oppressed' Irish Catholics features prominently in Irish Jacobite poetry, the often smug pamphlets and sermons of Protestant writers and preachers, and in Irish Jacobite *émigré* correspondence to the French and Stuart courts. The English Act of 10 William *c.*1 (1699) reduced the standing army in Ireland to twelve thousand and the actual number of soldiers in Ireland rarely numbered more than six thousand. Bartlett notes that men in uniform were still a much more common sight in Ireland than in England and the military force was widely distributed in no fewer than 263 barracks.[38] This and the strict disarming policy imposed against Catholics reinforced the Jacobite and Whig view that Ireland could make no

35 Fenning, *Dominican province*, p. 50.   **36** This is not to suggest that Catholicism would not have been feared (as it was in the reign of Charles II) had there not have been a pretender to the crowns of the three kingdoms.   **37** Kelly, review of Fagan, pp 151-2. The 'Jacobite question' is absolutely vital to the 'Catholic question' which Bartlett defines as 'the issue of the re-admission of Catholics to full civil, religious and political equality in both Britain and Ireland'; Bartlett, *Fall and rise*, p. 1. In spite of this, it is effectively ignored in his survey.   **38** Bartlett, 'Army and society', pp 174, 179.

contribution to the restoration of the Stuart king unless supported by an invasion force.

The lack of a comprehensive study of the Catholic church's relationship with the house of Stuart presents another gap in eighteenth-century historiography, only partially filled by Fagan's *Ireland in the Stuart papers* (1995).[39] This book does not seek to present an alternative history of Irish Catholicism or a pro-sopographical study of the Irish Jacobite episcopate. Nor does it attempt to suggest that Irish Catholics were all Jacobites. It does argue that Jacobitism had a pivotal place in the Irish Catholic ethos and that it percolated down to the lower echelons of Irish society.

The ties between Jacobitism and Catholicism were firmly established at the outset of James II's reign. Immediately after his accession to the throne in 1685, James II petitioned Pope Innocent XI for the right of nomination to bishoprics in his three kingdoms. James maintained this prerogative after his deposition in 1688 in spite of opposition from a few dissident Irish clerics who feared that the exiled king would attempt to anglicise the Irish church or that his right of nomination would bring further persecution on Irish Catholics. James II, Mary of Modena (acting as regent for her son) and the young 'James III' regularly exercised this right. Of 129 bishops and coadjutors appointed to Irish sees between 1687 and 1765, all but five were nominated by the Stuart kings. The Papacy recognised James III's regal pretensions. His long 'reign' and refusal to abjure the Catholic faith to succeed to the thrones of his ancestors ensured that he was viewed as the senior Catholic prince and martyr-king in the eyes of many European Catholics. It is no surprise, therefore, that he retained his role as the political conscience of many of the leading luminaries of the higher Irish Catholic clergy. Although the *de jure* King James III never had the chance to show his affection to those natives who had sacrificed everything in his cause, he jealously guarded and exercised this right of episcopal nomination to the Irish mission. As a result of this ideological hold, Jacobitism remained crucially relevant for Catholic Ireland. Rome rarely refused any of his nominations and the Irish clergy understood that it was to the Stuart court and not the Holy See that episcopal hopefuls had to make their representations.[40] Despite this, it has been effectively written out of the general history of eighteenth-century Ireland.

---

39 Keogh, review of Fenning, *Irish Dominican province*, pp 153-4; Barnard, 'Old Ireland', p. 917; Fagan (ed.), *Stuart papers*. **40** Giblin, 'The Stuart nomination of bishops', pp 35-47; Ó Buachalla, *Aisling Ghéar*, p. 216. Ecclesiastical promotions in the first half of the eighteenth century, a prosopographical study of the Irish Jacobite episcopate and an examination of patronage networks among Irish Catholics, Wild Geese and continental-based clergy, would provide a suitable Ph.D. topic.

II

Having offered a more positive gloss on Jacobite historiography and an alternative view of the relevance of Irish Jacobitism, it is necessary to explore the reason for its divergence from orthodox historical thinking. In this regard, Monod's study of English Jacobitism initiated a veritable Copernican revolution in Jacobite studies by directing attention to new sources and reinterpreting hackneyed material.[41] It provides a useful comparative model for Ireland. Particular attention should be given to the structure of the Irish Jacobite community. Quite apart from the links between Jacobitism and Catholicism, Irish Jacobitism became the most widespread form of Jacobite ideology in the three kingdoms in the late-seventeenth century. It also provided the greatest threat to the Williamite regime in the late 1680s and early-1690s. Contemporaries (and later historians) have criticised Richard Talbot, earl of Tyrconnell, and the Irish Jacobites for their preoccupation with the spoils of war before they had been won. It is often forgotten that Irish Jacobites alone had mobilised in great numbers in support of their king in 1688, in spite of the fact that they had already suffered from Stuart ingratitude on the restoration of Charles II in 1660.[42] Tyrconnell's transformation of the army in the mid-1680s ensured that he succeeded for a time in holding Ireland for King James.[43] James McGuire contends that Tyrconnell's lord deputyship was successful and that external factors beyond his control were ultimately responsible for his downfall. In spite of this, John Childs dismisses Tyrconnell's Irish Jacobite army 'as just about capable of hunting bandits', and contrasted the 'gentle' and 'effective' Protestant army with the 'thoroughly ill-mannered' reformed institution which emerged in the Tyrconnellite era.[44] It is worth remembering that James's English army was not reformed and it did not fire a shot in support of their king. Moreover, King James soon realised that the 'bandits' (rapparees) were fighting on his side. Recently Childs underlined the Irish Jacobite army's incompetence by asserting that its sole substantial defeat of the Williamite forces at Dundalk in 1689 resulted from a combination of poor weather and good luck. In doing so, he ignores William's defeat at the first siege of Limerick where he lost over 2,000 men and the havoc wreaked on the Williamite forces by the rapparees.[45]

Despite James II's inglorious flight to France, this poorly equipped and undisciplined army frustrated the ambitions of William of Orange and the League of Augsburg for three years. After the conclusion of the Treaty of

---

41 Monod, *Jacobitism*, passim. **42** Clarke (ed.), *Memoirs of James II*, ii, p. 354. **43** McGuire, 'Richard Talbot', pp 73-85. **44** Childs, *Army and James II*, pp 56-7, 67, 76. In contrast, Dickson points out that at the end of Charles II's reign the Irish army was an under-trained, under-equipped force with no active service experience, Dickson, *New foundations*, p. 21. **45** Bartlett and Jeffreys (ed.), *Military history of Ireland*, p. 188. Childs's is not an isolated view. Kenneth Ferguson believes that Tyrconnell made a mistake in arming the Catholics, although it was they who would later fight for his cause; Ferguson, 'Army in Ireland', p. 46.

Limerick, the Irish Jacobite army joined the army of William III's great enemy, Louis XIV. They went, according to their leader Sarsfield, 'to make another Ireland in the armies of the great king of France'.[46] The 'Wild Geese' and their successors, the Irish Brigades in France and Spain, remained pivotal to Irish Jacobite hopes and Protestant fears.[47] Although the Irish military in seventeenth-century Europe and their relationship with their homeland has been the subject of recent research, their eighteenth-century successors lack a modern interpretative history.[48]

This study does not seek to supply this, nor does it provide an extensive examination of the Irish exiles, the Irish Brigades in France and Spain or recruitment for foreign service, all topics worthy of separate monographs. For example, an examination of recruitment would involve a detailed discussion of the numbers joining the Irish Regiments in France and Spain in the eighteenth century. Arguments among contemporaries and historians over the exact numbers recruited for the foreign service have been as protracted as those relating to the imposition of the penal laws. In 1729, Sir Charles Wogan lamented that 100,000 Irishmen had died in the service of France since the 1690s.[49] Elsewhere, in a letter to Swift, dated 1733, he stated that 120,000 Irishmen had been killed in the service of France.[50] Writing in the early 1760s, Abbé MacGeoghegan put the figure at 450,000 for the period between 1691 and 1745.[51] Richard Hayes believed that MacGeoghegan's figures represented all those who served. However he assumes that those who served in the Irish Brigades were all of Irish origin. He arrives at a figure of 48,000 for the total casualties among the ranks of the brigade in this period.[52] In more recent times, Cullen put forward much smaller figures for recruitment for the Irish Brigades, suggesting that 'at its peak in the late-1720s and 1730s, enlistment in the French army reached, or did not fall short of, 1,000 per annum'. He also claimed that this influx did not taper off

46 McLaughlin and Warner, *The Wild Geese*, p. 5. Sarsfield promised that they would return with him the following year; Story, *An impartial history with a continuation thereof*, p. 259; Wauchope, *Sarsfield*, pp 257, 266, 280. One Irish *émigré* expressed frustration at the failure to realise this ambition; 'To the king's most excellent majesty' (1692 [?]) B.L., Add. Ms 28, 939, fol. 329. Others accused Sarsfield and the Irish leaders of blatant self-interest; N. Plunkett, 'A light to the blind' (Bodl., Carte Ms 229, fols 415, 431); Barry (ed.), 'The groans of Ireland', pp 131-2. In spite of this failure to return to Ireland an ideological cohesiveness survived between the *émigrés* and the Irish-based Jacobites; N. Plunkett, 'The most humble petition of the Irish abroad in behalf of themselves and of their compatriots at home' (N.L.I., Ms 477). See also Bodl., Carte Ms 229, fol. 46.   **47** Forman, *A defence*, pp 24-5, 30, 46.   **48** Henry, *Irish in Flanders*; Stradling, *Spanish monarchy and Irish mercenaries*; Ó Buachalla concurs: 'Tá leabhar le scríobh fós ar shaol na n-imirceach sin thar lear, ach is léir, fiú ar an mbeagán den chomhfhreagras atá pléite againn, is léir a lárnaí ina shaol a bhí an Stíobhartach, pé acu Séamas II, Séamas III, nó Séarlas Óg: is léir freisin a lárnaí ina gcuid machnaimh a bhí an stair – stair a muintire – agus a cheangailte a bhí an stair sin le dán na Stíobhartach'; Ó Buachalla, *Aisling Ghéar*, p. 432. McGurk makes the same point that the psychology of Irish military migration remains an untold story; McGurk, 'Wild Geese', p. 36.   **49** Charles Wogan to James III, 18 May 1729 (R.A., Ms 128, fol. 34). **50** Quoted in Petrie, *Jacobite movement*, p. 300.   **51** MacGeoghegan, *Histoire*, iii, p. 754.   **52** Hayes, 'Irish casualties in the French military service', pp 198-201. See also idem, *Biographical dictionary*, pp 181, 317; Hayes McCoy, 'Wild Geese', p. 339.

decisively until the 1740s.[53] Harman Murtagh states that 5,000 Irish soldiers accompanied Mountcashel to France in 1690 and sixteen thousand more left Limerick with Sarsfield after the Treaty of Limerick. Chevalier Geydon, a veteran of forty years service with Dillon's Regiment, claimed that it sustained losses of up to six thousand soldiers by 1738. Murtagh surmises that 'the experience of the other Franco-Irish Regiments cannot have been dissimilar'. Although conceding that recruitment peaked in the 1720s, he claimed that Dillon's regiment received eight hundred recruits from Ireland when stationed at Sedan in 1729. Information on prisoners captured after the 'Forty-five' would suggest that the rank and file was overwhelmingly Irish-born; a generation later, this figure had collapsed to 10%.[54] In a controle of Fitzjames's Regiment of Horse in the French army in 1737, Eoghan Ó hAnnracháin shows that 261 non-commissioned men out of 311 (80%) were Irish-born.[55] His more recent research on Clare's regiment shows that 131 out of 431 (30%) of the new recruits between the Battle of Fontenoy (1745) and Lafelt (1747) were Irishmen.[56]

Assessing recruitment numbers and their relationship to Jacobitism is a more complicated procedure than number-crunching in the Archives Nationales. Cullen argues that 'the large numbers of recruits for France which appear in reports from the countryside up to the mid-eighteenth century are invariably worthless figments of imagination'. Nevertheless, he makes the essential point that 'the fears behind these estimates were nourished by the multiple links created by trade, both legal and clandestine, and the emerging Catholic community in exile'.[57] An extensive trawl of the muster rolls in France and Spain would give a clear picture of the level of military emigration to France and Spain. One should, however, not lose sight of the fact that many others, including clerics, merchants and itinerant labourers, left for England, Europe, America and Canada (particularly the fisheries in Newfoundland). Their nervous Protestant neighbours would not have always been aware of their eventual destination. For example, in 1727 Archbishop Boulter claimed that lusty young fellows were quitting the country on the pretence that they were going to England for work.[58] Five thousand per annum were travelling from the southeast of Ireland to do seasonal work in the Newfoundland fisheries.[59] The actual numbers recruited cannot be easily dismissed. Cullen's numbers of one thousand per annum

53 Cullen, 'The Irish diaspora', pp 121, 124-5, tables (6.1) and (6.2), pp 139-40; Lydon, *Making of Ireland*, p. 219. It is hoped that recent proposals by the Scottish-Irish Studies programme to enter the muster rolls of the Irish Regiments in the French army onto a database will finally provide an accurate figure. **54** Murtagh, 'Irish soldier abroad', pp 297, 298, 312. Ó Buachalla shares Cullen and Murtagh's figures, concluding that twenty thousand Irishmen left the country between 1691 and 1692 and he takes fifty thousand as the lowest number who left Ireland for the service of France and Spain in the years 1720-2, 1724-30 and 1739-43; Ó Buachalla, *Aisling Ghéar*, pp 213-14, 336-7. **55** Ó hAnnracháin, 'An analysis of Fitzjames's cavalry', p. 254. **56** Ó hAnnracháin, 'The Irish Brigade at Lafelt', p. 2. I have found no other figures in print which question Cullen, Murtagh, Ó Buachalla or Ó hAnnracháin. **57** Cullen, 'Irish diaspora', pp 114-17, 119, 125, 129; table (6.2), p. 140. **58** Boulter to Newcastle, 19 May 1726, in Boulter, *Letters*, i, pp 57-60. **59** Smyth, 'Irish migration, p. 51.

would, and did, have huge consequences in terms of perception. However, the critical point is the contemporary belief that thousands were being recruited was as important as the reality. This common perception ultimately determined Catholic hopes and Protestant fears, upon which this study is based.

The geographical extent of the phenomenon within Ireland, the eventual destination of the recruits, the mechanism of recruitment and the existence of networks between colonel proprietors of regiments and their agents on the forfeited estates would also be worthy of further consideration.[60] Work also needs to be completed on a comparison with Scotland and other countries, which provided cannon fodder for the dynastic wars that ravaged Europe in the first half of the eighteenth century.[61] A case can be made for the existence of close links between the recruitment phenomenon and the Irish Jacobite polity at home and abroad. Many factors drove young men to seek their fortunes in foreign armies in the Jacobite period, a mixture of dynamism, persecution and poverty, to paraphrase Cullen.[62] The emergence of a cult of the Irish Brigades and the Wild Geese in Irish literature suggests that Jacobitism should be included among these reasons.[63]

Aside from their effects on Irish Jacobite and Whig opinion, these recruits supplemented a thriving Irish Jacobite diaspora in eighteenth-century Europe. Nevertheless, the disproportionately large influence exerted on the Irish polity by this exiled community remains another neglected area of study. Indeed the Irish historiographical tradition has considered the decapitation of St Ruth as the effective end of Irish Jacobite militarism. This belies the prominent part which Sarsfield's 'Other Ireland' played in the armies of France, Spain and the extent to which they retained a practical affection for their exiled king and their homeland. The *émigré* Irish should be considered a component part of what the early-eighteenth century Jacobite writer Nicholas Plunkett calls the Irish 'nation', on the authority of the Irish poets, the Irish diaspora and Protestant con-

---

60 An examination of recruitment and the Irish Brigades in the context of Irish Jacobitism sheds light on the mechanics and ritual of recruitment, the involvement of Catholic clergy, Catholic gentry and converts and its strong Jacobite dimension. See also Ó Buachalla (ed.), 'Irish Jacobitism in official documents', pp 128–38; *Aisling Ghéar*, pp 334-94. 61 Steve Murdoch and Alexia Grosjean have completed a study on Scottish soldiers in the Swedish and Danish armies between 1590 and 1707. They constructed an alpha-numeric database of over eight thousand officers of Scottish origin in these armies, which has allowed them to ascertain their geographical distribution, their preferred destination, the ideological, economic and political motivation behind their flight and their mobility within regiments and throughout the armies in question. A similar project could be undertaken using the French and Spanish military archives at Vincennes and Simancas, the Bibliothèque Nationale, as well as other private respoitories (including the Stuart Papers at Windsor Castle). This would answer many of the same questions posed by Murdoch and Grosjean; Murdoch, 'The database in early modern Scottish history', pp 87, 91-2; Grosjean, 'Scottish-Scandinavian seventeenth-century links', pp 105-21. 62 Cullen, 'The Irish diaspora', pp 114, 117, 121-2; Murtagh, 'Irish soldiers abroad', pp 310-11; Ó Buachalla, *Aisling Ghéar*, p. 337. Ó Buachalla's monograph provides the best recent examination of the phenomenon; ibid., pp 334-94. 63 Murtagh agrees that the ethos of the Irish Brigades in France and Spain was strongly Jacobite; Murtagh, 'Irish soldiers abroad', pp 307-10.

temporaries. Plunkett drew a cameo of this absent but vital Irish political interest in an unpublished pamphlet entitled 'The state of the nation'. He identified 'great numbers abroad and at home tho' not enjoying lands or inheritance, yet are worthy patriots and highly capable of serving their country'. He lavishly praised on 'those Irish whom the world owns to be constant to the Catholic religion, constant for their loyalty to their prince and noted for their natural courage'.[64] This self-righteous rhetoric would become the hallmark of Irish Jacobites, embellishing many letters from Irish émigrés to the court of their exiled king.

The Irish colleges on the continent also provided vital foci for the Irish diaspora during the Jacobite period and acted as tangents between the two sections of the Irish 'Nation'. The Collège des Lombardes provided thirteen bishops for Irish sees in the period between 1688 and 1715. Natalie Genet-Rouffiac also notes that 1214 students from the Universities of Paris and Toulouse-Cahors served on the Irish mission in the seventeenth and eighteenth centuries. Irish soldiers remained in contact with the expatriate clerics of their native diocese. They contributed to their upkeep when their fortunes allowed, and entrusted the exiled clergy with the education of their sons. The support given by the first and second generation of Irish *émigrés* is best exemplified by the proliferation of bursaries and educational foundations which they bestowed on the colleges, often with the object of providing education for impoverished clerics from their wider kinship circle, diocese or province. In return, the college clergy took care of the spiritual needs of their secular brethren; they became chaplains to the Irish Brigades and provided expatriate Irish noblemen with testimonies and certificates of noblesse.[65] On a practical level, the colleges acted as a useful port of call for Irish emigrants who were unfamiliar with the French language and French customs.

Historians of all persuasions have attested to the central place of the Irish diaspora in eighteenth-century politics. Lecky believed that 'the real history of the Irish Catholics during the first half of the eighteenth century is to be found in the countries of Europe' and he marvelled at the 'energy and ability of Ireland's soldiers and scholars put to the service of other nations'.[66] Hayes suggested that Paris was the capital of Catholic Ireland in the eighteenth century.[67] The cult of the Irish Brigades also flavoured later historiographical and literary accounts from Matthew O'Conor, Thomas Davis, J.C. O'Callaghan, Sir Arthur Conan-Doyle and William Butler Yeats.[68] However, those few historians who have tracked the eighteenth-century *émigrés* have focused on regimental histories

---

64 Plunkett, 'The state of the nation' (Bodl., Carte Ms 229, fols 70, 454). See also O'Donoghue, 'Jacobite threat', p. 34; Flood, *Wogan*, p. 136. **65** Swords (ed.), *Irish-French connection*, p. 63; Walsh, *Irish continental college movement*, p. 47; Genet-Rouffiac, N., 'La première generation', pp 290-3, 308-13. **66** Lecky, *Ireland*, i, pp 250, 413. Similar views are expressed by Matthew O'Conor and W.D. Griffin; O'Conor, *The brigades*, preface, vi; Griffin, *Irish on the continent*, pp 46-8. **67** Hayes, *Irish swordmen*, p. ix; idem, *Old Irish links with France*, p. 29. See also McLaughlin, 'A crisis for the Irish in Bordeaux in 1756', pp 129-47. **68** O'Conor, *Military history*, idem, *The Irish Brigades*, O'Callaghan, *Irish Brigades*. See above, fns 46-52.

of the Irish Brigades, continental colleges or religious houses, or biographical and prosopographical examinations of Irishmen who rose to high political, military and ecclesiastical office. The single most comprehensive source for the eighteenth-century Irish *émigré* community throughout Europe, the Stuart Archive in Windsor Castle, has been effectively ignored.[69] Following the pioneering endeavours of Louis Cullen, the ties between Ireland and its diaspora throughout the period merit further investigation, in particular the shared Jacobite rhetoric and persecution mentality.[70] Gearóid Ó Tuathaigh has stated that historians need to apply themselves more systematically to the study of popular historical consciousness over the *longue durée*. This could be done 'with a view to establishing what constituted this consciousness at different times, what factors shaped it, how did it manifest itself at different times, in different forms, to different purposes down through the centuries, what the evidence is for continuities and discontinuities'. He added that 'this would require careful attention to a wide range of sources and texts of a kind that many historians are not accustomed to handling'.[71]

The rapparees who rose in support of James II and the recruits who left Ireland to join the exiled Irish Brigades are an Irish equivalent of Monod's 'theatre of ex-officers' or the disbanded residue of James II's army in post-revolution England. Their activities were deemed to have more than purely mercenary motives, provoking serious concern in Protestant circles during the first half of the eighteenth century. Rappareeism and recruitment and the Irish Brigades feature prominently in official correspondence in those periods (1692, 1695-7, 1715-16, 1719, 1722, 1739-49, 1759-60) when a Jacobite invasion seemed most likely. The depositions of recruiters and enlistees who turned king's evidence offer an insight into the Irish Jacobite underworld, which conforms to the Monodian model of English popular Jacobitism. French officers, priests, merchants, converts, Catholic gentry and poets became implicated in this illicit activity. The depositions also uncover intricate recruiting networks between Ireland and Europe. Jacobite networks linked Calais, St Malo, Bilbao, Genoa and Leghorn, ports which retained links with Ireland through trade, privateering and recruiting.[72]

The dispatch of large numbers of rapparees during the Jacobite War, the execution of numerous recruits for the foreign service, the preoccupation with condemned and executed Jacobites in England and Scotland and the emerging

---

69 The neglect of this source has been stressed by the four reviewers of Fagan (ed.), *Stuart papers*. **70** Cullen, 'The Irish diaspora'; idem, 'The Galway smuggling trade in the 1730s', pp 7-40; idem, 'The overseas trade of Waterford', pp 165-78; idem, 'The smuggling trade of Ireland', pp 149-75; idem, 'Irish merchant communities at Bordeaux, La Rochelle and Cognac', in idem and Butel (ed.), *Négoc. et industrie en France et en Irlande aux xviiᵉ et xixᵉ siècles*, pp 51-4. Little has been written on popular historical consciousness. **71** Ó Tuathaigh, 'Irish historical revisionism', in Brady (ed.), *Interpreting Irish history*, p. 324. Griffin states that the Irish émigrés were a distinct element in European society; Griffin, *Irish on the continent*, pp 460-3. **72** Most major ports between Brittany and Cadiz housed an Irish presence; Smyth, 'Irish emigration', p. 50.

cult of the 'outlaw rapparee' in the Irish literary tradition would also suggest that Daniel Szechi's 'Jacobite theatre of death' should be extended to Ireland.[73] The ultimate platform for the articulation of the Jacobite ideology also grew out of the close association between Jacobitism and crime within the three kingdoms. Post-war dislocation in England and Scotland drove many ex-soldiers and highlanders onto and beyond the legal periphery. Condemned criminals and Jacobites enhanced this association and the scaffold, like the coffee-house or tavern, became a platform from which the Stuart cause and the illegitimacy of the new regime could be trumpeted. The association of Jacobitism with the Sussex smugglers and the Waltham Blacks in England, and with the proscribed clans and cattle-thieves of Scotland, had its equivalent in the contemporary Irish Protestant mind. Privateers, rapparees, foreign service recruits, priest-catching vigilantes, Jacobite mobs, Houghers[74] and Whiteboys fulfilled similar roles. The government utilised the spectre of Jacobitism as a cover for the judicial massacre of the MacDonalds of Glencoe in 1692 and to justify the notorious 'Black Acts'. Post-1745 banditry in Scotland was the excuse for what Allan Macinnes has described as 'genocide' against the Jacobite clans.[75] Similarly in eighteenth-century Ireland, the Catholic populace was often collectively punished for the misdemeanours of the tories. Tories and rapparees such as Éamonn an Chnoic, Seán Ó Duibhir, Redmond O'Hanlon, Pádraig Fléimionn, Cathal Mac Aoidh, Pilib Mac Giolla Gunna, Muircheartach Ó Suilleabháin Béarra and Séamus Mac Mhuirchidh all joined James III and Charles Edward as symbols of popular defiance in Irish poetry in the late-seventeenth and eighteenth centuries.[76] The thievery, banditry, privateering, levelling, vandalism and night-walking of the O'Donoghues of Glenflesk, the O'Sullivans of Beare, the O'Mahonys of Cork, the Houghers of Iar-Chonnacht and the Munster Whiteboys became associated in the Protestant mind with Jacobitism. The priest-hunter continually invoked the Jacobite spectre against the clergy in times of political unrest.

In view of the sectarian nature of the Jacobite war in Ireland and of William III's adoption of the role of Protestant champion of Europe, it might seem surprising to find Irish Protestant Jacobites. This study will consider the political discourse and mentality of a small, but influential and vocal, Irish Protestant Jacobite tradition in the context of the work of Monod, Murray

---

73 Szechi, 'The Jacobite theatre of death', in Cruickshanks and Black (ed.), *The Jacobite challenge*, pp 57-73. John Caryll, secretary to Mary of Modena and Thomas Lally, a prominent Irish Jacobite and colonel-proprietor of Lally's Regiment, had contact with the Sussex smugglers; Monod, *Jacobitism*, pp 111, 115. **74** Thousands of cattle were destroyed (houghed, that is, had their hamstrings cut) in an organised protest against the extension of large-scale stock-rearing in Galway, Clare and other western counties; Connolly, *Religion*, p. 219. **75** Thompson, *Whigs and hunters*; Winslow, 'Sussex smugglers,' pp 119–67; Cruickshanks and Erskine-Hill, 'The Waltham Black Act and Jacobitism', pp 358–65; Macinnes, 'The aftermath of the '45', pp 103–13; idem, *Clanship, commerce, passim*. Pittock claims that the smuggling acts of 1698, 1717, 1721 and 1745 were raised amid great anxiety over Jacobitism; Pittock, *Inventing and resisting*, p. 92. **76** The most recent appraisals of toryism in seventeenth and eighteenth-century Ireland are Connolly, *Religion*, pp 203-33 and Ó Ciardha, 'Buachaillí an tsléibhe', pp 59-85.

Pittock and Ian Higgins on contemporary England and Scotland. The Irish
Protestant Jacobite legacy is more significant for its quality than its quantity. As
well as supplying the evangelist of the non-juring tradition (Charles Leslie), the
conscience of English Protestant Jacobitism (James Butler, second duke of
Ormond), the Stuart king's admiral-in-waiting (George Camocke), three of the
principal English Jacobite leaders (Arran, Orrery and Barrymore), one of the
most fanatical of all the non-juring Jacobites (George Kelly) and two of the
seven men of Moidart (George Kelly and Thomas Sheridan), this small but
vibrant Protestant Jacobite tradition survived the Glorious Revolution and
lingered until the 1730s.

   Throughout this study, attention will also be focused on Protestant anti-
Jacobitism in order to provide further insight into the role of the Stuart claimant
in Irish political life. This perspective appears in the correspondence of government and local government officials and the prolific output of Protestant
preachers and pamphleteers. A direct relationship existed between Protestant
fears of the Pretender and Catholic expectancy; Protestant attitudes towards the
Stuarts fluctuated with the trajectory of European politics, ranging from fear
and paranoia to disdain.[77] This book seeks to rescue Jacobitism, the main
political culture on the island for the greater part of the century, from what E.P.
Thompson called 'the enormous condescension of posterity'.[78] This will be
achieved by examining the Irish Jacobite experience and the political literature
of the majority Irish-speaking community in its proper political context, free
from the distorting prism of hindsight.

                                    III

The lack of attention to Jacobitism as an aspect of eighteenth-century Irish
history is partly explained by the nature of the evidence. Eveline Cruickshanks
has described the difficulties facing the Jacobite historian. Stressing the need for
ciphers or fool-proof lines of communication with the Stuart court (a contact
discouraged by the Stuart king himself), she claimed that it would be naive of
historians to expect to find evidence of Jacobitism in private papers.[79] This problem has also been recently highlighted by Daniel Szechi:

       The natural exigencies of participation in eighteenth-century conspiracy
       necessarily militated against record-keeping and memoirs of this kind.
       Most of our sources for the inner history of the Jacobites and their cause
       derive from the records of the Stuart court in exile or the depositions of

77 As well as being central to British politics, the fear of Jacobitism moulded British policy at home
and abroad in the same period; Ó Buachalla, *Aisling Ghéar*, p. 259.   78 Thompson, *English working
class*, p. 13.   79 Cruickshanks (ed.), *Ideology and conspiracy*, p. 4.

witnesses, spies and informers of all kinds that pepper the official papers of the British, French and other governments who had to deal with them. Sensible Jacobites still resident in Britain generally tried to keep their business oral and burnt their correspondence whenever they feared the government of the day was about to embark on a Jacobite hunt. In consequence we have scant resources with which to construct a mental history of Jacobitism.[80]

These difficulties are exacerbated in Ireland where the majority population remained Irish-speaking and many of the Irish Jacobite aristocracy had moved to the continent. The tenuous position of the Catholic clergy, the extreme caution of the depleted Catholic aristocracy and gentry and the diligence of the government militated against treasonable correspondence. This apparent silence cannot be taken as a reluctance on the part of the Irish in contacting their spiritual *or* temporal masters in Rome. It is also absolutely vital that incidences of Jacobite sedition, illicit toasting and treasonable words should be measured against the fact that Irish was the main linguistic culture on the island. Much of what would have passed between monoglot Irish speakers, or in the presence of monoglot English speakers, was not recorded or detected. Many references to toasting and seditious words in the Irish tradition have only survived in the context of Irish literature and song.

Irish Jacobitism provided a corner stone of the political, cultural and religious life of Catholics and Protestants throughout the eighteenth century. The sources for examining its influence are varied, if necessarily vague, tentative and subjective. Understandably the state-papers, government records, legal depositions, anti-Jacobite pamphlets and sermons and other 'official sources' have been relied upon to provide the lion's share of the evidence. The loss of the eighteenth-century crime reports in the Four Courts conflagration in 1922 means that the Irish Jacobite historian does not have the diversity of material for a study on the scale of Monod's *Jacobitism and the English people*, replete with geographical and statistical analyses of activities such as illicit toasting and prosecutions for treasonable words. Yet, the Monodian model does have a comparative value.[81]

The Irish Jacobite historian must cast the net far and wide to glean information from the letter-books of the many lords lieutenant, lords justice and secretaries of state whose portfolios related to Ireland. This study of Irish Jacobitism is based on a rigorous use of official state papers, sixty years of newspapers, hundreds of pamphlets, sermons and broadsheets, as well as some correspondence in foreign archives. Far from there being a conflict between 'unofficial' sources such as poetry and song and 'respectable', 'official' documents, they com-

---

80 Szechi, 'George Lockhart of Carnwath', p. 979.   81 Ó Buachalla also expressed the belief that no scholar will be able to write a book on Irish popular Jacobitism as Monod has done for England; Ó Buachalla, *Aisling Ghéar*, p. 341.

plement each other in many ways, above all in revealing that in two completely different types of records James's return was considered a political reality.

The State Papers (Ireland), Archbishop King's extensive correspondence and collections of pamphlets, sermons and broadsheets relating to Ireland in the major repositories in England and Ireland have been relied on for an insight into Protestant attitudes towards Jacobitism. The importance of Archbishop King's correspondence is best exemplified by David Hayton: 'King was not a man of faction, he did not advocate partisan policies and Lord Lieutenant Sunderland came to rely on his correspondence to such an extent that on occasion their private correspondence usurped the function of official letters'.[82] The Stuart papers also represent a largely untapped source of over eighty thousand letters, which contains much relevant information on Irish Jacobitism, the Irish diaspora, the penal laws and the state of the Irish mission. Patrick Fagan has recently published a well-received two-volume collection of the letters relating to Ireland.[83]

Because no rising occurred in Ireland in support of the Stuarts, and due to the disparagement of Jacobitism by Irish historians, no comprehensive examination of the ideology exists. This is demonstrated by the paucity of references to Jacobitism in the indices of the *New history of Ireland*.[84] In spite of this, the Stuart claimant figured prominently in contemporary political discourse. The extensive selection of newspapers and broadsheets, often copies of their London counterparts, contain a small selection of local news. However, they kept a wide direct and indirect readership abreast of international politics. Ó Buachalla notes that from the beginning of the eighteenth century 'the Pretender' was a central character in the newspapers of the major cities and great interest was taken in himself and his supporters at home and abroad. 'Ó bhlianta tosaigh na haoise amach, ba charactar lárnach i nuachtáin na ceannchathrach é an Pretender. Cuireadh suim faoi leith, is cosúil, ina chuid taistil ar fud na hEorpa agus i ngníomhaíocht a lucht leanúna thar lear agus sa bhaile'.[85]

The adversarial Protestant pamphlet and sermon tradition brought the Stuart claimants periodically to the forefront of Irish political life. In spite of this, Cadoc Leighton is reticent on their value as a medium for understanding political events or social change, accusing the authors of being 'frequently ill-informed, nearly always tendentious, and uniformly lacking in the sense of proportion which only temporal distance gives'. Nonetheless, he does rely heavily on them in con-

---

82 Hayton, 'Ireland and the English ministers', p. 202. Connolly's influential *Religion, law and power* draws heavily on King's papers.   **83** See Ó Ciardha's, J. Kelly's, P. Kelly's and L. Irwin's reviews of Fagan (ed.), *Stuart papers*. However, Fagan's two volumes contain very little material relating to the Irish diaspora, an integral part of the Irish Jacobite 'nation'; Ó Ciardha, review of Fagan (ed.), *Stuart papers*.   **84** Richard Hayes's *Manuscript sources for the history of Irish civilisation* has very few references to Jacobitism in the subject indices.   **85** Ó Buachalla, 'Seacaibíteachas', p. 33; Ó Buachalla, *Aisling Ghéar*, p. 429. Munter claimed that the lower strata of society were subscribing in large numbers to the periodical press; Munter, *Irish newspaper*, p. 132.

structing the Irish Catholic mentality, and cites them as a useful source for anti-Catholic feeling.[86] In contrast, J.G. McCoy rebukes those who have disregarded the value of such printed sources in attempting to capture the spirit of the age, asserting that 'contemporaries considered such material as an essential part of the political culture'.[87] For an examination of popular Jacobitism, it is essential that the themes in pamphlet discourse, replicated in the didactic monographs and commemorative sermons of the Protestant clergy, are not dismissed as hollow sabre-rattling. The fact that they were continually emphasised by pamphleteers, preachers, clergymen, and occasionally by prominent political figures, reflected the Stuart king's media-value.

The activities of Irish Jacobites in exile have been examined in part by O'Callaghan, O'Conor, Hayes, Beresford, and more recently by Genet-Rouffiac. Nevertheless, there has been no attempt to correlate this material with its contemporary European, 'British' or Irish political context.[88] The existence of an exclusively Irish Jacobite mentality can be gleaned from a systematic examination of a wide array of sources as indicated above. These range from clerical and military correspondence in the Royal archives at Windsor, communications and memoirs of Irish officers in the Archives Nationales, the abundant depositions in official sources and the popular anti-Jacobite press and the poetry of the Irish Jacobite literati.

The neglect of Irish poetry as a source for eighteenth-century Irish history typifies the general treatment of Irish-language sources by historians. Francis John Byrne, one of the leading authorities on early Irish history, has commented that that the sympathetic historian 'must at least pay the subjects of his study the elementary courtesy of learning their language'.[89] James Lydon, the doyen of medieval Ireland, stressed the importance of a grounding in Irish for any Irish historian working up until the modern period, and highly commended the endeavours of the English historian Edmund Curtis who took the trouble to learn Irish.[90] His colleague Louis Cullen, the most prolific eighteenth-century historian of his generation, remarked that 'it is distressing that under-graduates now are unwilling or incompetent to read Irish language material'.[91] On the general neglect of Irish language sources, Kevin Whelan considered it remarkable that there is 'no conception that an understanding of the majority language of the island until the nineteenth century might be a necessary qualification for an Irish historian'.[92] On the matters of historical consciousness, of nationhood

---

86 Leighton, *Catholicism*, introduction, pp 16, 55.   **87** McCoy, 'Local political culture', introduction. **88** Christopher Duffy has found it a matter of great regret that the other Ireland remained all but unknown outside the practitioners of the military history of Ireland; quoted in D'Arcy, 'Exiles and strangers: the case of the Wogans', pp 171-85. See also O'Conor, 'Ireland and Europe', p. 13. Griffin has recently suggested that 'the history of the Irish people in the eighteenth century can be fully understood only in a European context'; Griffin, *Ireland on the continent*, pp 46-7. See also O'Conor, *Irish brigades,* preface, p. vi; Genet-Rouffiac, 'La première generation'.   **89** Quoted in Duffy, *Ireland,* p. 4.   **90** Duffy, 'A real Irish historian', pp 11, 13.   **91** Whelan, 'Watching the detective', p. 11.   **92** Whelan, 'Recent writing of Irish history', p. 30.

and nationality, its antiquity and manifestations, the leading nineteenth-century historian Gearóid Ó Tuathaigh states that 'it is difficult to see how a discussion of cultural or 'national' consciousness in Ireland in the early modern period can be conducted very sensibly by those who cannot comfortably handle sources'.[93] Tomás MacSíomóin has recently provided a Céitinn-like counterblast against the cultural colonisation and post-colonial linguistic apartheid inherent in much Irish history. He rightly deems it to be 'a serious lack in our current dominant historical narratives'. Indeed, he states that 'the linguistic dimension of this process suffers particularly in this regard, being pretty much a "no-go area" as far as the generality of historians are concerned'.[94]

In spite of the continued neglect of Irish-language material, it continues to be fertile ground for the intrepid explorer. The surviving literary output derives from three main areas of Irish and Scottish Gaeldom: firstly, the province of Munster; secondly, Oriel (Oirialla, representing most of the modern counties of Louth, Armagh, Monaghan and parts of Down and Meath); and finally the Mac Donald territories (the Isle of Skye, the outer Hebridies) and mainland Invernesshire in Scotland. The Irish poet remained one of the great reflectors (and to a lesser extent, moulders) of public opinion in Ireland until the close of the eighteenth century. Through the accumulating social, economic and political disasters of the Reformation, Tudor centralisation and anglicisation, the collapse of the Nine Years' War (1594-1603), the Flight of the Earls (1607), the Plantation of Ulster (1609), the 1641 rebellion and the Jacobite wars, he remained close to the heart of Irish political life and retained his role as political chronicler and conscience of the nation.

The importance of Irish poetry as a historical source was stressed as far back as Seathrún Céitinn's *Foras feasa ar Éirinn*. Compiled in the 1630s, it was the first book of the Old Testament of post-Tridentine Irish Catholic nationalist identity, what Hastings would term pre-French Revolutionary Irish nation-alism.[95] It became an invaluable reference book for many eighteenth-century Irish poets. Céitinn justifies his extensive use of poetry as a source for his history and stated that because the bones and marrow of history are found in poems, he deemed it proper to depend on their authority in reference to history:

> Do bhrígh gurab i nduantaibh atá cnáimh agus smior an tseanchusa, measaim gurab oircheas dam cinneadh mar ughdardhás air, ag tráchtadh ar an seanchus.[96]

---

93 Ó Tuathaigh, 'Irish historiographical revisionism', pp 317, 324. The founding fathers of the so-called 'revisionist' school of Irish history have expressed similar views; Lyons, 'The burden of our history', p. 92; Dudley-Edwards, 'An agenda for Irish history', pp 60, 62.   **94** Mac Síomóin. 'The colonised mind – Irish language and society', p. 44.   **95** Hastings, *Construction of nationhood*, pp 85-95.   **96** Quoted in O'Rahilly (eag.), *Five poems*, p. vii. See also Ó Buachalla, *Aisling Ghéar*, p. 513.

Edmund Spenser, one of Céitinn's main whipping-boys, clearly understood the importance of the language question in sixteenth- and seventeenth-century Ireland:

> The wordes are the image of the mynde, so as they proceding from the mynde, the mynde must needes bee affected with the wordes: So that the speech beinge Irishe, the harte must needes be Irishe, for out of the aboundance of the heart the tongue speaketh.[97]

Any attempt to probe the Jacobite mind or minds in the late-seventeenth and eighteenth centuries, or the ideology which it spawned, should at least engage with its literary heritage.

Énrí Ó Muirgheasa, who collected large numbers of poems and songs among the Irish speakers of Ulster, believed that 'the person who would try to understand the life and mentality of Gaelic Ireland during the eighteenth century must put aside the histories, forget all about the Irish parliament and come to live in spirit with McCooey [Art Mac Cumhaigh] and his contemporary poets'.[98] Ó Muirgheasa's advice is particularly relevant in relation to Jacobitism. Irish poets did indeed ignore Dublin and London and their parliaments. Instead, they focused on the machinations of James III and his confederates and prospective allies in Paris, Rome and Madrid and on the battles and sieges of the dynastic wars which ravaged Europe in the first half of the eighteenth century. They knew that it was from there, and not in Dublin, Edinburgh or London that the house of Stuart would be restored.

John Lorne Campbell noted the neglect of Scots-Gaelic sources by Scottish historians in his introduction to his *Highland songs of the '45*: 'It is astonishing that any historian should feel himself properly equipped to write the history of his country while remaining ignorant of the language spoken over half its area'.[99] Campbell pointed out that Scots-Gaelic literature had not been particularly well edited. This has been more than rectified in the last twenty years through the efforts of the Scottish Gaelic Texts Society. The same gap could not be said to exist in Irish literature due to the trojan endeavours of Risteard Ó Foghludha, Tadhg Ó Donnchadha, Pádraig Ua Duinnín, Énrí Ó Muirgheasa and a host of editors of the Irish Texts Society volumes. Little of this poetry has appeared in translation or has been properly appraised in a historical context. Thus, for instance, R.A. Breatnach apologised for even discussing the historical background in his survey of eighteenth-century poetry.[100] In more recent times, Cornelius Buttimer notes that 'the period 1700-1850 is the best documented phase of the Gaelic literary tradition' but adds that 'it is the least understood' and

---

97 Spenser, *View of state of Ireland*, quoted in Mac Síomóin, 'The colonised mind – Irish language and society', p. 47. **98** Ó Muirgheasa (eag.), *Amhráin Airt Mhic Chobhthaigh*, p. xxv. **99** Campbell (ed.), *Songs of the '45*, introduction, p. xviii. **100** Breatnach, 'The end of a tradition', p. 129.

lacks 'the informed critical commentary which one might expect for such a significant era'.[101] Ó Tuathaigh also lamented the lack of an integrated narrative of Irish poetry.[102] A basic chronological account of Irish politics between the 1690s and the 1760s allows us to examine the extent to which the Stuart claimant loomed large in the Irish Catholic and Protestant consciousness, in a manner which is beyond the confines of a more thematic approach. Much of the greater Catholic populace had little access to other aspects of the popular media such as newspapers and pamphlets. Internal and continental communication had obvious dangers. Poetry, therefore, was the principal medium through which Irish Catholics could articulate and disseminate their political sentiments with relative impunity. The fact that Jacobitism provides the dominant theme in surviving eighteenth-century Irish poetry has obvious implications for its survival among Irish Catholics. Ó Buachalla has made the same point, noting that while the Jacobite ideology manifested itself through many media in Britain, in pamphlets, sermons, orations, books, ballads (or indeed through iconography glass and and touch-pieces) it manifested itself in Ireland through the single medium of poetry:

> Ní hionadh sin freisin, mar bíodh gur saothraíodh an reitric Sheac-aibíteach i bhfoirmeacha difriúla (paimfléid, seanmóirí, óráideanna, leabhair, bailéid etc.) sa Bhreatain; in Éirinn bhí an reitric sin taobh, ar an mhórgóir, le haon mhéan amháin – véarsaíocht .[103]

The utilisation of Irish poetry as an historical source presents some difficulties. Monod underlined the lack of interest shown by historians in English political poetry. Having considered its advantages and disadvantages as a reflection of the 'voice of the people', he argued that 'to be silent on the subject of Jacobite poetry is to ignore a whole industry'.[104] Ó Fiaich stressed this same point in his 1973 edition of Art Mac Cumhaigh's poetry:

> Níor fhág pobal Gaelach an 18ú haois mórán scríbhinní ina ndiaidh seachas a gcuid filíochta; cuid mhór de na doiciméidí i mBéarla a bhain leo scriosadh iad i 1922. Na tuairiscí mar gheall orthu a d'fhág cuairteoirí ar Éirinn ina ndiaidh tá de mhíbhuntaiste acu gur mhinic a bhí teorann chreidimh nó teorann teanga idir a lucht scríofa agus an gnáthmhuintir.[105]

The thematic and ideological similarities between Irish, Scots-Gaelic and English Jacobite literature are striking and give further credence to Erskine-Hill's

101 Buttimer, 'An Irish text on the War of Jenkins's ear', p. 75.   102 Ó Tuathaigh, 'Hyde and the Hidden Ireland'.   103 Ó Buachalla, *Aisling Ghéar*, p. 333. See also ibid., pp 347, 555-6.   104 Monod, *Jacobitism* , p. 47.   105 Ó Fiaich (eag.), *Mac Cumhaigh*, p. 51.

concept of a 'rhetoric of Jacobitism'.[106] Common themes in Jacobite verse centre around the questions of hereditary right, the right of the lawful prince, disdain for the corrupting influence of foreigners and the inevitability of a Stuart restoration as the only solution to the nation's problems. Vincent Morley has recently compared Irish and Scots-Gaelic verse. He emphasises the contrasting political environments of the two areas. In particular, he noted the absence of bitter religious invective and overt nationalist sentiment in the Scots-Gaelic verse. Scots-Gaelic Jacobitism was a narrowly conceived ideology founded on the single issue of dynastic loyalty, while Irish verse shows the evolution from Jacobitism to Jacobinism.[107]

Daniel Corkery stressed that the Scottish poems were 'simple, homely, direct and that they were written to and about a living man on whom living eyes had rested with affection'.[108] Although the messianic cult of the Stuart prince provided a central theme to the Irish Jacobite literary genre, James III was a real and influential figure in popular political, ecclesiastical and literary circles for over fifty years.[109] Irish Jacobites were neither politically nor ideologically detached from their exiled brethren in Europe, or their Gaelic counterparts in Scotland. This is evident in their reaction to the changing fortunes of European Jacobite diplomacy, and the reporting of particular events that were likely to have implications for the Stuarts. Pittock and Donaldson have identified the importance of the Jacobite literary tradition in the development of the modern Scottish identity. Similarly the poetry of Douglas Hyde showed the extent to which the themes and messianic messages of Jacobite poetry could be evoked by Defenders, United Irishmen, Fenians and Sinn Féiners.[110]

One of the longest-running debates in eighteenth-century Irish historical studies has been the controversy surrounding Corkery's *Hidden Ireland* published in 1924. This has relevance for the use of Irish poetry as a historical source and the importance of Jacobite ideology. According to Cullen, Corkery's thesis was 'long established as an aspect of the interpretation of the eighteenth-century economic and social history of Ireland'.[111] Despite Cullen's much-quoted challenge to Corkery, the *Hidden Ireland* still has merit: eighteenth-century Irish historians have too readily used Cullen's challenge to Corkery's thesis to justify

---

106 Erskine-Hill, 'Literature and the Jacobite cause', pp 49-70; Pittock, *Poetry*; Mac Craith, 'Filíocht Sheacaibíteach', pp 57-75. **107** Morley, 'Idé-eolaíocht an tSeacaibíteachais in Éirinn agus in Albain', pp 14-24. **108** Corkery, *Hidden Ireland*, p. 130. Ó Buachalla takes issue with this opinion; Ó Buachalla, *Aisling Ghéar*, p. 417. For a general biographical note on Corkery; Connolly (ed.), *Oxford companion*, p. 321. **109** Ó Buachalla, 'An mheisiasacht is an aisling', pp 72-87. **110** Ó Tuathaigh, 'Hyde and the Hidden Ireland'; Pittock, *Poetry*, pp 207-42; Donaldson, *Jacobite song, political myth and national identity*, passim; O'Riordan, *Gaelic mind*, pp 7-8. One could add Thomas Davis, Charles Gavan-Duffy, Patrick Pearse, Thomas MacDonagh, Joseph Plunkett and Alice Milligan to those influenced by eighteenth-century Irish Jacobite literature. Indeed, Ó Buachalla suggests that it was not Tone or Connolly who shaped the Irish nation but the Stuarts, even if it was unknown to themselves; Ó Buachalla, *Aisling Ghéar*, p. 658. **111** Corkery, *Hidden Ireland*; for appraisal, see Cullen, *Hidden Ireland: a reassessment*, pp vii, 1.

ignoring Irish sources.[112] As for Jacobitism, it has remained as hidden to Irish historians as it was when Corkery first took up his pen in its cause. It is indeed ironic that Corkery's failure to explain the term 'Protestant Ascendancy' should serve as a launching pad for McCoy's most recent examination of the Protestant Ascendancy mind, while the original intention of Corkery's work remains lost on many Irish historians.[113]

Some of Cullen's criticisms are valid but they need to be modified, particularly in the light of the general consensus among English and Scottish historians regarding the significance of Jacobitism as a political ideology until at least 1750.[114] Difficulties do arise in assessing the real level of political alienation outlined in Jacobite 'aislingí' (allegorical poetry) and political verse. Nevertheless, a failure to utilise this literature as a means of exploring the eighteenth-century Irish Catholic mentality magnifies the dangers of reading Irish history from exclusively English-language sources and state-papers. Cullen has recently conceded that 'in a fresh look at the Hidden Ireland, politicisation would merit more attention than it received in my 1969 paper'.[115] Other scholars have highlighted the importance of literary sources for eighteenth-century Irish history studies. Ó Buachalla argues that too much attention has been directed to official state documents to the neglect of other sources, literary works, newspapers and ballads.[116] Ó Tuathaigh takes the view that these poems 'deserve closer scrutiny as they are, in many ways, all that we have of the voice of Gaelic Ireland in the eighteenth and early-nineteenth century'.[117] These observations highlight the need to move away from the preoccupation with, and exclusive reliance upon, 'official' manuscripts. Although no serious scholar would underestimate their importance it is becoming clear that there are more varied sources for the history of eighteen-century Ireland.[118]

Cullen's claim that many well-to-do Catholics disassociated themselves from the Stuart cause must be balanced against the real fears of those Catholics who struggled to retain their lands in the face of penal laws, Protestant discoverers, and the opportunism of those who converted to Protestantism. The suspect political loyalty of the latter group fascinated their Whig and Jacobite contemporaries and has come under the scholarly scrutiny of none other than Cullen

---

112 Connolly suggests that Cullen's reassessment offered 'a powerful critique of the limitations of Corkery's Gaelic literary sources as a guide to the realities of economic and social relationships'; Connolly, 'Approaches to Irish popular culture', p. 84. Nevertheless Cullen himself writes (in his 1988 reprint) that 'apart from the validity or otherwise of Corkery's concept, the use of literary material as historical evidence has considerable relevance to the historian's task in describing men and conditions as they were in their own times'; Cullen, *Hidden Ireland: a reassessment*, p. 4. For a recent retraction of his dismissal of the Hidden Ireland, see Connolly, 'Eighteenth-century Ireland', in Boyce and O'Day, *Modern Irish historiography*, p. 28.   113 McCoy, 'Local political culture', introduction.   114 Ó Buachalla's review of Cruickshanks and Black, p. 189.   115 Cullen, *Hidden Ireland: a reassessment*, p. 48.   116 Ó Buachalla, 'Seacaibíteachas', pp 30-1; Ó Buachalla, *Aisling Ghéar*, pp 333, 555-6.   117 Ó Tuathaigh, 'Gaelic Ireland, popular politics and Daniel O'Connell', p. 29.   118 The best recent survey of the new departures in eighteenth-century Irish history is Barnard, 'Farewell to Old Ireland', pp 309-28.

himself.[119] His choice of the work of the Irish poets Peadar Ó Doirnín, Piaras Mac Gearailt and Eoghan Rua Ó Súilleabháin as representative examples of Irish diffidence towards the Stuart prince cannot be taken as sufficient to undermine the political dimension of the 'aisling'. Despite Ó Doirnín's apparent disparagement of the Stuarts, they feature in many of his poems, which shows the extent to which they and their activities retained the attention of his peers. Even his satirical 'Tá bearád i Londain' appreciated the workings of European politics and the obligation of Ó Doirnín to address the Jacobite issue. Similarly, Piaras Mac Gearailt's retrospective criticism of the 'aisling' in 1767, eight years after Quiberon Bay (the last threatened Stuart invasion in 1759) runs counter to his earlier zeal for the fallen dynasty. Eoghan Rua's indications that the messianic dimensions of the 'aisling' should not be taken seriously were more a reaction to the not entirely misplaced confidence of his predecessors that deliverance was at hand. Eoghan Rua himself straddles the period between the Jacobite twilight and the explosion of the United Irishmen onto the political scene. By this time Irish literary figures such as Mícheál Óg Ó Longáin, Miles Byrne and Charles Teeling finally managed to divert the attentions of 'Gráinne Mhaol' (Ireland) from her 'Buachaill Bán' (Charles Edward).[120]

A close perusal of the 'aislingí' and other political poetry composed in the eighteenth century, particularly in the context of Irish, British and European politics, reveals that its Jacobite content was more than vacuous literary rhetoric. Although Cullen noted that the verse yearned for restoration and not revolution, the crucial point surely is that a return of the Stuarts represented the only realistic option for many Irish Catholics until the 1760s.[121] Cullen's other main criticism of the 'Hidden Ireland' rests on his assessment of the 'aisling' as merely a literary motif, lacking substantive political significance.[122] This criticism, however, leaves some questions unanswered. If this poetry was void of political content and confined to the upper classes of the literati, how does one explain its utilisation of the popular 'amhrán' metre, its transmission throughout Ireland in the oral and scribal traditions, and its employment of imported Jacobite airs such as 'The king shall enjoy his own again', 'Bonny Dundee', 'The White Cockade', 'Charlie come over the water' and 'Over the hills and far away'?[123] The poetic tradition became much more 'democratically-minded' after Aogán Ó Rathaille,

119 Cullen, 'Catholics under the penal laws', p. 32. See also Whelan, *Tree of liberty*, p. 6; Power, 'Converts', in Power and Whelan (ed.), *Endurance and emergence*, pp 101-28. **120** Cullen, *Emergence of modern Ireland*, p. 198; idem., *Hidden Ireland: a reassessment*, pp 10, 49. **121** Cullen, *Hidden Ireland: a reassessment*, p. 16. Michelle O'Riordan provides another recent analysis of the Hidden Ireland and the relationship between Irish history and literary criticism; O'Riordan, 'Historical perspectives', pp 73-82; idem., *Gaelic mind*, p. 301. See also Ó Buachalla, 'An mheisiasacht', pp 72-87; Ó Tuama, *Cúirt, tuath agus bruachbhaile*, pp 57-84. **122** Cullen, *Hidden Ireland: a reassessment*, pp 48-9; Having made an exception for the 1744-5 period, Cullen dismisses the Munster aisling as 'something of a mirage'; Cullen, 'Catholics under the penal laws', p. 32. See also Leighton, *Catholicism*, pp 55-7; O'Donoghue, 'Jacobite threat', p. 33. **123** Breatnach, 'Oral and written transmissions of poetry', pp 57-67.

as the poet increasingly functioned as the self-appointed spokesman of his peers.[124] Moreover, throughout the eighteenth century, much of Irish and Scottish-Gaelic poetic culture had a toasting and drinking dimension; the poetry was often addressed to Ireland in her various female guises, or to her aristocracy, gentry or people. The poets continually acted as media for the transmission of English war-news and the dramatic quality of the 'aisling' resembled an embryonic form of street theatre.[125]

Wading through dusty manuscripts and printed volumes of these poems, it is easy to forget that they were not composed as historical source-material. In editing two hundred Ulster songs, Ó Muirgheasa rightly remarked that they were not composed for reading but for recital and they are now without the music as a widow is without her husband:

> Chan le h-aghaidh léightheoireachta acht le h-aghaidh ceoltóireachta a cumadh na h-amhráin seo, agus níl ionnta mar tá siad annseo ná focla gan na fuinn – ach mar bheadh baintreabhach ann a mbéadh a céile pósta caillte aicí.[126]

The convergence of the Gaelic elite and folk culture is borne out in the more populist metre of contemporary poetic composition, and its survival in the midst of social deprivation. As Pittock has suggested: 'those who wished to defend a peculiarly Scottish (or Irish) high culture were forced into an alliance with their own folk culture as the only alternative to surrender to the standards of the British state'.[127] Ó Buachalla coined his memorable hierarchical analogy of three generations from a king to a spade ('trí ghlúin ó rí go ramhainn'), to represent the socio-economic decline of the literati in seventeenth-century Ireland – from Ó Bruadair through Ó Rathaille and Mac Cuarta to the hedge school-masters and scribes Ó Doirnín and Eoghan Rua Ó Súilleabháin.[128]

The bias towards Scottish airs in Irish Jacobite song added a pan-Gaelic dimension to Irish Jacobitism.[129] The form and metre of this poetry suggests that it was composed for a popular audience. Moreover, a cursory study of its content contradicts the opinion that it does not have a political dimension.[130] That popular songs are worthy of examination for political content is demonstrated in Zimmerman's collection of political ballads, or indeed by the popular ballad-culture of the nineteenth and twentieth-century loyalist and nationalist tradi-tions.[131] The nineteenth-century antiquarian T. Crofton-Croker made the

---

124 Leerssen, *Mere Irish*, pp 274-5.　125 See Ó Buachalla, *Aisling Ghéar*, pp 413-25, 604-13.　126 Ó Muirgheasa (eag.), *Dhá chéad*, réamhrá.　127 Pittock, *Poetry*, pp 6, 37; Culley, *Hidden Ireland: a reassessment*, pp 16-17.　128 Ó Buachalla (eag.), *Peadar Ó Doirnín*, p. 25.　129 de Blácam, *Gaelic literature surveyed*, p. 316. For Scottish airs in the English tradition; Monod, *Jacobitism*, p. 48.　130 I have not sought to discuss at any great length poetic *genres* or metres.　131 Zimmerman, *Songs of Irish rebellion*.

following astute observation: 'The songs of the people are always worthy of attention and it appears to me extraordinary that the most positive treason should for so long have been published without notice'.[132] Ó Muirgheasa attacked those who dismissed the political content of Irish poetry and song when he stated that the person who cannot see in these songs anything but harmless 'come all yes' is not only blind, but blind as the sole of your boot:

> Agus an duine nach dtig leis féiceáil ins na ceoltaí seo ach cineál 'come all ye', tá sé níos mó ná bheith caoch – tá sé chomh dall le bun do bhróige.[133]

Monod, Chapman and Pittock have stressed the importance of the street-singer in the Jacobite ideology of Scotland and England. It is unlikely that eighteenth-century Ireland would have been different, particularly in view of the importance of the oral tradition and because of the fact that it was one of the few media at their disposal for the articulation of Jacobite sentiment.[134]

Historians should not dismiss the repetitive rhetoric of the poem, song and sermon without attempting to integrate such material into the context of Irish, British and European politics, or to compare it to contemporary pan-Jacobite or Whig literature. The very fact that such Jacobite or anti-Jacobite rhetoric continually resounded from the pulpit, press or pew, or was fixedly rooted in the repertoire of the poet, is indicative of its popularity among audiences. It is also a further demonstration of the survival of the Stuart king as *bête-noire* and *messiah* in Irish political life for the first part of the eighteenth century. The reactions of the Irish poets to European affairs find almost identical reflections in the Protestant press, pamphlets and sermons. Nevertheless the political content of the poetry of the late eighteenth- and early-nineteenth-century poets Eoghan Rua Ó Súilleabháin, Tomás Ó Míocháin, Mícheál Óg Ó Longáin and Antoine Ó Raiftearaí has been effectively neglected. In spite of this, the frequently quoted narratives of Mrs Mary Delany and even Arthur Young are likely to contain less insight into Irish politics and the forces that shaped it.[135]

One characteristic of eighteenth-century Irish history that is demonstrated throughout this work is the close relationship between Irish Jacobite poets and the Catholic clergy. This has implications for the close links between Jacobitism,

132 Crofton-Croker, *Researches*, p. 329.   133 Ó Muirgheasa (eag.), *Dhá chéad*, réamhrá. Leerssen makes a similar point in relation to Moore's *Melodies* which are often seen as light-weight ditties. He stated that 'some of them did pack a political punch and evinced an uncowed and enduring sense of Irish national separateness'; Leerssen, *Remembrance and imagination*, pp 79, 82, 162-3.   134 Pittock, *Poetry*, p. 5; Chapman, 'Jacobite argument, pp 175, 203-4; Monod, *Jacobitism*, p. 47; Breatnach, 'Oral and written transmissions of poetry', pp 60-4; Sherry, 'Press coverage of political trials', p. 148; McCoy, 'Local political culture', p. 63.   135 Ó Muirithe (eag.), *Ó Míocháin*; Ó Donnchadha (eag.), *Ó Longáin*; Ó Coigligh (eag.), *Raiftearaí*. The severely sceptical attitude that some historians have adopted towards Irish poetry as a historical source contrasts with their uncritical use of the travel narratives of such monoglot and sometimes hostile outsiders.

Catholicism and the penal laws. Priest-poets such as Liam Inglis, Seán Ó Briain, Conchubhar Ó Briain, Domhnall Ó Colmáin and Uilliam Mac Néill Bhacaigh Ó hIarlaithe were the heirs of Seathrún Céitinn and Pádraigín Haicéad who had emerged as major political voices in the seventeenth century.[136] They promoted the Stuart cause, which was an intrinsic feature of Irish Catholic nationalist identity until at least 1760.[137] The Catholic church stepped into the breach created by the effective destruction of the Catholic aristocracy to patronise these formidable exponents and moulders of public opinion. The poets steadfastly supported their exiled king and outlawed church. The church appreciated their loyalty and, as Fr Conchubhar Mac Cairteáin recorded in his preface to the unpublished 'Agallamh na bhFíoraon', held it to be a national and spiritual duty to patronise the native culture.[138]

The Irish Catholic clergy's influence on the main themes and the diffusion of literary output throughout the greater Catholic community had consequence for the popularisation of the sentiments expressed in Irish literature. Although historians have neglected the seditious and treasonable output of Jacobite poetry, at least three poets were prosecuted for composing seditious verse, and a number of others expressed fears of prosecution. The allegorical language and cryptic nature of Irish verse presumably shielded many others, and the knowledge of Scots-Gaelic and Irish among the Scottish Presbyterian population of Ulster might be advanced as another reason why Ulster showed less enthusiasm than Munster for the exiled Stuarts.[139] Like its Scottish and English counterparts, Jacobite poetry in Ireland operated at two levels, and the educated ear knew exactly who the poet meant when he referred to 'The Blackbird', 'The Shepherd', 'The Little Branch' or 'The White-backed Heifer'.[140] That the bilingual poet based much of his political verse on material from local news-sheets shows his role in the diffusion of international war-news to an Irish-speaking public.

136 The most accessible examination of the relationship between literati and clergy in the eighteenth century are Ó Fiaich, 'Irish poetry and the clergy', pp 30-56 and Heussaf, *Filí agus cléir san ochtú haois déag*, passim. **137** For the purpose of this study I would agree with Seán Connolly's explanation of the difference between 'national consciousness, an awareness of belonging to one nationality or another, and nationalism, a political philosophy and programme for action built around the proposition that national consciousness finds its only proper expression in the achievement of a nation-state'; Connolly (ed.), *Oxford companion*, pp 378-9. I would also strongly subscribe to Adrian Hasting's opinion that 'if nationalism became theoretically central to western political thinking in the nineteenth century, it existed as a powerful reality in some places long before that'; Hastings, *The construction of nationhood*, p. 4; chapter 1. **138** MacCairteáin, 'Preface to Agallamh na bhFíoraon', in *Iris leabhar Muighe Nuadhad* (1913), p. 35, quoted in Breatnach, 'The end of a tradition', p. 133. See also Fenning, *Irish Dominican province*, p. 57; Ó Fiaich, 'Irish poetry and the clergy', pp 30-56. **139** In a recent biography of William Neilson, the Presbyterian Gaelic grammarian, Séamus Ó Saothraí has shown that five Scottish-born Scots-Gaelic-speaking Presbyterians preached and ministered in the meeting house in Dundalk. Native and bilingual speakers of Irish such as Neilson and his father Moses preached to Scots-Gaelic settlers and converts in Armagh, Down, Tyrone and Monaghan; Ó Saothraí, *An Ministir Gaelach*, pp 21-8; Ó Ciardha, 'review of Ó Saothraí, *An Ministir Gaelach*', pp 481-3. **140** Erskine-Hill, 'Literature and the Jacobite cause', pp 49-70; McCaughey, review of Cruickshanks, pp 113-15. Ó Buachalla makes the same point in relation to a poem by the Munster Jacobite poet Eoghan an Mhéirín Mac Cárthaigh in which

The 'Hidden Ireland' theory has also been the subject of recent criticism by Nicholas Canny. He contends that 'enthusiasts', eager to trace Ireland's nineteenth and twentieth-century 'restless dominion' status back through the seventeenth and eighteenth centuries, have used 'a Hidden Ireland of Irish literary and spiritual leaders to cultivate the concept of an Irish independence to attain these objectives by political means'.[141] Canny correctly warns against the teleological tendencies of the later republican and nationalist historiographical traditions, and questions the utility of nineteenth-century ballads and songs as historical sources. His commendation of recent revisionist historiography as disinfecting the received historical wisdom does not warn of the dangers of falling into the same trap as the 'enthusiasts'. The 'Hidden Ireland' and the historical usefulness of seventeenth and eighteenth-century Irish poetry cannot be ignored by the historian of Irish Jacobitism. A close examination of the activities of a treasonable Irish Jacobite episcopate and clergy, who owed their ecclesiastical dignities and secular allegiance to their Stuart master in Rome, shows that they did not cultivate Irish 'independence', but loyalty to the regal rights and pretensions of the exiled Stuart.

The neglect of poetry by historians has also been compounded by an overemphasis on its most despairing and unrealistic aspects. Canny, for instance, has judged it as being 'deeply pessimistic in its outlook'.[142] There is certainly evidence of dejection in some of the poetry. This pessimism was more than offset by optimism, centred upon the Irish Brigades in the service of France and Spain between the conclusion of the Williamite wars and the 1750s. This literary conceit reflected a political ideology which, although often idealistic or unrealistic, remained central to the politics of the former Stuart kingdom until the 1760s. Jacobitism dimmed and flickered rhythmically with the ups and downs of the diplomatic fortunes of the house of Stuart. The tradition was never totally extinguished but smouldered until it was transformed by the explosive conflagrations of the 1790s. By this time, Irish popular political consciousness made the transition from Jacobite to Jacobin and 'Bony' (Bonaparte), and later Daniel O'Connell, replaced the 'Bonny Prince' as the darling of the popular political consciousness.

he mentions 'the child' (Charles Edward); Ó Buachalla, *Aisling Ghéar*, p. 414. For a list of these popular literary pseudonyms for the Stuart, ibid., p. 556; see also Ch. 3, pp 170-1, fns. 240-52. **141** Canny, 'Irish resistance to empire', pp 288-9. **142** Canny, ' Formation of the Gaelic mind', p. 111.

CHAPTER I

'Caithréim Shéamais' agus 'Séamas an Chaca':[1] Irish Jacobitism, 1684-90

The 'Williamite War', 'the Jacobite War' the 'War of the two kings' or cogadh an dá rí' has often been portrayed as little more than an insular side-show in the continuing international conflict between Louis XIV and the forces of the League of Augsburg, or, as Canny phrases it, 'a struggle between two armies brought into the country from outside'.[2] While this presentation has obvious merits, it can diminish the insular dimension of the war, thereby minimising its dramatic impact on the Irish people.[3] Similarly, the excessive emphasis on the war itself has over-shadowed contemporary attitudes towards the Jacobite succession and the level of popular participation in the war effort in the late 1680s and early 1690s.[4] The first section of this chapter explores the contrasting effects of the Jacobite succession on the Irish Catholic and Protestant communities. Having considered the structure of Irish Jacobitism, it will show how the political events in England, Scotland and Europe created the conditions for Richard Talbot, earl of Tyrconnell's catholicisation of the Irish army in the era preceding the Williamite invasion of Ireland. Tyrconnell's decision to defy the new Williamite regime in London, and King James's French-sponsored invasion of Ireland, encouraged the popular mobilisation of the Irish Jacobite nation in the late 1680s and early 1690s, sponsored by the Catholic clerical, aristocratic and gentrified elite.

Although rapparees have featured luridly in the many military histories of the war, their political and military origins in the 1680s as a manifestation of popular Jacobitism have received less attention. The emphasis that contemporary Whig writers placed on the predatory, apolitical aspects of rapparee activity has obscured its Jacobite dimension. Historians have too readily accepted these prejudicial testimonies or viewed the rapparee as an Irish

---

1 Dáibhí Ó Bruadair, 'Caithréim an dara Séamais', in MacErlean (eag.), *Duanaire*, iii, pp 78-80; Ó Buachalla (eag.), 'Briseadh na Bóinne', p. 84. 2 Canny, 'Irish resistance to empire', p. 290. 3 These are ritually re-enacted by Unionists on the streets of Ulster and by their nationalist counterparts in dances such as 'The siege of Ennis' and the 'Walls of Limerick'. 4 Simms, *Jacobite Ireland*; Maguire (ed.), *Kings in conflict*; Doherty, *The Williamite war*. There is little emphasis in either of these works on ideology, popular attitudes to or popular participation in the war.

variant of the Hobsbawmian bandit. Section two traces the origins, evolution and nature of rapparee activity in the late 1680s and early 1690s. The close links between rapparee activity and the Jacobite war-effort became the most visible manifestation of popular Jacobitism in the Irish countryside. The Williamite army's tendency to kill hundreds, if not thousands, of Jacobites and innocent civilians as rapparees, and the government's propensity to levy crippling fines locally where rapparee activity occurred, cemented their close association with the greater Catholic community. A re-appraisal of rappareeism as a principal facet of popular Jacobite activity in the period serves as a background to the association between rappareeism, Jacobitism and the wider Catholic community which would long survive the 1690s.

The Irish poetic caste had declared their allegiance to the Stuarts on the accession of the Stuart dynasty to the thrones of the three kingdoms in 1603.[5] They remained steadfast throughout the trauma of the Interregnum and the recurring hysteria of the popish plot (1679) during the latter part of the reign of Charles II. Their verse showed that, after the exclusion crisis (1681) had been finally settled, the accession of James II ushered in a new era of hope for Irish Catholics.[6] The last section takes an analytical approach to the surviving literary sources, ranging from the 'court' poetry of the Munster poets Dáibhí Ó Bruadair and Diarmuid Mac Sheáin Bhuí Mac Cárthaigh, to the popular poems and laments of the folk-tradition. Consideration is also given to the cult of James II, which transformed itself from the messianic prince of Ó Bruadair's verse to the 'cowardly shite' of popular memory.[7]

I

In the period between the Jacobite succession (1685) and the outbreak of the war (1689), Irish Catholics and Protestants had an equally acute awareness of the prospect of a sharp reversal in their political fortunes. Post-succession popular dissension manifested itself in the immediate aftermath of the duke of Monmouth's (Charles II's natural son's) rebellion and precipitated a polarisation of political opinion on the eve of the war of the two kings.[8] Raymond Gillespie's examination of the relationship between Irish Protestants and James II propounds the view that Protestants remained loyal to him until after the Battle of

---

5 The 'Irish' lineage, to which the literati constantly referred in their fabricated genealogies of the Stuart kings (reaching back to the mythical Irish king Fergus), ensured that royalism remained a constant theme in seventeenth-and eighteenth-century poetry and prose; O'Flaherty, *Ogygia*, p. xiii; 'Address of Burghers of Kilkenny to James II', 22 Mar. 1689 (*H.M.C., Ormond*, vii, p. 389); Ó Buachalla, 'Na Stíobhartaigh agus an t-aos léinn', pp 81-134; idem, 'James our true king', pp 7-35; idem, *Aisling Ghéar*, pp 1-66; Murphy, 'Royalist Ireland', pp 589-604. 6 O'Callaghan (ed.), *Macariae*, p.15. 7 Ó Buachalla (eag.), 'Briseadh na Bóinne', p. 84. See below, pp 82-4. 8 Simms, 'The war of the two kings', p. 483 (T.C.D., Ms. 2055). See also U.L., Cambs. Add. Ms 1[c], fol. 64.

ie They were Hiberno-centric rather than British patriots

the Boyne.[9] Irish Protestant inaction during Monmouth's rebellion and the ninth earl of Argyll's invasion and their unwillingness to embrace William's cause until after his victory at the Boyne are used to justify his central thesis. He discounts evidence of accumulating sectarian tension in the period immediately after the Jacobite succession and the large concentration of military personnel in Ulster during unrest in England and Scotland. It should also be pointed out that it was unlikely that Irish Protestants would show their hand until King William had moved against the Jacobite regime in Ireland and showed his new subjects that he had a reasonable chance of winning, or until they were driven into his arms by the machinations of the Jacobite parliament which attempted to overthrow the Acts of Settlement, the bedrock of Protestant hegemony in Ireland.

An undercurrent of opposition to the new Catholic king had survived from the popish plot and exclusion crisis. Political opportunism among prominent Protestant political and religious figures in the post-war period, the obsessive emphasis on the heroics of Derry and Enniskillen in Protestant historiography and the influence of William King's *State of the Protestants* (published to justify Protestant abandonment of James II by citing his inability to protect his heretofore loyal Irish Protestant subjects) has ensured that this opposition has often gone largely undetected.[10]

The depuritanisation of the army and militia initiated under the lord deputy-ship of Richard, first earl of Arran, bore out his father's (the duke of Ormond's) longstanding distrust of the Ulster Presbyterians. It also demonstrated that the house of Stuart had sufficiently recovered its nerve after the popish plot and the exclusion crisis to harry its traditional enemies.[11] Nonetheless, news of the treasonable activities of 'non-conformists' and 'fanatics' continued to reach Whitehall. These reports had some foundation. In spite of his contempt for Ulster 'fanatics', Ormond would never have exaggerated Protestant disaffection to play into the hands of his increasingly influential adversary, Richard Talbot, earl of Tyrconnell, later James's lord deputy of Ireland.[12]

Although many Irish Protestants reacted positively to James's succession, it caused unease in some Ulster circles. Reporting from Newtownstewart, County Tyrone, in July 1685, William Stewart (Lord Mountjoy) reported that although the surrounding country remained quiet, the inhabitants were 'not quiet themselves'; the accidental burning of the Protestant citadel of Enniskillen had 'put them in great fear and makes many not sleep in their beds'.[13] The troop

9 Gillespie, 'Irish Protestants and James II', pp 124-34. 10 Dickson, *New foundations*; Bartlett, *Fall and rise* 11 Arran to Massereene, 4 July 1683 (Bodl., Carte Ms 40, fol. 94). See also N.L.I., Ms 2432, fol. 21; Bodl., Carte Ms 217, fol. 85; Gillespie, 'Irish Protestants and James II', p. 125. 12 Ormond to Sunderland, 10 Dec. 1684 (N.L.I., Ms 2441, fol. 103). See also Bodl., Carte Ms 216, fols 149, 155, 161, 164, 174, 188; N.L.I., Ms 2441, fol. 247; N.L.I., Ms 476, fol. 295. 13 Mountjoy to [Ormond?], Newtownstewart, 26 July 1685 (Bodl., Carte Ms 217, fols 220-1). Gillespie seems to contradict his central thesis that Protestants did not turn from James II en masse until after the Boyne when he states 'that it was not certain that the Protestants would respect James II's succession' and that

movements throughout Ireland, particularly in Ulster, and the backlash against potential rebels in the wake of the Monmouth and Argyll rebellions in England and Scotland heightened tension between the two communities.[14] Protestants increasingly became the victims of Catholic witch-hunts, especially through alleged treasonable utterances against James while he was still duke of York. Archbishop King claimed that 'no sooner had they [Irish Catholics] gotten judges and juries that would believe them but they began a trade of swearing and ripping up what they [the Catholics] pretended they [the Protestants] had said of his late majesty, whilst duke of York some years before'[15] One such incident in February 1685, immediately after James's succession, resulted in a fracas between William Warnock and Turlough O'Donnilie of Castlecaulfield, County Tyrone. Warnock allegedly called the new king 'a popish knave who would headon [heathen] us all'.[16] These retrospective treason charges concerned the new lord lieutenant, Henry Hyde, earl of Clarendon, because it caused a great 'damp' and 'uneasiness' 'in so much as many do every day go out of the kingdom'. He advised the king to 'quiet men's minds' by the issue of a proclamation 'whereby an end might be put to all the prosecutions for words pretended to be spoken many years since, which would contribute as much as any to make men easy at home'.[17]

Continued accusations of treason against Protestants, proclamations preventing treasonable words against the king and the resulting sectarian disquiet finally culminated in the total disarming of the Protestant militia. These had been arrayed, in King James's own words, 'in consequence of Otes' [Titus Oates] pretended plot'.[18] However, this disarmament policy encouraged an upsurge of

'Lord Mountjoy later contrasted the fear of his succession with the peacefulness of the event itself'; Gillespie, 'Irish Protestants and James II', p. 127.   **14** For example, see *C.S.P.D., J. II*, pp 113, 132, 137, 145, 152); Dickson, *New foundations*, p. 26. *Twenty-third report of the Deputy-keeper*, pp 41-2; Clarke (ed.), *Life of James II*, ii, p. 60; N.L.I., Ms 2443, fols. 309, 377; *H.M.C., Ormond*, vii, pp 377, 390; N.L.I., Ms 2444, fols 53, 229; N.L.I., Ms 2445, fols 7, 105, 201, 207; N.L.I., Ms 1793, fol. 205; Bodl., Carte Ms 217, fols 137, 144, 158, 160, 168, 173-4, 188, 202, 206, 208, 220; Connolly, *Religion*, p. 36; *Clarendon letters*, i, pp 33, 351; ii, pp 72, 84-6, 89, 114; Bodl., Carte Ms 229, fol. 324; *Anal. Hib.*, xxvii (1972), p. 175; xxxii (1985), pp 39-41); *H.M.C., Ormond*, viii, pp 343, 346, 351, 354; Wettenall, *Hexepla Jacobaea*, pp 11, 13-14; *A full and impartial account of the secret consults*, p. 49; Miller, *James II*, pp 211-12.   **15** King, *State of the Protestants*, p. 100. See also ibid., pp 161-2; N.L.I., Ms 1793, fols 211, 218-19; *H.M.C., Ormond*, viii, p. 344.   **16** The examination of Coronet Andrew Graham of Castlecaulfield, 2 Mar. 1685 (Bodl., Carte Ms 217, fols 119-20). A man was arrested for speaking traitorous words at the proclamation of James II. Elsewhere, a Presbyterian minister preached that the accession of a Catholic king removed bonds of loyalty and invited rebellion. The proclamation of James's succession was torn down in Belfast; Gillespie, 'Irish Protestants and James II', pp 127-8.   **17** Clarendon to the king, 22 June 1686, in *Clarendon letters*, i, p. 278. Contemporary correspondence contains other instances of seditious words against the king; ibid., i, pp 67, 78, 83, 120; B.L., Add. Ms 15, 894, fol. 77; *C.S.P.D., 1685, J. II*, p. 90; *H.M.C., Ormond*, viii, p. 440; *H.M.C., Egmont*, i, app iii, p. 369; Miller, *James II*, p. 173; Connolly, *Religion*, p. 36.   **18** *Twenty-third report of the Deputy-keeper*, pp 41-3. Also see Leslie, *An answer*, p. 75; King, *State of the Protestants*, pp 100-102; *Anal. Hib.*, xxvii (1972), pp 175, 178; N.L.I., Ms 1793, fol. 246; *C.S.P.D., 1685, J. II*, pp 90, 145, 149, 152, 184, 187, 314; *C.S.P.D., J. II*, p. 113 [28-9]; Proclamation for disarming the militia, 16 Oct. 1685 (N.L.I., Ms 1793, fol. 229). For an overview, see Kenyon, *Popish plot*. Concern regarding treasonable words, the close association between the disarming of the militia and the political dimensions of toryism provided the context for one of the most bizarre occurrences of the whole

toryism in Ireland which in turn precipitated the emergence of unofficial armed Protestant associations, later deemed to be a direct challenge to Tyrconnell's government.[19] The sectarian and political nature of some of this tory activity may explain the unwillingness of Catholics to pursue them or to allow some of the Protestants to be re-armed.[20] The loss of the militia was sharply felt among Protestants. Michael Boyle, archbishop of Armagh and lord chancellor of Ireland, informed Ormond that the army, 'although placed in convenient quarters, will not be able to prevent mischiefs in highways and holdings'.[21]

The continuing political unrest in the other two kingdoms fed these fears.[22] A letter allegedly 'dropped' at Christ's Church Cathedral in Dublin shed light on popular Protestant attitudes towards the volatile political situation in England. It presented a scenario in which the Jesuits, Dominicans and Franciscans were plotting with the queen (Mary of Modena), (Roger Palmer), earl of Castlemaine (James II's ambassador to Rome), the pope (Innocent XI) and Louis XIV (king of France), to endanger Protestant lives and estates.[23] Edward Wettenall, Church of Ireland bishop of Cork and Ross, considered the growing political awareness among the populace to be 'a great evil': 'all sorts of men are strangely commenced politicians, scarce a farmer, scarce a foreman of a ship but he can censure or dictate to the government'.[24]

Restoration period, the rise and fall of the tory-hunter 'Tory' Will Hamilton. Hamilton had been a prominent tory-hunter in Ulster but he fell out of favour with the Tyrconnell clique in the army and ended up on trial for treasonable words and involved in a duel with Sir Thomas Newcomen, a close associate of Tyrconnell. He was finally stabbed by one of his junior officers. Tyrconnell attempted to intervene in the trial; Bodl., Carte Ms 217, fol. 123; *C.S.P.D. 1685, J. II*, p. 160; Bodl., Carte Ms 167, fol. 71; Bodl., Carte Ms 144, fol. 125; Bodl., Carte Ms 40, fol. 407; *H.M.C., Hastings*, ii, pp 395-6; *Clarendon letters*, i, pp 78, 165, 341-2, 363-6, 378; Bodl., Carte Ms 217, fols 123, 219; N.L.I., Ms 2449, fol. 115; *H.M.C., Ormonde*, vii, p. 440; N.L.I., 2450, fols 157, 374; Kelly, *That damned thing called honour*, p. 34. Archbishop King also alluded to Hamilton's 'murder' and believed that Tyrconnell showed his vindictiveness against the killers of the tories Patrick Fleming and Captain Power; King, *State of the Protestants*, pp 31-3. Captain Augner, the slayer of the Munster tory Captain Power, suffered similar 'persecution'; Clarendon to Sunderland, 19 Jan. 1686, in *Clarendon letters*, i, p. 13. **19** Clarendon to the Treasurer, 19 Jan. 1686, in *Clarendon letters*, i, p. 13. See also *H.M.C., Ormond*, vii, p. 397; Bodl., Carte Ms 217, fol. 259; *H.M.C., Ormond*, viii, p. 397; *C.S.P.D., 1685, J II*, p. 404. Simms believed that the Protestants formed themselves into armed associations as a result of this breakdown of law and order; Simms, *Jacobite Ireland*, p. 54. See also King, *State of the Protestants*, pp 31-3, 111. Charles Leslie later put forward an opposite view; Leslie, *An answer*, p. 75. See also N.L.I., 2450, fol. 157. **20** Clarendon to the Treasurer, 19 Jan. 1686, in *Clarendon letters*, i, p. 13. **21** Boyle and Ormond to Sunderland, 5 Dec. 1685 (N.L.I., Ms 2447, fol. 175). See also *Clarendon Letters*, i, pp 15, 30-1, 85-6; *Anal Hib.*, i, p. 109. As will be shown below, rapparees constantly impeded the progress of the Williamite armies and the government achieved no success against them until the effective formation of the militia in June 1691; *C.S.P.D., 1691*, p. 280. **22** For an example of popular sectarian tensions and rumours of war, see 'Examinations of Ellinor Bishop and Elizabeth, wife of David Taylor', 17 July 1686 (B.L., Add. Ms 15, 894, fols 53, 54). See also N.L.I., Ms 2444, fol. 131. **23** 'Copy of the letter found in Christ's Church', 31 Aug. 1686 (B.L., Add. Ms 15, 894, fol. 158); See also N.L.I., Ms 2445, fol. 181; King, *State of the Protestants*, p. 189. Rumours of French excesses against the Huguenots after the revocation of the Edict of Nantes in 1685 exacerbated Protestant paranoia; B.L., Add. 15, 892, fol. 261. See also King, *State of the Protestants*, p. 19; Bartlett, *Fall and rise*, p. 15; Leslie, *An answer*, introduction; B.L., Add. Ms 32, 095, fols 146-7. **24** Wettenall, *Hexapla Jacobaea*, p. 15. See also *Anal. Hib.*, xxvii, 1972, pp 175, 178; *Clarendon letters*, ii, pp 12-13.

Irish Catholics, for their part, appreciated the changing balance of power at the English court in the last years of Charles II, in particular the rising influence of the duke of York. A Williamite pamphleteer in the late 1680s noted that in this period 'they [the Irish] were well assured that there would be no parliament while Charles lived, and they would frequently discuss with that liberty and boldness as if the duke of York had actually been seated on the throne'.[25] James's succession in February 1685 re-animated Irish Catholic hopes which had been dampened by the popish plot and the exclusion crisis.[26] John Brenan, Catholic archbishop of Cashel, drew attention to the significance of both events in a letter of April 1684: 'For six years so violent has been the storm of persecution that I have not been able to hold even a private visitation. For the same reason during the past seven years, I have not held an ordination'.[27] Within three years, however, the political climate had been totally transformed. In his report to Propaganda in November 1687, Brenan applauded the end of the long reign of persecution as a consequence of the succession of a Catholic king. He expressed delight at the appointment of the earl of Tyrconnell, as commander of the Irish army. Tyrconnell had immediately set about catholicising the army and taken the fortresses and civil offices of the judiciary and magistracy into Catholic hands:

> This long tempest of persecution has at length come to an end and the devine mercy has been pleased to comfort the faithful in these parts by the coming to the throne of our most pious king James who publically professes the Catholic and apostolic faith, and in exemplary manner exercises the christian virtues. Soon after his coronation he appointed as his viceroy of this kingdom the earl of Tyrconnell, a native of the land and a brother of the late archbishop of Dublin of happy memory. He is a sincere and zealous Catholic, very desirous to promote the glory of God and the splendour of the true religion and to advance the Catholic nobility and gentry to the public offices and wealth. He has made a good beginning of this by reforming the army of the kingdom in which formerly not a Catholic could be found even in the ranks of the soldiers who were all heretics, and now almost the whole army is Catholic, as well the commandants and officers as the common soldiers. The fortresses of the kingdom are almost all in the hands of Catholic officials. The civil offices – as the judiciary and magistracy and the like – are, for the most part, assigned to Catholics. The bishops and priests, whether in

25 *A full and impartial account of the secret consults*, p. 39.   **26** Tanari to the secretary of state in Brussels, 31 Aug. 1685, in Giblin (ed.), 'Catalogue', ii, vols 51-80, p. 103. See also Cibo to Tanari, 2 Feb. 1686, in Giblin (ed.), 'Catalogue', part 8, vols 137A-147C, p. 99; O'Flaherty, *Ogygia*, pp iii, iv; *The royal voyage*, p. 15; Connolly, *Religion*, pp 29-30; Barnard, 'Old Ireland', p. 911.   **27** Power (ed.), *A bishop of the penal times*, p. 77. For a recent appraisal of his career, see Breatnach, 'Archbishop J. Brenan, his life and work', pp 148-56.

public or in private, may wear the ecclesiastical dress. The religious, that is the Franciscans and Dominicans, appear elsewhere in their regular habit and have begun to repair their ancient monasteries and convents. The parish priests, even in the cities, are building noble chapels for the religious functions and many conversions are being made in various parts of the kingdom.[28]

Protestant political discomfiture further increased as rumours circulated that Tyrconnell was to be made duke of Leinster and marquis of Dublin.[29] These were not totally unfounded in view of his eventual appointment to the lord deputyship and his receipt of a dukedom on the arrival of James II in Ireland. One Protestant commentator surmised that 'I suppose by Candlemas day you will see wonders in the Protestant church, poor Ireland will be taken clear off the hinges'.[30] According to another hostile contemporary, the native aristocracy employed 'wretched scribblers to make barbarous songs in praise of Tyrconnell ... and prophetically decree'd him the honour of destroying the English church'.[31] Lord lieutenant Clarendon, the main political casualty of Tyrconnell's rapid rise to power, had some Catholics arrested who had openly declared that by Christmas day there should not be a Protestant left in the army.[32] A retrospective account from 1689 noticed that James's succession raised Catholic expectations of a total transformation of Irish political and religious life. It claimed that 'they began to prick up their ears and expect advantage beyond their abilities, publicly declaring that the day was their own and that the Protestant religion must go down'.[33]

---

28 Bishop Brennan's report to Propaganda, 6 Nov. 1687, in Power (ed.), *A bishop of the penal times*, pp 84-90. See also Philips, *The interest of England*, p. 12.   **29** Clarendon to Treasurer, 27 Feb. 1686, in *Clarendon letters*, i, p. 69. See also ibid., i, pp 329-30, 338-9, 351, 388; ii, pp 54, 72, 74-5, 84-6, 89, 100, 114; N.L.I., Ms 2452, fol. 27; Wettenall, *Hexepla Jacobaea*, p. 17; *A letter from a gentleman in Ireland*, p. 6; King, *State of the Protestants*, p. 59; *Sermon preached by a new father in the Jesuit chapel*, p. 1; *A full and impartial account of the secret consults*, p. 58.   **30** Peter Westenra to Thomas Bligh, 11 Jan. 1687 (N.L.I., Special List 298, Rossmore Papers, T. 2929/1/6).   **31** Quoted in Ó Buachalla, *Aisling Ghéar*, p. 162.   **32** Clarendon to Sunderland, 22 July 1686, in *Clarendon Letters*, i, p. 324. See also ibid., i, pp 329-30, 338-9, 351, 355, 388; N.L.I., Ms 2453, fol. 55; *The history of the war in Ireland between their majesty's army and the forces of the late King James*, p. 4; King, *State of the Protestants*, pp 59, 294-5. Moran (ed.), *Spicilegum Ossoriense*, ii, p. 270; Power (ed.), *A bishop of the penal times*, p. 88; N.L.I., Ms 1793, fols 264-5, 285; H.M.C., *Ormond*, ii, p. 371; Proclamation against disaffection and fiery spirits in the pulpit, 21 Feb. 1687 (N.L.I., Ms 1793, fols 260-1). Wharton's lampoon 'Lillibulero' ('Lile ba léire', an allusion to the seventeenth-century astrologer William Lilly who predicted that a Catholic would ascend the English throne and re-establish Catholicism), which Wharton boasted had 'whistled a king out of three kingdoms' contained a verse mocking Tyrconnell's elevation to lord deputy; Ó Buachalla, 'Lillibulero'; Simms, *Jacobite Ireland*, p. 32; Miller, *James II*, pp 154, 169.   **33** Anon, *A true and impartial history of the wars of Ireland, Flanders, on the Rhine and in Savoy*. See also Proclamation of James II, 11 Feb. 1685 (N.L.I., Ms 1793, fol. 181). The political transformation is best evident in a retrospective doggerel verse; 'Who was (had he Teague's cause maintained)/The best of kings that ever reigned/He did his brother mourn to the throne/ And once more Ireland is our own./Sly Peter now shall bear the sway, and popery shall be in play;/He shall new model all the nation/From college unto corporation'; *The Irish hudibras*; Simms, 'The war of the two kings', p. 478; Connolly, *Religion*, p. 35.

The growing awareness among Catholics also manifested itself from the pulpit. A sermon preached in County Longford in October 1686 extolled James II's accession to the throne, expressed distaste at the prospect of a Protestant succession and stressed the need for the consolidation of the Catholic interest before such an undesirable eventuality:

> blessing God for restoring us a king that has brought in the truth of religion and hath not only set aside all heretics out of all public command in the army but also hoped and did believe everyone should be restored to his ancient rights which have been taken off since Henry VIII's time. As also he said we have a good example of the rebel Cromwell, who gave our estates to his followers, and so enabled his followers to make their conditions with their lawful sovereign and left them the wealth of the nation. But said he, you will say, a heretic will succeed and we have but the breath of one man for it, to which I answer that we hope to be in a far better condition before that extirpation.[34]

This sermon reflected fears and opinions being expressed at the highest level in the new Irish Jacobite administration. The 'Coventry Letter', deemed by contemporaries to be a concise statement of Irish Jacobite policy, stated that 'if the king died, he would be followed, as the successions stood, by his Protestant daughter, Mary, and Catholics were likely to be worse off than ever'. The author (Sir Richard Nagle), advised that their only recourse was 'to make their position safe by securing a larger share of the land'.[35] This preoccupation with land evidently percolated down to the general populace. The aged duke of Ormond complained to his confidant Archbishop Michael Boyle that he had re-emerged as a hate figure among the Catholic clergy and the 'rabble' as a result of the failure of Catholics to obtain an act of indemnity for the restoration of their estates. He feared that their malice was such that his house would be burnt down:

> The Roman Catholics thereabouts have been put in mind lately that but for me they should long since have obtained an act of indemnity and restitution of all their estates. How great and ungrateful soever this lie is, yet it is taken with the rabble in which I comprehend for honesty and understanding most of their clergy and it is swallowed as the clearest truth, insomuch that my Irish servant is afraid that the Irish portion may become so strong and their malice so implacable that my house and all in it may be burnt.[36]

---

34 'Account of sermon preached at Ballamore, 14 Oct. 1686 (B.L., Add. Ms 15,894, fol. 265). Also see Gilbert (ed.), *Jacobite narrative*, pp 5, 9, 17, 20; Miller, *James II*, pp 127-8, 142, 162, 175; Millet, 'Survival and reorganisation', p. 60. Clarendon stressed the importance to the Irish of their having a king of their own religion; *Clarendon letters*, ii, p. 34.   **35** Quoted in Simms, *Jacobite Ireland*, p. 31. **36** Ormond to Boyle, 6 Oct. 1685 (*H.M.C., Ormond*, vii, p. 368). See also *C.S.P.D., 1685, J. II*, p. 73; *H.M.C., Ormond*, viii, pp 398-9. There are numerous other hostile portrayals of Ormond in the Irish

The unpalatable prospect of the 'heretical' succession of James's Protestant daughter Mary (later Queen Mary), and her husband (and cousin) the prince of Orange (later William III), the Protestant champion of Europe, also appeared at a popular level. Rumours circulated in England that James would alter the succession in favour of a Catholic, while a deposition of March 1686 expressed the opinion that James would legitimise his natural son, James Fitzjames, the teenage duke of Berwick. In March 1686 Theodore Cade of Carrookmaguigny, County Donegal, recalled what Patrick Coyle had told him: 'Mr Fitzjames would inherit the crowns of Scotland and Ireland, that the pope had raised a bill to make him legitimate and that he would receive the assistance of France and Spain and come to Ireland to be sheltered until the king's death'.[37] Another controversy in November 1686 involved the princess of Orange and 'Mr Fitzjames' when a Catholic priest refused to drink the former's health and professed that the pope would legitimise the latter to succeed his father.[38] Thomas Sheridan, Jacobite secretary of state and first commissioner of the revenue, alleged that Tyrconnell also shared these views. He (Tyrconnell) had argued that the Irish would be mad to submit to be governed by the prince of Orange or 'Hyde's daughters' (Mary and Anne, James II's and Anne Hyde's Protestant daughters), proposing instead that they might set up their own king with French aid.[39] Clarendon referred to a popular Irish Catholic notion of ultimate papal suzerainty over the kingdom of Ireland which they 'believed as much as they did their articles of faith'.[40]

The possibility of a Catholic succession moved closer to realisation with the news of the queen's pregnancy, proclaimed amid enormous enthusiasm in Dublin.[41] This Catholic ebullience was boosted by absolute confidence that the queen would have a son. This supreme confidence did not pass the attention of one contemporary Protestant pamphleteer:

> Before I take leave of our supposed prince of Wales's birth, I must not omit to acquaint our readers of the universal confidence of all the Irish in the kingdom that the queen (as soon as it was said she was conceived) was with child of a son. They were so certain of this that they would lay

---

Jacobite tradition; Gilbert (ed.), *Jacobite narrative*, p. 8; Sheridan, 'Political reflections on the history and government of England' [1709] (R.A., Ms 2499, p. 68); Bodl., Carte Ms 229, fols 223-4, 241; Bodl., Carte Ms 217, fols 178, 191, 196; Murray, *Revolutionary Ireland*, p. 60; Ó Ciardha, 'The unkinde deserter and the bright duke', pp 177-93. **37** The examination of Theodore Cade, 15 Mar. 1686 (T.C.D., Ms 1995-2008, fol. 419). Recent work has shed light on the contemporary political climate; Miller, *James II*, p. 126; Pillogret, 'Louis XIV and Ireland', p. 3; Simms, *Jacobite Ireland*, p. 39; Connolly, *Religion*, p. 28; Mulloy (ed.), *Franco-Irish correspondence*, iii, pp 135-7; Bodl., Carte Ms 229, fol. 388. The popular tradition also seized on this unusual alliance between William of Orange and Rome; Simms, 'Remembering 1690', p. 233. **38** 'Inscribed copy of a letter, 12 Nov. 1686 (B.L., Add. Ms 15, 894, fol. 311). See also B.L., Add. Ms 21, 128. **39** Sheridan, 'An historical account' [c.1702] (R.A., Ms 2499). See also Simms, *Jacobite Ireland*, p. 39; Beresford, 'Ireland', p. 11; Miller, *James II*, pp 217-18; Pillogret, 'Louis XIV and Ireland', pp 3-4. **40** Clarendon to the lord treasurer, 26 Dec. 1686, in *Clarendon letters*, ii, pp 139-41. See also ibid., p. 431.

you twenty guineas to one, or another wager in proportion to that, from the highest to the lowest among them.[42]

Indeed Irish expectation of a male heir later fuelled the warming-pan story that became the subject of anti-Jacobite propagandists prior to the birth of the prince of Wales.[43] Catholics celebrated the prince's birth on 10 June 1688 with bonfires, bag-pipe music and the drinking of 'healths' and 'confusions', forcing the English out of their beds and breaking open their doors. Those who refused to participate were called 'fanatics' and 'Oliverian dogs'.[44]

Political events in England quickly overtook this Irish Jacobite elation. English Protestant distaste at the prospect of a Catholic succession, James's flirtations with non-conformists and Catholics and his arrest of the seven Church of England bishops for their refusal to countenance his Declaration of Indulgence (1687) precipitated the invasion of his son-in-law, the prince of Orange. The king's subsequent flight to France led parliament to declare that he had abdicated, allowing it to bestow the crown on William and Mary. The Irish Jacobites then looked to France where the hitherto all-powerful Louis XIV faced the combined strength of the Augsburg alliance and could not possibly countenance William's bloodless coup in the Stuart kingdoms.[45] The 'Sun-King' opted to send James to Ireland as a spring-board to re-capture his errant kingdoms. Irish Protestant commentators stressed the buoyancy of Irish Catholic hopes at the potential arrival of a French force, headed by King James, 'their great friend and patron which carries them to those extraordinary heights of insolence wherein they now reign'.[46] This Irish Catholic joy at the king's arrival in Dublin manifested itself in popular hysteria from gentlewomen, friars, oyster-wenches, poultry and herb-women and the composition and rendition of English ballads, including 'The king shall enjoy his own again'.[47]

41 *Twenty-third report of the deputy-keeper*, pp 42-3; *A sermon preached by the Rev father in the Jesuit chapel;* N.L.I., 1793, fols 301, 313; Simms, *Jacobite Ireland*, p. 44. 42 *A full and impartial account of the secret consults*, p. 39. See also O'Callaghan (ed.), *Marcariae*, p. 201; *H.M.C., Ormond*, viii, p. 352; Burke, *Archbishops of Tuam*, pp 183-4; Simms, *Jacobite Ireland*, p. 44; Miller, *James II*, pp 181-2. 43 Proclamation of the prince of Wales's birth, 23 June 1688 (N.L.I., Ms 1793, fol. 327); *A continuation of some pretended reasons for his majesty issuing a general pardon*, p. 2; *Irish hudibras*, pp 70-1; King, *State of the Protestants*, p. 34; Sergeant, *Little Jennings*, ii, p. 383. Rumours abounded in contemporary England that James Francis Edward was a suppositious child smuggled into the queen's bed-chamber in a warming-pan. 44 *A full and impartial account of the secret consults*, pp 43, 125. Also see *H.M.C., 7th report*, app 2, pp 742-3; *H.M.C., 11h report, app 5*, p. 136; Risk, Poems of Seán Ó Neachtain', p. 454; Murphy, 'Royalist Ireland', pp 600-1. 45 Simms, *Jacobite Ireland*, p. 59. 46 *The sad and lamentable condition of the Protestants*, p. 6. Retrospective doggerel verse noted Catholic elation: 'But one thing first I must declare/Thou little dreams of in this war/The first that's thither blown/Shall come from Brest or Dunkirk town/With an armada which shall bring/with them an abdicated king'; *Irish hudibras*, p. 17. Also see Gilbert (ed.), *Jacobite narrative*, p. 37; *H.M.C., Ormond*, viii, p. 362; Clarke (ed.), *Life of James II*, ii, pp 329-30; Phillips, *Interest of England*, p. 5; Bodl., Carte Ms 229, fols 328, 333-5; Wauchope, *Sarsfield*, pp 43-5. 47 Ó Buachalla, *Aisling Ghéar*, pp 165-6.

The delay in the arrival of Williamite succour to the besieged Protestant strongholds of Derry and Enniskillen provided a confidence-boost to the Tyrconnellite war-machine. Felix O'Neill took solace from his belief that Holland desired its forces and fleet back home to obstruct Louis XIV's expected invasion of that kingdom at the head of 100,000 men:

> The states of Holland have not only writ pressingly, but sent deputies to England to call home their fleets and forces and in case of non-compliance threaten to accept the French king as their protector to prevent the ruin that they may expect from that king at the head of one hundred thousand men in the bowels of their country by the 20th of this month.[48]

The Catholic linking of Dutch security concerns and Dutch fear of leaving the European Protestant interest over-stretched drives home the underlying point that Irish Catholics projected European conditions unto how they themselves would fare domestically. Their optimism fuelled an exuberant, expansionist Irish Jacobitism, which vividly contrasts with the introspective picture presented by hostile contemporaries. Dismissing the prospect of English help for the besieged Irish Protestants, Irish Jacobites contemplated a re-conquest of the other Stuart kingdoms. The English Jacobite, John Stevens, noted the favourable reaction of Irish Jacobites to the inconclusive naval engagement in Bantry, the constant stories about French military might and inflated estimates of the size of the French navy:

> It was not thought enough to cry up the advantage of the French at Bantry over a single squadron of the English fleet, into a complete and glorious victory, though never a ship taken or sunk or the pursuit followed. Every day supplied us with fresh fables of the entire defeat of both English and Dutch fleets.[49]

Although Stevens chose to mock this misplaced Irish Jacobite optimism it was as realistic as Stevens's (or James's) Francophobic reaction to English naval reversals, or their grandiose delusions about English naval prowess, considering that the combined Anglo-Dutch fleet could not match the power of the French navy at this time.[50] As France ruled the English Channel, Maréchal Luxembourg, 'Le

48 Felix O'Neill to Helena, countess of Antrim, Jan. 1689, in Berwick (ed.), *Rawdon papers*, p. 298. See also U.L., Add. Ms 1[c], fol. 64; Molyneux, *A journal*, p. 6.   **49** Murray (ed.), *Journal of John Stevens*, p. 67. See also U.L., Add. Ms 36, 296, fol. 55; Clarke (ed.), *Life of James II*, ii, p. 460; *The sad and lamentable condition of the Protestants*, p. 6; *Villare Hibernicum*, p. 9; Molyneux, *A journal*, p. 6. For the contemporary political and military contexts; Blüche, *Louis XIV*, p. 352; Simms, *Jacobite Ireland*, pp 60, 95.   **50** James II was said to be mortified by the result of the naval engagement at Bantry. When told that the English had been defeated, he retorted 'it is the first time then', and comforted himself that it was out of loyalty to him that the English Navy behaved so much out of

Tapissier de Notre Dame', swept the Augsburg armies before him.[51] Stevens's derogatory allusions to the Irish Jacobite army were shared by the foppish Franco-Jacobite commander le duc de Lauzun, and the English admiral Sir Cloudsley Shovell. They ignore the fact that this unpaid and ill-equipped force managed to stay in the field for three years against a superior army of veterans, armed and funded by the English parliament.[52]

The unquenchable optimism of the Irish Jacobites fed off rumours of civil strife in England. The dissolution of parliament, successive losses against the French and William of Orange's delay in relieving the besieged Irish Protestants also fostered hopes of an Irish invasion of England.[53] This Irish Jacobite ardour attracted the attention of le comte d'Avaux, the Dublin-based watch-dog of Louis XIV, who reported favourably on the popular elation at James's arrival in Dublin.[54] He recognised that Irish aspirations to religious and political privilege had become totally wedded to the Jacobite cause. D'Avaux also registered Catholic fear of a Tyrconnellite accommodation with the new Williamite regime, while emphasising that their total aversion to the prince of Orange complemented their fierce anglophobia.[55] The Williamite diarist Colles provides a vivid description of popular anger against the usurping prince of Orange: 'Among the ceremonies they use at the mass-houses was that they made an effigy of the prince of Orange and having formally cursed it after their manner, they cut it into pieces and spit on it and then burned it'.[56]

In his speech at the opening of 'The Patriot Parliament', James fed such fervour by appealing to Irish steadfastness in the face of the looming invasion, stressing that Irish 'liberty' was inextricably linked to his 'rights'.[57] Although James resisted attempts to repeal the Act of Settlement and Poynings's Law and later blamed the Irish in his *Memoirs* for their obsession with recovering their

character; Simms, *Jacobite Ireland*, pp 67-8. **51** Simms, *Jacobite Ireland*, p. 69; Erlanger, *Louis XIV*, p. 253. **52** Sir Cloudsley Shovell to Nottingham, 15 Mar. 1690 (*H.M.C., Finch*, ii, pp 273-4). See also King, *State of the Protestants*, pp 62, 141; Murray (ed.), *Journal of John Stevens*, p. xlii. Simms declared that it was remarkable that such an impoverished army should have acquitted itself as well as it did; Simms, *Jacobite Ireland*, p. 71. Lauzun achieved notoriety in the Irish nationalist tradition for his jibe at the outset of the first siege of Limerick that the walls could be breached with roasted apples; B.N., 12, 161, fol. 5, N.L.I., mf. p. 112, translated by Hayes (ed.), 'Reflections of an Irish Brigade officer', pp 68-9. **53** *The sad and lamentable condition of the Protestants*, pp 6, 9. See also *The royal flight, An account of the present state of Ireland giving a full relation of the new establishment made by the late King James*, p. 14; Gilbert (ed.), *Jacobite narrative*, p. 50; Simms, *Jacobite Ireland*, pp 52, 65-6. **54** Hogan (ed.), *Négociations*, pp 71-2. See also Story, *An impartial history of the war in Ireland with a continuation thereof*, p. 3; Gilbert (ed.), *Jacobite narrative*, p. 46; Leslie, *An answer*, p. 125; Clarke, *Life of James II*, ii, pp 327-30; N.L.I., Ms 7862; Hogan (ed.), *Négociations*, p. 8; Simms, *Jacobite Ireland*, pp 63, 64, 71; B.L., Add. Ms 28, 939, fol. 329; B.N., Fonds Français, Ms 12, 161, N.L.I., mf. p. 112. Ó Buachalla, *Aisling Ghéar*, pp 158-66. **55** D'Avaux au Roy, 4 Apr. 1689, in Hogan (ed.), *Négociations*, p. 50; Macpherson (ed.), *Original papers*, i, p. 314; Simms, *Jacobite Ireland*, p. 51. **56** Colles's diary of events (*H.M.C., Ormond*, viii, p. 355). **57** *The speech of the late king James II*. See also Clarke (ed.), *Life of James II*, ii, pp 329-30, 636; Gilbert (ed.), *Jacobite narrative*, pp 46,143; O'Callaghan (ed.), *Macariae*, p. 11; Leslie, *An answer*, p. 47; N.L.I., Ms 7862; T.C.D., Ms 1184.

ancestral lands in the face of military adversity, some evidence suggests that he used the issue of land restoration to rally the Irish to his standard. *An extract of the journal of the proceedings in the Irish parliament* noted his response to a motion of adjournment for a holiday in the 'Patriot Parliament' of 28 May 1689. When informed that the holiday commemorated the restoration of his brother and himself', he responded that it were 'the fitter to restore these loyal gentlemen who had suffered with him and had been unjustly kept out of their estates'.[58] James availed of scare-mongering and the propaganda potential of land and religion to broaden the base of his Jacobite war-machine. He also armed a Roman Catholic militia of men aged between sixteen and sixty, a significant step toward his outright indulgence of pike-men and rapparees. [59]

Hostile contemporaries continually charged Irish Jacobites with an obsessive and selfish preoccupation with ancestral lands.[60] Anthony Dopping, Church of Ireland bishop of Meath and effective leader of the opposition in the 'Patriot Parliament', accused the Jacobites of 'trying to dispose of the skin before the beast had been slain', and derided the Irish officers who left their regiments to inspect their ancestral lands.[61] Irish Catholics had already sampled Stuart ingratitude in the Acts of Settlement and Explanation in the 1660s. Charles II, a *bête noir* of the Irish Jacobite tradition, 'gave the lands of those who fought for him to those who fought against him'; the same Irish who would again champion the cause of his hapless brother.[62] Their political commentators stressed that they alone were doing the fighting, a point emphasised by Irish *émigrés* who later resented James's expedient diffidence towards his Irish subjects.[63]

58 Murray (ed.), *Journal of John Stevens*, p. liii. Also see Clarke (ed.), *Life of James II*, ii, p. 354; Gilbert (ed.), *Jacobite narrative*, p. 193; N.L.I., Ms 476, fol. 535; Leslie, *An answer*, p. 125; *An account of the present state of Ireland giving a full relation of the new establishment made by the late King James*, B.L., Add. Ms 36, 296, fol. 66.   **59** Proclamation against invasion, 30 July 1689 (*H.M.C., Ormond*, ii, pp 407-8); *Twenty-third report of the Deputy-keeper*, pp 44-5; Wellwood, *An answer*, p. 12; *Indictment and arraignment of John Price*, p. 8; *Anal. Hib.*, xxxii (1985), pp 35-115; U.L., Cambs., Add. Ms 1[c], fol. 64.   **60** Murray (ed.), *Journal of John Stevens*, pp li, 61-2; Leslie, *An answer*, p. 125; O'Callaghan (ed.), *Macariae*, p. 42; Bodl., Carte Ms 229, fols 331-2; Clarke (ed.), *Life of James II*, ii, p. 354.   **61** Simms, *Jacobite Ireland*, pp 82-3.   **62** Prendergast, *Ireland from Restoration to revolution*, p. 15. This opinion pervades contemporary Jacobite literature; Bodl., Carte Ms 229, fols 236, 238, 240, 246-7; O'Callaghan (ed.), *Macariae*, p. 14; Reilly, *Ireland's case briefly stated*, pp 93, 100; Reilly, *Impartial history of Ireland*, p. 65; [O'Conor], *Case of the Roman Catholics of Ireland*, p. 45. This sense of Stuart ungratefulness also manifested itself in the *Memoirs of Miles Byrne*, p. 7.   **63** *An address given to the late King James by the titular archbishop of Dublin*, pp 11, 17, 27; Murray, *Revolutionary Ireland*, p. 87; O'Callaghan (ed.), *Macariae*, p. 42; N.L.I., Ms 7862; B.L., Add. Ms 28,939, fol. 329; Bodl., Carte Ms 229, fols 102, 136-7; *An account of the present state of Ireland*, pp 15-16; Miller, *James II*, p. 185. Indeed Irish Jacobites expected that Louis XIV would make good his promise to restore James II to his throne, a failure later cited by Irish Jacobite writers to explain the humiliation of the French king by the treaties of Ryswick (1697) and Utrecht (1713); Plunkett, 'A light to the blind', fols 450, 468.

II

The potential for an ideologically cohesive Irish Jacobite polity existed before the outbreak of war in Ireland. All sections of the Irish Catholic interest had focused on issues such as the king's heir and the potential for a French victory before William of Orange could establish his reign in the three kingdoms. They also preoccupied themselves with the restoration of ancestral lands and the re-establishment of the Catholic religion. However, an active Jacobitism required the war to cement self-perceptions at all levels within the Jacobite community. Irish Catholics were drawn into the war effort by their clergy, aristocracy and gentry or were later goaded into it by the predatory activities of the Williamite army and the coercive legislation of the government. In spite of this, contemporary Protestant accounts depicted Catholic mobilisation as little more than an unholy alliance between a deposed English monarch and an inveterate Irish foe who manipulated their unfortunate prince to their own selfish ends.[64] The *Anonymous letter from Schomberg's camp* analysed the pyramidal structure of this Jacobite 'nation'. It reserved pride of place for the Roman Catholic clergy and lawyers: 'the sworn vassals of France and Rome who endeavoured the extirpation of Protestantism and the return of church lands'.[65] The Catholic church, both hierarchy and clergy, played a crucial role in the diffusion of Jacobite rhetoric down to the lower orders, by mobilising the Catholic populace in support of the king and maintaining their morale at key points in the struggle.[66]

A self-righteous, anti-Protestant strain of Irish Jacobitism emerged in the late 1680s and survived in clerical correspondence until the end of the Jacobite period. It resonated through a sermon preached by Fr Edmund Dulany before King James in Christ's Church Cathedral, Dublin on Ash Wednesday 1689. He attacked the prince of Orange as the 'ever cursed impious and unnatural Absalom' who had embarked 'in an ocean of boundless ambition to usurp the king's throne and imbrue his hands in his blood'.[67] Reflecting the sentiments of later Jacobite writers, such as Nicholas Plunkett, Charles O'Kelly and John Sergeant, Dulany viewed the English as 'a thrice perjured people, seduced by a nobility drunk with the love of dissolution and riot, sucked from the corrupt principles of a restless religion'.[68] The political high-ground thus claimed is

---

64 *A letter from Schomberg's camp*, p. 3; *Irish willingness to throw off the English yoke/revenge*; Wellwood, *An answer to the late King James's declaration*, p. 5. **65** *A letter from Schomberg's camp*, p. 3. See also *The declaration of William and Mary, Mephibosheth and Ziba*, pp 17, 34, 47-8. **66** Murtagh, 'The war in Ireland', pp 64, 86; Murray, *Revolutionary Ireland*, p. 233. Charles Leslie later stressed their influence in urging Catholics to take an oath of allegiance to William and Mary; Leslie, *An answer*, p. 125. **67** Dulany, *A sermon*, p. 16; Gilbert (ed.), *Jacobite narrative*, pp 183, 251. This anti-Williamite rhetoric was evident in contemporary England; [Sargeant], *Historical romance*, pp 22-3, 35. **68** Dulany, *A sermon*, p. 16. There are many other examples of this rhetoric in Jacobite discourse: *An address given to the late King James*, pp 11, 17, 27; Gilbert (ed.), *Jacobite narrative*, p. 184; Bodl., Carte Ms 229, fols 3, 102, 136-8, 142, 143-52; N.L.I., Ms. 7862; B.L., Add. Ms 28,939, fol. 329;

defended with the ideological weaponry of hereditary right and divine providence, central to Jacobite ideology in the eighteenth century:

> Unfortunate man, how far does your ambition drag you against a king that derives his power from heaven and not from men? You turn your sacrilegious army, you devise your stratagems and to attain his crown you arrived in the height of iniquity, treading underfoot the laws of God, man and nature in an unjust and unnatural war.[69]

Dulany impressed on his congregation the absolute necessity of rallying to the king's standard and further cementing the close ideological links between Jacobitism, religion and Irish national identity:

> It were to be wished that such as are members of our army have a strong sense of honour and conscience and discharge their duties with courage, care, vigilance and circumspection ... Faults committed in that duty do tend to dishonour God, to dethrone the king, to expose him to the fury of his bloodthirsty enemies, to betray the country and banish religion.[70]

His superior, Archbishop Patrick Russell of Dublin, sought to rally the dispossessed aristocracy and gentry to his master's cause with the promise of restoration and future political stability. Evaluating the proposed position of Ireland, Scotland and France *vis à vis* the restored monarchy, he echoed orthodox Irish Jacobite political thinking and unwittingly described the actuality of Ireland's role as the repository of a large section of the Hanoverian standing-army in the eighteenth century:

> For never a Catholic or other Englishman will ever think or make a step for your restoration, but leave you as you were hitherto and leave your enemies over your heads to crush you at any time they please and cut you off root and branch as they now publicly declare; and blame themselves that they had not taken away your lives along with your estates long ago! I dare aver if Ireland were put upon such a foot by the king, he shall never fear a rebellion in England, especially if Scotland be faithful to him and France a friend, all which can now be well contrived and concerted.[71]

O'Callaghan (ed.), *Macariae*, pp 9, 42; [Sargeant], *Historical romance*, p. 73; *An account of the present state of Ireland*, pp 15-16; Murray, *Revolutionary Ireland*, p. 87; Miller, *James II*, p. 185; Flood, *Wogan*, pp 141-2. **69** Dulany, *A sermon*, p. 16. See also King, *State of the Protestants*, pp 295-303.   **70** Dulany, *A sermon*, p. 20. Similar sentiments are expressed in Gilbert (ed.), *Jacobite narrative*, p. 36; Bodl., Carte Ms 229, fols 98, 274, 321.   **71** Bishop Molowny [Moloney] to Tyrrell, 8 Mar. 1689, quoted in Murray (ed.), *Journal of John Stevens*, p. lii. See also Gilbert (ed.), *Jacobite narrative*, p. viii; Murray, *Revolutionary Ireland*, p. 87; *An address given to the late King James*, N.L.I., Ms 7862; B.L., Add. Ms 28, 939, fol. 329; Miller, *James II*, pp 212, 217.

The *Anonymous letter from Schomberg's camp* shed further light on the influential dispossessed aristocracy and gentry to whom Archbishop Russell had appealed. This group prefigures the Jacobite 'underground gentry' of eighteenth-century Ireland and their *émigré* counterparts in Europe.[72] It also contextualises the Protestant phobia surrounding recruitment for foreign service which became an enduring manifestation of Jacobite sentiment in the eighteenth century:

> Next comes the numerous part of the gentry and nobility who by their rebellion in 1641 forfeited their estates of which the Protestants are seized. These have gained some military experience in the foreign parts and they are the flower of the rebel army; their condition cannot be made worse by any improsperous event of war; dig they cannot and will not and they will not be easily persuaded to return to beggary; nothing less than a good part or a whole part of the estates they forfeited will be a bait for them.[73]

In his consideration of the husbandmen and common labourers, this pamphleteer also effectively diagnosed the nature of Irish popular Jacobitism during the war, in the later 1690s and the eighteenth century.[74] He noted the continued political influence of the clergy, providing both a precedent for the Irish Jacobite literati and his own anti-Jacobite scribal successors, as well as a political justification for penal legislation against the clergy, aristocracy and gentry in the late 1690s:

> As for the common soldiers, part of them have been dragooning Protestants in France, the residue have from their cradles lived by theft and robbery, are incapable of labour and industry. Did these and the former submit to being disbanded, protected and dispersed, they would be more dangerous than now together in arms, for they would fill the kingdom with particular murders, rapine and robberies, rendering the planting of it impracticable: they cannot be saved to any good use but they'll run to France to strengthen the enemy of mankind.[75]

---

72 Whelan, *Tree of liberty*, pp 3-59.   **73** *A letter from Schomberg's army*, p. 4. There are numerous other contemporary accounts of this dispossessed aristocracy and gentry interest; Danaher and Simms (ed.), *Danish forces*, pp 75-6; Murray (ed.), *Journal of John Stevens*, pp xliii, 63; King, *State of the Protestants*, pp 24, 161-2; *History of the war in Ireland between their majesties army and the forces of the late King James*, p. 3; *Anal. Hib.*, xxvii, 1972, pp. 156-7; Richard Cox, 'Discourse on the methods necessary for the speedy reduction of Ireland' (T.C.D., Ms 1180, fols 67-73); idem 'Aphorisms relating to Ireland, submitted to the convention of Westminster' (T.C.D., Ms 1181, fols 29-35).   **74** 'Such is the ascendant that the priests have over the consciences of that bigoted people that it will be difficult and very chargeable, if not impossible (whilst these remain amongst them), to keep them from rebellion on the least foreign encouragement as 130 years sad experience verifies'; *A letter from Schomberg's army*, p. 5.   **75** *A letter from Schomberg's army*, p. 4; see also Story, *Impartial history*, pp 16, 21, 62, 87, 99-100; *The history of the war in Ireland between their majesties and the forces of the late King James*, p. 4; Murray (ed.), *Journal of John Stevens*, p. 63; Barry (ed.), 'Groans of Ireland', p. 131; *Mephibosheth and Ziba*, p. 12. There are numerous references to popular participation in the war; *The mantle*

III

Pikemen, tories and rapparees provided the most visible manifestation of Irish popular Jacobitism between the invasion of Schomberg and the Treaty of Limerick. Their militaristic activities became associated with the Jacobite armies and the Irish Catholic populace from the outset. John Keating, the Jacobite chief justice, recognised this fact, emphasising that thieves and robbers had become more numerous and assertive in the late 1680s. He also lamented that their depredations were generally attributed to the Jacobite army. The contemporary pamphlet *The present dangerous position of Protestants in Ireland under the new order of Tyrconnell* (1688) took this analysis one step further, suggesting that rapparees had become incorporated into the Jacobite army:

> The judges have appointed circuits as usual but everybody laughs at them, knowing that they dare not go to them to threaten to hang all robbers but if they do so the king will have a very thin army.[76]

Similarly, the Williamite observer Bishop King of Derry quoted one contemporary who mockingly asserted that the catholicisation of the army 'has rid us of the tories for they are taken into the army'.[77] Anthony Hamilton's *True relation of the actions of the Inniskilling men* gives a vivid description of these pikemen or rapparees. Recruitment usually took place at public masses: 'hills were covered with multitudes of them, arming and enlisting themselves and they were quartered in our towns and private houses'. He asserted that 'all of them were armed of all sorts sexes and ages, the old women and young children provided them skeans [knives] and half-pikes which they cut before our faces and it was difficult to get a horse shod in our country, all smiths being taken up on fitting out this sort of armory'.[78]

thrown off, p. 11; *A reason for his majesty*, H.M.C., *Finch*, ii, p. 387; Danaher and Simms (ed.), *Danish forces*, pp 39, 51; N.L.I., Ms 476, fol. 607; *An account of ther present state of Ireland under King James*; *Great news from Ireland*; Wauchope, *Sarsfield*, p. 185. **76** *The present dangerous position of Protestants in Ireland under Tyrconnell*; *An apology for the Protestants of Ireland*, p. 4; *A letter of a gentleman in Ireland* (Dublin, 1688), p. 11. Also see Leslie, *An answer*, pp 17-26, 188; *Good news for England*, p. 5; Simms, *Jacobite Ireland*, pp 53-4; Murray (ed.), *Journal of John Stevens*, p. 63. This popular mobilisation resonated in contemporary Protestant doggerel: 'Let them raise men no matter how/Call Teague and Dermot from the plough'; *The Irish rendezvous or a description of Tyrconnell's army of tories*, p. 6. **77** King, *State of the Protestants*, pp 28, 31, 33, 56. 62, 340. He also alleged that there were fourteen notorious tories in Cormac O'Neill's regiment; ibid., pp 56, 62. See also N.L.I., Ms 1793, fol. 391. **78** Hamilton, *True relation of the Inniskilling Men*, p. vii. There are many other descriptions of the rapparees in contemporary political discourse: King, *State of the Protestants*, p. 55; *Tyrconnell's proceedings in Ireland*, (1), p. 17; Gilbert (ed.), *Jacobite narrative*, p. 58; *The popish champion*, p. 17; *An account of the present state Ireland is in and the deplorable condition of the Protestants*; H.M.C., *Ormond*, viii, p. 368; *Good news for England*, p. 5; Giblin (ed.), 'Catalogue'. part 3, vols 81-101, p. 23; P.R.O., S.P. 67/4, fol. 38; *An address to the late King James*, p. 17; Leslie, *An answer*, p. 17; Murray, (ed.) *Journal of John Stevens*, p. 62; *An apology for the Protestants of Ireland*, pp 4, 7, 8, 14, 20-2; *The indictment and arraignment of John Price*, pp 3, 7; Croker (ed.), *The historical songs of*

King James underpinned this association between rapparee depredations and the Jacobite war-effort by effectively condoning the existence of these armed bands of pikemen in the immediate aftermath of the landing of Schomberg's army.[79] He initially attempted to differentiate between Jacobite partisans and those bandits who merely 'rob and spoil their neighbours and steal great amounts of cattle and other goods under the pretence that the owners thereof are in actual rebellion'.[80] In a futile attempt to restore his political credibility among Irish Protestants he called on his subjects to hand over such bandits to the justices of the peace and to restore stolen booty to the sheriffs. His gesture was meaningless as his army had already become associated with their pillaging partisans in the Protestant mind. The diarist Colles stressed the political dimension of these half-pikemen and robbers in an attempt to undermine King James's government: 'till King James arrived, all had acted for themselves'.[81] Although James's ambivalent proclamation reluctantly accepted rapparees as potential if politically embarrassing allies, William dismissed them as 'many Irish Papists and other lewd and vagrant persons, disaffected to the government who wander up and down to the terror of his majestie's subjects'.[82]

Despite James's reluctance to alienate his Protestant subjects, the abrupt religious transformation of the army, judiciary and local government ensured that rapparee activity did not always meet with the full rigours of the law.[83] Likewise, with the arrival of Schomberg, a distraught James became less squeamish about rapparee abuses. Although he never lost hope of a 'rapprochement' with his Protestant subjects, his proclamation of 3 September 1689 highly commended the activities of 'those not being enlisted in our standing army who armed themselves with pikes, skeans and guns for the defence of our kingdom, on or near the border between Ulster and Leinster'.[84] He pleaded for restraint towards, and immunity for, his loyal subjects; yet he encouraged incursions into enemy quarters to destroy and weaken them upon all occasions. He assured their compliance by a royal grant of the benefit of the plundered goods.[85] In

Ireland, p. 24; *Great news from Ireland*; Simms, *Jacobite Ireland*, pp 53-4, 220; Maguire (ed.), *Kings in conflict*, pp 86, 88. **79** Proclamation (James R.) 25 Mar. 1689 (N.L.I., Ms 1793, fol. 403). **80** Proclamation (James R.) 25 Mar. 1689 (N.L.I., Ms 1793, fol. 403). Contemporary evidence also existed of the rapparees robbing their co-religionists, and the Jacobite army hunting rapparees: *C.S.P.D., 1689*, p. 231; B.L., Add. Ms 9716, fol. 99; King, *State of the Protestants*, pp 127, 137; Wauchope, *Sarsfield*, p. 173. **81** Colles's Diary of events, 30 Mar 1689 (*H.M.C., Ormond*, viii, p. 362). **82** Proclamation, 6 May 1689 (*C.S.P.D., 1689*, p. 92); ibid., p. 181; King, *State of the Protestants* (Cork, 1768), p. 415. **83** Murray, *Revolutionary Ireland*, p. 86. **84** Proclamation (James R.) 3 Sept. 1689 (N.L.I., Ms 1793, fol. 467). See also *H.M.C., Ormond*, viii, pp 196, 211, 366, 370; King called the rapparees 'newly commissioned officers'; King, *State of the Protestants*, pp 104, 118; Leslie saw the rapparees as a consequence of armed associations of Protestants; Leslie, *An answer*, pp 66, 83, 86; Murray (ed.), *Journal of John Stevens*, pp 61, 64; Dunton, *Teagueland*, p. 49; *Irish willingness to throw off the English yoke*, p. 5. See also *A Journal of what has passed in the north since the landing of the duke of Schomberg*; Murtagh, 'The war in Ireland', p. 82; Mullin, 'The ranks of death', p. 19. **85** Proclamation (James R), 3 Sept. 1689 (N.L.I., Ms 1793, fol. 467). Also see Murray, *Revolutionary Ireland*, pp 63, 340; King, *State of the Protestants*, pp 134, 137.

spite of these proclamations, the English Jacobite commentator John Stevens failed to appreciate the extent to which rapparee pillage had been incorporated into the Irish Jacobite war-effort: 'Yet amidst these enormities every mouth was full of religion and loyalty, everyone promising a happy success to the rightful cause as if it had authorised us in the practice of all sorts of villianies'.[86]

The popular Williamite stereotype of the mobilised Catholic populace, armed with scian (knife) and half-pike in attendance at mass featured prominently in contemporary Williamite accounts:

> The people of the north are constantly alarmed by their popish neighbours who by the persuasion of their priests have all left their farms and betaken themselves to mountains and fastnesses where they at present live by their cattle where they rob, steal and exercise themselves in arms.[87]

These half-pike men and rapparees soon made their military presence felt, harrying enemy supporters and avenging the plundering activities of the Williamite army. As a consequence of their activities Schomberg's soldiers had been given strict orders not to leave camp on pain of death:

> For they straggled abroad and plundered those few people who were left, and some of them were murdered by the rapparees, a word which we were strangers to 'till this time ... such of the Irish as are not in the army but the country people, armed in a hostile manner with half-pikes and skeans.[88]

Story later argued that the Jacobite administration deliberately encouraged rappareeism by discharging part of the army to fend for themselves:

> To give you a brief account of how the Irish manage this affair, to make the rapparees as considerable as they really were ... they let loose a great part of their army to manage the best for themselves ... to all these they give passes ... that they might not be dealt with as rapparees but as soldiers.[89]

---

86 Murray (ed.), *Journal of John Stevens*, p. 9. Contemporary sources also provide an alternative view: B.L., Add. Ms 36, 296 fols 51, 55; MacErlean (eag.), *Duanaire*, iii, pp 174, 182; O'Callaghan (ed.), *Macariae*, p. 96; Gilbert (ed.), *Jacobite narrative*, p. 67.   **87** *The present dangerous position of Protestants under Tyrconnell*. There are numerous contemporary descriptions of the rapparees; H.M.C., *Ormond*, vii, pp 360, 363; Hamilton, *Account of the actions of the Inniskilling Men*, pp viii, 6; *A true and impartial history of the wars of Ireland, Flanders, on the Rhine and in Savoy*, p. 31; *The indictment and arraignment of John Price esquire*, pp 3, 7, 24; *Good news for England*, p. 5; Bodl., Carte Ms 217, fol. 307; King, *State of the Protestants*, pp 30 61-2, 104, 114, 141; Story, *An impartial history of the war with a continuation thereof*, p. 21; Simms, *Jacobite Ireland*, pp 53-4; *The popish champion or life of Tyrconnell*, p. 27; *Anal. Hib.*, xxxii, p. 60. This cameo is also confirmed in the contemporary poetry of Diarmuid Mac Sheáin Bhuí Mac Cárthaigh and Dáibhí Ó Bruadair; MacErlean (eag.), *Duanaire*, iii, pp 94, 128.   **88** Story, *An impartial history of the war in Ireland*, 9 Sept. 1689, p. 16. Also see H.M.C., *Ormond*, viii, 381; C.S.P.D., *1690*, p. 155.   **89** Story, *A continuation of the impartial history*, pp 49-50. See also ibid., pp 62-3; *Narrative of affairs of*

Nevertheless he sought to prevent any historical rehabilitation of the rapparees:

> But after all, lest the next age may not be of the same humour as this
> and the name of a rapparee may be possibly thought a finer thing
> than it really is, I do assure you that in my style they can never be
> reputed other than tories, robbers, thieves and bog-trotters.[90]

Leaders on both side of the political divide continued to view the rapparees as
Jacobite partisans. Like James II and D'Avaux, they realised that, in spite of their
auxiliary nature, these mobile, dispersed and locally knowledgeable forces could
be extremely effective. D'Avaux was especially complimentary of McMahon's
heroic defence of Castleblaney, County Monaghan, with a regiment composed of
'creaghts'.[91] Schomberg's description of this Jacobite garrison in Castleblaney
would suggest that he also viewed these creaghts as a type of irregular Jacobite
soldiery. Recognising the strategic importance of Castleblaney, he advanced
towards Armagh to isolate Charlemont and 'hinder a small supply of soldiers that
have assembled at Castleblaney for bringing in provisions and ammunition'.[92]

The rapparees justified D'Avaux and Schomberg's views by continually
attacking Williamite forces in Ulster. A newsletter of September 1690 referred to
those 'who came over a bog and carried away horses, cows and men'.[93] This capture of men suggests more organisational sophistication than would normally be
credited to irregular pilfering bandits. Williamite attempts to destroy three
divisions of a Jacobite army marching towards Sligo and Ulster, one of which
was described as 'composed chiefly of rapparees', indicates that they were accom-
modated within, or were synonymous with, the Jacobite army.[94] Rapparees
dogged the tracks of the cautious old Williamite commander (Schomberg) on
his trek towards the Boyne, and his ranks, exhausted by sickness and hard

Sir William Parsons, 1687-9, [c.1691] (N.L.I., Special List 319 [1], Rosse Papers); *The indictment and
arraignment of John Price*, pp 24-27; Murtagh, 'The war in Ireland 1680-91', p. 82; Danaher and
Simms (ed.), *Danish forces*, pp 16, 62; D. and H. Murtagh, 'The Irish Jacobite army, 1689-91', p. 38;
Murray (ed.), *Journal of John Stevens*, pp 91, 112, 155-7; *A true and impartial history of the war in
Ireland, Flanders, on the Rhine and in Savoy* , pp 78-9. **90** Story, *A continuation of the impartial
history*, p. 50; The tory and rapparee feature prominently in the Irish nationalist tradition; Davitt, *Fall
of feudalism*, p. 14; O'Hanlon, *The highwayman*, passim; Ó Ciardha, 'Woodkerne', passim. **91**
D'Avaux au Roy, 25 Jan. 1690, in Hogan (ed.), *Négociations*, p. 632. D'Avaux seemed to make a
distinction between the creaghts in Ulster and the rapparees in the rest of Ireland; Hogan (ed.),
Négociations, p. 586. 'Creaght' is the anglicised form of the collective noun 'caoruigheacht' (pl.
'caoruigheachta') meaning a herd of cattle with its keepers. See also Murray (ed.), *Journal of John
Stevens*, p. 162; Mulloy (ed.), *Franco-Irish correspondence*, ii, pp 208, 234-5: *H.M.C., Finch*, ii, p. 452.
92 Schomberg to the king, 11 May 1690 (*C.S.P.D., 1690*, p. 8). See also *H.M.C., Ormond*, viii, p.
370; Story, *An impartial history*, 2 May 1691, p. 15; Macpherson (ed.), *Original papers*, p. 173;
Schomberg to the king, 11 and 12 May 1690 (*C.S.P.D., 1690*, pp 7-8); Danaher and Simms (ed.),
Danish forces, p.76; For an examination of the social bandit, see Hobsbawm, *Bandits*; idem, *Primitive
rebels*; Joseph, 'Latin-American bandits', pp 293-336. **93** Newsletter, 20 May 1690 (*C.S.P.D., 1690*,
p. 14). **94** Resolutions taken by Count De Solms, Major-General Scravenmoer and Baron Ginckel,
12 Sept. 1690 (*C.S.P.D., 1690*, pp 118-19). See also ibid., pp 120-7; B.L., Add. Ms 9709, fols 97, 84.

marching, constantly fell prey to their attacks.[95] Their military efficiency as a strike force is exemplified by their extraordinary elusiveness:

> When the rapparees have no mind to show themselves upon the bogs, they commonly sink between two or three little hills grown over with very long grass that you might as soon find a hare as one of them. They conceal their arms thus: they take off the lock and put it in their pocket or in a dry place. They stop the muzzle with a cork and the touch-hole with a small quill and throw the piece into a pond or running water. You may see one hundred of them and they look like the poorest slaves in the world and you can search till you are weary and you will not find one gun.[96]

The duke of Wurtemburg's Danish mercenaries, themselves continually accused of pillaging, feared the plundering 'schnaphanen' (rapparees).[97] A letter of September 1690 described Williamite cavalry 'being in action against four thousand rapparees, 'schnaphanen', Catholics who came together and plundered a lot of Protestants who wished to come under the king's protection'.[98] They continued their intermittent raids on Williamite armies and positions in Munster. Count De Solms underlined the extent to which they disrupted Williamite supply lines, captured men and depleted William's equestrian stocks.[99] They also disrupted the administration of the criminal justice system and created a multitude of inconveniences by 'stealing horses on the grass close to city' and disrupting postal services and killing couriers.[100] These rapparee activities also featured favourably in the correspondence from the Jacobite side, specifically Fumeron and Sarsfield.[101] These descriptions of the activities of the rapparees have to be viewed within the context of Jacobite (and Williamite) military tactics and the extent to which the Jacobites were forced to live off the land amid continuing economic deprivation, and after the departure of James II. The Jacobite soldiers who deserted and attached themselves to the rapparees in the Ulster theatre were joined in their pillaging by the regular Jacobite armies and their Williamite adversaries.[102]

95 Story, *Impartial history*, p. 104. **96** Story, *Impartial history*, p. 153. See also Munchgaar to Harboe, 11 Feb. 1691, in Danaher and Simms (ed.), *Danish forces*, p. 98. **97** Schomberg to the king, 14 Mar. 1690 (*C.S.P.D., 1690*, pp 509-10); Danaher and Simms (ed.), *Danish forces*, pp 17, 20, 23, 65. In his work on guerrilla warfare between Sweden and Denmark in the wars of 1657-8 and 1675-9, Alf Åberg has suggested that outlaws and farmers driven to desperation by the harshness of the Swedish occupying troops filled the ranks of the 'schnaphanen' in Skane, review of A. Åberg, *Snapphanarna*, p. 247. **98** Munchgaar to Harboe, 18 Sept. 1690, in Danaher and Simms (ed.), *Danish forces*, p. 78. See also T.C.D., Ms 749 [2], fol. 183-183a; B.L., Add. Ms 9709, fol. 31. Munchgaar also suggested that there were many in their ranks of genteel origin; Danaher and Simms (ed.), *Danish forces*, p. 78. **99** Count De Solms to the king, 14 Sept. 1690 (*C.S.P.D., 1690*, p. 120). **100** T.C.D., Ms 1180, fol. 133; Danaher and Simms (ed.), *Danish forces*, pp 84, 110. **101** Fumeron à Louvois, 2 May 1691, in Mulloy (ed.), *Franco-Irish correspondence*, ii, p. 279. See also ibid., ii, pp 203-4, 257-8, 333; *H.M.C., Finch Mss*, ii (1670-1690), p. 478.

Although rappareeism had originated in the mobilisation of the populace and wholesale disbandment from Tyrconnell's army because of lack of funds, the numbers steadily increased due to the poverty and parsimoniousness of the Jacobite regime.[103] The inadequate resources of the Jacobite soldiery, their bad quarters and their subsequent recourse to pillage and plunder were recurring themes in D'Avaux's extensive correspondence. The improper distribution of arms and James's apparent unwillingness to pay his men deepened Jacobite organisational difficulties.[104] Williamite abuse of their pillaging Jacobite adversaries as mere bandits became a stark reality as impoverished soldiers plundered the countryside: 'All plowing is abandoned, the officers and soldiers having seized upon the poor people's garrons [horses], robbing and taking away the very roots [potatoes] they had for their livelihood'.[105] Contemporary Williamite sources and London satire constantly reiterated the contemptuous equation of Jacobites and 'rapparees'.[106] Those who held Connaught for James in the aftermath of the Battle of the Boyne were dismissed as 'some few desperados with Jesuit priests and friars who have got to the other side of the Shannon with Tyrconnell and Sarsfield at their head'.[107] With the Jacobite armies in disarray, yet still sufficiently intact, the writer observed that 'the country is already so full of thieves and robbers that unless care may be taken by the magistrates, a 'tory-war' will begin'.[108]

In April 1691, Lord Longford commented on the extent to which the country groaned under the burden of rappareesim. He identified five different types of rapparee and the effects of their ravages on the country: 'firstly the general Irish rapparees, secondly some of the Irish army, thirdly and fourthly the English army and militia and fifthly some of the English army that fled from the county of Limerick for shelter'. He stressed that 'although a man may have a favour from some parties, it is impossible to be secure from all'.[109] Robert Huntington also realised the terrible economic cost of the war and of the suppression of the Jacobites. Describing the Williamite army, he complained that:

> We labour under our remedy as well as our disease and 'tis much alike to the impoverished whether they are rapperied and undone by the Danish,

102 Proclamation, 18 Aug. 1689 (N.L.I., Ms 1793, fol. 459). See also N.L.I., Ms 1793, fol. 467. **103** Sergeant, *Little Jennings*, ii, pp 471, 491. **104** D'Avaux à Louvois, 23 Apr. 1689 in Hogan (ed.), *Négocations*, p. 92; Hogan (ed.), *Négocations*, pp 2, 36, 50, 79, 85-86, 96, 99; Simms, 'The war of the two kings', p. 493. **105** D'Albyville to James II, 27 Oct.-6 Nov. 1690 (*H.M.C., Finch*, ii, pp 472-3). See also *H.M.C., Finch*, ii, pp 475-80. **106** Crofton-Croker (ed.), *Historical songs*, pp 46-7, 71-2 and 76-7. Evidently Irish Jacobite soldiers took great offence at being called rapparees; Wauchope, *Sarsfield*, p. 159. There are many references to the rapparee in contemporary doggerel: *Irish hudibras*, p. 10; *'James II', Jacobite hudibras*, p. 1; *The royal voyage*, pp 5, 7; *A new year's gift for the rapparees*; *A new year's gift for the tories alias the rapparees*; D'Urvey, *The triennial mayor, or the new rapparees*, quoted in Sweeny, *Ireland and the printed word*, p. 525. **107** Newsletter (London) 19 July 1690 (*H.M.C., Le Fleming Ms*, i, no 3881, p. 281). **108** Newsletter (London) 19 July 1690 (ibid., p. 281). See also Simms, 'The war of the two kings', p. 258; **109** Lord Longford to Ellis, 25 Apr. 1691 (B.L., Add. Ms 28, 877, fol. 16).

French, Dutch, English or by the Irish tories, only the wounds of a friend are the most unkinde, cutting and deadly.[110]

By their indiscriminate and coercive measures, the Williamite government also persecuted the wider Catholic community for rapparee attacks. In doing so they hardened Irish Jacobite resolve against the new regime. On 19 November 1690, the lords justice issued a punitive proclamation: 'if any of his majesty's Protestant subjects had their houses or haggards burnt or were robbed and plundered by the rapparees, such losses would be repaid by the popish inhabitants'.[111] In an attempt to pressurise Catholic priests into compliance, the government further ordered that 'if any rapparees exceeding ten were found in a body, no popish priest should have the liberty to reside in such a country'.[112] The Williamite commander, General Ginckel, first earl of Athlone, later defended widespread persecution of the Catholic populace for rapparee activity by claiming that 'the inhabitants were in daily contact, stealing and supplying them with horses'.[113] Such vindictive Williamite reaction against rapparee activities also left them open to the charge that innocent civilians were being slaughtered under the guise of persecuting rapparees. This is a constant difficulty in dealing with a popularly-based adversary who could strike out suddenly at the enemy and then melt back into the Catholic populace.[114]

Differentiating between these tories and rapparees and the plundering Jacobite soldiery presented problems, particularly regarding the treatment of prisoners. Reliable sources from either side of the political divide suggest that rappareeism was used as a cover for the systematic slaughter of hundreds, if not thousands, of innocent Irish Catholics. According to a contemporary account of the siege of Cahir on 29 September 1690, 'the garrison was about four thousand strong, half of them were schnaphanen [rapparees] and about one tenth were hanged'.[115]

110 McNeill (ed.), *Tanners letters*, p. 506. Murray suggested that English plunder encouraged rapparees; Murray, *Revolutionary Ireland*, p. 94. The duke of Schomberg dismissed the Inniskilliners as 'so many Croats'; quoted in Ferguson, 'King William's army in Ireland', p. 65. Also see T.C.D., Ms 749 (i), fol. 25; T.C.D., Ms 749 [ii], fol. 140. John Curry provides a useful appraisal of the rapparees from primary sources; Curry, *Historical and critical review*, ii, pp 161-3. **111** Proclamation, Sydney, 21 Dec. 1690 (N.L.I., Ms 1793, fol. 603); *Twenty-third report of the deputy-keeper*, p. 46; *A true and impartial history of the war in Ireland, Flanders, on the Rhine and in Savoy*, pp 126-7; N.L.I., Ms 11, 477 [2]; *H.M.C., Le Fleming, report 14*, app 7, p. 323; Leslie, *An answer*, p. 164. Contemporary satirical pamphlets mocked Irish reaction to this pillage; *Irish hudibras*, p. 10. **112** Proclamation, Sydney, 21 Dec. 1690 (N.L.I., Ms 1793, fol. 603). See also M. Campbell to A. Rawdon, 6 Dec. 1690, in Berwick (ed.), *Rawdon papers*, p. 328; Wauchope, *Sarsfield*, pp 200-5; Murray, *Revolutionary Ireland*, pp 242, 265-6; McGrath 'Securing the Protestant interest', p. 38. For the arrest of a priest on the appearance of French privateers and Edward Synge, bishop of Raphoe's, suggestion to hunt priests in the same manner as rapparees in the eighteenth century, see Burke, *Irish priests*, pp 113, 203. **113** 'Memorial of what General Ginckel submits for the king's definite orders', 22 May 1691 (*C.S.P.D., 1691*, p. 385). See also Wauchope, *Sarsfield*, p. 185; *A true and impartial history of the wars in Ireland, Flanders, on the Rhine and in Savoy*, pp 126-7, 170. **114** Story, *An impartial history of the war in Ireland*, pp 138-9. See also Leslie, *An answer*, p. 164; Wauchope, *Sarsfield*, p. 114. **115** Danaher and Simms (ed.), *Danish forces*, p. 84.

Charles Leslie concluded that the 'vast numbers of poor harmless natives were daily hunted up and down the fields, as they were following their labour, or shot immediately as rapparees'. He deemed this to be 'a most terrible scandal to the government, which the Protestants themselves attest ... and many country gentlemen, as likewise several officers, even of King William's army ... did abhor to see what small evidence or even presumption was thought sufficient to condemn men for rapparees'.[116] The Williamite historian George Story pointed to the huge number of rapparees killed during the war and admitted that 'vast numbers of harmless natives' were slaughtered as rapparees.[117] In an entry in his common place book for 11 August 1691 the Irish Jacobite poet Tadhg Ó Neachtain stated that there were few towns in Ireland that had not got heads spiked on their walls and that he had seen the heads of boys as young as twelve and sixteen impaled in County Wicklow.[118]

The rapparee tag was also used to target former Jacobite officials. A letter from Colonel William Wolsley relating to the pursuit of Irish tories in 1690 states that he killed between 80 and 100 tories. Among the casualties were Andrew Tuite, James Ledwich and Redmond Mullady, late sheriffs of King James, as 'they are no soldiers, nor have any commission for what they do and therefore I conceive are not to be treated other ways than tories and highwaymen'. Elsewhere he referred to Gerald Nugent, the present sheriff for King James for the county of Westmeath, as the head of the rapparees near Mullingar.[119] The Williamite army also pillaged the wider Catholic community.[120] Schomberg lamented to King William that 'if our Irish colonels were as capable in war as they are in pillaging and not paying their soldiers here, your majesty would be better served'.[121] The diary of Thomas Bellingham details the excesses committed by Schomberg's soldiery in the aftermath of the surrender of Charlemont:

> Yet the articles though signed by Schomberg were nevertheless most barbarously violated by the soldiers who without any regard to age, sex or quality disarmed and stripped the townspeople, forcing even women to run the gauntlet stark naked.[122]

116 Leslie, *An Answer*, p. 164. **117** Story; *A continuation*, pp 3, 50-80. **118** Quoted in Ó Buachalla, *Aisling Ghéar*, p. 378; Dickson, *New foundations*, p. 39. These were not isolated incidents. The 'agallamh filíochta' between Mac Cuarta and Mac Oireachtaigh (pp 94-5) also claims that many more were killed in the late 1690s. The diarist Elizabeth Freke noted in 1694 that Lord Chief Justice Pyne and Sir Richard Cox condemned 28 persons to be hanged, drawn and quartered; [E. Freke], 'Mrs Elizabeth Freke, her diary', p. 49. Captain Richard Walsh, commander of a French privateer, was executed in Dublin in April 1696 while nine other Irish privateers were executed in London between 1691 and 1696; Melvin, 'Irish soldiers and plotters in Williamite England', p. 356. **119** Gilbert (ed.), *Jacobite narrative*, pp 258-9. A Captain Redmond was hanged by Colonel Wolseley after incriminating papers were found among letters addressed to him in Mullingar; Raymond-Redmond, 'Military and political memoirs', p. 29. **120** Danaher and Simms (ed.), *Danish forces*, p. 90; Hogan (ed.), *Négocations*, pp 543-5; *C.S.P.D., 1690*, p. 155; Petrie, *Berwick*, p. 83. **121** Schomberg to the king, 12 Oct. 1689 (*C.S.P.D., 1689*, p. 288). He compared the Enniskilliners to 'Croats' and 'Tartars'; Murtagh, 'The war in Ireland 1689-91', p. 70. **122** Faulkner, (ed.), 'An Irish diary', p. 24; Story, *Impartial history*, pp 138-9; Leslie, *An answer*, pp 151, 164-5.

Rapparees further strengthened these links with the greater Catholic populace by cultivating their image as self-appointed protectors of defenceless papists. For example, they stalked and shot the foraging stragglers of Würtemburg's Danish contingent.[123] Although Munchgaar believed that plunder provided their primary motivation, he observed that rapparees differentiated between particular racial groups:

> They give no quarter to English Protestants but spare Danes, Dutch and French... Recently they captured a land constable with a Danish trooper in Dungarvan. The constable offered £100 that he might live long enough to write a letter to his wife but they would not allow it as he was a Protestant.[124]

Tyrconnell vindicated Williamite claims of a close association between rapparees and the Jacobite cause when he called on them to join the army in the period before the decisive Battle of Aughrim. His apparent influence over them was so great that 'a hot press' was on foot over the Irish quarters and all firearms were to be taken from the rapparees and given to the hard-pressed soldiers to fill the depleted regiments and complete the broken army.[125] This Jacobite dependence on the rapparees became a constant feature of Williamite propaganda: 'these are the hopeful sticks the commanders of the Irish army encourage and put weapons into their hands, to harass and destroy the countries under their majesties's obedience'.[126] While Tyrconnell had encouraged all Connaught rapparees to join the army, St Ruth ordered them to plunder cattle to maintain it: on his death, he was called the 'rapparee saint'.[127] In October 1691, Ginkel required that 'those known by the name of rapparees, volunteers or creaghts do return to their respective parishes, deliver up their arms and enter their names with some of his majestie's justices of the peace'.[128] That many rapparees availed of the terms of the Treaty of Limerick provided ultimate proof of their close links with the Jacobite war effort.[129]

---

123 Würtemburg to Christian V, 7 Jan. 1691, in Danaher and Simms (ed.), *Danish forces*, p. 95. See also Simms, *Jacobite Ireland*, p. 199; N.L.I., Ms 1793, fol. 591; Leslie, *An answer*, p. 164; Wauchope, *Sarsfield*, p. 54.   124 Munchgaar to Harboe, 10 Jan. 1691 in Danaher and Simms (ed.), *Danish forces*, pp 96, 98. There is some contemporary evidence of rapparees taking prisoners; Santons-Boullain à Louvois, 2 May 1691, in Mulloy (ed.), *Franco-Irish correspondence*, iii, [2010], p. 159; ibid., ii, [1201], p. 279.   125 'News from Ireland received from Major Scavanmoer', 27 May 1691 (*C.S.P.D., 1691*, p. 390). See also Ginckel to the king 8/18 Aug. 1691 (ibid., p. 475); *H.M.C., Finch*, iii, p. 212; Murray, *Revolutionary Ireland*, p. 191. According to Sergeant 'Tyrconnnell did not believe in the value of the rapparees and all unprejudiced critics on his own side agreed with him'; Sergeant, *Little Jennings*, ii, p. 491.   126 *A true and impartial history of the war of Ireland*, p. 125.   127 Story, *A continuation*, 15 June 1691, p. 92; [McOlero], *The rapparee saint; A diary of the siege of Limerick*, p. 9; Giblin (ed.), 'Catalogue', part 3, vols 81-101, p. 20.   128 Story, *A continuation*, Oct. 1691, pp 262, 269. Also see *A true and impartial history of the war in Ireland*, p. 125; Giblin (ed.), 'Catalogue', part 3, vols 81-101, pp 23-4; Danaher and Simms (ed.), *Danish forces*, p. 137.   129 *The civil and military articles of Limerick*, p. 25.

IV

Finally, this process of popular politicisation was powerfully aided by the Irish literati, another vital component of Irish Jacobitism in the 1680s and 1690s and throughout the eighteenth century. They lavished praise on their new king, they lauded his future lord deputy, Tyrconnell, and championed his continued erosion of the Protestant interest in the late 1680s. They show that Irish Jacobitism, like its Scottish counterpart, involved more than a mere blind loyalty to the Stuarts. Questions of law and order, Catholicism, the Irish language and literature, land and privilege clustered around the Stuart cause in 1686-7 where they would remain until at least the 1760s.

Thus, in the Munster poet Dáibhí Ó Bruadair's 'Caithréim an dara Séamuis', the true (Catholic) clergy were contented and untroubled and because of this powerful knight (James II), the clergy of Calvin could no longer pursue their persecution of popery. Ó Bruadair rejoiced as he contemplated Catholic priests surrounding the king at Whitehall. He also lauded Tyrconnell's transformation of the Irish judiciary. He joyously proclaimed that a Daly (Denis) and a Rice (Sir Stephen) sat on the bench and were being exhorted by a lawyer of the Nagles (Sir Richard) to hear the pleas of those who did not speak the stiff upper-lipped, simpering English tongue:

> Atáid bhar bhfírchliar sámh gan dímhiadh
> D'áis an chaoimhniadh chomhachtaigh
> is cléirche Chailbhín béar nach anaoibh
> gan pléidh a bpeataoi ar phópaireacht.
> atáid ar bínnse Dálaigh Rísigh
> sdá n-áileadh saoi do Nóglachaibh
> re héisteacht agartha an té nach labhrann
> béarla breaganta beoiltirim.[130]

James is also eulogised in the Irish literary tradition as the royal star ('an realta ríoghdha'), the proven prince ('prionnsa dearbhtha'), the beloved disciple of bravery ('dálta cléibh na cródhachta'), the stag and hero of Europe ('fiadh agus feinnidh Eorrapa'), the shield of the poor and leech of the miserable ('sciath na mbochtán liaigh na lorán'), taurine prince ('tairbhfheith'), duke ('diúc'), and ordained admiral ('Amairéil orduighthe'), bringing the herb of relief for those wounded and stricken to earth by the plotters of (Titus) Oates

---

130 Dáibhí Ó Bruadair, 'Caithréim an dara Séamuis', in MacErlean (eag.), *Duanaire*, iii, p. 88. Judge Daly earned the praise of the usually scathing Archbishop King; King, *State of the Protestants*, pp 64, 72, 168. Sarsfield incarcerated Daly on a charge of treachery but he was released by Tyrconnell on his return to Ireland and he later played an active role in the surrender of Galway; Wauchope; *Sarsfield*, pp 173, 175, 188, 193, 239. For a note on Nagle, see Hayes, *Biographical dictionary*, p. 209.

(the plotter) ('is táthluibh fhortachta a dtárla loitighte/ ar lár ó phlotaireacht Oates uile').[131] Elsewhere James is described by Ó Bruadair as the true king ('rí dáiríribh') and the lawful high-king ('ardrí ionmhain óirdhlitheach').[132]

Celebrating James's triumph over Monmouth and his treasonable associates, Ó Bruadair implored those leading troops in the service of King James, of the bright armour, or those in the command of hosts to their fellow Irishmen and to turn their strength on their fierce enemies:

> Gach cuid d'Éirinn nár Chromaolaidh
> tugsat d'aonghuth deonuightheach
> a gcuirp sa gceathra a ngoil sa ngaisce
> fá chur glaice an ghleobhile
> acht an taobh úd do lean traosún
> is tug faonchrú a bhfeola ris
> tugadar Alba turas nár dhearmad
> urraim is aire dá órduighthibh.[133]

Similarly his Munster colleague Diarmuid Mac Sheáin Bhuí Mac Cárthaigh urged his listeners to drink the health of the king's wife, Mary of Modena, whom he eulogised as the beautiful, languid-eyed branch of the pure palm of Modena, the sister (*sic*) of the pope and the generous alms-giving pious queen:

> Ólaidh sláinte Mháire an mhallaroisc
> ó Mhódéna, craobh don ailm ghlain
> Siur an phápa an chráibhtheach almsach
> banríoghain, diadha, chiallmhar, charthannach.[134]

Mac Cárthaigh's 'Céad buidhe re Dia' also celebrated the reversal of Protestant political and religious ascendancy and the emergence of Catholic triumphalism in the mid-1680s. He praised God for delivering the Irish from every storm that threatened and portrayed King James at Mass in Whitehall surrounded by priests:

> Céad buidhe re Dia i ndiaidh gach anfaidh
> sgach persecution chughainn dár bagaradh

---

131 Dáibhí Ó Bruadair, 'Caithréim an dara Séamuis', in MacErlean (eag.), *Duanaire*, iii, pp 78-80. Also see Leerssen, *Mere Irish-Fíor Ghael*, pp 255-60, 274-5, 447. **132** Ó Buachalla, *Aisling Ghéar*, p. 166. **133** Dáibhí Ó Bruadair, 'Caithréim an dara Séamuis', in MacErlean (eag.), *Duanaire*, iii, p. 84; 'A thrúipfir más múascailt ón mbaile hálgas/ar chúntas do phrionnsa go harmálta /...os fiú leis an gcumhacht dá fheartaibh ailne/an sciuirse do thionnlacadh feasta thársa/ciunnaighsi is dlúthaigh read dhearbhriáthair/is iompuigh do phionnsa ar do dheargnamhaid', Dáibhí Ó Bruadair, 'A thrúipfhir más múscailt', in MacErlean (eag.), *Duanaire*, iii, pp 38, 40. **134** Diarmuid Mac Sheáin Bhuí Mac Cárthaigh, 'Céad Buidhe re Dia', in MacErlean (eag.), *Duanaire*, iii, p. 110. See also Murray, *Revolutionary Ireland*, p. 60; *H.M.C., report* x, app 5, 1885-7, pp 203-5; *H.M.C., Finch*, ii, p. 310. Rumours abounded that Queen Mary was the pope's daughter, Miller, *James II*, p. 71.

rí gléigheal Séamus ag aifrionn
i Whitehall 's gárda sagairt air.[135]

He rejoiced that the tables had turned, that the Gaels were armed and that they had possession of gunpowder, ports and towns. Lauding the scattering of the Presbyterians, he invoked the devil's fart after the fanatics:

Sin iad Gaedhil go léir i n-armaibh
gunnaoi is púdar, púirt is bailte aca
Presbyterians féach gur treascaradh
is braidhm an diabhail i ndiaidh na bhFanatics.[136]

He exulted that John (the Protestant) was lost without his red coat, as Catholics no longer tolerated his intimidating 'who's there?' at the side of the gate:

Cá ngabhann Seon, níl cóta dearg air
ná 'who goes there?' re taobh an gheata aige.'[137]

Talbot's Catholicisation of the army delighted Mac Cárthaigh. The Protestant cat-call 'Popish rogue' was no longer countenanced and has been replaced by its Catholic equivalent 'Cromwellian dog'. The dreaded 'who goes there?' was heard without fear as the defiant 'I am Tadhg!' (a Catholic) concluded such interviews. Mac Cárthaigh triumphantly mocked the cheese-eating churls (the Protestants) who return to their trades, every long-legged one of them. He rejoiced that they were bereft of gun, sword or rapier, that their energy had evaporated and their hearts had sunk:

'You Popish rogue' 'ní leomhaid a labhairt sinn
acht 'Cromwellian dog' is focal faire againn
nó 'cia súd thall' go teann gan eagla
'Mise Tadhg' géadh teinn an t-agallamh.

135 Diarmuid Mac Cárthaigh, 'Céad Buidhe re Dia', in MacErlean (eag.), *Duanaire*, iii, p. 94. See also King, *State of the Protestants*, pp 15-16, 62; Moran (ed.), *Spicelegium*, ii, p. 279; Phillips, *The interest of England*, p. 13; *The Irish hudibras*, p. 12; Miller, *James II*, p. 173. **136** Diarmuid Mac Cárthaigh, 'Céad Buidhe re Dia' in MacErlean (eag.), *Duanaire*, iii, pp 96, 128. **137** Diarmuid Mac Cárthaigh, 'Céad Buidhe re Dia' in MacErlean (eag.), *Duanaire*, iii, pp 12, 94, 96, 128. See also Bodl., Carte Ms 229, fol. 47. Connolly dismisses these lines as 'the sentiments of a traditionally minded member of a disappearing class, expressing ethnic and cultural antagonisms of a kind which by this time were becoming less acute'; Connolly, 'The defence of Protestant Ireland', Bartlett and Jeffrey (ed.), *Military history of Ireland*, p. 244. This opinion flies in the face of hundreds of sectarian, anti-Protestant poems composed in the Jacobite period. Canny suggests that this role reversal (the catholicisation of the army) was welcomed by all Catholics 'as is clear from an examination of the poetry of Dáibhí Ó Bruadair who composed a chronology in verse in the period'; Canny, 'Irish resistance to empire', p. 303. Numerous other contemporary references would seem to justify Canny's claim. This Catholic reaction is typified by the reception of the new charter from James II for the town of New Ross in 1687; Vigours, 'An account of the reception of a new charter from King James II to the town of New Ross', pp 133–6.

Bodaigh an Cháise táid go hatuirseach
ag filleadh ar a gcéird gach spéice smeartha aca
gan ghunna, gan chloidheamh gan pinnse chleachtadar
d'imthigh a mbrígh is tá an croidhe dá ghreada aca.[138]

Apart from the poetry of Ó Bruadair and Mac Cárthaigh, a series of 'caointe' (laments) have survived both in manuscript and in the folk tradition.[139] These illuminate the major events of the war, James's arrival in Ireland in the spring of 1689 and his decision to issue the infamous brass money. They also chart the progress of the Jacobite army in Ulster in the autumn of 1689 (particularly Derry), the camp at Newry (County Down), the fever-ridden stalemate outside Dundalk (County Louth), the defeat at the Boyne (County Louth), the first siege of Limerick July-August 1690, the war in Munster in autumn 1690 (particularly Kinsale, County Cork), Clonmel, Carrick-on-Suir, Thurles (County Tipperary), the battle of Aughrim (County Galway), July 1691, and the second Siege of Limerick.[140] This diversity would suggest that the poetry was being heard by the greater populace. It became a medium whereby news of political and military events percolated down the social pyramid. The survival of this material in both the manuscript and oral traditions of Ulster and Munster suggests a flourishing Jacobite culture among the Catholic population. Its populist nature indicates that the poet retained his role as political chronicler. For example, the defeat at the Boyne was dismissed by one anonymous poet. He

---

138 Diarmuid Mac Cárthaigh 'Céad buidhe re Dia', in MacErlean (eag.), *Duanaire*, iii, pp 94, 98. See also ibid., pp 14-15. In his 'Tuireamh Mhurcha Crúis', the Ulster poet Séamas Dall Mac Cuarta notes his relationship to golden Tyrconnell who was the companion of King James, the most important adviser and spokesman in the region 'Is Tablóidigh an óir bhí i gcomhar Rí Séamas,/Ceannfoirt is comhairligh ba mhó ins na réigiúin-'; Séamas Dall, 'Tuireamh Mhurcha Crúis' (eag.), *Séamas Dall*, p. 35. There are other contemporary portraits of Tyrconnell; *A full and impartial account of the secret consults*, pp 43, 58, 71; *The Royal flight*, p. 39; Gilbert (ed.), *Jacobite narrative*, pp 5, 15, 17; Bodl., Carte 229, fols 48, 55; King, *State of Protestants*, pp 19-20, 97.   **139** In relation to these songs Ó Buachalla asserts (quoting Frank O'Connor) that 'for the first time we hear the voice of the plain people of Ireland, left without leaders or masters'; Ó Buachalla, *Aisling Ghéar*, p. 171.   **140** 'James's arrival, Spring 1689'. (Teacht Shéamais, Earrach 1689): King James came to us in Ireland/with his English shoe and Irish shoe/ and coined into money for our pay the bottom of brass cauldrons/Let the Gaill of Ireland have the old brass 'Do tháinig rí Séamas chughainn go hÉire/rena bhróg ghallda 's rena bhróg Ghaelach/tóin an oighin bhuí do leaghadh mar phay dhúinn/bíodh an t-athphrás ag Gallaibh na hÉireann'; 'An Cogadh in Ultaibh, Fómhair 1689'. Elsewhere, the poet curses the Protestant citadel of Derry: 'Londonderry', pox to you 'A Londain Doire, bolgach chugatsa'. He described other engagements in Ulster: At Newry our companies were crushed and at Dundalk our camp was stretched 'Ag Iúr Chinn trá bhí ár gcompáin cloíte/is os cionn Dhún Dealgan bhí ár gcampaí sínte'. He also uttered one hundred laments for the fever that took off my hair and left me without a wisp 'Céad léan ar an fiabhras do bhain mo ghruaig díom/is d'fhág sé maol mé gan aon ruinne', 'Briseadh na Bóinne, Iúil 1690'; 'Luimneach: An chéad Léigear Iúil-Lúnasa 1690'; 'An Cogadh sa Mhumhain Fómhair 1690'; 'Eachroim Iúil 1691'; 'Luimneach: An Dara Léigear, Fómhair 1691'; edited by Ó Buachalla (eag.), 'Briseadh na Bóinne', pp 89, 90, 91; For the death of prominent Irish Jacobites, including Donnchadh Ó Briain, in the 'Breda' in Cork Harbour in 1690; Conchubhar Ó Briain, 'Ar bhás Dhonnchaidh Uí Bhriain A.D. 1690', in Ó Foghludha (eag.), *Carn Tighearnaigh*, p. 11.

urged the Meathmen not to be upset about the harvest or the defeat at the Boyne since Sarsfield was strong and his troops disciplined and he would drive the churls out of Ireland:

A scológaí na Mí, ná goilleadh oraibh an fómhar
nó an mórchloí fuaramar ag briseadh na Bóinne;
tá an Sáirséalach láidir is a thrúpaí aige in ordú
le gunnaíbh is drumaibh leis na bodaigh a chur as Fódhla.
's seinn och! ochón![141]

Another poet explored the heart-searchings of the Irish boys, breaking their hearts walking the mountains, looking out from Ireland's ports and shedding tears because they campaigned without King James:

Is iad na buachaillí seo buachaillí Gaelacha,
ag briseadh a gcroí ag siúl na sléibhte,
ag amharc amach ar chuantaí na hÉireann
is ag sileadh na súl ag siúl gan Séamas,
is uch! uchón![142]

The elevation of Sarsfield in popular verse followed his emergence as the military hero upon whom the Irish placed their hopes in the immediate aftermath of the first siege of Limerick.[143] Ó Bruadair eulogised his heroic defence of Limerick and the destruction of the Williamite siege-train at Ballineety, County Limerick in his 'Caithréim Phádraig Sáirséal'. He gloated that Sarsfield had left nothing of their bombs and copper pontoons or anything bigger than a coin of their brass ordnance, all of which he blew away like a candle snuffed in open air:

Níor fhág bumba ná bád úmha
ná bánbhonn dá bprásghréithibh

---

141 Ó Buachalla (eag.), 'Briseadh na Bóinne, Iúil 1690', p. 91. For a representation of this sentiment in contemporary sources; Wauchope, *Sarsfield*, pp 111-13. The obvious delight of the Williamites in Ireland after their victory at the Boyne prompted a defiant Irish poem from a dragoon in King James's army; Anon, 'Goidé an sgléip seo ar ughdaraibh an Bhéarla', in Ó Muirgheasa (eag.), *Dhá chéad*, pp 21-2; Ó Buachalla (eag.), 'Briseadh na Bóinne', p. 100. Also see U.L., Cambs., Add. Ms 1 [c], fol. 66. There is evidence of Irish despair after the Boyne in Irish literature in English and Irish; Brían Ó Fearrghail, 'Is é lá na Bóinne do bhreoidh go h-éag mé', *Cat. Ir. Mss. in R.I.A.*, fasc. 1-5, p. 149; fasc. 6-10, p. 929; R.I.A., Ms 23.0.35; Risk, 'Séan Ó Neachtain', p. 55. See also Bodl., Carte Ms 229, fols 372-3; Gilbert (ed.), *Jacobite narrative*, p. 109; N.L.I., Ms 476, fol. 595; O'Callaghan (ed.), *Macariae*, pp 48-9, 52; H.M.C., *Finch*, ii, pp 358, 361-2; Clarke (ed.), *Life of James II*, ii, p. 408; Berwick (ed.), *Rawdon papers*, pp 346-8; Forman, *A defence*, pp 24-6.   142 'Luimneach: An chéad léigear' (Iúil-Lúnasa 1690), in Ó Buachalla (eag.), *Briseadh na Bóinne*, pp 91, 99. See also H.M.C., *Finch*, ii, pp 470-3, 478; Clarke, (ed.), *Life of James II*, ii, p. 393; Murray, *Revolutionary Ireland*, p. 252.   143 M. l'Abbé Gravel à M. De Louvois, 25 Dec. 1690, in Molloy (ed.), *Franco-Irish correspondence*, iii, p. 168.

i mBaile an Fhaoitigh gan a scaoileadh
mar ghal choinnle in ndáil spéire.[144]

However, these triumphs were short-lived. 'Eachroim an áir' (Aughrim of the
slaughter) made a searing impression on the Irish consciousness.[145] Another poet
lamented the hordes of strong courageous soldiers, young aristocrats and powerful men clad in green, black and red coats who had died for James at Aughrim.
He mourned that they took the first blow at the side of the Boyne and the
second at Moate and the third and heaviest blow at Aughrim which few
survived:

Is iomdha saighdiúir láidir meanmnach,
mac duine uasail is sárfhear ceannasach,
faoi chlócaí uaithne, dubha agus dearga
do chailleadh le Séamas thíos in Eachroim
och! ochón!

Thug sinn an chéad bhriseadh ag bruach na Bóinne,
an dara briseadh ag Móta Ghráinne Óige,
an tríú bhriseadh in Eachroim Dé Domhnaigh,
buaileadh buille dhroma linn is cha mór a bhí beo againn.[146]

While Sarsfield's star remained in the ascendant, James's popularity
suffered following his hasty flight after the Boyne. According to one folk tradition, Sarsfield was so disgusted with the behaviour of his sovereign at the
Boyne that he maintained that the outcome of the battle would have been
entirely different if the heads of the armies were reversed:

---

144 Ó Bruadair 'Caithréim Phádraig Sáirséal', in MacErlean (eag.), *Duanaire*, iii, pp 142-58. See also Ó
Buachalla (eag.), 'Briseadh na Bóinne', p. 91; U.L., Cambs., Add. Ms 1, fol. 95; Wauchope, *Sarsfield*, pp
144, 153. **145** It is in Aughrim of the slaughter where they are to be found, their damp bones lying
uncoffined 'Is in Eachroim an áir atáid ina gcónaí/Taise na gcnámh ar lár gan chónra'; Séamas Dall,
'Tuireamh Shomhairle Mhic Dhomhnaill'; Ó Gallchóir (eag.), *Séamas Dall Mac Cuarta*, p. 63. **146**
'Eachroim (Iúil 1691)', in Ó Buachalla (eag.) 'Briseadh na Bóinne', p. 94. See also 'Briseadh Eachdhruim',
in Ó Muirgheasa (eag.), *Dhá chéad*, pp 22-3. There is a reference in a contemporary pamphlet to the 'merry
boys' in County Wicklow; *The indictment and arraignment of John Price*, p. 3. Aughrim has loomed large
in the Irish tradition; Dunton, *Teagueland*, p. 14. Molyneux described the walls of human skulls at the
old Franciscan friary adjacent to Aughrim and the skulls scattered on the battlefield; T.C.D., Ms 883(II),
fols 73, 82. Charles Leslie claims that the Williamites butchered two thousand Irish Jacobites after they had
sought quarter; Leslie, *An answer*, pp 162-3. There are numerous other examples from Irish literature which
show the importance of Aughrim in the Irish Jacobite tradition. Two couplets, English translations from
Irish, lamented 'Our friends in vast numbers and languishing forms/Left lifeless in mountains corroded
by worms' and Ireland's undoing by the those unburied that 'are all overground' quoted in Ó Muirithe
(ed.), 'Tho' not in full style compleat', pp 93-103. Art Mac Cumhaigh decried the Irish of all classes who
died at Aughrim 'nó gur básadh in Eachroim gach aicme de na Gaeil'; Mac Cumhaigh, 'Agallamh le
Caisleán na Glasdromaine', in Ó Fiaich (eag.), *Mac Cumhaigh*, pp 82. See also idem, 'Aisling Airt Mhic

An lá úd a chuaidh muinne os cionn sruth Bóinne,
gé go raibh bombaí arda is grán linn á scaoileadh;
le athrú ceannphoirt throidfeamaois arís iad'
's och!, a choirnéil Sáirséal céad slán go dtí tú!
's seinn óch óchón[147]

Another recorded that when James II disparaged his cowardly Irish army for
fleeing the Boyne, Lady Tyrconnell mocked him for reaching Dublin well in
advance of them.[148] James's flight from the field is also remembered in the folk
tradition: One verse recounts James's muster at Donore and the besieging and
engaging of his host at Duleek. His subsequent flight is recounted by a woman
from Tara who mocked him that his pursuers were close on his trail:

Aige Dún Uabhair a buaileadh an droma leis,
Is aige Damhliag cuireadh siege ag troideadh leis;
dá bhfeicfeá rí Séamas is bean Teamhrach ag magadh air,
'sin chugat an tóir, chugat an tóir, chugat a tóir a Shéamais.[149]

The worthy knight had become 'Séamas an chaca' (James the shite) who,
with his one English shoe and one Irish shoe, had lost Ireland:

Séamas an chaca, a chaill Éirinn
lena leathbhróg ghallda is a leathbhróg Ghaelach.[150]

Another Irish poet also accused him of having one English and one Irish
shoe, causing misery all over Ireland and doing nothing to alleviate it as the
jack boots crushed the poor Gaels:

Chumhaigh', in ibid., p. 112; Bodl., Carte Ms 229, fol. 412; Ní Ógáin (eag.), *Duanaire Ghaedhilge*, i, p. 111.
Whig literature from the early-eighteenth century mocked this Irish fixation with Aughrim; Moffett,
Hesperi neso graphia, pp 15-16, 25-7.   **147** 'Slán le Sáirséal (Nollaig, 1691)', in Ó Buachalla (eag.), 'Briseadh
na Bóinne', p. 96. Simms states that Sarsfield cast this aspersion on James, Hardiman claims that it was Sir
Tadhg O'Reagan. See also Murray, *Revolutionary Ireland*, p. 227.   **148** James II: 'Your countrymen,
madam, can run well' and she (Lady Tyrconnell) replied, 'Not quite as well as your majesty for I see you
won the race'; Simms, *Jacobite Ireland*, p. 153.   **149** Ó Buachalla (eag.), 'Briseadh na Bóinne', p. 84.
There are many other references to James's cowardice in the popular literature and in the folk tradition;
ibid., pp 169-70; Ó Buachalla, *Aisling Ghéar*, p. 169.   **150** Ó Buachalla (eag.), 'Briseadh na Bóinne', p.
84. For other representations of this, see *The present state of Europe*, p. 81; Campbell, *A philosophical survey*,
Ó Cróinín (eag.), *Seanchas ó Chairbre*, p. 29; Ó hÓgáin, 'An stair agus an litríocht béil', pp 173-96; Teeling,
History of the rebellion of 1798, pp 103-5. Gerard Murphy provides a proper context for James's derogatory
nickname 'Séamas an chaca'; Murphy, 'Royalist Ireland', p. 603. Many of his contemporaries accused
James of partiality to the English interest: Plunkett, 'A light to the blind' (Bodl., Carte Ms 229, fols 342,
361, 366); Leslie, *An answer*, p. 125; [Sargeant], *Historical romance*, p. 39; *Conference between a Papist and
a Protestant concerning the present fears of Londonderry and Ireland; An apology for the Protestants of Ireland*,
p. 12; *A letter from a gentleman in Ireland*, p. 6; Miller, *James II*, pp 224-5; Simms, *Jacobite Ireland*, p. 82.

Nárb é do bheatha anall chughainn a rí ghil Séamas
red leathbhróg ghallda is red bhróg eile Gaelach
ag déanamh buartha ar fuaid na hÉireann
's nár thug tú bualadh uait ná réiteach,
cuirimse mo mhallacht ortsa, a rí Séamas
is iomdha mac máthara a d'fhág tú in éide,
fána stocaí geala is a gcarabhataí gléigeal,
is bróga móra fuiate ar chlann na nGael bocht.[151]

The king had become a liability to his Irish subjects. A Jacobite officer in Athlone reported that 'the dauphin was landed in England with a great army, the duke of Schomberg was dead and it was said the prince of Orange too. The king was gone to France, but it was no great matter where he was, for they were better without him'.[152]

However, the breach between James II and his Irish Jacobite subjects can be exaggerated.[153] His reputation in the Irish historiographical tradition has been distorted by an over-emphasis on derogratory popular verses in Irish literature relating to 'Séamas an chaca'. It has been further prejudiced by English-language source-material, including his own *Memoirs*, and the eighteenth-century Catholic writers who criticised the luckless king for their own political ends. As Ó Buachalla suggests, 'when James II returned to France [in the aftermath of his humiliating retreat from the Boyne in 1690], he sailed not into oblivion but into a well-defined niche in traditional Irish ideology – the rightful king who was banished from his kingdom, but who was destined to return and reclaim his patrimony'.[154] No sooner had he gone into exile than he became the toast of the Irish literati (writing in Irish and English). By this time, his historical rehabilitation had occurred in the Jacobite high political tradition, particularly evident in O'Kelly's allegorical *Macariae Exidium*, Plunkett's *Light to the blind* and Sergeant's hitherto ignored *Historical romance*. The responsibility for his disastrous flight at the Boyne and apparent betrayal of his loyal Irish Jacobites

---

151 Ó Buachalla (eag.), 'Briseadh na Bóinne' pp 85, 90-91. James in turn was less than flattering about his Irish soldiery; *H.M.C., Finch*, ii, pp 336-7, 361. George Story mocked James's flight: 'James II made haste to Duleek, and from thence to Dublin whither he got that evening by 9.00 and early next morning ... going towards Bray scarce looked behind him afterwards until he got to Waterford and so on ship-board to France leaving his poor Teagues to fight it out or do what they pleased for him'; Story, *A continuation*, p. 25. His cowardice in Ireland also featured in contemporary doggerel verse: 'We must confess we once run from ye/And turned our royal bum upon ye/ That bum, which to have made us come again/You should have kissed it and brought us home again'; *James II: Jacobite hudibras*; 'A hue and cry', in Lord (ed.), *Poems on the affairs of state*, v, p. 23; *The last will and testament of the late King James*. Charles Leslie notes that 'the generality of the Irish papists do at this day lay all their misfortunes on King James because he would not follow their measures; Leslie, *An answer*, p. 125. **152** Story, *Impartial history*, pp 99-100. See also *H.M.C.*, xiv report, app 7, p. 349. **153** Murphy, 'Royalist Ireland', p. 603; Simms, *Jacobite Ireland*, p. 153; Kelly, 'A Light to the blind', p. 432; O'Donoghue, 'Jacobite threat', pp 52, 202. **154** Ó Buachalla, 'Irish Jacobite poetry', p. 42.

shifted onto his corrupt and treacherous Scottish and English partisans. James became a messianic figure in whom all the hopes of the defeated Irish Jacobites were invested. He provided their only realistic hope until his death in 1701. Moreover, their belief in his return provided a balm for the wounds received at the Boyne and Aughrim, wounds which would be salted by the repressive legislation of the late-1690s and early-eighteenth century.

V

Irish politics in the era between the succession of James II and the Williamite invasion reveals underlying sectarian tensions which intensified in the immediate aftermath of the Monmouth and Argyll rebellions. This questions the received opinion that Protestants remained loyal to James II until his defeat at the Boyne. An analysis of the Irish Jacobite community on the outbreak of the war in 1689 shows that the clergy and the dispossessed aristocracy and gentry aided the ideological and military mobilisation of the Catholic populace in the 1690s. This pyramidal structure of the Irish Catholic Jacobite community, radiating down from the king, through the Catholic clergy, aristocracy and gentry would be replicated in the later 1690s and in the eighteenth century. Nevertheless, the final military reduction of the Irish Jacobite 'nation' in 1691 and the retreat of its army to France forced Irish Jacobites to divert their attention to the European theatre. This preoccupation with European politics and recurring Jacobite invasion rumours moulded Irish Jacobitism in the late 1690s and in the early eighteenth century. Their supreme confidence in a reversal of their political fortunes remained the most salient feature of Irish popular Jacobitism.

The rapparees who wielded half-pike and skean in support of their beleaguered monarch in 1688 provided the most visible manifestation of Irish popular Jacobitism during the 'war of the two kings'. Re-animating an earlier seventeenth-century tradition in which the depredations of their predecessors (the woodkerne and tories) had a political dimension, their activities were endorsed under the royal signet of King James himself. As a consequence of the bureaucratic, political and economic breakdown of the Jacobite war machine, plundering by the regular Jacobite army and rapparee partisans became closely linked. Rapparee attacks on the Williamite soldiers, their burning of the houses of their officers and their theft of horses for the Jacobite cavalry blurred the distinction between them and the regular soldiery and contributed to the wholesale slaughter of innocent Irish civilians. The Williamite government reinforced the association between the rapparees and the Catholic populace by their retaliatory assaults on the Catholic clergy and the wider Catholic community. Rapparees would remain a constant preoccupation for the Protestant interest in the latter part of the 1690s. This close relationships between rappareeism and the Jacobite cause served to politicise predatory crime in the seventeenth and eighteenth centuries, associating the rapparee with the 'Jacobite theatre of death' and the elevation of the 'outlaw rapparee' into the Jacobite pantheon in the later-1690s.

The Irish Jacobite poets who had lauded the triumphs of James, Tyrconnell and Sarsfield in the glory days of Jacobite political supremacy turned their attention to the heroic exploits of the Wild Geese in Europe or the residual activities of the rapparees in the late 1690s and eighteenth century. Finally, the cult of James II in the 1680s and early-1690s fluctuated with the vicissitudes of war from the elevated heights of the 'court' poetry of Ó Bruadair and Mac Cárthaigh in the 1680s to the disrespectful doggerel of the popular literary and folk traditions of the war period. Exile and death facilitated a rehabilitation of the discredited James and ensured the hero-worship of his son (James Francis Edward) in the eighteenth century. James's enigmatic position, and that of his exiled house, in Irish popular politics after 1690 is neatly encapsulated in a traditional aphorism recorded in Dinneen's (Ua Duinnín's) dictionary. This also epitomised the position of Irish Jacobites under William, Anne and the Hanoverians: 'Dá olcas Séamas, is measa bheith 'na éagmais' (As bad as James was, it is worse to be without him).[155]

---

155 Dinneen [Ua Duinnín], *Foclóir*, p. 1004. See also Ó Buachalla, *Aisling Ghéar*, p. 181.

CHAPTER 2

'An Longbhriseadh':[1] the Shipwreck, 1692-1702

Although the Treaty of Limerick had terminated the Irish war, nobody on either side of the Irish Sea or the North Channel considered the Jacobite cause to be totally lost. The armies of James II's ally, Louis XIV, continued to hold the line against the Grand Alliance in every European theatre. Indeed the army of Maréchal Luxembourg, (including the formidable 'Maison Du Roi' and the Irish Jacobite army which had followed Sarsfield into exile) inflicted humiliating defeats on William, in particular at the battle of Landen where he lost 12,000 men, eighty cannon and a multitude of standards. Between 1692 and the death of King James II in 1701, Britain and Ireland provided the focus of a possible French assault against the Augsburg alliance. For example, in spring 1692, 30,000 men, half from the Irish Brigades, had been assembled at Brest under the veteran French soldier Maréchal Bellefonds to accompany James to England in what has been dubbed the 'Ailesbury Plot'.[2] Louis XIV supplied a squadron of ships under Admiral Tourville to transport 10,000 men. On 19 May King James arrived at La Hogue to join the expeditionary force. Contrary winds delayed their embarkation until they were intercepted and destroyed at the battle of La Hogue by a superior force under Admiral Lord Edward Russell. The invasion was abandoned, the Irish Brigades were dispersed among the French armies and a despondent James II returned to the monastery of La Trappe.

Reckless Jacobite optimism and French desperation at recent military reversals spawned another invasion scheme in 1695-6 known as the 'Fenwick Plot.' In the period between the death of Queen Mary in 1694 and the spring of 1695, a group of English Jacobites, led by the earls of Arran and Sunderland, began making preparations for a rebellion. They despatched Captain Charnock, a fellow of Magdalen College, Oxford, to France to solicit an invasion force of 10,000 men (8000 infantry, 1000 dragoons and 1000 cavalry). Charnock proposed his plan to James II at St Germain in June 1695 but the French forces were too preoccupied with the European theatre to risk an invasion. However,

---

[1] Dáibhí Ó Bruadair, 'An Longbhriseadh', in MacErlean (eag.) *Duanaire*, iii, p. 164. [2] Szechi, *The Jacobites*, p. 55; Beresford, 'Ireland', pp 14-15; Genet-Rouffiac, 'La première génération', pp 126-7.

Louis XIV finally authorised the expedition in October. In the same month, the French admiral Pontchartrain proposed Yarmouth as the most suitable landing-point, although the Jacobite earl of Midleton opted for the area around Newcastle-Upon-Tyne. In February 1696 the duke of Berwick was despatched to England to evaluate the strength of Jacobite forces. James II proceeded to Calais at the end of the month to join eighteen battalions of infantry and thirty squadrons of cavalry that had been assembled under Lord Harcourt. However, this plot foundered on mutual distrust between the French king and the English Jacobites. Louis XIV was not prepared invade until a rising had broken out. The English Jacobites refused to revolt until the French king showed his hand. A Jacobite sub-plot to assassinate William III became associated with the invasion and caused serious embarrassment to James, Louis and Berwick. Despite the protestations of Berwick, Louis finally decided to postpone the invasion.[3]

Paul Hopkins has explored the extent of Jacobite intrigue in England and Scotland in the 1690s while Patrick Melvin has charted Irish involvement in English Jacobite plotting in the 1690s.[4] This chapter adds Ireland to the picture. Seditious Jacobite traffic with France and England and related lawlessness raised Irish expectations during the 1690s. This contradicts claims of Irish Jacobite amnesia in the late seventeenth and early-eighteenth century, as well as questioning the supposed 'shipwreck' of the Irish Catholic interest in the aftermath of the Treaty of Limerick.

Rappareeism, continued to preoccupy the minds of Protestant writers. Irish government officials and local political commentators associated rapparee activity with Jacobite expectation and advocated the persecution of Catholic clergy, aristocracy and gentry and the greater Catholic populace for their misdemeanours. The Williamite administration, although increasingly more confident with the political status quo, were nonetheless determined to highlight the need for vigilance by stressing the link between rappareeism and Jacobitism. In contemporary Scotland, banditry (real and imagined) was deliberately associated with political disaffection.[5] Lauded by some Irish poets as a Jacobite rearguard who would continue the struggle until the return of the 'Wild Geese', others dismissed the rapparees as ruffianly bandits who recklessly drew the wrath of the authorities on defenceless Catholics.

Catholic priests and Franco-Irish privateers also remained actively associated with Jacobite activity on the ground and treasonable Jacobite traffic with France and the Stuart court-in-exile. They continually attracted the attention of government officials, pamphleteers and Protestant clergymen. The displaced Catholic aristocratic and gentry interest remained preoccupied with the European

---

3 Szechi, *The Jacobites*, p. 56; Genet-Rouffiac, 'La première génération', pp 133-4.   4 Hopkins, 'Aspects of Jacobite conspiracy in the reign of William III'; Melvin, 'Irish soldiers and plotters in Williamite England', pp 256-67, 353-68, 271-86.   5 Macinnes, *Clanship*, passim.

war while a leaderless but seemingly unbowed peasantry made no secret of their affections for Louis XIV. Their expectations of a Jacobite invasion fed off successive invasion rumours and increased the unease of their Whig counterparts. These factors also explain the Protestant fears which led to the repudiation of the Treaty of Limerick in the later 1690s.

The Irish diaspora came to be seen as a Jacobite army, aristocracy and gentry-in-waiting in both the Jacobite and Whig camps in the later 1690s. By far the most numerous group among the Jacobite exiles from the 1690s onwards, their dominance within the exiled Jacobite army and the Jacobite regiments in the French army compensated for their weak political influence at the exiled court.[6] A vocal Irish lobby at the Stuart court, eternally hopeful of a restoration of the exiled dynasty and their confiscated estates, remained in regular communication with their Irish-based brethren in the 1690s. This forged durable links between the two main sections of the Irish Catholic Jacobite community and encouraged an emerging literary cult of the Irish Brigades in Irish and English. There is also evidence from the 1690s of a small but influential Irish Protestant Jacobite tradition, particularly among doctrinaire Protestant clergymen, disgruntled Tory landowners and converts from Catholicism.

I

With the war at an end and mopping-up operations in full swing against the rapparees, Lord Chancellor Porter underlined the need for dispersing the Jacobite armies. The safety-valve of transportation was once again deemed the most effective method of permanently closing the Irish theatre of war.[7] However, while levying these disbanded Jacobites for foreign service, the lords justice were careful 'to forbear naming any inferior officers to command lest those who should be out of hopes of employment should lead any of the disbanded and turn rapparees'.[8] The lords justice realised that the Jacobite officer corps comprised the remnants of the aristocracy and lesser nobility who were most likely to provide a leadership for rapparee bands. In spite of the caution displayed by the lords justice, Porter underestimated the dangers of Jacobitism and the disruptive potential of rappareeism, 'having no reason to apprehend danger but for some of them lurking rapparees which may be an inconvenience for some time on the country'.[9] Nevertheless the lords justice remained fearful of the possibility of French intrigue with the disbanded Jacobites who had filtered into

---

6 Rouffiac, 'Un episode de la présence britannique', p. 337, ch. ix; Genet-Rouffiac, 'La première génération', pp 331-78.   7 C. Porter to Nottingham, 9 Jan. 1692 (*C.S.P.D.*, *1695* [Addenda] *1692*, pp 175-6). See also ibid., pp 179, 221-2.   8 Lords justice to Nottingham, 1 Feb. 1692 (*C.S.P.D.*, *1695* [Addenda], *1692*, p. 178). Also see McGrath, 'Securing the Protestant interest', p. 32.   9 C. Porter to Nottingham, 9 Jan. 1692 (*C.S.P.D.*, *1695* [Addenda] 1692, pp 175-6).

the rapparees out of economic necessity. They regretted the failure of previous
disarmament measures and the retention of considerable arms by the obstinate
Irish.[10] The authorities employed the militia (ever the scourge of toryism in the
late-seventeenth century) to search houses for these arms. Their coercive
methods exasperated the general populace which had obvious advantages for
the remaining rapparees and tories, whose mobility left them outside the
clutches of their adversaries, and won them the sympathy of the persecuted
population.[11] The excesses of the militia bore heavily on the Catholic community and drove many more Irish into exile.[12]

The lords justice's correspondence with Secretary John Trenchard provides
another view of the links between rappareerism and Jacobitism and, more
importantly, an evaluation of their rebellious potential in the 1690s. In an
imitation of previous policy, the lords justice issued a proclamation in 1694 for
committing local priests and the relations, harbourers and abettors of the
rapparees until they were taken or killed.[13] On the receipt of information that
rapparee numbers had increased in any particular area, parties of horse and foot
were quickly despatched and orders were sent to the local governor of the militia
to send as many men as possible to participate in tory hunts. These exertions
had borne fruit as many rapparees had been captured and appeared before the
assizes where they were convicted and executed. However the lords justice concluded that there were many areas where there would always be rapparee activity,
In particular, they singled out County Cork where there were many mountains
and fastnesses, and where the rapparees were sheltered by the clergy, gentry and
commonality. They identified the range of people who filled rapparee ranks in
the 1690s, including degenerate soldiery, 'coshering' aristocracy and gentry and
those who were in liaison with French privateers:

> There will be always tories in serveral parts of the kingdom and no care
> or dilligence will be able to root them out. And it is not to be wondered
> at that after a war wherein many have been totally undone and others
> fear being dragged into prison and languishing there for debt or cause of
> action arisen during the war, many have gotten a loose way of living and
> cannot betake themselves to a laborious honest calling. Some perhaps
> receive private encouragement from abroad or concealed enemies at
> home to alarm the government and the country being so ill-planted
> there are more of this type of rogue than at any time.[14]

A proposal for reducing rapparees in south Kerry and west Cork in 1694,
surviving in the papers of lord justice Sir Cyril Wyche, bore out many of the

---

10 Lords justice to Nottingham, 14 May 1692 (*C.S.P.D., 1695* [Addenda], 1692, p. 187). Also see T.C.D.,
Ms 1178, fols 47, 50.   11 'For seizure of all serviceable horses', 27 May 1692 (T.C.D., Ms 1178, fols 51, 53).
See also *C.S.P.D., 1691*, p. 280; *C.S.P.D., 1693*, pp 442-3.   12 R. Southwell to King, 15 Dec. 1691 (T.C.D.,
Ms 1995-2008, fol. 194). Also see *H.M.C., Finch*, iii, p. 305.

observations of the lords justice and provided a microscopic view of the rapparee menace at a local level. The inhospitable nature of the local terrain and the fact that the tories were 'continually concealed and sheltered by their friends up and down through the fastnesses' called for extreme action. The author advocated sending three hundred heavily armed soldiers into the area encompassing Iveragh, Roughty-Bridge, Berehaven, Glengariff, Cumhulo and Cumer, Gougane Bearra, Iveleary, Agharus, Ballyvourney, Drumuckane, Cullin and Novahills, Killgarvan, Glenflesk, Coolmagort and Valencia, in Counties Cork and Kerry. The forty soldiers posted at Valencia and Berehaven would also prevent French privateers from 'landing any of their men and committing any more spoils in that part of the kingdom'. They were advised to provide a mounted strike force of forty local men, mainly operating in County Kerry, and one hundred and ten dragoons to operate from Skibbereen, Roscarbery, Macroom, Mallow, Castleisland and Tralee. He urged them to pay the soldiers fortnightly to give them no pretence for spoiling the country, and proposed providing pardons for those tories who helped hunt down their former confederates. He also advocated the imprisoning of the local chieftains and Catholic priests and holding them responsible for tory depredations in the areas where they were most active, stating that although the chiefs 'are not usually along with the tories in their villainy yet they have entertained them in their houses'. With regard to tory depredations in the area of Skibbereen, he noted their destruction of the livestock of Alderman Hore and several other gentlemen and their threats against the revenue collector. He concluded by warning that unless the authorities took this extreme action, 'no Englishman can propose any safety to himself either in his person or fortune, nor can any man without hazard of his life ride abroad a mile from his own house either about his own or the king's business'.[15] Lists of suspected harbourers of tories in Cork and Kerry included the names of surviving gentry and substantial middlemen which would suggest that toryism in the south-west retained a political and military character which marked it out from banditry elsewhere.[16]

Sir William Trumbull's letter to the lords justice of November 1696 sheds further light on the defiant activities of these Kerry 'tories', particularly the O'Donoghue of Glenflesk. The darling of the Munster poets, O'Donoghue's activities set a precedent for the quasi-Jacobite lawlessness of his neighbours, the O'Sullivans of Beare, in the early eighteenth century.[17] Relating his violent treat-

---

13 Lords justice to Trenchard, 27 Aug. 1694 (P.R.O., S.P., 63/336/65). See also *C.S.P.D., 1694*, p. 276; Bodl., Carte Ms 170, fol. 144. 14 Lords justice to Trenchard, 27 Aug. 1694 (P.R.O., S.P., 63/336/65). 15 'Proposals for reducing the tories, c. 1694' (N.A., Wyche 2/120); See also ibid., 2/121, 125; N.L.I., Special list 126, p. 33; *C.S.P.D., 1694*, pp 37, 76-7, 94, 276-8, 354; Bodl., Carte Ms 170, fols 97-8, 112-3; P.R.O., S.P., 67/1/403; *H.M.C., Bucc and Queens*, ii, part 1, p. 161; Giblin (ed.), *Catalogue*, iii, p. 47. There was also a great deal of tory activity in contemporary Ulster; T.C.D., 1178, fols 8-32. 16 Connolly, *Religion*, p. 208. 17 Sir W. Trumbull to the lords justice, 10 Nov. 1696 (*C.S.P.D., 1696*, p. 434). See also *C.S.P.D., 1696*, p. 439; T.C.D., Ms 750/1, fols 41-2; B.L., Add. Ms 28, 880, fols 241, 261; *H.M.C., Portland*, iii, p. 603; P.R.O., S.P., 63/359/241, 254.

ment at the hands of these Kerry 'tories', William Brewster, son of Sir Francis Brewster, reported that O'Donoghue had arrived at his house with 500 followers. His assailant, with four or five of his followers, forced his way into the house and proceeded to strangle Brewster 'with my cravat and his Irish thumbs' and 'went so near as to a miracle I escaped [*sic.*] forcing blood out of my ears'. Forced to flee after a small boy had escaped from the house and raised the alarm, O'Donoghue made his escape, 'roaring nothing but slaughter to the English' and repenting that 'he ever left any of the name of Brewster living in King James's time'. Among the twenty seven depositions taken after his arrest, one alluded to his defiant Jacobite rhetoric, including his boasts that Sir Francis Brewster's king [William III] 'was dead or had run away and my king [King James II] will soon be here and then I will hang you up'. Although imprisoned, O'Donoghue was surprisingly bailed by two of his tenants, notwithstanding a warrant, and he promptly presented himself at his victim's house, boasting that 'if he lived 'till May he feared no longer'.[18] At the same time, groups of ten, twenty and thirty tories were reportedly active in Tipperary. They not only robbed houses and travellers but stripped, beat and killed people. They surrounded fairs and attacked persons going and coming from them, inflicting serious damage on trade and commerce in the surrounding countryside.[19]

A spurious 'rapparee' proclamation from December 1694, attributed to Colonel Dermot Leary, Colonel John Hurly, Captain Edmond Ryan and Captain Matthew Higgins, also confirms the association between rappareeism and Jacobitism.[20] It attacked the members of the 'pretended privy council and loyal subjects to the arbitrary usurper, the prince of Orange' and his proclamations 'against the remaining part of King James's subjects, contrary to the conditions made at Limerick' which had obliged these 'rapparees to stand out upon their keeping in defiance of the present government to the ruin and destruction of their subjects'. The proclamation then offered a reward of £200 sterling to anybody who brought in any member of the Williamite privy council and a further reward of £50 for any of the chief officers of those 'rebels and traitors' who were 'still in arms against King James'.[21]

Rapparees and the politicisation of crime during the Jacobite war and in the later 1690s also interested contemporary Catholic Jacobite writers. Ó Bruadair's

---

18 William Brewster to William Trumbull, 24 Nov. 1696 (*H.M.C., Downshire*, i, part 2, p. 710). See also ibid., p. 711; Connolly, *Religion*, p. 208; Hickson (ed.), *Selections*, ii, pp 147-8. O'Donoghue figured prominently in the Irish literary tradition: Ua Duinnín (eag.), *Dánta*, pp xxvi, xviii, xx, p. 40; Ó Foghludha (eag.), *Cois na Ruachtaighe*, p. 13. Irish exiles in St Germain in this period expressed confidence that James would be restored; *H.M.C., Bath*, iii, 1908, p. 204; Cullen, *Emergence of modern Ireland*, p. 197. **19** Connolly, *Religion*, p. 204. **20** 'Col. Dermot Leary, Col. John Hurly, Capt. Edmund Ryan, Capt. Matthew Higgins, John Murphy and the rest of their adherents, a Proclamation', 24 Dec. 1694 Bodl., Rawl. Ms D. 921, fol. 98. See also *H.M.C., Downshire*, i, pp 508-9, 619-21; *H.M.C., Bucc and Queens*, ii, p. 205; *C.S.P.D. 1694-5*, p. 455. **21** Bodl., Rawl. Ms D. 921, fol. 98. This pseudo-proclamation is obviously based on a contemporary proclamation from the lords justice and council. The Captain Edmund Ryan in question is possibly 'Éamonn an Chnoic' ('Ned of the Hill') of the Irish literary

poem 'Geadh ainbhfiosach feannaire nár fhiar a ghlún' highlighted Catholic ambivalance towards the rapparees in the late 1680s and early 1690s. He castigated those who put thievery and pillage above the cause of their king. In the poet's opinion, the cause which scattered the learned men across the sea and plunged into misery those who stayed behind was the constant pillaging of the gentry and the unthinking disobedience of those who took to plunder:

> Cúis tar lear do scaip ár saoithe uainne
> 'sdo mhúch ar fhan fá shlait go fíorghruama
> drong dár bhfearaibh seanga ar síorbhuaile
> is drong re slad gan stad go místuama.[22]

Ó Bruadair's distaste for rapparee activity does not take the military and political composition of the Jacobite army in the 1680s into account. His verse does not consider the extent to which they became a manifestation of Irish popular Jacobitism in the period between the landing of King James in 1688 and the conclusion of the Treaty of Limerick in 1691, under whose terms the rapparees were included.[23] Ó Bruadair may also have frowned on post-Aughrim rapparee activity as their depredations could taint James's future cause.

Nicholas Plunkett reiterated these themes in his unpublished pamphlet 'The improvement of Ireland' when he deplored theft 'as the reigning sin of the nation which has brought a scourge on the Irish people'. Rewards should be offered to induce discoveries and these should be charged out of the country where the depredations took place. Plunkett also ignored the political aura which surrounded crime in the late 1680s and early 1690s, and the extent to which it was condoned by James II and the Jacobite authorities. He failed to note that his Catholic compatriots, particularly the clergy, continually bore the brunt of government retaliation for rapparee activity, and the fact that Protestants used it to extort money from Catholics in the 1690s. His suggestion that it should not be admired indicates that there were many Catholics who did just that.[24]

Rapparee motivation also provided the subject of a poetic contention between the Ulster poets Séamas Dall Mac Cuarta and Aodh Mac Oireachtaigh in the 1690s. It showed the extent to which the rapparee remained associated with Jacobitism and Irish literature, and an ambivalent attitude towards rapparees

tradition; *Irish Sword*, vii (1965-6), p. 79. See also Giblin (ed.), 'Catalogue', part 3, vols. 81-101, pp 44, 47. **22** Ó Bruadair, 'Geadh ainbhfiosach feannaire', in MacErlean (eag.), *Duanaire*, iii, p. 182. Ó Buachalla takes a similar attitude to this poem and also notes than Ó Bruadair castigated the soldiers of his former patron Sir John Fitzgerald who would not follow the Jacobite army to France; Ó Buachalla, *Aisling Ghéar*, p. 187. See also Ó Bruadair, 'An Longbhriseadh', in MacErlean (eag.), *Duanaire*, iii, p. 174; B.L., 36, 296, fols 48-55. **23** *The civil and military articles of Limerick*, p. 25; Story, *A continuation*, pp 268-9. **24** Plunkett, 'The improvement of Ireland' (Bodl., Carte Ms 229, fol. 52). Part of this has been edited by Patrick Kelly as 'The improvement of Ireland', pp 45-86. Also see Gilbert (ed.), *Jacobite narrative*, p. 67.

from some sections of the Irish community in the 1690s. According to Mac Cuarta, MacDaid (a rapparee) was the true heir of Guaire (a pseudo-historical king of Connacht who gave all his wealth to the poets) in respect of liberality, nobility and learning '('Sé is léir liom uaim gurab oighre ar Ghuaire, ar fhéile, ar uaisle is ar eolas').[25] Mac Oireachtaigh differentiated between these robbers and legitimate Jacobites such as Ó Néill, the true heir of Guaire, or Gordon Rua Ó Néill, from whom hosts fled, who had gone across the sea. The naked, hunted kern [tory, rapparee] ought rather to be ploughing or threshing instead of being talked up as military leaders in the place of the Irish aristocracy:

> Ó Néill ba dual bheith in' oighre ar Ghuaire,
> bheireadh buaidh gach comhraic,
> Nó Górdun Ruadh dá ngéilleadh sluagh,
> d'imthigh soir uainn thar bóchna;
> An Cheathern bhocht fhuar a mbíonn orthu an ruag
> a [ba] chóir bheith a' bualadh nó a' romhair,
> Gá dtarraing anuas mar cheann-phuirt sluagh
> 'n-áithidh dhaoine uaisle Fódhla.[26]

Mac Cuarta commended their prowess and courage, continuing to fight every day against kings, despite the fact that many were lost from their ranks with only one out of three surviving:

> Nach cumasach dhóibh 's gan cuideadh dá gcomhair
> bheith i gcogadh gach ló le ríghthe,
> 'S gurab iomdha neart slóigh a cailleadh dar bpór,
> 's gan duine theacht beo as gach triúr dhíobh.[27]

Mac Oireachtaigh further criticised their activities. He claimed that Eoghan (the rapparee) was not able for Billy (the Protestant) and his crew unless he stole sheep and cows. His four men would be carcases for the English instead (in the place of) of their music and merriment. Those who were killed in battle were the jewels of King James's army; they (the rapparees) cannot stop armed bands but avoid the highways and break into the byre of every house-holder at night:

> Níl cumas ag Eoghan le Billy is a shlóighe,
> muna ngoide sé bó nó caora;
> Béidh a cheathrar na bhfeóil ag Gallaibh go fóill

25 Mac Cuarta agus Mac Oireachtaigh, ''S is léir liom uaim', in Ó Tuathail (eag.), *Rainn*, pp 2-4.   26 Mac Cuarta agus Mac Oireachtaigh, ''S is léir liom uaim', ibid., p. 2. For a note on Gordon O'Neill, see Hayes, *Biographical dictionary*, p. 250.   27 Ibid., p. 2.   28 Ibid., pp 2-4. There are other examples of anti-government and anti-establishment sentiment in seventeenth- and eighteenth-century Irish poetry;

i n-áitidh a gceóil 's a n-aoibhnis;
Ní raibh insa tóir 'ar basgadh go leór
ach macnaidh na seód Ríogh Síomus;
Cha stopann siad shlóighe ach a' seachnadh na ród,
a' déanamh sladtha ar chró gach íocaidhe.[28]

Séamas Dall advised the mountain boys to stick together and keep to their isolated fastnesses until the Gaels come across the sea, blessed by the clergy, to
deliver the Irish:

'S a bhuachaillí an tsléibhe, cuidighidh le chéile
's cuinnighidh mur n-airgneach(?) uaignis,
Go dtiocfa na Gaedhil le guidhe na cléire
'ar thonnaibh i gcéin 'gar bhfuasgailt. [29]

Mac Oireachtaigh had the last word, and rejected them as weak and senseless
fools who supplanted the status of the gentry and suggested that many lies had
been composed about them simply for money:

Bodaigh gan chéill ag imtheacht i dtréas
dá gcur i gcéim daoine uaisle,
'S an iomadaidh bréag dá chumadh 'na ndéidh
mar gheall ar mhéadughadh duaise.[30]

II

Many Irish Catholics shared Séamas Dall's expectations and waited impatiently
for the return of their exiled sovereign in the early 1690s.[31] An early example is
provided by their reaction to the sighting of a fleet off the south coast in June
1692: they disarmed the local Protestants and took a stand on the coast which
alerted the military in Dublin.[32] Rumours circulated in summer 1692 and caused
disquiet in both high political and popular circles, resulting in the imprisonment
of several of the Catholic aristocracy and gentry and the disarming of Catholics
in general.[33] These preventative actions culminated in a proclamation calling for
a mobilisation against a possible French invasion, with a complementary assault
against rapparees, vagrants and cosherers,[34] perceived as the focus of residual
militant Jacobitism.[35] Lord Longford claimed that 'the Irish (the most

Gillespie and O' Sullivan (ed.), *Borderlands*, p. 87; Ó Buachalla (eag), *Cathal Buí*, p. 85; Ó Foghludha
(eag.), *Mil na hÉigse*, pp 89-90; Murray, 'The lament for Patrick Fleming', pp 75-92; Ó Fiaich (eag.),
Art Mac Cumhaigh, pp 93, 146-7. **29** Ibid., pp 2-4. See also Murray, 'The lament for Patrick Fleming',
pp 75-92. **30** Ibid., pp 2-4. **31** Bishop King of Derry received a report from a gentleman who

considerable of which have been for some time in town) the last week carried
their noses high and looked big'. However, he added that 'the latest packets,
bringing news of the defeat of the French fleet at Barfleur have made them
crestfallen'. Nathaniel Wilson, Church of Ireland bishop of Limerick, complained of 'the impudence of the Irish at this time', 'their confident expectations
of a turn' and 'their presumptuous carriage which makes the Protestants
discord'.[36] His episcopal colleague Edward Wettenhall, bishop of Cork, underlined commonly held feelings of discontent among Catholics at their inability
to maintain the struggle against the Williamites:

> 'Tis sure, only the power of our enemy is abated not their malice or
> bloody minds, I might add justly, not their pride or expectations. The
> common folk stick not to our face to tell us that they will have a day for
> it and they are as confident of an army from France as they ever were. It
> vexes no doubt, the considerable part of their whole nation, that they
> should have been able from the rebellion in '41 to maintain a war of
> twelve years, and yet that this, much more a universal effort of the whole
> nation to have shaken off forever the English yoke, of which they had
> such assurance, should be fruitlessly over in so few years. They are
> therefore, without question, busy to retrieve our confusions.[37]

During the period before the disastrous French naval setback at La Hogue in
1692, when a major invasion of 'Great Britain' was planned, Jacobites 'carried
their heads high'.[38] Their confidence may have been affected by the formal
contact which was maintained between Ireland and the exiled court in this
period. In May 1692 messages were allegedly sent and received by the senior

promised to endow a Jesuit school from the lands he would get 'as soon as the king came over'; T.C.D.,
Ms 1993-2008, fol. 219. This invasion threat also featured in contemporary Whig pamphlets; *Memoirs
concerning the campaign of the three kings*, pp 8-9 21; [Trenchard], *A list of king James's Irish and Popish forces
in France*, *A letter from a friend concerning a French invasion to restore the late King James*; *The present state
of Europe*, *Impartial enquiry into the causes of the present fears and dangers of the government*, p. 3; *James II:
Jacobite hudibras*. See also B.L., Add. Ms 28, 940 fol. 159.   **32** News from Dublin, 4 June 1692, in Giblin
(ed.), 'Catalogue', part 3, vols 81-101, pp 35, 39, 41; Beresford, 'Ireland', p. 14-17; N.L.I., Special list 329,
De Ros Mss, 13/82, 135, 137, 152-3, 161; N.L.I., De Ros Mss., report 126, p. 51.   **33** Sydney to Nottingham,
12 Oct. 1692 (*C.S.P.D., 1695*, [Addenda], *1692*, p. 212); *A letter from a friend*; T.C.D., Ms 1178, fol. 69;
P.R.O., S.P., 67/1 fol. 443 [223]; Macpherson (ed.), *Original papers*, i, pp 464-8; Giblin (ed.), 'Catalogue',
part 3, vols. 81-101, p. 39; McGrath 'Securing the Protestant interest', p. 65. At this time Dr Dermot Lyne,
an Irish Catholic landowner in Cork and Kerry, was incarcerated for relieving rapparees and tories; Lyne,
'Dr Dermot Lyne', pp 45-6.   **34** *Cóisir*, feast, festive party. In medieval and late medieval Gaelic society,
the higher nobility levied a rent-in-kind on their tenants by feasting and availing of their hospitality
which was always forthcoming, resembling the earlier cuddy or 'cuid oidhche', literally the night portion
of entertainment, food, drink and lodging which an Irish lord extracted from his vassals for himself and
his retinue.   **35** Sydney, Proclamation, 19 Dec. 1692 (N.L.I., Ms 1793, fol. 605).   **36** Quoted in
Connolly, *Religion*, p. 234.   **37** [Wettenhall], *A sermon preached on 23 October 1692*, p. 16.   **38** Quoted
in Connolly, *Religion*, p. 22. These invasion rumours also circulated in the press; *The present state of
Europe*, p. 477; *A letter from a friend*.

Irish members of James II's war-cabinet (including Randall MacDonnell, Patrick Sarsfield and Lord Clare) to Sir Donat O'Brien and their other friends in Connaught and County Clare. MacDonnell also sent an emissary to his native Ulster.[39] By January 1693, government attention was directed at Catholic officers and priests because of renewed rapparee activity.[40] An upsurge of privateer activity on the south coast undoubtedly facilitated the renewed transmission of optimistic continental war news from privateer ships. According to information sent from Skibbereen in July 1694, the crew of a French privateer which had anchored in Wexford after capturing a small vessel from Liverpool were 'very free in their discourse'. They boasted that 'Lord Galway [Henry de Ruvigny] had been taken prisoner to France, King William lay entrenched and would not fight them [the French] and twenty thousand men had been sent to reinforce [Maréchal] Luxembourg and that he would suddenly force us to a battle'.[41]

The information of Owen Banahan in August 1694 also reflected contemporary Jacobite optimism. He had served as a quarter-master in James II's Irish dragoons and spent eighteen months in prison after the king's 'abdication' for attempting to reach Ireland. Escaping to the continent, he eventually arrived at the Jacobite court of St Germain where he met Edward Nagle, one of James II's privy councillors in Ireland in the late 1680s. Nagle predicted that the French fleet would baffle its Anglo-Dutch counterpart, that the prince of Orange would fail to make peace between the Turks and the emperor and that the king of France would make peace with all except England after his conquest of Catalonia and Savoy.[42] On his capture in July 1695, the defiant Franco-Jacobite privateer Captain Vaughan claimed that the prince of Orange had already been beaten before Namur and that Dover would soon be reduced to ashes.[43]

The government feared the impact of such invasion rumours on Catholic expectations and moved against privateers, rapparees and other disturbers of the public peace. In February 1694 the lords justice stressed the need to secure key ports and prevent them from being used as possible landing places by the

---

39 Information of Turlough McMahon, 21 Oct. 1700 (P.R.O., S.P., 63/361/83). See also P.R.O., S.P., 63/361/81, 120; B.L., Add. Ms. 40, 775, fol. 283; MacDonnell, *Wild Geese*, p. 60; B.L., Add. Ms 21, 553, note 291. **40** Sydney to Nottingham, 5 Jan. 1693 (*C.S.P.D., 1693*, p. 3). See also ibid., p. 277; Murray, *Revolutionary Ireland*, p. 263; N.A., Wyche Papers 2, fols 120-5; Giblin (ed.), 'Catalogue', part 3, vols 81-101, p. 44; P.R.O., S.P., 63/355/79. **41** Information from Skibbereen, 23 July 1694 (N.A., Wyche 2, fol. 123). Privateers were extremely active off the coast in this period; Bodl., Carte Ms 170, fols 40, 63, 97-8, 112-3; *C.S.P.D., 1695*, (Addenda), *1693*, pp 181-2, 185, 193, 477-8; Giblin, 'Catalogue', part 3, vols 81-101, pp 36 40, 41, 46; *C.S.P.D., 1693*, pp 152, 200, 276-8, 364, 418; P.R.O., S.P., 63/357/2; *C.S.P.D., 1694*, pp 76-77; P.R.O., S.P., 63/356/46; *H.M.C., Downshire*, i, part 2, p. 480. A proclamation from 1692 attempted to discourage contact between fishermen and French privateers; *Twenty-third report of the Deputy-keeper*, p. 48. Melvin provides a contemporary political context and numerous other examples; Melvin, 'Irish soldiers and plotters in Williamite England'. pp 359–60. **42** Information of Owen Banahan, 16 Aug. 1694 (*H.M.C., Downshire*, i, part 2, p. 446). For a note on Banahan's career and his activities, see Melvin, 'Irish soldiers and plotters in Williamite England', pp 359-60. **43** Dr Richard Kingston to Trumbull, 15 July 1695 (*H.M.C., Downshire*, i, part 2, p. 507). See also *H.M.C., Stuart*, i, p. 103. Vaughan was finally executed in January 1697 (*H.M.C., Downshire*, i, part 2, pp 728-9).

invaders. In reply to the king's commands regarding the increase of the companies in those regiments designated for Flanders, Galway, Cork, Kinsale, Kerry and Dublin were identified as strategic positions from where soldiers could not be moved.[44] Further anxieties existed over the state of the army and militia. In July 1694, Lord Deputy Henry Capel stressed the urgency of calling a parliament. He deplored the decay into which the king's army had fallen, urged the need for regimenting the militia, and bewailed Ireland's inability to forestall invasion or internal dissent.[45] The Irish 'were never more insolent in these parts' and 'were ready upon all occasions to join them [an external enemy]'. Capel argued for legislation to disarm the papists, preventing them from keeping horses above the value of five pounds, restraining foreign education and for encouraging the taking of tories.[46]

The continued rumours and actual incidences of seditious traffic between Scotland, France and Ireland justified such fears. Although the nature of this interchange is seldom explicit, correspondence continued between the Irish Jacobites and the exiled court, often through the Catholic clergy, English Jacobites and French privateers who haunted the Irish coast. Sir David Nairne, a prominent Jacobite exile at the Stuart court at St Germain, referred to traffic between Dublin and the exiled court in the 1690.[47] Sir Robert Southwell expressed unease at the return of Catherine Newcomen, the wife of Simon Luttrell, former Jacobite governor of Dublin, whom he considered to be 'a very intriguing woman'.[48] In August 1694 Secretary Trenchard received information from the lords justice regarding several alleged spies operating in the north of the kingdom. From County Kerry, it was alleged that Sir Thomas Crosby continued to receive treasonable correspondence from his brother Walter in Flanders.[49]

An anonymous communication to de Chenailles, Secretary William Trumbull's correspondent in The Hague, disclosed a French-sponsored invasion plan of a type which constantly appears in the popular literature of the period. It proposed to land James II, and the 40,000 men camped at Brittany and Normandy, in Ireland. It also pointed to regular contact between Ireland and the French ports of St Malo, Brest and La Rochelle which contained sizeable Irish mercantile communities:

> Our main design is by sea where you know the great growth that has taken place. This is only to transport once more, if possible, King James

44 Lords justice to Trenchard, 20 Feb. 1694 (Bodl., Carte Ms 170, fol. 78).   **45** H. Capel to Trenchard, 14 July 1694 (*H.M.C., Bucc and Queens*, ii, part 1, p. 94).   **46** H. Capel to Trenchard, 14 July 1694 (*H.M.C., Bucc and Queens*, ii, part 1, p. 94). See also ibid., pp 105, 161; *H.M.C., Downshire Ms*, i, p. 508; Giblin (ed.), 'Catalogue', part 3, vols. 81-101, p. 44.   **47** N.L.S., Ms 14, 266. I would like to thank Professor Howard Erskine-Hill for making a microfilm copy of this available to me. See also B.L., Add. Ms 28, 939, fol. 85; *H.M.C., Finch*, iii, pp 355-7; P.R.O., S.P., 63/355, fols 19-21; T.C.D., Ms 1995-2008, fol. 317; *C.S.P.D., 1697*, pp 197-8, 243.   **48** D'Alton, *King James's army lists*, i, p. 213.   **49** Bodl., Carte Ms 170, fols 151, 154. See also P.R.O., S.P., 63/356/70i, 71i; P.R.O., S.P., 67/1/401 [201]; *H.M.C., Downshire*, i, part 2, pp 516, 518, 639, 650, 683-4, 708, 710.

to Ireland. The Toulon fleet is ready; it cannot be stopped passing the straits, the squadron of De Nemond and other vessels will meet and take it to Brest where all the ships will meet, one hundred in all. We have many transports and 40,000 men on the coast of Normandy and Brittany, part of which will be embarked while some of our ships amuse the enemy.... There are several Irish of all sorts at St Malo, Brest and Rochelle, some of whom have boats which cross to Ireland and are in touch with Ireland. Last Summer two of these boats went there, one was repulsed with loss, the other embarked men who were well received. They stayed some time, made some arrangements and returned with two hundred sheep.[50]

The Catholic clergy also provided a vital link between the two sections of the Irish Jacobite 'nation'. Lord Galway reported to Shrewsbury from the allied camp near Casal in July 1695 that two Irish Capuchins had passed through on their way back to Ireland. The older monk 'gossiped a good deal with the writer's people and apparently thought he had said too much as they both departed without calling for the money that had been promised them by the writer for their journey'. He suspected that their journey related to French proposals to the pope to re-establish James II as king of England. These monks, belonging to the neighbourhood of Carrickfergus and enjoying the shelter of the earl of Antrim, would have brought news of this continental intrigue to many impatient Irish Jacobites.[51]

The Downshire papers in this period detail the espionage activities of Colonel Maurice Hussey. These activities were sanctioned at the highest level in Whitehall and Dublin. Hussey was sent to Dublin to find out 'among other things, what are the correspondence between Irish Papists and France and what expectations they have'.[52] He received a letter from France which was forwarded and partially deciphered in March 1696. It bristled with Jacobite expectation: 'all our comfort is the expectation we have of friends abroad and their coming home safe and successfully and as triumph [*sic*] as the wind can carry them, and consequently enabling us at least to bugbear our enemies and keep them in apprehension'. It also made specific reference to 'Jennings and his comrade' (Lord Middleton and My Lord Chancellor [Fitton?]), 'Russmuillon' [duke of

50 Anon. to Monsieur de Chenailles, [8] 18 Feb. 1696 (*H.M.C., Downshire*, i, part 2, p. 619). Numerous contemporary sources allude to the possibility of an invasion in this period: P.R.O., S.P., 63/357/18; P.R.O., S.P., 63/358/4; *H.M.C., Downshire*, i, part 2, pp 598, 639, 650, 709, 717, 722; *H.M.C., Hastings*, ii, 1930, pp 256-7; Bodl., Ms 14, 266; Bodl., Carte Ms 229, fol. 476; N.L.I., Ms 477, fol. 21; Beresford, 'Ireland', pp 18-19   51 Galway to Shrewsbury, 25 July-5 Aug. 1695 (*H.M.C., Bucc and Queens.*, ii, pp 205, 252). 52 Trumbull to Southwell, 8 July 1696 (*H.M.C., Downshire*, i, no. 1, p. 496). There is evidence to suggest that Hussey had earlier received correspondence from France; ibid., i, no. 1, p. 490; ibid., i, no. 2, p. 707. In another letter Hussey expressed the belief that 'the Toulon fleet is all at sea' and stated that 'very few letters are suffered to come out of France; ibid., i, no. 2, p. 598.

Savoy [and 'Mr Kemp' [James II]. The cryptic and skeletal nature of Hussey's surviving correspondence to the authorities might suggest an unwillingness to incriminate his Kerry neighbours, while his refusal to take the Oath of Abjuration in 1708 justifies suspicions that he was a Jacobite sympathiser.[53]

William Brewster, who had allegedly suffered at the hands of O'Donoghue of Glenflesk, stressed at this time 'that the Irish were never so high or the English so low and that which makes me mad is to see most of the English courting and making friends with the Irish'. He lamented that 'my father [Sir Francis] is very melancholy and I believe he wishes that he had kept his money and not laid so much out here'. The Irish 'have some damnable design' as 'they meet so much and are so impudent', laying particular emphasis on the activities of 'Thomas Connor, the old plotter' who 'always goes to England in times of plots'. He concluded that 'he [Connor] has a great deal of money and credit from the Irish'.[54]

A contemporary analysis, attributed to one of the Southwells, presented both an overview of Jacobitism in the 1690s and a blueprint for the imposition of penal laws. Southwell analysed the structure of the Irish Jacobite polity and delineated the Irish Jacobite mentality. He believed that the outward loyalty of the Irish populace to the establishment was feigned. Their true loyalty lay with their banished king and the expatriate Irish, in spite of the loss of their aristocracy, clergy, lawyers and great men. They retained their veneration for King James and the 'pretended' prince of Wales, and were ready when the occasion presented itself for his re-establishment and the recovery of forfeited Jacobite estates:

> Though such of the meaner sort of Irish peasants as might be admitted to
> stay in their native country and may seemingly show a great respect and
> submission to the English as they have at all times usually done, yet we
> must remember that all this is but forced, so also but a feigned obedience
> ... These peasants secretly and amongst themselves will undoubtedly
> retain the same veneration for King James and the Irish gentry as ever
> and possibly more, considering the present distress they are in, purely
> beset them for the sake of the Irish interest and the popish religion and
> will therefore undoubtedly be ready when occasion shall offer to give their

---

53 Col. Maurice Hussey to [?], 12 Mar. 1696 (*H.M.C., Downshire*, i, no. 2, p. 639). Another letter from France contained the names of prominent Irish Jacobite exiles, including Daniel Arthur, the banker, Patrick Trant and Dr Sullivan, President of the Irish College; ibid., i, no. 2, p. 650. See also ibid., i, part 2, pp 496, 499, 516, 518, 722. David Nairne's diary describes traffic between Dublin and St Germain in this period: 20 May 1696, 7 Sept. 1697, 21 Sept. 1697; N.L.S., Ms 14, 266; Bodl., Carte Ms 209, fols 164-8. Having visited his Irish friends, Hussey reported the conditions under which they would support a Jacobite plot. These included a peace between France and the allies which excluded; *H.M.C., Downshire*, i, part 2, p. 726. Ua Duinnín and Hickson suggest that Hussey was a Jacobite and that he refused to take the Oath of Abjuration; Ua Duinnín (eag.), *Dánta*, p. xxiii; Hickson (ed.), *Selections*, ii, pp 129, 133-5, 143. **54** William Brewster to Trumbull, 20 Nov. 1696 (*H.M.C., Downshire*, i, part 2, p. 710). I have not been able to identify this Thomas Connor.

assistance for the establishing of one (the pretended prince of Wales) and recovering the lost estates of the other.[55]

Southwell identified the continental, pro-French dimension to Irish Jacobitism, which emerged in the 1690s, and survived for much of the eighteenth century. He feared a general European peace which would facilitate a French invasion, or a rapparee uprising in Ireland:

> If we consider the power and potency of the French king both in men and money and what an affinity there is betwixt those people and the French on the score of their religion and for the sake of King James which we conceive might be the issue of this, and if that king [Louis XIV] but make peace with the rest of his neighbours and were at leisure to attend only on the English war ... the numerous army of the French king being thereby idle, he would but make little scruple of picking a fresh quarrel with us on some pretence or another. How easy were it for them to pour three or four score or a hundred thousand ejected Irish or French, and considering the potency of his fleet as being able there to maintain them, which in conjunction with the ordinary natives (though but as rapparees) might make it more difficult to remove them than ever yet we have found.[56]

He harboured deep suspicions of the Irish soldiers in the French service, deeming them to be more than capable of returning to the country to lead a future rebellion:

> And whereas it may be supposed that such an employment of Irish papists abroad may be rather detrimental to the Protestant interest in Ireland by fitting men to be capable of leading a future rebellion in that country when time shall serve, I do not question that it might be so ordered as that but few private sentinels may be capable of returning and as for officers a provision might be made upon the greatest of penalties that none such should return to the country and if any might happen to return, I suppose they might soon be detected by Protestants. But if we should suppose that one thousand such officers or more should at any

55 'Discourse concerning the securing the government of the kingdom of Ireland to the interest of England' *c.*1695 (B.L., Add Ms 28, 724, fol. 4). Similar sentiments were echoed in a contemporary manuscript written by a disgruntled Jacobite *émigré* author entitled 'The groans of Ireland' which provides a glimpse of the socio-political prestige of the 'underground gentry'; Barry (ed.) 'The groans of Ireland', p. 134. See also *Mephibosheth and Ziba*, pp 18-19, 34-5, 37-8; B.L., Add. Ms 15, 895, fol. 15; B.L., Add. Ms 40, 775, fol. 126; B.L., Add. Ms 28, 881, fol. 6; B.L., Add. Ms 20, 311, fols 68-. 56 'Discourse' (B.L., Add. Ms 28, 724, fols 5-6). See also *H.M.C., Downshire*, i, part 2, p. 726; Plunkett, 'The king of France should make himself master of the sea' (N.L.I., Ms 477); Erlanger, *Louis XIV,* passim.

time gradually steal themselves into the country, yet if a due care be taken for ridding the country of all such idle vagabond persons upon whose assistance and forwardness to join in such rebellions, and upon whom the hopes of such officers must depend.[57]

In his exploration of the nature of Irish political nonconformity, Southwell pinpointed the Irish language as the key to the survival of English-Irish antipathy and, by extension, Irish popular Jacobitism.[58] Ironically, in his later advice to his son, the prince of Wales, James II had impressed upon him the need to 'wear out' the Irish language, the single most important vector of Irish Jacobitism:

> Great care must be taken to civilise the ancient families, by having the sons of the chief of them bred up in England, even to the charge of the crown where they have not the wherewithal out of their own estates to do it by which means they will have greater dependence on the Crown and by degrees may be weaned from their natural hatred against the English, be more civilised, and learn to improve their estates ... setting up schools, to teach the children of the old natives English, which would by degrees wear out the Irish language, which would be for the advantage of the body of inhabitants, whether new or old, and would contribute much to lessen the animosities that are among them.[59]

Against this background of continuing Jacobite activity in Ireland, constant communication with the court of James II and frequent rumours of a Jacobite invasion, the violation of the Treaty of Limerick and imposition of the penal code in the latter part of the 1690s becomes comprehensible, if not pardonable. In his commemorative speech to the House of Commons on 23 October 1698, John Travers defended the repudiation of the Treaty of Limerick and the imposition of penal legislation. His sermon reflected the relief of Protestant Ireland at England's inclusion in the Peace of Ryswick in 1697. This contrasted with the frustration of their Irish Catholic Jacobite counterparts who cursed the French for concluding the war without restoring the Stuarts:

> They don't, it seems, now so much conceal their enmity and I am glad of it that we may be better upon our guard and the more consultative of our safety. How long was it before they would believe the peace of last year or at least that we were to be included in it because they would not

---

57 'Discourse' (B.L., Add. Ms 28, 724, fol. 15). See also *C.S.P.D., 1697*, pp 197, 240, 243, p. 503; P.R.O., S.P., 63, 359 fol. 66; *C.S.P.D., 1698*, p. 54.   **58** 'Discourse' ... (B.L., Add. Ms 28, 724, fols 18, 31). The association between the Irish language and sedition figured prominently in English political discourse; Leerssen, *Mere Irish and Fíor-Ghael*, p. 52; Crofton-Croker, *Researches*, pp 181-2; Caball, 'Irish bardic poetry', pp 234-7; Quinn, *Elizabethans and the Irish*, Ó Buachalla, *Aisling Ghéar*, p. 513.   **59** Clarke (ed.), *Life of James II*, ii, pp 636-7.

have it so, and when they could no longer resist the evidence of it how far were they from being joy'd? Did they not curse the king of France and treat him ignominiously for sheathing his sword without the restoration of their king who would have destroyed us?[60]

Travers preached that Catholic loyalty to William III was 'from the teeth outwards' and 'to trust to it was to lean upon a broken reed'.[61] This opinion was rooted in contemporary political reality and the close relationship between Catholicism and Jacobitism in the late seventeenth century. Forged in the political and religious conflagrations of the late 1680s, it was promoted by the clergy during the mass mobilisation of the war period and sustained by the religious persecution of the late 1690s.

At the close of a most turbulent century, Sir Francis Brewster's *Discourse concerning Ireland and the different interests thereof* provided a retrospective view of the Jacobite wars, a sharp assessment of Irish Jacobitism and a defence of the coercive legislation of the post-war period. His description of Irish resoluteness against the Williamite regime, the emperor, the king of Spain and the Catholic princes of Europe during the Jacobite war surpassed in flattery even the most nostalgic of his contemporary Jacobite peers.[62] It provides an alternative opinion to those military historians who have recently dismissed the Irish Jacobite army as a fighting force and understated the significance of their struggle against the Williamite army. Even after Jacobite Ireland had been defeated in the late 1690s, its Irish Protestant counterpart viewed the Catholic populace and their *émigré* brethren in the French service with unrelenting suspicion:

> And notwithstanding that there has been all along the war considerable numbers of Papists in the French service many of which remain there this very day and the ruins of demolished towns and fortresses in Ireland and the vast heaps of bones of slaughtered men in many parts of that kingdom are but too sensible monuments of their villainy and cannot when we see them, but make us reflect upon their behaviour towards us. And remember how four years have passed since they were brought by downward dint of the sword, beaten into good manners.[63]

60 Travers, *A sermon preached at St Andrews Church*, p. 15. Also see N.L.I., Ms 476, fols 87-8; Gilbert (ed.), *Jacobite narrative*, preface, pp x, 192; N.L.I., Ms 477, fols 828, 872-3; Barry (ed.) 'The groans of Ireland', pp 130-6; Forman, *A defence*, pp 33, 46. Other Protestant commentators also noted their affection for the French king; *Discourse concerning Ireland*, p. 14; King, *State of Protestants*, p. 19. **61** Travers, *A sermon preached at St Andrews Church*, p. 15. **62** *Discourse concerning Ireland*, p. 14. There are numerous examples of this type of rhetoric; Gilbert (ed.), *Jacobite narrative*, p. 110; 'To the king's most excellent majesty' [1692/7?] (B.L., Add. Ms 28, 939, fol. 329); Clarke (ed.), *Life of James II*, ii, p. 466; Plunkett, 'Deserters of their country (Bodl., Carte Ms 229, p. 3); Forman, *A defence*, pp 30, 36. In Plunkett's opinion, 'His Most Catholic Majesty made a false step in letting the Irish war fall'; Plunkett, 'A Light to the Blind' (Bodl., Carte Ms 229, fol. 450); Hayes, 'Reflections of an Irish Brigade officer', p. 68; Flood, *Wogan*, p. 137. **63** *Discourse concerning Ireland*, p. 15. See also [Trenchard], *A list of King James's Irish and Popish forces*; *A view of the court of St Germain*, p. 12; Dunton, *Teagueland*, p. 14; *Some queries for the better understanding*

Brewster considered the dispossessed Catholic aristocratic and gentry class, momentarily restored in the glory days of Jacobite political triumphalism, and the Irish Catholic clergy to be the guardians of Irish Jacobite culture. As keepers of the Irish political conscience, they took an active interest in international affairs, particularly those of the French king and his young Stuart confederate, a concern shared by their *émigré* brethren. Brewster had no illusions about the possibility of their joining the enemies of England, the only means by which they might be restored to their estates:

> They think themselves too much gentlemen to put their sons to trade or breed them up to anything that is laborious ... but sometimes walk about ... inquiring for news, heretofore concerning the French king and his successes against the confederates, but now (I am sure) concerning the prince of Wales, what kind of spark he is like to prove ... They are always looking upon the least commotion to join the enemies of England and by the assistance of their clergy compel the poor ignorant common people to follow them to all mischief imaginable.[64]

King's *State of the Protestants*, the bible of popular Protestantism in the eighteenth century, also cast aspersions on this clandestine, but highly influential political interest:

> So they reckon every estate theirs that either they or their ancestors had at any time in their possession no matter how many years ago and by their pretended titles and gentility they have such an influence on the poor tenants of their own nation and religion who live on those lands that these tenants look on them still tho' out of possession of their estates as a kind of landlord and maintain them after a fashion in idleness in their coshering manner. These vagabonds reckon themselves great gentlemen and that it would be a great disparagement to themselves to follow any calling or trade or way of industry and therefore either support themselves by stealing or torying.[65]

of a list of King James II's Irish and popish force in France, A list of King James's Irish and Popish forces in France, quoted in Sweeny, *Ireland and the printed word*, p. 315; T.C.D., Ms 883 (II), fol. 73. For evidence that many Irish were returning or expected to return from France after the Treaty of Ryswick, see J. Vernon to Williamson, 26 Oct. 1697 (*C.S.P.D., 1697*, p. 444).   **64** *Discourse concerning Ireland*, p. 19. **65** King, *State of the Protestants*, p. 36. See also *Continuation of some pretended reasons for his majesty* [William III] *issuing a general pardon*, p. 2; *A view of the court of St Germain*, p. 12; Murray, *Revolutionary Ireland*, p. 58; N.L.I., Ms 476, fols 380, 743; B.L., Add. Ms 28, 939, fol. 329; N.L.I., Ms 477, fols 1, 6; *Mephibosheth and Ziba*, p. 34; Lord (ed.), *Poems on the affairs of state*, v, p. 407; B. N., Fonds Guerre, Ms 7487, fol. 283, N.L.I., mf. p.102; [T. Sheridan] 'Political reflections on the history and government of England [c. 1709]' (R.A., Ms. 2499); Trenchard, *An answer to the late King James's last declaration at St Germain*, p. 35. James II's 1693 declaration was discussed in the contemporary press; *The late King James second manifesto answered*; *A dialogue between King James and the prince of Conty*.

Catholics, for their part, resented what they deemed to be a gross violation of public faith. An Irish Capuchin, 'with tears in his eyes', told Cardinal Piazza of the miserable state of the Irish Catholics and 'the severe measures taken against them in spite of all the treaties made when the Irish submitted to the prince of Orange'.[66] Nicholas Plunkett went further, suggesting that the penal laws represented an unnatural violation of the rights of property, a vicious assault against a naked people, a provocation of God, an obstacle to trade and a disincentive to Catholics to improve their holdings. He also linked these laws and any future Irish Jacobite rebellion, claiming that the greatest consequence of the repudiation of the Treaty of Limerick would be that it would goad the Catholics into a rebellion 'to run out at defiance with the government and take revenge on the infringers of public faith'. Such an eventuality would result in the defeat of the Protestants of Ireland, 'who cannot defend themselves without the power of England'. Plunkett concluded that this violation would 'give occasion to the enemy abroad to stir the coals at home and raise a flame in the nation ... which would put England to her triumphs to quench such a fire'.[67]

III

The Irish diaspora in Europe became pivotal to Jacobite hopes for the restoration of the house of Stuart and the downfall of Protestant Ireland. They also fuelled the fears of those who justified the contravention of the Treaty of Limerick and the imposition of penal legislation in the 1690s. Despite the crushing disasters of Aughrim and the flight of the 'Wild Geese', Irish Jacobites did not lose hope in Sarsfield and the Irish exiles. In the aftermath of the second Siege of Limerick, the failure of French aid to materialise and the conclusion of a favourable Treaty, Sarsfield led the greatest portion of the Irish Jacobite army into the European theatre.[68] Although Sarsfield promised his men that they would return the next year, this proved to be the last direct intervention in Irish political life of the Irish Jacobite army and its successor, the Irish Brigades.[69] Nevertheless, the Irish Jacobite army provided the principal danger to the revolutionary settlement in the aftermath of the Treaty of Limerick. Redolent of Corkery's 'Hidden Ireland' or Whelan's 'underground gentry', this 'other Ireland' emerged as a vital focus of Catholic hopes and Protestant fears in the late 1690s. Sarsfield's metaphor was

---

66 Piazza to the secretary of state, 20 Feb. 1695, in Giblin (ed.), 'Catalogue', part 3, vols. 81-101, pp 47. See also pp 51-2, 63, 77.　**67** Plunkett, 'The state of Ireland in brief 'till 1703' (Bodl., Carte Ms 229, fols 133-4). See also Hayes, 'Reflections of an Irish Brigade officer', p. 73. Writing in the 1730s, Charles Wogan abhorred the contravention of the Treaty of Limerick; Flood, *Wogan*, p. 137.　**68** McLaughlin and Warner, *The Wild Geese*, p. 5. Matthew Henessy attributed this metaphor to William O'Connor, quoted in Genet-Rouffiac, 'La première génération', p. 351.　**69** Story, *Impartial history*, p. 259. See also Wauchope, *Sarsfield*, pp 257, 266, 280; Ó Buachalla, *Aisling Ghéar*, pp 186-7; 'To the king's most excellent majesty' 1692/7? (B.L., Add. Ms 28, 939, fol. 329).

appropriate as the Jacobite army and its successor the Irish Brigades became a microcosm of Irish Jacobite polity which had succumbed at Aughrim and Limerick. It provided a refuge on the continent for those who sought to overturn the revolutionary settlement, flee the penal laws or make military or ecclesiastical careers for themselves in France and Spain. Prominent Irish Catholic aristocrats and Jacobite generals (Sarsfield, Mountcashel, Arthur Dillon, Daniel O'Brien, third Viscount Clare, Andrew Lee, Donnogh Mc Carthy, earl of Clancarthy, Gordon O'Neill) retained their position at the head of this 'little Ireland'. Moreover, soldiers and emigrants from their spheres of influence were often drawn into their regiments.

The role of the Irish Brigades in contemporary Jacobite politics cannot be dismissed as the preoccupation of expectant Ireland-based Catholics and para-noid Protestants. A letter from Captain Charles O'Malley at St Germain to his son in Ireland before the abortive La Hogue invasion in 1692 shows that the exiles retained a role in the politics of post-Aughrim Ireland and eagerly awaited a return to their inheritance. He declined to confer the patents for his Irish property on his son and cautioned him against any participation in 'the court of claims talked of to be held'. O'Malley also informed him of the forthcoming Jacobite invasion in the ensuing spring, and of his hope that he might be restored to 'his dear wife, his son and his country'. A will drafted by Justin McCarthy, Lord Mountcashel, desired that he might be buried in Ireland and that his cousin Florence might inherit his empty titles. He also hoped that Florence and all those who came after him would endeavour to reconquer all that the English had taken from his family and that his future heir would devote himself to the service of the Stuarts and the king of France, his legitimate sovereigns.[70]

A cult of the Irish Brigades emerged in literary form as a significant feature of the Irish Jacobite experience in this period. The English Jacobite author John Sergeant provided the first example in his *Historical romance of the war between the mighty giant Gallieno and the great knight Nasonious* (1694). Lauding their heroics at the battle of Landen in 1693, Sergeant refuted the aspersions cast on their military prowess in Ireland and rejoiced that they had:

> won much credit for their courageous behaviour, breaking down all before them by which they convinced the world how slanderously the reports were that were spread of them in Utopia [Ireland], for then they were not inferior to the best of the Nasonians [Williamites] when well cloathed, armed and fed.[71]

---

70 Captain Charles O'Malley to Teige c.1692, in O'Malley (ed.), 'The O'Malleys', pp 32-46; Ó Buachalla, *Aisling Ghéar*, p. 188.   71 [Sergeant], *An historical romance*, p. 67. See also Costello, 'An Irish hero of France', p. 327; Bracken, 'Piaracy and poverty', p. 129.

Nicholas Plunkett boasted that 'our troops abroad, for these twenty years past, have raised the admiration of nations, because there was no bad conduct, no division and no treachery to thwart them'.[72] The heroics of Sir John Fitzgerald, lord of Clonalis, at the battle of Landen in July 1693 provided a lection to cure the deep gloom of his friends 'Is liachtain leasuighthe ar chiach do charadsa', according to his one-time poet Dáibhí Ó Bruadair. He also chided those rapparees who had refused to accompany Sir John to France after the Treaty of Limerick, promising that when he came home that they would be watching for him and seeking that mercy which they so little deserved:

> Triall tan tairgfir a hiathaibh eachtarann
> iaidhfid anamud nuaghnúis náir
> cliar ag salmchur briathra is beannacht libh
> rianfas t'aistear gan truailliughadh i dtrácht
> ar dtiacht chum baile dhuit biaidh do t'fhairesi
> ag iarraidh taise 's budh fuarchúis dáibh
> an chliath nár cheangail sibh dia na Carraige
> is iad re t'fhaicsin an uair úd tláth.[73]

The Treaty of Ryswick (1697) and the disbanding of the Jacobite army were crushing political and economic blows to the exiles. This provided the main theme for the memorial from one disgruntled Irish Jacobite to the French king. He reminded him that the Irish Jacobites 'had fought, during ten years in defence of their religion and their legitimate sovereign, with all the zeal and fidelity which could be required of them, and with a devotion unparalleled, except among those of their unhappy nation'. They had been totally undone by a peace which had not only failed to facilitate the restoration of King James but had also left his Irish followers 'deprived of their properties to which they had legitimate claims, but were likewise prohibited from returning to their country, under pain of death'. A letter from Walter Innes to Charles Leslie in 1698 added to this bleak picture of economic vulnerability and starvation among the Jacobite diaspora in St Germain in the immediate aftermath of the disbandment. He lamented that 'it would pity a heart of stone to see the court of St Germain at present, especially now that all the English, Scots and Irish troops are disbanded'. He claimed that there are now 'not only many hundred of the soldiery starving, but also many gentlemen and officers that have no clothes to put on their backs or shoes to put on their feet ...'. James II did not have the resources

---

72 N. Plunkett, 'Deserters of their country, the cause of its ruin' (N.L.I., Ms 477, fol. 9). See also idem, 'To his most christian majesty: the most humble petition of the Irish abroad in behalf of themselves and of their compatriots at home' (N.L.I., Ms 477, p. 1); idem, 'A state of the nation' (Bodl., Carte Ms 229, fol. 70); idem, 'A light to the blind' (Bodl., Carte Ms, fols 454-5)   73 Dáibhí Ó Bruadair, 'Is liachtain leasuighthe', in MacErlean (eag.), *Duanaire*, iii, pp 224-5.

to provide for their relief. Moreover, anti-Catholic legislation passed in the Stuart kingdoms exacerbated the situation; 'many to escape hanging at home are daily come here to starve'.[74]

IV

Irish Catholics and their exiled brethren did not have a total monopoly of Irish Jacobitism in this period. A Protestant Jacobite interest also emerged in the immediate aftermath of the Treaty of Limerick. This has been noticed by Irish historians, in isolation from the greater Irish Catholic Jacobite community. It has rarely been examined in the context of Jacobite high-politics in the 1690s. Sir Thomas Crosby, Jeremy Donovan and Sir William Ellis were all committed Jacobites who incurred the displeasure of the Williamite administration for actively participating in the 'Patriot Parliament'.[75] William Sheridan, Church of Ireland bishop of Kilmore, refused to take the oath of allegiance to William and Mary and became the only non-juror among the Church of Ireland bishops.[76] More recently, other Irish Protestant gentlemen and political figures with ambivalent attitudes towards the revolutionary settlement have been identified. Charles O'Neill, M.P. for Randalstown, County Antrim, retired from public life because of his scruples in relation to the Abjuration Oath. An unnamed Tory mayor of Galway proclaimed his commitment to the principles of non-resistance. Sir Arthur Forbes, second earl of Granard was the only Protestant supporting James II's cause who survived in politics into the reign of Queen Anne. Robert Saunderson, later M.P. for Cavan (1712) and Lord Ross, a son-in-law of Lady Tyrconnell, were expelled from parliament in 1696 for refusing to subscribe to an association to defend King William.[77] Charles Leslie typified this residual Irish Protestant Jacobite presence.[78] In 1696 Leslie and Lord Forbes drank King James's health and that of the queen, the prince of Wales and Princess Louise-Maria in London.[79] Other incidences of Protestant Jacobitism can be charted from the early 1690s. George Gregson, a prominent preaching Quaker in Lisburn, County

---

74 Henessy, *The Wild Geese*, p. 51, quoted in Genet-Rouffiac, 'La première génération', pp 380, 382.   75 Simms, *Jacobite Ireland*, p. 76.   76 Doyle notes that Sheridan's colleague Thomas Otway, Church of Ireland bishop of Raphoe, expressed doubts about the revolution but was saved from his fate by his colleague Anthony Dopping of Meath and by making a suspiciously formulaic declaration of allegiance to William III. One of his colleagues, the high-flying John Pooley of Cloyne had some problems with the Oath of Abjuration and condemned it in the House of Lords in 1703. Doyle also suggests that his successor Thomas Lindsay, friend of the Jacobite bishop Atterbury of Rochester, was 'distinctly non-committal' about the Hanoverian regime; Doyle, 'Politics', pp 165-6, 195-6.   77 Hayton, 'Ireland and the English ministers', pp 134-7. Doyle notes that John Methuen considered Ross to be 'an open Jacobite'. He provides a list of Protestants of dubious political loyalties, including Viscount Ikerrin, Lord Kerry and Baron William Worth; Doyle, 'Politics', pp 44, 196.   78 For biographical notes on Leslie, see Shirley, *History of Monaghan*, pp 148-51; W. Harris, *The whole works of Sir James Ware concerning Ireland revised and improved*, ii, p. 282.   79 'Information of Joe Cooper 6-10 June 1696 (*H.M.C., Bucc and Queens.*, ii, p. 346). This was not an isolated example; T.C.D., Ms 1993-2008, fol. 283, 301; *H.M.C., Bucc*

Antrim, had his windows broken and his buckets, wheel-barrows and farm implements burned for not making a fire on King William's birthday during the early 1690s.[80]

Some of these Irish-based Protestant Jacobites did not merely take a principled political or religious stance in relation to the Glorious Revolution. Walter Crosbie, son of Sir Thomas of Ardfert, was considered to be 'one of the most active of the Jacobite agents who carried on during many years an extensive correspondence with King James's secret friends in England' during the 1690s.[81] Other prominent Protestant figures, including Lord Granard and Colonel Cunningham, were also allegedly involved in Jacobite scheming during this period.[82] The abortive invasion of 1692 provides a context for the witch-hunt against the Protestant landowner and Clare magnate Sir Donat O'Brien in the early eighteenth century. He was accused by Patrick Hurley, former aide-de-camp to Patrick Sarsfield, of being a partisan of King James and being privy to Jacobite plots in 1692 and 1695. Although the veracity of these accusations rested on disreputable witnesses, they complement other evidence for the survival of Jacobite sympathies among a handful of Irish Protestants. The discovery of personal conflicts does not always deprive such testimony of its value in reflecting an atmosphere of sedition from which it derived its credibility. While stressing that the discovery of personal conflicts between litigants made such cases more difficult, Monod maintains that the government did not sanction political witch-hunts and these trials cannot be casually dismissed as a government ploy to root out Tories.[83]

Accusations concerning Sir Donat surfaced against the background of his Jacobite baronetage and war-record. The specific charges levelled against him included contacts with Lieutenant Charles McCarthy, Captain Christopher O'Brien and Christopher Butler, as well as known continental-based Jacobites such as Colonel Charles O'Brien, fifth viscount Clare, Sir Gordon O'Neill and Randall MacDonnell. He was allegedly engaged in oral and written communication with the court of James II, and was accused of having definite information regarding future invasion plans. This points to contact between Irish Protestant Jacobites and the exiled court in St Germain in 1692, if not by the accused, at least by the named witnesses, in no way an isolated incident in late seventeenth-century Ireland.[84] They also give credence to the alleged

and Queens., ii, part ii, p. 570; T.C.D., Ms 1489 (ii), fol. 65; Hayton, 'Ireland and the English ministers', p. 285. **80** Story, *An impartial history of the war in Ireland with a continuation*, p. 50; *The history of the war in Ireland between their majesties army and the forces of the late King James*, p. 112. James McGuire published a list of non-jurors in the late seventeenth and early-eighteenth century; McGuire, 'Church of Ireland and the Glorious Revolution', p. 149. **81** Grimblot, *Letters of William III and Louis XIV ... 1697-1700*, i, p. 403, quoted in Melvin, 'Irish soldiers and plotters in Williamite England', pp 361-2. See also P.R.O., S.P., 67/1/401, fols 201-2; Bodl., Carte Ms 170, fols 123, 151, 154. **82** Lord Galway to Vernon, 21 Oct. 1699 (*C.S.P.D.*, *1699-1700*, p. 269). **83** Monod, *Jacobitism*, pp 235-38. **84** Information of Turlough McMahon, 21 Oct. 1700 (P.R.O., S.P., 63/361/83).

flirtation of other prominent Protestants with Jacobitism, notably Arthur Forbes, second earl of Granard, Charles Butler, second earl of Arran and his brother the second duke of Ormonde himself.[85]

A hitherto unnoticed memorandum to Thomas Tenison, archbishop of Canterbury, written in June 1697, also makes accusations of counter-revolutionary activity against former members of the Jacobite political establishment. It questions the loyalty of recent converts and a number of Protestant landowners. 'Seven great managers' were identified, including Sir Stephen Rice, James II's chief baron of the exchequer, Judge Denis Daly, Colonel John Brown and his son, along with a number of unnamed Galway, Waterford and Dublin merchants. Their heinous activities, it was claimed, involved a clandestine attempt to undermine the Protestant interest in Ireland by cultivating divisions between Presbyterians and Episcopalians, breeding ill blood between England and Ireland, promoting the disbanding of the army and feigning conversion to Protestantism. The author's suspicion also fell on Protestant Jacobites, here represented by Sir John Edgeworth and Lord Strabane, who were conversant with some of these Catholic Jacobite suspects. These individuals, and other Irish Jacobites in south Munster, maintained contact with St Germain during this period.[86]

V

Irish Jacobitism survived 'Eachroim an Áir' and the 'Longbhriseadh' of the Irish Catholic polity in the 1690s. It remained closely linked to rappareeism, illicit traffic with French privateers and mainland Europe, and it thrived on recurring rumours of an imminent French invasion.[87] The unique relationship among the Catholic populace, their deposed and exiled aristocracy and clerical masters was

---

85 Ó Murchadha, 'The Moughra Affair 1699', pp 48-56; See also O'Donoghue, 'Jacobite threat', pp 73, 75-6; P.R.O., S.P., 63/361/81; Hayton, 'Ireland and the English ministers', pp 134-7; McGrath, 'Securing the Protestant interest', p. 47; Morley, *An crann os coill*, pp 15-29.   **86** Anonymous letter to Tenison, June 1697 (Lambeth Palace, Gibson Papers, vol. 7, fol. 38). See also B.L., Add. Ms 40, 775, fol. 284). During his reign as lord deputy, Henry Capel received complaints of the activities of 'some few creatures of my Lord Ormond', one of whom was Sir J. Edgeworth; Doyle, 'Politics', p. 33. A paper in the hand of Colonel John Browne was allegedly found in the papers of Patrick Tyrrell, Catholic bishop of Clogher, regarding a plot to assassinate William III; Murray, *Revolutionary Ireland*, p. 313. Other allegations of links between Ireland and St Germain survive in contemporary sources; O'Donoghue, 'Ireland', pp 154-5: *H.M.C., Downshire*, i, part 2, p. 710; *H.M.C., Bath*, iii, p. 204; Hickson (ed.), *Selections*, ii, p. 147; Cullen, *Emergence of modern Ireland*, p. 197. Accusations of treason were made against the fourth earl of Granard (Arthur Forbes), Colonel Cunningham, Madden, Brady, Broomfield and Toole in relation to a plot to kill William III: *C.S.P.D., 1699-1700*, p. 269; *C.S.P.D., 1697*, pp 360-1, 364. For a general overview, see Melvin, 'Irish soldiers and plotters in Williamite England'.   **87** Ó Buachalla makes the same point: 'Is deacair againne a shamhlú go bhféadfadh aon duine in Éirinn, d'aithle na Bóinne agus Eachroma, a bheith ag cuimhneamh ar an am 'when the rightful king is enthroned', ach tá seintimintí mar é coitianta sna foinsí comhaimseartha – ag Stevens, ag Ó Bruadair, sa véarsaíocht dhí-ainm agus ag údair eile; Ó

pivotal to Irish Jacobitism in the 1690s, and would remain central to the survival of the ideology in the eighteenth century. The impact of the European war, recurring Jacobite invasion scares in the 1690s and the imposition of penal laws against Irish Catholics further ensured the survival of Jacobitism at a popular level in the eighteenth century.

The Irish diaspora emerged as an integral part of the Irish Jacobite community in the 1690s and a cult of the Irish Brigades developed in contemporary Jacobite literature. Irish Jacobites, their *émigré* brethren and their political opponents on both sides of the Irish Sea increasingly viewed this 'other Ireland' as the main instrument of any future Stuart restoration. All shades of political opinion deemed a landing of Franco-Irish officers to be an essential catalyst for the outbreak of rebellion in Ireland. It provided a topic of urgent correspondence between James III and his supporters, with regard to diversionary action in Ireland in the lead-up to successive Jacobite invasions during the eighteenth century. This also explains the imposition of laws against recruitment for the foreign service in Ireland in the first three years of the eighteenth century. These laws were maintained, even during the honeymoon period of the regency of Phillipe d'Orléans and in the era of Cardinal Fleury, when George II had to bow to Irish Protestant uproar and renege on his promise to allow Louis XV to recruit for his Irish Brigades. Finally, the emergence of a small Protestant Jacobite interest in clerical, aristocratic and gentry circles in the aftermath of the Glorious Revolution provides a prelude for Protestant Jacobite activity among students of Trinity College Dublin, high-flying clergy and disgruntled Tory landowners in the latter part of Queen Anne's reign.

Buachalla, *Aisling Ghéar*, p. 185. See also Clarke to Nottingham, 7 Sept. 1690 (*H.M.C., Finch*, ii, pp 450-1).

CHAPTER 3

'Séamas an Tagarach' agus 'na leoghain tar tuínn'[1] Irish Jacobitism, 1702-16

Although Louis XIV had been forced to accept William III as *de facto* king of England, Scotland and Ireland by the terms of the Treaty of Ryswick in 1697, he refused to banish the *de jure* James II from his dominions. The death of three ailing monarchs (Charles II of Spain, James II and William III in quick succession) in the early years of the eighteenth century ensured that Europe enjoyed less than five years of peace before being plunged into another bloody dynastic conflict. This general European war soon propelled the Jacobite cause to the forefront of the political agenda. The death of Charles II impelled Louis XIV to accept the Spanish king's bestowal of his sprawling dominions on Louis's own grandson, Philippe duc d'Anjou (contrary to the terms of his partition treaty with William III of 1700).[2] Similarly, his pledge to the dying James II in 1701 and the death of his old adversary William forced him (against his better judgement) to recognise the young James Francis Edward Stuart as 'James III' of England, Scotland and Ireland. The last act was a direct violation of the Treaty of Ryswick and in defiance of the English Act of Settlement of 1701 (which settled the succession on the Electress Sophia, the grand-daughter of James I). It thrust Britain into the war on the side of the arch-duke Charles (later Emperor Charles VI), the Habsburg claimant to the Spanish throne. Facing the combined strength of Europe, hampered by the ailing Spanish monarchy, bereft of generals of the calibre of Turenne, Luxembourg and Condé, and confronting the combined military genius of Prince Eugene and the duke of Marlborough, France once again turned to the Jacobites.

At the beginning of 1705, Nathaniel Hooke ('Mr Hicky'), an Irish Jacobite convert from Protestantism and a trusted Franco-Jacobite agent of Louis XIV, accepted a commission as agent from the French court. He was to liase with

---

1 Ó Buachalla, 'Seacaibíteachas', p. 43; idem, *Aisling Ghéar*, p. 377; Ó Rathaille, 'Gile na Gile', in Ua Duinnín (eag.), *Dánta*, p. 20. 2 There were two partition treaties. The first divided the huge Spanish empire between the elector prince of Bavaria (who received Spain, the Indies and the Low Countries), the dauphin (who secured Naples, Sicily, the Tuscan ports and Guipuzcoa) and Archduke Charles (who acquired the Milanese). The second (signed in May 1700 after the death of the elector prince) gave Spain, the Low Countries and the Indies to the archduke and the rest to the dauphin; Petrie, *Berwick*, p. 114.

Scottish Jacobites to promote a Jacobite uprising as a prelude to a French invasion of the three kingdoms. Hooke was finally despatched in July 1707 and returned with numerous letters and a memorial for the French king; the Scots would raise 30,000 men if the French king provided them with 18,000 infantry soldiers, additional arms and a high-ranking general acceptable to King James III. After the signing of the Treaty of Union between Scotland and England on 27 January 1707, and its ratification by the English parliament on 17 March, the French ministry finally decided to organise an expedition in the following year. Louis promised to furnish 6,000 men and provide financial assistance. The pope pledged additional funding. The duke of Berwick was chosen to command the expedition. James III left St Germain on 9 March and joined the Jacobite leaders Perth and Midleton at Dunkirk. He fell ill with measles however and the flotilla was unable to embark until 23 March. Although Louis XIV began to doubt their chances of success, he allowed them to proceed. Hampered by adverse weather conditions they finally reached the Scottish coast at Inverness but failed to make contact with the assembled Jacobites at Leith. Deaf to James's entreaties, Forbain refused to allow the young king to disembark and they returned to Dunkirk on 7 April.[3]

The death of Queen Anne in August 1714 and the proclamation of George I as king of Britain and Ireland presented the Jacobites with another opportunity to attempt a restoration of the Stuarts. Although incapable of waging war on behalf of 'James III', and deterred from directly helping the Jacobites by the terms of the Treaty of Utrecht (1713), the ailing Louis XIV again undertook to aid the Jacobite cause. He promised substantial unofficial aid and authorised French half-pay officers and Irish volunteers to support a Stuart invasion of Scotland. He also encouraged his grandson Philip V to pledge 100,000 crowns to the Stuart king.[4] Philip donated 200,000 crowns, the duke of Lorraine provided 25,000 louis d'or and the pope bestowed 20,000 pounds. Berwick was the obvious candidate to lead the Jacobite forces but as a naturalised Frenchman he could not 'desert like a common trooper' to fight against a country at peace with France. Although a Jacobite by birth and inclination, Berwick was a soldier of the French crown and a man of honour. Undeterred, the Jacobites advocated a three-pronged strategy, whereby Ormonde and James III would lead an assault on the south-east of England with the object of marching on London. John Erskine, eleventh earl of Mar, would raise the clans in the Highlands to converge on Glasgow and Edinburgh; Jacobites on the English-Scottish borders would join the rebellion. However, the authorities were well informed of Jacobite invasion plans and they moved to arrest the chief insurgents. Ormonde reached the coast of Cornwall in the autumn but quickly returned to France.

3 Genet-Rouffiac, 'La première génération', pp 142-6, 237. Gibson, *Scottish card*, passim.   4 Genet-Rouffiac, 'La première generation', pp 142-6, 432. Gibson, *Scottish card*, passim.

After this fiasco Scotland emerged as the main focus of rebellion. Mar ('Bobbing John' of Jacobite legend) proceeded to Scotland and he raised King James's standard at Braemar on 6 September. He seized Perth, gathered a force of 12,000 men, and proclaimed James III as king in Aberdeen, Dunkeld, Perth, Montrose, Dundee and Inverness. A combination of chronic indecision and strategic incompetence allowed John Campbell (second duke of Argyll) to overcome the numerical superiority of the Jacobite forces and force a draw in the indecisive Battle of Sheriffmuir on 13 November 1715. By the time the Stuart king had arrived at Peterhead, the initiative had been lost, the clans had dispersed and the rebellion was over. James was keen to reassemble the highlanders but Mar advised him to return to France. The 'Fifteen' was over.

Ireland (or indeed Scotland) was not the main objective of the Jacobite invasion of 1715 but the 'rebellion' was certainly more than the non-event portrayed in Irish historiography.[5] Ireland's subsidiary role in Jacobite military planning would not have been lost on Irish Jacobites in the early-eighteenth century. All shades of political opinion were fully aware of the continental war which raged around them, and its possible implications for the revolutionary settlement of 1688. Troops were being ferried to and from Flanders and the newspapers abounded with European war-news and invasion rumours. French privateers preyed on allied shipping off the south coast of Ireland and recruits for the Irish regiments in French service left the country in large numbers, invariably to serve 'James III'. The invasion scares show Irish Jacobite and Whig awareness of political events on the continent and their effects on the popular political consciousness.[6] As Queen Anne's reign drew to a close, a Stuart exclusion or a Hanoverian succession were not considered by either friend or enemy as foregone conclusions.

Catholic expectation fed on the sustained contact between Jacobites in Ireland and the exiled community in continental Europe. These lines of communication, stretching across Catholic Europe, underpinned the far-flung geographical structure of Irish Jacobitism. Ireland-based Jacobites provided intelligence to French privateers on the movement of the British navy and the strength of the military establishment. These networks provided the basis for many of the reports to the Jacobite and French courts which advocated an invasion of Ireland. Some military advisors and political strategists at the Jacobite court held that Ireland had a vital diversionary role to play in any invasion of England or Scotland.

Catholic mob violence and the lawlessness of houghers, rapparees and recruits all heightened Protestant fears in this period of great uncertainty. Although a less significant and visible manifestation of popular Jacobitism than

---

5 The Scottish Jacobites, like their Irish counterparts in 1689, did not see themselves as rebels when they rose in support of their king in 1715.   6 Beresford provides the best account to date of Ireland's position in French military calculations over the eighteenth century; Beresford, 'Ireland', passim.

before, rappareeism retained a close association with Jacobitism, privateering and recruitment for foreign service. It continued to be viewed in some circles as a prelude to Catholic rebellion. As Hayton notes, 'tories and rapparees were a constant worry in this period; their membership was confined to the native Irish and their activities were occasionally invested with a political purpose'.[7]

Recruitment was the most visible manifestation of militant Jacobitism in the period before the Hanoverian succession. Historians have summarily dismissed the huge numbers routinely mentioned in contemporary correspondence. Nevertheless, many Irishmen did take shipping for foreign service, invariably, as far as they were concerned, for the service of James III. The terror of Irish Protestants and the expectations of Irish Catholics cannot be adequately represented by number crunching in the muster rolls of the Irish Regiments in Vincennes or Simincas. Protestant fears of these numbers prompted and maintained the more coercive aspects of Protestant Ascendancy legislation. Recruitment depositions also reflect an awareness of contemporary Jacobite politics. They refer to invasion plots and the machinations of the most prominent Jacobites on the continent. They reveal extensive and intricate lines of communication between Ireland and the continent, via Catholic priests, Irish soldiers and Franco-Irish privateers, Irish ship-owners and merchants.

The vibrant Irish Jacobite community on the continent animated Irish Catholic expectations at home and became the desired destination of many of these recruits. The developing links between the Irish diaspora and its indigenous brethren are revealed in the activities of privateers and recruits. The surviving correspondence of a number of Irish Jacobite agents (O'Connor, Hooke, Forristal) and the memoirs of continental Irish Jacobites show that these links permeated the highest echelons of the Jacobite court at St Germain.

Irish poets reflected the Jacobite preoccupation with European military and political affairs, particularly the activities of Irish generals and their triumphs on behalf of the Bourbon claimant to the Spanish throne. This period was a golden age of Irish political poetry, dominated by the cult of the messianic Stuart king. The Irish Brigades, as the Jacobite army-in-waiting, stimulated hopes of Irish Catholic salvation. The virulent reaction of the literati to the government's failed attempt to force Catholic priests to abjure the Stuart claimant in 1709 would suggest that the ideological cohesiveness of Irish Catholic-Jacobitism had survived from the 1690s.

The final years of Queen Anne's reign and the immediate aftermath of the Hanoverian succession also witnessed the emergence of a small but raucous Irish Protestant Jacobite interest. It flourished mainly in Dublin and maintained a more tenuous foothold in Galway, Kilkenny, Derry, and on the east Ulster estate of the earl of Antrim. It revealed itself in the taverns and coffee-houses of

7 Hayton, 'Ireland and the English ministers', p. 24; Beresford, 'Ireland', pp 36-7.

contemporary Dublin and reflected the seditious pamphlet and toasting culture of their Jacobite brethren in England and Scotland.

I

Hayton and Connolly correctly set the contemporary Irish Jacobite threat in the context of Whig and Tory political infighting. Connolly has also insisted that Protestant fears cannot be dismissed as paranoia. He underlined the 'considerable gulf' between the executive and the greater Protestant community, particularly in isolated areas with predominantly Catholic populations.[8] These well-documented attitudes towards the possibility of a European war and a Jacobite invasion, or the feasibility of a future Hanoverian succession, provide a crucial insight into the Irish Jacobite and anti-Jacobite mind-set. Protestant observers registered mounting anxiety within their own community at the possibility of a general European conflict. Even before the outbreak of the war of the Spanish succession, some Irish Catholics were reported to be 'very much up' on receipt of the news of a breakdown in relations between King William and parliament.[9] The presentation by Charles II ('the bewitched') of his sprawling Spanish dominions to Philippe, duc d'Anjou, caused some concern, prompting the general alarm and wholesale rearmament throughout Europe.[10] The Dublin press reported extensively on European politics and the possibility of Anjou's succession. All this contributed to Protestant unease, even at government level.[11] A proclamation by the lords justice of 28 February 1700 prohibited meetings, recommended papist disarmament and censured the 'many papists exercising ecclesiastical jurisdiction'.[12]

Archbishop William King (Ireland's equivalent to Bishop Burnet) reacted pessimistically to rumours of James II's death and apparent Dutch indifference at the prospect of a Jacobite succession in 1701.[13] He declined to credit these rumours, which were 'very convenient for the French designs', but surmised that 'if the young one [James III] should escape from France[14] and declare

8 Hayton, 'Ireland and the English ministers', pp 144, 180, 219; Connolly, *Religion*, pp 250-9. This fear, an obsession of eighteenth-century Irish Protestants, has been consistently neglected by historians; Leighton, *Catholicism*, pp 16, 55.   **9** Connolly, *Religion*, p. 234. 'The papists lately had more numerous and frequent meetings in several parts under the notion or pretence of devotion'; P.R.O., S.P., 63/361/162. See also T.C.D., Ms 750/2/2, fols 87-91; O'Donoghue, 'Jacobite threat, p. 156.   **10** J. Bolton to King, Lagore, 27 Feb. 1701 (T.C.D., Ms 1995-2008, fol. 766); Beresford, 'Ireland', p. 3.   **11** *The late king of Spain's will*; *A memorial presented by the count de Briond*; *The succession of Spain discussed*; *Anjou's succession considered*; *Anjou's succession further considered*.   **12** Proclamation, Berkeley and Galway, 28 Feb. 1701 (P.R.O., S.P., 63/361/162). King condemned the behaviour of some Kilkenny Catholics, deeming such 'outbursts of passion to be harmful to all concerned'; King to Baggott, 21 Mar. 1701 (T.C.D., 750/2/2, fols 87-91). See also Connolly, *Religion*, p. 234.   **13** King to Ezekiel Burridge, 28 Mar. 1701 (T.C.D., Ms 750/2/, fols 93-4). See also ibid., fol., 106.   **14** One of the great fears of the exiled Jacobite court was that the young prince would be kidnapped, taken to England and brought up in the

himself a Protestant, he might still have a chance [to succeed to the throne]'. By even contemplating the possibility of a Stuart restoration and criticising the forthcoming Hanoverian succession, King exhibited a xenophobic disdain for the house of Hanover, a disregard which would evolve into full-blown Jacobitism among a small section of the Irish Protestant community:

> I understand the duchess of Hanover is designed for succession but there is such a crowd of dependent, beggarly noblemen to come over with the succession that all the places and revenues in the realms of England would not satisfy them.[15]

Despite fears of war and incessant rumours of invasion, King remained uncomfortable with the prospect of a standing army due to its possible implications for a Stuart restoration.[16] Reflecting on the circumstances surrounding the previous restoration of Charles II in 1660, he believed that a standing army was 'the pretended prince of Wales's best card'. In doing so, he questioned the political intentions of the 'great deliverer' (William III) and his commitment to the Protestant succession in the house of Hanover. He also treaded perilously close to Jacobite comparisons between William III and Oliver Cromwell.[17] Rumours of alterations at court, military victories, the favourable state of trade and the treasury were all deemed to be 'so many stops' to bring in the 'prince of Wales' (James III).[18]

Anglican faith. Berwick's *Memoirs* and Clarke's *Memoirs of James II* note that William III had offered the crown to James Francis Edward on condition that he was brought up as an Anglican but both Mary and James refused his offer. See also Petrie, *The Jacobite movement, the first phase*, pp 112, 116; Genet-Rouffiac, 'La première génération', pp 136, 178.   **15** King to St George Ashe, bishop of Clogher, 21 Mar. 1701 (T.C.D., Ms 750/2/, fol. 103). See also T.C.D., Ms 1995-2008, fols 380, 908. A contemporary reference in the English Jacobite tradition mocked the '500 Germans all with empty purses'; quoted in Pittock, *Poetry*, p. 66.   **16** The lord lieutenant received information regarding the possibility of a 'French or Irish' landings at Kinsale and he called for reinforcements; lord lieutenant to Vernon, 22 Sept. 1701 (B.L., Add. Ms 40, 775, fol. 201). Vernon's correspondence also contains a letter from the lord lieutenant (Rochester) which suggests that Col. Hussey's intelligence regarding the possibility of a French invasion was being taken very seriously as two regiments were despatched to Galway and Limerick. It also contains a list of Irish Jacobite suspects in five [*sic*] counties of Munster and a reference to information received from Redmond Joy which related to the machinations of Lt. Col. Barry, Captain Randall Mac Donnell and Fr John Mulcahy on behalf of the French king; B.L., Add. Ms 40, 775, fols 283-4, 292. Edward Lloyd, another regular government informant in this period, claimed that 130 Jacobite officers had been sent to Ireland and England; P.R.O., S.P., 67/2/409 [205].   **17** King to St George Ashe, 12 Sept. 1701 (T.C.D., Ms 750/2, fol. 172). See also T.C.D., 750/2/3, fols 73-6. In 1713 King again evoked the spectre of General Monck's restoration of Charles II to demonstrate the validity of these fears. He also stated that the 'people of Ireland cannot put the Pretender out of their heads' and the fear of the Pretender 'distracts them and makes them do odd things'; T.C.D., Ms 2532, fol. 106. See also *Beware of the Pretender, Pretender's memorial to the French king*. On the Jacobite side, Nicholas Plunkett claimed that Louis XIV and William were colluding to restore James III; Plunkett, 'A Light to the blind' (N.L.I Ms 477, fols 900, 906); Plunkett, 'The calamity of the times' (N.L.I., Ms 477, fol. 17); Plunkett, 'A light to the blind' (Bodl., Carte Ms 229, fols 464, 475-6).   **18** King to Edward Southwell, 16 Feb. 1703 (T.C.D., Ms 1489 (ii), fols 155-6, 163).

The possibility of a French invasion featured in contemporary pamphlet literature and encouraged the demonisation of the Irish Brigades in contemporary Protestant discourse. Some were alarmed at an army of 'eighteen thousand Irish papists in France with King James at their head', ready to be transported to Ireland when called and to be received with open arms by seditious Catholics. Others dismissed the putative invading force as the worst of soldiers. Because these troops remained in the pay of the king of France, some Irish Protestants believed that his lending them to King James would amount to a declaration of war.[19]

Sir Robert Southwell, principal secretary of state for Ireland, asserted that Louis XIV's recognition of James III after William III's death 'is so much more than declaring a new war as his declaring never to have peace, for how can he be brought to renounce this or be believed if he ever does'.[20] The succession of Queen Anne (March 1702) was immediately followed by the proclamation of war with France, the mobilisation of Irish army regiments and the militia, amid calls for action against French privateers. Popular opinion would not have been oblivious to these developments: along with favourable war-news, these rekindled Irish Jacobites hopes.[21] Irish Catholics rejoiced at the prospect of a new war.[22] They maintained contact with Franco-Jacobite privateers, particularly on the south-west coast.[23] They circulated a rumour of a plot by the king of France to send 'the prince of Wales' to Ireland at the head of 16,000 men.[24]

The increasing activities of privateers on the south and west coasts (often manned by exclusively Irish Jacobite crews), their links with tories and their participation in recruitment figured prominently in government despatches and in the popular press. These sources preoccupied themselves with clandestine correspondence between France and Ireland and rumours of prospective invasions

19 *An exact survey of the duke of Ormonde's campaign in Spain*, p. 25; *The danger of France from the author of the duke of Anjou's succession.*   **20** Southwell to King, 29 Sept. 1702 (T.C.D., Ms 1995-2008, fol. 837). He had earlier expressed his relief at Anne's succession; T.C.D., Ms 1995-2008, fol. 890.   **21** Marsh and Drogheda, Proclamation, 18 Mar 1702 (N.L.I., Ms 1793, fol. 687). See also T.C.D., Ms 1489, fols 33-5; B.L., Add. Ms 37, 531, fols 1, 5, 7, 9, 12, 16, 17, 18, 28, 33-6. 83-4, 86, 90. The directions for the seizure of Father Bernardo O'Donnell on his landing in Ireland provides an example of the practical workings of this legislation; B.L., Add. Ms 15, 895, fols 189. See also ibid., fols 193, 203, 207, 211, 265; B.L., Add. Ms 40, 775, fol. 359.   **22** Beresford, 'Ireland', pp 31-8.   **23** The lords justice wrote to Lord Lieutenant Rochester on 9 June 1702 concerning the information sent by John Davies near Bantry, County Cork. This provided one example of the sustained contacts between local Catholics and French privateers; B.L., Add. Ms 37, 531, fol. 17. Privateers were also causing problems off the Galway coast, and they were frequently supplied with provisions off Kerry in this period; B.L. Add. Ms 28, 888, fols 294, 312. Privateer activity was rife off Waterford, Galway and there is evidence of Irishmen boarding privateers at Bantry, Dingle and Kinsale; B.L. Add. Mss 37, 531, fols 9, 12, 16-19, 35, 39. This prompted the sending of six men-of-war to the south coast; B.L., Add. Ms 15, 895, fols 239, 243. See also B.L., Add. Ms 37, 531, fol. 19; *H.M.C., Ormond,* ii , p. 468. In a letter to Sir Richard Cox, Charles Crow, Church of Ireland bishop of Cloyne, informed him of 'the great state of terror' in his part of the country as a consequence of the insults of French privateers. He claimed that three boats came into the Bay of Ballycotton and took provisions of sheep and lambs but left the Irish 'which I suppose they know by intelligence'. He asked for a company of foot and some dragoons; N.A. 2/447/17, fol. 25.

and internal disorder.[25] The lords justice proposed preventative measures, including the immediate return of all half-pay officers from England.[26] Although no concerted rebellion occurred in Ireland, individual actions sharpened Protestant anxieties; including the rescue of Maurice Donnellan, Catholic bishop of Clonfert, by a mob of 300 Catholics, attacks on priest-catchers, flagrant rappareeism in Limerick and Kerry and their shelter by the old Catholic gentry.[27] Scare-mongers such as Alan Brodrick, later Viscount Middleton, exploited attacks on Protestants in Mayo and Tipperary to suggest that Catholics intended to embark upon wholesale Jacobite rebellion.[28] Such appeals to popular Protestant fears show the continued potency of Jacobitism in contemporary political life.

An account of a design to invade Ireland from France in July 1702, emanated from a notorious discoverer named Redmond Joy. It outlined a proposal from the French king to despatch the prince of Wales to Ireland with a number of men and arms. Joy's evidence resulted in the arrest of six unnamed individuals who were questioned in Dublin by the lords justice and later sent to Limerick and Kerry to stand trial.[29] Whether these accusations had any basis in fact is of less importance than the effects they had on the political nation. That they prompted action at the highest level within the Irish political establishment should serve to caution historians against dismissing such depositions as being purely alarmist or mercenary, or in undermining their importance.[30]

24 For example see lords justice to Rochester, 9 June 1702; B.L., Add. Ms 15, 895, fol. 243). See also B.L., Add. Ms 37, 531, fol. 17.   **25** For an example of French privateers landing sixty men in Counties Kerry and Limerick, see Brady (ed.), *Catholics*, p. 5. The lords justice also reported on further French landings and links with Kinsale, Kilmare (Kenmare?), Duffy Island, Isle of Arran, Rathlin Island and Cape Clear; B.L., Add. Ms 37, 571, fols 17, 39. Privateers also landed men in Baltimore and Crookhaven, burned houses and plundered the country; B.L., Add. Ms 9716, fols 121, 135. See also B.L., Add. Ms 15, 895, fol. 235, 243; *H.M.C., Ormond*, ii, p. 468; *Dub. I.*, 11 Aug. 1702, 25 Aug.-1 Sept. 1702, 19 June 1703; Beresford, 'Ireland', pp 63-123.   **26** Lords justice to the lord lieutenant, 14 July 1702; B.L., Add. Ms 37, 531, fols 28, 35.   **27** Rescue of Maurice Donnellan, bishop of Clonfert, 30 Apr. 1703 (*H.M.C., Ormond*, ii, p. 473). Also see N.L.I., Ms 1793; P.R.O., S.P., 63/365/323-4; Brady (ed.), *Catholics*, pp 8, 15; P.R.O., S.P., 67/4/38; Connolly, *Religion*, pp 125-6, 208; T.C.D., Ms 1995-2008, fol. 1714; P.R.O., S.P., 63/363/39; B.L., Eg. Ms 146, fol. 38. Leerssen, *Mere-Irish and Fíor-Ghael*, p. 275; Ó Buachalla, *Aisling Ghéar*, p. 377. Colonel Maurice Hussey reported the contemporary abuse of toryism and rappareeism to extort money from the Catholics, 'a pretty law truly to destroy innocent people'; B.L., Add. Ms 34, 773, fol. 116. Jane Hanlon, the widow of Bryan Hanlon, murdered by the tories in County Armagh, was awarded £20 in March 1718. It was levied off the county. The £40 reward for taking the notorious Culmore in Armagh and the £30 for taking Parra Glas O'Connelly in Monaghan were also levied off the country; N.L.I., 11, 949. See also Moran, *Catholics under the penal laws*, p. 11; Hickson (ed.), *Selections*, ii, pp 137-9.   **28** Ormonde to Earle, 2 May 1704 (*H.M.C., 7th Report*, pp 770-1). Ormonde received notice of an invasion threat from the lords justice; N.L.I., Ms 2458, fols 469-78. See also P.R.O., S.P., 63/364/33. At this time the duplicitous Lord Lovat was using the Irish 'plot' to ingratiate himself with Mary of Modena; Macpherson (ed.), *Original papers*, i, pp 641-2. The Irish Protestant Jacobite Lord Granard warned the duke of Berwick against Lovat; B.L., Add. Ms 20, 311, fols 45. See also Beresford, 'Ireland', p. 40; Shield and Lang, *The king*, pp 82, 232.   **29** 'An account of a discovery made to the lords justice by three persons of a design to invade Ireland from France', *c.*July 1702'; B.L., Add. Ms 37, 531, fols 32-3. Also see ibid., fols 28, 36, 37; P.R.O., S.P., 67/2 280, fol. 141. I have not been able to determine the outcome of this trial.   **30** Lords justice to Rochester, 4 Aug. 1702; B.L., Add. Ms 37, 531, fols 36-7. See also B.L., Add. Ms 15, 895, fols 271-2. Redmond Joy (a co-author) later defied the council and showed an unwillingness to

While invasion reports (continually linked to the activities of rapparees and privateers) deepened popular Protestant anxieties, they had the opposite effect on Catholics.[31] Catholics reacted positively to the fluctuating course of the Wars of the Spanish Succession and the possibility of a Jacobite invasion.[32] William Harrison stated in 1701 that 'the good Catholics still believe James will never die and the advantages the Germans have in Italy are not so great as they are made'. He also claimed that 'they pretend to have intelligence from France that Mr [Maréchal] Villeroy is sent to Italy from the kingdom of Naples'.[33] Dublin Catholics built a mass-house and when the governor secured it, they claimed that they would soon regain possession of it: 'the Papists are very high but I believe by this time they are put down again'.[34] A memorial from John Blennerhasset and George Rogers, purchasers of a life interest in the forfeited estate of Nicholas Browne, second earl of Kenmare, noted that 'the priest Connellan, the other day, told his parishioners at mass that now they may with cheerfulness repair their old masshouse as their old master Lord Kenmare, meaning Sir Nicholas Browne, would soon have his estate again'.[35] In 1702 Edward Lloyd noted the reaction of Irish Catholics to the bravery shown by their compatriots at Cremona: it has 'added so much to their [Catholic Irish] insolency, that many Protestants apprehend they have some wicked project against the Protestants'. Lloyd later added that 'the Romans daily show their disaffection to the queen – by their observation of our weakness and their frequent discourses how to seize our garrisons, and the many wagers they often lay on the French side'.[36]

Sir Richard Cox's letter to Ormonde shows that these fears were taken seriously at the highest level within the political establishment. Disarmament proclamations had the two-fold purpose of deflating the rapture of the expectant Catholics and the fears of some of the Protestants. The revocation of Catholic firearm licences was absolutely necessary 'to encourage the English and stop the clamour of some of them', and 'to check the insolence of the Irish which is intolerable upon every foolish rumour of invasion which some of them expect with great impertinence'.[37]

appear upon summons which suggested either remorse or more likely a fear of intimidation; B.L., Add. Ms 37, 531, fol. 37; See also N.L.I., Ms 999, fol. 59. One contemporary described Redmond Joy as 'one of the greatest rascals in the kingdom'; Melvin, 'Irish soldiers and plotters in Williamite England', p. 281. **31** Mount Alexander to Southwell, 4 May 1704 (B.L., Add. Ms 9716, fols 137). See also P.R.O., S.P., 63/365/333-4, 257, 301; *I. I.*, 2 June 1705; *An express from Ross.* **32** Cox later noted Catholic exhilaration following reports of preparations at Brest for an invasion; N.L.I., Ms 2459, fols 59. Brest was a centre for Irish privateers in this period. **33** W. Harrison to Vernon, 5 Sept. 1701 (B.L., Add. Ms 40, 775, fol. 126). There is evidence of contemporary correspondence between Ireland and St Germain; O'Donoghue, 'Jacobite threat', pp 154-5. **34** J. Bonnell to Strype, 3 Oct. 1702 (U.L., Cambs., Add. Ms 4, iii, fol. 41. **35** Hickson, *Selections*, p. 124; Connolly, *Religion*, p. 234. **36** Lloyd to Ellis, 24 Feb. 1702 (B.L., Add. Ms 28, 888, fol. 77); Lloyd to Ellis, 30 Apr. 1702 (B.L., Add. Ms 28, 888, fol. 203). **37** Cox to Ormond, 20 May 1704 (N.L.I., Ms 2459, fol. 113). The south coast of Ireland sustained numerous privateer attacks in this period; P.R.O., S.P., 63/365/19. In one instance they managed to capture the packet boat; N.L.I., Ms 2468, fols 197; N.L.I., Ms 2469, fol. 141. Elsewhere French privateers plundered Innisboffin and Foxford, landed men and stole sheep. Pierce Arnop, a settler living near Crookhaven, was commended

As invasion rumours of this kind circulated, illicit trafficking and the machinations of potential traitors became a major concern in the government's intelligence reports. In 1702 the alleged Jacobite Sir Donat O'Brien had trimmed his sails to the prevailing political winds. He sent the lords justice evidence of a letter 'written from St Germains in France by an unknown hand which he thought it his duty to disclose as containing some treasonable matters though it seems in itself to be unintelligible'.[38] Robert Harley, first earl of Oxford, made inquiries about Lewis Gordon who had been incarcerated on suspicion of treasonable correspondence. In addition, evidence emerged of correspondence between Lady Tyrconnell and St Germain through Colonel Cusack.[39] Bishop King and Alan Brodrick also suggested that the Irish received accurate reports of European battles before they had arrived in Dublin.[40] Such contact undoubtedly exhilarated the Irish Jacobite community. In July 1704, a report claimed that French victories 'did so much exalt the papists in the kingdom so that they grew insolent and took liberty of talking more than ever they did since 1691'. They were 'as ripe for a new rebellion since the years 1641 or 1688', although 'the late successes against the Spaniards and Bavarians' had left 'their spirits somewhat depressed'.[41] Their expectations often revolved around the Irish Brigades in the

for his sterling service against the infestation of privateers. He blamed the local Irish for having informed the attackers of the weak state of his defences; P.R.O., S.P., 63/365/257, 301, 323-4, 333-4; Connolly, *Religion*, pp 236-7. Privateers also landed in Waterford and stole sheep; *I.O.*, 2 June 1705. See also T.C.D., Ms 750/3/2, fol. 32; B.L., Add. Ms 9717, fols 107, 116. The memoirs of a Huguenot refugee family in Berehaven in this period contains vivid insight into privateer activity and their intercourse with rapparees and the local Catholic populace in this period; Bigger, 'A Huguenot hero in 1704', pp 241, 288-9, 291, 296-7, 304, 306-7. See also 'Extracts from the letterbook of Joseph Ffrancklyn', p. 51. The French Huguenot, Reverend Jacques Fontaine, suffered the wrath of his Irish neighbours and French privateers in this period. Finally, in 1708 he was captured by a French privateer and his property was destroyed. His wife organised a ransom and the family moved to Dublin where he died in 1728; St. Leger, review of Ressinger, *Memoirs of the Reverend Jacques Fontaine*, p. 159. Rev. James Bland, archdeacon of Aghadoe and Philip Chamberlain, rector of Valentia, were also taken hostage by the French privateers; Hickson (eds.), *Selections*, i, p. 167. **38** This letter implicated Theobald Magee and Ambrose Moor in treasonable activity; B.L., Add. Ms 37, 531, fol. 19, 22-3. Hickson sheds light on the smuggling activities of Magee; Hickson (ed.), *Selections*, ii, pp 168-9. **39** Harley to Southwell, 2 June 1704; N.L.I., Ms 992, fol. 15. See Doyle, 'Politics', p. 246; N.L.I., Ms 99, fol. 169; *H.M.C., Portland*, iv, p. 93. Contemporary evidence exists of correspondence between St Germain, Ireland and the duchess of Tyrconnell; Bodl., Carte Ms 210, fols 64-6; Sergeant, *Little Jennings*, ii, p. 576-7. Indeed Sergeant has raised the possibility of Lady Tyrconnell being a Jacobite spy. This was not an isolated incident. The lords justice informed Southwell that they had received anonymous warning of a Jacobite rebellion; N.L.I., 2456, fols 469-73. See also N.L.I., 2459, fol. 29. In a letter from Limerick, Coursey Ireland warned the earl of Oxford, about the movements of Jane Hansard, 'a wicked and dangerous woman who was mixed up in a plot to kill King William'; *H.M.C., Portland*, iv, pp 102-3. **40** Connolly records two instances of European war news making its way to Cork before its arrival in Dublin; Connolly, *Religion*, pp 234-5. A proclamation in 1703 attempted to prevent fishermen and others from supplying French ships with provisions. Presumably they would have received European war-news along with these transactions; *Twenty-third report of the deputy-keeper*, p. 54. **41** Coursey Ireland to Harley, 18 July 1704; *H.M.C., Portland*, iv, pp 102-3. Protestant commentators also noted Irish reaction to the Battles of Almanza, Blenheim and the Jacobite invasion of Scotland. Hedges was outraged by the insolent villainous behaviour following news of the French victory at Almanza; Connolly, *Religion*, p. 234; O'Callaghan, *Irish brigades*, pp 203, 253-4; Flood, *A history of Irish*

French service. The prospect of 'eight thousand Irish cutting all the throats in England' became the main threat for some of their Protestant counterparts. They feared that if 'Mr H[ar]ly [earl of Oxford] had remained in government three days longer, the French might have landed at Thetford but there were now fifty ships in the channel to oppose them'.[42] These fears should not be dismissed from a position of hindsight. The negligent English policy created a situation in Ireland that the French and the Jacobites might have done well to exploit. France's failure to do so cannot be blamed on those Irish Jacobites who attempted to interest the Stuart and French courts in a diversionary attack on Ireland.[43]

That much is clear from contemporary reports from Jacobite Ireland which did manage to slip through the net. One important source for Irish Jacobite opinion at this time is the 1708 report from Fr Ambrose O'Connor, a native of Sligo, provincial of the Irish Dominicans and one of James III's secret agents. Fenning states that O'Connor's clandestine activities on behalf of the Stuart king 'may help to explain why there are long periods in his career during which he simply disappears from view'.[44] He had been despatched on a fact-finding mission by Mary of Modena as part of an invasion plan for contemporary Scotland. This scheme was the brainchild of Nathaniel Hooke who had twice visited Scotland to sound out the Scottish Jacobites on the possibility of a Jacobite descent.[45] Apart from characteristic exaggeration, O'Connor disclosed interchanges between Irish, English and Scottish Jacobites, while underlining the extent to which Irish Jacobitism remained oriented towards the continent. Likewise, his report sheds light on the ethos of Jacobitism throughout the country.

On his arrival in May 1708, he found that known Jacobite leaders had been imprisoned or deprived of their horses. Despite being hounded by the authorities, he managed to communicate with John, Lord Caryll, Mary of Modena's

music, p. 244; Doyle, 'Politics', p. 206. Richard Hedges, who reported Irish reaction to Almanza, incurred the wrath of Ó Rathaille: 'Gríofa's Heidges gan ceilg am sgeulaibh/a leabaidh an Iarla is pian 's is céasda!'; Ó Rathaille, 'An milleadh a d'imthigh air mhór-shleachtaibh na hÉireann', in Ua Duinnín (eag.), *Dánta*, p. 10.   **42** King to John Vesey, archbishop of Tuam, Feb. 1707 (T.C.D., Ms 750/3, fol. 189). See also *An exact survey of the duke of Ormonde's campaign in Spain*, p. 25. Plunkett's writings stress the homogeneity and efficiency of this force; Plunkett, 'Deserters of their country, the cause of its ruin' (N.L.I., Ms 477, fol. 6).   **43** Beresford, 'Ireland', p. 46; Ormonde to [?], 11 Feb. 1705 (P.R.O., S.P. 63/365/59). Also see N.L.I., Ms 2470, fol. 343; N.L.I., Ms 2465, fol. 479; P.R.O., S.P., 67/3/279 [140]. As Beresford has remarked: 'The pivotal role of the brigades in Irish political life in this period is manifest, even though no study of their socio-economic influence has ever been undertaken'; Beresford 'Ireland', p. 139. See also ibid., pp 52-3; Plunkett, 'Deserters of their country, the cause of their ruin' (N.L.I., Ms 477, fol. 9); Plunkett, 'To his most christian majesty, the most humble petition of the Irish abroad on behalf of themselves and of their compatriots at home' (N.L.I., Ms 477).   **44** Fenning, *Irish Dominican province*, p. 33.   **45** 'Mémoire à la Reine d'Angleterre par le Père Ambrose O'Connor, provincial des Dominicans Irlandois' (A.N., Fonds Guerre, Ms A1 2089, fol. 182, N.L.I., mf. p. 184). This has been translated in Nathaniel Hooke, *Secret history*, p. 105. See also Fenning, *Irish Dominican province*, pp 52-3; Beresford, 'Ireland' pp 53-6. For a biographical note on Hooke, see Petrie, *Jacobite movement*, p. 162. The Archives Nationales also contain a detailed account of a similar contemporary mission to Scotland by one Fleming; 'Relation du voyage du Sieur Fleming; et d' l'etat present de ce Royaume' (A.N., Fonds Guerre AI 2089, N.L.I. mf. p. 155).

secretary, and fulfilled his assignment by contacting the principal Jacobites in Connaught, including Lords Clanricard, Dillon, Bophin, Riverston and Colonel ('Counsellor') Terence McDonagh.[46] Clanricard and Bophin declined to meet him, pleading ill health, but Riverston professed his loyalty to James III. Two of the other senior Connaught Jacobites, Dillon and McDonogh, had been confined in Dublin. In Leinster, O'Connor received assurances of fidelity from major Catholic peers, including Thomas Dungan, Lord Limerick, Peter Plunkett, earl of Fingall, and Lord Trimbleston. They also stressed their willingness to contribute to James III's restoration. Lords Limerick and Fingall reported Irish readiness to hazard their lives and liberties for James III's service on receipt of arms and reinforcements. O'Connor felt inclined to reveal the nature of his mission more extensively but reconsidered in the aftermath of the abortive invasion of Scotland.[47] According to the testimony of Hugh McMahon, archbishop of Armagh, O'Connor's failure to properly cover his tracks ensured that he was recognised as soon as he landed. Details of his appearance were listed at every port in the country and a great reward was offered for him, dead or alive.[48]

O'Connor also sought intelligence regarding the disposition of 'the people of the north of Ireland called Scots'. He believed that their leaders were generally favourable and had gathered to toast James's health when he attempted to land in Scotland in 1708. While this seems wildly over-optimistic, independent evidence does exist of festering Presbyterian disillusionment with the Anglican political oligarchy - a discontent easily construed as disaffection by over-optimistic Jacobites. Sustained Jacobite sympathies existed among the tenants of the third earl of Antrim while non-juring Scottish Presbyterians frequently crossed over to Ulster.[49] Lord Fingall persuaded O'Connor that Randall MacDonnell, Lord Antrim, Bishop Patrick Donnelly of Dromore ('The Bard of Armagh'), and Colonel Con O'Neill remained well disposed to King James III.[50]

---

46 The following persons were committed to the Castle: 'The earls of Antrim and Fingall, Tremilston [Trimbleston] and Mountgarret, Sir Lawrence Esmond, Denis Daly, Colonel T. and W. Burke, Pool [Poole], Nangle, Butler, Westcourt and Kilcash, Col. Walter Butler, Wogan of Rathcoffey, Eustace and Hussey, Maj. Matthews, Daniel Mac Gennes [Magennis], Sir S. Rice. Edward and James Rice (sons), Mick. Fleming?, John Mapas, Rob. Nugent, Geo. Matthews, Butler of Bellicage, Mark Bacot [Baggott], Tho. Cook, [-] Elmore [Aylmer], Pat. Allen, Daniel Byrne, P. Bryan, Capts. Elmore [Aylmer] and J. Eustace, Dr Pat. Fitzpatrick, Garret Kelly, James Boylan, John Mapas, Lewis Moor [Moore], E. Nagle'; *Fau P.*, 15 Apr. 1708. **47** Lord Fingall was in contact with St Germain via one 'Mr White' in July-Aug. 1713 (Bodl., Carte Ms 211, fols 140, 148); Also see N.L.I., Fingall private collection, no. 6; R.A., Ms 195, fol. 53; Ms 212, fol. 145. **48** Fenning, *Irish Dominican province*, p. 53. **49** Dartmouth to Wharton, 11 July 1710 (P.R.O., S.P., 67/4/3r, 5r, 6r, 7). Contemporary sources contained other references to 'Presbyterian Jacobites' in this period (N.L.I., Ms 2467, fol. 147); *Presbyterian Jacobites*, Beresford, 'Ireland', pp 24, 39, 44, 46, 58; Hooke, *Secret history*, pp 39-40; Doyle, 'Politics', pp 235-7, 245-7. Nonetheless, Hayton might be closer to the mark when he states that these so-called Presbyterian Jacobites refused the Oath of Abjuration because of their reluctance to support establishment in church and state and not because of their loyalty to the house of Stuart; Hayton, 'Ireland and the English ministers', p. 291. **50** McRory, 'Life and times of Dr Donnelly', pp 3-33; Swords, 'Patrick Donnelly

They wished to hear personally from their king regarding any further invasion attempts on Scotland so that they could avoid imprisonment and hide their horses.

The closet Jacobite lawyer, Denis McNamara, supplied O'Connor with information on Munster and furnished a list of Jacobite sympathisers in Clare, Galway and Mayo. He assured him that the king could raise twenty thousand men provided that they could be supplied with arms. Thomas Dongan, Lord Limerick, advised him not to draw Protestant suspicion upon his own head and upon that of the second earl of Granard and promised to deliver King James III's message at another stage. All those who spoke to O'Connor were displeased at not being forewarned of the king's plan to land in Scotland. The abortive 1708 invasion had an important repercussion for Irish Jacobitism:

> The enterprise had produced at least one good effect that the lower classes of people who were kept in ignorance and were made to believe that there was no such thing as a prince who had just pretensions to the crown now know that there is a king who watches all opportunities of ascending the throne of his ancestors.[51]

The Irish Jacobite hierarchy assured O'Connor that Ireland remained ripe for an invasion, particularly in the overwhelmingly Catholic south-western part of the country where the garrisons had been heavily depleted. Their exiled countrymen and their Scottish and English brethren shared this collective optimism.[52] Upon the conclusion of his mission and with his curiosity satisfied regarding the zeal of the king's Irish subjects and the feasibility of a future invasion, O'Connor encouraged an Irish deputation to James III. The perilous nature of such a mission explains the lack of interaction between James and his Irish subjects. This was discouraged by James himself on the grounds of its hazards and the sufferings of his Irish supporters, who 'groaned under the tyranny of the heretick'.[53] Hooke's negotiations in Scotland in favour of the Stuart king in 1707, of which O'Connor's mission was a component part, reported that 'the Scots require, if his majesty pleases, that their k[ing] [James III] should be accompanied with 5,000 men' and that 'they would prefer the Irish troops that serve in France as being more accustomed to their manner of living and speaking the two languages of their kingdom'.[54] Indeed Hooke himself surmised that 'one may easily judge by the valour and irreproachable

---

1649-1719', pp 84-98. A report from the house of Commons in this period claimed that 'the common Irish have dependence on their lords and chiefs'; P.R.O., S.P., 63/366/300; O'Donoghue identifies the O'Neill mentioned in this memoir as Colonel Cormac of Shane's Castle, Country Antrim; O'Donoghue, 'Jacobite threat', p. 190.   **51** Quoted in Hooke, *Secret history*, p. 110.   **52** 'Mémoir au sujet de l'entreprise sur l'Irlande' (B.N., Fonds Français., vol. 7487, fol. 171, N.L.I., mf. p. 102); Beresford, 'Ireland', pp 20-3.   **53** O'Donoghue, 'Jacobite threat', p. 101. Later, in 1728, James expressed his unwillingness to give the usurper a new pretext to persecute Irish Catholics; Edgar to Mac Donogh, in Fagan (ed.), *Stuart papers*, i, p. 109.   **54** Hooke, *Secret history*, pp 5, 193.

conduct of the Irish regiments which serve in France what their countrymen would be capable of doing at home if they had arms'. He also claimed that Mr McClean, his Scottish contemporary, acting in concert with Colonel Dillon and the (Catholic) bishop of Waterford (Richard Piers), believed that the Irish 'had sufficient force to protect the Catholic counties and given time to arm and assemble they could send thirty thousand into the field'.[55]

Although nothing came of these contacts, information continued to pass between Ireland and the continent. In February 1709 Marc Forristal, a Roman Catholic from Dublin, informed the French authorities in St Malo that ten regiments had been transported from Ireland to England to join with another 20,000 English and Dutch troops for service in Flanders.[56] In May 1710 Fr Kennedy, an Irish priest, incarcerated in London on suspicion of being the archbishop of Dublin, managed to send a letter to Mary of Modena via another clergyman. He warned her about a spy named Captain Burke, the son of an executed sheep-stealer from Mullingar (an alias for Edward Tyrrell, the priest-catcher), who had turned informer against those who had raised him after his father's execution. He gave a vivid description of his appearance and noted that he had followed the Whig Lord Lieutenant Wharton out of Ireland and that he often used the pseudonyms Lord Enniskillen, Sir Edward Fitzgerald, Captain Brown, Conn O'Neill and Ensign Tyrrell.[57]

Contacts between Irish clergymen and their spiritual masters in Europe provide a parallel view of their links with the exiled Stuart court. Ambrose McDermott, Catholic bishop of Elphin, journeyed through Holland disguised as a Roman merchant. Another report to the Nunziatura de Fiandra claimed that 'the grace of God' saved Dr Hugh McMahon, archbishop of Armagh, from the 'snares' and 'traps' set for him. As a result of these 'persecutions', Cardinal Paolucci advocated 'sending as many Catholic clergymen as could live in hiding in the kingdom to help the Catholics, without being subject to the vexations which those who are known to the government have to endure'. On his arrival in Ireland, McMahon reported on the complexities of despatching news, while extolling his own secret method of getting information to the continent. Girolamo Grimaldi, abbot of St Maria, constantly experienced great inconvenience in procuring data from Ulster, which remained *terra incognita* even to the Irish in Flanders. Letters risked being intercepted, ensuring that many writers dared not trust their true sentiments to paper. This strategic silence should not be construed as a diffidence on the part of Irish Jacobites towards their spiritual or temporal masters.[58]

55 Hooke, *Secret history*, pp 191, 209. 56 Intelligence from Dublin, Feb., 1709 (Ministère de la Guerre, Séries Guerre, vol. 2186, fol. 3, N.L.I., mf. p. 186). 57 A letter from Fr Johnston to the queen about a spy and an extract of a letter from Fr Kennedy, 20 May 1710; Bodl., Carte Ms 210 [21], fol. 374; *Dub. I.*, 25 July 1710. A priest named Farrell provided information on other priests who had returned from France in this period without licence; P.R.O., S.P., 34/12, fols 43, 49. See also B.L., Add. Ms 20, 311, fol. 45. 58 Grimaldi to Paolucci, 9 Aug., 25 Oct. 1708, 12 Dec. 1709, in Giblin (ed.), 'Catalogue', part 3, vols. 81-101, pp 99,

Informal networks established by fishermen, ship captains and Franco-Spanish privateers constituted another major artery of communication between the Irish Jacobites and exiles. The brisk traffic in news is reflected in letters and reports intercepted by the authorities, including the postulation of the Derry clergy to James III of December 1709.[59] Numerous witnesses presented themselves before the government in this period, promising to give intelligence of illicit correspondence. A letter dated Dublin, July 1710 offered to shed light on 'the several disaffected persons of this kingdom who do hold unlawful correspondence with the court of St Germain by means of French privateers that come on this coast'.[60] Such links prompted a proclamation against correspondence with foreign ships.[61] Apart from the possibilities for oral exchanges, communications between Ireland and Europe were reciprocated. In 1702 Fr Christopher Martin was tried for binding, printing, publishing and selling a seditious libel, printed in France, which mentioned the late King James's queen and prince of Wales and prayed for their restoration.[62] In January 1712 an intercepted portmanteau from Norway contained unspecified prints and books of a treasonable nature. In February 1713 a routine search of a sea chest which had arrived in Mallow, County Cork, revealed several Catholic books and a genealogical dissertation on the Royal family of Stuart from Milesius to King James III.[63] For those that were intercepted by government officials it is reasonable to assume that many other escaped their attention, making their way into the country through returning clergy, recruits and privateers.

103-4, 107, 127, 129-30. See ibid., part 4, vols. 102-22, pp 7, 15-16, 18, 19, 24, 73.	**59** Ormonde forwarded the intercepted petition from the Catholic clergy of Derry to James III to Lord Dartmouth; Ormonde to Dartmouth, 23 Dec. 1709 (S.P. 67/4/38). In July 1710 the examination of Edward Rigby made reference to 'Lady Neal, a widow in Dublin who sent £150 per year to the Pretender in St Germain'; P.R.O., S.P., 67/4/7-8, 34. See also P.R.O., S.P., 67/4/15[9]; P.R.O., S.P., 67/4/11v; *Dub. I.*, 25 Feb. 1710; O'Donoghue, 'Jacobite threat', p. 113. Continual contact was maintained between privateers and the Kerry coast in this period; Hickson (ed.), *Selections*, ii, pp 163-7. A letter in the Carte papers shows that the double-agent Colonel Maurice Hussey was also in contact with the exiled court; Bodl., Carte Ms 210, fol. 66.	**60** Will. Jones to Henry Boyle, Dublin, 27 July 1710; P.R.O., S.P. 34/12/202. This information was sent to the lord lieutenant in Dublin; P.R.O., S.P., 67/4/8v-9r. Boyle believed that Jones's testimony was motivated purely by greed; P.R.O., S.P., 67/4/12v. The contemporary press contained evidence of privateer activity off Dingle, Berehaven and Dungarvan. Privateers captured sheep and cattle and maintained contact with 'the Irish'; *Dub. Gaz.*, 9 Oct 1708; 12 Mar. 1709; 14 June 1709; 18 Oct. 1709; *Dub. I.*, 25 Feb. 1709-10. In June 1711 the authorities issued a proclamation against privateers who concealed themselves in the kingdom; U.L., Cambs. Hib.o.711.3.	**61** Proclamation, Marsh and Freeman, *Dub. Gaz.*, 12 Mar. 1709. See also *Dub. Gaz.*, 14-18 June 1709; *Dub. I.*, 8 Oct. 1709; *Dub. Gaz.*, 18 Oct. 1709. The *Gazette* also carried a proclamation against tories and rapparees in this period; *Dub Gaz.*, 27-31 Dec. 1709.	**62** Fenning, 'Some broadsheets chiefly from Cork', pp 118-20.	**63** Lords justice to Southwell, 19 Feb. 1713 (N.A., Ms 3036, fol. 135); J. Dawson to B. Purdon, 13 Jan. 1712 (Bodl., Misc. Eng. Ms b 125, fol. 53). The book in question might have been Kennedy's, *Chronological, genealogical and historical dissertation of the royal family of the Stuarts*. See also *A letter from a gentleman in Cork to his friend in Dublin giving a full and true account of the whole trial and condemnation of Father Martin*. The executed Jacobite Sir James Cotter had a number of books in his library which could be considered seditious including *The hereditary right of the crowns of England*, *The life of James the second* and *The present state of Great Britain in 1718*; Ó Buachalla, *Aisling Ghéar*, p. 365.

The reaction within the Irish political nation to the abortive landing in Scotland in 1708 provided a context for this illicit traffic. For example, Robert, Viscount Molesworth, warned of the detrimental effect of 'ill-grounded' war-news from 'impertinent, disaffected persons' and 'false reports' of French victories in Spain and Germany.[64] Archbishop King's faith in Ireland's military inviolability and his supreme confidence in the British navy has been matched in Irish historiographical circles by an over-dependence on official source-material and the sweeping generalisations of hindsight.[65] Although aware of the ruinous state of Ireland's defences, King refused to believe that the French would risk an engagement with the superior forces of the British navy. The fact that events consistently proved him wrong is the main reason why his confident testimony should be balanced against Irish Jacobite optimism and Whig fears.[66]

While the lords justice engaged in frantic communication with Pembroke in March 1708, many Protestants in Ireland were gripped by panic.[67] The lack of communication from Westminster, the appalling state of the army and militia, the activities of privateers and the haughtiness of the Irish increased these apprehensions. King, not prone to exaggeration, informed Southwell that 'people here are almost frightened out of their wits with the fear of an invasion', an apprehension which was greatly enhanced by the late arrival of two packet-boats with English correspondence. He added that 'the justices and council have done what they think proper' but 'nothing near what some people would have done'. He also noted that 'the Irish according to their laudable custom are insolent and foolish and in truth we reckon our security rather in the weakness of our enemy than in our own strength'.[68] An alarmist report from County Derry regarding the Jacobite invasion of Scotland provided a local dimension for these apprehensions. It detailed a liaison between a local sloop and a ship bound for

---

64 R. Molesworth to his wife, 11 June 1707 (N.L.I., mf. p. 3752). There are other examples of such scare-mongering in contemporary Ireland; Williams (ed.), *Correspondence of Swift*, i, p. 72; *Fau. P.*, 29 Mar. 1708; Doyle, 'Politics', pp 206, 216. On the other hand, after Marlborough's spectacular defeat of the French at Blenheim, 'the dejection of some of the Irish (I mean such of them as I have seen) shown on this occasion is inevitable'; quoted in Connolly, *Religion*, p. 234.   **65** King to John Vesey, archbishop of Tuam, 16 Mar. 1707 (T.C.D., Ms 750/3, fol. 195). See also ibid., fols 139, 189; N.A., 2447, fol. 141. Others have taken the view that a Jacobite invasion at this time could have had profound consequences for contemporary British politics; Beresford, 'Ireland', pp 56-8; Gibson, *The Scotch card.*   **66** King to John Vesey, archbishop of Tuam, 16 Mar. 1707 (T.C.D., Ms 750/3, fol. 195)   **67** Lords justice to Pembroke, 13 Mar. 1708 (N.A., Ms 2447, fol. 141). Also see Giblin (ed.), 'Catalogue', part 3, vols. 81-101, p. 97; *Dub I.*, 9 Mar. 1708; *Fau. P.*, 7 Apr. 1708; *Dub. I.*, 10 Apr. 1708; *Fau. P.*, 29 Mar. 1708; Ó Buachalla, 'Seacaibíteachas Thaidhg Uí Neachtain', p. 33.   **68** King to Southwell, 13 Mar. 1707 (T.C.D., Ms 750/3/2, fol. 139). See also T.C.D., Ms 750/3/2, fols 126-7, 194; Brady (ed.), *Catholics*, p. 9. King's confidence was not shared by members of the establishment and the popular press. The miserable state of allied military affairs and the level of Catholic impudence prompted Sunderland's despairing suggestion 'to give up the game and submit to my Lord Marlborough's bringing in the prince of Wales [James III]'; B.L., Lansdowne Ms 1236, fols 236-8. Although this accusation of active Jacobitism against Marlborough seemed far-fetched, the memory of his intrigues in the 1690s would have been alive and it was indicative of the political temperature of the time; Doyle, 'Politics', p. 158.

Scotland which contained a handful of Irish aristocrats and companies of the Irish Brigades, who drank the 'prince of Wales's (James Francis Edward's) health.[69]

King's fluctuations between supreme confidence and unease reflected the political jitters which plagued Irish Protestants in this period. Despite dismissing the possibility of 'the Pretender' landing in Scotland and discounting a direct descent on Ireland, King still feared that the western ports of Ireland might become the focus of French interest on their return from Scotland.[70] He sought to strike a balance between avoiding panic and forewarning the country of imminent invasion.[71] Indeed, he advocated a campaign to limit the effects of the invasion scare on the Protestant community:

> I believe you will think it proper to encourage the country as much as we can. I do not mean that you should bear them in hand that there is not danger but that there is some but what we may with the help of God and due care can prevent.[72]

This policy of reducing the potential psychological damage of a Jacobite invasion did not find endorsement from the pulpit of Ralph Lambert in his London sermon to Irish Protestants in October 1708. Although the immediate danger had receded and papists had not openly espoused the Stuart cause, Lambert believed that their fasting and receiving the sacraments was a passive manifestation of popular solidarity for their exiled *liège*, whose embarkation from Dunkirk had been rumoured.[73] This verbal assault on Irish Catholicism cannot be dismissed as hollow sabre-rattling as the government attempted to reassure Protestants through a wholesale assault on Catholic worship. It tried to ban fasting and pilgrimages to holy wells and local shrines, thus demonstrating the fear of the military potential of these Catholic gatherings. The *Dublin Gazette* of 1 July 1710 drew attention to the 10,000 Catholics who had assembled at St John's Well, County Meath, who 'under pretence of religious worship may carry on dangerous designs to the great terror of her majesty's Protestant subjects'.[74] This harsh imposition of penal legislation affected all Catholics, a fact regularly alluded to in contemporary Irish poetry, correspondence to Propaganda Fide and the letters of the Irish diaspora to the Stuart court. These persecutions resulted in trying times for Irish Catholics, in particular the higher clergy and hierarchy.

---

69 *An express from Ballentoy near Londonderry.* These included Dunevald, Faren, Homes, Fitzgerald, Makarthy (McCarthy), Mackmahon (McMahon), Kiff (O'Keeffe), O'Sullivan, Makarthy jr., Conner, Mackmahon jr., Fitzmaurice, Boork (Burke), Prendergast, Clery, fifteen Irish lieutenants, five companies of the regiment of 'Bearne' and men of O'Brien's regiment (formerly Clare's).   **70** King to Charles Crow, bishop of Cloyne, 23 Mar. 1707 (T.C.D., Ms 750/2, fols 197-8).   **71** King to St George Ashe, bishop of Clogher, 23 Mar. 1707 (T.C.D., Ms 750/3, fol. 197).   **72** King to Clogher, 23 Mar. 1707 (T.C.D., Ms 750/3, fol. 196).   **73** Lambert, *A sermon preached to the Protestants of Ireland*, pp 12-3.   **74** One Tory expressed the opinion that 'they [the Whigs] so notably express the dangers of an insurrection in this

In December 1710 Archbishop King addressed continued Protestant fears of a Jacobite restoration. The queen's speech, the address and votes 'give great quiet of mind to all honest men who were, at least many of them, in mortal terror lest the Pretender should come in'. He attributed this terror to the proliferation of pamphlets that 'were scattered abroad, the stories that were whispered and the dismal representations that were industriously made'. A Stuart restoration weighed most heavily on 'the generality of the gentle' who 'are under an attainder by King James's parliament for lives and estates 'and 'any idea of the Pretender's return puts them out of their senses'.[75]

These fears manifested themselves at a local level. A 'pretender plot' in County Westmeath had been uncovered by a convert priest: he unsuccessfully attempted to implicate a Mr Miers, Mr Jones, Mr Shearns and Captain Newstead.[76] Rumours of this plot circulated in conjunction with a 'letter-dropping' incident outside the Four Courts which related to 'wicked and treasonable designs against her majesty's person and government'. The latter incident merited a proclamation offering a reward of £200 for the illusive Fr Murphy of Cavan.[77] Archbishop King appreciated the reciprocal links between these Protestant fears and their effects on Catholic expectation:

> The Pretender runs in the heads of most of the people of Ireland. The papists seem to have great hopes and the Protestants great fears and it is the business of some to persuade all that he is at the door ... and perhaps those men's suggestions is the cause of these expectations and fears.[78]

In another letter in February 1711, King aphorised that 'the great thing that frightens all the gentlemen of Ireland is the fear of the Pretender'.[79] He believed that 'the fear of the Pretender is so universal and has taken [such] a deep root in the hearts of all Protestants in Ireland that till that be removed or abated they

kingdom from a meeting of cripples and beggars at St John's Well'; quoted in Hayton, 'Ireland and the English ministers', p. 131. Efforts were also made to prevent papist devotion at St Kevin's shrine in Glendalough; Lecky, *Irel.*, i, p. 263. Kelly notes that a group of local Protestants, raised by the sheriff of County Wicklow, forcefully 'dispersed' the annual pilgrimage to Glendalough; Kelly, 'The impact of the penal laws', p. 152. In July 1715 Archbishop King also advocated a very tough line against pilgrimages to Lough Derg, calling for the destruction of the church site and the boats which brought pilgrims to the island; T.C.D., 2533, fol. 8.   **75** King to Mr. Annesley, 16 Dec. 1710; T.C.D., Ms 2531, fol. 238-9. See also T.C.D., Ms 750/4, fol. 13; T.C.D., 2531, fol. 316; N.L.I., Special List 337, O'Hara Papers; Hickson (ed.), *Selections*, ii, p. 136; O'Donoghue, 'Jacobite threat', p. 36.   **76** King to Dopping, 30 Dec. 1710 (T.C.D., 750/11/1, fol. 301); Brady (ed.), *Catholics*, p. 15.   **77** King to Dopping, 30 Dec. 1710 (T.C.D., Ms 750/11/1, fol. 301). See also Brady (ed.), *Catholics*, pp 15, 17; *Dub. Gaz.*, 12-16 Feb. 1711.   **78** King to Annesley, 12 Feb. 1711 (T.C.D., Ms 750/4, fols 10-11, 27-8). See also T.C.D., Ms 2531, fol. 316; T.C.D., Ms 2532, fol. 13. The danger to the Protestant succession, was the main theme of Whig propaganda in Wharton's viceroyalty (1708-10), became a constant clamour in the parliamentary session of 1711; Hayton, 'An Irish parliamentary diary', p. 108. The contemporary newspapers alluded to 'preparations' being made at St Germain'; *Fau. P.*, 22 Mar. 1711.   **79** Quoted in Hayton, 'Ireland and the English ministers', pp 29, 130.

have ears for nothing else'.[80] Elsewhere, he surmised that the Pretender was the 'true source of the zeal and violence of the Protestants of Ireland' and that if this fear was removed', you may lead them like a dog on a string'.[81]

Although treaty negotiations between France and the alliance had commenced at Utrecht in August 1712, the political climate in Ireland was comparable to that of 1687-8.[82] This calls into question accounts of the relative placidity of Irish political life and the political quiescence of Catholics in the aftermath of the Williamite conquest. As a senior clergyman, privy councillor and part-time lord justice, Archbishop King was more likely to underplay Protestant trepidation than exaggerate Catholic expectancy. His correspondence often soft-pedalled on the seriousness of the Jacobite threat. Nonetheless, in this period, he believed that Protestant fears outstripped even those of the Tyrconnell era:

> There are people that frighten the generality of Protestants here and if you look'd into the countenances of many you could not imagine their despondence to be greater in '86 or '87. This seems very unaccountable to me and I ascribe it much to the impudence of the papists who appear strangely cheerful. I reckon these naturally cause one another as in a dropsy, thirst causes drinking and drinking increases the thirst.[83]

Elsewhere, he stated that 'the papists are so exalted with the expectation of the return of the Pretender that till the peace appears and the terms provided in it for the Hanover succession with the disability of the others ever succeeding in his presence, cut off their hope, there is little probability of gaining on them'.[84] Some Protestants refused to countenance the possibility of a French invasion, while others were sufficiently 'malicious' as to construe the proclamation against James III 'as a prohibition to killing him because they are to bring him to a justice of the peace'.[85]

Rumours of Franco-Jacobite mobilisation deepened the apprehensions of others. John Puttock of Portaferry, master of the 'William and Mary', subscribed to rumours of 'the Pretender's' presence at Havre de Grace or Lorraine, and the possibility of his landing in Ireland or Scotland with 17,000 men which he had purportedly gathered at Nantes.[86] This scare-mongering also featured in the

80 King to Annesley, 23 Feb. 1711 (T.C.D., Ms 2532, fol. 13).   **81** Quoted in Lydon, *Making of Ireland,* p. 221.   **82** Proclamation regarding peace negotiations at Utrecht, 29 Aug. 1712 (U.L., Cambs. Hib.0.712.5).   **83** King to Tollet, 28 Aug. 1712 (T.C.D., Ms 2532, fol. 46).   **84** King to Annesley, 13 Nov. 1712 (T.C.D., Ms 2532, fol. 65).   **85** King to Story, 3 July 1714 (T.C.D., Ms 750/4/1, fols 312-13). Also see *Dub. Gaz.,* 3 July 1714; B.L., Add. Ms 47, 027, fol. 138; *A sermon preached to the Protestants of Ireland now in London, 23 October 1713; Observations on the report of the committee of secrecy,* pp 27-8; *Justice done to the late ministry,* p. 9; Davies, *Loyalty to King George;* Foster, *A sermon preached before the lords justice of Ireland,* pp 7-8; *Report from the committee of secrecy,* p. 7; *A letter to the clergy of the Church of England on occasion of the committal of the Rt Rev lord bishop of Rochester*   **86** Examination of James Puttock of Portferry, 4 July 1714 (S.P., 63/370/13). See also; P.R.O., S.P., 63/370/ 26, 28; T.C.D., 2536, fol. 4.

press. The contemporary pamphlet *Hanover or Rome* railed against the 'prospect of an invasion supported by the French and Irish cut-throats, fugitive criminals and beggarly desperate tories'.[87] The correspondence of Robert Molesworth, Archbishop King and the popular press resounded with news of the 17,000 Irish in the service of the ailing king of France, the possible machinations of the duke of Lorraine and the uncertainty of the Hanoverian succession.[88] Daniel Dering complained that 'the thing I dislike is to find many of our friends talk of the Pretender coming in as a matter that if it could be effected without blood, it might be well enough acquiesced and we continue a happy people, while at the same time will talk slightingly of the prince of Hanover's family'.[89] An incident at Kinsale, County Cork, reflected similar concerns at a local level. This deposition contained all the essential ingredients: a French privateer drinking James III's health, boasting about the recent disbanding of the English army and expressing his wish to cut Protestant throats as he did in the 1690s. Although it could be dismissed as a Whig fabrication or the delusions of a Frenchman in his cups, the account nonetheless reflected contemporary expectations at the prospect of a Stuart invasion.[90]

A further manifestation of these links between Jacobitism and crime is provided by the outbursts of the Houghers which coincided with the period between the attempts to impose an Oath of Abjuration and the period immediately preceding the death of Queen Anne.[91] Connolly has linked the Houghers to socio-economic issues but this would not have been so obvious to an uneasy Protestant populace.[92] King reported to Swift in 1712 the widespread belief that 'there is a deeper design under this practice and both the Whigs and the papists seem to suggest that the Pretender is at the bottom'.[93] Their spectacular actions undoubtedly contributed to the potentially explosive political climate.

Connolly himself points out that 'rural Ireland in the first half of the eighteenth century had its share of local disputes and individual acts of protest, the nature of which remain to be seriously examined'. This should be remembered in relation to contemporary Protestant anxiety. The political dimension of

---

87 *Hanover or Rome*, pp 3, 10, 15. **88** 'The house of Hanover seems to have a difficult game to play .... I hope God will direct and prosper them .... There is a great terror in the countenances as well as in the hearts of Protestants'; King to Molyneux, 3 Aug. 1714 (T.C.D., Ms 2536, fol. 4). See also T.C.D., Ms 750/4, fols 270-1; Molesworth Papers, N.L.I., mf. p. 3752; Blair, *Two sermons preached in Londonderry*, p. 19; Kirkpatrick, *A thanksgiving sermon preached in Belfast*, p. 31. **89** Dering to Perceval, 30 Mar. 1714 (B.L., Add. Ms 47, 027, fols 84-6). See also B.L., Add. Ms 47, 027, fol. 117. James proposes an opposite view; James, *Ireland in the empire*, pp 85-7. **90** 'Examination taken in Her Majesties behalf before James Dennis', 8 Dec. 1713 (P.R.O., S.P., 63/369/84). See also T.C.D., Ms 750/4, fols 240-41; T.C.D., Ms 2022, fol. 36; B.L., Add. Ms 47, 027, fol. 48; *Advice to the Protestants*, preface. **91** Ormonde, 'Proclamation against the maiming of cattle', 30 Nov. 1711 (U.L., Cambs., Hib. 0.711., 8, 9, 12, 3). See also Bodl., Eng. Hist. Ms b. 125, fol. 21; *Dub. I.*, 29 Mar. 1712. Regarding priest-catchers and privateers, see *Dub. I.*, 29 Mar. 1712; *Dub. Gaz.*, 29 Jan. 1712; 23-26 Feb. 1712; Brady (ed.), *Catholics*, p. 15. **92** King to E. Southwell, 11 Mar. 1712 (T.C.D., Ms 750/4/1/, fol. 6); Connolly, 'The Houghers', pp 139-62; Connolly, *Religion*, pp 215-19. **93** King to Swift, 16 Feb. 1712, in Williams (ed.), *Correspondence*, i, pp 289-90.

Hougherism was enhanced by its widespread popular support base, its particular zeal against the property of those who were 'not ancient inhabitants or natives' and rumours that it had links with the Irish regiments in the French army. Moreover, Catholics priests were being committed to prison in the areas where Houghers were most active.[94] John Vesey, Church of Ireland archbishop of Tuam, linked Hougher activities to popular Catholic expectations and the beginnings of a rebellion which would be supported by 'the common Irish', who are 'grown very saucy and uppish in their countenances of late'.[95] The fact that the general Catholic populace and clergy also incurred retribution for Hougher activity lent a popular and distinctively Catholic flavour to 'lawlessness'.

The activities of the O'Donoghues of Glenflesk and the O'Sullivans of Beare, two south Munster families with impeccable Jacobite credentials, illuminate this association between rappareeism, Jacobitism and rebellion in the early years of the reign of Queen Anne. Colonel Maurice Hussey reported that 'the rapps of Glenflesk was [*sic.*] the sure refuge of all the violence and villainies imaginable and it will always be so until nine parts of the O'Donoghue's followers are proclaimed and hanged on gibbets on the spot'.[96] Irish Jacobite poets, including Aogán Ó Rathaille and Diarmuid Ó Súilleabháin, celebrated O'Donoghue and his wild territory.[97] Ó Rathaille's praise for O'Donoghue stood in sharp contrast to his continual attacks on Dónall (Daniel) O'Mahony, head of the lawless 'Fairesses', who had established unchallenged mob law in the Dunloe area in the early-eighteenth century. A political dimension existed in contemporary rappareeism, smuggling and lawlessness, at least in the eyes of one of the Jacobite literati. Despite his continual affronts to the government, his impeccable genealogy and the poet's lament ('marbhna') for his second cousin John O'Mahony, Dónall's decision to take the Oath of Abjuration ensured the distrust and enmity of Ó Rathaille. It also merited his inclusion in Tadhg Dubh Ó Cróinín's 'jury of upstarts' in Ó Rathaille's 'Eachtra Thaidhg Dhuibh'.[98]

Queen Anne's death on 1 August 1714 coincided with the failure of a French invasion on James III's behalf.[99] Popular doggerel verse celebrated the Pretender's failure:

---

94 Connolly, 'The Houghers', pp 139, 142, 145. A shepherd in County Galway claimed that eight men, well-mounted and wearing white shirts over their clothes and with white linen bows on their heads (reminiscent of later descriptions of the Whiteboys), had killed some sheep; Lecky, *Irel.*, i, p. 363. J. Dawson states that he had examined a number of people under oath who suggested that the persons who travelled through the country in good clothes seemed to be Irish and French officers. He advised that Catholic priests should be committed to gaol in those areas where the Houghers were most active; Bodl., Misc. Eng. Hist. Ms b. 125, fol., 19, 21, 27; Lecky, *Irel.*, i, p. 364; Burke, *Irish priests*, p. 215.   **95** Vesey to Southwell, 22 Jan. 1711[12?] (P.R.O., S.P., 63/367/243).   **96** Ua Duinnín (eag.), *Dánta*, introduction, pp xxv-vi. **97** Aogán Ó Rathaille, 'D'Fhinnghín Ua Donnchadha an Ghleanna', in Ua Duinnín (eag.), *Dánta*, p. 40; Diarmuid Ó Súilleabháin, 'Do na Gleanntaibh', in Ó Foghludha (eag.), *Cois na Ruachtaighe*, p. 23. **98** Ua Duinnín (eag.), *Dánta*, ppxxvi-vii. Reports from 1714 noted but did not elaborate on the activities of Finin, David and John Mahony, their appearance in arms and their indictments for privateering, high treason and murder; Marsh's Library Z.3.1.1 [ix].   **99** King to Stearne, 10 Aug. 1714 (T.C.D., Ms 2536, fols 14-15).

Would we not let petit Lorrain
Our sham Pretender there maintain
Nor Philip dominate in Spain
This is not the time

...

Would we not have the Cat'lans slain
Nor France out trade us in the main
But down with proud Mardyke again

...

Would Perkin now he's lost his hope
Go straight to Rome to court the Pope
Or voluntarily take the rope. [100]

On the one hand, the swift proclamation of George I as king, allied to the disarming of Irish Catholics, removed the possibility of any immediate military opposition to the new Hanoverian regime. The celebratory Whig literature of the period shows considerable relief at his peaceful inauguration.[101] On the other, an upsurge in recruitment for foreign service and the increased incidence of toryism, particularly in Ulster, indicated Catholic Jacobite frustrations. Archbishop King equated this outburst of lawlessness and Catholic despair at the failure of a Stuart restoration:

> I suppose your excellency has an account of the great mischief done by vast numbers of robbers broke out in the northern counties of this kingdom of late. We formerly had vast numbers of those and had most severe laws against them ... but the great encouragement papists lately had of the Pretender's returning has given them new spirit and being disappointed they are mad and desperate and venture on these extravagances.[102]

An entry in the service book of Colonel Nassau's regiment of foot for 28 April 1716 bears testimony to the brutality of the government's reaction to this type of tory activity in the Fews, County Armagh. This was one of the hotbeds of toryism in the seventeenth and early eighteenth centuries and the preserve of 'Johnston of the Fews' (Seán an Fheadha), tory hunter *par excellence*. His brutal

---

100 *Alls out at last or see who's been in the wrong.* Also see *How stands your succession now?*; Contemporary sources stressed the connivance between Pretender and the duke of Lorraine; *Observations on the report of the committee of secrecy,* pp 27-8. See also B.L., Add. Ms 29, 981, fols 45, 104. 101 Proclamation of George I, 6 Aug. 1714 (U.L., Cambs. Hib. 0. 714. 7); Connolly, *Religion,* p. 143; *A poem on the happy arrival of his most serene majesty King George,* *The resolution of the states general of the United Netherlands for supporting the succession of the crown to the house of Hanover,* Blair, *Two sermons preached in Londonderry,* Kirkpatrick *A thanksgiving sermon preached in Belfast,* p. 19. 102 King to earl of Sunderland, 31 Dec. 1714 (T.C.D., Ms 750/4, fol. 238). See also T.C.D., Ms 2536, fols 162-3, 229-30, 231-2; T.C.D., Ms 750/4, fols 26-7, 29; *Dub. Gaz.,* 28 Dec. 1714.

methods ensured that he became the monster of the nationalist folk tradition of Oirialla, encapulated in the popular couplet: 'Jesus of Nazareth king of the Jews, save us from Johnston the king of the Fews'. This description of government brutality also makes the age-old correlation between the Irish language and treason (in this case Jacobitism) in the eyes of one British soldier:

> Sergeant Wilde of this corps stood for duty with six men at a redoubt of Blackbank, in the Fews, at the command of Mr Johnston, the constable of that wild country. Struck fear into the natives who call for the popish Pretender ... we razed their cabins to the ground and whipped the curs who cursed us in their Irish tongue.[103]

Whig euphoria soon evaporated with the real possibility of a Stuart invasion. In spite of the defection of the dukes of Ormonde and Leeds to Calais in July 1715, the Stuart claimant's vacation of Bar le Duc and continued French pandering to Jacobitism, King retained his pre-1708 scepticism.[104] Although not totally convinced of the dangers of an assault on Ireland from abroad, King harboured no illusion regarding the military competence of the expatriate Irish Jacobite General Arthur Dillon, whom he described as 'a very good soldier who has a great interest in that country [Connaught]'. King was sceptical of France's ability, 'though she espoused the matter with the utmost zeal', 'to find fleets and transports for so many different places and such long voyages'. Nevertheless, he believed that if they could land and raise a civil war. they might 'throw a few men into Connaught and if they brought arms 10-20,000 more, they might find hands to take them'.[105]

His opinion was not lost on one of his exiled Irish Jacobite contemporaries. Richard Bourke proposed an invasion of Connaught in this period. He suggested that Lieutenant-General Dillon 'of all his majesty's [James III] subjects that serves abroad is the only properest person to command such an expedition'.[106] Contemporary correspondence at the highest level within the Jacobite administration show that these fears were not unfounded. They were not lost on the Hanoverian administration in Ireland. Having taken the necessary and customary precautions against a possible invasion attempt, the government proscribed conventional assemblies of Catholics engaged in

103 Quoted in T. Harden, *Bandit country*, p. 78.   **104** Delafaye to King, 30 July 1715 (T.C.D., Ms 1995-2008, fol. 1690). His other correspondence contains numerous accounts regarding the invasion, particularly regarding Berwick; T.C.D., Ms 750/4/2, fol. 63. See also T.C.D., Ms 1995-2008, fols 1678, 1686-7.   **105** King to Molyneux, 30 July 1715 (T.C.D., Ms 2533, fols 37). The possibility of Dillon's descent featured in the popular press and other rumours of a French invasion; T.C.D., Ms 2533, fol. 39-42, 52-4; Davies, *Loyalty to King George, H.M.C., Stuart*, i, pp 511-2.   **106** Bourke to Bolingbroke, 25 Feb. 1716 (*H.M.C., Stuart*, i, pp 511-12). In Nov. 1715 his Whig contemporary Sir John St Leger was of the opinion that the Irish would rise in revolt in the event of any considerable success in Britain; B.L., Stowe Ms 750, fol. 136.

sporting or religious events.[107] This undoubtedly increased the resentment of Catholics at a popular level. They were reported to be 'insolent' at earlier rumours of the death of Queen Anne and they gave 'public expression of their sentiments', amid rumours of James III's arrival in Scotland.[108]

The succession of the Regent Philippe d'Orléans in France proved a decisive factor in allaying Protestant fears.[109] Despite this, King never lost sight of the continued threat that the exiled Stuart posed, a threat justified by the onset of the 'Fifteen' and the possibility of a diversionary invasion of Ireland. He believed that the Stuart claimant would 'watch all opportunity' and that 'once in every 3-4 years we must expect an alarm from him... whenever Britain is pressed by foreign or civil war'.[110] The correspondence of Sir Gustavus Hume acknowledged the Irish capacity for rebellion given favourable circumstances. Replete with the traditional throat-cutting scare-mongering, his memoir emphasised the need for a continental force to entice the Irish Jacobites into action.[111]

The country was generally quiet in the run-up to the landing of the Stuart claimant in Scotland. Nevertheless stirrings took place among Catholics in County Kerry. According to an intelligence report from Tralee in January 1716, Jacobites believed that 6,000 soldiers of the Irish Brigades would soon be landing in Ireland with Dillon at their head. A force of 3-4,000 men in Connaught, landed in ships in 2-300 at a time, would be joined by a further 20,000 within ten days. The familiarity of Catholics with the state of the king's forces and their tendency to ridicule the peace (Utreacht, 1713) enhanced the informant's fears:

> The people here I mean papists are so advanced that they will pay no money and the whisper is that 6,000 Irish abroad are to land this Spring in the kingdom and that General Dillon will be with them they find that there is no hopes of them coming in a body but the method is that they will come in small single ships by 2-300 at a time in different places upon the western coasts...What confirms me they have something in view there is not one of their heads but seems to have a particular account of the king's forces and seem to ridicule the force and if they

---

107 King to W. Nicholson, 30 July 1715 (T.C.D., Ms 2533, fols 40-2). See also *Dub. I.*, 2 Aug. 1715; T.C.D., Ms 9609, fol. 83, 98; P.R.O., S.P., 63/373/58; T.C.D., Ms 2533, fols 8, 43, 83-5, 94-5; Beresford, 'Ireland', p. 132; T.C.D., Ms 750/4/2, fols 60, 60a. 61; T.C.D., Ms 1995-2008, fols 1700, 1729; *H.M.C., 11th Report*, pp 184-5. **108** W. Caulfield to earl of Sutherland, 1 Aug. 1715 (P.R.O., S.P., 63/373/58). See also N.L.I., Ms 9609, fol. 83; T.C.D., Ms 1995-2008, fols 1704; B.L., Lansdowne Ms 352, fol. 5; B.L., Add. Ms 47, 028, fols 13, 51; B.L., Add. Ms 47, 027, fol. 160. **109** Delafaye to King, 17 Sept. 1715 (T.C.D., Ms 1995-2008, fol. 1726). See also *Secret memoirs of the new treaty of alliance with France*, pp 2, 7. Reference to this 'secret treaty' occurred in popular chatter; Fenning (ed.), *Fottrell papers*, p. 133. **110** King to Captain Flower, 23 Aug. 1715 (T.C.D., Ms 2533, fol. 62). See also T.C.D., Ms 2533, fols 115-17, 283; B.L., Add. Ms 47, 028, fol. 120; B.L., Stowe Ms, 228, fol. 142. **111** Sir Gustavus Hume to [?], 20 Oct. 1715; B.L., Stowe Ms 228, fol. 152. See also B.L., Stowe Ms 228, fols 164, 195; *H.M.C., 11th report*, app. iii, pp 184-5; P.R.O., S.P., 63/373/203.

could get 3-4,000 disciplined men they would in ten days have twenty thousand to join them.[112]

The arrival of James III in Scotland in December 1715 led to renewed calls from the lords justice for arms and ammunition, an augmentation of the armed forces in Ireland and an immediate militia array.[113] Catholics were disarmed and their prominent aristocrats imprisoned, including Lord Dillon and the earl of Antrim. News of the Jacobite invasion of Scotland also filled contemporary newspapers and pamphlets.[114]

The Irish diaspora remained buoyant in the aftermath of the ignominious collapse of the 'Fifteen'. Nor were the Jacobites in Ireland totally despondent. Contemporary reports of Jacobite 'insolence' in Dublin, centred around invasion rumours involving Charles XII, the warrior-king of Sweden, who was involved in a territorial dispute with the elector of Hanover. Although dejected at the news of the defeat of the earl of Mar, residual post-invasion Jacobitism in Dublin is attested to in anti-Georgian pamphlets and ritual celebrations of Ormonde's birthday.[115] These rumours of a Swedish-sponsored invasion of Scotland continued to surface in high-political circles.[116] King believed that Irish Jacobites, though less in number than their English counterparts, were much more violent.[117] The emigration of Presbyterian dissenters to the West Indies also dismayed Protestants as did the unceasing stream of young Irish Catholics departing for foreign service. King's correspondence constantly reflected the fears of their possible return, a continuing consideration in popular political circles during the next two decades.[118]

---

112 Extract of a letter from Tralee, 10 Jan. 1716 (P.R.O., S.P., 63/374/49; N.L.I., 9606, fol. 206). An examination of Ben Padfield in December 1715 related to Richard Devereux, master of the *Diana* of Dublin, and a ship laden with butter for Rotterdam and purportedly containing guns, swords and a popish priest; P.R.O., S.P., 63/374/28. Other contemporary sources contained rumours of the Pretender's invasion; P.R.O., S.P., 63/374/28, 42-9; N.L.I., Ms 9609, fol. 206; *H.M.C., Stuart*, v, p. 372.   **113** Lords justice to Stanhope, 13 Jan. 1716 (P.R.O., S.P., 63/374/26). Also see ibid., fols 42, 53.   **114** *A collection from three letters which arrived here from Edinburgh; Articles of impeachment against James, earl of Derwentwater;* St George Ashe, *A sermon preached in Christ's Church;* Forster, *Unanimity in the time of present danger;* N.L.I., 9609, fol. 185, 210, 212. Mark Kern noted that 'the seizure of Antrim struck dread upon the disaffected everywhere'; P.R.O., S.P. 63, 374, fol. 459. See also ibid., fol. 53.   **115** King to Story, 12 Feb. 1717 (T.C.D., Ms 2536, fol. 177). See also T.C.D., Ms 1995-2008, fol. 1813. Catholics were reported to be 'still very uppish notwithstanding the Jocks are beaten'; B.L., Lansdowne Ms 352, fol. 10. See also *The report of the judges of assizes of the north-east circuit of Ulster,* pp 13,16, 29.   **116** 'Mightily alarmed at the news of the intended invasion from Sweden'; see also Sir J. St. Leger to [Lord Macclesfield?], 21 Feb. 1716; B.L., Stowe Ms 270, fol. 244. Timothy Goodwin, Church of Ireland bishop of Kilmore believed that 'when Sweden is once brought low, the Tories will have nothing to keep up their spirits'; B.L., Lansdowne Ms 352, fol. 12. The duke of Mar considered using the Irish troops in Spain for a Swedish plot; *H.M.C., Stuart,* iii, p. 17. Sweden featured in Jacobite politics in Europe and Britain; *H.M.C., Stuart,* v, p. 412; McLysaght (ed.), *The Kenmare papers,* p. 104. The possibility of the Irish in France joining the Swedes in a Scottish invasion in 1717 cannot be discounted at this time; Beresford, 'Ireland', pp 136-7. The 'noble Swede' featured in Anglo-Scottish popular songs; Crawford, 'Political and protest songs', pp 11-12; Hogg (ed.), *Jacobite relics,* i, p. 110, ii, p. 44.   **117** King to Goodwin, 17 Nov. 1716 (T.C.D., Ms 750/11/2, fols 9-10).   **118** King to Wake, 6 Feb. 1717 (T.C.D., Ms 2535, fols 79-80).

II

Irish Jacobites were not content to sit and wait for the return of the 'Wild Geese'. Recruitment for foreign service emerged as one of the most salient features of popular Jacobitism in this period. The rhetoric of contemporary recruiting agents and the recruits themselves sheds light on the Jacobite ideology at a popular level. The exiled leaders of the Irish Jacobite nation featured prominently in the successive reports sent to the French and Stuart monarchs, the French government and the Jacobite court in St Germain. They also inspired Aogán Ó Rathaille, Seán Clárach Mac Domhnaill, Aodh Buí Mac Cruitín, their literary contemporaries and later nationalist writers and historians.[119] Fragmentary information survives on the motives and activities of the ordinary footsoldier who served in the ranks. One Galwayman, serving under a military banner in Europe, sent remittances to his father in Galway, sought tidings from home and returned information on his Jacobite compatriots to the Irish government. Like his Jacobite literary contemporaries, he also analysed European politics and their ramifications for the Stuart cause. He noted the contacts between the French and Turks and their implications for the reconquest of Spain by Phillip V, the Bourbon claimant to the contested Spanish throne. He also pinpointed the despair amongst the Irish exiles at the diffidence of their young king, describing Irish distrust of their Scottish and English compeers:

> It was by chance that I heard of a ship from Galway going to Nantes. I came several leagues on purpose to see how my friends were and to write you a line or two privately. The French court looks very great. We hear they are in alliance with the Turks and will put a great stop to the gaining of Spain but I assure you ye poor Irish are much down in the mouth by reason King James has dayly conference with gentlemen from Scotland as well as with the English and he has privately discussed amongst them that he is at making of underhand articles; if so they will tye his hands that it will not be in his power to do any good for Catholics. I remember my father told me that such of ye Irish Roman Catholics as followed King Charles ye second into France and left all their substance behind them to demonstrate their love and allegiance to him, when he was restored he was tyed up to such a degree that he could not show them any favour and fear now ye case will be the same.

He also warned of the dangers of divulging the contents of his illicit correspondence:

---

119 Mullin, 'The ranks of death' (T.C.D., Ms 7108, p. 76); Ó Buachalla, *Aisling Ghéar*, p. 432.

I hear very privately of a decent man from this kingdom designed for
the west of Scotland or the Isle of Inch in ye north of Ireland or both, the
time or issue I know not ... I met with four gentlemen that came from
Versailles with designs very soon for England with some ill design. The
ringleader is one Carthy who swore he would never part London till he
should do something that should be talked of hereafter. He will go under
the name of Campbell there. He is a lusty tall black man ... I would
rather go under the mercy of a Protestant government that under the
mercy of a blue bonnet government ... Give my father my duty but let
him not know or any man in Galway know a word of what I write to
you. I have altered my hand and name. If any body here should know a
word of this coming from me it might be my destruction.[120]

The melancholy which affected the Irish diaspora, vividly described by this
Nantes informer, featured in the writings of his Irish Jacobite predecessors, con-
temporaries and successors. Overall, Irish Jacobites remained buoyant but they
were often depressed by James II and James III's favouritism towards their
English and Scottish subjects or by the vicissitudes of European politics. The
anonymous Jacobite officer, who dedicated his 'Groans of Ireland' to William
III, most forcefully articulated it. This acerbic work castigated Sarsfield and
General John Wauchope for 'building their fortunes in France on the ruins of the
Irish'. It bewailed the deplorable condition of the 'poor gentlemen and the
women and children who were invited to go along with them to the continent
who are now begging their bread from door to door'.[121] Similarly, on receiving
news of James II's death, Nicholas Plunkett lamented that 'a great part of the
Irish nobility who had the honour to serve his majesty in the state and war at
his being in that kingdom were stabbed to the heart at the dismal intelligence'
because 'he could call them by their names and call them fellow sufferers'. He
believed 'that the case is somewhat altered with the enthronement of James III for
unto him they are strangers'.[122] An (anonymous) Irish Brigade officer also
complained to his son during the reign of Louis XIV that the Irish had not the
pleasure of approaching the person of their prince [James III] because they spoke
bad English and although they had sacrificed everything for his cause, political

120 Information from Nantes, 16 Aug. 1710 (P.R.O., S.P., 63/366/122).   **121** Barry (ed.), 'The groans of
Ireland', p. 131.   **122** [N. Plunkett], 'A light to the blind' (N.L.I., Ms 477, fol. 743).   **123** 'Lettre d'un
officier Irlandais à son fils' (B.N., Fonds Français, Ms 12, 161, fols 7-8, N.L.I., mf. p. 112). This was edited
by Hayes as 'Reflections of an Irish Brigade officer', pp 68-75. See also Plunkett, 'To the Irish nobility at
St Germain: a memorandum' (N.L.I., Ms 477 pp 1, 3, 4, 6); idem, 'To the Catholics of Ireland: a memorial for the defence of their country' (N.L.I., Ms 477, fol. 113). A memorial to James II expressed similar
sentiments; 'To the king's most excellent majesty', [c.1692(7)?]; B.L., Add. Ms 28, 939, fol. 329. The
Stuart papers continually bristled with this Irish self-sacrifice mentality. Catholics were occasionally
reminded of Stuart duplicity in the press; *A letter to the clergy of the Church of England on occasion of the
commitment of the Rt Rev Lord Bishop of Rochester.*

expediency dictated that he preferred the English and the Scots.[123] These misgivings existed during the Jacobite war, as a consequence of James's vacillations and his partiality for his English and Scottish advisors. They re-emerged after his ill-advised declaration of 1693 from St Germain, in which he promised that the Act of Settlement would not be repealed. They remained a feature of Irish popular Jacobite political dogma throughout the Jacobite period.

Recruitment depositions can also be examined for overt political sentiments. A case in point is the deposition of William Lehy of Waterford city, concerning the recruiting activities of Toby Butler, a lieutenant in the regiment of Piers Butler, third viscount Galmoy. As a consequence of this information, Butler was proclaimed as a tory and a bounty of £200 was placed on his head, a further manifestation of the close links deemed to exist between recruitment, toryism and rappareeism.[124] He had emphasised to the recruits that their service would be to James III, from whom Butler had a commission, and he promised them that they would return within a year to root out Protestants. As usual, the formal business concluded with the ritual drinking of James III's health.[125] Lehy laid particular emphasis on the arms, clothes and money promised to recruits on their arrival in France and the extent and covert nature of contemporary conscription. He also stressed the corollary between Jacobitism and a hatred of the English language:

> Met one Toby Butler who listed this depondent for the service of the Pretender and was to go on board a ship that was at the Little Island and that when the said Lehy was on board the said Toby Butler would give him £3 8s 8d and when he was landed in France that he should have clothes and arms. When he first listed him, the said Toby said it was for Newfoundland but immediately afterwards he said it was to go to France to serve the Pretender and bid him for his life not to tell anybody of it and declared to the said depondent that he had been fourteen years in the same service and that he would bring them all over here in a year's time and when the depondent said to him if he would list anybody who had no English, the said Butler replied "Damn the English for I am going to root them out' ... The said Butler told them that when he arrived in France, he should have £4 in advance and 4d more than any French soldier had ...There were forty others that had commissions from the Pretender listing men all over the kingdom.[126]

124 Proclamation, Shrewsbury and council, 2 Feb. 1714 (U.L., Cambs., Hib.0.713.12); *Dub. Gaz.*, 6 Feb. 1714.   **125** Examination of William Lehy, Three-mile Bridge, County Waterford, 26 Jan. 1714 (P.R.O., S.P., 63/370/219, 222). See also T.C.D., Ms 2022, fols 105-6. One Plunkett was convicted at the assizes in Maryborough in November 1714 for trying to seduce people to serve 'James III'; Brady (ed.), *Catholics*, p. 111; ibid., p. 311; Ó Buachalla, 'Irish Jacobitism in official documents', p. 128.   **126** 'The deposition of Michael Lehy of Killoloran, in the liberties of the said city of Waterford', 26 Jan. 1714 (T.C.D., Ms 2022, fols 105-6); 'Proclamation by the lord lieutenant and council', 2 Feb. 1713 (U.L., Cambs., Hib.O.713.12).

This recruiting was often associated with communal activities such as sporting occasions, religious services, oath-swearing and health-drinking. They involved a cross-section of the community including priests, publicans, aristocrats, gentlemen and labourers.[127]

The information of John Brady (dated Dublin, February 1714) contained even more explicit data on the Irish Jacobite network via Dover, Bristol and Calais to France. It also linked the recruiting officers with influential continental Jacobites, including the duke of Berwick, his son, Viscount Tinmouth, and the Irish Jacobites, Viscount Galmoy and General Dillon.[128] Brady had previously met Irishmen who joined Queen Anne's army in Spain and who now served the French king. On his arrival at the Collège des Lombardes (the Irish College) in Paris he met 'a great many Irish young priests, among them one or two out of the neighbourhood of one Philip Gaffney of the parish of Currin [County Monaghan] and a great many more from Cavan, Monaghan and Ireland'. They tried to persuade him to join the French army.[129] In common with many Irish *émigrés*, they anticipated a timely return to their native land. The realisation of their hopes seemed imminent amid rumours of an agreement between the emperor and the king of France and the resulting marriages of the king (James III) and Maximilian, eldest son of the elector of Bavaria, with the emperor's sisters. These *émigrés* were optimistic that the offshoot of these proposed marriages would be a new confederacy of Catholic princes, financed by the papacy, which would restore James III. The Irish clerics differentiated between Irish and English Protestants. The latter 'were not like the hell-hounds of Ireland' and that as a result 'the king had three friends [in England] for every one in Ireland'. It was an optimistic but by no means inaccurate distinction. Further evidence of links between France and Ireland identifies a priest from Cavan communicating via London through the person of none other than Thomas Sheridan, later one of the seven men of Moidart.[130] Despite the eventual proclamation of peace and the publication of terms regarding the succession of the electress of Hanover and the exclusion of James III, recruitment for the foreign service continued and many of the recruits 'declared that they would serve the Pretender'.[131]

127 Ó Buachalla, 'Irish Jacobitism in official documents', pp 128-58; idem, *Aisling Ghéar*, p. 339.   **128** 'Extract of a letter written by John Brady,' Dublin, 8 Feb. 1714 (P.R.O., S.P., 63/370/169). See also T.C.D., 2022, fol. 227. Brady's name was associated with plotting in England in the 1690s; Melvin, 'Irish soldiers and plotters in Williamite England', p. 276. Communication to the Stuart court-in-exile from such Jacobite agents as Ambrose O' Callaghan, Sylvester Lloyd, and James McKenna later reflected these clandestine links between Ireland and the continent.   **129** 'Extract of a letter written by John Brady, dated Dublin, 8 Feb. 1714 (P.R.O., S.P., 63/370/169). The charge that Catholic priests encouraged recruitment continued to be levied throughout the Jacobite period.   **130** Ibid. Also see T.C.D., Ms 2022, fol. 227. Michael McDonogh, Catholic bishop of Kilmore commended the loyalty of Sheridan and his family to King James II and the Milesian line; Fenning (ed.), *Fottrell papers*, p. 137. For a profile of Thomas Sheridan, see Bruns, 'Some details on the Sheridans', pp 65-6; idem, 'The early life of Sir Thomas Sheridan', pp 256-9.   **131** 'By the grand jury of the county of Dublin', 15 June 1713 (P.R.O., S.P., 63/369/175). See also *Dub. Gaz.*, 26-30 May 1713; U.L., Cambs. Hib.O.713,.fol. 43; U.L., Cambs. Hib.O.714. fol. 1.

The pillorying of a Jacobite for sedition revealed themes prevalent in orthodox Jacobite literature and high-political discourse. In July 1714 a tanner called Cusack was presented to the Dublin Grand Jury for expressing solidarity with those who recruited for the Stuart king in the hope of being restored to their lands. He condemned the lowly origins of Protestant settlers 'in their wooden shoes and leather breeches who now rode in the coaches' of the dispossessed Irish. Immortalised in 'Pairlement Chloinne Tomáis', in the poetry of Mac Cárthaigh and Ó Bruadair, and in the writings of Nicholas Plunkett and Charles O'Kelly, this motif remained a major theme in later Jacobite literature until the age of Eoghan Rua Ó Súilleabháin, the last of the great Jacobite poets.[132]

Rumours emanating from The Hague in April 1714 of a French-sponsored invasion of Scotland in favour of the Stuart king and his Irish army claimed that 'the king of France will encamp in the Low Countries with an army of 60,000 men' and that 'an army of 10,000 will be given to the Pretender who will bear the name of Irishmen and will be landed in Scotland where there is a strong party for him'.[133] This coincided with a French recruiting drive in Ireland, invariably for 'the Pretender' in contempary depositions. The (exaggerated) estimated numbers (10,000 and 20,000 are mentioned by King), the impotency of preventive proclamations, the difficulties of incarcerating offenders and successive rescue attempts by the mob kept recruitment at the forefront of contemporary political discourse. Although mindful of the mercenary motives of the trade in cannon fodder with France, King recognised the potency of the Stuart king and the Jacobite cause as a recruiting standard. He noted the duplicitous use of Jacobitism by the agents who ferried recruits to France, and stressed Irish zeal for their exiled *liège* and their desire to participate in his restoration:

> We have vast numbers everyday going off for service in France. 'Tis supposed that near ten thousand have gone this year and truly I have been told by the merchants that men are the best commodity that they can carry to France. Those that carry pretended commissions promise to carry them [the recruits] to King James III and that they shall come back with him at their head within a year. This is a fact which cannot be doubted but in my opinion it is only a pretence to inveigle the poor people who firmly believe it and are in hopes to see it performed which they earnestly desire and would venture anything to effect it, but the truth is I believe they are to recruit to the Irish Brigade in the French service to which they would not be so willing to go as to bring home their king, as they call him, for an Irishman loves to be in his own country and nothing encourages them so much to list themselves as the hopes

---

132 Brady (ed.), *Catholics*, p. 311. This reflects Micheál Baclámhach Mac Cárthaigh's derogatory allusion to 'the swaying scoundrels in knots and cocked beavers' who sit in our heros estates', in Ó Muirithe, 'Tho' not in full stile compleat', p. 94.   **133** Pelham from The Hague, 9-20 Apr. 1714 (*H.M.C., Portland*, v, p. 412).

given them to return within the year. However I can't think it prudent to suffer so many to go to serve in France where if there should be any opportunity, they will be ready and trained to serve the interests of the chevalier.[134]

King remained concerned by the large numbers leaving Ireland to exercise themselves in arms, a worry shared by many of his contemporaries.[135]

The sentiments outlined by King also had a popular dimension. In May 1714, Thomas Purcell, a yeoman, from County Cork, claimed that he resolved to go into foreign service having lost all his 'wearing clothes and linnen' and subsistence. Along with one Anthony Dillon, a broken soldier of Major-General Wade's Regiment, he was administered an oath by a commissioned officer named John Reilly 'who has since taken the name of Brady upon him'. He assured them that they would go to Lorraine to serve James III; they were also promised a speedy return to their native land with 'the Pretender or the duke of Berwick' and a reward of land. On their arrival in France, they would be reviewed by Mary of Modena, the queen dowager, and given a gold coin each.[136]

Active participation in recruitment by Catholic merchants and ship-owners in Dublin is identified elsewhere. In July 1714 Alderman Reilly and Seagrave, a merchant, were arraigned on this charge. James Gildart, a Catholic merchant and ship-owner, was accused of corresponding with the Stuart court. It was proposed to try him in the county rather than in the city of Dublin as the authorities doubted whether he could be found guilty in a city where the merchants had great influence.[137] William Carroll, the brewer, was allegedly 'one

---

134 King to Annesley, 27 Apr. 1714 (T.C.D., Ms 2532, fol. 271). See also T.C.D., Ms 750/4, fol. 271[157]. In June 1714, he also claimed that 'men have gone from thence on this account almost in every ship since August to the number of at least ten thousand, some think twenty thousand'; T.C.D., Ms 2532, fol. 290. Also see T.C.D., 2532, fol. 303; T.C.D., 750/4, fols 303-5. Shrewsbury reported an attempt by a mob of over one thousand rioters to rescue prisoners who had been jailed for recruiting for the foreign service; P.R.O., S.P., 36, 370, fol. 82. In May 1714 Robert Robnett described this attack by a three thousand strong mob of Irish papists on the ten soldiers and forty constables who escorted the prisoners from Kilmainham; P.R.O., S.P., 36/370/84. See also T.C.D., 750/4/1, fol. 296; T.C.D., 2534, fols 3-5; U.L., Cambs. Hib.0.7.14.2; See also Cullen, 'The Irish diaspora', pp 120-4, 135.   **135** This theme continued in both King's and Archbishop Hugh Boulter of Armagh's correspondence throughout the 1720s and 1730s. Distrust of their motives and his call for the disbandment of the Irish regiments in the French service was again reiterated later in the 1720s by King, Boulter and contemporary pamphleteers including Charles Forman and Caleb D'Anvers. **136** 'The examination of Thomas Purcell', 16 May 1714 (P.R.O., S.P., 63/370/86). In May 1714 William Maguire reiterated Reilly's promise that 'they would return back next year and get free land or estates and that they were to come back with the Pretender or the duke of Berwick'; P.R.O., S.P., 63/370/88. See also ibid., fols 90, 92; T.C.D., Ms 2022, fol. 331. The Portland manuscripts contain an account of the arrest of [Alderman] Reilly and Mr Seagrave, the merchant; Newsletter from 20 July 1714 (*H.M.C., Portland*, v, p. 473). A report from July 1714 to Perceval implicated one Reilly, a merchant and King James's alderman, in listing for the Pretender; B.L., Add. Ms 47, 027, fol. 140. See also P.R.O., S.P., 63/370/169; T.C.D., 2022, fol. 227-31. The State papers have accounts of attempts to prevent recruiting for the foreign service generally; P.R.O., S.P., 63/370/66, 167, 241.   **137** Connolly, *Religion*, p. 226.

of the Pretender's chief managers by his own papers and that he knew more than any that have been taken up'.[138]

The names 'Jean McDonnell' and 'Jean Naughton', the former possibly Seán Clárach Mac Domhnaill, the latter probably Seán Ó Neachtain, the Irish Jacobite poets, appear on a contemporary deposition relating to recruitment. Tadhg Ó Neachtain, son of the above-mentioned Seán, was also another likely participant.[139] Proclamations against recruiting proved ineffective as droves of recruits opted for foreign service. According to Shrewsbury, 5,000 men (rumoured by some scaremongers to be as high as 50,000) departed overseas with the prospect of a 'triumphant return to enjoy their ancient claims'.[140] King believed that Whigs used the spectre of recruitment for political expediency while others felt that the proposed execution of recruits amounted to judicial murder. He revealed that the execution of two recruits for the foreign service was 'ridiculed in the public newsletters, lampooned and abused and even after all some men do not stick to say that if these men be executed, they will have had hard measure, nay been murthered'.[141] In spite of these concerns, Protestants fled Dublin amid mounting papist audacity. King asserted that 'the generality of Protestants are of the opinion that the succession is not secure without some prince of that house [Hanover] to appear'. Daniel Dering also asserted that 'men's hearts melt for fear and many are

---

138 D. Dering to Sir J. Perceval, 29 June 1714; B.L., Add. Ms 42, 027, fol. 138. See also B.L., Add. Ms 47, 027, fol. 140; P.R.O., S.P., 63/370/169. 139 À leurs excellencies les seigneurs justiciers d'Irlande, 13 May 1714 (P.R.O., S.P., 63/374/314). See also U.L., Cambs., Hib. 0.714 [2]; B.L., Add. Ms 42, 027, fol. 138; B.L., Add. Ms 47, 027, fol. 140; P.R.O., S.P., 63/370/169; Ó Héalaí, 'Seán Clárach', pp 80-100. Contemporary reports from the Scottish highlands suggested that priests gave Jacobite songs to recruits; Pittock, *Poetry*, p. 197; Ó Buachalla, *Aisling Ghéar*, pp 381-2, 721. 140 Shrewsbury to Matthew Prior [in Paris], 1 July 1714 (*H.M.C., Portland*, v, pp 468-9). See also ibid., pp 471-2; P.R.O., S.P., 63/370/33-4, 44, 60, 66, 241; *Dub. Gaz.*, 5 June 1714; *Dub. Gaz.*, 3 July 1714; T.C.D., Ms 2532, fol. 303; T.C.D., Ms 750/4/, fols 304-5, 349-51; B.L., Add. Ms 47, 027, fol. 138. The introduction provides a discussion of the issue of numbers recruited, pp 32-3. 141 King to Molyneux, 17 June (T.C.D., Ms 2532, fol. 303). There are numerous references to recruits being sentenced to death. There is enough evidence in contemporary sources to suggest that many of these sentences were carried out. Five men were hanged, drawn and quartered on the charge of houghing cattle in 1712, along with a man executed on a charge of treason; *Dubl. I.*, 21 June 1712. The State papers noted that three more were executed for enlisting on 27 June 1714; P.R.O., S.P., 63,370, fol. 44. In July 1714 36 men were tried and found guilty for enlisting of the Pretender; P.R.O., S.P., 63,370, fol. 22. It is possible, but in no way certain that these included some of the twenty-one men who were executed on one day in July 1714 for enlisting for the Pretender; Ó Buachalla, *Aisling Ghéar*, p. 338; B.L., Add. Mss 47,027, fol. 140. Between fifty and sixty detainees in Dublin prisons were 'condemned for high treason' according to a letter from the duke of Shrewsbury to Matthew Prior; *H.M.C. Portland*, v, pp 468-9. A number of high-profile executions relating to Jacobitism took place in this period and they featured in the press, contemporary broadsheets and Irish poetry. These included John Reilly, Alexander Burke and Martin Carroll in 1714; Ó Buachalla, *Aisling Ghéar*, pp 338, 382. Joseph Sullivan, Felix Hara and Robert Whitty suffered the death penalty for enlisting in Nov. 1714; Brady, *Catholicism*, p. 311. King mentioned a recruit who 'declared at the gallows that he died with a cheerful mind because it was for his service to his lawful king'; T.C.D., 2536, fol. 191-2. In March 1715 Christopher Everard and Walter Eustace, under sentence of death for recruiting, escaped from prison and were subsequently proclaimed with a reward of £100 on their heads; U.L., Cambs., Hib. 0.714.19. King also informed Delafaye that 'several of the Pretenders men are under sentence of death'; T.C.D., 750/4/2, fol. 50a-b.

at their wits end ... most of figure are leaving the city, many go to England and in the meantime the papists crowd in on us'.[142] Dering asserted that 'people here are in the greatest uneasiness', 'every packet brings in something that adds to their alarms and they are daily put in fright by the insolence of the papists in marking peoples houses at night as if they intended mischief, in posting up written papers, some of which I saw myself which threatened destruction on the Protestants if the Pretender's men [the recruits] suffered'.[143] The government's difficulty in dealing with recruitment in this period, the want of sheriffs to execute the acts, and the large numbers being tried at the assizes, unnerved Irish Protestants.[144]

The joint deposition of 21 June 1714 from Thomas Gascoigne, master of the *Content of York,* Thomas Wells, mate of the same ship, and Henry Barnard, mariner, provides evidence of the continuing traffic in recruits. This deposition also highlighted the delicacy of contemporary Jacobite diplomacy, particularly in view of the declining health of Queen Anne. Six or seven ships had left Dublin with 700 recruits, it was also claimed that 500 others had been brought to the French ports of Nantes and St Malo. One of these ships had been freighted by a Dublin merchant named Fitzsimons. It contained eighty recruits, who were landed at Havre de Grace in France, expressing their wish to serve James III and the duke of Berwick. Their intention to return shortly to their homeland domi-nated the text. However, it reported that William Wadden of Waterford, master of another brigantine of thirty-five tonnes which had brought 160 recruits from Ireland's Eye, had stressed to these recruits the need to 'step statly and softly for if they should go over to England too soon, as they would deprive the queen of her rest'. This apparent softening towards 'Lear's second daughter' reflected high-political Jacobite thinking.[145]

Stuart loyalty manifested itself in an escalation of rappareesim and in recruitment for foreign service.[146] King recalled the last words of a participant in the burgeoning Jacobite theatre of death, a condemned Jacobite recruit who 'dyed with a cheerful mind because it was for his service to his lawful king James III who he owned to be the rightful king of these realms'. King later notes that

---

142 King to Molyneux, 17 June 1714 (T.C.D., Ms 750/4, fols 304). Also see T.C.D., Ms 750/4/, fols 305-6, 349-51.   **143** D. Dering to Perceval, 24 June 1714; B.L., Add. Ms 47, 027, fols 132, 115.   **144** Lords justice to Bolingbroke, 27 June 1714 (P.R.O., S.P., 63/370/44). Also see P.R.O., S.P., 63/370/22, 24, 33-4; *Advice to the Protestants,* p. 9.   **145** 'The joint examination of Thomas Gascoigne, Thomas Wells and Henry Barnard', 21 June 1714 (T.C.D., Ms 2023, fol. 31). See also P.R.O., S.P., 63/370/33-4; T.C.D., Ms 2023, fol. 28.   **146** King to Dean Story, 25 Jan. 1715 (T.C.D., Ms 2536, fol. 177). See also T.C.D., 2536, fols 20-24, 162-3, 178-9; U.L., Cambs., Hib.o.714.17; T.C.D., 2537, fol. 229-30. King's Papers highlight the continued association between, and prosecution of, rapparees, robbers and the Pretender's men; T.C.D., Ms 750/4, fol. 245. In a deposition from County Kilkenny of September 1714, Anthony Range informed on a recruiter named McKenny who had duped him and twenty others to Havre de Grace to serve in Lee's Regiment; P.R.O., S.P. 35/1,fol. 131. Later, in 1716 there were six proclamations against tories and rapparees which might signify either frustration at the abortive rebellion or represent an outlet for the energies of frustrated recruits for the foreign service; *Twenty-third report of the deputy-keeper,* p. 60.

'thirteen more were transported by the king's mercy' and that 'thirty more were to be tried next month for the same crime'.[147]

Recruiting trials continued unabated. William Carroll, a brewer from Dublin, was 'proved by several wittnesses to have provided men he enlisted for the Pretender's service with meat and drink'. Two witnesses were allegedly 'sworn by him to be true to the Pretender, by the name of James III'. Nevertheless, Carroll managed to prove that Thomas Harper, the most material witness against him, was 'a vagrant and noted thief'.[148] The examination of William Headen and Patrick Irreen at the Wexford assizes in July 1715 had all the hallmarks of the traditional recruitment deposition. There were inducements to recruits that they would serve James III, follow his standard into England and return to Ireland for the harvest. These expectations combined with the popular anticipation of a French invasion. Likewise the orchestrated witch-hunt against Francis Colclough demonstrated the fear among his Whig contemporaries that streams of ambitious recruits intended to join the Pretender in Lorraine:

> Francis Colclough, gentleman, brother of Caesar and one Luke Ford, son to Andrew Forde, a captain in the late King James's army, enlisted a great number of persons ... in May-June 1715 in order to go to Lorraine for the service of the Pretender ... Luke Ford told him he would have five pistols [pistoles] when he landed in France and they would not fight a battle 'til they landed in Ireland and England ... or serve none but James III.[149]

In another instance, recruits feared the possibility of deception in their efforts to join their exiled king: Fitzsimons, the recruiting agent, immediately took a glass of liquor and 'wished that it might be poison' to convince them that they would be going to Lorraine and not to the West Indies. In another instance Luke Ford assured the doubters that they would be brought to France and not Newfoundland.[150]

---

147 King to Charlett, 19 Feb. 1715 (T.C.D., Ms 2536, fol. 191-2). The contemporary proclamation against two escapees from Kilmainham Jail, Christopher Everard and Walter Eustace, both of staunch Jacobite stock and under sentance of death for high treason, was related to ongoing recruitment for the foreign service; U.L., Cambs. Hib.o.714.9; Recruitment and the Oath of Abjuration also became topics of contemporary pulpit politics; Story, *A sermon preached before his excellency the lord lieutenant.* **148** Lords justice to Sunderland, 30 July 1715 (N.L.I., Ms 9606, fol. 65). See also N.L.I., Ms 9606, fol. 65. A report from July 1715 stated that Morgan Field and Francis Callaghan enticed recruits to go to Lorraine to serve King James III; P.R.O., S.P., 63/373/ 8-9. In June 1715 William Carroll, the brewer, was described as 'one of the Pretender's chief messengers'; B.L., Add. Ms 47, 027, fol. 138. **149** John Forster's report of examination of William Headen alias Harding and Patrick Irreen regarding listing for the Pretender; N.L.I., Ms 9609, fol. 69. See also N.L.I., Ms 9606, fols 63, 66, 73. Headen declared that 'he would not stay to be a slave here since he would return again in the harvest'; quoted in Connolly, *Religion*, p. 244; see also *The report from the committee appointed by several of the late judges and other proceedings in relation to the election of magistrates from the city of Dublin*, 6 June 1716. **150** Examination of William Taylor and W. Doran, July 1715 (N.L.I., Ms 9609, fol. 73); Morley, *An crann os coill*, p. 46.

III

The Irish diaspora in Europe, which had emerged as the main stay of Irish Jacobite hopes in the 1690s, remained pivotal to Irish Catholic expectations at this time. It also became the destination of large numbers of recruits who left Ireland in the same period. They actively pursued Irish Jacobite interests at the Stuart and French courts by arguing that Ireland had an important diversionary role in any future Jacobite military strategies.

In July 1709 one contemporary Franco-Jacobite maintained that the English were France's most formidable enemies and a diversionary expedition to Britain and Ireland could provide the key to breaking the acute pressure on French forces in Flanders and the military impasse in Europe. For the success of such a venture, he stressed the need to send all the Irish in Flanders (amounting to as many as 50,000, plus the Irish reformed officers), with James III at their head, as an expeditionary force. Irish soldiers in France and Spain would provide the initial impetus to a successful invasion and subsequent rebellion among the Irish in Ireland. Such a force, furnished with extra supplies of arms, ammunition and ordnance, money and biscuit would raise 50,000 men in fifteen days and neutralise 'Princess' Anne's skeletal garrison force of 4,000 men. To justify such a heavy French investment in Ireland, he pointed to the Jacobite war and the extent to which the Irish theatre had sapped the strength of England and frustrated the League of Augsburg for three years with only limited French expenditure. Ireland provided an obvious invasion target because Catholics were the dominant group within the country, many of whom remained loyal to the Stuarts and upheld their traditional antipathy towards the English.[151] A memorial to the Marquis de Torcy of August 1710 shed light on the political disposition of the Irish:

> Their disposition has always been the same with regards to their lawful soverign, founded upon interest, liberty and religion and it may be added that the Catholics, who are at least 6:1 Protestant, are reduced to such despair by the last persecution of the English government, and are more disposed than ever to hazard all, and to undertake everything to free themselves from the oppressions they suffer.[152]

A treatise among the papers of Cardinal Luigi Gualterio, cardinal protector of Britain and Ireland, advocated an invasion through the ports of the south-west of Ireland. It mentioned in particular Castlehaven, Crookhaven, Bantry, Cork, Kinsale (County Cork), Kenmare, Valentia, Ventry, Dingle and Smerwick

---

151 'Invasion plan', July 1709 (B.N., Fonds Français, 7488 fol. 228, N.L.I., mf. p. 102); Beresford 'Ireland', pp 20-2.   152 A Memorial to the marquis de Torcy, of 29 Aug. 1710, in Macpherson (ed.), *Original papers*, ii, pp 165-6; McLynn, *France and the Jacobite rising of 1745*, p. 82; Miller, *James III*, p. 246.

(County Kerry). The Irish Catholic clergy, its hierarchy and the heads of the great families, who were well represented among the French king's army, would be essential to lead the people as, according to the treatise, all Catholics were governed by the lay heads and their religious.[153]

Another invasion plan entitled 'Mémoire au sujet de l'enterprise sur l'Irlande' [c.1706-8] furnished a list of those prominent exiled Irish aristocrats and gentry from each province who would wish to go to Ireland. These included Gordon O'Neill, Magennis (Lord Iveagh), Maguire (Lord Enniskillen), O'Donnell (Lieutenant Colonel in Fitzjames's Regiment), Henry O'Neill, O'Reilly and MacMahon (Ulster); Lord Brittas, Eugene McCarthy, MacCartie Spanach (Mac Cárthaigh Spáinneach), O'Sullivan, O'Callaghan, MacAuliffe and MacDonogh (Munster); Nugent (Brigadier and Colonel of the Regiment of Nugent), Colonel Cusack, Colonel Gaydon and other officers in Nugent's Regiment (Leinster) and Lieutenant-General Dillon, O'Gara, Lieutenant-General O'Shaughnessy and Captain O'Conor (Connaught). It proposed sending an invasion force of 6-8,000 men to the province of Ulster (the vicinity of Derry) in the harvest time. It would be accompanied by the reformed Irish officers in the French army who could head the regiments raised in Ireland. These forces (furnished with additional arms, a train of twenty or thirty cannon of different gauges, six mortars, 2,000,000,000 of an unspecified currency for the subsistence of 10,000 men for six months, a sufficient quantity of all types of munitions, including bullets, powder, ball and grenades) would also bring an additional quantity of arms for a further 20,000 men. The need to send bridles, harnesses and equipment for two cavalry regiments and 4,000 dragoons was also stressed.[154]

A similar memorandum from Gordon O'Neill, colonel (reformed), chief of the family of O'Neill, to the king of France, proposed that the only way to ensure a French victory was by placing the rightful king of England on his throne. An invasion of the north of Ireland with 5-6,000 thousand men was a necessary prerequisite for an invasion of Scotland and O'Neill advocated furnishing these soldiers with arms, ammunition and subsistence for the first six months. The French were to provide the necessary arms, uniforms and money to raise a further 30-40,000 Irish or Scots who were ready to take up arms for the service of their king. To fully bind the Irish and Scots to the king's service, he advocated affording them the same immunities, rights and privileges, while ensuring that the Protestants enjoyed full liberty of conscience. All

---

153 'Memoir on the means of affecting a rising in Ireland' [c.1703-07]; B.L., Add. Ms 20, 311, fol. 68). His assessment of the usefulness of a landing of the Irish exiles would be justified during the 1745 rebellion with the forced return of the duke of Cumberland's army from Flanders and the influence of a smaller force of Franco-Irish piquets and highlanders. Although Bonnie Prince Charlie's force failed to inspire confidence among his father's English, Irish and the majority of his Scottish supporters, his march through England precipitated political and economic chaos. **154** 'Mémoire au sujet de l'enterprise sur l'Irlande' [c.1706-8] (B.N., Fonds Français, 7487, fol. 171, N.L.I., mf. p. 102).

inhabitants of Ireland should enjoy free trade whereby they might no longer be forced to ship or disembark their merchandise through English ports, a great prejudice to the king's Irish subjects and his Irish revenues.[155]

Following his examination of such Franco-Irish invasion memoranda, Marcus Beresford concluded that French interest provided the primary motivation for an Irish landing, which amounted to little more than a diversionary strategy in a two-pronged invasion of Scotland or England.[156] Yet the main intention of these 'invasion memoirs' was to convince a sceptical French king of the tangible bene-fits of an invasion on behalf of the Stuarts. James III's preoccupation remained his English kingdom. His father had warned him of the dangers of throwing himself on the dependence of his Irish subjects and he regarded an Irish landing as a *pis aller*.[157] The Jacobites who urged a French or Spanish-sponsored invasion of Ireland necessarily stressed the advantages of such a campaign for France or Spain in an attempt to persuade these countries to invest both men and money.[158]

In August 1716, William Drummond hoped that the Irish subjects of King James III would spearhead any invasion of England and that Ireland would also make a diversionary contribution to James III's impending invasion:

> The people of England expect that the king has many thousands of Irish subjects as will serve for England though they judge it proper that some people should go to Ireland to hinder troops from coming from that country'.[159]

Ireland's role in any Jacobite rebellion was being discussed at the highest level within the Jacobite political establishment. In a letter to Francis Atterbury, bishop of Rochester, the titular duke of Mar urged him to include Ireland in any invasion plans:

> You cannot forget to think of Jones [Ireland], for, if some commodities [arms and soldiers] be not likewise sent to him to set up the trade

---

155 (B.N., Fonds Français, 4747, fol. 173, N.L.I., mf. p. 102). Beresford dates these invasion memoirs to the war of the Spanish Succession by pointing out that Justin McCarthy and Patrick Sarsfield, 'two generals of proven ability who would have been serious contestants for the leadership of any attempt to invade Ireland', are not mentioned in the memoirs and that they were both dead by 1694; Beresford, 'Ireland', pp 20-2. **156**, Beresford, 'Ireland', pp 5, 11, 144-5. O'Donogue alluded to the lack of reference to Ireland in Ormonde's letter-books in 1719; O'Donoghue, 'Jacobite threat', p. 130. See also Connolly, *Religion*, p. 245. **157** Beresford, 'Ireland', p. 131. See also *H.M.C., Stuart*, vii, p. 393. Aside from the memoirs listed here, the successive invasion plans of the duke of Berwick, John Drummond, fourth earl and first titular duke of Perth, John Erskine, first titular duke of Mar, General Arthur Dillon, Sylvester Lloyd, Charles Boyle, fourth earl of Orrery, Sir Charles Wogan, Patrick D'Arcy, [?] Redmond, Daniel O' Carroll, Ulick Burke, Dominic Heguerty, Thomas Lally, Fr Bernard Rothe and Ricardo Wall always stressed the benefits for the countries who would be investing their resources. **158** Beresford, 'Ireland'. The same could be said of Wolfe Tone's endeavours in the 1790s. **159** Memorandum by William Drummond, 25 Aug. 1716 (*H.M.C., Stuart*, iv, p. 57). See also ibid., iv, pp 71-2, 82-4.

[rebellion], I see not how it will be in his power to do it to any purpose for he is barehanded, and the other traders [Hanoverian establishment] in his part full of money and all the necessary commodities.[160]

An anonymous communication to Mar in September 1716 described a similar enterprise, while exhibiting considerable awareness of the numerical and political strength of the Irish Jacobite community. It advocated sending Ormonde and a group of Irish officers with 3,000 stand of arms as a precursor to an Irish Jacobite rising. The specified auxiliary numbers are realistic when one considers the disproportionate influence of 800 Franco-Irish picquets on the 1745 rebellion. That this anonymous author had direct intelligence from Ireland is suggested in the letter:

> As to the Irish affair laid before you I have it from an old gentleman lately come from thence who served in the late revolution with the king's party and who knows the exact present state of that kingdom.[161]

The failure of James II to avail of the potential of the Scottish theatre in 1688 provided one reason for the collapse of the Scottish Jacobite counter-revolution. In the same way, the subsequent neglect of the Irish theatre (despite the best intentions of Scottish and Irish Jacobites alike) had implications for the collapse of the 'Fifteen'. This same theme dominated General Arthur Dillon's post-invasion report to James III, which shared the popular analysis of native Irish Jacobites and those of the Irish regiments in the French and Spanish service. The failure to send money, arms and reinforcements to the insurgents prevented a successful assault on the Hanoverian state.[162] However, Dillon's emphasis on the political and military importance of the Irish Brigades in France and Spain also dovetailed nicely with the need to curry the political patronage of their

---

160 Mar to Rochester, 2 Oct. 1716 (*H.M.C., Stuart*, iii, p. 13). See also ibid., iii, p. 10. **161** Anonymous to the duke of Mar, 10-21 Sept. 1716 (*H.M.C., Stuart*, ii, pp 71-2). See also ibid., ii, pp 447, 465-6. Captain Richard Bourke, writing to Bolingbroke from in Douai in Feb. 1716, suggested that 'it was necessary to choose a skilful officer of sense and known probity of each province to be sent on such an expedition, capable to give the commander a perfect idea of the country, of the persons fit to be employed at home and those to be sent thither, of the harbours that arms and ammunition can be safely landed'; ibid., i, pp 511-2. The Irish diaspora in turn may have kept some of their compatriots in Ireland informed of ongoing Jacobite invasion plans in this period. A cryptic letter from Patrick Sarsfield in Ostend to Dominic Sarsfield in Cork, although cloaked in Jacobite mercantilist metaphors, may contain references to invasion plans; N.L.I., Sarsfield papers, report coll., 309 fol. 2401. 'Sarsfield esqr.' is included in a list of persons who had a cipher accorded to them by the Stuart court in 1725; Fagan (ed.), *Stuart papers*, i, p. 64; See also 'Records of the Sarsfield family of County Cork'. Other instances of traffic between the Jacobite court and Ireland exist from the period; 'Abstract of what money has been laid out on account of the King's late expedition'; *H.M.C., Stuart*, iv, p. 27. A report from Ratisbon mentioned the possibility of an invasion of Ireland and the traffic of officers and priests between Ireland and the continent; Extract of a letter from Whitworth to Lord Townsend, 1/21 May 1716 (P.R.O., S.P., 67/6/296 [149]). **162** Dillon to James III, 26 Sept. 1716 (*H.M.C., Stuart*, iv, pp 77-8). For a biographical note, see Hayes, *Biographical dictionary*, p. 59.

princely employers. He believed that the commanders of these troops could be prevailed upon to defy their employers in support of their legitimate king. This was not lost on those commentators and pamphleteers who believed that the loyalty of these Irish soldiers in France and Spain was first and foremost to the house of Stuart:

> Your majesty knows that there are five battalions and a horse regiment of your subjects in France and five battalions with two regiments of dragoons in Spain. It appears to me an essential point that you should take measures in time to obtain these troops or at least the best part of them… 'Tis to be presumed this will depend on the occurrences and on the situation of the interests of the princes who have power to give us succours. But, on the supposition of a refusal, in my opinion it will be indispensably necessary to have recourse to the only remaining expedient, which is to engage the chief commanders of the said troops underhand and even to command them on their allegience to obey such orders as shall be commissioned to that effect. You cannot doubt the obedience and submission of the said officers in everything relating to your service. If you be reduced to take this expedient you must employ nobody but judicious persons of prudence and credit. As to Ireland, a little project for that country can be made with small charges.[163]

In spite of numerous examples to the contrary, Irish historians have left Ireland out of the Jacobite equation. For example, Connolly has dismissed Ireland's importance as a target for a French or Jacobite invasion: 'As a springboard for a reconquest of Great Britain, it [Ireland] had little to offer. An invasion force, aided by the Catholic population, might well overwhelm local resistance. But when it had done so there would still be an invasion of the mainland to be attempted against an enemy which had now time to mobilise its land and naval forces'. Liam Irwin followed suit: 'In so far as Ireland ever figured in Jacobite plans it was merely to encourage rebellion there with the sole aim of distracting England's attention'.[164] The rationale behind these opinions ignores the popular belief in Jacobite circles at home and abroad that Ireland was the arsenal of the Hanoverian polity. Many memoirs to James III and the king of France stressed the need for detachments of the Irish Brigades to be sent to Ireland to rally the loyal Irish Jacobites and prevent the British government from

---

163 Ibid. Also see ibid., iii, p. 13. This idea of French collusion in the 'Fifteen' features in the *Secret memoirs*, p. 7. These *Secret memoirs* contain contemporary evidence of Jacobite contact with the west of Ireland; ibid., iii, p. 161. Hector MacDonnell claims that Hannah Roche brought letters to Irish Jacobites in 1716; MacDonnell, *The Wild Geese*, p. 71. The fate of the Irish in the French service was a constant source of worry to *émigré* Jacobites; *H.M.C., Stuart*, iii, pp 203, 260, 282, 323, 333-4, 388, 418. See also; T.C.D. 2536, fols 297-9. **164** Bartlett and Jeffreys (ed.), *A military history of Ireland*, p. 240; Irwin, review of Fagan (ed.), *Stuart papers*, p. 477.

transferring forces from Ireland to deal with Jacobite rebellion in England and Scotland. The south-east of England, and specifically London, was the real target of all prospective Jacobite invasions. The 'Fifteen' and 'Forty-five' must be seen for what they were; a subsidary, diversionary manoeuvers of a larger three-pronged assault on the Stuart kingdoms and a desperate gamble undertaken after the failure of landings in the south of England.

IV

Irish poetry provides another vivid insight into the nature of Irish Jacobitism in the early decades of the eighteenth century. It reflects Irish Catholic expectations during the War of the Spanish Succession and the 'Fifteen' and mirrors the Jacobite rhetoric in contemporary recruitment depositions. It also reinforces the pivotal role of the Irish exiles and the 'Wild Geese' in contemporary Irish Jacobite discourse. The poets fostered the emerging messianic cult of the Stuart monarch, the true spouse of Ireland. They lauded his impeccable genealogy and bemoaned the pathetic state of the country and its people in his absence.

The Irish literati remained trenchantly Jacobite and scathing in their condemnation of those who failed to espouse this cause. Feardorcha Ó Dálaigh's satire on Dr John Whalley, the almanac-maker and quack, composed in 1701, and the anonymous poem on the death of William III entitled 'Ó bhreith Chríosd i mBeithil bhínn', are examples of a triumphant, anti-Williamite literature. This literary genre was also prevalent in contemporary England and Scotland.[165] Irish poets kept their audience fully aware of the main incidents of the war, especially the exploits of Irish Jacobite generals and their implications for the Stuart cause. Having already lamented the death at Marsaglia in 1693 of Domhnall Ó Briain (Daniel O'Brien), fourth viscount Clare, Aodh Buí Mac Cruitín grieved for Séarlas Ó Briain (Charles O'Brien), fifth viscount Clare, who died at the battle of Ramillies in 1706. His poetry reflects continued fascination with the activities of the Irish diaspora and the hopes that they would ultimately spearhead a Stuart invasion of Ireland.[166] Mac Cruitín's efforts were

165 O'Donovan (eag.), *The tribes of Ireland*, introduction p. 3. The Jacobite priest-poet Fr Conchubhar Ó Briain also attacked Whalley in 1690; Ó Foghludha (eag.), *Carn Tighearnaigh*, p. 2. Whalley had been in the pillory for sedition in James II's reign. The Jacobite poet Diarmuid Mac Sheáin Bhuí Mac Cárthaigh wrote a satirical poem for the occasion; Ó Donnchadha (eag.), *Amhráin Dhiarmada*, pp 7, 45. See also 'Ó bhreith Chríosd i mBeithil bhinn', in *Cat. of mss in R.I.A.*, fasc. 16-20, p. 1980; R.I.A., Ms 23 A. 45, fol. 62. In contrast James assumed the mantle of the 'wronged king', abused at the hands of the usurping knave William, in the Jacobite tradition; Gilbert (ed.), *Jacobite narrative*, pp 94, 98, 100; Bodl., Carte Ms 229, fols 331-2; O'Callaghan (ed.), *Macariae*, pp 42-3, 49, 52. 166 Morley, *An crann os coill*, pp 15-29; Ó Buachalla, *Aisling Ghéar*, p. 218. Aodh Buí also hoped that Lord Clare's son Charles (sixth viscount, later maréchal of France, would return to claim his father's inheritance; Ó Buachalla, *Aisling Ghéar*, p. 218. Mac Cruitín composed poems in praise of the Uí Bhriain when he was serving in their regiment in Flanders, ibid., p. 342; Morley, *An crann os coill*. For notes on the fifth and sixth viscounts Clare; Hayes, *Biographical dictionary*, pp 31-2.

complemented by the biting sarcasm of Seán Ó Neachtain's mock-elegy 'Do bhris Mórbleu mo shluasaid' (France? has broken my shovel), occasioned by the death of the hated Whig admiral Sir Cloudsley Shovell off the Scilly Isles in 1707. Ó Neachtain joked that he believed that the god of the Saxons was all-powerful but now he saw that the god of Rome is more brave:

> Shíl mé riamh go mba láidir
> Dia ró-ádhmhar na Sagsan,
> Anois do chím gur cródha
> Dia na Rómha go fada.[167]

Ó Neachtain's 'Jacobides agus Carina', a commentary on the war of the Spanish succession in the allegorical Jacobite tradition of *Macariae Exidium* and John Sergeant's *An Historical Romance*, also exhibited a sharp awareness of European politics upon which Stuart fortunes depended.[168] The prose work is based on the contemporary War of the Spanish Succession. Its hero was James Fitzjames, duke of Berwick, hero of Almanza and saviour of the Bourbon Philip V of Spain. He was the main actor in a fanciful tournament in which Germanicus (the holy Roman emperor), Briotan Mór (Great Britain), Holandus (Holland), Saborius (Savoy), Galinus (France), Almansides (Spain), Babherius (Bavaria) and Jacobides (Berwick) all partake.[169] Two other poems by Ó Neachtain, one in English and one in Irish, greatly praised Berwick's military prowess, provided vivid detail of his military feats in Europe and ensured the young duke's emergence as a hero among the Irish Jacobite poets in the first fifteen years of the eighteenth century:

---

167 Ó Buachalla, *Aisling Ghéar*, p. 270. See also Ó Neachtain, 'Do bhris Mórbleu mo Shluasaid'; B.L., Eg. Ms 139, fol. ii, 88; Risk, 'Seán Ó Neachtain, p. 160, This poem contained many cryptic allusions to prominent Whig and Jacobite personalities, and references to the ongoing war in Europe; Churchill (duke of Marlborough) 'Mag an Teampuill' destroyed by the Cockerel (French) 'loigthe ag an choileach'; Charles (the arch-duke, later Emperor Charles VI) 'Cathaoir Ríoghdha'; a lustful thought born from my father (the duke of Berwick) 'Dúil do gheineadh ó m'athair', the earl of Galway 'Gaille', the earl of Peterborough 'fuachais Plandair', strong Victor Amadeus and the Emperor 'Sabhoi tréan is an t-Impir'; Risk, 'Ó Neachtain', p. 492. The Dublin press contained a report on Shovell's funeral; *Dub. Gaz.*, 30 Dec. 1707. **168** Ó Neachtain, 'Jacobides and Carina', in Flower, *Cat. of Ir. mss in B.L.*, ii, p. 93; Ó Neachtain, 'Muse help to blaze the flame of Berwick Grand', in Risk, 'Ó Neachtain', p. 154; Ó Buachalla, *Aisling Ghéar*, pp 269-70. Cathal Ó hIsleanáin also composed a poem of forty-six stanzas in 1706 on the recovery of the duke of Berwick, entitled 'Adhbhar gáire d'Inis Fáil', *Transactions of the Iberno-Celtic society*, p. ccix. The Protestant satirist William Moffett realised Berwick's position in the Irish popular Jacobite tradition: 'Then Berwick's duke was not forgot,/To him each man drank off his pot'; Moffet, *The Irish hudibras: Hesperi neso graphia*, p. 18. This satire was first published in 1716 and re-issued in 1724; Welch (ed.), *Oxford companion*, p. 243; see also N.L.I., Joly pamphlets, J.P. 6264. Berwick also figured in the contemporary English Jacobite literary tradition; B.L., Add. Ms 29, 981, fol. 46. His name was also associated with recruitment in later depositions; 'The joint examination of Thomas Gascoigne, Thomas Wells and and Henry Barnard', 21 June 1714 (T.C.D., Ms 2023, fol. 31). **169** Seán Ó Neachtain, 'Jacobides and Carina' (B.L., Eg. Ms 165, article 4). Berwick also figured in contemporary pamphlets published in Dublin; *An express from the earl of Galway with the particulars of the late bloody battle fought with the duke of Berwick; An express from Holland with an account of the duke of Berwick being dead of his wounds.*

Muse, help to blaze the fame of Berwick grand
That worthy is the worldly orb's command
Whose great exploits, anxious toyle and care
Whose prudent conduct, deeds without compare
Whose strategems, whose will, whose management
Whose valour, lead by wisdom excellent

...

Portugal tell truth – do not dissemble
At his success did the soyle all tremble?
Did not the king, the peer, the all I say
Dreading his dent, disordered run away?

...

My prayer is, and evermore shall be:
O're all his foes God send him victorie.[170]

The Irish poets also commented on the government's increasingly tough stance against Jacobites. In 1707, the government moved to impose the Oath of Abjuration against the Stuart claimant. This presented a major grievance for the poets and many other Irish Catholics in the early-eighteenth century. The question of abjuring the Stuarts and the penal laws remained inextricably linked with the Catholic question until the end of the 1770s. Catholic responses to the attempted imposition of the oath further illuminates the nature of Irish Jacobitism. The Irish literati reaffirmed their solidarity with their king and the church to which he stubbornly adhered.[171] The clerical poet William Daly described the grief and anguish which troubled his breast because of the great tyranny which had descended on the Irish Church. He lamented that no shelter existed for the gentry as every ignorant upstart was writing that Anne had a right to the possession of the three crowns:

---

170 Seán Ó Neachtain, 'Muse help to blaze the fame of Berwick Grand', in Risk, 'Ó Neachtain', pp 154-9; Ó Buachalla, *Aisling Ghéar*, pp 269-70. Seán Ó hUaithnín's poem 'Ar dhearbhú na hEaglaise' probably dates from this period. He expresses hope that the Chevalier will be coming back with strength to his own, accompanied by Berwick and O'Mahony (hero of Cremona). Monsieur (the French king, or possibly the Dauphin) and Barrier (the elector of Bavaria) also figure in his reckoning; Ó hAnluain (eag), *Seon Ó hUaithnín*, p. 42. His reference to the Cavalier might suggest that the poet was aware that James III fought in the War of the Spanish Succession under the incognito of 'The chevalier de St George.
171 Plunkett's attitude towards the imposition of the oath features prominently in his writings; Gilbert (ed.), *Jacobite narrative*, pp 186, 190; Plunkett, 'Deserters of their country, the cause of its ruin' (N.L.I., Ms 477, fols 3, 6). The Nunziatura de Fiandra also contains evidence of the reaction among Irish Catholics; Giblin (ed.), 'Catalogue', part 3, vols 81-101, pp 110, 112; part 4, vols 102-22, pp 8, 9, 11, 12, 13, 14, 20, 29. Fagan's, *Divided loyalties* (pp 22-48) provides the most recent examination of the abjuration question. See also Kelly's study of the effects of the penal laws in the archdiocese of Dublin; Kelly, 'The impact of the penal laws', pp 145-50.

> Mo scíos, mo lagar mo scairteacha im chlí breoite
> an tíoradh trasna so ar eaglais Chríoch Fódla
> gan díon dá maithibh is gach teallaire mí-eolach
> ag scríobh gurb d'Anna is ceart sealbh na dtrí gcoróineach. [172]

Aogán Ó Rathaille castigated the treasonable, treacherous wolves who banished and enslaved the clergy. He grieved that the son of Charles (I) (that is, James II), who was the true king, had been hounded into his lonely grave and his true heir banished. He also deplored the audacious perjuries brandished before the faces of our clergy and nobles which denied James's family (James III) the free possession of the three kingdoms:

> An truagh libh faolchoin an éithigh 's an fhill duibh
> Ag ruagairt na cléire as dá léir-chur fá dhaoirse?
> Mo nuar-sa go tréith-lag mac Shéarluis ba rígh aguinn,
> a n-uaigh curtha an' aonar, 's a shaor-dhalta air díbirt!
>
> Is truaillighthe, claonmhar, 's is tréason do'n droing oilc,
> Cruadh-mhionnna bréige fá sheula 's fá scríbhinn,
> 'G a m-bualadh re beulaibh ár g-cléire as ár saoithe,
> 'S nár dhual do chlainn Shéamuis coróin shaor na d-trí ríoghachta.[173]

His contemporary Aodh Buí Mac Cruitín was even more defiant. He promised that the blade-bearing Louis (XIV) and the pious prince (James III) were mobilising energetically and that they would liberate those who followed the true faith, while the degenerates who swore the false oath would have soiled trousers:

> Atá Laoiseach leadarthach, lannardha, líonmhórga
> is an prionsa paidreach ag preabadh go prímh-bheoga
> chum saoirse a thabhairt dá leanfadh an fíorChóimhdhe
> is beidh bríste salach ag meathach na mímhóide.[174]

Seán Ó Neachtain likewise vented his wrath against the twelve men, and a piper who deserted the ancient faith and took the oath in Aglish, County

---

172 Quoted in Morley, *An crann os coill,* p. 25. Many English Jacobites had no difficulty recognising Queen Anne; Monod, *Jacobitism,* p. 256. A doggerel verse in the Carte manuscripts mocked the cavalier attitude of those who abjured the Stuart claimant: 'Our Fathers took oaths as husbands took wives/For better or worse for the rest of their lives./Now like common strumpets we take them for ease/And whores and rogues part whenever they please'; 'Verse on the Oath of Abjuration' (Bodl., Carte Ms 209, fol. 457). **173** Aogán Ó Rathaille, 'Tarngaireacht Dhoinn Fhírinnigh', in Ua Duinnín (eag.), *Dánta,* p. 158. On the theme of restoration, Edmund Bingley hoped that 'it [a speedy restoration] may be the beginning of many happy years that we are to be blessed with under the king's peaceable reign over the three kingdoms'; R.A., Ms 192, fol. 57. Also see R.A., Ms 157, fol. 156. **174** Aodh Buí Mac Cruitín, 'A shaoi is a shagairt tá ag seasamh go síorchróga', quoted in Morley, *An crann os coill,* p. 26.

Westmeath, ('Dhá fhear dhéag, as píobuire d'eagluis Iathair-Mhidhe do thréig creideamh na seans agus tug móide mórmhíonna'.)[175] When Dean Burke of Ennis was before the magistrate Blood, the poet Seon Ó hUaithnín (at the instigation of Conor O'Brien) addressed him. His advice to this cleric showed awareness of the 'bed-pan' mythology in Ireland; Swear not oh priest without cognisance to your cause since I do not know who is his father, the red brick-layer who was spiked in London or the son of the king of England (James II), nobody knows:

> A shagairt ná dearbhaigh gan fios do chúise
> Is gan a fhios againn cia is athair do mhac an Phrionnsa;
> An bricléir dearg bhí tamall ar sparra in Londain
> nó mac rí Saxan be acu é cá bhfios dúinne.[176]

An anonymous correspondent told the Ulster poet Ragnall Dall Mac Domhnaill to shun forever the oaths that are false and treacherous ('seachain go bráth a Raghnaill, na mionnaí tá claon'). Likewise the Munster priest-poet Conchubhar Ó Briain attacks the perjured band ('gasra an fheill') in his poetic reply to Donnchadha Caoch Ó Mathghamhna's eulogy on James III's proposed arrival in Scotland.[177]

The motives which prompted penal legislation, its enforcement and effects have generated considerable controversy among Irish historians.[178] Whatever the reality, despair at the lot of the Catholics of Ireland poured forth from the pen of Nicholas Plunkett, one of the most prolific ideologues of Irish Jacobitism.[179] Catholics were treated 'not as subjects, but in the quality of slaves; they are barr'd from employment in the state, in the army, in the church, in the treasury, in the judicature and in all civil status, deprived of all the laws in the realm' and had

---

175 'Dhá fhear dhéag, is píobuire d' eagluis Íathair-Mhídhe do thréig creideamh na Seans agus tug móide mórmhíonna', in Flower, *Cat. of Ir. mss in B.L.*, ii, p. 36; Risk, 'Ó Neachtain', pp 460-3. See also 'Where learned authors hold it safe to swear', in *Cat. of Ir. mss in R.I.A.*, fasc. 16-20, p. 2481; 'You prelits of the nation what is your explanation? [c.1709], in Flower, *Cat. of Ir mss in B.L.*, ii, p. 411; Risk, Seán Ó Neachtain, p. 460. In contrast, Aogán Ó Rathaille advised Donnchadh Ó hIcí to emigrate to England and shun the troublesome oath which has brought sorrow on your country 'Tréig do thalamh duthchais/déin air choisde Lundain/ag seachaint móide an amhgais/do chur do thír fá bhrón'; Aogán Ó Rathaille, 'Chum Donnchadha Uí Ícidhe', in Ua Duinnín (eag.) *Dánta*, p. 136. Only 30 of the 1,089 registered priests in Ireland were prepared to abjure the Stuart claimant; Aogán Ó Buachalla, *Aisling Ghéar*, p. 279. Fagan notes that there were presentations against priests in Kilkenny, Carlow, Kildare, Westmeath, Offaly, Tipperary, Cork, Galway, Sligo, Roscommon and Leitrim for refusing the oath, Fagan, *Divided loyalties*, pp 44-5. **176** Ó hAnluain (eag.), *Seon Ó hUaithnín*, p. 15. See also B.L., Add. Ms 27, 946, fol. 692; Flower, *Cat of Ir. mss in B.L*, ii. p. 692. **177** Ragnall Dall Mac Domhnaill, 'A Chreagáin Uaibhrigh', quoted in Murray, *History of Creggan*, p. 10; An t-Athair Conchubhar Ó Briain, 'Is mac de Mars an Mar seo in Albain thuaidh', in Ó Foghludha (eag.), *Carn Tighearnaigh*, p. 29. See also Murphy, *Killaloe*, p. 32. There were attacks on a priest who took the oath; Connolly, *Religion*, p. 275. Thirteen priests were presented in March 1711 for saying mass without having taken the oath; Brady (ed.), *Catholics*, p. 15. Leading Catholics took the Oath in Dublin during the 1715 rebellion; *Dub. I.*, 30 Aug. 1715. For the popular Protestant view of the oath; Story, *A sermon*, p. 17. **178** Introduction, pp 27-30. **179** Kelly, 'The improvement of Ireland'; idem, 'A light to the blind' pp 431-62.

'lost their country tho' they live in their country'. By virtue of the laws against property, 'they are further enslaved by being debarred of their natural right in disposing of their real estates as they shall think fit'. Apart from the threat of life imprisonment for their refusal of the Oath of Abjuration, 'they are wholly barred from exercising their religion which reaches even to the dying man unless the priest can steal to preserve the deceasing person from death'.[180] Many Irish Jacobite poets from Aogán Ó Rathaille to Eoghan Rua Ó Súilleabháin echoed this acute sense of grievance, grievances which many historians have ignored when writing about the penal laws. In 1709, Fr Conchubhar Ó Briain lamented that every year is worse than the last year, that the clergy were without churches and suffered death-threats and persecution and were forced to go over the sea by successive acts of parliament:

> Gach bliadhain ag teacht is measa atá againn
> Is ár gcliar gan chealla ach bagar báis is broid'.
> 'n-a ndiaidh gach seal go gcaithfid trácht tar muir
> le riagail reachtmhar Achta an Phárlimint.[181]

However he hoped that the following year promised restoration and the rule of parliament would be overturned:

> Tá an bhliadhain ag teacht le calm-thráth chugainn
> bliadhain do gheallas ceart is cáil-chothrom.
> Bliadhain do leagfar reacht an Phárlaimint.[182]

His colleague Aindrias Mac Craith alluded to the hard laws of the Whigs which banished him to the edge of the country on his own ('dlíthe cruadha na Whigs do ruaig mé in imeall tuaithe im aonar') in his poem 'Is ceasnaidheach cásmhar atáim 's is léanmhar'. Liam Inglis later hoped that on the arrival of Charles Edward the poets will not be afraid to speak their treason ('is nár bh'eagal don éigse a dtréason d'innsint').[183] Seán Clárach's verse on his own pitiful state provided a metaphor for the plight of many Irish Catholics. Since the royal buck (James II) had quitted the field, he was left alone; his cattle shelterless, his plough team untied, the people in misery with the elbows out of their clothes, a price frequently on his head from the lords of the state, his shoes perished and no money in Irish hands:

---

180 Plunkett, 'The case of the Roman Catholics of Ireland [1710] (N.L.I., Ms 477, fols. 1, 7, 18).   **181** Eoin Ó Callanáin, 'Don Athair Ó Briain', in Ó Foghludha (eag.), *Carn Tighearnaigh*, p. 19. A translation of an Irish poem complained that 'Their laws has enacted are points in progression/To stifle confiteor and holy confession'; Ó Muirithe, 'Tho' not in full stile compleat', pp 94, 99.   **182** Muiris Múinte Ó hEachthigheirnn, 'Tá an bhliadhain ag teacht le calm-thráth chugainn', in Ó Foghludha (eag.), *Carn Tighearnaigh*, p. 17.   **183** Aindrias Mac Craith, 'Is ceasnaidheach cásmhar atáim 's is léanmhar', in Ó Foghludha (eag.), *Éigse na Máighe*, p. 193; Inglis, 'Atá an fhoireann so'; Ó Foghludha (eag.), *Cois na Bríde*, p. 36.

Atá mo chóraid gan fuithin
Is mo chuingir gan féar gan fás
Atá anshógh ar mo mhuirear
Is a n-uilinn gan éadach slán;
Atá an tóir ar mo mhullach
 go minic ó thiarna an stáit
Atá mo bhróga-sa briste
Is gan pinginn dá bhfiacha im láimh.[184]

Another anonymous poet asked how long would our mass be under the branches of a tree? ('An fad a bheidh ár n-aifrinn fé ghéagaibh crainn?')[185]

This persecution mentality also dominated the stream of letters from expatriate Irish Catholics to the Stuart court and the Propaganda Fide in Rome. They continually referred to the tribulations of the 'poor oppressed' Catholics of Ireland. Hugh McMahon, Catholic bishop of Clogher, later archbishop of Armagh, described their condition in the latter years of Queen Anne's reign and noted the 'general desolation' in Ireland and more specifically Ulster. He bemoaned the exclusion of lay Catholics from all political and military posts and the denial of their right of citizenship. The clergy 'of all grades, in order to live, go secretly from house to house and rely on the generosity and charity of their people who have been reduced to poverty'. This benevolence was not without its own particular hazards as they 'in turn exposed themselves to the inevitable confiscation of what little they possess' and the proliferation of enemies, bribes and spies 'could shake the constancy of the Catholics themselves'. Communication with Rome or St Germain was fraught with difficulties as it was considered treason by the government. Many of those who dwelt on Irish Catholic woes believed that the restoration of the house of Stuart provided the only real hope for the alleviation of the penal yoke.[186]

Aogán Ó Rathaille, the Dryden of Munster and Irish Jacobite poet *par excellence*, reflected on the destruction wrought on the Catholic gentry classes in the post-Williamite period. In his classic 'An milleadh d'imthigh air mhór-shleachtaibh na h-Éireann', he painted a vivid picture of the decay which infected Irish society with the true king in exile. He reaffirmed the age-old functions of the poet as medium between the king and his kingdom, personified

184 Seán Clárach, 'Isé do leónuig mo chumas', in Ó Foghludha (eag.), *Seán Clárach*, p. 53. Ó Muirithe has edited an English version of Seán Clárach's poem from a manuscript in the R.I.A.; Ó Muirithe, 'Tho' not in full stile compleat', p. 96. Eoghan Rua Ó Súilleabháin observed in a revealing couplet that it was not being sunk in misery all the time that was the worst, but the scorn that accompanied it ('Ní ins an ainnise is measa linn bheith síos go deo, ach an tarcaisne a leanas sin' nach leigheasfadh na leomhain), quoted in Whelan, *Tree of liberty*, p. 14. **185** Quoted in Whelan, *Tree of liberty*, p. 11. Tadhg Gaelach Ó Súilleabháin composed a poem on his incarceration in Cork jail for treason; Tadhg Gaelach, 'Céad slán chon bárrachach Cois Bríde'; Ní Shéaghdha, *Catalogue*, fasc. *xii*, p. 99. See also Cullen, 'Patrons, teachers and literacy in Ireland', p. 35. **186** Copy of a letter from Hugh McMahon, alias Nelson, bishop of Clogher to [Grimaldi], *c*.1 Dec. 1707, in Giblin (ed.), 'Catalogue', part 3, vol. 81-101, pp 90-93.

as a beautiful woman. In a typically eloquent passage, he described Ireland as a country devoid of the shining blood of Éibhear, under the persecution of the foreigners, trampled under the feet of tyrants, distressed, deserted and crucified in great sorrow, devoid of men and women, without motion, vigour and heedless and with no justice for the poor of late:

> Tír gan triath do ghriain-fhuil Éibhir!
> Tír fá ansmacht Gall do traochadh!
> Tír do doirteadh fá chosaibh na méirleach!
> Tír na ngaibhne – is treighid go h-eug liom
>
> Tír bhocht bhuaidheartha, is uaigneach céasda!
> Tír gan fear gan mac gan céile!
> Tír gan lúth gan fonn gan éisdeacht!
> Tír gan chothrom do bochtaibh le déanaí![187]

While primarily the chronicler of Ireland's woes, Ó Rathaille explored the multi-dimensional nature of the Jacobite consciousness. He became the most skilful practitioner of the 'aisling' and in another poem, named after this favoured literary genre, a belief in Stuart deliverance counterbalanced his despair. Ó Buachalla has rightly stated that it was easy to appreciate the hope and despair in these 'aislingí' as rumours would have been widespread in contemporary Ireland (1707-8) that the Stuart was on his way: 'Ní deacair idir dhóchas is éadochas na n-aislingí sin a thuiscint. Bhí ina scéal reatha is ina ráfla coiteann ar fud Éireann sna blianta sin 1708-9 go raibh an Stíobhartach is a lucht leanúna ar a slí'.[188] Ó Rathaille explored the fluctuating expectations of Irish Jacobites in response to continental wars, rumours of internal rebellion and their possible implications for the Stuart cause. In his poem 'An Aisling', he encountered Aoibheall (the ancestral Munster goddess), lighting three candles at every harbour in the name of the true king (James III) who would soon return to claim his inheritance as sovereign of the three kingdoms. In this particular case, however, the poet's dream, which represented political reality for many of his Irish, English and Scottish contemporaries, evaporates before his eyes, leaving him sorely afflicted in the morning before Titan (the sun) had stirred his feet:

> D'fhreagair an bhrighid Aoibhill nár dhorcha snuadh,
> Fachain na d-trí gcoinnle do lasadh air gach cuan,
> A n-ainm an rígh díograis bheas aguinn go luath.
> A g-ceannas na d-trí ríoghachta, is dá gcosnamh go buan.

---

187 Aogán Ó Rathaille, 'An milleadh d'imthigh air mhór-shleachtaibh na hÉireann', in Ua Duinnín (eag.), *Dánta*, p. 6.   188 Ó Buachalla, *Aisling Ghéar*, p. 277.

As m'aisling do shlím-bhíodhgas go h-athchumair suas,
Is do mheasas gur bh-fhíor d'Aoibhill gach sonas dár luaidh;
Is amhlaidh bhíos tím créachtach doilbhir, duairc,
Maidion sul smaoin *Titan* a chosa do luadhaill.[189]

Like his predecessors, Ó Bruadair and Mac Cárthaigh, the reinstatement of the Catholic church was a major preoccupation for Ó Rathaille. In his optimistic 'Tairngreacht Dhoinn Fhírinnigh', the Stuart restoration would result in Ireland becoming playful, her forts merry, the Irish language celebrated by the poets, and the eclipse of the boorish English tongue. The poet also promised that James and his court would give patronage to the Gaels. The Lutheran bible and its black heretical teaching would be banished across the sea to Holland, along with the troop responsible for the persecution of the true clergy. Louis (XIV) and the prince (James III) should instead hold court and assembly:

Beidh Éire go súgach 's a dúnta go h-aodharach,
As Gaodhailg 'g a scrúdadh go múraibh ag éigsidh;-
Beurla na m-búr n-dubh go cúthail faoi néullaibh,
As Séamus 'n chúirt ghil ag tabhairt cungnta do Ghaodhlaibh.

Beidh an bíobla sin Lúiteir 's a dhubh-theagasg éithigh,
'S a bhuidhean so tá cionntach ná humhluigheann don g-cléir chirt,
'G a n-díbirt tar triúchaibh go Neuu-land ó Éirinn;
An Laoiseach 's an Prionnsa beidh cúirt aca 's aonach![190]

Ó Rathaille's poem also explored the balance of power in Europe immediately before the Treaty of Utrecht in 1713. According to the poet, the thunder (war) would stop by the power of the sun (Louis XIV, the Sun-King) which would scatter the mists surrounding the people of Ireland. The emperor would shed tears and Flanders would be in bondage which would facilitate the return of the 'Brick-layer' in King James's stead:

Stadfaidh an tóirneach le fóirneart na gréine,
As sgaipfidh an ceo-so do phór-shleachtaibh Éibhir;

---

189 Aogán Ó Rathaille, 'An Aisling', in Ua Duinnín (eag.), *Dánta*, p. 22. **190** Aogán Ó Rathaille, 'Tairngreacht Dhoinn Fhírinnigh', in Ua Duinnín (eag.), *Dánta*, pp 158,60. This theme figured prominently in Irish and Scots-Gaelic literary discourse; Campbell (eag..), *Songs of the '45*, pp 14-16, 172; see also Connolly, *Priests and people*, p. 13; Froude, *The English in Ireland*, i, p. 533. Contemporary Irish poetry contains specific derogatory references to the English language; idem (eag.), *Seán Clárach*, p. 76; Ó Foghludha (eag.), *Cois na Ruachtaighe*, p. 17. In stark contrast to this utopia, Fr Liam Inglis lamented that the English language is esteemed without the vigour of Irish 'Is araid atá an Béarla is gan tapaidh 'san Ghaeilge'; Inglis, 'm'atuirse traochta na fearachoin aosta' Ó Foughludha (eag.), *Cois na Bríde*, p. **41**.

An t-Impre beidh deorach as Flóndrus faoi dhaor-smacht,
'S "an bricléir" go modhmharach a seomra Rí Séamus.[191]

When one considers the bloody campaigns of the British hero Marlborough
and Prince Eugene, the Atlas of the Holy Roman Empire, and their implications, both for the survival of the empire and for the fate of the Protestant
succession in England, Ó Rathaille's observations amount to more than the
sentimental rantings of a 'file faoi sceimhle' or a disgruntled Kerry bard.[192]

Ó Rathaille's sarcastic use of the Whig nickname of 'Bricklayer' for James III
indicated his contempt for those who dared question the impeccable genealogy
of the Stuart claimant. This, and the belief that James would rescue the Gaels,
also permeated his Ulster contemporary Raghnall Dall Mac Domhnaill's 'A
Chreagáin Uaibhrigh' in November 1715. Tracing James's lineage back through
Mary Queen of Scots and Henry Stewart, Lord Darnley, to Fergus I, the Irish-
born king of Scotland, the poet reiterated the prophecy of the truly religious
Ultan which foretold the delivery of the Gaels from captivity:

> Trí coróna do ghaibh Séamus Cia dhaoibh nár fheachas air an scéal linn,
> do labhradh air aon oileán de na h-oileanaibh sin. Agus is amhlaidh
> thainic an Séamas sin; Ríoghain mhórdha mhór-ghairmithe darbh' ainm
> Máire, agus fós árd-fhlaith uasal onóireach ó gheinealach na h-Alban ó
> thréibh Fhearghusa mhóir mhic Earcha mhic Eochaidh mhuinreamhair
> ... darbh' ainm duke of Lennox agus do rug sí mac meadhach mór
> mhéanach darbh ainm James the first agus is ón tSéamas sin a thainic an
> dá Shéarlas, Máire agus Anne mar aon leis an Seabhac fíor-ghlic, fíor-
> eolach do bhláth luibhghoirt na fineamhna, an réalt suaithnidh solas-
> ghlan, an dreagún tréan, díogbhalach, an nathar nimhneach, neart-chal-
> ma, an bheithir bhríoghmhar, bratallach agus an leomhan cródha
> casgarthach gníomh-eáchtach, cath-bhuadhach le bhfuasgailtear an
> Gaedheal ó dhaoirse agus ó dhaoir-phionoid eachtrann, mar a deir an
> fáidh fíor-naomhtha Ultan.[193]

---

191 Aogán Ó Rathaille, 'Tairngreacht Dhoinn Fhírinnigh, in Ua Duinnín (eag.), *Dánta*, p. 158. Other
contemporary sources contain references to the 'Bricklayer'; *H.M.C., Portland, 13th report*, part 3, p 159;
Miller, *James II*, p. 187. **192** Ó Tuama, *Filí faoi sceimhle*, pp 83-184. **193** Raghnall Dall Mac Domhnall,
'A Chreagáin Uaibhrigh', in Murray, *A history*, pp 56-9. Ó Buachalla dates this poem to 1715; Ó Buachalla,
Aisling Ghéar, p. 305. In his allegorical poem 'Tionól na bhfear Muimhneach' Ó Rathaille dismissed the
calumnies regarding the parentage of 'James III'; Ua Duinnín (eag.) *Dánta*, pp 108-9. Fr Conchubhar Ó
Briain in his poem 'A Alba ó shealbhais an Rí cóir cirt' [1719] castigated the foreign puck-goats who
maintained that you were a bastard who had not descended from the brave king 'Na gall-phoic do
dhearbhuigh go díchórach,/Gur bhastard thú nár sreabhadh d'fhuil an Rí chródha'; Ó Foghludha (eag.),
Carn Tighearnaigh, p. 29. The optimistic sentiments in Raghnall Dall's poetry are reflected by his Scottish
contemporary Sìlis na Ceapaich's 'Do Rígh Séamus' (A song for King James). This was composed in the
run-up to the 'Fifteen' to the Irish tune 'Mo Mhailí bheag ó'; Sìlis nan Ceapaich 's, 'Do Rìgh Séamus',

These recurring invasion hopes continued to regularly feature in contemporary Irish poetry. In his poem 'Gile na Gile', the normally pessimistic Ó Rathaille hoped that Ireland's heroic lions from across the sea would support James III, the most fine thrice over of Scottish blood, against the black, horned, foreign, hate-crested crew:

'S an duine badh ghile air chine Scoit trí h-uaire,
Ag feithiomh air isi bheith aige mar chaoin-nuachar

...

Mo threighid! mo thubaist! mo thurrainn! mo bhrón! mo dhíth!
mo shoitseach mhuirneach, mhiochaisgheal, bheól-tais, chaoin,
ag adharcach fuirionn-dubh miosgaireach cóirneach buídhe;
's gan leigheas 'na goire go bh-fillid na leoghain tar tuínn.[194]

The poet's ridicule of the horned Hanoverian monarch was not a unique reference in the Irish literary tradition to George I's cuckoldry. Ó Buachalla also uncovers an allusion to three horns and a penis ('trí hadharca is feam') in Ó Rathaille's poem; 'Tionól na bhFear Muimhneach'.[195] An English verse in a contemporary Irish manuscript also mocked the infidelity of the consort of George I:

At vast expense the Britons would adorn
The Hanoverian with one single horn
To his consort his merit better knew
At small expense has furnished him with two.[196]

Seán Clárach's 'Comhracann mo mhacaomh' (an Irish version of the Scottish-Jacobite Song 'My laddie can fight') promised to 'drive the mad bull (King George) from the fair forest and pluck his cursed horns off his thick skull' ('Seól fam bulla na buile as an gcoill/Is adharca na mallacht is maith stracfam dá mhaoil').[197]

The peace of Utrecht (1713) and the death of Louis XIV (1715) were severe blows to the Stuart cause.[198] However, Irish Catholic Jacobites were not totally

Ó Baoill (eag.), *Bàrdachd Shìlis nan Ceapaich*, pp 16-19 See also her four poems on the earl of Mar and on the battle of Sheriffmuir; ibid., pp 26-50; See also 'The landing in Scotland'; B.L., Add. Ms 29, 981, fol. 107. The metaphor of the oak ships figured in the English Jacobite tradition; Pittock, *Poetry*, p. 50. **194** Aogán Ó Rathaille, 'Gile na Gile', in Ua Duinnín (eag.), *Dánta*, p. 20. Ó Buachalla pointed out that while Nicholas Plunkett (and Ó Rathaille) alluded to the nobility (the Irish in St Germain or 'the lions over the sea') Irish poets often referred to them as individuals and in a local context; Ó Buachalla, *Aisling Ghéar*, pp 200, pp 205-6. **195** Ó Rathaille, 'Tionól na bhfear Muimhneach', in Ua Duinnín (eag.), *Dánta*, p. 108; Ó Buachalla, *Aisling Ghéar*, p. 296. **196** Ó Tuama, 'At vast expense the English would adorn'/'Cia Chaitheadar Gaill a saidhbhreas óir le puimp', in *Cat. of Ir. mss. in R.I.A.*, fasc. 1-5, p. 292. A translation from Irish mocked the cuckhold who has late come over which has caused our prince to turn a rover; Ó Muirithe, 'Tho' not in full stile compleat', p. 100. **197** Seán Clárach, 'Comhracann mo mhacaomh', in Ó Foghludha (eag.), *Seán Clárach*, p. 60. **198** 'Obituary of Louis XIV', Mac Domhnaill, in *Cat. of Ir.*

despondent in this period. D.G. Boyce claimed that they did not even grumble in 1715 when the Scottish and a minority of the English Jacobites rose in support of their exiled monarch.[199] However, Boyce's opinion of Irish Jacobite passivity is not borne out by the level of Catholic Jacobite expectation, contemporary recruitment depositions or in Irish Jacobite literature. The elation of the literati at the outset of the 'Fifteen' made itself apparent in the literary outpouring regarding the earl of Mar, self-styled standard-bearer of James III.[200] Seán Ó Neachtain's contemporary 'Welcome to George I' contains double-meaning words and allusions including 'Fál teith' (welcome, flee Ireland, hot wall), 'sláinte/slán, teith', (welcome, Goodbye, flee), 'neamhchumtha' (heavenly, misshapen), 'anfhlaith' (great prince, tyrant), 'andúil' (great love, monster), 'ní maith' (a good thing, don't like), 'an meadhg' (whey, Hanoverians), 'ar an ccách' (everyone, on the shit), 'a cheart do Sheoirse (George's right, George's desert), 'an bhréig-Phretender' (James, or George).[201] Aodh Buí Mac Cruitín best captured the mood of the moment when hopes were high for a Stuart restoration in the period immediately preceding the Hanoverian succession. He urged Ireland not to consider that her warriors were dead, however many have been lost across the sea, as some of that group lived and would return and avenge the blood of her snow-white body:

> A Bhanba ná meastar leat ár laochra Fáil,
> cé easpa dhuit a gcailleamhain gur éag an táin,
> mairid cuid den aicme sin ar téacht tair sáil
> do chaithfeas fuil do shneachta-choirp 'na n-éiric d'fháil.[202]

The anonymous poet who penned an undated lament on the exile of the Uí Néill and its effects on Ireland was similarly confident of their timely return. He decried the exile of Clann Néill across the sea and Ireland's heartbroken state since their departure. However, he assured his listeners that these eggs would produce many eagles wherever they were hatched:

---

mss. in R.I.A., fasc. 1-5, p. 454; 'Peace concluded and men broke', Flower, *Cat. of Ir. mss in B.L.* ii, p. 217. **199** Boyce, *Nationalism in Ireland*, p. 98; Beckett, *Making of modern Ireland*, p. 161. For contemporary rumours of an impending Jacobite landing in Ireland in 1715 and Marlborough's presentation of a paper to parliament on the state of the country; Beresford, 'Ireland', pp 128-9.   **200** Donnchadh Caoch Ó Mathghamhna, 'Más mac do Mhars an Mar so a n-Albain aoird' and An tAthair Conchobhar Ó Briain, 'Más mac de Mars an Mar seo in Alban uaidh', in Ó Foghludha (eag.), *Carn Tighearnaigh*, p. 29; Anon, 'Ó deirig Mar mar Mhars a nealaibh thuaidh', in *Cat. of Ir. mss. in R.I.A.*, fasc. 1-5, p. 80. Ó Buachalla provides a description and context for these poems on Mar's rising in Scotland and his struggle with Argyll; Ó Buachalla, *Aisling Ghéar*, pp 308-9. Ó Rathaille is also credited with composing a poem on James's arrival in Scotland; [Ó Rathaille?], 'An lá tháinig an prionnsa (Séarlus) go h-Albain', in Ua Duinnín (eag.), *Dánta*, p. 139.   **201** Seán Ó Neachtain, Fál teith S[h]eaáin Uí Neachtuin', in Risk, 'Seán Ó Neachtain', pp 41-6, 462. Ó Buachalla provides a context for Seán Ó Neachtain's poem and other examples of such word-play; Ó Buachalla, *Aisling Ghéar*, pp 292-3. Flood recorded the following English verse which dated to this period: 'Let our great James come over/And baffle the prince of Hanover/With hearts and hands in royal bands/We'll welcome him at Dover'; Flood, *Irish music*, p. 245. **202** Morley, *An crann os coill*, p. 45.

D'imthig clanna Néill thar sáile
'S tá Éire cráidthe ó d'imthigh siad.
Ach deánfaidh uibheacha iolair iolraidh
Cibé an áit i ngorthar iad.[203]

Even after the collapse of the 'Fifteen', Seán Clárach Mac Domhnaill's song 'Ar thulaigh im aonar', composed to the tune 'A bhean a' tighe shéimh', is saturated with impatience for their king's long-awaited arrival. He assured his audience that James would come although he was long delayed by the spite of the Swedes and the artful (Philippe d'Orléans) Regent (of France). He promised that Philip V and holy Clement (Pope Clement XI), the champion of the weak, and King Louis (XV) of the war-like Bourbons would bring bright Caesar (James III) back to us:

Tiocfaidh bhur Séamas cé gur moilleadh a theacht
Le mioscais na Suedes is Régent cliste na gcleas
An fhuireann so is téachtmhar tréanmhar tuillte dhe neart
Ní coimirc dóibh sléibhte réidhteacht muingthe ná scairt.

Pilib is Clément naomhtha, cuisle na lag
Is Isacus Réx de thréanfhuil Bhurbon na gcath
Tiocfaid le chéile is deanfid iorghail treas
is cuirfid na Caesair ghléigeal chugaibh tar n-ais.[204]

V

Although Catholics predominated in the ranks of Irish Jacobitism a small Protestant Jacobite interest emerged in the early eighteenth century. George Dodington remarked in 1707 that 'you would hardly believe that there should be such a creature as an Irish Protestant Jacobite and yet 'tis certain that there are a great many such monsters'. Although, as Hayton has suggested, Dodington was an English Whig with little understanding of Irish politics, his observation was not unfounded.[205] Carried over from the residual high-Tory and non-juring Jacobitism of a small group of Irish Protestants in the 1690s, it flourished in the coffee-houses and taverns of Dublin, particularly during Ormonde's last lieutenancy in Ireland. It retained a foothold in Trinity College and was reflected in the mob politics of Dublin during the initial years of George I's reign. It also

---

203 Quoted in Hyde, 'Eagles in exile', p. 47. **204** Seán Clárach Mac Domhnaill, 'Ar thulaigh im aonair', in Ó Foghludha (eag.), *Seán Clárach*, p. 52. There are other references to political flirtations between the Stuart court and Sweden, Russia and the pope; *H.M.C., Stuart,* iv, pp 444-5; ibid., iv, p 473; ibid., v, pp 133, 446; ibid., i , p. 85; ibid., vii, pp 56, 302; B.L., Stowe Ms 232, fol. 51; Beresford, 'Ireland', pp 134, 136-7; B.L., Stowe Ms 250, fol. 37; R.A., Ms 61, fol. 121; Miller, *James III*, pp 163, 181.

managed a final flurry of seditious pamphleteering and toasting before vanishing into high-church and Protestant literary circles.[206] Given the nature of Jacobitism and the dangers of overt Jacobite displays, it is not surprising that, in spite of the electioneering of Sir James Cotter and some contact between Jacobite students in Trinity College and the Dublin 'mob', there is little evidence of interchange between Catholic and Protestant Jacobites. Evidence of surviving Irish Protestant Jacobitism reflects its English Protestant counterpart and shows the flexibility of the ideology and its ability to act as an easily comprehended cultural platform with which many social, political and religious groups could identify.

This Irish Protestant Jacobite interest has received little attention by historians. James McGuire concluded that 'a besieged Protestant colony could not afford the luxury of a non-juring party in Ireland'.[207] F.G. James argued that the Pretender had very few active supporters among Irish Tories and that the disaffection of Ormonde and his lord chancellor, Sir Constantine Phipps, gave the Whigs an opportunity to attack all high Tories.[208] More recently James Kelly has stated that Irish Jacobitism was overwhelmingly if not exclusively Catholic.[209] David Hayton, Seán Connolly and Tom Doyle point out that the high-flying sentiments of some Irish Protestant clergy found little expression among the Protestant laity. Hayton correctly concludes that the Protestant gentleman with scruples about the revolution was 'a curiosity'.[210] Nevertheless references exist to the occasional Scottish-Protestant or indigenous Protestant clergyman who refused to take the oaths or who were forced to recant non-juring principles.[211] The Dublin press attacked those Protestants who flirted with Jacobitism. *An essay upon the interest of England in the present circumstances of affairs* (1701) vented its spleen against an active Protestant Jacobite group. It believed that they 'fondly flatter themselves that a boy banished by England almost as soon as he was born, who with his milk suckled in popery and an aversion to England which has been strongly inculcated in him to the age of 13 by two of the most zealous, stubborn and vengeful parents, will not forget that his great-grandmother and grandfather had their heads cut off by the people of England'.[212] The popular press occasionally catered for this Protestant Jacobite group. The detention of Patrick

---

205 Dodington to [?], 14 Aug. 1707 (S.P., 63/366/230-1); Hayton, 'Ireland and the English ministers', p. 151. For some examples of Protestant Jacobitism; T.C.D., Ms 750/3/2/, fols 229-30; *Dub. I.,* 29 June-4 July 1710, 4 July 1710, 19 Aug. 1710, 11 Nov. 1710, 18 Nov. 1710; *Dub. Gaz.,* 27 June-1 July 1710, 15-19 Aug. 1710.	**206** Hayton provides the best general survey of this period; Hayton, 'Ireland and the English ministers'.	**207** McGuire, 'The Church of Ireland and the Glorious revolution', p. 149.	**208** James, *Ireland in the empire,* pp 85-7.	**209** Kelly, 'The glorious and immortal memory', p. 32.	**210** Hayton, 'Crisis in Ireland', p. 195.	**211** For examples, see R. Echin to Ormonde, 26 Dec. 1705 (N.L.I., Ms 2467, fol. 147). Robert Johnson reported the case of a Protestant minister who was forced to renounce his Jacobite views; N.L.I., Ms 2471 [505] fol. 963. See also *H.M.C., Ormond,* viii, p. 292.	**212** *An essay upon the interest of England.* See also *The pope's speech to the college of cardinals.* Another pamphleteer believed that 'it is unreasonable for one who resolves to live a Protestant that a popish priest might rule over him as that a man should employ a wolf for his shepherd or an eagle to protect and secure his dovehouse'; *Discourse concerning Ireland and the different interests thereof,* p. 39.

Campbell in the north of Ireland, for printing and distributing Andrew Bell's *An enquiry into the causes of the miscarriage of the Scots at Darien*[213] suggests evidence of a seditious interest on the earl of Antrim's estate during the first years of the eighteenth century. The Scotsman 'Honest' Lewis Gordon had also set up a seditious club in this period. Hostile Whig observers perceived their activities as opening divisions between Protestants and promoting the interests of the 'pretended prince of Wales'.[214]

George Faulkner, 'the prince of Dublin printers', was prosecuted in 1708 and 1709 for printing popish prayer-books. He was also accused of reporting the burning of Wicklow by the French, and for printing a 'seditious' and 'scandalous' pamphlet. However a carefully packed jury failed to pass a guilty verdict.[215] The coffee-house owner and printer Edward Lloyd attempted to publish *The memoirs of the chevalier de St George* (James III) and other works, showing the extent to which Dublin provided a base for such seditious pamphleteering, particularly during the lord chancellorship of Sir Constantine Phipps. Lloyd's case became a *cause célèbre* and prompted Whig-Tory infighting because he was recommended to the queen's mercy while the Whig agitator Dudley Moore felt the full force of the law.[216] Moore, the younger brother of a prominent Whig M.P., had been charged following an affray at a Dublin theatre on King William's birthday. He disrupted the performance of the favourite Whig play *Tamerlane* because the prologue, a strong attack of the Treaty of Utrecht, had been banned by the lords justice. Moore mounted the stage and recited the prologue himself, for which minor offence an information was filed against him.[217]

Lloyd's prosecution for seditious pamphleteering was not exceptional. The printer Richard Pue, closely connected to Lloyd, was arrested on a number of occasions for verses which 'highly reflected on the late House of Commons'.[218] The prosecution of the printer Edward Waters for publishing a libel against the government called *England's Eye*, and the 1714 indictment of his colleague

---

213 This ill-fated Scottish settlement at Darien was projected by William Paterson and sanctioned by the Scottish parliament in 1695. An expedition sailed in 1698 but English commercial opposition scuttled the scheme, ruining many investors and further deepening Scottish discontent with the Williamite regime. A pamphlet published in 1746 gives a good account of this; *The Thistle*, p. 16.   **214** Jersey to lords justice, 30 Jan. 1700 (P.R.O., S.P., 67/2/280 [141]). See also N.L.I., Inchiquin papers, interim report, fol. 1. Campbell was also indicted for printing and publishing seditious libels 'decrying the Queen's hereditary right and placing it with the Pretender'; *The argument of one of the Queen's Council against Mr. Dudley Moor*.   **215** Munter, *A dictionary*, p. 283. Munter provides evidence of another Tory publisher being pardoned for printing and advertising a Jacobite tract; ibid., p. 245.   **216** J. Stanley to Shrewsbury, 24 Dec. 1713 (P.R.O., S.P., 63/369/34, 47). See also B.L., Add. Mss 34,777, fols 76-9; N.L.I., Thorpe p.12; Bodl., Eng. Hist., Ms *c*.42, fol. 63.   **217** Hayton, 'An Irish parliamentary diary', pp 121-2. Hayton describes the lengthy proceedings of the committee formed to look into the cases of Lloyd and Moore; ibid., pp 134-5; idem, 'Ireland and the English ministers', p. 284.   **218** Munter referred to Lloyd as 'the notorious Jacobite coffee-house proprietor'. When Ormonde ordered the charges to be dropped Lloyd began publishing *Lloyd's Newsletter*. He was later forced to flee to London after Ormonde's replacement; Munter, *A dictionary*, pp 168, 220.

Dickson for a ballad entitled 'Tis time to come over' showed that a market survived for seditious literature.[219] Another printer named Campbell was also acquitted of the charge of printing and publishing 'two impudent and seditious libels'.[220] Deliberations in the Irish House of Commons regarding a pamphlet by J. Drake entitled *The memorial of the Church of England humbly offered to the consideration of all true lovers of our church and constitution* (London, 1705, repr. Dublin, 1711) also concluded that it contained paragraphs which were deemed to be 'highly reflecting on her majesty, the late King William and the Hanoverian succession'.[221]

Catholic Jacobite printers also involved themselves in this illicit pamphleteering. The activities of James Malone, formerly printer to James II, bears out Hayton's assertion that 'the Catholics had their own underground press in contemporary Dublin'.[222] Malone was sentenced to nine years in prison in 1703 for publishing *The memoirs of James II*, a work later burned by the common hangman. According to the *Journals of the House of Commons*, James Eustace of Yeomanstown, County Kildare brought a copy of the *memoirs* to Malone from England. The printer John Brocas was also arrested for printing a further two hundred and fifty copies (Malone later confessed that five hundred copies were produced). Some of these had been sent to Limerick and Galway, including one to the son of the former Jacobite lord chancellor Sir Stephen Rice and another to Nicholas Lynch (-FitzAmbrose). Eustace absconded before his arrest and the messenger of the sergeant-at-arms found that his closet and papers had been tampered with before they could be searched. The Dublin historian, J.T. Gilbert, identified a seditious religious work, also published by Malone and Luke Dowling, containing 'certain prayers for the late King James and his queen and also for the Pretender'. These were dispersed 'about the time of the late invasion intended by the French king on North Britain with the intent to be dispersed in order to influence and encourage the papists'. Malone and Dowling were fined forty shillings for each copy of a manual of devout prayers, and that they paid the fine and continued their trade. They were also forced to take the Oath of Abjuration. Malone's case was not an isolated incident. The publisher responsible for the *Flying Post*, a contemporary Catholic newspaper, was lambasted as 'an Irish newsmonger and Paris gazette-gelder who continues to impose on the public by false and sham news for which he hath lately been indicted at the quarter-sessions in this city'. He was described as 'a tool to the papists by keeping them in heart and hopes of great matters'.[223] Malone and

219 Newsletter, 22 June 1714 (*H.M.C., Portland,* v, p. 460). Waters was again prosecuted in February 1715 and in 1720; Williams (ed.), *Correspondence,* ii, p. 240.   **220** *The argument of one of the queen's council against Mr Dudley Moor,* Munter, *A dictionary,* p. 268.   **221** Hayton, 'An Irish parliamentary diary', p. 119.   **222** Hayton, 'Ireland and the English ministers', p. 22.   **223** Munter, *A dictionary,* pp 36, 181 The executed Jacobite Sir James Cotter also had a copy of these memoirs in his library; Ó Buachalla, *Aisling Ghéar,* p. 365. See also *Journal of the House of Commons,* ii (1692-1713), pp 367-70. Gilbert, *Streets of Dublin,* pp 27, 597-8.

Dowling also printed 'a manual of devotions, with a form of prayer for the pretended prince of Wales by the name of James III'.[224] One hundred and fifty copies of a seditious *Life of James II* were produced in 1712 and 1713.[225]

Contemporary evidence exists for the importation of 'several papist books and a genealogical dissertation of the royal family of the Stuarts from Milesius to James III of England and Ireland'.[226] One newspaper editorial related this seizure of seditious literature to Protestant apprehension and papist elation, which stemmed from reports of the Pretender's imminent arrival:

> Whereas John Hallridge, esq., a gentleman of this kingdom, did lately wait upon Secretary Southwell with a letter he had received from Ireland dated from Castlehyde in the County Cork, and without a name but supposed from Mr Arthur Hyde esq. giving an account of the great apprehensions the Protestants of that country were in from papists being 50:1 that they were forced to be on their guard that many priests were lately come over, said mass publically and then put on their swords, either as daring or making it unsafe to punish them; that a trunk was seized near Mallow in the said county, containing several popish trinkets, books and letters, directed to several persons in this kingdom, encouraging the papists here by letting them know the Pretender would soon come over and that the said trunk was given to Mr Archdeacon, a popish merchant of Cork, by a nobleman lately arrived from France and that Mr Hyde gave an account of the said letter to the government but was not thought worthy of an answer.[227]

Protestant Jacobite rhetoric occasionally surfaced in high-flying Protestant sermons. The sermon preached by Jonathan Wilson, chaplain to Sir Constantine Phipps, on the anniversary of the restoration of Charles II, may have been intended as an allegorical reference to his bohemian nephew. The tyrant Absalom, referred to in the sermon, could as readily be identified with William III as with Cromwell. Absalom, the son who deposed his father, remained synonymous in both the English and Anglo-Irish Jacobite tradition with King William:

> His royal son, the heir both of his crown and sufferings, for no other cause than he was the son of such a father, proscribed and banished as a common traitor to make room for one of the most flagitious tyrants and usurpers that ever scourged the land … On the other hand did Absalom

---

224 *A short account of the late proceedings of the University of Dublin against Forbes*, pp 11-12; Phillips, *Printing and book-selling in Dublin*, p. 31.   **225** Phillips, *Printing and book-selling in Dublin*, pp 68, 284.   **226** Lords justice to Southwell, 19 Feb. 1713 (N.A., Ms 3036, fol. 135).   **227** Brady (ed.), *Catholics*, p. 19. See also *A letter from a gentleman in Cork to his friend in Dublin giving a full and true account of the trial of one Christopher Martin*. See also Bodl., Eng. Hist. Ms b. 125, fols 53-5.

by malicious invectives against the government raise faction and rebellion in the state by the arts of adulation and popularity his fair and cajoling speeches to the people, to steal their affections from their lawful king.[228]

This cryptic jargon also appeared in some contemporary Tory pamphlets and broadsheets. Ormonde's re-appointment as lord lieutenant in 1710 was the subject of a triumphalist ode, which had distinctively Jacobite undertones:

As the famed oak by wonder doomed to wait
Decayed or blooming, on the Stewart's fate
But true the Butlers to the royal line.[229]

Another pamphlet published in contemporary Dublin taunted Whig duplicity in relation to the Oath of Allegiance sworn to James II and on the question of the legitimacy of 'his son', 'the prince of Wales'. Asserting that Whig 'aversion to the Pretender is not so deep ground as they would have you believe', the author related the tale of the old Whig who said 'that he could not deny but when they were all introduced in all of the corporations of the nation by King James II, they promised to stand by him and his son with their lives and fortunes' and 'consented to the legitimacy of the birth of the prince of Wales'.[230]

Drinking clubs and coffee-houses supported a residual Protestant Jacobite interest in the first fifteen years of the eighteenth century. In their work on Tory political thought and Jacobite political argument in contemporary England, Goldie and Chapman have stressed the importance of the broadsheet, pamphlet, ballad, and coffee-house for the clandestine diffusion of unorthodox political ideas and news.[231] Ireland was no different. A small covert group of Protestant Tories, whose loyalty lay with the exiled scion of the royal Stuarts, were *habitués* of some Dublin coffee-houses, providing a readership for both locally produced and imported Jacobite works.[232] Archbishop King claimed that coffee-house literature provided themes for the sermons of the different clerical factions.[233] The role of the coffee-house is encapsulated in a doggerel verse on

---

228 Wilson, *A sermon preached at Christ's Church.* See also Monod, *Jacobitism*, pp 36, 52. **229** *The church and monarchy secured by the return of his grace the duke of Ormonde.* Ormonde purportedly donned a white rose on James's birthday; O'Callaghan, *Irish Brigades*, p. 282. Another contemporary pamphleteers represented Ormonde as the 'Butler' and James as the 'Steward'; *The complaint of a family.* The Jacobite writer Nicholas Plunkett believed that Ormonde would put the government of the House [of Commons] in 'honest hands'; Bodl., Carte Ms 211, fol. 114. Dr Whalley's *Decree for the stars* was directed against this particular political species, 'those curs who vent their spite' and 'show their teeth but cannot bite'; [Whalley], *A decree for the stars.* **230** *Beware of the Pretender*, p. 3. **231** Goldie, 'Tory political thought', pp 34-5, 39, 42; Chapman, 'Jacobite political argument', pp 10, 192-3, 203-5. **232** *Dub. Gaz.*, 16-20 Dec. 1712. Lloyd's coffee-house was considered the seat of Jacobitism in Dublin; 'The Swan Tripe Club in Dublin: A satyr' ... Apr. 1706 (B.L., Add. Ms 23, 904); Munter, *Dictionary*, p. 168. **233** King to Jenkins, 20 Feb. 1712 (T.C.D., Ms 2532, fol. 119).

Richard Pue, a staunch supporter of the Tory interest: 'Ye Quidnuncs who frequently come to Pue's/To live on politics, coffee and news'.[234]

Jacobite activities in Dublin centred around a number of particular taverns and coffee-houses, including The Globe (a favourite haunt for Trinity students), Lloyd's coffee-house at Cork Hill and the Swan Tavern. The Swan provided the subject of a Grand Jury presentment at Michaelmas 1705 as one of the Brodrick Whig faction claimed that seditious toasts were drunk there. Dr Francis Higgins, 'the Irish Sacheverell', one of its principal members, was later tried and acquitted of being 'a disloyal subject and a disturber of the public peace'. In his *Postscript to Mr Higgins's sermon* (inscribed 'printed by Edward Lloyd and sold at his coffee-house'), Charles Leslie denied rumours that a clergyman of the 'Swan Tripe Club' had asserted that it was time to call home the young gentleman from St Germain ['James III']'.[235] These activities enable us to glimpse the Irish Protestant Jacobite tradition and its ideological links with its English counterpart.[236]

Occasional references also allude to Protestant Jacobite sedition. In June 1711, a Mr Whitway M.A., a member of Trinity College Dublin, was accused of using unfavourable words against the memory of King William. His case was referred to Archbishop King of Dublin. He later wrote to St George Ashe, bishop of Clogher, vice-chancellor of the University to inform him that he had examined three witnesses and found the defendant guilty as charged.[237] Another indictment suggests the existence of Jacobitism within the armed forces. It involved two soldiers of eleven years who asserted that they would fight for the Pretender, or the prince of Wales ('James III').[238] In August 1715 two displaced officers who were informed against for drinking the Stuart king's health, and for endeavouring to enveigle another man to go and serve him, purportedly declared that 'James III was their king and they would own no other'.[239] Sir Richard Cox prosecuted

234 Munter, *A dictionary*, p. 220.   **235** *Grand Jury presentment*, 25 May 1705; 'The Swan-Tripe Club in Dublin, a satyr April 1706'; B.L., Add. Ms 23,904). A printed copy survives in the Gilbert collection; *The Swan-Tripe Club in Dublin: a satyr*. See also Doyle, 'Politics', p. 199; Gilbert, *Streets of Dublin*, p. 498; Leslie, *Postscript to Mr Higgins's sermon*. Dr Travers attacked the malicious and groundless insinuations of Tripe clubbers; *Dr Travers, his defence of King William of glorious memory*. Given the clientele which frequented the premises, it is not surprising that Mr Butler, owner of the Swan Tavern, refused to deliver the said adjoining ground to her majesty for the use of the public; Bodl. Engl. hist. b. 125, fol. 4.   **236** Harley to Southwell, 2 June 1704 (N.L.I., Ms 992, fol. 15); O'Donoghue, 'Jacobite threat ', p. 139; Pittock, *Poetry*, p. 77; Monod, *Jacobitism*, p. 251.   **237** Accusations were made against Mr Whitway for insulting the memory of King William on 24 June 1711; *H.M.C Portland*, v, 1899, pp 21-2. Parson (George) Kelly, one of the seven men of Moidart, was reportedly expelled from Trinity in this period because of his Jacobite sentiments; Hayden, 'Prince Charles Edward's Irish friends', p. 95. In 1710 a student was reproved for omitting reference to the revolution in a 5 November oration. He answered that he did not say anything of it for his class fellows would hiss him if he said anything to its advantage and he should not be able to live in the college, quoted in Connolly, *Religion*, p. 240.   **238** Information of John Hallard, 6 May 1713 (P.R.O., S.P., 63/369/62). See also *H.M.C., Ormond*, viii, p. 340.   **239** W. Perceval to Sir J. Perceval, 27 Aug. 1715 (B.L., Add. Ms 47,028, fol. 63). Similarly, three Irish soldiers in England, Joseph O'Sullivan, alias Silver, a sergeant in Colonel Pail's company of guards, Felix O'Hara and Robert Whitty port-major Thomas Wyndham and commissary John Birch at the Cork assizes in July 1713 for drinking the memory of James II and the health of James III and his Catholic allies in Europe. Whether this resulted from an over-indulgence in alcohol or whether it is a case of *in vino veritas*, it shows that there was a distinct Jacobite dimension to contemporary Whig/Tory political infighting.

Cox's prosecution directs attention to a seditious culture in which the cryptic toast provided, as in the case of the state banquet, the central protocol. The toast to '£3. 14s. 5d.' (James III, Louis XIV and Philip V) ranks, in terms of ambiguity and ingenuity, among the finest in the Anglo-Irish and Gaelic traditions.[240] Others include the three Bs (The Best Born Briton, James III),[241] Sorrell (the horse which threw William III to his death),[242] 'An druimfhionn donn dílis' (the little white-backed cow, James III or Charles Edward),[243] 'An Féinics' (the phoenix, James III or Charles Edward),[244] 'Gille Mear' (Charles Edward),[245] 'An tÚrghas Óg/An Craoibhín Aoibhinn' (the young sapling/the little flowery branch, Charles Edward),[246] 'An Seabhac Siubhail' (the wandering warrior/ hawk,

suffered the death penalty for enlisting for the exiled Stuart king. As part of the recruiting ceremony, they swore allegiance to James III, abjured the pretender (George I) and drank confusion to those who would betray King James, asserting that 'George would be glad to get back to Hanover on Ormonde's arrival at the head of three thousand men'; Bodl., Rawl. Ms *c*.743, fol. 38. See also Linebaugh, *The London Hanged*, p. 95. **240** The case of Thomas Wyndham and George Birch 21 July 1713 (N.L.I., Ms 2476, fol. 349). These cryptic toasts also occurred in the Irish tradition. For example: 'Four first and double one and mouse in the language of learned men [Latin]' (that is, 4 +(1 x 2) = 6 (Sé) + Mus= Séamus) 'Ceathair ar dtúis/is dúbail aon annsoin/is i na dteangain na n-úghdar múinte glaoidh ar luich'; in Piaras Mac Gearailt, An file agus Aibigeál Brún', in Ó Foghludha (eag.), *Amhráin Phiarais Mhic Gearailt*, p. 52. A number of other variations of this Jacobite equation survive in the Irish tradition; Ó Buachalla, *Aisling Ghéar*, pp 352-3. See also O'Grady, *Cat. of Ir mss in B.L.*, i, p. 607. **241** For toast to the three 'Bs' (Best Born Briton); Examination of Hartpole Fitzgerald, 20 May 1715 (P.R.O., S.P., 63/372/111). **242** For allusion to toasting Sorrell; 'The Swan Tripe Club, a satyr...' April 1706; B.L., Add., Ms 23, 904). See also Bodl., Carte Ms 209, fol. 457; Kelly 'The glorious and immortal memory', p. 33. A song penned in Cloyne, County Cork, in response to 'The Boyne Water' praised 'the sorrell horse which revenged the wrong on him who caused the slaughter; Ó Muirithe, 'Tho' not in full stile compleat', p. 100. This toast to Sorrell survived in Irish political discourse. On 4 Nov. 1745 Lord Lieutenant Chesterfield gave a toast to the glorious and immortal memory of the great and good King William who delivered us from brass money, popery, slavery and wooden shoes. 'I'll drink your toast', said the Catholic gentlewoman Lady Moll Nugent, who was one of the company, 'but with a trifling addition if you will give me leave'. 'Certainly', said the viceroy. 'I shall add the memory of the Sorrell horse that kicked his brains out', quoted in O'Reilly, *The Irish abroad*, p. 270. See also U.L., Cambs., Madden 25, fols 3,4,5. In a country with no moles, the classic English Jacobite toast to the 'little gentleman in the velvet waistcoat' (the mole which dug the hole that tripped Sorrell and threw King William, causing him to sustain the broken collar-bone which hastened his death) had little relevance; Monod, *Jacobitism*, p. 146. **243** 'An druimfhionn donn dílis, in Ní Ógáin (eag.), *Duanaire*, i, p. 69. **244** 'An Féinics flaith de phór Gaedhil'; Ó Tuama, 'Móirín Ní Chuillionáin', in O'Daly (eag.), *Poets and poetry* (1849), p. 60; Ó Buachalla, *Aisling Ghéar*, p. 233. **245** Seán Clárach Mac Domhnaill, 'Bímse buan ar buairt gach ló', in Ó Foghludha (eag.), *Seán Clárach*, p. 45. **246** Seán Ó Tuama, 'Cuisle na h-Éigse', in O'Daly (eag.), *Poets and poetry*, p. 60; Another poems by Liam Inglis uses the cryptic name 'An Craoibhín Aoibhinn'; Inglis, 'Atá an fhuireann so thall gan amhras díleas', in Ó Foghludha (eag.), *Cois na Bríde*, p. 36. The motif of Charles Edward as the 'young sapling', shooting from the withered (royal) oak, was popular in contemporary political discourse and in the Jacobite medallic tradition; Monod, *Jacobitism*, pp 78, 83. The seditious speech of William King, Jacobite rector of St Mary's College Oxford, at the opening of the Radcliffe Camera in Oxford contained the words 'Redeat ille Magnus Genius Britanniae'; ibid., p. 36.

Charles Edward),[247] 'An t-Óg Mhaoidhear' (the young stewart, Charles Edward),[248] 'the Blackbird' (James III),[249] 'Ristín, Risteard' (little Richard, Richard),[250] 'Mac an Cheannaí' (the Merchant's son, James III, the duke of Berwick),[251] 'An Cíoná' (the 'fingers', five of trumps, the penultimate card in the popular Irish card game 'twenty-five').[252]

Jacobite Irish Protestant voices came to a final crescendo in the aftermath of the fall of the Tory ministry and the defection of Ormonde to the Jacobite cause. It echoed in the halls of Trinity College and in the recesses of the tavern and coffee-houses and amid the flurry of treasonable papers circulated by the supporters of the Stuart claimant. In 1715 King gloated to Dean Story that 'the virulent pamphlets that are spread against his majesty you need not wonder at them...losers will talk and their game is lost, and despair finds them on all little efforts that they think will vex their enemies'. The seditious publication *English advice to the freeholders of Ireland* led to the arrest of a group of printers (including John Hyde, John Brookes, Sarah Waters, Edward Waters, John Perry, John Anderson, Thomas Thorne, John Edwards, John Harding and Richard Stave). It later became the subject of a lengthy controversy and over a dozen examinations.[253]

The ripples of suspicion eventually reached Jonathan Swift, dean of St Patrick's. Although Swift's writings suggest that his sympathies were high-Tory rather than Jacobite, an appreciation of the volatile nature of contemporary Irish politics and a perusal of his life justify some of these suspicions.[254] His intended dedication of his *Abstract of the history of England* to King Charles XII of Sweden and its anti-Hanoverian dedicatory letter to Count Gyllenbourg, the Swedish Ambassador, implicated in a Jacobite plot, was sailing close to the wind for the

---

247 Muiris Ó Gríobhtha, 'An Seabhac Siubhail', (*c.*1753-8), in Ní Ógáin (eag.), *Duanaire*, ii, p. 9. 248 'Mo chéile ceart, an tÓg Mhaoidhear' (My proper husband, the young steward), in Walsh (eag.), *Reliques of Irish Jacobite poetry*, p. 103. 249 This song is dated by Flood to 1707. A copy was given to Alan Ramsay in 1724 for his *Tea table miscellany.* Flood maintained that the Blackbird was purportedly used as a name for a horse belonging to the earl of Thomond; Flood, *A history of Irish music*, p. 244. See also Mac Quoid (ed.), *Jacobite songs and ballads*, p. 18; 'The Royal Blackbird' (U.L., Cambs., Madden 24, fol. 634). 250 Ó Buachalla states that the Irish literati were possibly aware that 'Richard' was a common cipher for James III; Ó Buachalla, *Aisling Ghéar*, pp 350-1. 251 Ó Buachalla, *Aisling Ghéar*, p. 345. 252 Ó Buachalla, *Aisling Ghéar*, p. 355. Ó Buachalla has catalogued a whole series of such pseudonyms for the Stuarts; Ó Buachalla, *Aisling Ghéar*, p. 554. 253 [F. Atterbury], *English advice*, T.C.D., MS, 2536. Also see T.C.D., Ms 2536, fols 187-9, 207-8; T.C.D., Ms 1995-2008, fols 1602; P.R.O., S.P., 63/372/1-31. King also deplored the continued scandal of libels, virulent pamphlets aimed directly against the king himself as opposed to his ministers; T.C.D., MS 2536, fols 282-5. Eveline Cruickshanks has suggested that Arthur Charleton of Northumberland wrote most of *English advice* under the direction of Atterbury, Bolingbroke and possibly Ormonde. I would like to thank Dr Cruickshanks for bringing this to my attention. 254 Ó Buachalla also takes a similar view: 'Bíodh nárbh fhéidir a áiteamh gur Sheacaibíteach é Swift, fós is cinnte gur chabhraigh a chuid scríbhinní féin le hamhras, le ceistiú, le ciontacht fiú, i dtaobh na réabhlóide a chothú. Thug sé féin le tuiscint gur mhó a chabhraigh teacht Sheóirse I le cúis na Seacaibíteach ná aon tarlang eile; dá bharr, a dúirt sé 'seven millions are said to have changed their sentiments'; Ó Buachalla, *Aisling Ghéar*, p. 300. 255 Swift, *Works*, xiii, p. 325; Higgins, *Swift's politics*, pp 79, 86. Gyllenbourge was later arrested for his part in a Swedish-Jacobite plot.

cautious Dean.[255] Higgins and Pittock have noted the Jacobite innuendos and anti-government sentiments in Swift's works. These included his 'Ode to Dr William Sancroft' (non-juring archbishop of Canterbury), *The tale of a tub*, *Gulliver's travels* and his revealing anti-revolutionary annotations on Bishop Gilbert Burnet's *History of his own time*. He also suggested that there was ambivalence in his dedication to 'Our eldest hope, divine Iulus' (Frederick, prince of Wales or his Jacobite counterpart Charles Edward) in his *On poetry: a rhapsody*.[256]

Aside from these passive manifestations of Swift's Jacobite leanings, he also maintained links with individuals of dubious political pedigree. During the last Tory ministry, Swift had regular contact with key figures including Robert Harley, earl of Oxford, Henry St John, viscount Bolingbroke, John Barber, Charles and Mary Caesar, Sir John Hynde-Cotton, Lord Lansdowne, the duke of Ormonde, Sir Constantine Phipps, and Francis Atterbury, Church of England bishop of Rochester. Even after the Hanoverian succession and the impeachment of Ormonde and Bolingbroke, and despite his constant disavowal of the Pretender, Swift retained contact with many Jacobite sympathisers and fellow-travellers. These included the gazetteer Charles Forde, John Barber, the duchess of Ormonde and her chaplain Arthur Charleton, Alexander Pope, the fourth and fifth earls of Orrery, Knightley Chetwood, Thomas Carte, Sir Charles Wogan and Robert Leslie.[257] He also received a letter from Ormonde after his flight to France.[258] King, not considered a witch-hunter, connived at the seizure of Swift's correspondence and believed him to be a Jacobite.[259] Swift reacted fiercely to King's innuendo and hypocrisy in the aftermath of Bolingbroke's arrest. The post-master was still opening his letters in 1722.[260]

As in contemporary England, Ormonde's birthday provided the occasion for residual Tory and Jacobite displays in Dublin. The arrival from England of an increasing number of libellous pamphlets against George I and his government caused concern in government circles.[261] A customs official intercepted a packet of seditious material in the possession of Jeffreys, agent of John Hartstonge, the

256 Higgins, *Swift's politics*, chapters 3 and 4; Pittock, *Poetry*, pp 119-28; For evidence that Swift and Sheridan were acquainted with the talkative Robert ('Robin') Leslie; Williams (ed.), *Correspondence*, ii, pp 62-3, 393, 425; iii, p. 331; ibid., ii.   **257** Williams (ed.), *Correspondence*, ii, pp 143, 163, 184, 188 216, 306. See also S.P., 63, 372, fol. 42.   **258** Nokes, *Swift*, p. 223. See also Higgins, *Swift's politics*, pp 7-8, 18-19, 23, 67, 75, 77.   **259** O'Donoghue, 'Jacobite threat', p. 167.   **260** Nokes, *Swift*, pp 223-4, 228, 271; Williams (ed.), *Correspondence*, ii, p. 172.   **261** John Sterne, bishop of Dromore to King, May 1715; (T.C.D., Ms 1995-2008, fol. 1655). King stated that 'virulent libels against the king and his ministry are every day sent over and handed about'. He tied associated this traffic with the 'great doings' of the previous Saturday on the duke of Ormonde's birthday; T.C.D., Ms 2536, fol. 263.   **262** King claimed that there were 'two letters of the bishop of Derry which were not very prudent, I confess'; T.C.D., Ms 2536, fol. 293. See also T.C.D., Ms 2536, fol. 291; N.L.I., Ms 9609, fol. 36. He suggested that his successors in Derry, Hickman and Hartstonge, had Jacobite leanings; T.C.D., Ms 2535, fols 88-91. Bishop Nicholson of Derry complained that four or five of his clergy had left out the customary collect used in times of war and tumult in 1715 and 1719 quoted in Connolly, *Religion*, p. 241. As late as March 1717, a

Church of Ireland bishop of Derry.[262] These included *Sir William Wyndham's Case, A Ballad on the late Lord Wharton, English advice to the freeholders of England* (by Arthur Charleton) and an assortment of Jacobite lampoons.[263] At this time, King informed Joseph Addison that 'many libels and virulent pamphlets are sent from your side and secretly handed out amongst the party here'.[264]

This proliferation of literary imports suggests that Irish Jacobites, particularly those of the Tory variety, retained a political voice in contemporary Dublin. John Sterne, Church of Ireland bishop of Dromore, believed that the pamphlet onslaught against George I in the Tholsel surpassed any against his predecessors and was only matched by the vigilance of the Whigs:

> Every reign has been attacked by numbers of very virulent libels and if his majesty seemed to have suffered more that his predecessors 'tis owing I hope to the commendable vigilance of those he has employed under him and who have taken more care to discover them. [265]

The attacks on the statue of King William on College Green from 1700 onwards and the vandalism committed on three tapestries of George I amounted to more than the drunken revelry of boisterous Trinity students. Monod has depicted this type of activity in contemporary England as individual Jacobites waging war on counter-symbolism.[266] The attack on the tapestries of George I was a direct retaliation by Jacobites against the removal of the arms of the attainted duke of Ormonde from Christ's Church.[267] Trinity College, like Oxford, provided a centre for a short-lived, muted but no less acrimonious Protestant opposition to the elector of Hanover. The libellous Jacobite songs 'Nero II' and the favourite royalist and Jacobite anthem 'The king shall enjoy his own again' circulated freely in the college. Derogatory political catch-cries resounded against King William and the Whigs. Students sang the praises of the Tories, particularly Bolingbroke and Ormonde.[268]

---

disgruntled Protestant clergyman claimed that Derry abounded with the 'slavish doctrines of non-resistance and indefeasible hereditary right'; N.L.I., Ms 9610, fol. 22. The Jacobite agent Sylvester Lloyd claimed that Derry is in 'such a way of thinking that the government has not been able for some years past to get a Whiggish mayor or sheriffs elected', quoted in Fagan (ed.), *Stuart papers*, i, pp 67-8. In 1715, the duke of Berwick advised his half-brother (James III) to send for the Church of Ireland bishop of Derry (Hartstonge) on his arrival at Dover ; *H.M.C., Stuart*, i, p. 370. **263** Examination of George Houghton, 3 May 1715 (P.R.O., S.P., 63/372/41, 49-50, 111-17). See also N.L.I., Ms 9609, fol. 31; T.C.D., 750/4/2, fols 47-8, 259. **264** King to Addison, 14 May 1715; T.C.D., Ms 750/4, fol. 255. See also T.C.D., Ms 750/4/2, fols 47-8; Monod, *Jacobitism*, pp 173-82. **265** John Sterne, bishop of Dromore to King, 23 May 1715 (T.C.D., Ms 1995-2008, fol. 1644). See also T.C.D., Ms 750/4/2, fols 47-8, 51a-52. **266** Kelly, 'The glorious and immortal memory', p. 32; O'Donoghue, 'Jacobite threat', p. 145. For contemporary English comparison; Monod, *Jacobitism*, p. 120. **267** Gilbert, *Streets of Dublin*, p. 583; 'Proclamation by the lords justice and council of Ireland', 22 Oct. 1714 (U.L., Cambs., Hib.0.714.12[7]). **268** For the Jacobite ballad 'Nero II', see Examinations of Sam From?, Henry Corner and John Kearney, 12 May 1715 (P.R.O., S.P., 63/372/115). See also P.R.O., S.P., 63/372/111-4.' For the singing of the Jacobite

Xenophobic propaganda against 'Dutch rogues' dominated allegations concerning Philip Neymore, 'a senior and sophister' of Trinity College Dublin. While Neymore's alleged wish to become a papist may indicate exaggeration, his possession of brass money from the 1690s is a precursor to the later Jacobite medallic and touch-piece tradition. His cryptic Jacobite toasts to 'The man in the black wig', 'The man that's far away' and 'The king before George' had their counterparts in contemporary Irish, Scots-Gaelic and English Jacobite popular culture.[269]

The evidence against Neymore contained a mixture of Tory and Jacobite themes including xenophobia and anti-Presbyterianism. A number of collegians toasted Ormonde and called Marlborough 'a villain who ought to be walked to the gallows'. Neymore stated that 'the Church of Rome was as pure and as holy as the Church of England' and that he would rather be put in orders by the pope than a Church of England bishop. He claimed that King William 'encouraged Presbyterians in Scotland', 'employed Dutch rogues' and 'the Pretender was King James's son'. He concluded by stating that 'King William ought not to have been crowned king while Queen Anne lived'.[270]

Other Dublin Jacobites shared the hopes of their English Protestant Jacobite counterparts that James would become a Protestant.[271] Hartpole Fitzgerald's evidence of May 1715 reflected this view.[272] Hearing his rendition of 'The king shall enjoy his own again', he asked George Malley to elaborate on his principles. Malley replied 'that the Pretender would be king of England and those of his [Malley's] principles would fare well' and that 'Dr Lesly [Charles Leslie] was with the Pretender and would make him a Protestant'. Fitzgerald also described a meeting which took place in the Globe Tavern before Ormonde's birthday which was attended by Edmund Bingley, Digby (a senior), Lehunt, Smith, Gunning and Jepson. He specifically mentioned drinking the health of the three 'Bs' (the Best Born Briton/James III).[273]

anthem 'The king shall enjoy his own again' in Trinity College; P.R.O., S.P., 63/372/117. It had been sung when James II arrived in Dublin in 1689; Simms, *Jacobite Ireland*, p. 64. A contemporary Scoto-Whig poem mocked 'The duke of Ormonde, the joy of poor Teague'; Hogg, *Jacobite relics of Scotland*, i, p. 417. See also Monod, *Jacobitism*, p. 181. **269** Examination of Robert Cook, 14 May 1715 (P.R.O., S.P., 63/372/112). See also B.L., Add. Ms 29, 981, fols 45, 100; Crofton-Croker (ed.), *Researches*, p. 201. Jacob Twisleton was arrested in Dublin at this time for carrying Jacobite medals; O'Donoghue, 'Jacobite threat', p. 148. **270** Examination of Bate Cook, 14 May 1715 (P.R.O., S.P., 63/372/116). **271** Goldie, 'Tory political thought', p. 312. **272** *A pill to purge the state melancholy, or a collection of excellent new songs* contained and advertisement for a number of political ballads including the Jacobite song 'Let joy in the medal with James III'. It contained the following seditious verse: 'Let joy in the medal with James III's face/And the advocates that pleaded for/'Tho' the nation renounces the popish race/Great Louis of France will restore him', quoted in Petrie, *The Jacobite movement*, p. 187. See also Hogg (ed.), *Jacobite relics*, i, p. 359. The songs in this collection were sung to such popular political tunes such as 'Lillibulero' and 'Bonny Dundee'. **273** The examination of Hartpole Fitzgerald, 20 May 1715 (P.R.O., S.P., 63/372/111). See also P.R.O., S.P., 63/372/115. The contemporary deposition of William Markham contained a similar cryptic rhyme: 'Confusion to those who keep him out, the devil turn him inside out that would not turn the family out'; P.R.O., S.P. 63/372/113-4. The possibility of James's conversion to Protestantism had appeared

Jacobite sedition in Trinity College remained a great source of embarrassment to the provost and fellows. They observed a transformation in the popular political life of the college from traditional high-church Toryism to unabashed Jacobitism.[274] The defection of its chancellor, Ormonde, and the importation of libellous pamphlets from England were among the contributory factors. The Globe Tavern and Lloyd's coffee-house in Cork Hill, regular haunts of Trinity students, remained centres of Jacobite activity. The material which circulated among Irish Protestant Jacobites in this period is characterised by the contents of a package sent from London to George Houghton, the controller of the ordnance. It contained material 'of the most treasonable nature in favour of the Pretender's right to his majesty's crowns', including 'a great number of seditious pamphlets and verses'. These included: 'A copy of the Pretender's declaration', 'A letter from Bolingbroke to [Simon], Lord H[arcourt]t', 'libellous verses in the hand of one Will Wight, late of the regiment commanded by Lord Windsor', and the 'Epilogue to Lady Jane Grey'.[275] In one of the accompanying Jacobite lampoons, the traditional Jacobite rhetoric is invoked to consign the wicked old peer [Manwaring?] and a bishop [Burnet?] into hell where they consort with 'Old Nick' (the devil).[276] The other contained the following seditious lines:

> His Lord Germans G[eorge] was forced to leave
> that he might Britain's diadem receive
> his faithful subjects wept by fame we hear
> and envoy'd us their prince's presence here
> justice and mercy there bore equal share
>
> ...
>
> but sure his clemency he left behind
> for we in Britain cannot justice find
>
> ...
>
> Britons be kind, compassionate the tears
> His Hanoverians shed and heard their prayers

in the press as early as 1710; *Fl. P.*, 22 Mar. 1711. It remained a popular rumour; *An historical essay upon the loyalty of the Presbyterians of Great Britain and Ireland*, p. vi; *Advice to the Protestants*, pp 9-10; *A letter to the Protestant dissenters of Ireland*. In a letter to her brother in June 1713 Henry Boyle's sister wrote that 'the Pretender shows much coldness and indifference every day than others to the Romish church'; N.L.I., Special List 206[1] Shannon papers. The press also contains references to Leslie's endeavours to convert the Stuart king to Protestantism; *Hanover or Rome*, pp 11, 15; *Fau. P.*, 22 Mar. 1711; Miller, *James III*, p. 144; Shield and Lang, *The king*, p. 193. Genet-Rouffiac suggests that Leslie cultivated an Anglican cult when he arrived at the Stuart court; Genet-Rouffiac, 'La Première génération', p. 210.   **274** King to Stearne, 27 May 1715 (T.C.D., Ms 2536, fols 297-9). See also T.C.D., Ms 2533, fol. 15; B.L., Stowe Ms 750, fol. 104.   **275** Examination of John Whalley of the city of Dublin, before William Whitshead, 9 May 1715 (P.R.O., S.P., 63/372/56). See Hayton, 'Ireland and the English ministers', p. 109. Another contemporary reference suggests that 'The Globe Tavern' was a Jacobite meeting house; P.R.O., S.P., 63/372/111. Edward Lloyd, 'the Dublin coffee-man', was later implicated in an Oxford riot; T.C.D., Ms 1995-2008, fol. 1734; Munter. *A dictionary*, p. 168.   **276** George Houghton, 3 May 1715 (P.R.O., S.P., 63/372/49-51).

But let their much lov'd sovereign turn again
and bless them with his mild and prudent reign
But let the Germans not ungrateful prove
But give the Britain's too the king they love
Give us the hero of the martyr's line
To whom the crown belongs by right divine.[277]

'The epilogue to Lady Jane Grey' drew inspiration from the failed usurpation of the crown from the Catholic Mary I ('Bloody Mary', the anti-hero of the Protestant tradition). It was unequivocally Protestant in sentiment and strongly anti-Hanoverian in tone. It urged James III to renounce the Roman Catholic doctrine of transubstantiation, embrace the Protestant faith and assume the throne of his ancestors:

Tonight usurping tyranny attend
and reap your fate in whineing Jenny's end
when crowns and sceptres are by fashion given
shall royal idiots plead a right from heaven
...
What W[illia]m was, G[eorg]e is and J[ame]s shall be
When aune was and set the nation free
yet J[ame]s be Br[?]ck is one thing alone
Renounce the wafer G[od]? and mount thy throne
Shall things else confess the Stewart line
And rule in mercy with a right divine.[278]

Popular Jacobitism percolated downwards from Trinity College to the Dublin 'mob'. This was already apparent in the turbulent election of 1713 when an election mob was headed by the luckless Sir James Cotter.[279] It later featured in the rescue of captured recruits and the annual celebration on 10 June (the birthday of James III).[280] In June 1715, when the authorities pilloried 'young Tooley for riot in the Tholsel and [—] Rock for scandalous words against his majesty', they were not only spared the usual indignities of being fully secured at the pillory and the customary egg-throwing. Indeed, they even enjoyed the encouragement of a raucous Jacobite crowd. Edmund Bingley, the collegian,

---

277 'Examination of George Houghton, 3 May 1715' (P.R.O., S.P., 63/372/49-51). A copy of 'Nero II' was found in Knightley Chetwood's pocket-book; O'Donoghue, 'Jacobite threat', p. 141. Contemporary Jacobite lampoons contained numerous attacks on Dr Gilbert Burnett, bishop of Sarum; B.L., Add. Ms 29, 981. 278 'Examination of George Houghton, 3 May 1715' (P.R.O., S.P., 63/372/49-51). See also ibid., III-17; N.L.I., Ms 9609, fol. 31; P.R.O., S.P., 63/372/41; T.C.D., Ms 750/4/, fols 255, 257; T.C.D. 1995-2008, fol. 1643. 279 Cullen, *Modern Ireland*, p. 198. 280 King to Samuel Molyneux, 25 Apr. 1714 (T.C.D., Ms 750/4/1, fol. 296). See also T.C.D., Ms 2536, fols 303-5, 313-14, 315-16; P.R.O., S.P., 63/370/84, 86, 88; P.R.O., S.P., 63/374/314.

was less fortunate. He was tied to the pillory and whipped for crimes which included treasonable utterances against William III, Queen Anne, and King George, as well as for his distribution of the seditious poem 'Nero II' among impressionable Trinity students.[281]

On 23 May 1715 George I's birthday was also an occasion for civil unrest. The Jacobites routed the loyalists, extinguished their bonfires and many were injured on both sides. The trained bands and the constables seized eighteen of the insurgents for breaking windows and drinking unlawful toasts. On the following Sunday, the anniversary of the restoration of the royal family (1660), the tumult increased and seditious toasts were drunk including 'high-church and Ormonde', 'no foreigners', 'no king but a Stuart' and 'down with Cromwell and Calvin'. [282] King believed that 'the seed and pest of Jacobitism had been nursed in the college these last seven years'.[283] Although he continually made representations against the election of a seditious Fellow called Edward Forbes, the provost and fellows refused to take action and King was vigorously libelled for his troubles.[284] The authorities finally expelled Forbes for describing King William as a 'murderer and traitor and for speaking words which called into question Queen Anne's right to the throne'. His case became a *cause célèbre* in Dublin and (together with the Sacheverell trial in England) provided an impetus to other Trinity students to declare their aversion to the revolution. Another College fellow, William Thompson, declared at a public feast that there was little difference between Cromwell who took off the father's (Charles I) head and William who dethroned the son.[285] The riots on Ormonde's birthday forced

281 *Whalley's N.*, 29 June-11 July 1715; See also P.R.O., S.P. ,63/372/115. Edmund Bingley allegedly 'corrupted' the youth of the college and asserted that King William and Queen Anne were usurpers; T.C.D., Ms 2536, fols 297-300. Despite being disowned by his father, Bingley persisted in his Jacobitism, becoming secretary to the Jacobite duke of Wharton and the duke of Ormonde in Spain. He continued to collect Jacobite poems, ballads and portraits of the Stuart princes; R.A., Ms 160, fol. 79; R.A., Ms 162, fol. 112; R.A., Ms 168, fol. 204; R.A., Ms 172, fols 177, 184; R.A., Box 3, fol. 58. Thomas Lewis was tried, convicted and stood in the pillory for seditious words while another unnamed man was pilloried as a result of words relating to the defacing of King William's statue in College Green; *Dub. I.*, 4 July 1710. Similarly, James Doyle, a Protestant clergyman from Gorey, County Wexford, was also pilloried for sedition in April 1716; T.C.D., Ms 2533, fol. 191. See also T.C.D., 2533, fols 205-8. 282 *Dub. I.*, 11 June 1715. See also B.L., Stowe Ms 750, fol. 104; Monod, *Jacobitism*, pp 150, 167; *Dub. I.*, 7 June 1715. 283 King to William Nicolson, bishop of Carlisle, 16 July 1715 (T.C.D., Ms 2533, fol. 15). Contemporary Whig opinion deemed Trinity College to be 'a nest of Jacobites, a garrison holding out for the Pretender'; quoted in Hayton, 'Ireland and the English ministers', pp 134-5. 284 King to William Nicolson, bishop of Carlisle, 16 July 1715 (T.C.D., Ms 2533, fol. 15). See also T.C.D., 750/3/2, fols 229-30. Forbes interrupted a toast to William III and compared him to a highwayman; Doyle, 'Politics', p. 200. For bibliographical notes on Forbes and attempts by the English ministry to make capital out of the incident and to discredit Trinity College; Williams (ed.), *Correspondence*, i, pp 93-5; O'Donoghue, 'Jacobite threat', p. 19; T.C.D., Ms 2022, fol. 226. 285 Hayton, 'Ireland and the English ministers', pp 134-5; *A short account of the late proceedings of the University of Dublin against Forbes*. Trinity College might owe its magnificent eighteenth-century 'Long Room' indirectly to Jacobitism since King believed that the Whigs financed the new library as an enticement to stick to the principles of the revolution; Kinane, review of McDonnell and Healy, *Gold-tooled bookbindings*, pp 157-8. See also Connolly, *Religion*, p. 81; Doyle, 'Politics', p. 179; T.C.D. Ms 2533, fol. 15; *H.M.C., Eight Report*, app. 1, 1881, p. 59; B.L., Stowe Ms 750,

the hand of the governing body, although the flight of two other culprits and the conviction of Bingley did not prevent calls for the latter's pardon.[286] King remained adamant that the proliferation of Jacobite mobs, seditious catch-cries and general disaffection in Great Britain and Dublin, and more particularly at Oxford and Trinity, was due to the lack of punitive legislation.[287]

The strong-handed tactics subsequently employed by the Whig administration did not totally overawe the Protestant Jacobites. Amid rumours of the French king's death and fears of a French invasion, King noted that 'many friends of the late government are now openly Jacobites'. He also deplored the renewed vandalism of King William's statue and believed that such activity was prompted from within the college.[288] In a letter to the dean of Ossory, King noted that 'the Protestants of the town are as disaffected as papists, a clergyman's son was implicated in defacing King William's statue'. He claimed that 'the friends of the duke of Ormonde do him harm by their conduct and the Tories being dismissed from office were becoming Jacobites'.[289]

Such evidence of popular Jacobitism persists throughout the eighteenth century, often directed against priest-catchers and Quakers, annually resurfacing on James III's birthday.[290] Rumours of impending invasion and the popular chatter of the seditious pamphlet industry continually fed the political ferment on the eve of the 'Fifteen'. The Stuart king's manifesto, printed locally in Dublin and posted in several parts of the city, including the parliament house, became the subject of a proclamation offering a reward for the printer's identity.[291] Other seditious material circulated in the country. A copy of this proclamation and *The late duke of Ormonde's letter to all true lovers of the Church of England and their country, urging them to restore the ancient monarchy and constitution of England* can be found in the papers of the earls of Shannon.[292] A text of James III's proclamation, along with Budgell's *To all the nobility, gentry and commonality of Ireland* was posted in several parts of the city.[293] In spite of these,

---

fol. 104; B.L., Lansdowne Ms 352, fols 11-12. The Whigs suggested that the money granted by Queen Anne's government to the university was their reward for their swift action against the antics of Forbes; Hayton, 'Ireland and the English ministers', p. 139.   **286** King to William Nicolson, bishop of Carlisle, 16 July 1715 (T.C.D., Ms 2533, fol. 13). See also T.C.D., Ms 2533, fols 3-4, 9-10; T.C.D., Ms 2536, fols 319-20.   **287** King to Nicolson, 6 July 1715 (T.C.D., Ms 2533, fols 3-4). Also see T.C.D., Ms 2536, fols 313-14; B.L., Lansdowne Ms 352, fol. 11; T.C.D., Ms 750/11/3, fols 214-7; T.C.D., Ms 750/5/, fols 14-15. Ironically King later boasted that there had not been a single riot since George's accession to the throne and dismissed what had happened on Ormonde's birthday as mere drunken revelry; T.C.D., Ms 2533, fol. 43. John St. Leger noted that 'there was no mob on the Pretender's birthday ... the arm of the civil power is too strong ... and the magistrates are vigilant'; B.L., Stowe Ms 750, fol. 104. See also T.C.D., 1995-2008, fol. 1701.   **288** King to the dean of Ossory, 1 Sept. 1715 (T.C.D., Ms 2533, fols 72-3).   **289** King to Ossory, 10 Sept. 1715 (T.C.D., Ms 2533, fols 79-81). See also T.C.D., Ms 2533, fols 103-4.   **290** King to Sterne, 17 Sept. 1715 (T.C.D., Ms 2533, fols 88-90). Also see T.C.D., Ms 2533, fols 52-4, 88.   **291** Sir Gustavus Hume to [?], 25 Oct. 1715; B.L., Stowe Ms 228, fol. 164); *Whalley's N.*, 26-9 Oct. 1715; See also T.C.D., Ms 2533, fol. 64.   **292** N.L.I., misc. papers, private collection no. 393, fol. 2797.   **293** B.L., Stowe Ms 228, fol. 164, 197. See also *Whalley's N.*, 26-9 Oct. 1715.

King rejoiced that 'a stop [has been] put to the great number of libels and virulent pamphlets that were scattered about to poison the people'.[294]

Protestant Jacobitism was not confined exclusively to Dublin. Residual strains survived elsewhere in Ireland. The authorities suspected that the third earl of Antrim maintained contact with his rebel kindred in Scotland. He allegedly colluded in shipping victuals to the rebels and received a visit from the rebel Clanranald after the battle of Dunblain. Accused of persecuting his Whig tenants, his imprisonment dampened the spirits of the disaffected elements on his estate.[295] Charges of continued disaffection among Antrim's tenantry featured in *The report of the judges of assizes of the north-east circuit of Ulster.* Whether this indicated ongoing friction between Anglicans and Dissenters, or a genuine manifestation of Jacobitism, is less significant than the fact that highchurchmen still provided targets for such Jacobite slurs. Mr [-] Fanning allegedly toasted the duke of Ormonde, 'the best person that was in the kingdom'. When this was opposed, Fanning proposed alternatively the health of 'poor James Butler now begging in France' and expressed regret at the fall of the late ministry. He also cast the usual Tory aspersions on the Whig ministry 'which would cheat the king and pocket the money' and finally declared that the late Tory ministry was 'always just' and that 'the duke of Ormonde was one of the finest men in the world'.[296] The work of Seán Connolly and William Neely has broadened the picture, showing the extent to which Derry, Galway, Waterford and Kilkenny, as well as clerical circles, remained centres of residual Irish Protestant Jacobitism.[297] The survival of such an interest in these areas can be explained by the political leanings of the respective Church of Ireland bishops and, in Kilkenny's case, the influence of Ormonde and, possibly, his brother, Lord Arran. As Connolly himself notes, the use of Jacobitism as a political weapon signified much more than a mere device used by the Whigs to taunt their Tory adversaries.

294 King to W. Wake, bishop of Lincoln, 2 Nov. 1715 (T.C.D., Ms 2533, fols 111-13). As late as February 1717 King remarked that 'the virulent pamphlets against the king are a result of despair'; T.C.D., 2536, fol. 177. **295** Lynn to Stanhope, 27 Dec. 1715 (N.L.I., Ms 9609, fol. 185). See also P.R.O., S.P., 63/374/147; N.L.I., Ms 9609, fols 104-5, 185; P.R.O., S.P., 63/374/459; P.R.O., S.P., 67/4/3r, 67/4/7. The Stuart papers suggest that Antrim was in contact with St Germain in 1716; H.M.C., *Stuart*, ii, pp 289-90. See also 'The deposition of the Revd Mr James Smith of Balentoy in the County Antrim, 28 February 1716' (Marsh's Library Z.3.1.1 [xii]); MacDonnell, 'Jacobitism and the third and fourth earls of Antrim', pp 50-95. **296** *The report of the judges of assizes of the north-east circuit of Ulster*, pp 13,16, 29. **297** In 1716 Archbishop Synge referred to strong parties of disaffected Protestants in Kilkenny, Derry, Waterford and Galway. The lords justice complained of 'the neglect of most of the clergymen here to mention his majesty and their royal highnesses in the prayer before their sermons'; quoted in Connolly, *Religion*, pp 239-42. See also Neely, *Kilkenny*, pp 139, 144.

Catholic Jacobitism in this period, mirroring Protestant apprehensions, thrived during the War of the Spanish Succession. It was nurtured by the ties which existed between Ireland and the continent. However, linguistic considerations and the difficulties involved in corresponding with the Stuart court and Irish exiles ensure that the historian only has access to the written material which the government intercepted or which survives in foreign archives. Such records are often tentative and one can only speculate on the nature or extent of oral communications. Isolated outbursts from Catholics, the arrival of known and suspected Jacobite spies and military personnel from France, and the interception of ciphered correspondence from St Germain, shows that Jacobitism retained a strong attraction for many Irish Catholics. This fascination survived the disappointment generated by the abortive Scottish invasion of 1708 and the failure of the 'Fifteen'. The war itself increased contact between Ireland and Europe and raised Jacobite hopes. More formal and semi-formal links between Ireland and the Stuart court emerged at the end of the first decade of the eighteenth century. Correspondence between Ireland and France show that lines of communication remained open, usually through the good offices of recruiters, Catholic clergymen and privateers. These channels would again prove vital to the survival of Jacobitism after the Hanoverian succession.

Although no thorough examination has been made of James Francis Edward's impact on the Protestant political consciousness, and despite the fact that political infighting between Whigs and Tories encouraged Jacobite scaremongering, clearly Catholic hopes and Protestant fears directly influenced each other in this period and for much of the eighteenth century. Protestants continued to view Catholic public displays such as pilgrimages, fastings and sporting activity as the harbingers of rebellion. Recruitment to the Irish Brigades, mob violence, rescues of priests and captured recruits, and continued rapparee acctivity reminded them of their vulnerability.

Militant Jacobitism manifested itself most visibly in recruitment for foreign service. While the related depositions must be treated with caution as they are subject to exaggeration, they provide valuable information on Jacobite activities. The majority of these relate to the French service and often refer to prominent international Jacobite figures. They reveal intricate lines of communication between Ireland and centres of *émigré*-Irish interest involving Catholic priests, Franco-Irish soldiers, Irish ship-owners and Dublin merchants. Recruitment re-emerged as a major issue in Irish politics in the 1720s and 1730s when Spain provided the most likely ally of the exiled Stuarts. Whig politicians used the links between recruits, rapparees, privateers and the Catholic populace to claim that they intended to embark on wholesale rebellion. The depositions also reflect a surprisingly accurate grasp of Jacobite high-politics. The continual promises of a speedy return were supported by evidence of Jacobite invasion plans. The affidavits placed special emphasis on commissions received directly from the Stuart claimant, the need for taking an oath to serve him, and not to reveal the recruiter's identity. Recruits were assured that they would only serve King James and would return within one year to receive lands and titles. Proceedings normally concluded with a toast to the exiled king.

The expatriate Irish Jacobite community in Europe provided the greatest hope of the Irish-based Jacobites and their poets in the 1720s. Although Ormonde and the Irish regiments in Spain actively engaged in a Jacobite invasion attempt in post-1715 period, the French-based Irish Jacobites participated in Jacobite espionage and the French government could not vouch for the loyalty of the Irish Brigades. It was forced to move them from strategic coastal areas from where they might be able to join a Jacobite invasion. These invasion scares ensured that Jacobitism retained a pivotal place in Irish political life.

A small Protestant Jacobite interest existed in Dublin city, particularly Trinity College, as well as the estate of the third earl of Antrim, and the cities of Kilkenny, Galway and Derry. Centred on the coffee-house and tavern within the capital, these Jacobites engaged in seditious toasting and singing, pamphleteering and in assaults on Whig counter-symbolism of a type which was prevalent in contemporary England. Their enthusiasm sometimes spilled onto the streets, inciting a Jacobite mob which would continue to make an annual appearance on the Stuart king's birthday.

With George I somewhat precariously on the throne in 1716, despite the passivity of the Irish during the 'Fifteen', a combination of indigenous and *émigré* Jacobite optimism, and interrelated Protestant fears, ensured that the Jacobite threat remained central to Irish political life for the next twenty years.

CHAPTER 4

'Séamas Mac Shéamais is an Diúc thar lear':[1] Irish Jacobitism after the 'Fifteen'

After the death of Louis XIV in 1715 and the succession of his sickly five-year old great-grandson Louis XV, control of war-weary France fell to the regent Philippe, duc d'Orléans. He was eager to strengthen his position in case of a succession crisis, thwarting the ambitions of his main dynastic rival King Philip V of Spain (who had been forced to renounce his claim to the French throne under the terms of the Treaty of Utrecht). The regent cultivated the friendship of George I and concluded the anti-Spanish Anglo-French alliance of 1716 (which became the Tripartite Alliance when joined by the United Provinces in 1717 and the Quadruple Alliance with the inclusion of Austria in 1718). With the stroke of a pen, the Jacobites lost their most powerful prospective ally (France) but gained the friendship of Spain, the greatest loser at the Treaty of Utrecht.

Fired by the ambition of Philip V and his wife Elizabeth Farnese, and re-invigorated by the machinations of their chief minister Cardinal Alberoni, the Spanish invaded Savoy and seized Sardinia and Sicily in 1717. This naked aggression, compounded by further threats to Naples, led to the outbreak of war with Britain and Admiral Byng's destruction of a Spanish fleet at Cape Passaro in the same year. In spite of this serious setback, Alberoni still counted on the support of Charles XII, the warrior-king of Sweden, who was locked in territorial conflicts with the elector of Hanover and whom Alberoni hoped would invade Scotland. However, this scheme was frustrated by Charles's death at Frederichall in 1718. Undaunted, Alberoni fell back on the traditional idea of an armada. In February 1719 Philip V published a manifesto in favour of the male and Catholic line of the house of Stuart. James III himself reached Catalonia from Italy and soon entered Madrid. Philip and Elizabeth received him in state and presented him with 25,000 pistoles and a service of silver plate valued at 60,000 pistoles. A considerable military force, most of them Irish, was allocated for his service. A select detachment of Spanish infantry, accompanied by several prominent Scottish noblemen and Irish officers, had already sailed

1 Liam Rua Mac Coitir, 'Caitlín Ní h-Uallacháin', quoted in Ó Buachalla, *Aisling Ghéar*, p. 324.

for Scotland in early March. The landed at Kintail, in Scotland, to await the arrival of Ormonde in England at the head of a flotilla which had sailed from Cadiz. This fleet consisted of five men-of-war and twenty transports, containing 5,000 soldiers under the command of Don Balthazar de Guerra. However, it was dispersed by a storm off Cape Finisterre and Ormonde abandoned the enterprise. The mobilisation of a French invasion force (ironically led by the duke of Berwick) forced the beleaguered Spanish to sue for peace.

Without question the main dangers to the Hanoverian regime in Ireland during this period were external. Nevertheless, the level of contact between Ireland and the exiled Jacobite interest does not bear out the image of overwhelming apathy and passivity with which post-Aughrim Irish Jacobites were allegedly infected. The successive invasion scares, the tendency of priesthunters and informers to use Jacobitism to bait their prospective victims and the continued activity of Jacobite mobs showed that Jacobitism remained a significant factor in contemporary politics. The invasion threats and partial application of the penal laws focused Jacobite and Whig attention on European politics and the possibility of a Spanish-Jacobite restoration. These factors also helped to sustain recruitment for foreign service.

Two domestic crises in Britain and Ireland, 'Wood's Half-pence' and the 'Atterbury plot', also affected Irish Jacobitism in the aftermath of the failure of the 'Fifteen' in Scotland. While the potential allies of the Stuarts continually changed throughout the period, the mainstays of Irish Jacobitism – Catholic clergy and gentry, recruits for foreign service, Irish poets and converts – remained intact. The main adversaries of the Jacobites within Ireland railed against such people and the Protestant press obsessively followed the movements of the Stuart claimant and his confederates throughout Europe, keeping him at the forefront of the Irish political consciousness. The official despatches and ceremonial shibboleths of the ruling oligarchy consistently reacted to, and reflected, popular protest, shedding further light on the exiled king's role in Irish political life. A Protestant Jacobite interest still manifested itself in Dublin, exhibited in a residual, seditious pamphlet tradition and among a raucous mob who gathered to celebrate the exiled king's birthday. It also occasionally revealed itself in Protestant literary circles among the converts who were accused of recruiting for the foreign service and those who opposed Wood's Half-pence.

I

In August 1717, Archbishop King expressed confidence that the peaceful state of international affairs had isolated the exiled Stuart court and forced it to fall back on the Jacobite interest in the three kingdoms:

The Pretender's hopes are chiefly grounded on the strength of his party in Britain and Ireland and for ought I can see the report goes current in foreign parts that we are already engaged in a bloody civil war and the Pretender has no more to do than to land and head his party. If this be his notion, he will be miserably mistaken. I find it among the papists ... the great number of the nobility and gentry of the kingdom are deserting their country and going into France ....[2]

Irish Protestant confidence also dominated the popular press, which mocked the Stuart claimant's diplomatic isolation and the weakness of his potential allies:

> Meanwhile regardless of the royal cause
> His sword for James no brother sovereign draws.
> The pope himself surrenders with alarms
> And though he hears his darling son complain
> Can hardly spare one tutelary saint
> But lifts them all to guard his own abodes
> And in ready money coins his gods.
> The dauntless Swede, pursued by vengeful foe
> Scarce keeps his own hereditary snows
> Nor must the friendly roof of kind Lorraine
> With feasts regail our garter'd youth again.[3]

While dismissive of contemporary Irish Jacobite expectations, King was worried by the emigration of the Catholic nobility and noted its effects on the respective political interests within Ireland.[4] The assassination in 1717 of Henry Luttrell, one of the *bêtes noires* of Irish Jacobites, threatened to bring the wrath of the administration down upon the general Catholic population through the harsh implementation of the penal laws.[5] Enforced or not, the penal legislation remained a Damoclean sword in the Catholic consciousness.[6]

Luttrell's name was synonymous in Jacobite discourse with treachery; he was arrested for communicating with the Williamites in the latter stages of the Jacobite war and accused of duplicity at Aughrim and Limerick. He later accepted a pension from the Williamites and his children conformed to

---

2 'King to Charles Delafaye, 6 Aug. 1717 (T.C.D., Ms 750/4, fol. 268). 3 *An epistle from a lady in England to a gentleman at Avignon.* 4 King to Charles Delafaye, 6 Aug. 1717 (T.C.D., Ms 750/4, fol. 268). 5 Francis Annesley to King, 28 Aug. 1718 (T.C.D., Ms 1995-2008, fol. 1873. See also T.C.D., Ms 750/5/, fols 10-13; *Pue's O.,* 14-18 Apr. 1719; *The whole tryal and examination of Thomas Caddy and Richard Wilson,' who were try'd at the King's Bench the 4th of this instant February for the murder of Henry Luttrell; The whole account of the arraignment and confinement of Thomas Grace, Coll. Luttrell's cousin, who is now fast and double boulted in Newgate for perjury'.* Two proclamations were issued against the murderers of Luttrell; *Twenty-third report of the deputy-keeper,* p. 66. 6 Da Cunha letters, 30 Nov. 1717; in McLysaght (ed.), *Kenmare papers,* p. 101.

Protestantism in order to acquire the estate of his brother Simon, a former governor of Dublin who had followed James II into exile. References to Luttrell's treachery abound in the Irish tradition. In his poem 'Ba mhinic tú ag díol na steanncán', Seán Ó Tuama reminded his audience that it was Luttrell who sold Limerick. An English song, to the Irish tune 'Síle Ní Ghadhra' about the second Siege of Limerick, censured 'Blind' Henry Luttrell and (Robert) Clifford for 'betraying like hangmen their country and people'. O'Callaghan records a satirical verse on Luttrell's assassination:

> If heav'n be pleas'd when mortals cease to sin-
> And hell be pleased when villians enter in
> If earth be pleas'd when it entombs a knave
> All must be pleased now Luttrell's in his grave.[7]

However, greater problems than an isolated assassination troubled the Dublin and London administrations at this time. In early 1718, rumours of a Spanish-Jacobite invasion, headed by the exiled Ormonde, circulated in Whitehall and Dublin. The authorities made provisions for the proper security of the kingdom, including the imposition of a bounty on Ormonde's head, a reinforcement of the Limerick and Ulster garrisons and an examination of all suspected persons.[8] These activities attracted the attention of Irishmen of all political creeds. Papist mobs, and the dangers incurred in suppressing their activities, concerned even the normally complacent Archbishop King.[9] Nevertheless, King remained confident that an invading army 'would get nothing but blows'.[10]

The contemporary political climate proved hazardous to those harbouring Jacobite sympathies. Disreputable Protestant discoverers, including James Goyn, John Garcia and William Goggins, brought charges of treason against Cornelius Martin (whose niece had also allegedly been raped by Goggins). Their use of Jacobitism to accuse this Catholic gentleman, and in Goggins's case to deflect attention from his own heinous crime, indicates the shock-value of Jacobitism and the exposed legal position of Irish Catholics. The depositions also uncovered recruitment networks for foreign service and magnified local 'traitorous' assemb-

---

7 Aindrias Mac Craith, 'Ba mhinic tú ag díol na steanncán', in Ó Foghludha (eag.), *Éigse na Máighe*, pp 132-3; Ó Muirithe, 'Tho' not in full stile compleat', pp 97-8. See also de Brún (ed.), 'Two Breifne manuscripts', pp 426-37. Luttrell's skull was taken out of his tomb in 1797 and smashed with a pick-axe by a labourer named Carthy who was later hanged for his part in a plot to assassinate Luttrell's grandson Lord Carhampton, a character no less detested in the 1790s than his grandfather had been; O'Callaghan, *Irish brigades*, pp 102-4. Similar verses were written on the death of Dr Gilbert Burnet, the Whig bishop of Sarum; B.L., Add. Ms 29, 981.   8 Bolton to the lords justice, 14 Jan. 1718 (N.A., Ms 2447, fol. 205).   9 'I have been so harassed every day for near a fortnight in putting the army and militia in a posture against the threatened invasion', King to Annesley, 29 Mar. 1718 (T.C.D., Ms 750/5, fol. 129). See also T.C.D., 750/11/3, fols 111-3; T.C.D., MS 1995-2008, fol. 1858; *H.M.C., 2nd Report*, p. 255; T.C.D., 750/11/3, fols 119, 145; Bartlett, *Fall and rise*, p. 49.   10 King to Mr Annesley, 29 Mar. 1718 (T.C.D., Ms 750/5, fol. 143).

lies of Catholics for personal gain. Although contemporaries and later historians have dismissed such depositions as the products of discredited witnesses,[11] their admittedly exaggerated information often reflected actual Jacobite preparations, which were borne out in later evidence.[12] Martin was brought to trial, and the lords justice petitioned Secretary Bolton to have the rape charge dropped against Goggins, thereby showing the lengths to which the authorities were prepared to go to prosecute one Jacobite.[13] At this time King also made a well-established correlation between contemporary rapparee activity and the encouragement given to Irish Jacobites by Spain's preparations for an invasion. He also noted that many of the Irish country gentlemen showed favour to the 'tories'.[14]

His communications with Edward Southwell in Paris retailed alarming tales which circulated in contemporary Dublin, including Alberoni's favourable reception in France, a proposed Catholic crusade against Protestantism and a restoration of 'the Pretender'. Such themes remained a constant feature of contemporary Irish Jacobite poetry and Irish *émigré* correspondence with the Stuart court. They undoubtedly filtered back through the clergy, merchants and recruiters for foreign service who were active among Catholics, and through those who received remittances from their families in Ireland or exercised powers of attorney on behalf of clients and relations on either side of the English Channel.[15]

The rumours which circulated in contemporary Dublin were not without foundation. In mid-January 1719, Secretary James Craggs received a report from Abbé Dubois, the French minister, regarding James III's overtures towards Ormonde and a group of Irish officers in Spain 'who wished to liberate their oppressed brethren in Ireland'. A further letter to Craggs from Genoa provided him with a report of three Spanish men of war and thirteen transports, laden

---

11 Edmund Byrne, Catholic archbishop of Dublin referred to John Garcia's testimony as of 'the perjured evidence of a Spanish Jew'; Giblin (ed.), 'Catalogue', part 4, vols 102-22, p. 83; Burke, *Irish priests in penal times*, pp 314-15; Walsh, 'Glimpses of Ireland', p. 294; Wall, *Catholic Ireland in the eighteenth century*, p. 25. **12** F. Panton to Mar, 23 July 1718 (*H.M.C., Stuart*, vii, p. 80). James III remained absolutely confident of the loyalty of his Irish subjects in the service of the king of France; ibid., p. 559. **13** Examination of James Goyn [Goggins?]', 24 May 1718 (P.R.O., S.P., 63/376/35). See also; ibid., fols 39-40, 47, 49. Goggins later proved unwilling to prosecute despite a penalty of £40 imposed by Lord Chief Justice Whitshed; P.R.O., S.P., 63/377/133. See also P.R.O., S.P., 63/376/49. Goggins may have suffered from a guilty conscience or may have been subject to intimidation. I have not found any evidence of Martin's fate or whether Goggins had his rape cases quashed. **14** King to Lord Fitzwilliam, 12 July 1718 (T.C.D., Ms 750/11/3, fols 211-12); King to T. Coote, 19 Nov. 1718 (T.C.D., Ms 750/5/, fol. 64). See Marsh's Library Z.3.1.1. [xxiv]; T.C.D., Ms 750/11/3, fol. 211-12. Ironically, rumours of an armed uprising in Ireland also circulated in high Jacobite circles in Europe, based on news, from Vienna; *H.M.C., Stuart*, vii, p. 91. Philip V showed his affection for Irish Catholics by declaring that no confiscations or reprisals be made against them (ibid., p. 475). For a biographical note on Redmond and his relationship with the Stuart court, see Hayes, *Biographical dictionary*, p. 274. **15** King to Edward Southwell, 10 Jan. 1719 (T.C.D., Ms 750/5, fols 245-7). Remittances were sent to Ireland from exiled Jacobites; R.A., Ms 41, fol. 49; T.C.D., Ms 2011, fol. 70; Swords (ed.), 'Irish material in the files of Jean Framont'. There are numerous other examples; deBreffny, 'Letters from Connaught to a Wild Goose', pp 81–99; Swords, 'Calendar of material in the files of Jean Framont', passim.

with five thousand men, allegedly to carry 'the Pretender' to Ireland. Another claimed that 'many Irish officers have steered the same course as the duke of Ormonde'.[16] The press and private correspondence resounded to rumours of a forthcoming invasion attempt on Ireland and Ormonde's appeals to his country-men in France to join the king of Spain.[17] The *Flying Post* stated that 'the late duke was to have landed in Ireland with ten thousand Spaniards and arms for twenty thousand men ... and the late king of Sweden in Scotland with fifteen thousand Swedes and arms for thirty thousand men'.[18] The *Dublin Impartial Newsletter* also noted that preparations were afoot in Spain to resist a French invasion: 'the Spanish army is full of French-Irish and German officers [deserters] who flatter themselves that the French will not find them'.[19] *Pue's Occurrences* claimed that 'the later duke of Ormonde has written to several of his friends inviting them to come and serve the king of Spain'.[20] These reports were based on information from the highest levels of the British establishment. Lord Stair, the British ambassador in Paris, passed on intelligence from the (French) Regent regarding possible Swedish involvement with the six Irish regiments in an invasion of England, Scotland or Ireland.[21] A proclamation published in the same paper for 17-20 February 1719 gave official notice that 'the late duke of Ormonde, after a short stay at Madrid, did embark from Spain with an intent to land in this kingdom in order to incite a rebellion therein'. Precautionary measures, including the customary raising of the militia, were initiated.[22]

Throughout February 1719, the Protestant press stressed Jacobite intrigues in Spain.[23] Continual and accurate reports of Irish officers in France and Spain joining Ormonde's impending Irish invasion featured in correspondence to Whitehall from the continent. These led to calls for the embarkation of troops for Ireland.[24] The lords justice received detailed orders to secure the kingdom.[25] The government also moved hastily to disarm and dismount Catholics and impose the Oath of Abjuration. These preparations took place amid conflicting rumours of Ormonde's landing and the Stuart king's incarceration in the castle of Milan.[26] Exacerbated by sensationalist scare-mongering, these allegations

16 Extract of a letter from Abbé Dubois to Secretary Craggs, 16 Jan. 1719 (B.L., Stowe Ms 247, fol. 78). See also B.L., Stowe Ms 247, fols 81, 90. This manuscript contains much correspondence regarding the possibility of a Jacobite invasion of Ireland and the likely participation of the Irish Brigades; ibid., fols 80-98. **17** *Pue's O.*, 17-20 Jan. 1719; *Dub. Cour.*, 20 Jan. 1719. **18** *Fl. P.*, 3 Feb. 1719. **19** *Dub. Imp. N.*, 7 Feb 1719. **20** *Pue's O.*, 17-21 Feb. 1719. **21** Lord Stair to Secretary Craggs, 11 Mar. 1719 (B.L., Stowe 247, fol. 84). **22** *Pue's O.*, 17-21 Feb. 1719; 'Despatch to Lord Castledurrow', 14 Mar. 1719 (N.L.I., Ms 11, 481, [2]). See also *Harding's N.*, 17 Mar. 1719, *Need. P.*, 19 Mar. 1719. The political activity in Europe and the ever-optimistic *émigré* hopes permeated Colonel Francis Bulkeley's contemporary despatch to Mar: 'Providence will make use of the ferment that all Europe seems to be in to accomplish the king's restoration and his subjects happiness'; R.A., Ms 42, fol. 9. For similar sentiments, see R.A., Ms 42, fol. 18. **23** *Dub. I. News.*, 7 Feb. 1719; *Dub. I.*, 21 Feb. 1719. **24** 'Extract of a letter from Consul Henshaw, Genoa, 28 Feb. 1719 (B.L., Stowe Ms 247, fols 80-1). See also B.L., Stowe Ms 247, fols 84-6; *H.M.C., Polwarth*, ii, pp 83, 94-5; *Pue's O.*, 25-8 Apr. 1719; *Pue's O.*, 22-4 Mar. 1719. **25** Bolton to the lords justice, 7 Mar. 1719 (N.A., Ms 2447, fol. 207); Lord Stair to Secretary Craggs, 11 Mar. 1719 (B.L., Stowe Ms 247, fol. 84). **26** This particular edition carried news relating to Ormonde's invasion from Dublin,

coincided with troop movements to England and caused continued consternation through March 1719.[27] The press remained obsessed with Ormonde's
activities in Spain, in particular his intended invasion of Britain and Ireland
with the soldiers of the Spanish-Irish regiments. Continual reports of James's
arrival in Spain, his close political links with Philip V, and the preoccupation
with ongoing troop movements and militia arrays heightened Protestant fears.[28]

The government's preparations against a Jacobite invasion affected all levels
of Irish Catholic society, further underlining the link between Jacobitism and
Catholicism. As was customary in periods of political turmoil or threatened
invasion, the authorities curtailed Irish Catholic communal activities, including
horse-racing, football, hurling and 'commoning' (shinty/winter-hurling) and
other sports, as well as visits to holy wells and pilgrimages. By reinforcing the
association between Jacobitism, popular activities and the Catholic religion the
Jacobite ideology appears to have been drawn into the conscience of many Irish
men and women:

> And whereas we have received information that great numbers of papists
> and reputed papists and others disaffected to his majesty have of late met
> in divers parts of this kingdom under pretence of horse-racings and
> football matches whereby the peace of the nation and the safety of the
> government may be endangered ... suppress all meetings and horse-rac-
> ing ... and all tumultuous and numerous meetings under the pretence of
> football playing, hurling and commoning and other sports ... and unlaw-
> ful meetings at wells or other places of pretended pilgrimage.[29]

In 1721 the authorities intercepted a cache of illicit Jacobite correspondence. At
the same time one local government official was alarmed by 'the very extra-

---

London and Paris; *Pue's O.*, 21-4 Mar. 1719. The following week's edition reported a wholesale
embargo on shipping as a consequence of the Ormondist invasion fear; 24-8 Mar. 1719. A
proclamation was also published in Dublin on 31 April calling for the disarming and dismounting of
papists who refused to take the Oath of Abjuration; *Pue's O.*, 14-17 Mar. 1719; 28-31 Mar. 1719. News
from Madrid from 17 March stated that the fleet had left Cadiz to support an invasion of Ireland;
Dub. I., 31 Mar. 1719; Brady (ed.), *Catholics*, pp 29-30.　**27** King to Annesley, 24 Mar. 1719 (T.C.D.,
Ms 750/5, fols 42-3).　**28** *Pue's O.*, 8 Apr. 1718; 19 Apr. 1718; 13 May 1718; 9 Sept. 1718; 21 Oct. 1718;
16 Dec. 1718; 20 Dec. 1718; 23 Dec. 1718; 1 Feb. 1718; 10-14 Mar. 1719; *Harding's Imp. N.*, 10 Feb. 1719;
19 Mar. 1719; 2 June 1719; 13 June 1719; *Dick. I.*, 14 Feb. 1719; 21 Feb. 1719; 14 Mar. 1719; 21 Nov. 1719;
1 Dec. 1719; 5 May 1719; 22 Aug. 1719; *Hume's Cour.*, 9 Mar. 1719; 31 Mar. 1719; 4 Apr. 1719; 8 Apr.
1719; 10 Apr. 1719; 15 Oct. 1719; 7 Nov. 1919; 11 Dec. 1719; 23 Jan. 1720; 21 Apr. 1719; 6 May 1719; 25
May 1719; 8 Aug. 1719; 5 Aug. 1721; *Need. P.*, 11 Mar. 1719, 13 Mar. 1719; 23 Mar. 1719; 30 Mar. 1719;
4 May 1719; 25 May 1719; 1 Dec. 1719; *Whalley's N.*, 25 Mar. 1719; 28 Mar. 1719; 4 Apr. 1719; 14 Dec.
1719; 19 May 1720; *Hume's P.*, 4 Apr. 1719; 8 Sept. 1719; 14 Dec. 1719; 22 Jan. 1720; 10 Aug. 1719;
Toulman's Dub. P., 8 Apr. 1719; 1 Dec. 1719; *Harding's Imp. N.*, 7 Nov. 1719; 28 Nov. 1719; 7 Jan. 1720;
3 Sept. 1720; 1 Oct. 1720; *Fl. P.*, 7 May 1719; *General Postman*, 20 July 1719.　**29** *Dub. I.*, 31 Mar. 1719.
See also J. Craggs to the lord lieutenant, 30 Apr. 1719 (P.R.O., S.P., 67/7/87).

ordinary devotions, fastings and other penances among the Irish all over the country'. He claimed that 'hundreds went barefooted daily to the church, that men who had long been confined to their houses or their beds now joined in the devotions'. These pieties were deemed to have a Jacobite dimension. When asked the reason for their fervour, 'they replied that they were commanded to do it for the good of their souls and the advantage of another person'.[30] By striking at the roots of their religious, social and cultural lives, these measures show the intermittent but indiscriminate imposition of the penal laws upon all sections of the Catholic community, not just the recusant land-holders and clergy. The psychological effects of these laws lie well beyond the narrow confines of recent studies of the effects of penal legislation.[31]

The Ormondist threat dominated the popular press in the early summer of 1719. A report in the *Dublin Courant* of 6 April 1719, brought by Captain Daniel Morrison from Cadiz, concerned six gentlemen boarding a ship in disguise, two of whom were thought to be James III and Ormonde. Morrison asserted that 'the Spaniards in Cadiz expressed great joy that the poor Catholics of Great Britain and Ireland would soon be relieved'. This could only increase Irish Catholic affection for the Spanish king and raise their hopes of a timely invasion. This was presumably only one of the many such reports which made their way to Ireland through maritime trade.[32] Letters from Madrid confirmed that a Spanish fleet had sailed from Cadiz, consisting of eight men-of-war. These were to be joined by two others which sailed from Port Passage, 'on one of which the late duke of Ormonde embarked'.[33] The *Dublin Postman* also carried news that two men-of-war were landing war-like stores at Corunna and that two persons of distinction were coming from Madrid. They were expecting some more men-of-war and fifty transports from Cadiz with soldiers and stores; Irish, English and Spanish officers in Cadiz were ready to make a descent on some part of Britain or Ireland. The report claimed that 'an order is come for an Irish pilot married in this place and the consul who is also an Irishman to embark on board the said ships'.[34]

The popular press confirmed the scattering of the Spanish fleet. Nevertheless the threat partially materialised with the arrival on Irish soil of Patrick Sarsfield, second earl of Lucan, with a group of Spanish-Irish officers to assist him.[35] Although little light can be shed on Sarsfield's activities, the subsequent proclamation involved the now customary witch-hunt against the Catholic hierarchy, friars and popish priests, and calls for petty officials to be more diligent in securing the public peace in their respective territories. At the same time, Lord

---

30 L. Osborne to Busteed, 12 Dec. 1721, quoted in Lecky, *Irel.*, i, p. 414.   **31** Introduction, pp 27-30.   **32** *Dub. Cour.*, 6 Apr. 1719.   **33** *Pue's O.*, 7-11 Apr. 1719.   **34** *Dub. P.*, 8 Apr. 1719. The Dublin press reported that James had allegedly been fêted by Philip V of Spain as the 'Linea masculina y Católica de la Casa Sturda'; *Pue's O.*, 11-14 Apr. 1719.   **35** *Dub. Cour.*, 11 Apr. 1719; *Dub. I.*, 11 Apr. 1719; *Pue's. O.*, 11-14 Apr. 1719.

Chancellor Middleton claimed that 'the Irish are very insolent in the remote parts of the kingdom and they as little believe that the designed invasion is in great measure defeated as they formerly pretended to believe any such thing was intended'. Irish Catholics were probably inclined to talk down the chances of a descent from Europe, with the possible motive of deflecting any possible government backlash.[36]

The 1719 invasion scares did not have a direct military effect on Ireland but the landing in Scotland continued to feature in the press. A proclamation in April 1719 called for the apprehension of William Murray, marquis of Tullibardine, George Keith, late earl marschial of Scotland and William Mackenzie, late earl of Seaforth, whom the authorities expected to flee to Ireland after the collapse of the 'Nineteen'.[37] Particular emphasis was placed on the numbers of Irish papists in their ranks and rumours of a rebellious 'plot' among their native brethren.[38] Ormonde's preparations unnerved the Whigs and raised the expectations of their Catholic contemporaries. Irish Jacobite anticipation of Ormonde's proposed invasion was such that 'they could not help being discovered and the people were well-affected to the king [James III]'.[39]

Although Archbishop King felt vindicated in the aftermath of 1719 by the failure of the Irish to support the Scottish insurgents, his analysis of Irish Jacobite impotence ignored the need for the appearance of a sizeable invasion force as a necessary prerequisite to an uprising. This was always seen by native and *émigré* Jacobites as a necessary stimulus to concerted action. Throughout the greater part of this period, Catholics remained totally disarmed, many of their leaders were exiled and those who remained were incarcerated at the first sign of trouble:

> 'Tis somewhat to the honour of the Protestants of Ireland that notwithstanding we have 6-7 papists for one of us, we have kept our country quiet when Britain is now under the fear of a second rebellion. I believe a little good management might have prevented any trouble in the one as easily as in the other.[40]

This smug assertion from a senior member of the political establishment should not be used as a yard-stick to measure popular Catholic expectations or Protestant fears of a Jacobite invasion, nor can it be taken out of a local,

---

36 Connolly. *Religion*, pp 235-6; Coy, 'Local political culture', p. 201; Petrie, 'Ireland in the French and Spanish strategy', p. 161.   37 *The Postman*, 13 Apr. 1719. These Scottish fugitives were 'the same who sailed under a convoy of two men-of-war from Port Passage and were to have made a diversion in Scotland at the same time the rising was to have been in Ireland'; *Pue's O.*, 25-28 Apr. 1719. James Spaight, surveyor of Carrickfergus, claimed that a man had seen the earl of Seaforth and the late Clanranald's brother board a vessel in the sound of Mull; P.R.O., S.P., 63/377/269. See also Williams (ed.), *Correspondence*, ii, p. 312.   38 *Pue's O.*, 2-5 May 1719; *Dub. Imp. N.*, 2 June 1719.   39 Quoted in O 'Callaghan, *Irish brigades*, pp 318-20.   40 King to William Nicholson, Bishop of Derry, 28 May 1719 (T.C.D., Ms 750/5, fol. 163). The strength of the Irish establishment is discussed in the Introduction, pp 29-30.

contemporary political context which abounded with invasion rumours and landings of Scotland-bound Spanish ships. It should also be contrasted with another dispatch from King on the same day which alluded to a Spanish vessel of sixty guns and 400 men which docked at a place called the Black Saddle on the west coast of Ireland. Two men who boarded these were carried off and set down seven leagues from the Black Saddle. King claimed that they were bound for Scotland to join the rebels. It was accompanied by another vessel which had became separated. King concluded that 'we are not yet at the end of the invasion'.[41]

Despite the failure of Ormonde's descent to materialise, the Stuart claimant remained the bogeyman of the Protestant tradition. The press coverage given to the abortive 1719 invasion, which had in no way abated by the summer of that year, reflected this fact. By September 1719, incidental reports of the Stuart claimant's marriage in Rome and Ormonde's failure to raise Irish recruits in France for a British invasion seemed less menacing than those relating to a possible landing from Spain.[42] The actions of the rapparees at home were quite a different matter, focusing attention on the defiant demeanour of the papists.[43] Their potential to avenge the proposed branding of Catholic priests prompted an infamous letter from the duke of Bolton to Secretary Craggs of 25 August 1719, advocating the castration of Catholic priests, arguably the single most shameful proposal of the 'Protestant Ascendancy'. Historians have been quick to point out the impractical nature of this legislation and suggested that the most ferocious clauses may have been deliberately inserted to ensure its defeat. Yet, public thanksgivings took place in all the chapels of Galway and most others in the kingdom after the castration bill was rejected, showing that the threat was taken seriously by many Catholics. It should warn historians against the dangers of understating the psychological effects of penal legislation on Irish Catholics.

> The Popery Bill as it came from the House of Commons inflicted no greater punishment on the priests of the Romish religion than that of burning of the cheek, but it being observed that when the punishment was exercised in this kingdom in other cases, the rapparees in their robberies made it a common practice to burn innocent persons with that

41 King to Col. Foley; 28 May 1719 (T.C.D., Ms 750/5, fol. 164). Other Spanish ships engaged in naval manoeuvres off the coast in this period, allegedly attempting to supply the Jacobite forces in Scotland; N.L.I., Ms 9610, fols 139, 141; P.R.O., S.P., 63/377/216, 253; *H.M.C., Polwarth*, ii, p. 173; *Pue's O.*, 30 June- 4 July 1719.   42 *Dub Imp. N.*, 7 June 1719; *Pue's O.*, 20-3 June 1719; 30 June- 4 July 1719; 26-9 Sept. 1719; 21 Nov. 1719.   43 Great crowds flocked on the road from Crumlin to Dublin to see the captured rapparee Captain Fitzgerald; *A full and true account of the surprising and apprehension of Captain Fitzgerald*, 5 Dec. 1717; *The speech of Captain Fitzgerald*, 25 Dec. 1717. Contemporary broadsheets suggested an association between rapparees and recruits for the Pretender's service; Finnmore, *The Pretender's foot exercise*; idem, *The Pretender's exercise to his Irish dragoons*; *The last speech and dying words of Captain McDermott who was formerly concerned in listing men for the Pretender and was hanged and quartered at Cavan, 30 March 1725.*

mark in order to destroy the distinction it was intended for, and that nothing less than a very severe punishment would be effectual to prevent the frequent arrival of priests here, it was thought proper by the privy council to deter them with the penalty of castration.[44]

The need for solidarity among Protestants in the face of the 'strict union of the papists among themselves with their apparent interest and attachment to the Pretender' provided a useful rallying call for the lord lieutenant in the early days of July 1719.[45] This cannot be dismissed as hollow rhetoric given that the continued threat of a Spanish invasion precipitated preventive action at the highest level of the Irish administration.[46] Measures included the deployment of three men-of-war off the Irish coast, the speedy cantonment of troops before 20-21 November, and the array of four full regiments of foot near Athlone.[47] The *London Flying Post* mocked the Jacobites and papists and attacked Ormonde:

> Your quondam duke of Ormond has met with disappointment in his design to raise rebellion in France for that he had voluntarily put a padlock on his sword ... a person so loaded with perjury and treachery is never like to be blessed in any of his undertakings till he repent and reform and in that case he must abandon your odious party. If he be capable of thinking, he would consider what a different part he acts this November when he threatens his native country with an invasion on behalf of popery and tyranny, from what he acted in November 1688 ... and from what he did in 1702 when he attended the late Queen in her procession from St Paul's ... You had better content to call him [The Pretender] knight or cavalier to a Polish lady in Polish dress.[48]

When the immediate threat of another Ormondist invasion had finally passed, attention switched to the fallout from the trial and execution of the high-profile Irish Jacobite Sir James Cotter, deemed to have been one of the most traumatic political events of the first half of the century in Ireland.[49] Cotter was a prominent member of the Munster Catholic gentry and a son of Sir James

---

44 Duke of Bolton to Craggs, 25 Aug. 1719 (N.L.I., 9610, fol. 201); (S.P. 63/378, fols. 42-4); Brady, *Catholicism*, p. 34; Dickson, *New foundations*, p. 80.   **45** 'They deceive themselves who imagine that the designs of the enemies of our peace do not extend to Ireland as well as the rest of his majesty's dominions...a good agreement and union among all the Protestants will greatly contribute to this end and the number as well as the strict union of the papists among themselves, together with their apparent inclination and attachments to the interests of the Pretender'; *Pue's O.*, 30 June-4 July 1719.   **46** 'All the letters from Madrid dated 24 October bring an account that the late duke of Ormonde was sailed from St Andero with 7 men-of-war or frigates having on board eighteen hundred men and ten thousand arms with a design to make a descent in England, Scotland or Ireland'; *Pue's O.*, 3-7 Nov. 1719.   **47** E. Webster to Bolton, 5 Nov. 1719 (P.R.O., S.P., 63/378/135); Webster to Bolton, 10 Nov. 1719 (P.R.O., S.P., 63/378/ 141); King to Molyneux, 10 Nov. 1719 (T.C.D., 750/5, fols 208-9, 245-7).   **48** *Dub. Gaz.*, 21 Nov. 1719; *Pue's O.*, 12-15 Dec. 1719.   **49** Cullen, *Emergence of modern*

Cotter, knighted by Charles II after his assassination of the regicide John Lisle in Basle in 1664. He inherited his father's Jacobitism and was accused of festooning his horses and hounds with white roses, as well as engaging in other defiant anti-government and pro-Jacobite activities in Queen Anne's reign. In 1713 the House of Commons ordered his detention by the sergeant-at-arms for his part in a Tory mob's attempt to intimidate Whig voters. Although he managed to evade arrest on this occasion, he was indicted in 1718 for allegedly raping his mistress, a Quaker named Elizabeth Squibb. Cotter strongly denied the charge but was tried, convicted and executed. Catholic opinion believed that the trial was politically motivated; Miss Squibb was purportedly drunk at the time of the alleged assault, she allegedly continued to travel with Cotter after the supposed rape and several days had elapsed before she made a complaint.

Whether or not Cotter was guilty of the rape or vested interests colluded in his judicial murder, his execution had a traumatic effect on Catholic opinion in the south of Ireland. Seán Clárach Mac Domhnaill, Éamonn de Bhál, Liam Rua Mac Coitir, Piaras Mac Gearailt and many other leading Jacobite poets composed laments for him. According to Froude, Munster 'burst into a wail of rage'. The Quakers (who rallied around Miss Squibb) were singled out for particular retribution. They could not show their faces in the streets. Placards covered their walls and Quaker girls were threatened with being 'cottered'. The mayor of Cork appealed in vain to the recusant clergy to restrain their flocks. This Catholic intimidation of the Quaker community had an unmistakable Jacobite dimension. A revenge note posted on the door of a Quaker meeting-house demonstrated Jacobite anger:

> Vengeance belongeth to me; I will repay, saith the Lord. Now look to it, ye hell-born crew. Cotter's life shall be a sting to your cursed carcases that shall be meat for dogs, and your cursed souls to burning Acheron, where they will burn in flames during eternity. Fenn, look sharp, and other bursengutted dogs besides, the which were instruments of taking Cotter's breath. Other blackguard dogs look sharp. God save King James III of England, to whom you will soon pay anguish and punish in this matter.[50]

Ireland, pp 199-200; Bartlett, 'Review article', p. 216; Hogan and Ó Buachalla (ed.), 'Letters of James Cotter', pp 66-96. See also P.R.O., S.P., 67/7/80v; *Whalley's N.*, 7 May 1720; T.C.D., Ms 750/6, fol. 135; Brady (ed.), *Catholics*, p. 34. **50** Ó Buachalla, *Aisling Ghéar*, p. 363. See also ibid., pp 186-7; Brady (ed.), *Catholics*, p. 34. Swift states that 'the ballad upon Cotter is vehemently suspected to be of Irish manufacture; and yet is allowed to be sung in our open streets under the very nose of the government'; Swift, *Works* (Dublin, 1769), iv, p. 40. A proclamation was issued after Cotter's death to prevent Quakers from being insulted; *Twenty-third report of the deputy-keeper*, p. 61. *Whalley's Newsletter* of 7 May 1720 noted that a Quaker's House in Meath Street was gutted with the result that six or seven priests were arrested for promoting riot. All but one Catholic chapel remained closed the following Sunday, Kelly, 'The impact of the penal laws', p. 153. A recent appraisal of the Squibb rape

Although Cotter's fate has loomed large in recent historiography, Ormonde's abortive landings and the contemporary political climate to which it was closely linked have been written out of eighteenth-century Irish history, or taken as a watershed for the terminal decline of Irish Jacobitism. According to Connolly, the great age of Jacobite expectation was already over in the period after Ormonde's failed invasion attempt.[51] It is similarly dismissed by Bartlett: 'Admittedly as long as the Pretender remained a threat, Protestants could not rest entirely easy; but the penal laws, Protestant self-assurance, the assumed goodwill on England, and after 1714, the remoteness of a dynastic upheaval all combined to render a Catholic resurgence more of a bugaboo than a direct threat'.[52] Although there are some official sources which suggest that Irish Protestants were dismissive of the dangers of Jacobitism, many others support an opposite opinion. To over-emphasise one opinion is to provide a blinkered view of eighteenth-century Ireland. These views certainly have some validity in relation to contemporary Jacobite high-politics and reflect the self-confidence of some sections of the 'Protestant Ascendancy'. Nevertheless, they can blind us to the fact that Jacobitism (like royalism in Interregnum England) was an ideology founded on unquenchable optimism. These conclusions also underestimate the seriousness of the danger later posed to the brittle Hanoverian state by the 'Forty-five'. They also reflect an over-reliance on official government sources which are no less subjective as historical source-material than the partisan poetry of the Irish literati, or the optimistic memoirs of the Irish diaspora. The poetry's relevance for the greater Catholic community is also neglected, as is the elusive 'Hidden Ireland' in its two manifestations, the popular-Jacobite culture and the continental (no less Jacobite) Ireland in exile.[53]

The links between the two sections of the Irish Jacobite community were maintained by recruitment for foreign service in the 1720s. Recruits often had more than merely mercenary motives for running the gauntlet of capital punishment; mere mercenaries would hardly have risked execution to follow the hazardous profession of soldiering.[54] The authorities received reports of incessant recruitment and clerical participation therein. A letter to Henry Ievers in County Clare expressed horror at the great number of unregistered priests in

trial denies the judicial murder claim; Kelly, 'Abduction of women', pp 15-16. Ó Buachalla's examination of Cotter's background, his upbringing and education contests Louis Cullen's claim that Cotter was 'a reckless Jacobite' who showed a 'truculent and provocative Catholic attitude towards Protestants'. He also examines accounts of his death and the numerous laments composed by the Irish literati; Ó Buachalla, *Aisling Ghéar*, pp 361-9. See also Ó Buachalla, 'The making of a Cork Jacobite', pp 469-98. The refusal of the lord lieutenant to grant a reprieve may have depended less on Cotter's political or religious credentials than the fact that Cotter's father had been lavishly rewarded for the assassination of the viceroy's wife's grand-father; Garnham, *The courts, crime and criminal law*, p. 263. **51** Connolly, *Religion* , p. 236. **52** Bartlett, *Fall and rise*, p. 35; O'Donoghue, 'Jacobite threat', p. 131. **53** Introduction, pp 33–6; 38–51. **54** Introduction, pp 32–5. Reports in the press that the Spanish attempted to encourage desertions from the French and allied armies also had implications for Jacobitism among

the kingdom who refused to take the Oath of Abjuration; they were engaged in 'several pernicious and traitorous practices', as well as 'encouraging and promoting the enlisting of men for the service of the Pretender'.[55] As was customary with all rumours of internal revolt, external invasions and recruitment for foreign service, Catholic clergy were prominently implicated and their actions deemed to have official sanction from the Stuart court. One contemporary report claimed that 'the Jacobites are now retiring to St Germains. The only motion they are making at present is sending Irish priests into Ireland in disguise to raise recruits'.[56] Lord Carteret claimed that 'popish priests pass over daily in disguise from France to raise recruits'.[57]

This resulted in the rigorous imposition of penal legislation against Catholics in 1723 and 1724 typified by a new bill entitled 'A bill for explaining and amending the acts to prevent the further growth of Popery and for the strengthening of the Protestant interest'. This threatened the Catholic clergy with the ultimate punishment of high treason and was deemed by Lecky to 'rank with the most infamous edicts in the whole history of persecution'.[58] The rumoured arrival of fifteen hundred such clergy from the continent in March 1722 led the government to suspect 'some design extraordinary to be on foot to disturb and distract the minds of ignorant and unthinking people'.[59]

The close relationship between rappareeism and recruitment also featured in contemporary political discourse. One account from Dungarvan, County Waterford claimed that 2,000 recruits were lurking in the surrounding countryside waiting for an opportunity to carry them to Spain.[60] The commissioners of Oyer and Terminer (Court of Admiralty) wrote from County Cork in 1721 to complain that 'the papists who have of later been enlisted for the foreign service have appeared in such great numbers and in so public a manner that we are apprehensive the civil power alone will hardly be able to disperse them'. They asked for troops to be sent, especially to the sea coasts; 'we have reason to believe that at least twenty thousand have been of late and are now ready to be shipped off'.[61] Philip Perceval in County Cork also stressed this association:

> 'Tis generally believed that a great deal of the mischief which has been done in the country was owing to a great number of men who have listed for the Spaniards and can't get an opportunity of going off. They say that there are many hundreds of them and for my part I think the best way would be to let them go.[62]

Irish *émigrés* in this period; *Dub. Imp. N.*, 7 June 1719. There are many other examples in this period of concerted attempts to encourage defections from the British armies; O'Callaghan, *Irish brigades*, pp 219, 243, and 245.   **55** W. Hay to H. Ivers, 20 Feb. 1721 (N.A., Iever's papers, 1720-52). See also P.R.O., S.P., 67/7/124.   **56** 'Extract of a letter from Mr Crawford at Paris', 24 June 1722 (B.L. Stowe Ms 250, fol. 85). See also Ó Buachalla, *Aisling Ghéar*, p. 339.   **57** Carteret to lords justice, 28 June 1722 (P.R.O., S.P., 67/7/124).   **58** Lecky, *Irel.*, i, p. 164.   **59** Brady (ed.), *Catholics*, p. 35.   **60** Cartaret to Grafton, 22 June 1721 (P.R.O., S.P., 67/7/85).   **61** Lecky, *Irel.*, i, p. 419; introduction, pp 31-2.   **62** Percival to Sir J. Perceval, 20 Feb. 1721 (B.L., Add. Ms 47, 029, fol. 50). Five hundred men who had

The authorities did not make the same deduction. Acts were passed in Ireland both for the suppression of tories, robbers and rapparees and to prevent recruitment for foreign service.[63]

Extensive reporting of the trial of Captain Francis Fitzgerald at Cork in April 1722 (for enlisting men for foreign service), reflected a continued fascination with 'Wild Geese' and their association with the rapparees. It further highlighted the deep-seated suspicion that such recruitment was ultimately for 'the Pretender'. In March 1721, the *Dublin Intelligence* reported that Fitzgerald, having denied that he had 'Wild Geese' on board, allegedly shot a passenger who had tried to get onto the ship's deck. Although Fitzgerald's victim may have been pressed into the service or proved a reluctant participant, the newspaper claimed that the service of their exiled king provided the main motivation for some of his associates. When requested to enlist directly for the service of Philip V on their arrival in Spain, these recruits purportedly threw down their money and refused to enroll until reassured by a crucifix-bearing priest that they would only serve James III.[64] This report was corroborated by the British consul in Bilbao who commented on the large numbers arriving in Spain from Ireland:

> I could hardly believe it myself if it were not made so plain to me and confirmed by many people that it was impossible to bring such numbers of men from Ireland for the Pretender's service ... I gave your lordship an account from Corunna of about four hundred and fifty and now I am to inform you that many hundreds have landed in the ports of Biscay and Asturias. I cannot get an exact account of the numbers ... I can give your lordship a pretty good rule at their numbers, which having made two entire battalions of Sherlock's Regiment, there were some hundred remaining who were ordered to the Irish Regiments in the king of Spain's service. They threw down their pay and declared that they would serve no other prince but King James for whom they were listed in Ireland. I

listed themselves in County Cork for the service of the Pretender had waited in a body for passage to Spain but quickly dispersed when an order was issued to apprehend them, 10 Jan. 1722; Brady, *Catholics*, p. 312. In July of that year Moses Nowland was arrested for attempting to ship two hundred men for foreign service; ibid., p. 312. See also *Harding's Weekly I. N.,* 13 Jan. 1722; Ó Buachalla, 'Seacaibíteachas', p. 36; B.L., Add. Ms 47, 029, fol. 112.   **63** P.R.O., S.P., 63/382/114; *Dub. Cour.,* 23 Jan. 1722.   **64** The *Dublin Intelligence* and *Whalley's Newsletter* reported on the trials of Captain Fitzgerald, Standish Barry and Nathaniel Hayes, see *Dub. I.,* 3 April 1722; *Whalley's N.,* 9 April 1722. The examination of Morish Hayes states that Captain Fitzgerald had attempted to transport one hundred men to Spain. Recruited by Sir Peter Stafford, who had his knighthood conferred on him by 'the Pretender', he drank the health of the Stuart claimant under the name James III, 20 Jan. 1721; P.R.O., S.P., 67/7/109. For the strong Jacobite sentiments of those who arrived in Spain; B.L., Stowe Ms 250, fols 88-90. The State Papers France also contain a reference to the contemporary recruiting activities of Nathaniel Hayes; *List and index society,* vol. 119, S.P. 78, State Papers France, 1723-7, pp 128-9. A proclamation was issued in 1722 for his arrest after he had escaped from jail; *Twenty-third report of the deputy-keeper,* p. 61. The *Twenty-third report* also carried a description of one Menzies, also engaged in smuggling recruits into France, see ibid., p. 105.

spoke to many of them and they freely owned it, they are kind of prisoners for fear they should run away ...[65]

In July 1722 Sir Peter Stafford was named as an agent for the Stuart king in Spain. He had been knighted by 'the Pretender' on his visit to Spain and 'it was certain that he had some cash both to debauch our soldiers and aid such as come from Ireland or suffer for the cause'.[66]

Fitzgerald and Captain Henry Ward were finally executed for enlisting for the Pretender's service in Spain. A report in the *Dublin Courant*, purportedly based on a letter written by Fitzgerald after his conviction, reveals attitudes towards the condemned recruiter and the existence of an Irish Jacobite 'theatre of death'. Fitzgerald's accusers claimed that he received a British half-crown from Father F[rancis] Q[uinn] to drink James III's health, swore an oath of loyalty to the Stuart king and had the priest's sworn promise of an ensign's commission. Its publication attempted to pre-empt the impact of a posthumous speech published after his execution:

> I think it reasonable and proper to publish the above copy of a letter to me from Francis Fitzgerald after his conviction and sentence that the world may not be amused by a speech published [as his] the day of his execution.[67]

As in contemporary England, some condemned recruits used the scaffold as a political platform, and their last speeches were circulated by Irish Jacobites. A popular lament for seventeen men taken on a sloop for enlisting for the Pretender evidences a sympathetic attitude towards these condemned recruits.[68] The attempted assassination of key witnesses in the trial of Standish Barry, Edward

---

65 [Parker?] to [Carteret?], 10 Aug. 1722 (B.L., Stowe Ms 250, fol. 90). 66 *Appendixes referred to in the report from the committee*, p. 19. See also; B.L., Stowe 250, fol. 88. Stafford's name also occurs in relation to the abortive Jacobite invasion from Spain in 1719; Dickson, *The Jacobite attempt of 1719*, p. 135. 67 *Dub. Cour.*, 24 Apr. 1722. This Henry Ward was named by Sir Anthony Wescombe in a letter to Lord Carteret as the master of a sloop called the *Hopewell*; *Appendixes referred to in the report from the committee*, p. 19. The *Dublin Courant* carried these accusations against Francis Quinn; *Dub. Cour.*, 24 July 1722. The English government proved unwilling to execute a condemned soldier-turned-highwayman for fear of the fallout from his last speech, quoted in Fagan (ed.), *Stuart papers*, i, pp 34-5. Swift made a collection of printed dying speeches of Irish culprits, annotated with his own comments; Crofton-Croker, *Researches*, p. 183; Introduction, pp 36-7. 68 *A new song called the sorrowful lamentation for Anthony Bulger ... taken on board a sloop at the bar of Dublin who were supposed to be listed for the Pretender*. Tadhg Ó Neachtain was preoccupied with the trials and executions of recruits; Ó Buachalla, *Aisling Ghéar*, pp 374, 382-3. The British Library contains a broadsheet entitled *The last speech and dying words of Captain McDermott who was formerly concerned in listing men for the Pretender and was hanged and quartered at Cavan, 30 March 1725*. This is the only last speech I have found relating to a recruiter executed outside Cork or Dublin. A man named James O'Connor was hanged in Magheracloone, County Monaghan on a charge of recruiting for the

Barry and Charles Doran, implicated in enlisting in May 1722, showed that solidarity with the accused extended to more than the occasional pathetic lament:

> As to the state of affairs here I don't find we have reason for any disturbance at present, though several of the Irish who were listed (if for the king of Spain's service) in the Pretender's name and are now upon their trial in Cork and will swing for it. Many papist gentlemen in that county of estates have been informed against, among the rest Mr Standish Barry, the evidence [witness] against whom was shot out of a window at Cork but it happened to wound him only in the knee'.[69]

These recruitment depositions occasionally expose the machinery of contemporary recruitment. In March 1721 the British consul at Corunna uncovered links maintained between Ireland and Spain through the activities of 'Colonel Sherlock and his wife and some of their emissaries who manage the affair there'. He resented their abuse of diplomatic privilege, stating that although 'they came under British colours, they took no notice of me, and in an insulting manner have given to understand they will pay no consulage'. He described the antipathy towards the English community in Corunna, which sharply contrasted with the esteem in which the local Spanish population held the Irish: 'they look on these people as martyrs for their religion which makes them so insolent that I am apprehensive of some insult to my person'.[70] Sir Anthony Wescomb also stated that about four hundred and fifty men had arrived in Corunna from County Cork as recruits for (Sir) Peter Sherlock's Regiment. Sherlock was 'a sort of a farmer' in Ireland but now is 'a sort of agent' for the Pretender in Madrid. Sherlock was also a relation and supporter of Sir Peter Stafford.[71] A further report suggested that a vibrant, vocal and assertive Irish Catholic community resided in Bilbao:

> There is no town in Spain so favourable to the Jacobites and their cause as this is, the great liberty the country enjoys and their having no public person from Britain and the great numbers of Irish papists dwelling here are very great encouragements to the Jacobites to lay their designs that way. The town, tho' not very big, is very populous and one half are Irish papists. The few English merchants that live here are cowed and stand in awe of them to a degree that is ridiculous.[72]

Pretender; Rushe, *History of Monaghan*, p. 61. It is highly unlikely that these were unique occurrences. **69** Perceval to Sir John Perceval, Dublin, 19 May 1722 (B.L., Add. Ms 47, 029, fol. 122). Also see *Trial of Mr Standish Barry, 20 May 1722*; *Whalley's N.*, 9 Apr. 1722; Crofton-Croker, *Researches*, p. 201; *Dub. Cour.*, 24 July 1722, 1 Oct. 1722; O 'Callaghan, *Irish brigades*, p. 161. **70** Extract from Mr Parker, his majesty's consul at Corunna to the post-master general, 22 Mar. 1721 (P.R.O., S.P., 67/7/84). See also B.L., Stowe Ms 250, fol. 89. **71** *Appendixes referred to in the report from the committee*, p. 19. These also report that many hundreds more arrived for 'the Pretender's' service in Ireland; ibid., p. 23. A contemporary intelligence report made an association between Sir Peter Sherlock and McCarthy Mór in contemporary recruitment deposition from Ireland; P.R.O., S.P., 67/7/133. **72** [Parker?] to [Carteret?],

Some of the large numbers of Irish in Bilbao at this time may have been assembled there as a consequence of Ormonde's invasion scheme. Wescombe also presumably meant that half the foreigners in Bilbao were of Irish origin. He later claimed that after Ormonde had been recalled to Madrid 'the Jacobites that were flocking from all parts of Spain to these coasts were gone back to their lurking holes again'.[73] Evidence in Larrauri's *Historia del Consulado de Bilbao* suggests that there was a considerable expatriate Irish community in Bilbao:

> Now a very considerable trade was carried on between the ports of Dublin and Bilbao. In fact there was a very large Irish colony in Bilbao which included many from Dublin, Shees, Philips, Seagraves, Jordans and Dorans, these last from Rush. There too the Irish Dominicans conducted for long a hospice not far from the famous shrine of Nuestra Senora de Begona. From Bilbao Dublin took large quantities of iron and in return Bilbao took salted meat, butter, fish, grain, raw-hides and tallow candles. In 1734 Dublin took 13,488 quantities of iron and in 1749-50, 3,352.[74]

The seizure of a large number of swords inscribed 'for James and my country' enhanced fears of a possible Jacobite landing in May 1722. The mutinous state of the king's forces and endemic absenteeism among the Protestant gentry contrasted with the numerical superiority of the papists and the Irish regiments in foreign armies. The threat to trade and business, which resulted in poverty and desperation, was sharpened by the sending of military reinforcements to England, amid fears of intended invasions centered on Lord Charles O'Brien, sixth viscount Clare's regiment in Dunkirk.[75] The destination of these recruits

---

16 Aug. 1722; (B.L., Stowe Ms 250, fol. 95). Cullen, *Hidden Ireland: a reassessment*, p. 18.   **73** [Wescomb] to [Carteret?], 13 July 1722 (B.L., Stowe 250, fol. 88). See also *Appendixes referred to in the reports*, p. 18.   **74** Quoted in Meagher, 'Glimpses of eighteenth-century priests', p. 146. The Dominicans had a hospice which served as a temporary shelter for those going and coming between Ireland and Spain; Fenning, *Dominican province*, p. 65 A further examination of Larrauri's two-volume work shows that Bilbao traded with many other Irish ports in eighteenth-century Ireland, including Bantry, Belfast, Berehaven, Cork, Drogheda, Dublin, Dungarvan, Galway, Killybegs, Kinsale, Derry, Sligo, Waterford, Wexford and Youghal; Larrauri, *Historia*, ii, pp 395-410.   **75** For reference to the inscribed swords; O'Donoghue, 'Jacobite threat', p. 176. See also Carteret to the lords justice, 10 May 1722 (P.R.O., S.P., 67/7/120); *Fau. P.*, 21 May 1722. The State papers also reported on the embarkation of six regiments from Ireland to Bristol, unrest in Ireland, orders for officers to repair to their regiments, fear of insurrection and danger from outlawed, banished men; P.R.O., S.P., 67/7/120. Regarding the possibility of unrest in Ireland; T.C.D., Ms 750/7, fols 108-11, 119-20, 122-6. A popular song considered the possibility of a Jacobite invasion of Ireland from Italy or Spain; *Upon the fringes, 16 July 1722*; See also *H.M.C., Various Collections, Mss of M.L.S. Clements of Ashfield Lodge, Co. Cavan*, viii, p. 342. A correspondent to the Stuart court stressed the necessity of sending at least 8,000 stand of arms to Ireland so that Ireland might have a share of the royal favour; Fagan (ed.), *Stuart papers*, i, p. 36. Lord Clare's regiment at Dunkirk caused unease in political circles; *H.M.C., Polwarth*, iii, pp 137, 177, 181; B.L., Stowe Ms 250, fols 76, 83, 95. In his correspondence to Carteret of April 1722, Sir Luke Schaub reported that many Irish officers, under pretence of going to

provides a measure of popular Jacobitism in contemporary Ireland, indicating that the standard of James III possessed a more powerful allure than those of the kings of Spain or France.[76] King described the disturbance caused by 'thousands' of Wild Geese in a letter to Lord Kingston, who had been implicated in recruiting. Indeed Kingston's association with Jacobitism demonstrated the vulnerable position of Catholic converts:

> I suppose your Lordship is apprised how the country has been disturbed by a sort of people called the Wild Geese and that some thousands have been listed for the service of the Pretender. This cannot be denied since it is manifest beyond contradiction. Whether they were really intended for that service is not the matter but that those who enlisted them designed it so, and were persuaded that they were to be so, can be no doubt, but if your lordship gave no encouragement then you are in no danger. [77]

Although unwilling to accuse Kingston of treason, the lord lieutenant cast doubt on his loyalty to the Hanoverian regime in 1724. He had been freed from jail 'upon entering into recognizances of forty thousand pounds', while the case against his son who had fled to England and remained there was still pending. Although the lord lieutenant stressed the 'gross prevarications and false accusations' of the witnesses, he still believed that Kingston and his son 'are not so free as might be wished of having favoured these treasonable practices'.[78] A similar question-mark hung over another Protestant Jacobite suspect, Sir Knightley Chetwood, accused of enlisting for the Pretender's service. Convinced that some private malice lay behind the charge, Grafton nonetheless believed that Chetwood 'doth not give any strong testimony of his affection for the government'.[79]

An intercepted packet from James Horan and his solicitor Francis Glascock (Glascoe) to James Wogan at the college of Navarre in Paris in July 1724 provided evidence of the continued traffic between Ireland and Jacobite Europe. It also uncovered an Irish dimension to the 'Layer Plot', which took place in contemporary England. The packet contained letters from the prominent *émigré*

---

their regiments, were drawing to the sea coasts; *Appendixes referred to in the report from the committee*, pp 3, 5.   **76** King to Lord Kingston, 9 June 1722 (T.C.D., Ms 750/7, fol. 128). See also T.C.D., Ms. 750/7, fols 142, 205-6; B.L., Stowe Ms 250, fols 88-9.   **77** King to Lord Kingston, 9 June 1722 (T.C.D., Ms 750/7, fol. 128). In a letter to Annsley, King asserted that 'the affair of the Wild Geese is costly and troublesome'; T.C.D., 750/7, fols 208-9; See also P.R.O., S.P., 63/383/133. King also noted the magnitude of the task facing Chief Justice Cox in examining recruits; N.L.I., Ms 2056. For Kingston's Jacobitism, see O'Donoghue, 'Jacobite threat', pp 62,154; Murphy, 'Irish Jacobitism and Freemasonry', pp 75-83.   **78** Grafton to Carteret, 2 Apr. 1724 (P.R.O., S.P., 63/383/133). A list of correspondents with the exiled court from 1700 included his name; O'Donoghue, 'Jacobite threat', p. 154.   **79** Grafton to Carteret, 2 Apr. 1724 (P.R.O., S.P., 63/383/134); Petition of Knightley Chetwood, 29 Nov. 1723 (P.R.O., S.P., 63/383/135). A copy of the Jacobite ballad 'Nero II' was found

Jacobites, Sir Charles Wogan and his brother Nicholas, including a typically cryptic 'mercantilist' Jacobite message which Glascock dismissed as an apolitical reference to dealings with the Mississippi Company.[80] The authorities charged Glascock with high treason and committed him to Newgate for possessing three letters from Sir Charles. No information has survived regarding the exact nature of Glascock's activities and he successfully petitioned for bail.[81] His association with the Jacobite plotter Christopher Layer is suggested by intercepted Jacobite correspondence left at Glascock's house on Arran Quay, Dublin, and by a further communication to Robert Dillon at his house in Latus Court, London.[82] King confirmed his knowledge of Glascock activities and asserted that he had seen the original letters which he considered 'very foolish if not downright treasonable'.[83]

Layer's association with the shadowy Jacobite plot, contemporaneous with another related Jacobite scheme which derived its name from Francis Atterbury, bishop of Rochester. It reminded the Protestant oligarchy and the reading public of the capacity of their Irish papist counterparts for traitorous intrigue. More importantly, they show that Irish Jacobites were not totally oblivious to the machinations of Jacobite high-politics.[84] Atterbury's arrest became a *cause célèbre* in the Dublin press and resulted in the apprehension of vagrants and street-hawkers who circulated seditious ballads about the incarcerated bishop.[85] In

in Chetwood's pocket-book; O'Donoghue, 'Jacobite threat', p. 141. **80** The examination of John Burke of the city of Dublin, gentleman, July 1722 (N.L.I., Ms 9611, fol. 56). This is obviously the John Bourke, 'an attorney' from Ireland, who was arrested on his way to Paris to see some of his clients, discharged and re-arrested as a result of the contents of a letter from Francis Glascock, 2 Aug. 1723, *Appendixes referred to in the report from the committee*, p. 41. See also N.L.I., Ms 9611, fol. 58; P.R.O., S.P., 63/380/106; T.C.D., Ms 750/7, fols 227-8; T.C.D., Ms 750/7, fol. 243; D'Arcy, 'Exiles and strangers', pp 171-85; Flood, *Wogan*, pp 21, 99. During his trial George Kelly told the court that his many trips to France related to his dealings in Mississippi stock; *Memoirs of the life, times and transactions of Rev George Kelly*, p. 3. **81** Lords justice to Carteret, 17 Sept. 1722 (P.R.O., S.P., 63/380/117). See also P.R.O., S.P., 63/380/123, 125. **82** Copies of Jacobite letters connected with Layer's conspiracy, 18 Aug. 1722, 7 Sept. 1722 (*H.M.C., 11th report, appendix iii, Jacobite papers and letters, 1703-27*, p. 191); B.L., Stowe Ms 250, fol. 34; *A report from the committee appointed by order of the House of Commons to examine Christopher Layer, Appendixes referred to in the report, papers relating to Ireland*; For sensationalist journalism regarding the 'Leare Plot', see *Dub. Cour.*, 1 Oct. 1722; *Undeniable reasons for suspending the Habeas Corpus Act 10, November 1722*. Layer was associated with Lord North and the Atterbury Plot; Cruickshanks, 'Lord North, Christopher Layer and the Atterbury Plot', pp 92-106; Cruickshanks and Erskine-Hill (ed.), *The Atterbury Plot* (forthcoming). **83** King to Annesley, 8 Oct. 1722 (T.C.D., Ms 750/7, fols 227-8). See also ibid., fol. 243. **84** King to G. George, 16 Feb. 1722; T.C.D., Ms 750/7, fol. 305. See also T.C.D., Ms 750/7, fols 316-6. Treason charges were brought against Augustine Nugent in 1722; *H.M.C., 2nd report, papers of the Rt. Hon. the earl of Granard*, p. 235. Ó Buachalla charts the involvement of the Galwayman Rev George Kelly and the Roscommon man Captain Dennis Kelly in the Atterbury Plot; Ó Buachalla, *Aisling Ghéar*, p. 330. **85** 'This town is in great ferment about sending the bishop of Rochester to the tower'; King to William Wake, archbishop of Canterbury, 28 Aug., 1722 (T.C.D., Ms 750/7, fol. 200). See also Sherry, 'Press coverage of two political trials in the 1720s', p. 148. Christopher Layer's associated plot, and in particular the involvement of the Rev George Kelly and rumours of General Dillon's role in the forthcoming invasion, featured prominently in Dublin press; ibid., pp 143-57. Allusions to the

March 1722 *Whalley's Newsletter* reported that 'Mr Fitzgerald, who kept a
printing-house in Mountrath Street, was bound to appear at the quarter-sessions
for printing and selling a seditious ballad for which two men who were singing
it with roguish intent are now in Newgate'.[86]

Dismissing any possibility of a Jacobite landing, King focused on the earl of
Orrery's arrest for his part in Atterbury's activities. Although mindful of the
'many thousand trained men who would return from foreign service' and the
'many others who would list themselves if they had any head to draw to', he
discounted the feasibility of such an invasion as 'no foreign power had countenanced this conspiracy'.[87] Swift also considered Orrery's involvement in the
plot in a letter to the former Tory and Jacobite suspect Robert Cope of 9
October 1722. He ridiculed the new 'brazen' equestrian statue of George I on
Essex Bridge before turning to the plight of his friend Orrery, expressing the
hope that 'my brother Orrery has loved his land too much to hazard it on
revolution principle'.[88] A deposition regarding seditious words spoken by
Edward Gillet, mayor of Youghal, County Cork, suggests that Orrery's influence
was not exclusively confined to English Jacobite high-politics. Gillet dismissed
the plot as a Presbyterian design or a contrivance of the king to get money from
parliament.[89]

King discussed the recurrent recruitment problem and the refusal of Protestants and zealous Whig juries to return guilty verdicts. He questioned the
integrity of the witnesses, compared the trials to the popish plot in the reign of
Charles II:

> The vermin commonly called Wild Geese, I mean persons listed for the
> pretender, gives us infinite troubles and yet the Irish evidences who
> inform against them are much more vexatious. You have heard of the

Atterbury plot, and in particular the role of General Dillon and Kelly in contemporary Jacobite
intrigue also featured in the Dublin press; *Cato's vision; Cato's letter to the bishop of Rochester.*   **86**
Quoted in Phillips, *Printing and book-selling in Dublin*, p. 55. Seditious ballads were also common in
contemporary popular England; Monod, *Jacobitism*, pp 8, 46.   **87** King to Hopkins, 10 July 1722
(T.C.D., 750/7, fols 153-5). The popular press also noted Orrery's involvement with Layer, George
Kelly and Ormonde; *Carson's intelligence*, 16 Mar. 1723; *Harding's Imp. N.*, 23 Mar. 1723; 30 Mar. 1723;
Hume's. Cour., 3 Apr. 1723. Among the papers of the earl of Orrery in Harvard, there is a derogatory
indictment of the crowned heads of Europe, 'the savage monsters crowned with vice polluting every
throne, I mean all kings except our own'. When one considers that George I kept two mistresses,
the king excepted from these vices could be James III; 'Verses by Dean Swift which ought to have
been in the Rhapsody if it had been safe to print them' (Harvard Eng. Ms. 218.2, ii, fol. 115, N.L.I.,
mf. p. 786). The final published version of Swift's *Rhapsody* contained a number of equally suspect
lines: 'Fair Britain in thy monarch blest/Whose virtues bear the strictest test'; Swift; *On Poetry: a
rhapsody*, line 415.   **88** Swift to R. Cope, 9 Oct. 1722, in Williams (ed.), *Correspondence*, ii, pp 434-
5. Robert Cope, Tory M.P. Loughgall, County Armagh, had been arrested in 1715 as a suspected
Jacobite; Higgins, *Swift's politics*, p. 151. See also Simms, 'Dean Swift and Armagh', pp 131-41.   **89**
'Examination of Penny Mills', 2 Aug. 1722 (P.R.O., S.P., 67/7/138); 'Information of Charles Ray', 10
Aug. 1722 (P.R.O., S.P., 67/7/139). Orrery's family had a long association with Youghal; Barnard,

popish plot in King Charles II's time and what work the Irish evidences did then but those were saints and sages to some of those who now appear.[90]

He also commented on a widely-held Catholic belief 'which greatly pleases them and on which they depend for certain' of the French king's coronation obligation 'to extirpate all heresies' and 'declare for the Pretender as the most effectual means to destroy the Northern heresies'.[91]

These rumours were not exclusively confined to official government correspondence or the Protestant press. Owen Daly, a captured recruiter who turned king's evidence accused senior Catholics in south Munster of Jacobite trafficking. This underlined the continuing dangers facing the surviving Catholic aristocracy and gentry, Protestant converts and the residual Tory interest in times of political adversity. Daly alluded to trafficking between Ireland and England, and the exchange of sizeable sums of money as well as making references to Ormonde and James III. These depositions also contained evidence of disguised visits and clandestine political trafficking with several prominent Catholics. Those whom he implicated had already incurred government suspicion and their political loyalties were in question. The toasts and treasonable words attributed to these magnates contained allusions which are replicated in contemporary Irish poetry, in official sources, and in the seditious toasts which are recorded in contemporary English Jacobite circles. Daly, for example, accused O'Sullivan More (Ó Súilleabháin Mór) of recruiting men for the service of the Pretender under the name of James III, promising recruits that he would soon make a descent on Britain to dethrone King George and that the force which was to come would bring arms with them. He drank the health of James III and damnation to his Hanoverian adversary.[92]

The information against McCarthy More (Mac Cárthaigh Mór) is even more compelling and refers to letters sent by him to Sir Peter Sherlock, already implicated in Spanish recruitment, and to Sir Toby Bourke of Bilbao, one of the most influential Irish Jacobites in Spain 'who would soon come back with the Pretender to dethrone King George'.[93] Daly also alleged that Sir Thomas Crosbie used the pretence of going to fight the Moors to enlist men for the foreign service; he referred to 'the Pretender' as King James III and promised

'Youghal and the Boyles', pp 1-5. **90** King to Southwell, 22 Dec. 1722 (T.C.D., 750/7, fol. 264). One of his correspondents, William Linegar, underlined the king's initial unwillingness to issue a general pardon to the Wild Geese; W. Linegar to King, 13 Sept. 1722 (T.C.D., Ms 1995-2008, fols 2015-16). **91** King to Hopkins, 6 Nov. 1722 (T.C.D., Ms 750/7, fols 232-5). See also P.R.O., S.P., 67/7/134). The existence of a 'popish' plot occasioned a proclamation in the *London Gazette* which was also printed in its Irish counterpart; *Dub. Cour.*, 3 Nov. 1722; *Fau. P.*, Nov. 1722. **92** Information of Owen Daly against Mr. O'Sullivan More (Mór), 9 Oct. 1722 (P.R.O., S.P., 67/7/133). **93** Information of Owen Daly against Mr. McCarthy More (Mór), 9 Oct. 1722 (P.R.O., S.P., 67/7/133); Marquis Mc Sweeny, 'Sir Toby Bourke and Dr J. Higgins'; M. Walsh, 'Sir Toby Bourke,

conscripts that they would return in August to dethrone King George. Sir Thomas stated that the Protestants and the Romans would by this time have joined together to bring James III home.[94]

Daly linked Sir Thomas Fitzgerald, Knight of Glin, to the Quaker Nathaniel Hay who had been executed for his part in this illicit trade with Spain. In conjunction with references to a possible massacre in England, a Spanish plot and the groundswell of support for the Pretender in Britain and Ireland, Fitzgerald reputedly reiterated popular Catholic hopes that the king of Spain and the young French king, when crowned, would assist the Pretender.[95] Daly also accused Valentine Brown (third Viscount Kenmare) of promising that those who went to Spain would return with the Pretender before August and bring arms for many more. Kenmare allegedly said that 'now was the time to give a helping hand to the business'; 'many persons of great worth in England supported him [James III]' and also he referred to the sum of £2,500 and a letter for the attainted Ormonde.[96] It is no surprise that the major landed Catholic figures mentioned in these depositions were patrons of the most important Munster Jacobite poets of the period. Cormac Spáinneach Mac Cárthaigh patronised Seán na Ráithíneach Ó Murchú, Valentine Browne and Mac Cárthaigh Mór extended their largesse to Aogán Ó Rathaille Ó Murchú, while Ó Súilleabháin Mór funded the literary endeavours of Diarmaid Ó Súilleabháin.[97]

Thomas Biggs, an Irish friar who had come from Louvain to renounce the Catholic religion, suggested that economic considerations also motivated this recruitment. He had met two Irish Brigade officers, Sir John Hurly (Hurley) of Berwick's Regiment and Bernard O'Calachan (O'Callaghan) of Dorrington's on his return from the continent. They had been recruiting in County Cork for the Irish Brigades, and 'both knowing me for a friar and thinking me designed for the mission, made no scruple of opening their minds'. They informed him that 'they ran the risk of being taken but sent one hundred and thirty men from Cork': October and November was the best time for transporting recruits, the wine trade provided a useful decoy, and that 'many Irish farmers lived by what they were allowed from abroad for deluding young fellows to the foreign service'.[98]

politician and diplomat', pp 143-55.   **94** Information of Owen Daly against Thomas Crosbie, 9 Oct. 1722 (P.R.O., S.P., 67/7/134).   **95** Information of Owen Daly against Mr Fitzgerald, 9 Oct. 1722 (P.R.O., S.P., 67/7/134); *Whalley's N.*, 9 Apr. 1722.   **96** Information of Owen Daly against Lord Kenmare, 9 Oct. 1722 (P.R.O., S.P., 67/7/133-4). Browne's name was included on a list of persons who had a cipher accorded to them in the Stuart papers; Fagan (ed.), *Stuart papers*, i, p. 64. Lord Carteret suggested that the Dalys were disreputable witnesses; P.R.O., S.P. 67/7/141. See also T.C.D., Ms 750/7, fols 246-9, 253, 264-5, 269-72; P.R.O., S.P., 63/384/36. Ó Buachalla provides the most recent overview of such recruitment depositions; Ó Buachalla, 'Irish Jacobitism in official documents', pp 128-38.   **97** Ó Buachalla, *Aisling Ghéar*, p. 343.   **98** Delafaye to Hopkins, 6 June 1723 (P.R.O., S.P., 67/7/147). The previous year an unnamed Catholic priest who turned king's evidence also promised to impeach a number of prominent Catholic gentlemen; *Dub. Cour.*, 27 Oct.

The activity of these 'farmers', utilising their local reputations and the standard of the exiled king to recruit impressionable young men into the Irish Brigades, shows the continued social prestige of the surviving Catholic aristocracy and gentry. It also suggests a widespread deference towards the Stuarts among the greater Catholic community in many parts of the country. Although continually dismissive of the capacity of Catholics to lend assistance to their exiled king, King never doubted their willingness to do so. Indeed his comparison of the Irish Catholic gentry with the English Cavaliers provides a good insight into the nature of Stuart Royalism in the respective kingdoms. Both were clandestine political ideologies which were powerless to oppose the superior forces of the state and were therefore ultimately dependent on external intervention or an internal Protestant *coup d'état*.[99]

King spoke of the 'infinite trouble with persons listed for the Pretender' and expressed the certainty that 'several thousand have been spirited away to Spain by this argument'. They would be 'entertained in his service and when they are trained to arms, they will return with their king at their head to invade England'. He was under no illusion that when given the opportunity they would 'answer the ends of their enlisting'. He questioned the policy of 'suffering so many desperate fellows to be trained with arms in their hands of whom we are assured that upon any breach they would be ready to attack us and be more dangerous than thrice as many foreigners because they are acquainted to the country and accustomed to the climate'. He concluded that 'King William was a wise man who upon the peace of Ryswick [1697] stipulated that the Irish battalions in the French service should be broke'.[100] He also noted that there was a contemporary dimension to recruiting. The ban on allowing poor tenants to enlist for the foreign service meant that 'the strong turn robbers and rapparees and the weak beg. As a proof of this the streets and all places are crowded with beggars and the jails with malefactors'.[101] Swift's caustic satire *A modest proposal* also made the link between poverty, recruitment, Spain and 'the Pretender':

> The mothers instead of being able to work for their livelihood are forced to employ all their time in strolling to beg sustenance for their helpless infants, who as they grow, end up either turning thieves for want of work or leave their dear country to fight for the Pretender in Spain or sell themselves to the Barbadoes.[102]

The stream of recruits to join their brethren in the Irish regiments of France and Spain offset Catholic military impotence at home. King harped on about

1722.   **99** King to Grafton, 6 Nov. 1722 (T.C.D., Ms 750/7, fols 230-1).   **100** King to General George, 8 Jan. 1723 (T.C.D., Ms 750/7, fol. 274). See also *H.M.C., Polwarth*, iii, p. 225.   **101** King to General George, 6 Apr. 1723 (T.C.D., Ms 750/7, fols 331-2). See also T.C.D., Ms 2537, fols 81-2; T.C.D., Ms 750/7, fols 337-9, 340-42.   **102** Swift, *Works*, iv, p. 341. For reference to recruitment in

the dangers of allowing so many Irish enemies to be trained in arms and the certainty of their willingness to return with their king at their head.

Contemporary high-political Jacobite activity provided a context for recruitment in the early 1720s. Similarly, the threatened imposition of penal legislation was linked to the fallout from the 'Atterbury Plot' and the alleged links between Jacobitism and Catholicism. A letter from Giuseppe Spinelli, abbott of Saint Caterina, to Cardinal Agnese in November 1723 shows that news had reached the continent that the Irish Catholics again faced the prospect of a rigorous imposition of the penal laws. Spinelli attributed this to their refusal to abjure the Stuart king. He spoke of the pope's sorrow at the recent decision by the Irish parliament to banish all those priests who refused to take the oath 'against the Catholic religion and King James'. He deemed this to be a blatant violation of the Treaty of Limerick which made conditions 'worse than in Cromwell's time'.[103] This refusal to subscribe to the Oath of Abjuration provided a vital material link between Catholicism and Jacobitism. At this time, allegations of clerical complicity in recruitment constantly featured in contemporary government correspondence: 'the vast swarms of Romish priests who infest the kingdom are continually negotiating against the government, particularly in listing men for the foreign service, in which they have exerted their influence'.[104]

In spite of the dangers, Irish Catholics maintained direct links with the continent and their exiled king, with much of the correspondence pertaining to James III's exclusive right to nominate the Catholic hierarchy. This emphasised his pivotal role in ecclesiastical and political life, and his prominent place in the Irish political consciousness. He laid particular emphasis on the wishes of the clergy and laity when making his choice, and the smoothness and efficiency of episcopal appointments in the eighteenth century depended on the Stuart king:

> Indeed were it not for these Stuart kings in exile, the appointment of Irish bishops during the eighteenth century would not have taken place so smoothly and so efficiently. It is due to them in great part, that the persecuted Catholics of Ireland had a sufficient number of bishops to strengthen and guide them when consolation and encouragement were so directly needed.[105]

---

contemporary London, see 'Deposition of John Cunningham, 28 June 1723 (P.R.O., S.P., 63/385/249). **103** Spinelli to Cardinal Agnese, 26 Nov. 1723; Giblin (ed.), 'Catalogue', part 4, vols 102-22, pp 109, 114-15.   **104** Grafton to Carteret, 15 Nov. 1723 (P.R.O., S.P., 63/382/16). 'On Wednesday last several prisoners were apprehended by some of the king's officers on suspicion of being concerned in a gang many of whom 'tis reported are going off for the Pretender or other foreign service ... 'tis said there was among them two clergyman of the church of Rome'; *Dub. I.*, 15 Oct. 1726.   **105** Giblin, 'The Stuart nomination of bishops', pp 35-47. There are other examples of Irish episcopal recourse to the king [James III] in this period; R.A., Ms 86, fol. 5; Ó Buachalla, *Aisling Ghéar*, p. 216; Irwin, review of Fagan (ed.), *Stuart papers*, p. 477. Irish Whigs believed that popery and Jacobitism constituted 'their greatest and most implacable

Moreover, his influence over the Irish Catholic episcopate, and his insistence on the presentation of postulations in favour of episcopal candidates signed by the clergy and laity of their respective diocese, enhanced his pivotal role in Irish ecclesiastical and secular politics in the first half of the eighteenth century. The cryptic nature of Bishop Ambrose O'Callaghan's communications to James III's secretary in 1724, including his references to 'the patron's [King James III's] kindness', 'your house' (Ireland) and 'the farms' (diocese) of Dublin and Kildare showed the dangers of such intercourse. The allusion to additional oral data to be supplied by the messenger has tantalising implications for the diffusion of information between Ireland, its diaspora and the Stuart court.[106]

The practical and psychological effects of the penal laws also had a popular dimension. An incident in Magherafelt, County Derry, illustrates the extent to which apparently innocuous manifestations of religious devotion (the raising of money at wells and mass-houses) and the activities of itinerant preachers were perceived to provide a cover for extensive Spanish recruitment. They also served to buoy up Catholic expectations which were purportedly unprecedented since James II's reign:

> Some time since when great numbers were inlisted in this kingdom for the service of the Pretender and sent into Spain, most of those who engaged were not only influenced but even actually enlisted by popish priests. One of which was executed for treason had an ample testimonial of his merits for their zeal on this occasion from one of their titular bishops or his vicar-general and another of them who made his escape and against whom a proclamation issued appeared to have been an itinerant preacher under different names in most parts of the country and to have listed men, marched them through the country as their officer and to have billeted them on popish houses in this way. [107]

The official reaction typified the Protestant attitude towards popular Catholic worship, the potential in these large religious gatherings for civil unrest and the continued links between Catholicism, recruitment and Jacobitism.

William Smith, an itinerant Catholic priest, had allegedly drawn crowds of 2-3,000 people, and considerable public notoriety, when he ministered in the open fields of Kerry, Limerick, Meath, Tyrone and Derry. Two hundred people armed with staves and stones pursued six or seven men at arms who assisted in

enemies', quoted in Ó Buachalla, *Aisling Ghéar*, p. 217.　**106** O'Callaghan to Col. Hay, 22 Feb. 1724 (R.A., Ms 80, fol. 73); Fagan (ed) *Stuart papers*, i, pp 50-1; 100-101. For other cryptic correspondence and the dangers involved, see R.A., Ms 169, fol. 21; R.A., Ms 178, fols 147, 170; de Breffny, 'Letters from Connacht to a Wild Goose', pp 81, 82, 91; Fagan (ed.), *Stuart papers*, i, pp 44, 100, 128, 129, 159, 165, 184, 276, 285; ii, pp 4, 51.　**107** 'Thomas Morlay to Hove, 17 Apr. 1725 (P.R.O., S.P., 63/385/199). See also P.R.O., S.P., 63/385/176-85; N.L.I., Ms 9612, fols 48-80; Larkin (ed.), 'Popish

the attempted execution of a warrant against Smith. He was accused of preaching sedition and rebellion. His virulently anti-Protestant sentiments mirrored seventeenth and eighteenth-century Royalist and Jacobite poetry and prose. Smith regularly discoursed on Calvin, Luther and Satan, claiming, among other things, that the devil attended Calvin and Luther at their bedsides. He claimed that those who were not of the Roman Catholic church were heretics. Tracing the woes of Irish Catholics from the reign of Henry VIII (who founded the Protestant religion), his daughter Elizabeth (who established it) and James VI and I (who confirmed it),[108] he vented particular spleen upon Non-Conformists, Presbyterians and Quakers whom he considered 'to be in the possession of the devil'. Having issued the call to arms for religion, accompanied with the promise of eternal reward, Smith reminded his listeners of the sufferings of Oliver Plunkett, the martyred archbishop of Armagh, the loss of Catholic abbeys, benefices and monasteries, and of the absurdity of expecting alms from heretics. He also hoped that the Roman church would again be a glorious church restored to all former dignatories, abbeys and monasteries.[109]

Walter Bell repeated many of these accusations against Smith. He laid special emphasis on Smith's assertion 'that the Romans were depressed and obliged to 'go to ditches and glens to celebrate mass and the fact that the Church of Rome was so much under in the twelve [*sic.*] counties of Ulster'.[110] The priest promised that if they (Catholics) shed their blood for the church they would go to heaven and 'the sectaries would not be a mote before them'.[111] Smith's seditious message apparently reverberated through the country from Limerick to Derry and provided grist to the mill of Protestant unease. Not only did Catholic men and women frustrate twelve armed men who attempted to arrest him, but Lord Lieutenant Carteret believed that they showed an 'insolence' unprecedented since the days of James II:

> I am concerned the papists are so uppish and barefacedly insolent, preaching up sedition and blasphemy, making collections, raising money at mass places that the softest construction the most intelligent here can put on it is that the papists design once more (if they can find an O'Neill to head them) to play over the same? 41.[112]

riot in South Derry', pp 97-110.   **108** Lecky noted the activities of Bourke, a native of Connaught, who had appeared in Kerry and preached to crowds of over two or three thousand people; Lecky, *Irel.*, i, p. 256.   **109** Deposition of William Ussher, 5 Apr. 1725 (N.L.I., Ms 9612, fol. 55). See also ibid., fols 58, 59, 63, 64, 65, 69, 71, 72.   **110** Deposition of Walter Bell, 5 Apr. 1725 (N.L.I., Ms 9612, fol. 60). This questions the tendency to dismiss the cameo of the mass-rock and the hunted priest as a figment of nineteenth-century nationalist imagination. The historiography of the penal laws is treated in the introduction.   **111** Deposition of Walter Bell, 5 Apr. 1725 (N.L.I., Ms 9612, fol. 60). See also O'Donoghue, 'Jacobite threat', p. 101.   **112** Lord Carteret to Delafaye, 22 June 1725 (N.L.I., Ms 9612, fols. 48); Deposition of Thomas Newe, 5 May 1725 (N.L.I., 9612, fol. 50) See also ibid., fols pp 49-80. At the same time, Edward Nicholson, Church of Ireland bishop of Derry, maintained that 'the

Smith was pilloried, whipped and branded with a B, but Catholics flocked to visit the jailed priest and gave him money.[113]

A contemporary poet expressed similar sentiments to Smith. He asked how long will the fanatics be tearing down churches? how long will they be haunting the hills with short swords? how long will our monasteries be denuded and roofless? how long will our masses be held under the branches of trees?

> An fada bheid na fanatics ag réabadh ceall?
> An fada bheid ag seasamh cnoic le faobhar lann?
> An fada bheid ár mainistreacha maol gan ceann?
> An fada bheid ár n-aifrinn fé ghéagaibh crann?[114]

Contemporary Irish poetry showed a particular concern for the religious question. The repeal of the penal code and the punishment of Protestants were continually associated with a Stuart restoration. Domhnall Ó Súilleabháin pledged that Luther's crew would be destroyed ('In éinfheacht, beidh léir-scrios ar aicme Liútair').[115] Piaras Mac Gearailt promised that Charles and his armed fleet were coming across the sea with help to save us and that Luther's clan would be forgiven nothing ('Tá Carolus 's a lannsa 's a chobhlach gléasta/Ag tarraingt thar abhainn le cabhair d'ár saoradh/Is ní mhaithfidh súd bonn do chlann Liutaerius').[116] His contemporary Aindrias Mac Craith guaranteed that the true church will regain its churches ('Beidh a gcealla ag an eaglais fhíre').[117] In another verse he expressed the belief that Calvin's gang would be in trouble ('Do gcuirfeadh sliocht Chailbhin i bponc') in the event of a Stuart restoration.[118] In a poem composed on the outbreak of The War of Jenkins's Ear (1739), he prophesised that on the arrival of an invasion force from the west, the psalm of the dead will be sung on Tara without any emphasis on the [Protestant] minister. ('Beidh psailm na marbh á dTeamhair dá gcanadh 's gan beam ar mhinisdir').[119] Later, during the 'Forty-five', Tadhg Gaelach Ó Súilleabháin assured his audience that Protestant rubbish would be under pressure ('a bhrúghfas an brúscar san Liútar is Sheáin').[120]

present insolence of our popish clergy is unspeakable'. In spite of the Oath of Abjuration, he claimed that four or five masses has been said in his diocese over the corpse of an executed rapparee, 'whose funeral rites were celebrated with as pompous and numerous attendance as if a man had been knight of the shire', quoted in Donnelly, *Ardstraw West*, p. 68. Lecky noted that 'great numbers flocked to see an imprisoned priest called Neal Boyle in Galway Gaol and some had offered as much as one thousand pounds to bail him'; Lecky, *Irel.*, i, p. 258.   **113** J. Parnell to Carteret, 24 Aug. 1725 (N.L.I., Ms 9612, fols 105-8).   **114** Anon., 'A fhir chalma san teangain sin na nGaedhal', in Ó Foghludha (eag.), *Míl na hÉigse*, p. 57.   **115** Diarmuid Ó Súilleabháin, 'Beidh radharc súl nach tinn liúm', in Ó Foghludha (eag.), *Cois na Ruachtaighe*, p. 49.   **116** Piaras Mac Gearailt, 'Duan na Saoirse' [A.D. 1758], in Ó Foghludha (eag.), *Amhráin Phiarais Mhic Gearailt*, p. 25.   **117** Aindrias Mac Craith, 'A Dhalta nár dalladh le dlaoithe' (A.D. 1746), in Ó Foghludha (eag.), *Éigse na Máighe*, p. 204.   **118** Aindrias Mac Craith, 'A bhile den fhuirinn nach gann', in Ó Foghludha (eag.), *Éigse na Máighe*, p. 174.   **119** Aindrias Mac Craith, 'Léir-ruathar Whiggonia', in O'Daly (eag.), *Poets and poetry* (1849), p. 78.   **120** Tadhg Gaelach, 'Cúrsa na Cléire' (A.D. 1745), in Ó Foghludha (eag.), *Tadhg Gaelach*, p. 109; These sentiments proliferate in Art Mac Cumhaigh's poetry which contains derogatory references

In Dublin, much sedition and mob violence remained clearly Jacobite in nature, particularly around celebrations of James III's birthday on 10 June. The continued observance of this most sacred of Jacobite festivals shows that Jacobitism was neither a formulaic convention in Irish poetry or a folkloric residue but a vibrant ideology. Disturbances in June 1724 culminated in the fatal beating of a Quaker and other loyalists who had incensed the Jacobite mob by wearing red roses. A riot ensued in which the Jacobites, festooned with white roses, gained the upper hand on their loyalist counterparts. The symbolic white rose worn by the Jacobite loyalists featured in the English Jacobite tradition, as did the catch-cry of 'Ormonde and the High-church'. The reference to the white woman on horseback echoed the allegorical 'aisling' tradition, reflecting a potent fusion of indigenous and external political symbolism. This exhibition of Jacobite counter-symbolism did not take place under a tree as in the classic 'aisling' tradition or in a monoglot Irish-speaking environment but on St Stephen's Green, in the heart of the capital. These well-to-do Jacobite loyalists could afford to wear white roses, their catch-cries were distinctively high church Protestant in tone and their ability to manipulate local vagrants and 'the mob' suggests an ideological cohesion in contemporary Dublin Jacobitism:

> On Wednesday night last, being that on which 'tis thought the Pretender was born a crowd of his friends met at St Stephen's Green, their usual place of rendezvous, on that night and eminently distinguished themselves by wearing white roses and almost murdering one poor loyal Quaker for carrying the ensign of the adverse party, being a red rose. 'Tis further reported that there was a sort of a procession around the green, a thing like a woman dressed in white on horseback appearing to be the chief person in the same. There was another skirmish besides that of the friends in which several heads were broken given and manfully received till at full length the white roseonians being more superior in numbers and having more vagrants appeared masters of the field. We hear that several of the eminent gentlemen who distinguished themselves on the Pretender's birth night in the mob at St Stephen's Green by breaking the loyalists, and roaring out 'High Church and Ormond', 'Down with King George' and 'Long live the Pretender' etc., and learning that some of their antagonists are about giving an account of their names and occupations have thought fit to set out on pilgrimage lest they should be taken out and made examples to the rest of their comrades.[121]

to Luther, Calvin, Henry VIII, and Anne 'Bullin'; Mac Cumhaigh, 'Tagra an dá Theampall', in Ó Fiaich (eag.), *Art Mac Cumhaigh*, p. 84. **121** *Dub. I.*, 13, 17 June 1724. The report in *Needham's Postman* claimed that the mob had 'fallen upon a Quaker and some others who were beaten so badly that their lives are despaired of'; *Need. P.*, 11 June 1724; *Dub. I.*, 13 June 1724. Riots between soldiers and the Dublin mob were a regular feature in contemporary Dublin; B.L., Add. Ms 47, 030 fol. 103;

Jacobitism also reared its head in other unlikely circles during this period. The obsessive long-term preoccupation with Jacobitism in the Protestant consciousness is exemplified by attempts to link it to the Wood's Half-pence controversy.[122] Marmaduke Coghill, judge of the prerogative courts, believed that 'nothing but the Pretender could create more unease in this kingdom than these half-pence'.[123] Primate Hugh Boulter feared that the universal dissatisfaction had generated unprecedented and unwanted intimacies between Whigs, Jacobites and papists. While this alarmism can be considered a political ploy to quell rising opposition to the half-pence, it indicated the stigma which Protestants attached to Jacobitism.[124]

The 'Half-pence' controversy provided a major theme in 'The extract of a letter from Dublin written to Dutton [General Arthur Dillon] by a person of credit and well versed in the state of his country for the farmer's [James III's] use'. It was written by Sylvester Lloyd (bishop of Killaloe, 1728-39 and later Ferns, 1739-44) and sought to make political capital from the Wood's Half-pence controversy by trying to interest the Stuart monarch in an Irish invasion. Travelling for most of the summer in the west of Ireland, Lloyd was heartened by the almost universal zeal for the Jacobite cause, and the readiness to assemble around the Stuart standard. Rosy with Jacobite optimism, his treatise also reflected mounting hopes in high-political Jacobite circles, and provided corroborative evidence for the buoyancy in Irish Jacobite literature.[125] Lloyd examined the structure of the Irish Jacobite community and identified three main support groups. The first of these had remained unwaveringly loyal to King James:

> The first are infinitely the greatest number and such as you may entirely depend on if you will give me leave to except some few, perhaps not absolutely in the whole, whose possessions are the right of some persons

P.R.O., S.P., 63/387/ 208; Fagan, 'Dublin Catholic mob', pp 133-42; Monod, *Jacobitism*, p. 210. Quakers had become the whipping-boys of Irish Jacobitism since the execution of Cotter. **122** In the early 1720s, the scarcity of small specie prompted the British ministry to grant George I's mistress, the duchess of Kendal, a patent to issue a large quantity of copper coins which she sold to an ironmaster called William Wood. **123** Marmaduke Coghill to Southwell, 18 Aug. 1724 (B.L., Add. Ms 21, 122, fol. 15). Earlier, in 1721 the economic slump known as the South Sea Bubble also resulted in open hostility to King George's government. King had lamented that 'few will even drink the king's health'; T.C.D., Ms 750/6, fols 209-11; T.C.D., Ms 750 /7, fol. 338. Hostility towards the directors infused the Dublin press. For example, *Jack Ketch*, a pamphlet published in Dublin suggested that the directors of the South Sea were fellows 'so swollen with guilt that poor Derwentwater and Kenmure [two Jacobite leaders executed after the 'Fifteen'] his last two customers were babes and petty larceners to them'; *Jack Ketch. His letter to the directors of the South Sea*, p. 4. 'Jack Ketch' had been earlier used as a pseudonym by John Price for the publication of his *A hue and cry after the Pretender*. **124** Boulter to Annesley, 19 Jan. 1725 (P.R.O., S.P., 63/385/15) Attempts were also made to lumber 'The Drapier' with the stigma of Jacobitism; P.R.O., S.P., 63/385/1. In this period Boulter feared the possibility of Jacobite dissent in Trinity College; P.R.O., S.P., 63/385/61. **125** Extract of a letter from Dublin written to Dutton ... 15 Jan. 1725 (R.A., Ms 79 fol. 50). See also Fagan (ed.), *Stuart papers*,

in your circumstances, and whose avarice stifles the sentiments of virtue,
but they are of such mean character, that they are worth nobody's while
to mind them.

The second group, comprised of Protestant converts, had temporarily deserted
the king's cause for reasons of political expediency:

> As to the second class of men who have changed their way of thinking,
> they are numerous and of the most powerful in the kingdom. A great
> deal is to be expected from them and I dare confidently say that all are
> rather willinger to serve you than any of those mentioned in the first class
> and is certainly more in their power to do so, being men of fortune,
> qualified by the laws to possess what implements may be necessary for
> you [ie. guns/horses], as they are old natives that still retain the affections
> of the people. I can firmly assure you from my own knowledge of several
> amongst them they are more impatient than any to see you; the consci-
> ousness of their faylure, together with the impossibility as the case now
> stands of retrieving it otherwise than by supporting your claim, adds a
> spur to their friendship and makes them more earnest than ever to serve
> you.[126]

Other Jacobite commentators shared these views. Recent examinations of this
particular interest group have similarly emphasised their distinctiveness from
the existing political regime.[127] As a result, converts remained a constant source
of suspicion among orthodox Protestants.

Finally the third group identified by Lloyd were those whose Jacobitism was
essentially opportunistic, due to their dissatisfaction with government policy,
particularly regarding Wood's Half-pence. It contained several persons of
honour 'at the head of whom I would place the old earl [John Bourke, ninth earl
of Clanrickarde] who continued always very steadfast to you and will remain
your friend to his dying day'. The more fickle political interest within their ranks
may have been influenced by such anti-government literature as Swift's *Drapiers
letters*. Lloyd viewed them as a mixed blessing for the Jacobite cause. While their
boisterousness helped confidence, their lack of caution brought the wrath of
government on their devoted brethren:

---

i, p 49.   **126** Extract of a letter from Dublin written to Dutton … 15 Jan. 1725 (R.A., Ms 79, fol. 50);
Also see Fagan (ed.), *Stuart papers*, i, p. 49; Synge, *A sermon preached at St Andrew's on 23 October 1725*,
p. 65; Hutchinson, *Advice concerning the manner of receiving popish converts*, p. 3. Evans, the Church
of Ireland bishop of Meath, suggested that 'these pretended converts are the great darlings of the
disaffected party [that is, Catholics and Jacobites], their political notions are entirely with them';
quoted in Hayton, 'Ireland and the English ministers', p. 27.   **127** Cullen, *Emergence of modern
Ireland*, pp 195-6; Power, 'Converts', p. 124; Hayton, review of Whelan and Power (ed.), *Endurance*

These are men of interest, capable to lead a great part of the multitude. The rest are guided by hopes of having better interest from you in point of trade, which they all follow. They are very zealous to drink your health and indiscreet to babble a great deal, which though useful in some measure to keep up spirits, yet certainly does more hurt than good, for by this indiscretion they alarm your enemies and give handles by their folly for oppressing your real friends and making new rules to disable them from ever serving you. Though I should not advise to depend on the humour of the latter sort, animated at present against Wood's coin, if not set to work in such a temper yet there will remain a twain not to be despised.[128]

James's only opposition would come from those who had received 'illegal fortunes' [during the revolution of 1688] which they were sure to lose if you gain the lawsuit'. His disdain for this group occasioned recourse to the favoured Jacobite concept of 'legitimacy', and derogatory references to these persons of 'low' and 'mean' character. At the same time, the Protestant Jacobite, Lord Orrery, emphasised the need to create a diversion in Ireland, as a necessary precursor to a successful invasion of either of the other two kingdoms. Although aware of the military impotence of the Jacobite community in Ireland, he believed that they would eagerly embrace rebellion if furnished with officers, men and money; an opinion shared by many of his predecessors and compeers, and constantly reiterated by his Whig counterparts.[129]

In February 1726 Lloyd repeated his main themes in another lengthy memoir on the state of the Irish Jacobite community despatched to Colonel Daniel O'Brien, a leading luminary among the expatriate Irish Jacobites. He supplied details of the numerical strength of the Hanoverian army ('twelve thousand effective men, all on the Irish establishment – though not all at this time in the kingdom').[130] He also questioned the prospective loyalty of the Royal Scotch regiment 'commonly called Orkneys who are, to a man, officers and soldiers, the king's friends and have been therefore quartered and continued in Ireland since

and emergence, p. 450; Murphy, *Killaloe*, p. 62; Power, *Tipperary*, pp 82-4; James, *Ireland in the empire*, p. 179; Simms, 'Connaught in the eighteenth century', pp 129-30; Leighton, *Catholicism*, pp 7-8; Smyth, *Men of no property*, p. 13.   **128** Extract of a letter from Dublin written to Dutton…, 15 Jan. 1725 (R.A., Ms 79, fol. 50); For an opposite view; T.C.D., Ms 750/8, fol. 13.   **129** Orrery to James III, 7 May 1725 (R.A., Ms 82, fol. 18). See also R.A., Ms 96, fol. 17; R.A., Ms 200, fol. 102; R.A., Ms 81, fol. 95; R.A., Ms 107, fol. 150. An invasion memoir presented to James III in 1737 by Daniel O'Carroll claims that he had impressed on Orrery the absolute necessity of a diversionary Jacobite operation in Ireland; R.A., Ms. 200, fol. 112. In a letter to Secretary Delafaye of 5 April 1724, Walter Shee proposed to give 'a perfect relation of the whole designs of the wicked intrigues which were carried on in Ireland in order to dethrone his majesty and place a popish Pretender in his stead'. It is unclear whether Shee was an adventurer or whether he had information regarding the machinations of Lloyd, Orrery or other Irish Jacobites; Shee to Delafaye, 5 Apr. 1724 (P.R.O., S.P. 35/49).   **130** Introduction, pp 29-30. The Irish establishment remained at twelve thousand until

the insurrection in Scotland' ('the Fifteen'). He re-stated his opinion that the bitter controversy surrounding Wood's Half-pence had encouraged defections to the Jacobite standard. Assured of the loyalty of the Catholic hierarchy and lower clergy to the Jacobite cause, he again earmarked the convert class as a potentially powerful Jacobite bulwark in Ireland:

> Their followers or clans, as being old natives, are vastly superior in numbers to the Old English Protestants as they are called, who are still looked upon as being strangers and aliens by the common people and they are demonstrable for that reason better able to serve the king than the English Protestants are, though their estates may be otherwise greater. This the government is so well convinced of and alarmed at that they have in the present session of parliament set a law on foot, which has already passed the House of Commons, to prevent as they term occasional conformity to papists and whereby they intend to disable all converts from the popish party to the Protestant religion from bearing any employments civil or military, from sitting in parliament or pleading at the bar 'til after seven years probation.[131]

His report stressed the greater wealth and interest enjoyed by this class, their prestigious status among the general populace, and the extent to which they were mistrusted by the government of the day. These suspicions help explain the optimism of a committed and ambitious Jacobite, eager to impress his stoical lord.[132] Although Lloyd can be accused of exaggerating the strength and extent of contemporary support, it should be remembered that the Jacobite ideology (like Royalism in post-revolutionary France or Russia) sustained itself on extravagant hopes. Lloyd deduced that 'his majesty's interest is not so low in Ireland but that a great deal may be expected from us in case his majesty's service may require it'. He believed that 'we should at least be able to employ 12,000 of the usurper's best troops which would be no small service while his friends have a push elsewhere'. Like many other Jacobite observers who had furnished the exile court with invasion plans, he advised that 'a few officers of good conduct be sent beforehand into the respective parts of the kingdom where they are natives', who would soon 'make a universal commotion and the king would soon find as many men as he had arms to give them'. Lloyd believed that 'nothing would be more easy than to surprise the Barracks and Castle of Dublin where there are ordinarily one regiment of horse and two of foot, and where there are arms and ammunition for several thousand of his majesty's friends'. The landing should be made in Waterford (the capital of his own diocese) which

---

1767; Bartlett and Jeffreys (ed.), *A military history of Ireland*, p. 216.   **131** Sylvester Lloyd to Daniel O'Brien, 4 Feb. 1726 (R.A., Ms 90, fol. 70); Fagan (ed.), *Stuart papers*, i, p. 65. See also R.A., Ms 99, fols 28-9; R.A., Ms 262, fol. 187; P.R.O., S.P., 63/409/58, 66.   **132** Sylvester Lloyd to Daniel O'Brien,

had a navigable river system (the Barrow, Nore and Suir), in close proximity to Bristol, the Jacobite heartland of Munster and the strategic citadel of Athlone.

In conclusion, he returned to the issue of Protestant participation in Jacobite rituals, and identified a number of Protestants, the residue of the old Ormondist Tory interest who retained an affection for the exiled Stuarts; 'they drink his [King James III's] health every day, and will, I'm sure, fight for him on occasion'. These included the earls of Anglesley and Granard, Thomas Vesey, bishop of Ossory and 'creature of Ormonde', (James Barry), the fifth earl of Barrymore, Sir Richard Cox, Peter Browne, bishop of Cork, Lord Charlemont, Sir Arthur Brownlow and Lords Athenry and Mayo.[133]

The covert survival of this Protestant Jacobite interest provides a context for the fate of Swift's friend, Thomas Sheridan. He was stripped of his chaplaincy for his use of an inappropriate theme ('sufficient unto the day is the evil thereof') in a sermon on the anniversary of the succession of George I.[134] Swift dismissed it as a proverbial slip of the tongue. However, Sheridan came from acknowledged Jacobite stock. He shared the company of suspected and known Jacobite sympathisers and Tory fellow-travellers, including the earl of Orrery, 'Robin' and 'Harry' Leslie, sons of Dr Charles Leslie, Alexander Pope, Thomas Carte and Peter Browne, Church of Ireland bishop of Cork. There may be Jacobite undertones in Sheridan's ciphered correspondence to Carte in which he asserted that 'we never fail to remember (14) and (17)'.[135] Swift later urged the embattled

---

4 Feb. 1726 (R.A., Ms 90, fol. 70). **133** For Granard's Jacobitism, see B.L., Add. Ms 20, 311 fol. 45; *H.M.C., Stuart*, vii, p. 87; Shield and Lang, *The king*, p. 232. Barrymore wrote a letter to James III from Paris; R.A., Ms 122, fol. 128; See also P.R.O., S.P., 63/406/151; B.L., Add. Ms 47, 004B, fol. 31. Accusations of Jacobite sedition were made against Cox; O'Donoghue, 'Jacobite threat', pp 36, 205, 212, 221. Daniel O'Carroll, in presenting an invasion memoir to James III in 1737, claimed that he had paid a visit to Ireland and called on Lords Mayo and Atherny; R.A., Ms, 200, fol. 112. Orrery's correspondence in Harvard has reference to the bishop of Cork as Orrery's and Pope's mutual friend in Cork; Orrery to Pope, 10 Aug. 1735 (Harvard Ms Eng. 218 2f vol. 7, fols 6, 8, 100, N.L.I., mf. p. 786). See also the Jacobite duke of Wharton's letter to Peter Browne, bishop of Cork; N.L.I., Crossle Ms 496, fol. 104. Browne had gained notoriety in the early-eighteenth century as a consequence of his pamphlet controversy with Edward Synge in relation to drinking the memory of King William III; Browne, *Of drinking the memory of the dead*; Browne, *A second part of drinking in remembrance of the dead*. For an edition of Lloyd's letter with biographical notes, Fagan, (ed.), *Stuart papers*, i, p. 70. Fagan has also drawn attention to another list of Irish ciphers from this period which he believed could be taken as Jacobite sympathisers or persons of interest at the Stuart court; 'Thomas Power esq., Lord Mayo, Lord Bermingham [Lord Atherny], Browne of Oneal [the Neale?], O'Maley, Fitzgerald, Sir Kary Linch Blake Esqr., Lord Trimbleston, Lord Carloton[?], Lord Bellew, Sir John Bellew, [?] Talbot Esqr., Lord Gormanston, Hussey Esq., Lord Netherfield, Esmond Baronet, Esmond esqr., Lord Montgomery, Sarsfield esqr., Stephen Copinger, esqr., Kenton esqr., Lord Kilmare [Kenmare], Col. Butler of Kilcash, Mathews esqr., of Anfield, Lord Ker, McMahon of County of Clare'. This list also includes the names of at least two other possible Protestant Jacobite sympathisers, Lord Mayo and Lord Bermingham; Fagan, (ed.), *Stuart papers*, i, p. 64. A biographical study of this group of individuals and their English and European links might shed light on the existence of obscure Jacobite networks. **134** Kelly, 'The glorious and immortal memory', p. 34. Connolly has noted another seditious sermon of this nature. In 1719, a clergyman in Kilkenny chose as the text of his sermon on the anniversary of George I's succession 'Thou shalt not set a stranger over

Sheridan 'to take the oaths to the powers that be and not to discover your disloyalty in the pulpit'.[136]

The links between disillusionment with Wood's patent, the survival of a Protestant Jacobite interest in the aftermath of the succession of George I and Swift's cautious advice to Sheridan may be reflected in the 'Verses by Dean Swift which ought to have been inserted in the Rhapsody if it had been safe to print them'. Jacobite sympathies evidently circulated through a literary circle which included Sheridan, Swift and Orrery. These individuals corresponded with such known Jacobites as Thomas Carte and the Oxford cleric William King. One of these verses 'Upon the omission of the "Dei Gratia" on Wood's Half-pence' drew on the age-old ideology of the divine right of kings to question the legitimacy of George I's reign:

> No Christian king that I can find
> However queer or odd
> Excepting ours has ever coined
> Without the grace of God.
> By this acknowledgment they show
> The mighty king of kings
> as whom from whom the riches flow
> from whom their grandeur springs.
> Come then Urania and my pen.
> The patent's cause assign
> all other kings are mortal men
> But George, 'tis plain 's divine.[137]

Swift's 'Drapier' even threatened that the Irish might have to turn to Jacobitism on account of Wood's Half-pence.[138] The Stuart king was continually assured of Swift's loyalty to his cause and received copies of *Gulliver's travels* from Michael McDonogh, Catholic bishop of Kilmore, as well as a copy of Swift's *Complete works* from Charles Wogan. These loyal subjects of the Stuart king assured him of Dean Swift's eagerness to see him and his zeal in satirising the government.[139] As

---

thee', quoted in Connolly, *Religion*, pp 241-2. **135** Sheridan to Carte, 28 Nov. 1732 (Bodl., Carte Ms 227, fol. 287). See also Bodl., Carte Ms 227, fols 47-8. Monod argued that Thomas Carte was James's 'principal liaison with the Tories in the 1730s and 1740s'; Monod, *Jacobitism*, p. 103. Cruickshanks has suggested that while Carte was held in high esteem, he was considered to be indiscreet. I would like to thank Dr Cruickshanks for bringing this to my notice. See also Higgins, *Swift's politics*, pp 8, 24. Lilliput was used in Jacobite circles to denote Hanover; *H.M.C., 10th report, appendix 1 and 2*, p. 479; Harvard, Eng. Ms 218 2f vol. 7, fols 6, 8 and 100, N.L.I., mf. p. 786. Thomas Carte asserted that he knew the 'D[ean] O[f] S[aint] P[atrick's]' very well and he is my friend'; *H.M.C., 10th report*, appendix 1 and 2, p. 485. **136** Swift to Sheridan, 11 Sept. 1725, in Williams (ed.), *Correspondence*, iii, p. 93. **137** 'Upon the omission of the Dei Grata on Wood's half-pence.' (Harvard, Ms 218.2, vol. 3, fol. 116, letters, essays, poems and other performances, [N.L.I., m.f. 786]); Swift, *On poetry: a rhapsody*. It is not clear whether these lines provide tantalising evidence of Swift's covert Jacobite sympathies or whether they were

late as 1738, Swift daringly praised (and hoped for the return of) Ormonde and he execrated Hanoverian tyranny. He later was pleased that the Irish Jacobite plotter, Rev George Kelly (later one of the seven men of Moidart, 'so valuable a company'), had become Ormonde's chaplain.[140]

The fears of the political establishment could also be fuelled at local level, as indicated by the examination of Edward O'Connor from the barony of Clanmaurice, County Kerry in October 1725. O'Connor bore all the hallmarks of a man eager to cash in on his sensational evidence. With access to confidential, high-level Jacobite intelligence, he identified a litany of prominent Jacobites including Sir Toby Bourke, Admiral Thomas Gordon, Sir Henry Stirling, Admiral Saunders, Robert Gordon, Francis Bulkeley, Rev George Kelly, William Walters, James and William Hore [Sir Henry Goring] in places as far afield as Madrid, Kronstadt, St Petersburg, Rotterdam and Bordeaux.[141]

His intelligence was taken seriously at the highest level of the Hanoverian establishment. Charles, second viscount Townshend interviewed O'Connor and conceded that he liked him 'better than I expected because I find he is plain in what he says and does not pretend to have more knowledge than he really has'. However, he cautioned against employing him 'in any place where he may be either a danger to himself or be liable to be sooner known to have made this discovery'. He warned against sending him back to Spain ''tho he should run no risk there for it was not expected by those who delivered the letters that he should carry them thither himself'. Townsend also informed Captain Deane 'that the king has signed a warrant for O'Connor's pardon but advised him [Deane] to keep it as it would be very wrong for him to have a paper about him'.[142] Townsend also requested the mobilisation of Sir Robert Walpole's spy-network to obtain copies of the correspondence of Waters, Hore and Gordon in France while 'his man' in Leiden attempted to intercept the letters of John Archdeacon and Creagh, merchants in Rotterdam and Amsterdam.[143]

The Kerry historian Mary Hickson charted the inglorious career of Timothy Sylvester O'Sullivan, another of the Munster spies of Sir Horace Walpole, the

composed by Orrery and attributed to the master. **138** Pittock, *Inventing and resisting*, p. 82. **139** J. Edgar to M. McDonogh, 19 May 1728 (R.A., Ms 116, fol. 48). See also R.A., Ms 118, fol. 116; R.A., Ms 157, fol. 10; Fagan (ed.), *Stuart papers*, i, pp 82-3, 109, 120. **140** Higgins, *Swift's politics*, p. 19. On the one hand, Swift described James II in a letter of 1735 as 'a weak, bigoted papist, desirous like all kings of absolute power, but not properly a tyrant'. On the other, he predicted in another letter to his Jacobite friend John Barber that 'without some unexpected assistance from heaven, many thousands will see [England] governed by an absolute power'; Higgins, *Swift's politics*, p. 67. Erskine-Hill has recently noted that Swift took ten copies of Brooke's *Gustavus Vasa* (published in 1739) which contained 'every sign of sedition that a drama of its time could display'; Erskine-Hill, *Poetry of opposition and revolution*, pp 129-32. **141** The examination of Edward O'Connor, 7 Oct. 1725 (P.R.O., S.P., 63/386/50). See also P.R.O., S.P., 63/386/153; P.R.O., S.P., 63/382/5, 49. The William Hore referred to in this deposition is most likely Sir Henry Goring. I would like to thank Dr Cruickshanks for this information on Goring. **142** Townsend to Capt. Deane, 8 Oct. 1725; P.R.O., S.P., 63/386/153. O'Connor finally became a member of Walpole's all-encompassing European spy-network; P.R.O., S.P., 63/386/155. **143** Townsend to Sir R.

British Ambassador to Paris. Walpole recruited this well-placed exiled Cork Jacobite, a correspondent of the Princess d'Auvergne and Fanny Trant (daughter of Sir Patrick Trant, one of King James II's revenue commissioners), to spy on smugglers, privateers and recruits in 1729. He went to Ireland under the guise of recruiting for the Irish regiments in France. However, his plan became unstuck when he accidentaly dropped a letter addressed to Sir Horace Walpole at a convivial gathering at Port Magee, County Kerry. He had promised in the letter to acquaint 'his majesty King George' with the activities of privateers and smugglers off the south coast. His O'Sullivan blood saved him from an angry mob and he was conveyed to nearby Killarney where he penned a letter to Dublin Castle providing an account of his adventure.[144]

These activities should be seen in the context of the short-lived Alliance of Vienna between Austria and Spain in 1725-7, and rumours of a Spanish-Imperialist plot to put James III on the throne of England. The arrival of Russian ships in Limerick and the rumours of gun-running and attempted landings in Scotland and Ireland fuelled these reports:

> Two letters from Mr Beare, collector at Limerick and Mr Madden, coast officer at Kilrush, contained an account of those Muscovite ships, two of which put in at Limerick and the third of which is said to have put in at Galway ... I have received intelligence that there were persons in the kingdom very busy listing men for the foreign service.[145]

These 'Muscovite' ships, in conjunction with recurring recruitment for the foreign service, interested the press, which also reported Ormonde's favourable reception at the Spanish court, the continued links between 'the Pretender' and Spain and the possibility of another Spanish-sponsored invasion:

> We hear from Spain that the duke of Ormond is mightily caressed there and there is talk that he is to get a grand commission to go on some enterprise but how to believe it we can't say. However, the Pretender keeps a good correspondence with that court and 'tis likely that they may make some attempt in the approaching trouble if there be no stop put to their designs.[146]

Walpole, 15 Oct. 1725 (P.R.O., S.P., 63/386/155). **144** Hickson (ed.), *Selections*, ii, pp 177-84. There are other examples of Walpole supplying intelligence regarding Ireland; P.R.O., S.P., 63/382/49; P.R.O., S.P., 63/382/51, 62. **145** 'Carteret to Newcastle, Nov. 1725 (P.R.O., S.P., 63/386/316). Contemporary reports survive of Jacobite and Spanish attempts to coax France into an alliance with the emperor and put the Pretender on the throne. The state papers contain intelligence reports regarding the export of ammunition from the north of Ireland to the Scottish highlanders; *List and index society*, vol. 119, pp 165, 195; P.R.O., S.P., 63/386/286. Spanish officers were also reported to be active in Ireland in this period; P.R.O., S.P., 63/387/36; P.R.O., S.P., 67/8/31; P.R.O., S.P., 67/8/107. **146** *Dub. I.*, 29 Jan. 1726. A report in the local press alluded to the capture of fifty or sixty recruits

II

Lloyd and Orrery's links with the Irish diaspora and O'Connor's emphasis on the Jacobite activity of Irish merchants and Jacobite agents on the continent showed that the exiled community had emerged as the main hope of their Irish-based counterparts in the early-eighteenth century. They played a pivotal role in indigenous Jacobite communications with the Stuart court and took an interest in the political fortunes of their co-religionists at home. For example, Luttrell's death and the threat of a backlash against Irish Catholics reached the ears of General Dillon and the duke of Berwick on the continent.[147] Dame Mary Butler, abbess of the Irish Benedictines at Yprès, writing to both her spiritual and secular masters in Rome, encapsulated the persecution mentality of the *émigrés* and their interest in the plight of their brethren. She complained to Pope Clement XI in 1714 that she and her community had to 'leave their fatherland and give up all they owned to freely practice the Catholic religion'; Catholics who would not convert to Protestantism were 'being persecuted more and more every day and deprived of whatever little goods remain in their possession'.[148] Dame Butler's themes are consistent with indigenous Irish Jacobite sentiments.

Some Irish Jacobite exiles did more than bemoan the fate of their Irish Catholic co-religionists. Sir Patrick Hume (Lord Polwarth) deplored a prospective invasion by Ormonde and the Jacobite exiles, a concern deepened by news of the departure of many Irishmen from the French to the pro-Jacobite Spanish service.[149] The correspondence of the Jacobite duke of Mar, and George Kelly's trip to Ireland on behalf of Ormonde suggest that Ireland had a place in contemporary high-Jacobite intrigue. Mar's correspondence shows that both England and Ireland were expected to provide much-needed finances to support the continental-based Jacobite war-machine. General Dillon informed James III on 25 May 1717 that George Kelly had arrived back from Ireland 'with several letters for Ormonde and D. 17 [Dillon?]' and the promise of 'a pretty good succour in money from thence'. This clandestine intercourse continued throughout this period, further reinforcing the ideological homogeneity between Ireland and the Jacobites exiles.[150] The secrecy with which the participants pursued these contacts partly explains the apparent inactivity of Irish Jacobites, which historians have been too quick to ascribe to passivity.

In 1718 Irish Jacobites sought to interest their exiled king in an assault on Ireland. The Franciscan Ambrose O'Callaghan (Jacobite agent and future

on 'The Mayflower' in County Cork; *Dub. Post.*, 24 Jan. 1726; *Dub. J.*, 25 Jan. 1726. **147** Lieut. Gen. Dillon to Mar, 25 Nov. 1717 (*H.M.C., Stuart*, v, p. 233). In a letter to his son the duke of Liria relating to the assassination of Luttrell, Berwick remarked that 'there is the end of a great rogue but he had courage withal', quoted in Petrie, *Berwick*, p. 318. **148** Abbess of Yprès to Clement XI, *c*.1714, in Giblin (ed.), 'Catalogue', part 4, vols 102-22, p. 67. See also Fagan (ed.), *Stuart papers*, i, pp 178, 207, 215-7, 295, 308-9. **149** Lord Polwarth to Mr. Jeffreys, 21 Mar. 1719 (*H.M.C., Polwarth*, ii, p. 106); *Dub. I. News*, 1 Feb. 1719. **150** Mar to Captain H. Straiton, 3 Jan. 1718 (*H.M.C., Stuart*, v, p. 358). See also

bishop of Ferns) excused the inactivity of Irish Jacobites during the 'Fifteen' and provided yet another invasion proposal for the stoical James III. He stressed that 'the want of a diversion in Ireland contributed to the ill success of the king's affairs in Scotland in 1715, and it was impossible for the well-affected in Ireland to do anything for want of arms'. One of O'Callaghan's correspondents – 'Robin' Leslie, of Glaslough, County Monaghan, assured him that the gentlemen of the north would join the Jacobites, and he advocated the seizure of Enniskillen, Derry, Carrickfergus and Charlemont.[151] James III rejected this scheme, which he deemed was the brainchild of 'mad Robin' Leslie.[152] Although James was content to send O'Callaghan to Ireland on a fact-finding mission, he had no intention of assigning a role to the headstrong Leslie in any future plans.[153] General Dillon agreed with Ormonde on the impracticability of the plan but advised James to consult Lord Granard.[154] Although this scheme proved impractical, it is significant that an Irish Protestant Jacobite was using a prominent Irish Catholic cleric and Jacobite agent as an intermediary to try to interest his stoical monarch in an invasion plan and to cast aspersion on his non-Irish followers. Before Leslie's invasion memoir is dismissed outright, it should be remembered that Charles Edward's hare-brained scheme was also impractical but it shook the Hanoverian monarchy to its foundations. Leslie was not willing to disclose his ambitious plan to Mar or Nairne but only to Sir Charles Wogan who was in his confidence. His fears may not have been totally unfounded when one considers the activities of 'Bobbing John', earl of Mar and his later betrayal of the Jacobite cause. Leslie's links with Wogan also provide a context for depositions relating to the Catholic lawyers and gentlemen who had earlier been accused of maintaining a correspondence with Charles and Nicholas Wogan and Ormonde in the run up to the abortive Ormondist invasion in 1719 and 1722. This illicit contact may be one reason why the scheming Leslie had moved from his native Glaslough to take up permanent residence in Dublin.[155]

---

ibid. v, p. 479; P.R.O., S.P., 67/7/134; *H.M.C., Stuart*, iv, p. 274. **151** James III to Lieut. Gen. Dillon, 6 May 1718 (*H.M.C., Stuart*, vi, p. 406). Rochester similar views of the English Jacobite capacity to revolt; ibid., vii, pp xxv-vii. **152** Charles Leslie accompanied the Stuart king to Italy in 1717. Fearing for his health, he returned to Paris two months later. The duke of Mar commented: 'I imagine his son Robin [Robert] did not like the place, there being little stirring there for his stirring spirit'. This is the same 'Mr Leslie' who came to Venice from Florence in March 1717 and who was described as being 'as mad as ever', quoted in Ingamells, *Dictionary*, p. 597. Charles came back to Ireland to die in 1721; Clark, *English society*, p. 144; Rushe, *The history of Monaghan*, p. 15. Swift also wrote a parody on Rev Leslie's sons 'Robin' and 'Harry'; Faulkner, *Swift's works*, xiii, p. 325. **153** James III to Dillon, 6 May 1718 (*H.M.C., Stuart*, vi, p. 406). Leslie's failure to get a hearing at the Stuart court may have influenced his decision to return to Ireland with his ailing father in 1721; Rushe, *The history of Monaghan*, p. 15. James III's scepticism regarding an Irish invasion was best represented by the Irish Protestant Jacobite Admiral George Camocke's assertion that 'Scotland and Ireland signify not a fifth wheel of a coach to your majesty's affairs, old England is to pay the piper and, for God's sake, dance to the tune of the bishop of Rochester' (*H.M.C., Stuart*, vii, p. 393). **154** James III to Dillon, 6 May 1718 (*H.M.C., Stuart*, vi, p. 406). See also ibid., vii, p. 87; D'Arcy, 'Exiles and strangers. The case of the Wogans', pp 171-85. **155** Whyte and Whyte, *On the trail of the*

While invasion rumours filtered into Ireland through maritime trade and through the recruiters who had the Stuart king's permission through their colonel-proprietors to levy men for the foreign service, more direct intercourse between Ireland and the exiles also existed. Captain Galway, an Irishman at Cadiz, brought news to Galway of Ormonde's contact with General Dillon in relation to the procuring of 10,000 stands of arms for an invasion of Ireland.[156] Ormonde's letter to Lord Landsdowne formed part of intercepted Jacobite correspondence which had been sent under the cover of Daniel Arthur, the Parisian banker. This also shed light on the activities of the Rev George Kelly and James Talbot, an Irish officer in the Spanish service.[157] Suspicions regarding the association between recruitment and Jacobitism were not unfounded. James III's contacts with the lieutenants of the Franco-Irish Jacobite regiments in March 1722, on the eve of another possible invasion of England, provided further proof of his surviving prestige, and the extent to which his exiled Irish subjects pursued the Stuart agenda in their adopted lands. These communications provided an effective *carte blanche* to the leaders of the Irish regiments in the French and Spanish armies to use the Jacobite standard and have the blessing of the exiled king to recruit in Ireland:

> The particular zeal and forwardness you expressed for my service some years ago assure me that you will not be less desirous now in contributing to its advancement in the manner which will be further explained to you by Mr. Dillon. I heartily wish for my own sake that you will be able to give your personal assistance on this great occasion, but at least I hope it will be in your power to render some of your officers and soldiers of your regiment in assisting in this great undertaking ... [158]

It is no surprise that Recruitment depositions emphasise the importance of the authenticity of warrants and commissions received directly from James III.[159]

Jacobites, p. 67. According to Peter Collins, Robert was living in Islandbridge at the time of his death in 1743; Collins, *County Monaghan sources*, p. 57.   **156** Lettre à Monsr. Dumville dans une lettre addressée à Monsr. Thomas Wilmore, chez Monsr. Stockoer, libraire à Charing Cross, Londres 23 Apr./4 May 1722 (B.L., Stowe Ms 250, fol. 3). A contemporary report even rumoured that Ormonde was in Ireland; B.L., Add. Ms 47, 029, fol. 50.   **157** To Mr Digby (Landsdowne or Dillon) under cover of Mr Arthur, banker at Paris (B.L. Stowe 250, fol. 25[46]). See also; B.L. Stowe 250, fols 6, 25, 27, 29, 33. Genet-Rouffiac explores the association between banking and espionage and Daniel Arthur's links with the Stuart court and Ireland in 'La première génération', pp 575, 577, 583.   **158** 'Copy of the king's [James III] letters to Generals Michael Rothe, Andrew Lee, Christopher Nugent, Mr [Andrew?] Shelton [Sheldon], General Daniel O'Donnell, Cooke, Charles O'Brien, Viscount Clare and Lieut. Gen. Dillon, 1722, 10 Mar. 1722 (R.A., Ms 58, fol. 66). See also; *H.M.C., Stuart*, vii, p. 559. James encouraged recruitment for Irish regiments in France and Spain, in *List and index society*, vol. 119, State papers, France, 1723-7, p. 164). Contemporary reports suggest that Irish priests were being sent from St Germain to recruit in Ireland; *Appendices referred to in the report*, p. 15; P.R.O., S.P., 67/7/147. James also appreciated the exiled Lord Clancarthy's influence among the tenants of his forfeited estate; R.A., Ms 59, fol. 28.   **159** Ó Buachalla, 'Jacobitism in official documents,' pp 128–38;

The Irish *émigrés*, however had to content themselves with more passive manifestations of Jacobitism in the aftermath of Ormonde's abortive invasion attempts. These included the pursuit of healing medals for the king's evil (scrofula), the collection of portraits and Jacobite songs, and the sending of Christmas and New Year's greetings to their exiled king.[160] They continually sought the king's adjudication in matters pertaining to family honour. Frequently, they petitioned him for financial relief and his letters of reference remained essential for securing commissions in continental armies.[161]

Colonel Christopher Nugent showed that a reciprocal dependence characterised the relationship between the exiled king and his expatriate Irish subjects. In 1723 Nugent expressed delight at his ability to facilitate Lady Brittas's son with a commission in his regiment, and thus oblige James III to whom he owed his position in the French military elite and French *ancien régime* society.[162] The Stuart papers also abound with compliments to James III and Queen Clementina on the birth of Charles Edward, prince of Wales, in December 1720. While this flood of congratulations to the Stuart court had a distinctly aristocratic component, the communal elation of the Irish exiles was most succinctly expressed by Wogan who lauded the succession of 'the most ancient royal line in the world'.[163]

The exiled brethren continued their correspondence with King James III in the immediate aftermath of the failure to organise a Spanish-sponsored Jacobite invasion. They commented on European affairs and their possible ramifications for the Stuart cause. Material considerations also motivated these links with the exiled king. Madame Marie McMahon's letters to James III of September 1723, seeking preferment for her husband in the French army, showed the benefits of her continued loyalty to Jacobitism. Her exiled king enabled this expatriate

idem, *Aisling Ghéar*, pp 339-40. **160** Dillon to James III, 7 Oct. 1720 (R.A., Ms 49, fol. 38). See also R.A., Ms 54, fol. 111. There are other references to the 'king's evil' from a later period; R.A., Ms 216, fol. 85; R.A., Ms 414, fol. 89; R.A., Ms 50, fol. 96; R.A., Ms 64, fol. 128. There are other examples in the Stuart papers relating to the collection of portraits and Jacobite songs and the sending of new year's greetings; R.A., Ms 50, fol. 96; R.A., Ms 64, fol. 128. The plight of these exiles is encapsulated in contemporary verse: 'Tho' much you suffer, think I suffer more/Worse then are exile on my native shore./Companions in your master's flight you roam/Unenvy'd by your haughty foes at home/For ever near the royal outlaw's side/You share his fortunes and his hopes divide/On glorious schemes and thoughts of empire dwell/And with imaginary titles swell'; *An epistle from a lady in England*. **161** J. Nagle to James III, 14 Jan. 1723 (R.A., Ms 64, fol. 128). See also R.A., Ms 69, fol. 125; R.A., Ms 70, fol. 45; R.A., Ms 68, fol. 21; R.A., Ms 66, fol. 139; R.A., Ms 70, fol. 43; R.A., Ms 106, fol. 113. **162** Col. Nugent to James III, 28 Oct. 1723 (R.A., Ms 71, fol. 120); See also R.A., Ms 72, fols 33, 124; R.A., Ms 111, fol. 12; R.A., Ms 124, fol. 105; R.A., Ms 136, fol. 104; R.A., Ms 200, fol. 175. **163** Charles Wogan to James III, 20 Feb. 1720 (R.A., Ms 52, fols 26, 52, 78, 83, 120; R.A., 122, fol. 113; R.A., Ms 200, fol. 102. Irish *émigrés* were also jubilant at the birth of Henry, duke of York; R.A., Ms 81, fol. 45. The exiles continued to observe the health and diversions of the princes; R.A., Ms 168, fol. 204; R.A., Ms 169, fol. 30; R.A., Ms 172, fols 177, 184; R.A., Ms 51, fol. 142; R.A., Ms 52, fol. 79; R.A., Ms 53, fol. 129; R.A., Ms 56, fol. 6. In Dublin, the Jacobite poet Tadhg Ó Neachtain, also recorded the births and genealogies of the Stuart princes in his commonplace book; Ó Buachalla, 'Seacaibíteachas Thaidhg Uí Neachtain', p. 43.

Fermanagh aristocrat to gain the intercession of James's half-brother the duke of Berwick, a maréchal of France, and Maréchal Villars, the two most influential soldiers in the French army. The longevity of Jacobitism among the Irish in Europe and, by extension, among their brethren in Ireland, can be understood better in terms of such practical benefits.[164]

The mercenary motives of such correspondence often conceal a strong sense of exile, as is evident in Roger O'Connor's letter to John Hay (later titular earl of Inverness), James III's minister, in November 1723. Commenting on rumours of the French regent's death 'which will very likely produce great changes, in the government of France but in all Europe which may contribute to his majesty's restoration', he wished 'to get our bread from him [James III] as his loyal subjects in his own dominions and without being continually troublesome to him abroad'.[165] The desire to return home gives credibility to the expectant optimism of the Irish Jacobite literati. The wished-for brevity of the Irish *émigrés'* sojourn abroad also appeared in correspondence from Lord Inverness to Captain O'Mahony. Commending O'Mahony's steadfastness, Inverness desired that the king might soon have an occasion of 'putting their loyalty and attachment to tryal' and that 'after so many years in a foreign country', O'Mahony might 'at last have the satisfaction of putting the king in possession of his own'.[166]

The Stuart court believed that the Irish *émigré* officers, like the episcopate, had an obligation to encourage Jacobite sentiment among James III's exiled Irish subjects. This belief was reinforced by the hierarchical structure of Jacobitism, percolating from the king, through the officer corps to the regular forces of the Irish regiments and, by extension, through the Jacobite episcopate, the Irish mission and the recruiting mechanism, and finally down to many indigenous Irish Catholics.

III

The Jacobite sentiments in recruitment depositions and in the surviving correspondence between the Stuart court and Irish Jacobites are reflected in contemporary Jacobite poetry. The poets preoccupied themselves with contemporary European politics and its implications for the Stuart cause. They sang the praises of King James III, his military leaders and his Spanish ally. George I, the French regent and prominent Irish Whigs provoked their ire. They mourned

---

164 Madame Marie McMahon to James III, 26 Sept. 1723 (R.A., Ms 71, fol. 102) See also R.A. 71, fol. 120; R.A., Ms 66, fol. 9; R.A., Ms 79, fol. 19; R.A., Ms 80, fol. 40; R.A., Ms 69, fol. 110; R.A., Ms 82, fol. 93; R.A., Ms 182, fol. 112; R.A., Ms 170, fol. 139. **165** Roger O'Connor to Hay, 20 Nov. 1723 (R.A., Ms 71, fol. 72). **166** Lord Inverness to Captain O'Mahony, Albano, 20 June 1725 (R.A., Ms 83, fol. 46). For other examples of this *émigré mentalité*, R.A., Ms 80, fol. 40; R.A., Ms 92, fol. 55; R.A., Ms 184, fols 81-82; R.A., Ms 111, fol. 126; T.C.D., Ms 2011, fol. 69; R.A., Ms 122, fol. 113; Fagan (ed.), *Stuart papers*, i, p. 41.

the death of Mary of Modena in 1718, and completed the political rehabilitation and literary beatification of the deceased James II.

Ormonde's pivotal role in Jacobite invasion plans, and his subsequent demonisation in Irish Protestant circles, contributed to his emergence as a dominant figure in Irish literary tradition in the 1720s. Apart from the Stuart claimant himself, Ormonde was the principal bogeyman of the authorities and the main hope of the Jacobites.[167] In his 'Marbhna Sheagháin Bhrúin', Aogán Ó Rathaille noted that Brown was of the blood of the duke, of his race and his kinfolk ('d'fhuil an Diúic, dá chrú, is dá chomhgus'). The 1720 marriage of Valentine Browne, third viscount Kenmare to Honora, daughter of Thomas Butler of Kilcash, a grand-niece of Ormonde, provided the subject of Ó Rathaille's 'Epitalamium do Thighearna Chinn Mara'. The poet rejoiced that Browne had espoused the star of Munster, near in blood to the duke from Kilkenny (ó 's céile don mBrúnach í, Réalt ón na Mumhan/'s gaol gearr don Diúc ó Chill Choinnigh). Ó Rathaille also included the duke and all his relations ('an Diúc 's a ghaolta sin uile') in his allegorical assembly of Munstermen, ('Tionól na bhfear Muimhneach'). Similarly, Seán na Ráithíneach Ó Murchú's poem 'Is fada mo thart' refers to the hereditary Butler duke ('an Diúc ghluin Bhuitléarach'), while Donnchadh Rua Mac Conmara lavishes his praise on the 'Leinsterman', Tiobóid Buitléir, Butler of the dukes ('Buitléaraigh na nDiúicí'). [168]

Irish poets were fully aware of the changing fortunes of Jacobite diplomacy in this period and appreciated the impossibility of French succour after the death of Louis XIV, the succession of Orléans and his political courtship of George I.[169] They turned their attention instead to Spain where the enigmatic Cardinal Alberoni presided over the kingdom's political resurgence, and showed no hesitation in using Jacobitism to twist the British lion's tail. Even before the abortive landing of Ormonde in 1719, Seán Ó Neachtain's elegy on the death of Mary of Modena in April 1718 ('Fáth éagnach mo dheór, Tuireadh ar bhás mhná an dara Rí Séamas') shows that Irish Jacobite hopes had already switched to Spain and Rome where James III now resided. Queen Mary had been the toast of Diarmuid Mac Sheáin Bhuí Mac Cárthaigh in the 1680s and her generosity to the exiled Irish was well known.[170] The deadly cause of Ó Neachtain's tears

---

167 Ó Buachalla, *Aisling Ghéar*, p. 324.　168 Ó Rathaille, 'Tionól na bhfear Muimhneach', in Ua Duinnín (eag.), *Dánta*, pp 52-3; Ua Duinnín (eag.), *Dánta*, introduction, xv, appendix, pp 48-59, 106-110, 164-6; Seán na Ráithíneach/Éamonn de Bhál, 'Is fada mo thart', in Torna (eag.), *Seán na Ráithíneach*, p. 150; Ó Foghludha (eag.), *Donnchadh Ruadh*, pp 41-2; Ó Ciardha, 'The unkind deserter and the bright duke', pp 177-93; Hogg (ed.), *Jacobite relics*, i, p. 417.　169 The Regent's banishment of James featured in the contemporary Dublin press; *Secret memoirs of the new treaty of alliance with France*. It was also celebrated in doggerel verse: 'Inconstant Orléans still we mourn the day/That trusted Orléans with imperial sway/For o'er the Alps our helpless monarch lands/Far from the call of his despondent friends'; *An epistle from a lady in England*.　170 Mac Sheáin Bhuí Mac Cárthaigh, 'Céad Buidhe re Dia', in MacErlean (eag.), *Duanaire*, iii, p. 110. The Stuart queen continually showed her concern for the exiled Irish (*H.M.C., Stuart*, i, pp 87, 95, 100, 107, 109, 110, 114, 117, 118, 121, 124, 125, 126, 129, 131, 132, 137, 139, 140, 141 143, 144, 145, 153, 154, 160, 168, 169, 171,

1 *(Right)* Sir Godfrey Kneller, *James II*, 1684,
National Portrait Gallery, London.
2 *(below)* Alexis Simon Belle, *Prince James Francis
Edward Stuart, 'James III'*, 1712, National
Portrait Gallery, London.

3 *(left)* Artist unknown, *Prince Charles Edward Stuart, 'prince of Wales'*, 1748, National Portrait Gallery, London.
4 *(below)* Artist unknown, *James Fitzjames [Stuart], duke of Berwick and Liria.*

5 *(right)* François de Troy, *Richard Talbot,
earl of Tyrconnell,* 1690,
National Portrait Gallery, London.
6 *(below)* Rigaud (attr.),
Patrick Sarsfield, earl of Lucan,
National Gallery of Ireland.

7 *(above, left)* Artist unknown, *Thomas Fitzgerald, 19th knight of Glin.* Fitzgerald was accused of trafficking with Jacobite exiles, private collection.

8 *(above, right)* Randall Mac Donnell, *4th earl of Antrim,* copyright Randall Mac Donnell, private collection. Randall received a ring from James Francis Edward which contained a lock of his sister Princess Lousia's hair. He was in communication with St Germain and Scotland during the 'Fifteen'.

9 *(left)* Joseph Michael Wright, *The Irish Chieftain or Sir Neill O'Neill,* Tate Gallery, London. O'Neill was mortally wounded when attempting to prevent William of Orange from crossing the Boyne.

10 *(above, left)* Engraving after Alexis Simon Belle,
Revd Charles Leslie, National Gallery of Ireland.
11 *(above, right)* William Sherwin [engraver],
*William Sheridan, non-juring bishop of
Kilmore and Ardagh*, private collection,
12 *(right)* Hans Hysing, *Charles Butler, 2nd earl of
Arran*, Dúchas and the Courtauld Institute of Art.

13 *(above, left)* Artist unknown, *Charles Boyle, 4th earl of Orrery, 1707,* National Portrait Gallery, London.
14 *(above, right),* Engraving by M. Ford after Ottway, *John Barry, 4th earl of Barrymore*
15 *(left)* Artist unknown, *Major-General Charles O'Brien, 5th Viscount Clare,* private collection. Colonel of Clare's Regiment, he was killed at Ramilles in 1706.

16 *(above, left)* Bartholomew Dandridge,
Nathaniel Hooke, National
Portrait Gallery, London.
17 *(above, right)* Artist unknown,
James Butler, 2nd duke of Ormond,
Dúchas and the Courtauld Institute.
18 *(right)* Nicolas de Largeillière (attrib.),
Lieutenant-General Michael Rothe,
colonel-proprietor of Rothe's Regiment
('The Pretender's Footguards'), Dúchas.

19 *(above)* Engraving attributed to Jean Sorieul and Earnst Meyer, *The Irish Brigades in France. Soldiers of the Regiments of Clare, Dillon, Lally and Roth,* National Library of Ireland.

20 *(below, left) The Kylemore Flag,* Kylemore Abbey. Captured by Lord Clare's Infantry at the battle of Ramilles in 1706 and presented to the cloisters of the Irish Benedictines at Yprès.

21 *(below, right) Colour of the Regiment of Dillon, Irish Brigade,* National Museum of Ireland.

22 *(above, left) Thomas Lally, comte de Tollendal,* Lally led the Irish on the field in their greatest single triumph against the English at Fontenoy and was decorated after the battle by Louis XV in person. He became a close confidant of the elusive Stuart prince and continually advocated an assault on England in support of the Jacobite cause.
23 *(above, right)* Artist unknown, *Charles O'Brien, 6th Viscount Clare, 9th earl of Thomond. Maréchal of France (1757) and governor of Languedoc,* private collection. Lord Clare commanded the Irish at Fontenoy and later played a key role in negotiating the Treaty of Fontainbleu. He was commander of an abortive French invasion force in 1759.
24 *(right)* Artist unknown, *Sir Charles Wogan,* National Gallery of Ireland. Attainted for his part in the abortive rebellion of 1715, he was knighted and made a member of the Roman senate for his daring rescue of Clementina Sobieska. Wogan remained a devoted Jacobite until his death in 1753.

25 Pierre Lefant, *Bataille de Fontenoy, 11 Mai 1745*, Réunion des Musées Nationaux.

26 *(above)* Engraving by J.D. Reigh (1889), after Horace Vernet, *After the Battle of Fontenoy*, National Library of Ireland. The subtle changes to Vernet's original (see front cover) provides a powerful visual representation of the de-Jacobitization of the Irish nationalist tradition. The captured union jack has been altered to include the cross of St Patrick (post-1800); the Irish have acquired green uniforms and are now fighting under a republican flag.

27 *(below)* Engraving by J.D. Reigh (1886), *Revenge! Remember Limerick!; Dash down the Sassenach*, National Library of Ireland. 'Marchez conntre les ennemis de la France et les vôtres. Ne tirez que quant vous aurez la point de vos baionnettes sur leur ventres', attributed to Lally at Fontenoy; in Voltaire, *Fragments sur l'Inde*.

this is Seán Mc Donnells translation into Irish of
the Scotch Jacobite song the "Black Loddy."

Seaghan Clárach Mac Domhnaill ccc

To the air . "the Black Loddy."

My Loddy can fight, and my Loddy can sing,
As fierce as the northwind, as sweet as the spring.
His face was destined for no less than a King
Such Graces shine on my Black Loddy.

Cómapcán mo Macaoiñ, iſ catháy cóiñ biñ
le h-éunlaiɣ an eyplaiɣ, cóiñ ɲeán leɲ an n-ɣaoɩt;
Tŋ fépoɩɲ oa a caoán ɣan é beɩt ɲa Ríɣ,
Tá an uɲpeaó ɲiŋ ɲɣéiŋ aɲ mo Macaoiñ.

Of soft down of Thistles I'll make him a bed,
With lillies and roses I'll pillow his head;
And with a tuned Harp so gently I lead
To ease in sweet slumbers my Loddy.

Cóiɲeomɲa leabaó le ɲeóćáy ɣo miŋ,
le lile iſ le ɲóɣa aɲpeoɩó cóaɲ a éɲŋ;
ſiŋɣeaŋ ɣo ɲeólta aɲ ceol-éɲuɲ ɣo biñ,
Cum ɲuaɲ éup ɣo ɲuaɲe aɲ mo Macaoiñ.

Let Thunderbolts rattle thro' mountains of snow,
And Hurricanes over old Caucass' blow.
Let all things go right on Earth here below
When we shall get home our black Loddy.
Aɲ ɲléɩbɩe an tſneaća buó coɩɲneáć oo ɲɩoɲ
Iſ ~uaɲćaŋ aɲ ɲuaɲ éɲoc Caucaɲ ɣan bɩɲé
Fać ŋ maɲ aɲ oeaɲ aɲ an tſɲeoɣal ſo bɩoó
Ŋ uaɩɲ ćeabáṁŋa a baɩle aɲ Macaoiñ.

28 RIA Ms.23, E.1, p.5. Part of Seán Clárach Mac Domhnaill's translation into Irish
of the Scottish-Jacobite song 'The Black Laddy', in the form of a barántas.

A poetic Translation of Part of a Newspaper in the Year 1744.

Seaghan (Clárach) Mc Domhnaill cct.

Eisdidh le'm ghlórta, a mhór-shlíoċ Mhiléſuſ,
Buſ dibſe bo deónaċ mo ſgeól do ſgaipeadh,
Buſ ſcoiꞇe ce leónadh, buꞃ leóġan, iſ buꞃ lóċꞃa
a ꞃCꞃuoc iniſ Fódla, Ɡan Fód na ꞅeꞬaꞃ:
Táꞃ Báꞁle le pilib 'Ɡ mꞃꞁꞃ iſ aꞁꞃ ꞇꞁꞃ,
Snꞁ ꞇáꞁꞃe do ꞇꞃꞁlle dá Fꞃꞁꞁꞃ má'ꞅ Fꞁoꞃ,
Beidh ſꞁꞁmle 'Ɡuſ ſólladh co'Ɡ Fóꞁpꞃeaċ an éꞁꞃliꞬ,
iſ Dꞁoltuſ an comáꞃaꞁcc Ɡaċ ló dá leaꞬan .

I.

Tá Fóꞁpꞃeaꞇ, iſ Fóꞃſa Ɬuſ ſóꞁꞃſe Ɬuſ ſéꞁdꞁ,
iſ Dꞁꞃ-Ɬeaꞃꞃadh Dꞃólaꞃ Ɬaċ ló lé Fada,
AꞬ ſꞁoꞃ-ſꞃeadadh cſeóꞁꞃſe Ɬo ꞇꞃeóꞃaċ Ɬan ꞇꞃóꞁadh,
ꞇá'n Fꞁꞇ bꞃꞁſde, bꞃeóꞁꞇe ſ nꞁ'l Fóꞁꞃꞁnꞇ aco:
An méꞁd ſꞁn dá bFꞃꞁꞁꞃ aꞁꞁmꞁꞬ ꞁ ꞬCꞁan,
iſ léꞁꞃ, ná'ꞃ leꞁ.eadh lon Dꞃꞁne 'co nꞁaꞃ,
Beꞁd cꞃꞁmne Ɬo Deó co'Ɡ Ɡleó ċeꞬꞇáꞬ.ena,
ꞅꞬ ſlꞁobadh dá ſeóꞁꞇaꞁꞁ ꞁſe póꞃꞇ Sebꞇaſꞇꞁan.

2.

Tá Babáꞃꞁa comáꞃaċ aꞬCꞃóꞁꞃ iſ ꞁꞬCéꞁmꞁb
An ꞁmpꞃe ſan eóꞃoꞁꞃ, ſꞁn ſꞬeól ná meaſadh,
AꞬ ꞁꞃꞬéꞇanꞇ a ſlóꞁꞬꞇe aꞬ Bóꞃoꞁb Bꞁéꞃa
ꞇá'n RꞁꞬ-bean Ɬo deóꞃ-Fꞁꞁꞇ, ſa ꞇóꞁꞃ dá ꞇaFan:
ꞇá ceꞁbꞁꞃꞁulleꞃ Ɬan cumaſ, Ɬan Cꞃꞁc,
AꞬ Sꞁſꞁlꞁ cꞃꞁꞃeadh an bꞃꞁſeadh ſ á bcoꞁn:
ꞇá pꞃuſꞁa Ɬuſ pólanꞁ a bpóꞃꞇaꞁ Sꞁleſꞁa
Sꞁn coꞁbce ſꞁoꞃ leópaꞁld Fá ceó na mallaſ.

3 .

---

29 RIA Ms.23.D.8, p. 277. Seán Clárach Mac Domhnaill's poetic translation of
a part of a newspaper in the year 1744, 'Eistighidh l'em ghlórtha, a
mhór-shliocht Mhilesius' (pp 277-80).

30 RIA Ms. 23, B.38, p. 237. One folio of Aogán Ó Rathaille's 'Mac An Cheannaí' [The Merchant's son], who many scholars believe to be the duke of Berwick (pp 228–9).

As ʋo Aonʈa cSeaʒʋin ʋ ʈrʋmx
Aon ıſ ʋó fá ʋó 'n mo pʋıſſe, ʋ oıʋ
S ʒo ʈʋeun na nʋeóıʒ 4 ſeól ʋa ſʒınfeaʋ tʋuſ
tʋo leun naċ fóʒnan cʋóʋaʒ ſʋoıʈe bʋʋc
Don Rex, a nʋóʋʈ ʒo ıʒólľfaʋıſ na ʈóıʋc.
(1)aıċ.

Dá ċon, ʋá ʋó ʒo ʒlúpʋnʋʋ, ʒʋoıſeaċ, ʒʋc,
Sna pʋıʋ ʋuʈ leó, ſan ſeóla ſʒċoılfeaʋ tʋuſ,
Dá nʋBeıʋaċ ʋʒCʋoıʋ le fóıʋ neʒʈ cloıʋʋm aʒʋʋñ,
Nó ċon ʋa póʋ, ſe ʋ fóıʋfeaʋ ʒʋoıʋıl ʒo bʋʋoſʒ.
2.

Aon 4 ċon, ıſċon na cceañ ſoıʋ cʋıʋ,
Aon, ċon ʋá nʋeıſ, ıſ feuc na ʋʈeañʈa tʋuſ,
Aon an ċon4, cé ʒuʋ ʒañ an cuıʋ,
ıſé pıʋ Reʒſ le ʈʋeun cuʋ ʒall ʈ4 tʋʋʋ.
3.

A Dó pʋıʋ ċon, ıſ ċon beaʒ ʒʋeıʋeanaċ ʒʋc,
ıſ, ſeúlfaʋ ċon na nʋeʒ fá meıʋʒ aʒ pʋc:
fóʋ ʈʒ ċon na beul, m4 ʒpeıʋm aʒ tʋuſ,
8ıʋ Seóıʋʋſe ʋċoʋ, an Reʒſ na ʈeıʒean ʈ4 tʋʋʋ.
4.

N.B. For each of the four Verses above,
John Enemy won a Bowl of Punch
Wager from Father George Brown
in the County Limerick, who obliged
him to compose the two last of
Single Aces, which were double
the two first Verses.

Sıʋ ċon, ıſ ċon, ıſ ċon, ıſ ċon ſıʋʒıl,
ıſ leıʒım ċon beaʒ 4 ʒaċ ʈċoʋ ʋon bıċ:
ʋo neıʒıʋ an Reʒſ, ʋ ʈʋeaʋ lú ċeıʋ ʋo pʋc,
S ʋſʋʋʒ pʋeıʋ ſʋoſʋmʋʋ ʈʋeʋʈ ʒaʋ Reıʋı 4bıc.

31 RIA Ms. 23.D.8, p. 282: a whole series of cryptic verses
containing the name of the Stuart king (see p. 170).

32 *(above)* William Hogarth, '*Calais Gate*' *and the* '*Roast Beef of Old England*', Tate Gallery, London. Hogarth's powerful anti-Jacobite piece contains the picture of the scrawny, starving, ragged Irish soldier ('Wild Goose'), supping watery French soup and gazing with covetous eyes on the roast beef. This picture contrasts sharply with the fearsome reputation of the Irish Brigades as manifested in the pamphlets of Charles Forman and John Keough.

33 *(left)* Stephen Slaughter [*c.*1745], '*The king over the water*', private collection. One of the earliest Irish conversation pieces it shows two men at a tripod table drinking glasses of wine in a toast. Closer scruitny shows that the bottle actally contains water and the subjects are in fact drinking to 'The king over the water'. The seditious nature of the piece is compounded by the oak leaves under the table, symbolic of the royal oak of the house of Stuart. It compares very closely to the Jacobite portrait of 'Benn's Club', Sharp, *Engraved Record*, p. 271.

and eternal grief which had left the Irish under a cloud was the death of a generous supplier of alms, a lofty fount of piety and bounty, a generous princess of jewels and a venerable loss for the youth who now lay without vigour under a stone. He bemoaned the sorrowful news that had recently arrived and lamented that Spain had been left half-drowned in grief:

Fáth éagnach mo dheór
d'fhág Gaedheala fa cheó
bean riartha na n-iarrach
scuith-dhiadha, cheart, chóir,

Flaith fialmhar na seód,
Creach-fhianach na n-óg
gan bhíodhgadh fa líogadh,
 m'fháth caointe go deóidh!
...
So an Mhaire gan ghó
Rinn' bás de mo bheó
An rígh-bhean a d'íoc súd
A chíos leis an an gcró

'S tearc ádhbhar as mó,
Ná ádhbhar mo ghleó
Sgéal cráite do thárla
San áit seo go nódh.

Tá gártha i ngach ó,
Tá i gcáirdeas don Róimh,
Na Spáinne mar fágbhadh
léar-bháidhte mo dhóigh.[171]

At the same time Ó Neachtain also promoted the political and spiritual beatification of Mary's deceased husband. He believed that the consort of King

---

175, 196, 203); see also ibid., vi, p. 423; R.A., Ms 194, fol. 153; Genet-Rouffiac, 'La première génération', p. 179. **171** Ó Neachtain, 'Tuireamh ar bhás mná an dara rí séamas', in Ní Fhaircheallaigh (eag.), *Filidheacht*, p. 22; Ó Buachalla, *Aisling Ghéar*, pp 212-3; A 12-page lament for James II in the papers of the earl of Fingall from September 1701 also extols the virtues of his wife (*H.M.C., 10th report*, 1885-7). News of her death also preoccupied Protestant Ireland. Robert Molesworth rejoiced that 'two hundred and fifty thousand pounds sterling had died with her and that she did not leave a farthing to him [the Pretender] which madds the Jacobites'; Molesworth to his wife, 6 May 1718 (N.L.I., Molesworth papers, mf. p. 3752). See also McLysaght (ed.), *Kenmare papers*, p. 105. King also showed interest in her last will, asking Edward Southwell that 'if you can't come by a copy of it [the will] there must be some reason for keeping it secret'; N.L.I., Ms 2056, no. 2. Rumours of her disavowal of her son featured in the Dublin press; see *A dialogue between Dr Lesly and the Pretender; A letter from Paris giving an account of the death of the late queen-dowager*.

James (II), greater than Caesar of the hosts, and the wise, pious king who was most faithful to Rome would both be active amongst the saints and virgins while the family of Milesius (the Irish) were laid low in their wake:

> Frae Séamas ba mhó
> Ná Caesar na slógh,
> An ríogh-fhlaith ba naomhtha
> 'S ba dílse don Róimh
>
> 'Measg naomh agus ógh,
> Tá an dís seo ba gnó
> Sliocht Mhíleadh go híseal
>   Fa dhaoirse 'n-a ndeóidh.[172]

Ó Rathaille, on his death-bed in 1729, attributed his afflictions to King James's removal. He added to the emerging cult of the martyr king in the Irish Jacobite literary tradition. He lamented that his brain trembled, his greatest hopes had dissolved, his innards were wounded and a lance had pierced his intestines as Catholic wealth, means and share of gold were mortgaged for a penny to a crew from the land of Dover (England) since the knave (William III) won the game against the crowned king (James II):

> Do thonn-chrith m'inchinn, d'imthigh mo phríomhdhóchas,
> poll am ionathar, biorann trím dhrólann,
> ár bh-fonn, ár bh-foithin, ár monga, 's ár míon-chomhgus,
> a ngeall re pinginn ag fuirinn ó chríoch Dover
> ...
> Ó lom an cuireata cluiche ar an Rígh coróineach.[173]

His colleague Aindrias Mac Craith observed how contemporary European diplomacy had begun to isolate the Jacobite movement. He grieved at the piercing wound to his heart from the poison caused by the deceitful link between the lion (Britain) and the empire (Holy Roman Empire). He believed that had the ships been launched by (Cardinal) Alberoni and 'The Kite' (George Keith, the earl marschal), they would be forever under the moderate rule of the true king (James III). He warned that the exiled prince would come back with

---

172 Ó Neachtain, 'Tuireamh ar bhás mhná an dara rígh Séamas', in Ní Fhaircheallaigh (eag.), *Filidheacht* p. 22. Reference to James's devotion to the Catholic faith appears in contemporary political discourse, see Fenning (ed.), *Fottrell papers*, p. 137. The Scottish poet Rob Donn McKay noted James VII and II's steadfastness in matters of the faith 'Nach è Seamus an Seachdamh/Dhearbh bhith seasmhach 'na inntinn?', Rob Donn, "Oran nan casagan dubha', in Campbell (eag.), *Songs of the '45*, p. 244. See also *The pope's speech to the college of cardinals*. A verse in the Nairne papers reflected Ó Neachtain's sentiments; 'Behold the monument to James the just/Which makes each atom of his sacred dust/As he lies abandoned and alone/Greater than Alexander on his throne'; Bodl., Carte Ms 208, fol. 419.   173 Ó Rathaille, 'An

a vengeance and George would be forced to flee with a rabble of his followers. In Ireland, Brodrick would not have a chance and Evans's status as lord would be gone:

> Isé abhar cnead is mó agum, do chealg beó mo chroí-se,
> Síonta an Athar chóchtaigh dá gcur gach ló ar ríne,
> Trí nimh an cheangail chórda tá idir an León 's an tImpre,
> Ná sílim flaith lem fhóirthint ar feadh na hEorpa timpeal.

...

> Dá mbeadh 'na shathach seólta Ailbiorón, 's an Scíteach,-
> Go brách ná deachtaig teóra le gealla ró-fhada an rí chirt!

...

> Casfa ar ais is fóirfig an flath tá ar fó go fíochmhar,
> Is rachaig seacha Seóirse agus gramaisg mhór dá mhuintir;
> Craithfig flathas Fólla ré dteacht trí fómhar timpeal
> Is beig malairt *chance* ag Bródraic 's gan gairm lórd ag Ivans.[174]

file ar leaba a bháis ag scríobhadh gus a charaid iar n-dul a n-éadóchas a g-cúisibh airighthe', in Ua Duinnín (eag.), *Dánta*, p. 110. Pádraig Ó Súilleabháin uses the same metaphor in his poetic contention with Seán Ó Murchú in the 1720s: An expulsion (of James II) which has been made/ since the knave (William of Orange) was played on the ace (James II)/and the game was played harshly without reversal 'Ar ionnarba atá ó tugadh an mádh/'s an cuireata i ndeáidh an aéin leis/Do rian an cluiche go dian gan filleadh'; Torna, *Seán na Ráithíneach*, p. 130. Erskine-Hill has recently suggested that card-games were an understood form of witty comment on international affairs; Erskine-Hill, 'Literature and the Jacobite cause', p. 54. Cryptic allusions to Jacobite politics in eighteenth century literature are 'spadillio' (Louix XIV), 'the rebel knave' (William III/the duke of Monmouth), 'Queen of Hearts' (Queen Anne), 'the king unseen' (James III); idem, *Poetry of opposition and revolution*, pp 77-82. Card-playing metaphors pervaded Irish Jacobite literature and the Stuart, particularly the notion of the Stuart prince as 'the fingers', or 'the five of trumps', the best card in the popular game twenty-five; Ó Buachalla, *Aisling Ghéar*, pp 354-5. For the transformation from James the Shite 'Séamas an chaca' to the brave king 'an rí códha'; An tAthair Ó Briain, 'A Alba ó shealbhais an rí cóir chirt [1719]', in Ó Foghludha (eag.), *Carn Tighearnaigh*, p. 28. A verse in the Irish literary tradition lamented: The second King James ('tis he that) is in the earth laid beneath the sod/[he] to whom England submitted and that was powerful o'er in Scotland./Oh stone what should make the greater king to be beneath thy surface,/and no single being of his race beside him?/Get the answer from thy father/for it was he that had his head cut off mss. 'An ndara rí Séamus is é atá a dtalamh faoi fhód//Saxan dar ghéill is ba thréan ar Alban fós/A leacsa cá dobhéarfadh réx na Breatan as mó,/A dtaisce fá thaobh is gan aonneach ina aice dá phór an freagradh/dá athair bain sgéal ós é dar gearradh sgóig'; O'Grady, *Cat. of Ir. mss. in B.L.*, i, p. 621. Also see 'An elegy on the death of James II' (*H.M.C.*, *Fingall*, pp 200-3). Mac Mhaighisdir Alasdair, noted the consequence of an act of parliament which took the crown from your (James II's) head 'De thrusdar de dh' acht pàrlamaid/a dh' fhoil an crún múd' cheann'. He added that William who dealt you this blow was a usurper himself 'An tUilleam rinn an tachd-sa dhuit/Gum b'eucorach é-féin', A. Mac Donnell, 'Oran a rinneadh sa bhliadhna 1746', Campbell (eag.), *Songs of the '45*, Monod, *Jacobitism*, p. 55. This cult of the 'wronged king' survived in Irish and Scots-Gaelic poetry and this is evident in the work of Art Mac Cumhaigh, even after he had lost hope in the Stuarts; Mac Cumhaigh, Moladh Shéamais Pluincéad, in Ó Fiaich (eag), *Art Mac Cumhaigh*, p. 129. **174** Rahilly (eag.), 'Deasgan Tuanach', p. 656. Ó Buachalla takes an 'Scíteach' (the kite) to be George Keith, the earl marschal; Ó Buachalla, *Aisling Ghéar*, p.

Alan Brodrick, the object of MacCraith's spleen, personified the archetypal political beneficiary of the Glorious Revolution. Appointed solicitor-general under William III in 1695 (an office he retained under Anne), he later became speaker of the Irish House of Commons and attorney-general; he was created Baron Brodrick of Midleton by George I in 1715 and Viscount Midleton two years later. A poem composed in the same period by an tAthair Conchubhar Ó Briain, entitled 'Más dóchas ár ndóchas i mbliadhna mheath', also longed for the flight of the Brodricks and Crofts ('Ná Bródraic do shéoladh 'n-a ndiaidh is Crafts').[175] Similarly, Dónall na Buile' Mac Cárthaigh vented his spleen against Brodrick, while Piaras Mac Gearailt deemed him to be a wrecker of churches and temples, who had made walls and stables from their stones ('badh ghnáthach le Bródric réamhráighte bheith ag brise 's aig leaga seanchealladh, teampaluibh, ag déunamh balluidhe iothlan, stábluidhe is luibhghort dá gclocha').[176] George Evans's receipt of the ancient title of Lord Carbery also drew the ire of Diarmuid Ó Súilleabháin.[177]

Ua Duinnín believed that Ó Rathaille's contemporary allegorical poem 'Tionól na bhfear Muimhneach' referred to the abortive Jacobite invasion of 1719-22.[178] Liam Rua Mac Coitir's poem 'Is briathra leamha ar óll-bhaois' also placed his hopes on the exiled warrior in Rome of the shining, illustrious blood of the McCarthys of Cashel ('an gliadhaire catha ar deóraidheacht sa Róimh/ mhín fí choimirc chách de ghrian-tsliocht Chaisil cheól-chaoin is fós ní bhfuil fuil is fearr').[179] Uilliam Mac Cairteáin an Dúna surmised that if an invasion would come from Spain to Ventry or Beare, they would be joined by a valiant troop from Munster: ('Dá dtagaidh a dtracht ón Sbainn invasion. Go cailaith Fhinn Tragh nó'n bádh sin Bhéarra. Bá chalma an trúp Do rachadh ón Mhumhan'). Ó Buachalla has recently drawn attention to a proliferation of pro-Spanish Jacobite poetry in the period from Seán Clárach Mac Domhnaill, Seán Ó Tuama and Liam Dall Ó hIfearnáin, among others.[180]

Their optimism proved short-lived. Aogán Ó Rathaille's 'Mac an Cheannaí' (the merchant's son) provided a personal insight into the poet's despair after Ormonde's abortive landing in 1719. The poet encounters the maiden 'Éire' (Ireland) and hears of her longing for 'Mac an Cheannaí'.[181] He informed her of

690. Mac Craith's 'cheangail chórda' or tied knot (the Quadruple Alliance) was described by Count O'Rourke, James's representative in Vienna, as 'a gordian knot so fatal to your majesty's affairs'; R.A., Ms 71, fol. 90. **175** Conchubhar Ó Briain, 'Más dóchas ár ndeochas i mbliadhna mheath', in Ó Foghludha (eag.), *Carn Tighearnaigh*, p. 30. **176** Ó Buachalla, *Aisling Ghéar*, pp 310, 652. **177** Diarmuid Ó Súilleabháin, 'Mo chiach atúirseach an treascairt', in Ó Foghludha (eag.), *Mil na hÉigse*, p. 294. **178** Ó Rathaille, 'Tionól na bhfear Muimhneach', in Ua Duinnín (eag.), *Dánta* , p. 106. **179** Liam Rua Mac Coitir, 'Is briathra leamha ar óll-bhaois [1719]', in Ó Foghludha (eag.), *Cois na Cora*, p. 26. **180** Ó Buachalla, *Aisling Ghéar*, pp 312-14. **181** Dudley-Edwards, 'Who was Mac an Cheannuidhe', pp 55-78; Ó Cléirigh, 'Cérbh é Mac an Cheannaí', pp 7-34; Mac Craith, 'Filíocht Sheacaibíteach na Gaeilge', p. 60. All these authors opt for 'Mac an Cheannaí' as a figurative representation of the Stuart cause. Ó Buachalla chose the duke of Berwick as the most likely candidate for 'Mac an Cheannaí'; Ó Buachalla, *Aisling Ghéar*, p. 686, fn. 50. Elsewhere, James II is

his death in Spain. The poet described her reaction on hearing this: the maiden's visage was transformed and she screeched and her soul departed with one high leap, leaving the poet in sorrow at her terrible state:

adubhart léi , iar chlos a sgéal,
a rún gur éag ar chleacht sí,
Thuas 'san Spáinn go bh-fuair sé bás,
is nár thruagh le cách a h-aicíd;
Iar g-clos mo ghotha, a bh-fogas dí,
chorruig 'a cruit, 's do sgread sí;
Is d'éalaigh a h-anam d'aon phreib airde;
mo léan-sa an bhean go lag-bhríghach.[182]

The Irish poets and the general populace retained a fascination with Jacobite high-politics. On the coming of age of Louis XV in 1722, Archbishop King reported that 'a notion has gotten into the papist's heads that the king of France swears at his coronation to extirpate all heresies and that when he is crowned his confessor will press him in pursuance of his oath to declare for the Pretender as the most effectual means to destroy the northern heresies'. He claimed that 'they [the papists] greatly please themselves with this and depend on it as certain'.[183] The death of the French regent in November 1723 did not go unnoticed among the Irish literati. In the aftermath of Louis XIV's aggressive foreign policy and France's economic breakdown, Orléans, Abbé Dubois and later Cardinal Fleury, had soft-pedalled on the restoration question, to the chagrin of the continental Jacobites and the extreme displeasure of the Irish poets.[184] Tadhg Ó Neachtain castigated the memory of Fleury in 1743 in his poem 'Mian gach mórdhacht claoidheann cró' (Death destroys every desire of greatness); Donnchadh Caoch Ó Mathghamhna toasts the demise of Orléans, the wretched dog, who

---

the called 'The Merchant' in high-political Jacobite discourse, Clarke (ed.), *Life of James II*, ii, p. 528. If this poem was written in 1706/7, 'Mac an Cheannaí' could indeed be the duke of Berwick as he fits all the criteria mentioned by Dudley-Edwards and he was rumoured dead (like Mac an Cheannaí) after the battle of Almanza (in Spain); *An express from Holland with an account of the duke of Berwick's being dead*. Berwick had already figured prominently in the Irish tradition. If 'Mac an Cheannaí' was written *c*.1716, it could be seen to represent Berwick's betrayal of the Jacobite cause which figured in the press; *Secret memoirs*, pp 9, 19 and his death in the poem could be a figurative representation of his disavowal of the Stuart cause. Moreover it could serve as a warning from over-enthusiastic Jacobites on the arrival of his son, the duke of Liria, in Ireland in 1720; Mac Craith, 'Filíocht Sheacaibíteach', pp 60-1, fn. 8. Liria's arrival also featured in contemporary newspapers; *Harding's Imp. N.*, 1 Oct. 1720; *Hume's C.*, 5 Aug. 1721. **182** Quoted in Ó Buachalla, *Aisling Ghéar*, p. 277. **183** King to Hopkins, 6 Nov. 1722 (T.C.D., 750/7, fol. 234-5); Connolly, *Religion*, p. 236. See also Information of O. Daly, 9 Oct. 1722 (P.R.O., S.P., 67/7/134). Black noted that the Anglo-French alliance was very fragile in this period and that the Jacobites hoped that their cause would be advanced by the majority of Louis XV, the death of Orléans, Bourbon or Fleury; Black, *British foreign policy*, p. 141. **184** 'The Regent is generally thought to be the king's greatest enemy'; *H.M.C., Stuart,*

destroyed King James's cause ('A mhadra bhoicht lear loiteadh cúis Shéamuis'). He hoped that he would not rest a foot until the body and soul of the regent was in the pound/pen of the black monster (Hell) (''s ler leagadh an chos gan sos ba rún naofa ar leacaibh na losc i loc na duphéiste anam is corp go docht an Diúic Regent').[185] Orléans also attracted the sharp-tongue of Seán Clárach who accused him of being a wolf in sheep's clothing. He abused the grim reaper for his tardiness in snatching Orléans, lamenting that he did not have the regent in darkest captivity nine Christmases ago, asserting that his funeral would have been a great cause of joy and no cause of apprehension to the fettered Gaels who were waiting for news of the arrival of the true Caesar. The poet's exploration of the relationship between Regency France and the Jacobite court in exile portrayed Orléans as the tyrannical leader whose evil deed was the single most destructive act for all men and the single stumbling-block which prevented the coming of Caesar (James III):

> Is é an donas duit, a éig oirdhreic', nár thraoch i gclais
> é i ndoircheacht naoi Nolaig ó shoin faon i nglas;
> fé shonas do b 'é a shochraid, níor bhaoghal teacht
> nGaedhal gcosrach lé torannaibh um Chaesar ceart.
>
> ...
>
> Ár Rex oirdhreic is é a thostuigh mo léan thar lear
>
> ...
>
> Is a ghné dhonais an t-aondochor san do chéas gach fear
> An t-aonphosta san ler obadh ar ár gCeasar teacht.[186]

IV

A Jacobite bias in contemporary pamphlets and broadsheets suggests that a residual Protestant Jacobite interest survived during George I's reign. This mirrored developments in contemporary England as uncovered by Paul Chapman.[187] Cornelius Carter of Fishshamble Street, one of Dublin's most active printers of sedition, stood indicted at the King's Bench for a satiric elegy on the assassinated Henry Luttrell in 1717. Rev William Harris claimed that

---

vi, pp 503-4. See also ibid., v, p. 12; ibid., vii, pp 56, 474-6. **185** Donnchadh Caoch Ó Mathghamhna, 'A mhadra bhoicht lear loiteag cúis Shéamais', Flower, *Cat. of Ir. mss. in B.L.*, ii, pp. 409-10; Breatnach, 'The end of a tradition', p. 147. For the satire on Fleury; T. Ó Neachtain, 'Mian gach mórdhacht claoidheann cró', in *Transactions of the Iberno-Celtic Society*, i, part 7, p. ccxxix. In the latter part of the eighteenth century, Míchéal Óg Ó Longáin dismissed the Regent as a joker who took English bribes to betray our prince [ie. the Pretender] 'cladhaire ghlac breab ón Sagsanach agus do rin feall ar ár bPrionsa .i. an Pretender'; quoted in Ó Buachalla, *Aisling Ghéar*, p. 318. **186** Seán Clárach, 'Ar bhás Regent na Fraingce' (Lá Nodlag 1723), in Ó Foghludha (eag.), *Seán Clárach*, pp 69, 17; Ó Buachalla, *Aisling Ghéar*, p. 319. See also Beresford, in 'Ireland', p. 142. **187** Chapman,

Carter had sent his servant Sweeny to ask him to write the lampoon. He pleaded ignorance of Luttrell's career, but Carter furnished Harris with a paper which stated that 'Harry and Simon were brothers, that Simon had stood firm for King James and went to France with him and died there but the said Henry forsook his master at Aughrim and Limerick'.[188] Carter also desired him to compose a lament for John Hartstonge, late Church of Ireland bishop of Derry who had been accused of Jacobite sympathies.[189] Apprehensions about an Ormondist invasion in 1719 were apparently whipped up by sections of the press, including Cornelius Carter, 'the father of Irish yellow journalism'.[190] According to the testimony of John Whalley, the Tory printers Cornelius Carter, John Harding and Richard Pue were forced to go to ground for printing sensationalist reports in their 'jackish news-papers' that the king of Spain had proclaimed the Pretender [as the true king of England]. They also reported that Captain George Cammocke, another prominent Irish Protestant Jacobite, had offered the Whig admiral Sir George Byng 100,000 pieces of eight and a dukedom, and a reward of £10,000 pounds for every captain that would come over to the Pretender.[191]

Jacobite sympathies within the Protestant community was not confined to the press. While the Catholics reacted optimistically to news from the continent, faint murmurings of support for an Ormondist invasion emanated from the territory of the closet Jacobite, Alexander MacDonnell, third earl of Antrim.[192] In 1718 David Higgins reported from Downpatrick, County Down, on the activities of ensign Murray who had indiscreetly voiced his 'aversion to King George and an affection to the Pretender'. Murray hoped that 'the late duke of Ormonde when he invaded the kingdom would set up a standard and declare for the church'. He drank confusion to regicidal Presbyterians and assured his hearers that he 'would never imbue his hands in the blood of a king [James III]'. He also made 'several other base sayings concerning the invasion now and formerly talked of from Spain'. Higgins claimed that if Murray obtained a *noli prosequi*, 'the Jacobites whereof there is a great plenty in this place will speak against the king and constitution'.[193]

'Jacobite argument', pp 175, 192-3, 202-4.   **188** Although it seems that this seditious elegy has not survived or may never have been printed, a contemporary deposition sheds some light on its contents, 'The examination of Rev Mr William Harris of Fishamble Street taken before Hon. William Caulfield on his majesty's kings bench', 30 Oct. 1717 (Marsh's Library Z.3.1.1 [cxii]). For a profile of Carter; Munter, *A dictionary*, p. 50; Phillips, *Printing and book-selling in Dublin*, p. 60.   **189** pp 172-3 262.   **190** Munter, *A dictionary*, p. 50.   **191** *Whalley's. N.*, 4 Apr. 1719. The exact details of Camocke's activities compare very favourably with this report; Charnock, *Biogrphia Navalis*, 6 vols, iii , pp 221-30. See also *H.M.C.*, *Stuart*, i, 371-2, 382, 430; ii, 364, iv, 7, 492; v, 63-4; vi, 213, 302, 397, 400, 432; vii, 312, 393, 661); MacDonnell, *The Wild Geese of the Antrim MacDonnells*, pp 78, 81-2, 83, 85. Edward Waters, the printer, was tried in 1720 while Harding again appeared before Chief-Justice William Whitshed in 1724; Williams (ed.), *Correspondence*, ii, pp 240, 375. Harding eventually died in custody for printing Swift's *Letter to the whole people of Ireland*; Higgins, *Swift's politics*, p. 159. Paul Chapman sheds light on Jacobite ballad-culture in contemporary England; Chapman, 'Jacobite political argument', pp 203-6.   **192** Mac Donnell, 'Jacobitism and the third and fourth earls of Antrim', pp 50-5.   **193** David Higgins to Craggs,

The catch-cry of 'Ormonde and the High Church' among the Dublin mob also points to a continued Protestant Jacobite contribution to the popular political life of the city, and to the importation of orthodox English Jacobite slogans.[194] Although King confidently reported in summer 1718 that Trinity College students were no longer 'mainly' Jacobite and that Jacobitism received no 'great' encouragement therein, three students fought with English soldiers who objected to their singing 'The king shall enjoy his own again'.[195] Although King reiterated Irish Protestant solidarity against the Pretender, he admitted to the existence of a residual 'Tory' element which intermittently manifested itself in the Jacobite mob and in the printing industry. Other commentators on both sides of the political divide suggest that sympathy for the Stuart cause survived among members of the old Tory interest (Chetwood, Brownlow, Barrymore, Annesley, Granard, Charlemont, Athenry and Mayo), Protestant converts (Kingston and McCarthy) and a literary circle which included Orrery, Swift, Sheridan, Cope, Browne and Harry and Robin Leslie. Its survival has to be measured against the fact that the Tory party had been completely demoralised in Ireland following the attainder of Ormonde and the removal of Arran (!) Longford, Phipps Orrery and Barrymore and Phipps to England. Residual Protestant Jacobitism was less likely to show itself publicly in the bleak climate of early-Georgian Ireland. As Connolly has observed, 'allegations of Jacobitism or fellow travelling, damaging enough in England, were much more so in Ireland'.[196]

V

Jacobitism remained associated with all aspects of Irish Catholic life in this period. Priest-catchers, informers and other dissolute witnesses hoisted the Jacobite scarecrow at every opportunity and the laws against the Catholic clergy aristocracy and gentry were imposed during periods of threatened invasion. The greater Catholic community also suffered from the resulting curtailment of Catholic worship, the ban on visits to local shrines, wells and places of pilgrimage and the prohibition of popular sporting events. These oppressions, along with Catholic expectations and recruitment, kept Jacobitism alive at a popular level during the political stagnation of the late 1720s and 1730s.

---

20 Apr. 1718 (P.R.O., S.P., 67/7/84). At the same time the soldiers quartered at Waterford were withdrawn by their officers from the Cathedral Church on the grounds that the preaching of the bishop tended to alienate them from the establishment; Lecky, *Irel.*, i, p. 423. **194** *Pue's O.*, 2 -6 June 1719; Mac Craith, 'Filíocht Sheacaibíteach', pp 61-2. **195** King to Molyneux, 12 July 1718 (T.C.D., Ms 750/11 3, fols 214-5). King rejoiced that 'idlers and Jacobites have no great encouragement in the college'; T.C.D., Ms 750/5, fols 14-5. In spite of these assurances, Archbishop Hugh Boulter of Armagh feared the menace of Jacobitism in the college as late as 1727, Connolly, *Religion*, p. 240. **196** Connolly, *Religion*, p. 86.

Recruitment remained as a central tenet of Irish popular Jacobitism. Witnesses habitually raised the Jacobite bugbear with regards to recruiting; key members of the surviving Munster Catholic aristocracy and gentry, prominent Protestant converts, unregistered Catholic priests, rapparees, smugglers, gun-runners and privateers also remained associated with recruitment. Recruiters placed great emphasis on 'commissions' received from 'the Pretender' and some recruits refused service to any but 'James III'. These depositions often contained precise information on impending Jacobite invasions and vivid detail on important Jacobite exiles. The allusions to active Jacobite agents in Spain suggest more than coincidental knowledge of Jacobite high-politics and recruitment networks. It remained a major preoccupation of the government in the period before the outbreak of a general European war in 1742 and the Irish Brigades, their ultimate destination, was seen by many as a Jacobite army-in-waiting.

The exiles stressed Ireland's diversionary role in the re-conquest of the other Stuart kingdoms. Influential exiles also advocated an invasion in the late 1720s, while clerical Jacobite agents kept them informed of the strength of the Irish establishment and the state of the indigenous Jacobite community. Further-more, reports from British officials in Spain and the independent evidence of those recruits who turned king's evidence, uncovered numerous contacts between the exiles and their native land as carried through Irish sea-captains and ship-owners. The surviving correspondence of Ambrose O'Callaghan, Sylvester Lloyd, James McKenna and lesser members of the Catholic clergy confirm the involvement of the Catholic clergy in Jacobite espionage.

Irish poetry reflected the nuances of contemporary Jacobite politics. Having been cast adrift by their French confederates, Philip V of Spain became the new hero of the Irish literary tradition. Cardinal Alberoni and Spanish-based Jacobites such as the earl marischal and the duke of Ormonde replaced Mar and Berwick in the affections of Irish poets. The failure of Ormonde's successive invasions resonates in Irish Jacobite poetry. They turned their attention to mourning the death of the queen-dowager Mary of Modena, the cult of the 'martyr-king' James II and the woeful state of their son's political affairs. This set the stage for the hitherto unthinkable despair of Seán na Ráithíneach Ó Murchú.

In spite of the flagging fortunes of contemporary Jacobite diplomacy, the Irish exiles featured prominently in the output of Jacobite poets and Protestant pamphleteers alike. Their correspondence with the Stuart court included optimistic commentaries on European politics, requests to James III for pensions, pedigrees, titles, preferments, petitions for medals, touch-pieces for the king's evil, prints and pictures of the royal family. All this was vital to the sur-vival of their Jacobite identity in a period of diplomatic isolation and inactivity. The links maintained between Ireland and the continent were crucial to the elaboration, maintenance and survival of a Jacobite ideology until the end of the 1750s.

CHAPTER 5

'Agus briseadh go deo ar Shéamas':[1]
Jacobitism in the doldrums, 1725-39

The Anglo-French alliance of 1716 secured the Hanoverian succession in Britain and Ireland, protected Hanover and thwarted the political ambitions of Philip V of Spain. It remained the corner-stone of European diplomacy until 1731, effectively isolating the Jacobites. Nevertheless there were periods of tension during the 1720s when relations between France and Spain temporarily improved and threatened to transform the international situation to the advantage of the Stuarts.[2] To the general amazement of Europe, Austria and Spain negotiated a treaty in July 1725 which prompted James III to observe that 'the affairs of Europe seem now to be in such a situation as to promise us soon some happy turn in our favour'. The possibility of a league between France, Spain and Austria was no fantasy in 1725.[3] In 1726 the Jacobite representative in Vienna presented a memoir to Prince Eugene of Savoy guaranteeing the Pragmatic Sanction (Emperor Charles VI's proposal for the succession of his eldest daughter Maria Theresa) and supporting the Ostend Company in the event of a restoration of the Stuarts. In return, the Austrians were asked to provide 6,000 men to aid a Jacobite invasion.[4]

Other powers also emerged as possible allies of the Stuart king. As early as 1724, the Jacobites believed that the czar of Russia would attempt something in their favour.[5] Later, in 1727, they hoped that Czarina Catherine would send her troops to attack Hanover. Between 1733-5, many expected that Louis XV's mobilisation in support of the claims of his father-in-law Stanislas Leszczynski during the War of the Polish Succession, and his subsequent attack on Austria, would precipitate Britain's entry into the conflict. This raised the possibility of

---

1 Seán na Ráithíneach Ó Murchú, 'Do dhearbhadh linn', in Torna (eag.), *Seán na Ráithíneach*, p. 130. 2 Black, 'British foreign policy 1731-35', in Cruickshanks and Black (ed.), *Jacobite challenge*, pp 142-60. 3 Black, 'British foreign policy 1731-35', p. 145. 4 Eugene told him that assistance for the Stuart cause was useless unless there was strong internal support; Black, *British foreign policy in the age of Walpole*, pp 146-7. 5 Black, *British foreign policy in the age of Walpole*, p. 143. Hoadly, *An enquiry*, pp 31-3. Contemporary Irish *émigré* Jacobite hopes rested on the czar, the king of Spain and the duke of Lorraine; R.A., Ms 72, fol. 104.

open Bourbon support for the Jacobites. French naval and military activity was in marked contrast to Britain's total lack of preparation for war.[6]

Irish Jacobites carefully monitored these diplomatic developments which impacted on all sections of the Irish community. The Stuart claimant and his confederates regularly featured in the press in the immediate aftermath of the abortive Spanish invasions of the early 1720s. Newspapers reported extensively on rumours of Austro-Spanish and Russian plots, as well as incidences of Jacobite gun-running and privateering. Catholic Jacobite activity and related lawlessness complemented the sustained official contact between Ireland and the exiled court through the Jacobite episcopate. Jacobite recruitment to the Irish Brigades in the French service ensured that many on both sides of the political divide viewed the brigades as a Jacobite army-in-exile. The enduring links between Ireland and the continent guaranteed the survival of Jacobitism during the diplomatic paralysis of the later 1720s and 1730s.

I

The Irish press reported on the short-term flirtation between Bourbon Spain and the Imperial Hapsburgs in 1725-7. It seethed with insinuations of Jacobite intrigues and kept the activities of 'the Pretender' and his cohorts firmly in the public domain. It retained a particular (almost fanatical) preoccupation with Ormonde and Wharton, two of the more senior Jacobite figures on the continent in the later 1720s.[7] Cardinal Alberoni's frequent visits to Clementina Sobieska, the estranged wife of James III, were also reported, as was a plot to send James and his sons to Ireland or Scotland in the spring of 1727 with the assistance of the king of Spain and the emperor. The news-sheets also alluded to a diversionary

---

6 Black, *British foreign policy in the age of Walpole*, pp 147, 150, 152-3. Stanislaus had been elected by the Polish Sejun in 1733 after the death of Augustus II. Aside from the fact that Stanislaus was the father of the queen of France, the French had traditionally protected Polish independence; Petrie, *Berwick*, p. 321. The possibility of combined Bourbon support for the Stuart cause was considerably enhanced by the birth of a dauphin in November 1733 and Philip V's admission that his claim to the French throne was unrealistic.   7 The Dublin press remained totally obsessed with the activities of Ormonde and Wharton; *Dick. I.*, 2 Apr. 1726, 19 Apr. 1726, 23 Apr. 1726, 30 Apr. 1726, 22 Oct. 1726, 5 Nov. 1726, 3, 7 Jan. 1727, 13-18 May 1727, 10-13 June 1727, 10-17 June 1727, 13 June 1727, 10 Apr. 1728, 15 Apr. 1729, 13 May 1729, 10 June 1729, 1 July 1729, 19 July 1729, 25 Nov. 1729, 29 Nov. 1729; *Dub. Week. J.*, 6 Aug. 1726, 20 Aug. 1726, 26 Nov. 1726, 3 Dec. 1726, 11 Mar. 1727, 20 Apr. 1728, 1 June 1728, 13 July 1728, 21 Sept. 1728, 2 Nov. 1728, 28 Feb. 1729, 22 May 1731, 12 June 1731; *Fau. Dub. J.*, 24 May 1726, 5 Aug. 1726, 15 Oct. 1726, 29 Oct. 1726, 26 Nov. 1726, 3 Jan. 1727, 4 Mar. 1727, 8 Mar. 1727, 25 Mar. 1727; *Need. P.*, 4 Apr. 1726, 16 Aug. 1727; *Walsh's Mer.*, 22 Apr. 1726, 26 May 1726, 10 Aug. 1726, 9 Mar. 1727; *Dick. P.*, 22 Apr. 1726; *Walsh's Cas. Cour.*, 5 Aug. 1726, 3 Oct. 1726; *Dub. Gaz.*, 5 Aug. 1726, *Fa. Post.*, 1 Sept. 1726; *Whitehall Gaz.*, 3 Oct. 1726; St *James's Evening Post.*, 31 Oct. 1726; *Fau. Week. J.*, 8 Jan. 1727; *Weekly Post*, 10 Feb. 1729; *Fl. P.*, 16 May 1729; *Walsh's Dub. P.*, 9 Nov. 1730. The Jacobite suspect Knightley Chetwood also alluded to Wharton's activities, rumours of the breach between Walpole and the duke of Argyll, the Pretender's arrival in the Hague and rumours of war; 'Chetwood Letters', pp 100-6, 381-6, 410-15.

expedition by George Keith, the ninth earl marischal, into Scotland. The recall of Scottish regiments from Ireland made the Jacobites 'prick up their ears'.[8]

Benjamin Hoadly, published *An enquiry into the reasons of the conduct of Great Britain with relation to the present state of affairs* in 1727, criticising the machinations of Austria and Spain, whom he believed owed so much to King George. The bishop reminded Irish Catholics and Protestants alike of the Pretender's continued relevance in British and Irish politics.[9] He explored the intrigues of James III's minister in Vienna, and the meetings between the renegade Wharton and an unnamed Russian minister. Appalled at the welcome given to Ormonde and Wharton at the Spanish court, he cautioned against the tendency among Protestants to dismiss the Jacobite threat as a political bugbear:

> I know very well how easy and how common it is to laugh at the name of the Pretender whenever it is mentioned upon some occasions as a political bugbear or scarecrow; a mere word of alarm or a puppet to be played by statesmen at their pleasure. But it is important for Great Britain and will end in total ruin for ourselves and our posterity, if those who are at the helm should suffer themselves at the pleasure of such who wish them no good to be laughed out of that care and watchfulness their king and country require of them.[10]

Calling for renewed vigilance, Hoadly highlighted the preparations of 12,000 men at Galicia and Biscay and the arrival at Cadiz of Spanish ships with 5,000 stand of arms destined for the Pretender. The *Dublin Intelligence* reported that Spain intended to organise another Ormonde-led invasion attempt.[11] The press and official government correspondence hummed with accounts of recruitment, in particular the case of a Franco-Irish officer named John O'Connor 'who had been very active in taking men out of the country'. His incarceration had prompted the direct intercession of Count de Broglie, French ambassador to Britain.[12]

8 *Walsh's Cas. Cour.*, 27 Jan. 1727; *Dub. I.*, 10 Jan. 1727; 14 Feb. 1727; 28 Mar. 1727; 18-22 Apr. 1727. See above pp 235-6.   **9** Hoadly, *An enquiry*, p. 3. Reports of the engagements entered into between the king of Spain and the emperor circulated in pamphlets and broadsheets; *Humble address of the right honourable lords spiritual and temporal, January 1726*; *A letter from Count Sinzendorff, sent to M. de Palm, the emperor's resident at the court of the king of Great Britain*; Hoadly, *An enquiry*, p. 21. Black has alluded to contemporary fears of Austria and Prussia acting against Hanover in this period; Black (ed.), *Walpole*, p. 147.   **10** Hoadly, *An enquiry*, pp 3, 17-18, 20, 27 and 29. Another contemporary pamphlet commented on the machinations of France and Spain; *Reasons of the utmost importance*, pp 3-4. The fragility of the Hanoverian state on the arrival of Charles Edward in 1745 justified Hoadly's (and Prime-Minister Walpole's) warnings to the political establishment against such complacency. **11** In a letter to the House of Commons, George I claimed that the British government had intercepted correspondence between Ormonde and Mar which stated that the Spanish were sending deserters of all nations to Catalonia and that a great intercession was being made with the king of Spain in order to arm the Pretender for another invasion; *Dub. I.*, 2 Apr. 1726.   **12** *Need. P.*, 24 Jan. 1726; *Dub. Week. J.*, 10 Apr. 1726; *Dub. I.*, 18 Apr. 1726. Another report stated that 'many others are

The diplomatic flirtations between Russia and the Jacobite court ensured that considerable attention was given to the three Russian men-of-war off the Irish coast in July 1725, their attempted embarkation for Scotland and eventual detention at Limerick and Galway in July 1725. In November Lord Lieutenant Carteret ordered revenue commissioners to send accounts of all arriving ships and he commanded General Pearce, governor of Limerick, to strengthen the garrison there. Carteret believed that these ships were linked to recruiting for foreign service and despatched Captain Townsend of the *Success* in Waterford and Captain Rowley, commander of the *Lively*, to send intelligence of departing recruits. He further believed that these Russian ships had come to encourage dissaffection within the kingdom or to convey intelligence or arms. It was claimed that they had earlier put in at the Isle of Lewis in Scotland on their way from Spain with naval stores, and Carteret surmised that they had come to encourage disaffection in the kingdom, to land arms or gather intelligence.[13]

At the same time a ship from Rotterdam landed at Killybegs, County Donegal. It was laden with small arms, muskets, swords, pistols, two or three hundred small barrels of gunpowder, ball, shot and trumpets, allegedly bound for Africa and commanded by Captain William Doyle of Waterford. Suspecting that Doyle harboured Jacobite sympathies, a local government official tendered him the oaths of allegiance to King George, which he readily took. Nonetheless Thomas Hammond, Thomas Lindell and John Keynell, all members of Doyle's crew, alleged that he held Jacobite sympathies, and a commission from the emperor or the king of Spain (possibly procured by Ormonde), four commissions from 'the Pretender' and four sets of colours.[14] He had not been given clearance from Rotterdam, and was 'surely' in the Pretender's interest, having been forced to flee Hamburg after Lord Townsend had issued orders for his arrest. Furthermore Doyle had allegedly called the Pretender 'James III' and commanded a ship in Spain's service. He also had connections with a Jacobite named Richard Reeves in Ireland and Dominic Sarsfield at Ostend.[15]

constantly plying their trade about this city [Dublin] for lusty fellows under the notion of recruiting the Irish Regiments in France'; *Dub. I.*, 7 May 1726. The State papers abounded with depositions regarding the recruiting activities of a ship called the 'William and Catherine' of Portsmouth in County Cork in April 1726; P.R.O., S.P., 63/388/11, 13, 15, 17, 23, 69. For French diplomatic intervention in O'Connor's case; P.R.O., S.P., 63/387/176. According to one informant O'Connor had brought many recruits out of the country; P.R.O., S.P., 63/387/178. Eleanor O'Connor claimed that he had abducted her husband for the French service; P.R.O., S.P., 63/387/178, 182.   **13** Extract from a letter by John Madden, coast officer, 12 July 1725; P.R.O., S.P. 67/8/81. See also; P.R.O., S.P., 67/8/81, 107; P.R.O., S.P., 63/386/286, 316.   **14** The high-political context is discussed in the chapter introduction.   **15** John Donnell to Nicholas Foster, church of Ireland bishop of Raphoe, 10 Apr. 1726 (P.R.O., S.P., 63/387/146). See also P.R.O., S.P., 63/387/134, 142, 154, 156, 167. He had purportedly applied to the grand duke of Tuscany for a patent for two privateers to hunt down pirates but turned a pirate himself. For his contemporary links with Richard Reeves; *H.M.C., Polwarth*, iv, p. 223. He also had contact with Dominic [Patrick, according to one of these letters] Sarsfield in Ostend; R. Daniel to Marchmont, 14-18 Apr. 1725, in *H.M.C., Polwarth*, iv, pp 280, 285. Port officers reported all ships that touched Irish harbours; P.R.O., S.P., 63/387/136. Dominic Sarsfield was no stranger to

The Stuart court was alerted to Doyle's incarceration in another report on the state of the Irish Jacobite community from Bishop Sylvester Lloyd in May 1726. Lloyd reported to Daniel O'Brien, James III's representative in Paris, that he had just visited the Jacobite heartland of Munster 'where you have many friends [who are] very impatient to see you'. James's supporters in Munster were fully aware of the latest developments in European diplomacy and the rumours of a Jacobite invasion. He assured O'Brien that 'I will miss no opportunity that I can with prudence lay hold of to promote your interest'. He also guaranteed that 'one thing you can depend on, that whenever you commence your suit, you will not want witnesses to prove your title, so impatient are all your own neighbours to see you restored to your rights'. He reiterated the time-honoured claim of Irish Jacobites at home and abroad: 'Arms and officers are all we want. I shall make use of all means that art and providence can suggest to dispose our friends in Dublin to do their duty if any army should be intended'. He did, however, have a number of novel proposals for the effective reduction of Dublin: 'We must endeavour to seize the Bank of Dublin and the small port of Waterford, and other places, if matters be indiscreetly managed. There will be no impossibility in this'. In conclusion, he referred to the fate of Captain Doyle:

> A ship of 4 and 20 guns commanded by one Doyle, an Irishman, has lately been seized at a place called Killibeg, a harbour in the north of this kingdom, on suspicion that he came with an evil design on our coast. The captain was brought under a strong guard and is actually a prisoner in the castle [Dublin]. I am told he says he is bound from Holland to the West Indies and only just came into Ireland to take provisions. What the end of this affair will be I can't tell but we are in great fright. The great God give our friend a blessing.[16]

The stalwart Lloyd communicated regularly with the Stuart court in Rome, re-assuring the exiles of the strength of the Jacobite community within Ireland, and keeping Irish Jacobites abreast of European politics. He arranged for correspondence from Jacobite circles as far afield as Sweden to come through the post office in Bordeaux to a Mr Pine in Dublin.[17] Lloyd also reported the

seditious traffic (p. 149, fn. 161). Daniel O'Brien later recommended a similar gun-running voyage to the Madagascar pirates as a blue-print for the importation of arms into the Scottish highlands in October 1727; R.A., Ms 111, fol. 2. For a note on O'Brien; Hayes, *Biographical dictionary*, p. 214. **16** Lloyd to Col. O'Brien, 25 May 1726; R.A., Ms 114, fol. 137; Fagan (ed.), *Stuart papers*, i, pp 77-8. For the emphasis on prudence in the pursuit of King James affairs, see below, fn. 116. **17** Copy of Lloyd's letter to Colonel Daniel O'Brien, 6 May 1726; R.A., Ms 93, fol. 82. He also sent a complete list of horse and foot; R.A., Ms 99, fols 28-9. Lloyd's diocese [Killaloe] was one of the biggest in Ireland, some 150 miles in circumference and crossing the borders of four countries. He preached and ministered in every corner of it; Ó Buachalla, *Aisling Ghéar*, p. 641. At this time, his episcopal colleague Ambrose O'Callaghan, bishop of Ferns, trafficked in pig-tail (tobacco) with the Stuart court; R.A., Ms 140, fol. 71; see also; R.A., Ms 157, fol. 10; R.A., Ms 160, fol. 122; R.A., Ms 191, fol.

deep-felt rage of Irish Catholics at parliament's attempts to introduce coercive legislation, and the scandalous rumours in Dublin regarding James's rupture with his consort Clementina.[18] Although these reports of James's marital difficulties also abounded in the press Tadhg Ó Neachtain deemed them too sensitive for inclusion in a common-place book which he compiled from contemporary newspapers.[19]

Irish Catholic Jacobite expectancy of impending war surfaced in another missive from the redoubtable Lloyd in June 1726. While his exaggerated accounts need to be treated with considerable caution, they revealed the trepidation caused by the diversion of troops to England. He reported that since his landing in Ireland he had seen multitudes of his majesty's Catholic and Protestant friends. He underlined their willingness to serve the Jacobite cause: 'It is impossible to express the impatience they are in to do him service. The rumours we have of an approaching war have made many who I never believed sincerely in his interest declare themselves in the most honest and resolute manner'. He also reflected Whig concerns at the movement of troops from Ireland: 'Let the matter be as it will our enemies here are in the greatest consternation. Four regiments of foot have been shipped off for the west of England. General McCartney is come over hither and 'tis said the remaining part of our troops are to form a camp near Athlone, a place on the river Shannon in the centre of the kingdom'. He then noted the administration's extraordinary caution in imposing the Oath of Allegiance on Catholics.[20]

This official apprehension contrasted sharply with the high spirits of the Dublin Jacobites who unrestrainedly celebrated James III's birthday in 1726. The customary wearing of white roses resulted in a riot between the Jacobite mob and the lord mayor's forces, in which four people were injured and over thirty arrested. Boulter understated the level of trouble by dismissing the annual fracas between the papist 'rabble' and the Whig 'mob'. He did concede that the papists had come out in strength and were more animated than usual at the prospect of war in Europe. The involvement of eighty government troops and the arrest of thirty combatants would suggest that this was a wholesale riot:

> As we had some trouble in the town last night, I thought it my duty to give your lordship a short account of it to prevent it being taken for a greater affair than it proved. As there had been various reports spread about the town that the papists intended to make a rising about 10 June,

154; P.R.O., S.P., 67/9/141. **18** Lloyd to Col O'Brien, 25 May 1726 (R.A., Ms 114, fol. 137); Fagan (ed.), *Stuart papers*, i, pp 77–8. See also R.A. 93, fol. 82. **19** *Dub. I.*, 13 Sept. 1726, 17 Sept. 1726, 1 Oct. 1726; *Dick. I.*, 16 May 1727; *A letter from the Lord W[har]ton to the earl Cad[o]gan*. Ó Buachalla, 'Seacaibíteachas', p. 48. James's marital difficulties also caused great heart-searching the Scottish writer George Lockhart; Szechi, 'George Lockhart of Carnwath', p. 989. **20** S. Lloyd to J. Hay, 1 June 1726 (R.A., Ms 94, fol. 54). 'All Europe in agitation once more'; Hoadly, *An Enquiry*, p. 21. See also Fagan, *Dublin's turbulent priest*, p. 126.

though we had no reason to apprehend any such thing would be attempted we thought ourselves obliged in prudence to give the proper direction to forces here ... All things were quiet till yesterday evening when a very numerous rabble assembled in St Stephen's Green as the usually have done on 10 June ... Upon complaints the lord mayor attended with a number of constables came on the green to disperse the rabble but meeting with opposition they were assembled with staves and bricks ... at first the rabble would not disperse but upon wounding three or four of them about thirty of them are taken and imprisoned. They will very speedily be examined and we are not without hope of finding some gentlemen who by some circumstances are thought to have had a hand in occasioning these disturbances ... But at present we don't find much in it other than the papist rabble coming down to fight the Whig mob as they do on that day. On the prospect of war the papists here are better in heart so they might come in greater numbers.[21]

In July 1727, Lloyd sent Colonel O'Brien a list of 'queries' circulated among Dublin Catholics in relation to an approach to the new king (George II) from leading 'Pale' gentry (including the earls of Westmeath, Carlingford, Fingal and Lord Trimbleston) on behalf of their Catholic brethren. In their judgement, Jacobitism had become an increasingly intolerable millstone around the neck of Irish Catholicism. This incident provides evidence of the first major rupture in the relatively cohesive if politically redundant Irish Catholic polity.[22] The earl of Westmeath, an absentee based in London, organised a meeting on 8 July 1727 of some of the principal Irish Catholics at the 'Lyon Inn' (Werburgh Street, Dublin). He informed the assembly that their proposed approach to King George II had the support of Cardinal Fleury, the French prime-minister. Lloyd attested that when they had been suitably plied with alcohol they were encouraged to put their names to an address to King George. He claimed that many of those who signed had returned the following morning, demanding that their signatures be removed from the petition.

The Irish ecclesiastical forces of the exiled monarch quickly mobilised to neutralize this affront to his dignity. The first of Lloyd's 'queries' questioned whether 'three or four lords and about twenty gentlemen without election or

---

21 Boulter to Newcastle, 11 June 1726, Boulter, *Letters*, i, p. 65. For similar sentiments, see lords justice to the lord lieutenant, 11 June 1726 (N.L.I., Ms 2446). See also P.R.O., S.P., 63/387/208; *Dub. J.*, 11 June 1726; *Dick. I.*, 11 June 1726; *Fau. Dub. J.*, 11 June 1726; *Dub. Cour.*, 5 July 1726; *Dick. I.*, 10 June 1727; See also *Dub. I.*, 13, 17 June 1724; Boulter, *Letters*, i, pp 80-1; T.C.D., Ms 750/8, fols 231-2; *Dub. I.*, 14 June 1729. A proclamation was issued against those involved in this rioting; *Twenty-third report of the deputy-keeper*, p. 64. Ó Buachalla provides further information on the Jacobite drinking-culture in the Irish language and suggests that the poet Tadhg Ó Neachtain was part of a Jacobite drinking club; Ó Buachalla, *Aisling Ghéar*, pp 390-1. **22** The best recent account of this approach to George II is Fagan, *Divided loyalties*, pp 63-74.

deputation from the Roman Catholics can in any honest sense be understood to be the Roman Catholics of Ireland'.[23] Some historians claim that the views expressed in Lloyd's riposte were no less representative of Irish Catholic opinion than the pronouncements of Westmeath and his colleagues. These bishops were appointees of the pope, almost all were nominated by James III and they would have wielded greater influence through the lower clergy and greater Catholic community than a coterie of absentee Catholic lords who had effectively disengaged from active politics.

Lloyd's second and third queries asked 'whether in their meeting at the Lyon on the 8th of July the proper parties concerned were all present' or whether such an address was not 'precipitate', 'passionate' and 'presumptuous'. The fourth query asserted that the oath was 'injurious to the sentiments of the holy mother church and dishonourable to the renowned fidelity of an Irishman', while the fifth viewed the penal laws as a continuing popular grievance, despite the ingratiating rhetoric of self-serving Catholic lords. Lloyd claimed that certain obsequious language in the address 'wiped away our tears without removing the cause' and dismissed this fawning approach as 'vile and nauseous flattery'. He reminded Catholics of their indispensable religious duties and reiterated Irish loyalty to God's anointed. Finally, he rejected as irrelevant the common distinctions between loyalty to the *de jure* and *de facto* king by emphatically stating that 'allegiance in our language and laws' means 'more than mere fidelity'. Given the evident influence of the Stuart king on the Irish mission, this distinction between *de jure* and *de facto* is less marked in Catholic Ireland than in any other of the Stuart kingdoms. The bishop challenged 'the junta' to answer these queries 'to all Irishmen before they presume to present their heinous address in the name of the whole kingdom'.[24] This 'irrelevance' is realistic when one considers the lack of Catholic participation in contemporary Irish political life and the influence of the Stuart king over the Irish mission. Bishop Ambrose O'Callaghan's assurances of Irish loyalty to the Stuart king reinforced Lloyd's claim to speak on their behalf. O'Callaghan believed that James III merited such

23 Lloyd to Col O'Brien, 15, 20 July 1727 (R.A., 108, fols 80, 99); *Dub. J.*, 25-7 July 1727. Bishop Stephen MacEgan stated that 'not above sixty or a few more had signed'; Fagan, *Divided loyalties*, pp 63, 107. **24** Lloyd to Col. O'Brien, Dublin, 20 July 1727 (R.A., Ms 108, fol. 99); Fagan (ed.), *Stuart papers*, i, pp 97-8. Other Irish clerics made loyal postulations in this period; R.A., Ms 102, fol. 106. Another Catholic prelate Stephen MacEgan of Meath referred to this approach to George II as a 'Machivellian scheme'; R.A., Ms 112, fol. 36. Elsewhere Lloyd referred to it as a 'scandalous affair'; R.A., Ms 114, fol. 136. A report in the Nunziatura di Fiandra described those who subscribed to the oath as unrepresentative of the broader Catholic community; News from London, 24 June 1727, in Giblin, 'Catalogue', part 4, vols 102-2, pp 121-2; Fagan (ed) *Stuart papers*, i, p. 108; R.A., Ms 130, fol. 99; Fagan, *Dublin's turbulent priest*, p. 127. In spite of these statements from influential Catholic bishops, Boulter stated that this oath caused 'great heats and divisions among those of that religion here' Boulter, *Letters*, i, pp 150-2. Maureen Wall also claimed that Catholics, for the most part, were quite content to swear a simple oath of allegiance to George II; Wall, 'Catholic loyalty to king and pope', p. 18. See also Fagan, *Divided loyalties*, pp 62-5. Two members of the Irish diaspora reacted with hostility to what one claimed to be a betrayal of 150 years of Irish Catholic loyalty, in Fagan (ed.), *Stuart papers*, i, p. 100; R.A., Ms 126, fol. 12.

devotion as his 'concern for their welfare deserves that return from them' and he promised that his 'endeavours for their relief will not be found wanting'.[25]

This conciliatory approach to the throne prompted Edward Synge, Church of Ireland archbishop of Tuam, to offer an olive branch to the Irish Catholics. He utilised the work of a noted Catholic theologian, Dr Franciscus Martin's *Iberno Galviensis,* to induce Irish and English Catholics to renounce their doctrine of passive obedience.[26] Synge's hostile treatment at the hands of Dublin's Whig balladeers showed that they, like George II, were not yet ready to conciliate Catholics:

> Most are at a loss to find out his true meaning
> Whilst others of some dark design are complaining.
> Some think he's for Martin
> Some for Jack his heart in
> But most do agree he's for Peter 'tis certain.
> O S[y]nge who would think thou were bred at St Germains
> Who reads what opinions you've preached in your sermons.
> Now who will not say you are for the Pretender
> When you oppose the true faith and the faith's true defender.[27]

The struggle for the conscience of Irish Catholicism between Hanoverian conformists and Stuart royalists coincided with the prospect of renewed war in Europe in 1727. The Spanish-Imperial alliance and Spain's hostile pretensions towards Gibraltar caused a fall in stock prices in England and yet another flurry of optimistic correspondence between the Irish exiles and James III.[28] Their Irish-based contemporaries were similarly aroused and Boulter noted that the 'papists eagerly took up reports that Gibraltar had fallen'. His episcopal counterpart Sylvester Lloyd informed Daniel O' Brien that 'we are in the great hurry on account of a rumour that Gibraltar is besieged'. He also noted the concern caused by the delay in the arrival of the 'pacquet boat' and the arrival of several principal officers to raise four new regiments and to ship four others to the 'straights' (of Gibraltar). He concluded that the country would, with the exception of the militia, be denuded of troops.[29]

25 O'Callaghan to James III, 12 June 1731 (R.A., Ms 146, fol. 194). See R.A., Ms 147, fol. 37. **26** Synge, *Sermon preached at St Andrew's,* p. 68. For a consideration of Synge's toleration sermons; Lecky, *Ireland,* i, pp 304-5. See also Fagan, *Divided loyalties,* pp 53-5. **27** *An excellent new song to a good old tune.* Fagan claims that 'an anti-Catholic majority dominated the House of Commons and the voices of moderation (Synge, Clayton and Berkeley) were drowned by a rabid and vocal majority'; Fagan, *Divided loyalties,* p. 75. **28** R.A., Ms 112, fol. 142; R.A., Ms 99, fols 59; R.A., Ms 99, fol. 172; R.A., Ms 102, fol. 62; R.A., Ms 108, fol. 124; R.A., Ms 113, fol. 151; *H.M.C., 11th report,* app. ix, ii, p. 199. Ambrose O'Callaghan expressed horror at the possibility of peace between England and Spain over Gibraltar; R.A., Ms 119, fol. 135. In a later despatch to James, he hoped for peace between France and Spain; R.A., Ms 122, fols 70, 73. **29** Connolly, *Religion,* p. 236; Lloyd to Daniel O'Brien, 5 Jan. 1727, in Fagan (ed.), *Stuart papers,* i, p. 91.

They provided a context for the alleged Jacobite toasting of an English ship-captain Michael Bath 'in the company of three or four gentlemen of the country, all papists' in Ballinskelligs, County Kerry, in March 1727. Bath drank the health of 'Jemmy' several times. When asked the identity of Jemmy, 'he replied laughing a son of his in England'. Rebuked for his villainous intentions, he defiantly declared 'Damn his blood if he valued a half-penny any who heard him, that he meant King James III and accordingly drank his health and struck a gentleman in the company who drank King George's'. He informed the assemblage 'that he had the Pretender on board his ship and had landed him once'. He hoped to 'once again to land his dear Jemmy among his friends, that his dear Jemmy had two thousand men as clever fellows as any in England, ready to engage for him at his command'.[30] Irish opinion remained susceptible to such imported rhetoric, which further reinforced and preserved the Jacobite ideology. Consistent reporting in the newspapers also kept the exiled Stuart at the forefront of Irish political life.[31] Even the normally unperturbed Archbishop King expressed his mistrust of Spanish intentions; he deplored their piratical assault on English trade to America and returned to the old bugbear of endemic recruitment for foreign service.[32] This unease contrasted sharply with Catholic elation at the death of George I and the prospect of the Tories coming to power in England.[33] Boulter was dismayed at the demoralised state of the Protestant interest in Ireland and the relative weakness of the armed forces. The emissaries of the king of Spain were active among the Catholics and he lamented that the government had failed to prevent Spanish recruitment.[34] Dr Marmaduke Coghill also despaired at the apparent partiality of the English parliament towards Catholics, in defiance of the Protestant interest. He specified the private bill in favour of the sons of the deceased Jacobite General Arthur Dillon, 'who are persons the Irish have long wished for and on whom they have always depended on to lead and support them when occasion offered'.[35] The possible restoration of Robert McCarthy,

---

30 F. Chute to the chief commissioner of the revenue, Ballinskelligs, 29 Mar. 1727 (P.R.O., S.P., 63/388/210). Boulter noted that recruits were still going off to France and Spain; P.R.O., S.P., 63/388/208. 'I cannot help further suggesting that we have too many here who want neither the disposition or the opportunity to give an account to the enemy of our nakedness to Spain and that it may be a temptation to the enemy, if it only be for the disgrace of the thing to come and insult us in the very harbour of Dublin', Boulter, *Letters*, i, p. 126. **31** *Dub. I.*, 28 Mar. 1727; *Dub. I.*, 18-22 Apr. 1727, 26 Apr.-6 May 1727. **32** King to Annesley, 6 May 1727 (T.C.D., Ms 750/7, fols 194-6). Recruiting and privateering continued to feature in the press; *Fa. Post.*, 7 Mar. 1727; *Need. P.*, 9 Mar. 1727; *Dub. J.*, 27 June 1727; *Dick Fl. P.*, 13 July 1727; *Dub. I.*, 28 Sept. 1728. **33** Boulter to Carteret, 29 June 1727, in Boulter, *Letters*, i, pp 138-9. Orrery claimed that great changes were now talked of; Sir Robert Walpole was to be demolished, the duke of Newcastle's head taken off and the duke of Ormonde recalled, in 'Letters upon various occasions to and from John, earl of Orrery' (Harvard Ms Eng., 218.2, vol. i, N.L.I., mf. p. 786). **34** See Boulter, *Letters*, i, pp 118-19, 121-22, 126, 138-9, 179. **35** Dr Marmaduke Coghill to Edward Southwell, 11 Mar. 1728; B.L., Add. Ms 21, 122, fol. 68. See also B.L., Add. Ms 21, 123, fol. 104. James remained confident of the young Dillon's loyalty; N.L.I., Ms 22, 321, fol. 26 [2]; R.A., Ms 160, fol. 149. In 1738, James informed Mrs Dillon of a zealous letter from 'young Dillon' [in Ireland?]; N.L.I., Ms 22, 323. I have not managed to locate this letter in the Stuart papers.

fifth earl of Clancarthy, to his huge estate in 1735 prompted contrasting reactions from opposite ends of the political spectrum. Seán Clárach rejoiced that the earl of Clancarthy was coming with authority from the crown ('Tá Iarla Chloinne Carrtha le hádhbhar ag teacht ón gcoróinn').[36] It caused consternation in Protestant circles. Orrery informed Swift that 'we live under perpetual terror that Lord Clancarthy's thunderbolt will destroy half our most wealthy neighbours; like chickens in a farmyard, we tremble at the kite above us'.[37]

Numerous examples abounded of increasing Catholic 'insolence' in this period. Catholics insulted the king's officers, their priests were increasingly immune from prosecution, women of fortune fell prey to Catholic abductors and thrifty 'papists' undercut Protestants in the lease market. Presbyterians emigrated in droves, further weakening the Protestant interest. Despite the 'non-political' nature of these activities, they should be considered in assessing the defiant optimism in contemporary Irish literature. As King reported to Southwell:

> I remember something of Ireland for 60 years and made some obser-
> vation on the state of it but I cannot call to mind that the papists seem
> to be so much indulged and favoured since King James time. They insult
> the king's officers everywhere that are concerned in the revenue, nobody
> dares accuse their priests or hinder their insults for by their mobs they
> either maim them or knock them in the head. They take away women
> of fortune by force and they depend on popish embassies for a pardon.[38]

In spite of these fears, however, some Protestant writers dismissed the Jacobite threat. Indeed, once the immediate prospect of a Jacobite landing had receded, the Stuart king emerged as a pathetic, comic figure in contemporary Protestant discourse. One report mockingly described the pope's presentation of a crown to the Stuart claimant, and his regret that he did not have a kingdom to go along with it:

> The Pretender is at present in so great favour with the pope that his
> holiness is continually sending for him. Yesterday, having entertained
> him he took him into his great presence chamber wherein stood a crown
> of beaten gold weighing about 16 oz. and adorned with jewels to a great
> value which the Pretender viewing and much admiring its beauty and

---

36 Seán Clárach Mac Domhnaill, 'Tá Iarla Chloinne Carrtha', in Ó Foghludha (eag.), *Seán Clárach*, p. 106. Ó Buachalla also notes the expectation and elation among the Irish literati at the earl of Clancarthy's ongoing attempts to regain his estate; Ó Buachalla, *Aisling Ghéar*, pp 589, 591. **37** Orrery to Swift, 11 July 1735, in 'Letters written in Ireland 1735-7' (Harvard Ms 218 2f., vol. 7, N.L.I., mf. p. 787); McLynn, 'Good behaviour', p. 49. **38** King to Southwell, 27 Apr. 1728 (T.C.D., Ms 750/9, fols 58-60). See also N.L.I., Ms 2056. Boulter's correspondence sheds light on the fears generated by large-scale emigration to the colonies, Boulter, *Letters*, i, p. 209.

richness asked the pontiff for whom it was designed. The pope, smiling, answered [for] yourself putting it on his head and said it became him tho' not so well as if it had a kingdom to answer it.[39]

Another newspaper reported James's death, ridiculing his royal pretensions and his close association with the pope, Jesuits, and those priests and friars he had sent to Ireland:

> His highness the chevalier de St George, commonly called the Pretender, thro' long expectation of being once more invited to these kingdoms and despair of ever doing any good for himself should he even get safely to any of these, took all so impatiently to heart as threw him into a violent disease which is assumed to have killed him in a few days, notwithstanding all the hopes that could be given him by his holiness, the pope or his physicians or to the contrary from the working underhand of so many Jesuits, priests and friars as have clandestinely been sent to these parts, particularly Ireland.[40]

Samuel Madden's portrayal of the Stuart king in his *Memoirs of the twentieth century* (1728) typified this sarcastic Protestant self-confidence. Describing his 'encounter' with the lineal descendants 'of one of our ancient kings [James II] who abdicated the throne because of his aversion to the northern heresy', Madden deployed all the abusive associations between 'the Pretender', 'his good patrons the Jesuits' and popery.[41]

---

39 *Dub. Gaz.*, 15 Mar. 1729. Elsewhere, the press reported that 'it is now said that the Princess Clementina Sobieski will not go to Rome but that the chevalier de St George will return thither immediately after the Easter holidays'; *A supplement to the Dublin Newsletter*, 20 Mar. 1729. Another claimed that 'some letters from Rome mention that the pope and college of cardinals had several long conferences with the Pretender and made him divers presents and ordered his whole family to come to Rome and reside there, which causes great speculation'; *Walsh's Dub. Week. Imp. N.*, 21 Mar. 1729. A report in *Hussey's Weekly Post* claimed that 'they write from Bologna that not a day passes but some domestic and baggage of the chevalier de St George set out for Rome which makes us conclude that they will be followed by the Princess Sobieski and her two sons'; [*Hussey's*] *Week. P.*, 9 Apr. 1729. **40** *Dub. Gaz.*, 15 Mar. 1729.   **41** Madden, *Memoirs*, pp 51-2. Although the Stuart claim had dissolved long before the twentieth century, some of Madden's predictions had an uncanny accuracy. 'Henry IX's' prefectship of the college of cardinals realised the Pretender's imagined portfolio of valet-de-chambre to his holiness. While Charles Edward had little truck with the Jesuits or any religious order, an illegitimate daughter (Charlotte, later duchess of Albany) became his sole successor, the theatre rather than the opera provided the prince's main diversion and his retinue eventually took on an eerie resemblance to that anticipated by Madden. The nunnery gave sanctuary to his mother, his mistress and his wife in the final tragic chapters of the Stuart saga. By the time that Madden managed to go to press with this work (1733-4), however, the rumblings of the War of the Polish Succession had considerably altered the political situation in Europe in favour of the exiled Stuarts. This transformation, the quasi-Jacobite activities of the hero and his indirect criticism of the ministry in a book which Madden dedicated to Frederick, prince of Wales (to whom he may have acted as a tutor), might explain why he destroyed over one thousand copies before they could go into circulation. For an alternative view, see Wilson, *History of the future*, pp 135-6.

Nevertheless, the Jacobite faithful still managed their annual display in the late 1720s and early 1730s. In July 1730 the lord mayor of Dublin took precautionary measures against 'meetings of a seditious character', and doubled the guard to prevent 'any celebration marking the birthday of the Pretender'. The report asserted that 'evil-intentioned people assembled at various places wearing white roses and insulted those passers-by whom they thought to belong to the opposite party'. It added that 'they did not even spare the officers of justice and many of the rebels were injured, killed or arrested by the soldiers'. The disturbances continued for three nights.[42]

Irish Jacobites were much more likely to engage in this type of aggression against their enemies when they visited continental Europe. Leghorn, which contained a vibrant Irish exile community, provides a useful microcosm of interchange between the exiles and their native land.[43] A Whig merchant named Clarke abused King James III, Queen Clementina, the royal family and their Jacobite retainers as 'beggars and scandalous people', before unsheathing his sword and defiantly throwing down the gauntlet to the assemblage. This challenge was eagerly taken up by a native of Waterford named Murphy. He 'had lately came from thence with his ships and he endeavoured to pass into the conversation with a strong resolution to bring Clarke to account for what he had said.' A fatal confrontation was prevented by the man of the house and his servants.[44] Aside from describing this abrasive political exchange, these letters catalogue the continued traffic between the two sections of the Irish Jacobite community, exposing an *émigré* Jacobite underworld of toasting, ballad-singing and music which mirrors the Irish literary tradition.[45]

---

42 Report from Dublin, 19 July 1727, in Giblin (ed.), 'Catalogue', part 5, vols 123-32, p. 14; see also P.R.O., S.P., 63/392/154. As late as June 1735, the lord mayor of Dublin published a proclamation against the wearing of white roses; *Country Journal*, 9 June 1735.   **43** Cullen, *Emergence of modern Ireland*, p. 33.   **44** Paul Kearney to Thomas Tyrrell, Jan.-May 1734 (R.A., Ms 170, fol. 150). Nick Duff, a native of Dublin and captain of the 'Elizabeth', also defended aspersions cast on James II; R.A., Ms 185, fol. 130.   **45** Kearney to Tyrrell, 9 Aug. 1734 (R.A., Ms 172, fol. 74). Kearney informed Tyrrell that one Burn, the captain of an Irish ship, had a poor country woman and her child on board his ship 'going to Rome to claim his majesty's usual clemency'; R.A., Ms 178, fol. 78. He also informed him that a 'a private gathering' (a collection?) was made for one Mr O'Neile who was seeking passage to the papal port of Civita Vecclia; R.A., 181 fol. 48. Another man named O'Neile returned to Ireland to do an errand for Colonel McMahon; R.A., Ms 182, fol. 84. Captain Redmond, a ship's captain from Dublin, had the opportunity to kiss the prince of Wales's hand when he was lodged in a convent in Genoa. Lord Dunbar warned Redmond not to tell people on his return to Dublin that he had seen the prince in this dress 'for it was somewhat effeminate', a possible allusion to Charles Edward's use of female attire nearly ten years before his adaptation of the persona of Betty Burke in the aftermath of the 'Forty-five'; R.A., Ms 197, fol. 16. Kearney sent his thanks to Tyrrell for his receipt of a ballad he had sent him; R.A., Ms 209, fol. 48. A small child named Netterville, accompanied by a Dominican friar, brought Scotch snuff, pig-tail, '*usquebagh*' (whiskey) and butter from Ireland; R.A., Ms 213, fol. 91. An Irish piper 'played his bags and surprised the whole theatre who had never heard the like music'; R.A., Ms 213, fol. 154. Kearney's correspondence from October 1740 also had news of food riots in Dublin; R.A., Ms 226, fol. 179. See also R.A., Ms 172, fol. 107; Fagan (ed.), *Stuart papers*, i, pp 162, 168. Such displays of Jacobite solidarity were not exclusively confined to Leghorn. In his macaronic poem composed in Newfoundland 'As I was walking one

Murphy's exhibitionist Jacobite display in Italy would have been impossible in the stifling Irish political climate described by Dr Christopher Butler, Catholic archbishop of Cashel in April 1734. Butler warned of the hazards of correspondence from Ireland 'where all letters going out of the country and coming in are opened and brought to the government'. A disturbance had been caused by 'a poor priest' (John Henessy, parish priest of Doneraile, County Cork) who had been dismissed from his ministry by his bishop (Tadhg Mac-Cárthaigh Riabhach, Catholic bishop of Cloyne) because of his scandalous life and for invading a neighbouring parish. He appealed to the civil authorities and claimed that the archbishop of Cashel was collecting money for the Stuart king. His story was all the more readily believed when a paper written by a prominent Catholic solicitor, Patrick Nagle, was found in Mac Cárthaigh Riabhach's papers. This comprised a list of those who had subscribed money to be used for a campaign to soften anti-Catholic legislation. The upshot of this discovery was the appointment of a special committee of the House of Commons which required that the laws be put into execution against Catholics. Fenning claims that the outburst, which ran from December 1733 to April 1734, showed 'unusual severity'. Ambrose O'Callaghan wrote in March that 'the sham was the most terrible and shocking since Oliver's day [Oliver Cromwell or Oliver Plunkett]'.[46] This incident exposed the uncertain position of the higher Catholic clergy and their association with the Stuart court. These facts have been too readily disregarded by those old-style Catholic historians – such as Daniel MacCarthy, William Burke, Patrick Moran and Reginald Walsh – who have tended to concentrate on the dissolute nature of the witnesses and gloss over the 'treasonable' relationship between the higher clergy and the exiled Stuart king.[47]

Bishop Butler's colleague, bishop-elect Stephen Dowdall, displayed no such timidity on his appointment to the see of Kildare in December 1733. Writing

evening fair', the Irish Jacobite poet Donnchadh Rua Mac Conmara called on his listeners to 'Come drink a health my boys to royal George, our chief commander 'nár orduigh Críost' [not ordained by Christ]; Ó Foghludha (eag.), *Donnchadh Ruadh*, p. 36. There are numerous examples of this type of toasting in the Irish literary tradition; pp 170–71; pp 306–7.   **46** Fenning regarded this as 'the most severe persecution of the century which began in December 1733 and did not subside until the following April'; Fenning, *Irish Dominican province*, pp 142-3, 201. This opinion fits rather uncomfortably with Bartlett's description of the penal laws as 'an inherited system of petty oppressions'; Bartlett, *Fall and rise*, p. 29.   **47** Archbishop of Cashel to the Nuncio in Brussels, 12 Apr. 1734, in Giblin (ed.), 'Catalogue', part 5, vols 123-32, p. 40. See also R.A., Ms 178, fol. 147; R.A., Ms 169, fol. 21. Fears were expressed of letters being intercepted in this period; Fagan (ed.), *Stuart papers*, i, pp 170, 195, 210, 247, 275. See also *A report from the committee appointed to inspect original papers*, pp 4, 6, 16. Irish *émigrés* knew the trials of Irish Catholics in 'that poor oppressed country'; R.A., Ms 180, fol. 114; Fagan (ed) *Stuart papers*, i, pp 186-8, 193-5, 207, 211, 215-7, 340. Ambrose O'Callaghan described a conspiracy against a prominent Dublin merchant and one Walker, a reputed popish priest; R.A., Ms 167, fol. 101. Bishop Stephen MacEgan sent a coded letter from Dublin and expressed fears that his letters would be opened; R.A., Ms 178, fol. 170. See also Fagan, *Divided loyalties*, p. 60. In May 1734 Isiah Hort, the church of Ireland bishop of Kilmore, feared 'private cabals among the papists', quoted in McCoy, 'Local political culture', p. 202.

from London, where his passage to Ireland had been disrupted by the activities of Fr John Henessy Dowdall showed the extent to which James III remained in the conscience of many of the Irish Catholic episcopate. His missive also sheds light on their two-pronged role in the ecclesiastical and political life of contemporary Ireland. He stressed the continued loyalty of his flock for the Jacobite cause and their hopes for James's restoration to the throne:

> The indispensable duty I own [*sic*] your most sacred majesty and indeed my inclination for the service of the royal family always led me to give the best proofs in my power of my loyalty and attachment to your sacred person ... I shall make it my principal duty to do your majesty's subjects all the good I can both spiritually and temporally and with the greatest zeal for your service instruct the people in my care in the duty and loyalty due to your majesty and your royal family. I should have been earlier in my acknowledgement for your majesty's most gracious favour to me, but being in London at this time it was notified to me that your kingdom of Ireland then labouring under new oppressions and tyrannies, it was thought fit by your majesty's good subjects in that country that I should stay some time in London to solicit some relief for them by means of the foreign ministers ... This is all that afflicted Catholics can hope for there, till it pleases God to restore your most sacred majesty to the throne of your royal ancestors ... May the Almighty God illuminate by his grace the minds of your rebellious subjects to see the errors and the madness that has possessed them for so many years ... to give to God what belongeth to God and to Caesar what belongeth to Caesar [48]

Dowdall's embarkation for Ireland coincided with the arrival of Toby Butler with the express permission of James III.[49] Ireland at this time was awash with rumours of Louis XV's mobilisation in support of his father-in-law's claim to the

---

[48] Stephen Dowdall, Bishop of Kildare to James III, 23 Apr. 1734 (R.A., Ms 169, fol. 183). Dowdall's royalist sentiments echoed contemporary Jacobite rhetoric as 'Caesar' remained a popular pseudonym for the exiled James. See also R.A., Ms 202, fol. 96; Fenning (ed.), *The Fottrell papers*, p. 87; R.A., Ms 209, fol. 74; R.A 230, fol. 133; Murphy, *Killaloe*, p. 70; Giblin, 'Stuart nomination of bishops', pp 35-47.　**49** James III to Fr Clark, 6 Sept. 1734 (*H.M.C., Fifteenth report*, p. 238). Donnchadh Rua Mac Conmara lavished his praise on the 'Leinsterman', Tiobóid Buitléir, Butler of the dukes 'Buitléaraigh na nDiúicí'; Donnchadh Rua Mac Conmara, 'Teastas', in Ó Foghludha (eag.), *Donnchadh Ruadh*, p. 42. This is most likely Toby Butler, synonymous with that person who comes as a messenger to Ireland 'A dhuine seo thagann mar theachtaire ar Éirinn'; Donnchadha Rua Mac Conmara, Eachtra ghiolla an amaráin', in Ó Foghludha (eag.), *Donnchadh Ruadh*, p. 28. Toby Butler, a lieutenant in Lord Galmoy's regiment, was proclaimed in 1713 with a reward of £200 for his capture, for enlisting for the service of the Pretender; U.L., Cambs. Hib.0.713.12; P.R.O., S.P. 63/370/222. At the same time, Thomas Fitzgerald embarked for Ireland from the Stuart court to encourage 'as many young gentlemen as he met for the service of the king'; R.A., Ms 178 fol. 120. Edmund O'Donovan, uncle to John O'Donovan, editor of the *Annals of the Four Masters*, was imprisoned in 1736 for recruiting for the foreign service; Hayes; 'A famous Irish war correspondent'.

Polish crown and 'the Pretender's making a very rich livery in order to shine at a certain foreign court [France]'.[50] Protestant diatribes against the Pretender and the traitorous tendencies of his Irish supporters rained down from Church of Ireland pulpits on the anniversary of the 1641 uprising. Pamphlets and sermons were filled with foreboding at the rumblings of Europe's latest dynastic war. In a sermon preached in Christ's Church in 1735, Thomas Rundle, Church of Ireland bishop of Derry, repeated the earlier warnings of Hoadly, and cautioned against Catholic treachery and Protestant complacency:

> We should always remember that popery hath still the same principles, the same love of power, the same acts of zeal and cruelty, the same resentments ... They nourish hope from the very treasons and esteem them such merit, as should engage the popish powers to restore and support them ... They still have a view to one at Rome whom they call their civil sovereign.[51]

During the War of the Polish Succession, Boulter reported that 'French successes against Austria left the papists more than ordinarily insolent'.[52] It is surely significant this 'insolence' also manifested itself in contemporary poetry. Aodh Buí Mac Cruitín censured Russia and Austria for their invasion of Poland in 1734. According to the poet, 'Caesar' (Charles VI, the holy Roman emperor) entered the crooked game with madness and the Russian (czar) engaged with violent fury against the person (Stanislas Lesczynski, king of Poland) to whom the state and the clergy had unanimously submitted, to furiously expel him from his realm. Aodh Buí believed that the warrior of the violent feats in Paris (Louis XV) would ultimately prevail and that he (Louis) would establish his dad [father-in-law] (Stanislas) in a free status without oppression:

> 'S le mire do théid Séasar san mbáire fiar
> 's an Ruiseach le fraoch éigin' 'na pháirt ag triall,
> an duine dar ghéill d'aontoil an stát' 's a chliar
> go gcuirfid as réim éisean le dásacht dhian
> ...
> Atá curadh na n-éacht n-éigneach i bPáras triath
> ... is do shuidhfeas 'na chéim saorchairte a dháid gach chiach.[53]

---

50 *A supplement to the Dublin Impartial Newsletter*, 18 Sept. 1734. One newspaper made a thorough examination of the background to the cause of the war and the seeds of the War of the Austrian Succession; *Dalton's Dub. Imp. N.*, 19 Oct. 1734. A pamphlet published in Dublin compared the French monarch's assistance of Stanislas and his endeavours for the Pretender; *Reasons for a war from the imminent danger with which Europe is threatened*. Irish émigrés expressed optimism at the outbreak of war; R.A., Ms 182, fol. 87. See also R.A., Ms 177, fol. 103; R.A., Ms 179, fol. 176; R.A., Ms 176, fol. 131. **51** Thomas Rundle, bishop of Derry, *A sermon preached in Christ's Church*, pp 25-6. **52** Connolly, *Religion*, p. 236. **53** Quoted in Morley, *An crann os coill*, p. 112.

II

The popular press, seditious correspondence between the two sections of the Irish Jacobite community, and the struggle for the conscience of Irish Catholicism between Hanoverian conformists and doctrinaire Jacobites in the late 1720s kept the Stuart claimant at the forefront of contemporary political discourse. Recruitment also survived as a prominent manifestation of Irish popular Jacobitism in the 1720s and 1730s. Political correspondence and press reports throughout the latter part of 1726 carried numerous accounts of recruiting and noted the expectations of Irish Jacobites.

Commenting on their prodigious fasting and praying, Primate Hugh Boulter targeted clerical involvement in this recruitment and noted the use of migrant harvesting in England as a cover for potential recruits. He also commented the bias of recruits for the Spanish service and the possibility of a mischievous design among the Roman Catholics:

> Lusty young fellows are quitting the country on pretence that they are going to England to work such as here have occasion to employ many hands feel the effects of this description but nobody here questions but that these really are going to the foreign service. We shall not be wanting in our endeavours to keep everything quiet here but as accounts from all hands seem to forebode some mischievous design among the papists. I am very apprehensive that before some months are past there will be a necessity of putting the militia here in good order…nor shall we attempt anything of that nature 'till the designs of the papists clear up farther and we are able to make a proper representation on the state of the nation.[54]

The arrest of Cornelius O'Leary in Cork city in May 1726 reflected these apprehensions at a more local level, and revealed the discomfort which returning 'Wild Geese' caused in Protestant circles. O'Leary purportedly came back to Ireland for medical reasons after twenty-five years in the Franco-Irish regiments of Lieutenant-General William Dorrington and Lieutenant-General Michael Rothe. However others claimed that he was a priest who had come over to raise recruits for foreign service.[55] This was not the only example of the association

---

54 Boulter to Newcastle, 19 May 1726, in Boulter, *Letters*, i, p. 57-8. Contemporary newspapers and official correspondence contain many accounts of recruiting from all over the country, often involving large numbers: *Need. P.*, 24 Jan. 1726; *D.J.*, 25 Jan. 1726; *D.I.*, 18 Apr. 1726; 7 May 1726; 15 Oct. 1726; 3 Dec. 1726; P.R.O., S.P., 63/387/192; Boulter, *Letters*, i, pp 57-8, 60.   **55** The examination of Cornelius Leary, 15 May 1726 (P.R.O., S.P., 63/388/29). The lords justice suspected that he was listing men for the Pretender; P.R.O., S.P., 63/388/5. Although claiming to be an officer in Rothe's regiment, he was also accused of being a priest; P.R.O., S.P., 63/388/30. A letter to Lord Lieutenant Carteret from one Crawford in Corunna in June 1722 stated that 'the only motion they [the Jacobites at St Germain] are making at present is sending Irish priests in disguise to raise recruits', in *Appendixes*

between recruitment and Catholicism. The lords justice claimed that 'listing and carrying young men into the foreign service is proclaimed with great industry since the papists have been injoyned in such extraordinary fasting as has not been known since the year the Pretender was in Scotland'. They also alleged that 'their priests have in several places preached sermons tending to stir up their congregations to sedition'.[56]

The last speech, confession and dying words of Moses Nowland (executed for recruiting for the foreign service), circulated in newspaper and broadsheet, kept the recruitment issue to the forefront of Irish political life and provided one of the best documented incidences of the Irish Jacobite 'theatre of death'.[57] Nowland, hanged, drawn and quartered in St Stephen's Green in June 1726, had admitted in his last testimony – circulated before his execution – that he had enlisted men 'to enter themselves in the service of Spain under the notion that it was for the Pretender, a bait which the ignorant readily swallow and by which they are easily deluded'.[58] If this was a Whig fabrication, it anticipated the views of Forman and other contemporary pamphleteers who believed that recruiting agents used the Jacobite cause to entice the ignorant populace into the foreign service. However, the *Dublin Intelligence* alluded to a more authentic version of this purported address, in which the condemned man denied committing any crime or that he had issued the false declaration which had already been circulated:

> Wednesday last Moses Nowland condemn'd for enlisting men with a traitorous design for the service of the Pretender was brought from Newgate accompanied by a troop of guards to St Stephen's Green and there pursuant to his sentence was executed, his bowels being burnt, his head cut off etc ... He made little declaration at the gallows saying in particular only he dy'd for no crime and that he made no speech, the scandalous lies that were printed as such of his being only the invention of the publishers but had he thought he should really have dy'd he would have made a declaration at large.[59]

referred to in a report, p. 15. Daniel McGrath was associated with Francis Quinn and Standish Barry, who both stood trial for recruiting for the Pretender ; pp 196, fns 64; 197, fn. 67; P.R.O., S.P., 63/387/88, 194; P.R.O., S.P. 63.388/67, 71, 79, 91; N.L.I., Ms 9612, fol. 153. One commentator stated that 'I am satisfied that the people called Wild Geese are assembling in the farthest part of the kingdom'; P.R.O., S.P., 63/388/25. There are other examples in contemporary sources of discomfort caused by returning Irish Brigade officers; *List and index society*, vol. 119, pp 207, 213; R.A., Ms 200, fol. 102; Cullen, 'Politics of Caoineadh Airt Uí Laoire', p. 15; Ó Buachalla, *An Caoine*, passim.   **56** Lords justice to lord lieutenant, 28 May 1726 (P.R.O., S.P., 63/387/202); *Dick. I.*, 15 Oct. 1726   **57** Introduction, pp 36–7.   **58** *The last speech, confession and dying words of Moses Nowland*; *The whole trial and execution of Moses Nowland*.   **59** *Dub. I.*, 9 July 1726. See also *Dick. I.*, 2 July 1726; *Dick. I.*, 28 July 1726. News of Nowland's execution reached the Stuart court; R.A., Ms 96, fol. 50.

Although Nowland paid the ultimate price for his association with recruitment and Jacobitism, the threat loomed large for many of his Catholic Jacobite contemporaries. Aeneas Daly, arrested while recruiting in County Kerry, implicated a number of prominent south Munster gentry, including Valentine Browne, third viscount Kenmare, Captain Roger O'Donoghue, Colonel Sherlock, O'Sullivan More (Ó Súilleabháin Mór) and McCarthy More (Mac Cárthaigh Mór). Daly accused them of promoting recruitment, having commissions from the Pretender, and enlisting men in order to assist the king of Spain to invade the three kingdoms in favour of the Stuarts. These activities had been spear-headed by a Spanish-Irish captain named James McGragh, whose accomplices, John Fahy and Richard Fitzgibbons, both purportedly held commissions from James III and daily enlisted men for his service in County Kerry.[60] Although no further action was taken against these prominent Catholic figures, this manipulation of evidence showed their vulnerability at the hands of mercenary informers and unscrupulous or self-serving local officials.

Additional information from Charles McDonogh related to Thomas Grogan who told McDonogh that he had come from France (although McDonogh later found out that he had come from Spain). Grogan had stated that 'they would soon be in this country [Spain] in a condition to help his friends ... that the design of besieging Gibraltar was to make the king [George I] draw his forces there and that James III would make a descent into this country'. Elsewhere, McDonogh came into the company of John Butler of 'Luin', County Clare. Butler informed him that he was a major in the Spanish service and that if he could raise twenty to thirty men for the Spanish service, Butler would secure him a commission in that army. Butler intimated to him that he already had one hundred men ready for embarkation. On the same day Grogan brought McDonagh a gentleman who called himself Barry but whose real name Callaghan O'Callaghan. O'Callaghan claimed that he had authority to list men for King James III. McDonagh believed that his letters were being opened and noted the hesitant collusion of local gentlemen with recruitment, despite its lucrative returns.[61] He also mentioned the recruiting activities of James Barry, at the post-office in Cork, who was a captain in the Spanish service, and David Connor, a victualler in County Cork. He told McDonogh that 'he would soon put him in a way of paying his debts; if the examinant could do any service in encouraging men to list in the service of James III that he could give him a guinea per man'.[62]

60 Information of Aeneas Daly, 31 Jan. 1727 (P.R.O., S.P., 63/388/176); see also P.R.O., S.P., 63/388/ 172, 175, 178.   61 Information of Charles McDonogh, 4 Feb. 1727 (P.R.O., S.P., 63/388/175); Examination of Charles McDonogh, 11 Mar. 1727 (P.R.O., S.P., 63/388/192). McDonogh also attempted to incriminate Lord Killmare [Kenmare?] and Roger O'Donoghue; P.R.O., S.P., 63/388/ 176. In an (intercepted?) letter from John Butler to James Barry, Butler (who apparently used the name Charles McDonogh for correspondence) suggested that 'the good gentlemen of this country assist me as much as their fear will allow them they being well assured of a descent'; P.R.O., S.P. 63/388/194. 62 'Examination of Charles McDonogh, 11 Mar. 1727 (P.R.O., S.P. 63/388/192).

Charles McCarthy (Cormac Spáinneach Mac Cárthaigh), Protestant convert and patron of the poet Seán na Ráithíneach Ó Murchú, provided a target for the informer Owen Sweane in the same period. McCarthy purportedly patronised a hurling match as a cover for recruitment, and was accused of playing host to a popish priest who administered a Jacobite oath of fidelity to the prospective recruits:

> He was sworn by Charles McCarthy, Carrignavar [County Cork], at a public house there with 16 others, to enlist ostensibly for service in Spain, but in reality for the Pretender. All except two (who would go voluntary) were given some money (various types of coin). He was also sworn by a priest to be faithful to James. I was also sworn by a priest (who lives in MacCarthy's house) to be faithful to James [III]. He adds that there was a great assembly on 24 June which this examt. believes was contrived on purpose to bring persons together in order to be enlisted for there had not been any hurlyings suffered by the said Charles McCarthy on his lands on any 24 June since the time of his turning Protestant which was in the year 1720, except the said day. [63]

Ó Murchú composed an eulogy for Cormac Spáinneach in the 1720s, rejoicing at his release from a false court ('Ar saoradh mo mháighistir agus mo thighearna díoghraiseach dúthaighe Cormac Spáinneach ó chóir bhréige'). He was also praised by Seán Clárach Mac Domhnaill and Eoghan an Mhéirín Mac Cárthaigh.[64] Seán Clárach's verse on Cormac Spáinneach refers to his royal blood and his kinship with the 'generous kings' (possibly James II/III).[65] Eoghan an Mhéirín rejoiced at Major General McCarthy's return to Ireland ('Fáilte is fíche i gcrích Fáil, do Major Cormac Mac Cárthaigh'). He praised him as the bright hawk and the sweet flowering sacred tree ('An seabhac sultmhar, subhach sámh, an binn-bhile bhláith').[66]

Contemporary recruitment was not exclusively confined to south Munster. Concern about the phenomenon in County Sligo in 1729 prompted Brigadier-General Owen Wynne to hold an investigation. One witness interviewed suspected a townsman named Thady Hart of enlisting for 'the Pretender'. However, he was unable to prove any overt acts. Nevertheless, he gave General Wynne a confidential letter he received from Hart which he claimed referred to recruit-

---

63 Information of Owen Sweane, 28 July 1726 (P.R.O., S.P., 63/388/41). The lords justice alluded to the recruiting activities of pretended converts and unregistered priests; N.L.I., Ms 9612, fol. 161. 64 Ó Donnchadha (eag.), *Seán na Ráithíneach* , pp xiii–iv; Seán na Ráithíneach Ó Murchú, 'Ag guidhe 's ag dáil', in ibid., p. 22; 'Beannacht Sheáin Uí Mhurchadha chun Seáin Chláraigh agus Cormac Spáinneach an teachtaire'; Seán na Ráithíneach Ó Murch, Beannacht le searc', in ibid., pp 254, 284. 65 Seán na Ráithíneach do Chormac Spáinneach', in Ó Foghludha (eag.), *Seán Clárach*, p. 67. Ó Donnchadha suggested that Seán Clárach visited Cormac Spáinneach in 1743. Furthermore, he believed that both were involved in a Jacobite plot in 1745; Ó Donnchadha (eag.), *Seán na Ráithíneach*, pp xiii, 464. 66 Ó Foghludha (eag.), *Eoghan an Mhéirín*, p. 70.

ment. He believed that 'shipped goods' was the cant phrase for dispatching recruits for the Pretender.[67]

Recruitment also preoccupied senior members of the Irish, British and French political and military establishments at this time. Controversy surrounded French proposals to obtain official permission to recruit for the Irish regiments in the period between the Jacobite scares of the late 1720s and the outbreak of the War of the Polish Succession in 1734. This refutes Samuel Madden's dismissal of the importance of the Stuart cause in Irish politics. It also indicates that recruitment remained one of the single most important manifestations of Irish Jacobitism in this period of political stagnation.[68] One doggerel published in contemporary Dublin made a connection between recruitment and Jacobitism:

> How he [Walpole?] and the pope a project did forge
> To get tall Irishmen to fight for King George
> An army to make for the Popish Pretender
> Against the good king, of our faith the defender.
> The recruits which the French from Dunkirk do demand
> For all that they yet have pulled down on that strand
> 'Ere many years pass may attempt to come over
> As they tried once before from Dunkirk to Dover.[69]

Similarly, a verse attributed to an anonymous Irish officer in the French service enhanced the cult of the Irish Brigades. He described the hordes of warriors whose hostility would never abate, spread over Europe without wealth, clothes or good stock. Their reversal of fortune and unquenchable hostility stemmed from the exile of James II and their possible return was inexorably linked with the fate of his son:

> Nach léir duitse Gaoidhil bhochta sa glan-áille,
> Na héacht-choin nach ngéilleann dá n-eascáirdibh,
> Spréidte fá'n Earoip 'na sealbhánaibh
> gan spré ghlan, gan éadach, gan deagh-tháinte.[70]

Given the continued *détente* between France and England, as well as the relative tranquillity of Ireland, the French government was confident that permission would be given to recruit in Ireland for the Irish Brigades. The arrival of French recruiters in the early 1730s caused uproar among Protestants, forcing George II to renege on commitments given to his ally Louis XV.[71]

---

67 O'Rorke, *Sligo*, i, p. 237.   **68** The best account of recruitment is Beresford's, 'Ireland', pp 145-57.
69 *The squire and the cardinal*.   **70** Quoted in de Blácam, *Gaelic literature surveyed*, pp 275-6.   **71**
Boulter to Carteret, 20 May 1729, 20 Aug. 1729, in Boulter, *Letters*, i, pp 247-8, 256-7. See also P.R.O.,

The arrest and execution, in spite of French ministerial intervention, of Martin Mooney for recruiting, and the furore at the possibility of a pardon, became a *cause celèbre* in Anglo-French diplomatic circles. The refusal of the Irish Protestant Ascendancy to back down in the face of British government pressure on recruitment shows the extent to which it remained a live issue in Irish politics. Mooney had received permission from the adjutant-major of Nugent's regiment to return to Mullingar, County Westmeath, for a six-month period.[72] He had been arrested immediately after landing in the country and committed to Wexford Gaol on suspicion of recruiting.[73] After examining Mooney's papers, Thomas Marlay announced that he had indeed been guilty and should be denied bail. The arrest on a similar charge of William Hallian, of The Black Lion Tavern on the Blind Quay (George's Quay, Dublin), Mooney lodgings and the forwarding address for his correspondence, compounded Marlay's suspicions.[74] Mooney was finally convicted 'on the fullest and plainest evidence of not only enlisting men who had a mind to go into the foreign service but also forcing men away and carrying men against their will, even Protestants'.[75]

The French immediately intervened at the highest diplomatic levels to secure Mooney's acquittal, and their initial success prompted Berwick to express his thanks at the mistaken belief that the British authorities had released him.[76] However, this intervention floundered on the rocks of Irish Protestant intransigence. When the justices of County Dublin heard of Mooney's reprieve they fell into 'great heats and came to a resolution to draw up a representation of the many dangerous consequences which might follow if the criminals, and particularly Mooney should be pardoned'. The Irish Protestants wished to make an example

---

S.P., 63/393/1; B.L., Add Ms 36, 137, fols 186, 199; P.R.O., S.P., 63/392/80. The *Dublin Intelligence* reported the acquittal of one Murphy for recruiting in May 1729; *D.I.*, 17 May 1729.   **72** Certificate by the adjutant-major of the regiment of Nugent, 11 June 1729 (P.R.O., S.P., 63/391/216).   **73** The humble petition of Martin Mooney (P.R.O., S.P., 63/391/226). See also P.R.O., S.P., 63/391/218-9; 'Mooney and McGurk were executed at St Stephen's Green. Mooney left behind a paper stating that he had been well educated, and formerly a servant to Thomas Fortescue, Esq. He afterwards became a farmer in County Wexford, until he entered into Nugent's Horse. Being disappointed in a commission he left that regiment and went into the duke of Berwick's Foot where he was promised a lieutenancy upon condition that he would bring 20 men from Ireland to fill up some companies .... He died in the 23rd year of his age .... MacGurk had formerly been a schoolmaster, went to France, listed in Dillon's Regiment, soon made a sergeant, but having a quarrel with two persons whom he wounded he made his way to Ireland and set up a school again .... He died in the 29th year of his age'; Brady (ed.), *Catholics*, p. 52.   **74** *Dub. I.*, 18 Nov. 1729. See also P.R.O., S.P., 63/391/218; Brady (ed.), *Catholics*, 26 Sept. 1730, p. 313.   **75** Extract of a letter from Sir Ralph Gore, 20 Dec. 1732 (P.R.O., S.P., 63/395/337; *Dub. I.*, 18 Nov. 1729. Mooney was accused of abducting Henry Whitehead, a Protestant, into the duke of Berwick's regiment; P.R.O., S.P., 63/395/337.   **76** Carteret to Newcastle, 18 Nov. 1729 (P.R.O., S.P., 67/10/88). See also *Lists and index society*, vol. 205, pp 7,18. Waldergrave believed it was unlikely that Berwick would insist on Mooney's release; Waldergrave to Delafaye, 21 Jan. 1733 (*Lists and index society*, vol. 205, p. 44). He described the difficulties involved in releasing him; ibid., vol. 205, p. 45. Similarly the duchess of Berwick attempted to secure the release of Lieutenant (Luke) Barnwell, imprisoned for recruiting; ibid., vol. 205, p. 58; *Dub. Week. Jnr.*, 20 Apr. 1734. It is unclear whether she was successful.

out of Mooney.[77] He was finally executed along with McGurk on 17 February 1733, leaving a paper to be read at the scaffold.[78]

The pamphleteer Charles Forman's *Letter to Sir Robert Sutton for disbanding the Irish regiments in the French army* (1728) described English and Irish Protestant anxiety in relation to recruitment. He assessed the political role of the Irish Brigades and their importance to the survival of Jacobitism. Reflecting the sentiments of other contemporary pamphleteers, including Caleb D'Anvers and John Keogh, his treatise effectively prophesised their role in Maréchal Saxe's abortive invasion of 1744 and their disproportionate influence in the 'Forty-five':

> As long as there is a body of Irish Roman Catholic troops abroad, the chevalier will always make some figure in Europe by the credit they give him; and being considered as a prince that has a brave and well-disciplined army of veterans at his service tho' he wants an opportunity to employ them at present, which he expects time and fortune will favour him with. Should France grow wanton with power, forget her engagements and obligations to Britain, can she anywhere find such a proper instrument as the Irish regiments to execute such enterprises she may undertake in favour of the chevalier's pretensions when they square with their own interests and private views?[79]

Forman's treatise provides an important reflection on the influence of the military diaspora in eighteenth-century political and literary circles. He assessed the merits of the Irish Brigades and their suitability for a prospective invasion of Britain, as well as reciting a litany of their military triumphs from Cremona to Almanza, Barcelona to Ramillies.[80] The poems of the Irish Jacobite literati, the letters of the Irish exiles to the Stuart court, and the popular press tradition of the Whigs in Ireland, outline the extra-political motivations with which Forman credited the officer corps and general proprietors of the regiments. He claimed that 'some of whom by inclination but most by interest, as the case stands, are entirely devoted to the chevalier and the hopes of their being restored to their estates'.[81] Forman argued that the links forged between recruitment and Jacobit-

77 Thomas Tickel to [?], 13 Jan. 1733 (P.R.O., S.P., 63/396/1, 3). See also *List and index society*, vol. 205, p. 70.   78 Brady (ed.), *Catholics*, p. 52 (above, fn. 73); For recruiting generally; *Dub. Week. Jnr.*, 9 Feb 1734; 20 Apr. 1734; 8 June 1734.   79 Forman, *A letter to Sir Robert Sutton*, p. 17. See also D'Anvers, *The craftsman's first letter*, p. 1. *The Craftsman* was published in Dublin; *Dub. Daily P.*, 25 Aug. 1739. See also *The squire and the cardinal*. Correspondence to the Stuart court held that these pamphlets influenced George and his party; R.A., Ms 141, fol. 138. Dillon called Forman a 'rogue and a villain'; R.A., Ms 128, fol. 151. See also Chapman, 'Jacobite political argument', pp 20, 76, 110.   80 Keogh recounts the tale of the British Colonel Gower who complained to the duke of Marlborough after Blenheim that he had lost his regiment against the Irish Brigade. At the same time, another English colonel present said he wished he had been there with his regiment'. 'I wish you were', said Gower, 'for I would have a regiment and you would not'; Keogh, *A vindication*, pp 93-4.   81 Forman, *A letter to Sir Robert Sutton*, p. 20.

ism explained its endurance as a popular ideology in Ireland. The recruiters and colonel-proprietors made unscrupulous use of Jacobitism to entice Irishmen into the Brigades:

> They daily make recruits in London and several parts of Ireland tho' surrounded with difficulties which one would think ought to be insuperable under a ministry so celebrated for its vigilance and ability .... Their methods of recruiting is certainly as base as it is savage and void of all sentiments of humanity and the gallows is too mild a punishment for the vile lies they tell the poor ignorant creatures they spirit away. To support the vanity and splendid equipages of about twelve Irish colonels, pretendership is kept up and a whole nation exposed every year to the just severities attending the resentments of their provoked sovereign.[82]

Forman believed that if these Irish regiments were dispersed into the regular French and Spanish armies 'that military nursery of inveterate enemies to his majesty's title will be entirely broken and dispersed'. As a result of this, 'the officers will be too much dispersed to be brought together on occasion without giving too much alarm and will not readily obtain the connivance of the French or Irish colonels for deserting their colours when the chevalier may have occasion for their service'. These measures would also serve to stifle recruitment: 'the private men will also, for want of recruits, dwindle in a very few years to too inconsiderable a number to be any ways serviceable to the chevalier or formidable to us'.[83] Only a comprehensive examination of the muster rolls of the Irish Regiments in France and Spain, in conjunction with Irish recruitment networks and an appraisal of the ideology which underpinned the officer corps of these regiments will enable us to properly evaluate the links between recruitment and Irish Jacobitism.

The Irish government was not totally oblivious to the sentiments expressed in Forman's pamphlets, and to the sensitivity of the recruitment issue. Having initially co-operated with George II's decision to permit the French to enlist for the Irish regiments in the late-1720s and early-1730s, they later (in the face of Irish Protestant opposition) established strict conditions upon which the French musters might take place. The Brigades raised men without any beat of the drum, great care was taken to avoid causing offence, the numbers did not exceed seven hundred and fifty, and the musters terminated after three months. The recruiting officers were expected to behave in such a manner as not to make

---

Similar sentiments are manifest in other pamphlets from the period; D'Anvers, *The craftsman's first letter*, p. 1; D'Anvers, *Craftmans extraordinary*; Forman, *A defence*, pp 8, 13-14, 17, 19, 24, 50; Keogh, *A vindication*, pp 93-5. For the use of the Irish regiments as a political threat; Reilly, *The impartial history of Ireland*, pp 140-1. On the cult of the Brigades generally; Flood, *Wogan*, pp 136-41. **82** Forman, *A letter to Sir Robert Sutton*, pp 21, 36. See also D'Anvers, *The craftsman's first letter*, p. 1; Linebaugh, *London hanged*, p. 95. **83** Forman, *A letter to Sir Robert Sutton*, pp 35, 36-7.

themselves obnoxious to the laws or to incur the displeasure of the government.[84] Charles Delafaye, British ambassador to Paris, castigated the Irish Brigades for their continued use of the livery of the king of England and English marching tunes. His counterpart, the French ambassador, le comte de Broglie, denied that the Irish troops had ever been looked upon as the army of the exiled James II. He proposed 'to avoid any colour of objection', that 'it need not be mentioned in the letters of licence that these men are for recruiting the Irish regiments'.[85] In spite of these precautions Archbishop Boulter feared that 'all the recruits raised here for France or Spain are generally considered as persons that may some time or another pay a visit to this country as enemies'.[86]

Recruiting re-emerged in 1735 as a problem for the administration: ninety recruits were held in Dublin for trial, pending the intercession of the French minister.[87] Meanwhile the heroic exploits of the Irish Brigades in the service of France, the ultimate destination of those detained, were described in the *Dublin Gazette*. According to a Parisian despatch, the Irish were disgusted at their neglect by the French press covering the French army's retreat during an engagement of the War of the Polish Succession. While Boussleur's brigade had refused 'so hot a service' and the other French brigades showed minimal enthusiasm, Lord Dillon volunteered the Irish Brigades to cover the retreat of the army and serve his most christian majesty in his hour of need:

> Marshal Coigny was extremely chagrined at the damp on the spirits of his troops until Lord Dillon came up and told his excellency that the Irish troops had always looked on it as an honour to serve France and should now esteem it a much greater one to make good the rear against the Germans. His lordship was taken immediately at his word. Boussleur's brigade changed post and Sir Garret O'Lally, brigadier-general at the head of Dillon's, Berwick's, Bulkeley's and Rothe's Regiments, kept the Germans in exercise 'til the French army got to a post of safety ....

84 Newcastle to the lord lieutenant, 11 Aug. 1730 (P.R.O., S.P., 63/393/1). **85** C. Delafaye to the attorney-general, 31 Oct. 1730 (B.L., Add. Ms 36, 139, fol. 203). See also P.R.O., S.P., 63/393/26-30; Boulter, *Letters*, ii, p. 28-9, 31. Colonel Henessy, the chief recruiter, exercised 'great prudence' during his stay in Ireland; P.R.O., S.P., 63/393/32. See also P.R.O., S.P., 63/395/108. At this time, twenty or thirty men were committed to jail in Birr, County Offaly, on a charge of high treason for enlisting for the foreign service; *Dub. Jnr.*, 2-5 Jan. 1731. Another body of men were taken by the king's barge off Bray, County Wicklow, on suspicion of going into the foreign service although it later transpired that they were going off to Wales to cut bark; *Fau. Dub. J.*, 20-23 Mar. 1731. **86** Boulter to Newcastle, 14 Oct. 1730, in Boulter, *Letters*, ii, p. 27. Boulter believed that this recruiting would cause unease; Boulter, *Letters*, ii, pp 25-6. The press reported on the build-up of 15,000 French soldiers at Dunkirk and the arrival of the Pretender in France; *Dub. P.*, 12 July 1731. It also carried news of the construction of new fortifications along the French coast; *Dub. P.*, 26 Aug. 1731. *Émigré* hopes dominated Irish correspondence to the Stuart court in this period; R.A., Ms 146, fol. 151; Ms 166, fols 141, 160; Ms 161, fol. 65; Ms 170, fol. 111; Ms 180, fol. 35; Ms 181, fols 14, 113; Ms 174, fols 19, 35; Ms 163, fol. 166. **87** Thomas Tickell to Walter Cary, 12 May 1735 (P.R.O.N.I., D. 207/A/1/7, N.L.I., special list, Shannon papers 206[i], p. 30). See also ibid., p. 31; *Pue's O.*, 7-10 June 1735.

For such a piece of service they think it hard not to be allowed even a line in the *Paris Gazette*.[88]

While this may have been a deliberate attempt by the Protestant press to discourage recruitment and lower the French king's stock in Irish Catholic opinion, it served to reinforce the special influence of the 'Pretender's foot-guards' in the popular political consciousness. Dillon displayed an impetuosity which undoubtedly invigorated Irish Jacobites. This chivalrous bravado inspired a heroic literary tradition of the Irish Brigades, which included contributions by Ó Bruadair, Ó Rathaille, Aodh Buí, Seán Clárach, Seán na Ráithíneach, Liam Rua, Aindrias Mac Craith and a host of Jacobite poets until the end of the Seven Years War.

In a virulent anti-Whig poem from the period, Aodh Buí left no doubt as to his motives for joining the Brigades. The poet supposed that if he put on the red coat and went with the Brigades across the sea with their sails spread and their silken banners displayed, they would receive no justice or recompense from the foreigners until they took possession of their dwellings and hanged King George with a knotted rope to the melodious music of the harp:

> Is dóigh má ghabhaimse an cóta dearg so,
> leo go rachad tar sáile,
> a scóda leathna, 's seolta scartha,
> 's a sróll 'na mbratachaibh árda;
> cóir ná ceannach ní gheobhaid ó Ghallaibh
> go dtógaid sealbh a n-áitreabh,
> is Seoirse a thachtadh le córda casta,
> 's is ceolmhar a screadfas an chláirseach.[89]

This poem reflected the extreme Jacobitism and anti-Hanoverian sentiments of his *émigré* brethren, and those who ran the gauntlet of capital punishment to join the Irish Regiments in France and Spain. John Ragg described the hatred of Britain among the members of General Andrew Lee's regiment stationed at Calais, suggesting that Aodh Buí's sentiments would have been well received in their ranks:

---

88 *Dub. Gaz.*, 30 Dec. 1735. The Dublin press closely followed the careers of the Wild Geese in foreign armies; *Fau. Dub. J.*, 5 Mar. 1739; 8 May 1739; 24 June 1740; 29 July 1740; 16 Sept. 1740. **89** Aodh Buí Mac Cruitín, 'Is grinn an tsollamháin chím fán Nollaig seo', quoted in Morley, *An crann os coill*, p. 103. Morley suggests that the 'screaming' harp allusion may refer to the emblem on the regimental flag of Lord Clare's regiment. I would like to thank Dr Morley for sharing his views with me. Seán Ó hUaithnín, the Clare Jacobite poet, also joined these ranks in the period (1721); Ó hAnluain (eag.), *Seon Ó hUaithnín*, p. 20; Ó Murchú, review of Ó hAnluain, pp 199-200. Also see Litton, 'Daniel Huony, admiral of the Royal Navy in Spain', pp 51-9.

I was taken up by force at Calais by one who was recruiting there for this regiment, brought to Belhume and obliged to serve as a soldier in Captain Francis Mandeville's company in General Lee's regiment of Irish foot which is now garrisoned in that place. It is not possible for me to express the hardships of this service .... In a word, I would rather be under the slavery of the Turks than in the condition I am, under pretended Christians by an implacable hatred against all such as are not like themselves, mortall enemies to the Isle of Britain and its present happy constitution.[90]

When these sentiments are taken into consideration the Regent's caution in sending the Irish regiments away from the Channel coast on the threat of a Spanish-sponsored Jacobite invasion may have been justified.

While Mac Cruitín's verse exuded confidence at the possibility of a Franco-Irish invasion, the poetic contention between Pádraig Ó Súilleabháin and Seán na Ráithíneach Ó Murchú provides evidence of Irish Jacobite despair in the late 1720s. It also contains the contrasting strands of thought evident among the literati in Ireland. These included the close association between Jacobitism, Catholicism, recruitment and the Irish Brigades. Ó Súilleabháin's opening verses are imbued with dejection often evident in the poetry of Ó Rathaille. He lamented the fact that the Irish were left weak and exhausted without regard or attention and James III was vanquished forever.[91] By his ingenious use of the classic Jacobite card-playing metaphor, in this case the popular Irish game of 'twenty-five', he traced Catholic woes to the revolution in 1688; the knave (William of Orange) was played on the ace (James II), the game was lost, and thousands were ruined between the Boyne and Cork. For poetic effect he repeated the couplet which emphasised his woe at the eternal destruction of James at the end of each verse.[92] Ó Súilleabháin chided Ó Murchú for his literary inactivity in spite of the fact that he had been given the prize by the whole country in the prophecy of the druids (a reference to the fact that he was head of 'Dámhscoil na mBlarnan', the Munster school of poetry).[93]

Ó Súilleabháin's supposition was that he had gone across the sea with a troop (as a recruit) to bring the treacherous hordes to suppress us which would be appropriate for him since he did not write accurate history (poetry) about a

90 J. Ragg to Lord Polwarth [10] 21 Jan. 1723 (*H.M.C., Polwarth*, iii, p. 225). See also Beresford, 'Ireland', p. 132. **91** 'D'fhág fann lag sínn, gan mheabhair gan chrích,/ná beann ar Chrích Éibhir; /'s is dearbh an sceól, mo thuirse gach ló/an briseadh go deo ar Shéamus'; Ó Donnchadha, *Seán na Ráithíneach*, p. 130. **92** 'Ar ionnarba atá ó tugadh an mádh/'s an cuireata i ndeáidh an aéin leis,/Do rian an cluiche go dian gan filleadh,/mo chiach, lér milleadh na céadtha./ón mBóinn aníos go seól Chorcaighe 's go Móir-thigh cruinn tug léirscrios;/'s is dearbh an sceól, mo thuirse gach ló,/an briseadh go deó ar Shéamas'. Ó Donnchadha, *Seán na Ráithíneach*, p. 130. **93** 'Is iongnadh línn tú id chodladh mar taoi,/ 's gur bronnadh ó'n gcrích an chraobh dhuit,/Let fheabhus chun grinn i bhfáistin na ndraoi/ag labhairt ar Chloinn Mhilésius,/a seanchus cruinn ó'n gcéad-ghein, scaoil/Ó

woman without a spouse (aisling poetry).[94] Ó Murchú retorted that he had no intention of going overseas with a troop although the Irish have long waited impatiently for help from King James.[95] He conceded that the Irish were not a powerful body and their appetite for heroism had been diminished for fear of their blood being spilled and due to the fact that the anger of the all-powerful king (God) was unabated and their own sins were unremitted.[96] He lamented that Ireland was in the iron grip of the English, the Catholic church was silent and bereft of her buildings, her princes overseas and abandoned and every poet and wandering musician foresaken.[97] He deplored their long wait for legion of the brave lions (the Irish Brigades) without lands, farms, possessions or wealth. He claimed that the land of Ireland was withered and dried up after every injustice and every section of the community was oppressed.[98] The poet's conclusion left little room for optimism: Every Englishman was in peaceful possession of the living of every noble of the royal provinces of Ireland. The Irish elite who were always generous to the poets were scattered or suffering every disaster with little relief. There was little option for the poet except to concede that George was king and the Eoghan's seed (the royal house of Munster from whom the Stuarts were descended) was withered.[99]

III

Charles Wogan's observations on the possibility of an Irish invasion in 1729 contrasted with Seán na Ráithíneach's despair. He re-emphasised the political

---

Scotia chaoin, an dé-bhean'; Ó Donnchadha, *Seán na Ráithíneach*, p. 131. **94** 'Is eaglach línn go ndeachais tar tuinn,/mar tuigthear badh cuibhdhe é dhuit, chun sluaighte an fhill do thabhairt d'ár gclaoidhe, /monuar is sínn traochta /san chás nár scríobhais árd-stair ghrinn/ ag trácht ar mhnaoi gan chéile; /'s is dearbh mo sceól, mo thuirse gach ló, an briseadh go deó ar Shéamas', Ó Donnchadha, *Seán na Ráithíneach*, p. 131. **95** 'Agam níl rún taistil na dtrúp 's do neartuigh mo chumha an scéal guirt /ciodh fada gan fonn do chlannaibh chirt Niúil/ ag fanamhaint le congnamh Séamais'; Ó Donnchadha, *Seán na Ráithíneach*, p. 131. **96** 'Is eaglach liom nach neartmhar an drong/ chun cais-meartha i gcúigibh Éireann,/nó, is dearbh a ndúil gaisce bunscionn/ le heagla a gcrú do thaoscadh;/nó, is feargach riú Feartach na ndúl/'s ar bpeacadh gan chúiteamh tréimhse/ 'sé ndeara nárbh umhal a dtaisteal tar srúill/go hathchumair chughainn d'ár n-éileamh'; Ó Donnchadha, *Seán na Ráithíneach*', p. 132. **97** 'Tá Banba i bpudhair cheachartha chumhaing/ ag Sacsaibh gan súil a réidhtigh;/ár n-eaglais ciúin, gan chealla gan chúil,/'s ár bhflatha thar triúchaibh tréigthe;/'s gach eagarthach ciúil, nó seanchadh siubhail,/go hairgthe, cúis mo dhéara;/'s gan agamsa súil atharrach úird/d'fhaicsint go scumhaidh mo shaoghal'; Ó Donnchadha, *Seán na Ráithíneach*, p. 132. **98** 'Is fada le feitheamh air leigion na bhfíor-leógan/gan fearann, gan feirm, gan feiste gan puinn tóice,... /M'atuirse an t-eibear d'fheicsin ar chrích Fódhla/go seargtha seirgthe ar leirg gach mí-chóthruim, /'s an aindeise ar deireadh dá gcreimeadh, mo dhíol deóire,/i n-anbhroid leigthe gach eite d'ár mbuidhin chródha'; Ó Donnchadha, *Seán na Ráithíneach*, p. 133. **99** 'Gach Sagsanach preicill i seilbh go síthe óilte/I mbeatha gach cleite badh threise i ngach rí-chóigeadh;/is na seabhaic, ná céileadh ar fheile gach suim seide,/go dealbh ar teicheadh, nó i n-eibior gach líobóide ... /'s nífheadar-sa a dheireadh, acht go ndeirim gur Rí Seóirse,/'s gurab airgtheach ceisnimh an beile do shíol Eóghain'; Ó Donnchadha, *Seán na Ráithíneach*, 133.

motivation of the Irish Brigades, and supported the commonly-held belief that salvation would only come with the return of these 'lions over the sea'. Like O'Neill, Berwick, Dillon, O'Callaghan, Lloyd and Orrery before him, Wogan began by assessing the numerical strength of enemy forces in Ireland. He stressed the age-old necessity of sending a Franco-Irish expeditionary force, furnished with extra arms and accoutrements, to raise rebellion in Ireland and prevent troops from being sent from Ireland to counter the main attack on England.[100] Wogan based his memoir on information received from Irish *émigrés* recently returned from Ireland. He emphasised the suitability of Connaught and Munster for such a landing:

> I have heard from gentlemen of good sense lately returned from Ireland relating to the two provinces of Munster and Connaught, where they have been all last Winter about their domestic affairs. Your majesty knows that the great security of the present government in Ireland consists in the number of about 10,000 men that are on the establishment (for tho' they are counted 12,000 they do not amount to near that which I speak of) and in the barracks for horse and foot at proper distances all over the kingdom to frighten the inhabitants from any notion of rising but all this severity would be very precarious if while the main descent or rising was in England, about 8,000 men could be sent to Ireland to land in Cork and the others in the neighbourhood of Galway in order to make a diversion and hinder the troops upon the establishment to be sent as a reinforcement to England.[101]

Wogan highlighted the resilience of the Irish Jacobites, their willingness to avail of any opportunity to throw off their tyrants, and the iron grip which the Catholic clergy exerted on the conscience of their flocks:

> Now as to the country the people are almost under the absolute domination of their parish priests who generally keep a list of their parishioners of body, strength and spirit and could be masters to send them to any rendezvous.[102]

The links between Catholicism and Jacobitism should never be ignored, nor should the extent to which Irish Jacobitism retained the hierarchical structure already evident in the popular mobilisation of the 1680s. The exiled Stuart king provided the apex of this Jacobite pyramid, his chosen episcopal nominees

---

100 See pp 122-3, 134, 147-50, 212-4. **101** Wogan to James III, 10 May 1729 (R.A., Ms 127, fol. 152); Introduction, p. 29. **102** Wogan to James III, 10 May 1729 (R.A., Ms 127, fol. 152). This clerical influence remained a constant preoccupation with his Protestant contemporaries, as one pamphleteer suggested that 'their priests make all things lawful'; *Seasonal advice to Protestants*, p. 36.

occupied the next tier and they transmitted the Catholic Jacobite message down through the secular clergy to the Catholic populace. The military structure of the Franco-Irish and Spanish Brigades on the continent replicated this hierarchical structure and Wogan's treatise shows the potential links between the two.[103]

Wogan suggested that the recruiting privilege recently granted to the Irish Brigades could be covertly used to evaluate militant Jacobitism in the kingdom, showing that the suspicions of many within the Irish Protestant Ascendancy regarding the extra-political dimensions of recruitment were not totally without foundation. He proposed that officers related to the local gentry should be sent to Ireland with French passports and commissions. With the co-operation of local clergy and under the guise of recruiting, they could easily ascertain precise numbers of those ready to serve King James. Having emphasised the dubious loyalties of the converts to the present establishment, he highlighted their undiminished sway over their tenants and their willingness to 'shake off the yoke from their consciences' by embracing the Jacobite cause:

> Now tho' an attempt of this kind needs no preparative except the landing of some men and arms as the French-Irish have leave to recruit there and do it with a high hand in this time of great amity between France and England, if 5-6 officers with French passports and commissions and related to the gentry of those parts could be sent thither to transact with the clergy of sense (for there is zeal enough) so as to mark the numbers of men ready to serve under pretence of recruiting for the Irish-French regiments, to bargain for horses here and there, to have them ready at Cork and to contrive ways of securing the barracks.[104]

Wogan's preoccupation with his native land was a recurring theme in his regular correspondence with James III. His great regard for his exiled countrymen and appreciation of recent developments in European politics dominated another letter of 18 May 1729. He vented his spleen against France for her duplicitous friendship with England, and lamented the huge losses which the Irish Jacobites had sustained in the service of a French king who had betrayed their cause:

> But with all this England is sick at heart, as France is rotten. Would to God we could see that the former made the latter pay dearly for her ill-placed and ill-timed friendship. There was a time and we have seen it when France was entirely in the power and at the disposal of England, her old but too generous conqueror and the sinister use France has made of the life and liberty allowed her upon too easy terms made me often

103 Fagan has spoken of a chain of command from the pope to the laity in the eighteenth-century church. The Stuart claimant, who appointed the hierarchy, must be included along with the pope at the top of the chain; Fagan, *Divided loyalties*, pp 79-80.   104 Wogan to James III, 10 May 1729 (R.A., Ms 127, fol. 152).

sorry that she was spared at that time. I speak as a private man. It may appear bold of me to look on France with such indignation. I cannot help but when I see the exile of the royal family sacrificed for her and the graves of one hundred thousand of our countrymen who died bravely without having been of any use in the cause that banished themselves and designed to fight for.[105]

Wogan was not an isolated figure crying in the Jacobite wilderness. Henry O'Neill of the Fews, County Armagh, wrote to King James III on 29 June 1731 also giving precise expression to the Jacobite sentiment among Irish exiles. He stressed his sufferings and those of his countrymen 'that have sacrificed all for the royal cause', and let James know that 'there were some of them still in a condition to serve him after an exile of forty years'. He deemed himself to be one 'of the number and the head of a family that had the good luck to render the king, his father of blessed memory, considerable service during the late wars in Ireland' and offered him 'with zeal what I have learned during forty years in a foreign prince's service'.[106]

Alexis O'Sullivan was indignant at James Edgar's (James III's secretary), refusal to intercede with his exiled master on the petitioner's behalf despite his sacrifices and those of his illustrious forebears, 'the most noblest, ancientest and heroickest Milesians', for the cause of King James II.[107] His letter contained all the gratuitous Jacobite flourishes displayed in the correspondence of the Catholic clergy to James II in the late 1680s or the writings of Nicholas Plunkett. It also embodied their resentment of their exclusion from the Stuart court already evident in the 'Groans of Ireland' (*c*.1693) and the 'Memoir of the Irish officer to his son' (*c*.1715). O'Sullivan assailed the Scots for their treachery towards Charles I and James II in blatant contrast to Irish fidelity:

> His majesty King James III is my king for he is king of Ireland as well as he is king of Scotland or England and the Irish, especially the Milesians, have been far better subjects and ten times more faithful and loyal to the family of the Stewarts than ever the Scotch have been. This is well known and proved by all records and histories that the Scotch began the war against Charles I (of blessed memory) and afterwards sold him to the

---

105 Wogan to James III, 18 May 1729 (R.A., Ms 128, fol. 34). Wogan hoped that the crowned heads of Europe would suffer retribution for their sins against James; R.A., Ms 112, fol. 102; Flood, *Wogan*, pp 135-6, 141-2. Count Berehaven attacked the 'infatuated court of France'; R.A., Ms 141, fol. 157. Other contemporary references to French ingratitude appear in the Stuart papers; R.A., Ms 96, fol. 66; R.A., Ms 177, fol. 127. **106** Henry O'Neill to Dr Cosen, 29 June 1731 (R.A., Ms 146, fol. 108). O'Neill went to France with James II and spent many years in the French and Spanish-Irish regiments. There are numerous other examples of this rhetoric in the Stuart papers; R.A., Ms 130, fol. 167; R.A., Ms 146, fol. 107; R.A., Ms 188, fol. 197; R.A., Ms 191, fol. 20; Daniel O'Carroll to James III, 5 Sept. 1737 (R.A., Ms 200, fol. 112); Fagan (ed.), *Stuart papers*, i, p. 314. **107** A. O'Sullivan to James III, 14 July 1739 (R.A., Ms 216, fol. 85).

English. The Scotch fanaticks kept Londonderry from James II (of blessed memory).[108]

Such self-riteous indignation infused a manuscript written down by the Jacobite heir of the confiscated estate of the Waddings of Ballycogley, County Wexford, sent to his son Thomas Wadding in Tenerife. It provided a 'a true copy of deeds and indentures of the ancient inheritance of the Wadding's of Ballycogley to which Thomas was the lawful heir'. This document had been sent to Thomas by his sister Delphina after the death of his brother Luke. He urged his son to take care of it 'penning down at foot thereafter your posterity for although we enjoy nothing but the bare title having lost all for our loyalty and Catholic religion (to the glory of our family)'. He asserted that 'it was both reasonable and necessary that parents should leave their posterity some light of their predecessors'. He also urged his son to guard it in anticipation of a Stuart restoration, when the 'Cromelian rebbles' would be displaced and the Waddings restored to their rightful position.[109]

The activities of Daniel O'Carroll (of Ely O'Carroll, County Offaly), Thomas Lally (Count Tollendall, formerly Tollendaly, County Galway), John Redmond and the Abbé Thomas Tyrrell in this period provide further evidence of the Irish diaspora's involvement in the affairs of Ireland. They reflect the beginnings of the breakdown of the Anglo-French alliance and the distant rumblings of a general European war. Although O'Carroll's letter bristles with formulaic Irish Jacobite rhetoric, his reference to dealings with Lords Ormonde, North, Orrery and the Irish Jacobite general Sir Arthur Dillon, James III's most trusted Irish confidants, would seem to indicate that he knew the main powerbrokers in the exiled Irish Jacobite community. He also claimed that he had journeyed to Ireland to consult a number of prominent Irish-based Jacobites and to inspect military installations with a view to Ireland's possible role in a diversionary action on behalf of the Stuart cause:

> For this reason I took a journey to Ireland, under the pretence of visiting
> my parents, to the Lords Mayo [Theobald Bourke, viscount Mayo] and
> Athurny [Francis Berminghan, fourteenth Lord Atherny] and several
> other relations; the people there from a long peace were grown rich by

---

108 A. O'Sullivan to James III, 14 July 1739 (R.A., Ms 216, fol. 85). O'Sullivan was an impoverished Irish soldier and according to his own account a Jacobite exile. The Stuart papers contain numerous examples of Irish Jacobite self-righteousness; R.A., Ms 157, fol. 19; R.A., Ms 157, fol. 150; R.A., Ms 176, fol. 68; R.A., Ms 244, fol. 28; R.A., Ms 247, fol. 163; R.A., Ms 194, fol. 147; R.A., Ms 249, fol. 53; Flood, *Wogan*, pp 141-2. A general reflection of these sentiments pervaded the works of Nicholas Plunkett; Plunkett, 'A Light to the blind' (N.L.I., Ms 476, fols 166-7); idem, 'For the reinthroned king: a method for governing England, Ireland and Scotland' (N.L.I., Mi 477, fol. 2) See also Barry (ed.), 'The groans of Ireland', pp 130-6; 'Lettre d'un officier Irlandais à son fils' c. post 1715 (B.N., Fonds Français., Ms 12, 161, N.L.I., mf. p. 112) Hayes as 'Reflections of an Irish Brigade officer', pp 68-75. 109 'The ancient inheritance of the Waddings of Ballecogley', 18 Sept. 1733 (N.L.I., 5193, fols 154-9); Whelan, *Tree of liberty*, p. 11.

industry and numerous, and capable of making a strong diversion, new converts and all honest to a man. I reviewed all the places of action and I forded the Suck and Shannon in several places which raised the hopes of multitudes and I saw it gave some easiness to others. I returned to England after three months stay.[110]

Little information has survived on the exact details of the machinations of Tyrrell, Redmond and Lally. However, Ulick Burke, a son of the ninth earl of Clanricarde and a colonel in the French service, prepared a comprehensive invasion plan based on a trip to Ireland in 1737.[111] It included an appraisal of contemporary English, Scottish and Irish politics. He advised James that Ormonde should lead an invasion of England; 'the Irish might easily be brought in, which would prevent bringing over troops [to England and Scotland] which proved so fatal to Scotland in the year 1715'. The Irish and Scots would support the house of Stuart but 6,000 arms would have to be sent to West Connaught, to the earl of Clanricarde's estate for the purpose of arming the Irish Jacobites.[112] Bourke himself, acting as deputy to his kinsman, the young earl of Clanricarde, would surprise the garrisons of Galway and Athlone. He also promised that his friends would capture Limerick and make James III master of the whole area west of the Shannon.

To 'make people's duty suit with their interest' Burke advised King James to consider a number of key political changes, some of which reflect orthodox high-political Jacobite thinking and wholly Irish Jacobite sentiments. James should 'settle a union or association between Scotland and Ireland so as to make them entirely subject to your majesty' and a 'check on any rebellious subjects in England'. He also proposed that 'all the estates forfeited by the late unhappy revolution and since be restored to the proper owners' and 'that the union between Scotland and England be dissolved and that Scotland and Ireland be allowed such a body of troops on foot of their own natives for the security of his majesty's person and government'. He recommended the repeal of Poynings's

---

110 O'Carroll to James III, 5 Sept. 1737 (R.A., Ms 200, fol. 112). Lord Mayo and Lord Atherny's name appearned on a list of Irish ciphers in the Stuart papers; R.A., Box5/163; Fagan (ed). *Stuart papers*, i, p. 64.   111 John Redmond visited Ireland in 1737 to discover the strength of the Jacobite party; O'Donoghue, 'Jacobite threat', p. 193. In the same year, after the death of his father Sir Gerard, Thomas Lally visited Scotland and England to assess Irish Jacobite power. He then crossed to Ireland and visited his ancestral home, and studied places along the coast for landing foreign troops; Hayes, *Irish swordmen*, pp 232, 236. In 1740 Abbé Thomas Tyrrell informed the Jacobite secretary James Edgar that 'if I can be anyway useful to his majesty in making a transitory journey to England and Ireland to take a short and sharp view of the present situation of affairs, so as to be capable at my speedy return here to give you a clear or profitable account thereof, I willingly will perform without one halfpenny being chargeable to the king ...', in Fagan (ed.), *Stuart papers*, i, pp 294-5. It is not clear if Tyrrell ever made his journey to Ireland. 112 Ulick Burke to James III, 19 Aug. 1737, in Fagan (ed.), *Stuart papers*, i, pp 262-6. O'Carroll had also pointed out that 'Ireland was become the nursery of the English troops' (R.A., Ms 200, fol. 102); introduction, p. 29.

Law (vigorously opposed by James II in 1689),[113] and the granting of the same liberty of conscience to Catholics as they had enjoyed under Charles II (which had been guaranteed under the 'broken' Treaty of Limerick). Finally, he advocated the restoration of those rights to Roman Catholics peers and gentry which they held before 1641, and the total repeal of the penal laws which had been imposed against the Catholics since 1691.[114]

The Irish *émigrés* also interceded on behalf of Irish clergymen for vacant sees in Ireland. These episcopal hopefuls still had to canvass among the native gentry and clergy, displaying the potency of secular influences on the king's prerogative.[115] Dr Robert Lacy, appointed to the see of Limerick in 1737, was reminded by James III of the twin ecclesiastical and political characteristics of episcopal appointments. The Stuart monarch also emphasised the need for 'zeal' and 'prudence' in Lacy's performance of his duties towards God and his prince. James's particular emphasis on 'prudence' helps explain the caution with which the Irish episcopate advised their flocks during the tumultuous 'Forty-five'. This reticence would have met with the approval of James himself, who showed a greater interest in the spiritual welfare of his Catholic kingdom than in its participation in a hopeless Jacobite uprising. In view of James's despair at the recklessness of Bonnie Prince Charlie's landing in Scotland, Irish passivity cannot be taken to indicate Catholic indifference towards their exiled king.[116] Similarly, the Abbé Dunne saw no inconsistency between loyalty to James III and living quietly under the present government. In a letter to John Hay, Lord Inverness, Dunne thought it 'not inconsistent with our tenets to live quietly under a government that protected them, and await favourable opportunities without undertaking anything that may bring a persecution on them from the government until they could find themselves in a situation to assert their right'.[117]

This thinking was in line with the attempt by English Catholics to formulate an oath of submission to the Hanoverians in 1715. It was inspired by their efforts to 'safeguard Catholics against persecution, not to make them loyal to George I'. Monod notes their 'terrible dilemma': maintaining allegiance to the Stuarts

---

113 This law was introduced by Sir Edward Poynings in 1494. It required the lord deputy and council of Ireland to seek the king's permission to summon an Irish parliament and his approval of draft bills. The king and English privy council sent back a licence to hold parliament and his approval of proposed draft bills. Its object was to curb the power of Garret More Fitzgerald, eight earl of Kildare who had supported the Lancastrian pretender Lambert Simnel. The law provoked much controversy in the sixteenth and seventeenth centuries. James II resisted attempts by the 'Patriot' Parliament' to repeal it; Connolly (ed.), *Oxford companion*, pp 458-9.   **114** Ulick Burke to James III, 19 Aug. 1737, in Fagan (ed.), *Stuart papers*, i, pp 262-6.   **115** For examples, see A. Dunleavy to James III, 19 Aug. 1726 (R.A., Ms 96, fol. 67). See also R.A., Ms 102, fol. 106; Ms 197, fol. 149; Ms 198, fol. 17; Ms 200, fol. 183; Murphy, *Killaloe*, p. 70; R.A., Ms 243, fols 84, 179; Ms 198, fol. 58; Ms 201, fol. 150; Ms 202, fol. 101; Ms 209, fol. 97; Ms 215, fol. 82; Ms 216, fol. 9; Ms 222, fol. 114; Ms 226, fol. 34; Ms 232, fol. 119; Ms 243, fol. 84; Giblin (ed.), 'Catalogue', part 6, vols 131-5g, pp 100-101; de Breffny, 'Letters to a Wild Goose', p. 82.   **116** James III to Dr R. Lacy, 27 Nov. 1737 (R.A., Ms 202, fol. 96); See above, fn. 16; R.A., Ms 202, fol. 164.   **117** Quoted in Fagan (ed) *Stuart papers*, i, pp 83-4, 293.

led to further persecution, but disowning the exiled line meant a betrayal of their deepest sentiments.[118] Chapman has also highlighted this caution and the pivotal importance of passive obedience to English Jacobite political argument. He argues that 'the people were not envisaged as embarking on a spontaneous restoration of themselves' and that 'they were to support their prince when he required it, that is when he raised his standard on British soil'.[119] Ireland was no different in this regard. This close association between Jacobitism and Catholicism was the one issue which had the potential to cause a rift between James III and the Irish Catholic clergy. By instructing his clergy to avoid open politics, the Stuart claimant ensured that they did not attract the unwanted attention of the government and thereby put a strain on their loyalty. This also enabled them to act with relative impunity as the agents and correspondents of James and his Irish agents in Europe. They would also serve as useful allies against the machinations of O' Conor, Trimbleston and the Catholic Committee in the late-1750s and 1760s.

IV

Irish Jacobitism survived the comparative paralysis of Jacobite diplomacy between the mid-1720s and the outbreak of a general European war in the early 1740s. Irish clergymen acted as agents for James III and corresponded with Rome regarding episcopal preferments, and stressed their spiritual and secular obligations to James III. They scuttled any attempts to come to an accommodation with King George II in 1727, and kept the exiled court informed of the strength of the Irish Jacobite community. Passive manifestations of popular Jacobitism provided a context for active demonstrations of solidarity, which included attacks on Whigs and riots on the Stuart king's birthday. Jacobite activity was sporadic, tentative and clandestine. Links with the continent were retained through the usual channels, informing the Irish at home about Jacobite high-politics. This awareness is evident in a multiplicity of contemporary sources.

The state of Jacobite Ireland in the lean years of the 1720s and 1730s can also be viewed through the eyes of their Irish Whig contemporaries. When the long-awaited Jacobite challenge to the revolutionary settlement failed to materialise in the 1720s, the Irish Protestant community reverted to monitoring the activities of 'the Pretender' in Rome. They rejoiced at his marital difficulties, and continually stressed his close relationship with the pope, that other arch-villain of the Protestant tradition. At the same time, a certain flippancy entered Protestant discourse in relation to the Pretender as depicted by Madden's *Memoirs of the twentieth century* in 1728 and numerous derogatory references to 'the

118 Monod, *Jacobitism*, pp 132-3.   119 Chapman, 'Jacobite political argument', pp 274-5, 276-7.

Pretender' and his court in the popular press. The Protestant backlash against French recruiting in Ireland in 1730, and the eventual breakdown of the Anglo-French *détente*, shows that Jacobitism was still perceived as a significant threat to the existing regime. It emerged from the doldrums in the late 1730s and early 1740s as rumours circulated of French military successes and a possible invasion. The French king again resumed his role (along with the pope and the Stuart king) as an inveterate enemy of the Irish Protestant tradition. The activities of 'the Pretender' and those of his agents were carefully scrutinised by Irish Protestants, especially their flirtation with foreign powers. When the numerous invasion scares receded, Protestants retained a more relaxed interest in his activities, movements and marital difficulties while countless sermons deployed the old rhetoric of popery, arbitrary power, brass money and wooden shoes.

Recruitment to the Irish regiments in the French and Spanish armies pre-occupied Irish poets, Protestant pamphleteers and official correspondents. This interest reflected the continued importance of the Irish Brigades in Jacobite high politics, which would again manifest itself in the 1740s and 1750s. Jacobitism also survived among the Irish exiles during this period. They constantly appealed to their exiled Stuart king in Rome, seeking preferment both in the church and the military. James III remained a potent force in Irish ecclesiastical politics. He retained the loyalty of the majority of the Irish Catholic episcopate who themselves had, the finger on the pulse of Irish political, social and cultural life. In *ancien régime* Europe, where Catholicism, honour and pedigree were deemed to be important, Jacobitism provided the Irish diaspora with useful practical, cultural and psychological baggage in foreign countries. It was a badge of loyalty which would have been easily carried and provided a sheet anchor in the uncertainty and dislocation of exile.

A more active Jacobitism emerged in the period immediately preceding the outbreak of the War of Jenkins's Ear, when prominent Irish exiles and Jacobite agents returned to their native land on reconnaissance missions, and advised King James on Ireland's suitability for a diversionary invasion.

CHAPTER 6

'Séarlas in Alba ag gearradh na méirleach':[1] Ireland and the 'Forty-five'

The era from the outbreak of the Spanish-British colonial conflict known as the War of Jenkins's Ear in 1739 to the Treaty of Aix-la-Chapelle in 1748 provides another high-point in the history of Irish Jacobitism. Dormant Jacobite spirits in Ireland and on the continent revived with the outbreak of war in 1739, and the emerging crisis across Europe. The death of the Holy Roman Emperor Charles VI on 20 October 1740 precipitated Frederick the Great of Prussia's invasion of Silesia two months later in direct defiance of the Pragmatic Sanction which had guaranteed the succession of Charles VI's eldest daughter Maria Theresa. The War of the Austrian Succession had begun and it was only a matter of time before Britain and France entered the fray. The subsequent military stalemate in Europe restored Jacobitism to the forefront of European politics. Britain and Ireland again became the focus of a possible Franco-Jacobite invasion on behalf of Charles Edward Stuart, James III's eldest son and the great hope of the Jacobites. Although Ireland was not the direct target of these French invasion plans and 'the big dog' did indeed 'fail to bark in the night', the effects of the abortive Franco-Jacobite invasion of 1743-4 and subsequent Jacobite rebellion of 1745 reverberated through all levels of the Irish community.[2]

The poets turned their eyes to Europe and placed their trust in the Bourbon kings of France and Spain, and the 'Wild Geese' in the service of both monarchs. Their poetry provides an accurate chronological account of the main incidents of the European war and the 'Forty-five'. Bonnie Prince Charlie replaced his father as the lawful suitor of 'Éire' in Jacobite verse, as the poets prematurely heralded the long-awaited humiliation of Irish Protestantism. The Irish exiles also reacted positively to the transformation in Jacobite political affairs. They had already sensed the impending disintegration of the Anglo-French *détente* in the late 1730s, reacting with a spate of invasion plans and reconnaissance missions to Ireland. They assured their king of their willingness to join the prince in Scotland. Many of those who failed to cross the English

---

1 Seán Clárach Mac Domhnaill, 'Gach Gaoidheal geal greanmhar', in Ó Foghludha (eag.), *Seán Clárach*, p. 72. **2** The metaphor is Murray Pittock's; Pittock, *Jacobite politics and literature*, p. 188.

Channel lobbied the French and Spanish courts, and eagerly sought news of the prince's progress.

Rumours of French preparations and Charles Edward's remarkable campaign in Scotland reached the ears of the greater Catholic populace, primarily through their clandestine links with France and the poems and songs of the Irish literati. Although a terrible famine had recently devastated the Jacobite heartland of Munster, the 'common people' from Cork to Donegal eagerly watched for French ships on the horizon and reacted positively to news from Scotland.

Despite this reawakening, Ireland has hardly featured in reappraisals of Jacobite historiography of this period. Although 'Jacophiles' and 'Jacosceptics' alike have seen the 1745 rebellion as a watershed in eighteenth-century British history, it has seldom featured in eighteenth-century Irish historiography.[3] According to F.G. James, the last Jacobite rising produced almost no reaction from Irish Catholics.[4] Although this is true in a purely military sense, the inactivity must be assessed in the context of Catholic military impotence, the absence of any invasion force from the continent (the essential ingredient for a general uprising in any of the Stuart kingdoms) and the relative strength of the military establishment in Ireland. It should also take into account the catastrophic effects of the 1741 famine which wiped out a quarter of the Catholic population (particularly in Munster).[5] James's opinion that 'the complete absence of overt Jacobite sympathy among Irish Catholics soon quieted suspicions and led to a new spirit of toleration on the part of many Protestants' belies what actually happened.[6] In a pan-British context McLynn has berated the dismissive extrapolations of historians 'worshipping the God of historical inevitability'.[7] Historians, over-impressed by Ireland's quiescence during the 'Forty-five', have understated the latent strength of Irish Jacobitism.[8]

This attitude is typified by Canny's dismissal of Ó Buachalla for 'mistaking rhetorical flourish [in Irish Jacobite poetry] for a serious political message', and

---

3 Linda Colley warns that the 'romantic aura that still hovers around his [Charles Edward's] memory should not obscure the seriousness of the invasion'; Colley, *Britons*, p. 80. Ó Buachalla criticises the tendency to contrast the primitive rustic highlanders (who won most major battles of the 'Forty-five') with the progressive modern armies of George II (many of whom were raw levies); Ó Buachalla, *Aisling Ghéar*, p. 405. See also Black, *Culloden and the '45*, pp 66-7; idem., 'Could the Jacobites have won? pp 24–30'. Michael Wagner believed that the survival of the Hanoverian dynasty and the rule of the Whigs was a, close call indeed, saved by the crass stupidity of the Jacobite leaders; Wagner, 'Scotland in the late 18th century', p. 148. For similar views, see McLynn, *Bonnie Prince Charlie*, chapters 7-17, p. 551; Erskine-Hill, *Poetry of opposition and revolution*, p. 146.   4 James, *Ireland in the empire*, p. 144. See also Boyce, *Nationalism*, p. 98. Mc Lynn states that 'not a flicker of support for the Stuarts was discernable in Ireland'; McLynn, 'Good behaviour, pp 47–8.   5 The great famine of 1741 ('Bliain an Áir') is the subject of a modern treatment; Dickson, *Arctic Ireland*.   6 James, *Ireland in the empire*, p. 186; Lecky, *Ireland*, i, p. 269. An opposite view is provided by O'Callaghan; *Irish brigades*, p. 417.   7 McLynn, *Bonnie Prince Charlie*, pp 124, 63.   8 James, *Ireland in the empire*, pp 174-81; O'Brien (ed.), *Catholic Ireland in the eighteenth century*, pp 56-7. Connolly provides the best recent survey of Irish passivity in this period; Connolly, *Religion*, pp 244-6. For the strength of the establishment in 1745, see O'Callaghan, *Irish brigades*, p. 413; O'Donoghue, 'Jacobite threat', p. 153; Beresford, Ireland', p. 173.

his [Ó Buachalla's] assumption that 'anybody in Ireland or elsewhere believed that a French invasion of Ireland in support of the exiled cause was a practical possibility in the eighteenth century'.[9] Likewise, it is a central element of Connolly's treatment of eighteenth-century Ireland that the state faced credible internal and external challenges which explain the repressive penal laws which it adopted. In contradiction of this thesis, he discounts the Jacobite threat after 1715 and dismisses the existence of a serious political message in contemporary Jacobite poetry.[10] Kelly, in his recent analysis of Protestant attitudes towards the 'Forty-five', claimed that 'Bonnie Prince Charlie posed Irish Protestants no threat but his early military successes terrified them'.[11]

While the prince himself might not have posed a direct threat to Ireland in 1745, Maréchal Saxe certainly did in 1744. The possibility of a French invasion did not totally recede with the onset of the 'Forty-five' and proved a major factor in hindering the suppression of the Scottish rebellion.[12] The public commemorations between Charles Edward's invasion of Scotland in July 1745 and his defeat at Culloden in April 1746 produced a greater participation by all strata of the Irish Protestant community. This and the subsequent proliferation of 'Cumberland', 'Culloden' and 'Hanover' societies shows that many Protestants took the 'Forty-five' seriously. The failure of the Irish to rise during the 'Forty-five' should also be viewed in the context of the inactivity of the English Jacobites. It should also consider the unwillingness of even loyal Scottish Jacobites, including Donald Cameron, Randal McDonald of Clanranald, Sir Alexander McDonald of Sleat or the unscrupulous Simon Fraser (Lord Lovat), to join the prince until they received assurances of French support, titles and pledges of compensation for their lands, or until they had fallen under the personal spell of the prince's persuasive personality.[13] Therefore to contend that Irish Jacobite poetry of the period lacks a real political message or political relevance is as unrealistic as to deny the importance of the many Jacobite plots and invasion plans which were hatched throughout the eighteenth-century. The corollary of this argument – that Irish Protestants suffered an enormous collective paranoia for the greater part of the century – is equally unacceptable.

9 Canny, review of Ó Buachalla, 'Na Stíobhartaigh agus an t-aos léinn: Cing Séamas', p. 280; Liam Irwin has reiterated the view that 'eighteenth-century Irish poetry, with its obsession about the Stuarts as saviours of Ireland, was divorced from reality'; Irwin, review of Fagan (ed.), *Stuart papers*, p. 477. **10** Connolly, *Religion*, p. 248; Barnard, 'Old Ireland', pp 916, 919. **11** Kelly, 'The glorious and immortal memory', p. 39. Tensions in Ireland in 1745 were in fact greater than Lecky implied in his history; Cullen, *Emergence of modern Ireland*, pp 13, 198; see also Petrie, 'Ireland and the 'Forty-five', p. 275. **12** Cumberland's campaign against Charles Edward was hampered by rumours of a French invasion of England, Black, *Culloden and the '45*, p. 72; Ó Buachalla, *Aisling Ghéar*, p. 403. **13** Erskine-Hill, *Poetry of opposition and revolution*, pp 146-7. Indeed, the majority of the Jacobite clans did not turn out in the 'Forty-five'; Macinnes, *Clanship, commerce*, pp 159-88, 246.

I

The output of Irish Jacobite poets matched the outpouring from Irish Protestant Hanoverian royalism uncovered by Kelly.[14] Despite this, their repertoire has been consistently ignored by many who claim to explore contemporary Irish Catholic political sentiment in the seventeenth and eighteenth centuries. This poetry provides an uncanny insight into Catholic Jacobites attitudes throughout the decade from the outbreak of the War of Jenkins's Ear until the Treaty of Aix-la-Chapelle. Its vivid detail on the European conflict and its affirmation of the cult of Charles Edward Stuart reflects the hopes of many Irish Catholics at home and abroad within a traditional Jacobite literary context. Liam Dall Ó hIfearnáin's poem 'Caitlín Ní hUallacháin' proclaimed that peace would not come from the trouble in Spain which would facilitate the unsheathing of swords for war. He hoped that the foreigners would be laid low by the strength of Irish hands and that the son of the king (James III or Charles Edward) would be wedded to 'Caitlín Ní hUallacháin' (Ireland):

> Ó measaimíd nach calma rinn, den bhuairt seo i Spáinn
> Acht mealladh slighe chum catha cloidhimh do thabhairt i dtráth;
> beidh Galla arís dá leagadh síos le lúth ár lámh
> Is mac an ríogh ag Caitlín Ní hUallacháin.[15]

Seán Clárach also anticipated a Spanish-sponsored Jacobite invasion in this period. He informed his listeners that there was a story of great joy which he happily accepted that James was coming across the sea along with a Spanish force:

> Do b'é a labhairt scéalta aitis
> Tré n-ar ghlacas gáirdeas
> Go raibh Séamas ag teacht tar muir
> mar aon le fuireann Spáinneach.[16]

---

14 It certainly runs counter to McLynn's claim that there was no opportunity for Irishmen sympathetic to Jacobitism to counter the propaganda offensive mounted by the ruling elite. Indeed, this offensive would have been irrelevant to many Irish Jacobites who did not read or understand English, McLynn, 'Good behaviour', p. 53. **15** Liam Dall Ó hIfearnáin, 'Caitlín Ní hUallacháin', in Ó Foghludha (eag.), *Ar bhruach na Coille Muaire*, p. 40. Liam Prút has suggested that the duke mentioned in the line 'Roimh Shéamas Mac Shéamais is an Diúic thar lear' was Henry, duke of York, and that when this poem was composed it was not necessary to mention Charles Edward by name; Prút, 'Liam Dall Ó hIfearnáin', p. 195. Ó Buachalla argues that the duke in question is the second duke of Ormonde and that the poem dates to 1718-9; Ó Buachalla, *Aisling Ghéar*, p. 324. Liam Dall sent copies of his poems to Donal Dinneen at the Irish College in Toulouse; Walsh, *Irish continental college movement*, p. 132. The best recent analysis of Liam Dall's poetry is Prút, 'Liam Dall Ó hIfearnáin', pp 185-214. **16** Seán Clárach Mac Domhnaill, 'Oidhche an aonaigh d'éis a fhliuchta'; Ó Foghludha (eag.), *Seán Clárach*, pp 94-5.

Elsewhere he hoped that the white Spaniard (Philip V) would come with men across the turf ('Dá dtagadh an Spáinneach bán le fearaibh thar móin').[17] In his poem 'Léir ruathar Whiggonia', Aindrias Mac Craith assured his listeners that an unstoppable band was approaching the Shannon and boasted that when the band (Irish Brigades) came across the ocean Whiggery would be trounced:

> Tá fuirionn ná cuirfear ar g-cúl
> Ag druidim le ciúbhar na Sionnaine
> Nuair thiocfas an fhuirionn tar abhainn
> Is deimhin go b-planncfam Whiggiona.[18]

Seán Ó Tuama's 'A Cuisle na h-éigse', specifically mentioned Philip, the illustrious James and their hordes ('Pilib 's Séamas glé, 's a sluagh').[19] An anonymous Ulster poet also toasted Philip V in this period. He called for his listeners to take a full glass in each hand and drink a health to King Philip and the child (Charles Edward) who was ever absent. He lamented that the Irish have long been under a thick mist of gloom and if they were not relieved France and Spain would be destroyed:

> Bíodh cárt i ngach láimh agus gloine,
> Is ná dearmad iad a bheith lán,
> Go n-ólfamuid sláinte Ríogh Philip,'
> 'S a leinbh seo 'riamh ar fán;
> Is fada faoi smuid 's gan síomad,
> gan dalta 's gan aoibhneas le fagháil,
> 'S muna dtóigfear an brón-sa dínn feasta
> Creacfam an Fhrainnc is an Spáinn.[20]

He prayed to God that the Stuart would come across with Lord Clare, that the Gaels would be joyful and elevated and that the yellow foreigners would be left with nothing:

> Guidhim feasta Rí Geal na n-aingeal,
> An aicme seo chlaoidheadh i dtráth,

---

17 Seán Clárach Mac Domhnaill, 'A ainnir is áilne lámh', in ibid., pp 100-1.   **18** Aindrias Mac Craith, 'Léir ruathar Whiggonia', in O'Daly, *Poets ands poetry of Munster* (1849), p. 78. The version of this poem which Ó Buachalla quotes from alludes to a storm passing over the Shannon, Ó Buachalla, *Aisling Ghéar*, p. 412.   **19** Seán Ó Tuama, 'A Cuisle na h-éigse', in O'Daly (eag.), *Poets and poetry of Munster*, p. 60. Buttimer has recently edited an Irish prose text based on contemporary newspapers which was obviously intended for an Irish-speaking audience; Buttimer, 'An Irish text on the war of Jenkins's ear', pp 75-98.   **20** Anon, 'Sláinte Ríogh Philib', in Ó Muirgheasa (eag.) *Dhá chéad*, pp 19-20. O'Daly suggests that the child who is forever absent ('an leinbh seo 'riamh ar fán') refers to Charles Edward; O'Daly, *Poets and poetry of Munster* (1849), p. 116.

'S a ndíbirt ón mhnaoi tá faoi sgamaill
Ar a mbaistimíd-inne Innse Fáil
An Stíobhart dá dtigeadh tar chalaith,
'S gan dearmadadh Tighearna an Chláir,
Béidh Gaedhil bhocht 'le haoibhneas i ngradam.
Is na Gaill bhuidhe arís le fán.[21]

The emphasis on Spain shows that it cannot be dismissed as formulaic literary convention. These poets were acutely aware of recent diplomatic developments and knew exactly who the most likely ally of the house of Stuart was at the end of the 1730s.

Liam Rua Mac Coitir also anticipated the possibility of a Bourbon-Jacobite alliance and a Scottish uprising in support of the Jacobite cause. He stated that troops from Ireland, a great band from Spain, a tidy band from Britain, the shield-bearers of Scotland's sweet sod, Louis of France and the exiled warrior in Rome would all rally to the cause of Móirín Ní Luingheacháin (Ireland):

Beidh Fianna Fearainn fód Fhloinn is mór-bhuidhean do thig ón Spáinn
Glain-chliar ó Bhreatain fós maoidhim go ngeóbhaid linn i gcoinne chách;
Lucht sciath ó Albain fhóid-mhín is cóir Laoisigh chliste cháidh.
'S ná hiarr-sa teacht 'na cómhair síos ar Mhóirín Ní Luingheacháin
Tá gliadhaire catha ar deoraidheacht sa Róimh mhín fí choimirc chách.
De ghrian-tsliocht Chaisil cheól-chaoin is fós ní bhfuil fuil is fearr,
Beidh an triath 's a mhac le fórsaibh ag ródaidheacht go hInis Fáil
'S a bhliadhan seo ag teacht ag tóraidheacht ar Mhóirín Ní Luin-
gheacháin.[22]

Liam Inglis's 'M'atuirse traochta na fearchoin aosta', composed in 1742, also appreciated the radical transformation of the Jacobite position, in particular France's incorporation into the anti-British camp. He hoped that the banishment of the tyrants would free Irish towns from high rents (possibly quarterage) and end the use of nicknames for Prince Charles. His arrival and the reduction of the swarthy Johns (the English) would return all the lost churches, reverse the status of the English and Irish languages and end the enforced silence of the poets. Charles Edward would speedily come across the sea and 'yellow John' would be put in his place:

Do ghlanfadh a Éirinn mar dhanair na méirligh
'S ár mbailte a shaoradh ó árd-chíos;
...s is mairg do bhéarfadh leas-ainm ar Shéarlas
Do bhainfeadh a réim cheart de Sheán Buidhe.

21 Anon, 'Sláinte Ríogh Philib', in Ó Muirgheasa (eag.), *Dhá chéad*, pp 19-20.　**22** Liam Rua Mac Coitir, 'Móirín Ní Luingheacháin', in Ó Foghludha (eag.), *Cois na Cora*, p. 26.

...

Do cailleadh le tréimhse ár gcealla le chéile
Ó d'eascair na faoil-choin i bhFáil chrích
Is araid tá an Béarla 'is gan tapaidh 's an Ghaedhilg
Is balbh ár n-éigse ar gnáth-chaoidh

....

Go dtagaidh lá éigin tar farriage Séarlas
A bhainfear a réim ceart de Sheán Bhuidhe.[23]

Muiris Ó Gríobhtha responded to these lines, promising that the honourable prince of the blood of the MacCarthys of Cashel (Charles Edward) would crush the English Whigs and make the swarthy Johns howl:

Gur dhearcas prionnsa d'fhuil Chaisil Chuirc ionnruic
Ar shleasaibh na srúill thóir ag rámhaidheacht;

...

Is geallaid go mbrúghfaid an gall-whig ciontach
Is bainfid sin liúgh as na Seáin Bhuidhe.[24]

Seán Clárach Mac Domhnaill lauded the triumphs of the French, Spanish, Prussian, Polish and Bavarian forces who opposed the Austrian/British/Dutch alliance during the War of the Austrian Succession. He gleaned his war-news from the local *Limerick Journal*, translated it into Irish, and often set it to a popular Jacobite tune for public delivery.[25] The mediating role of the Irish poet and song-writer in the diffusion of European news to an Irish-speaking public parallels the role of the ballad-singer in contemporary England.[26] It also questions the too neat distinction often made between 'oral' and 'literary' forms. Seán Clárach's expectations contrast sharply with Whig fears which were expressed at the highest levels within the political establishment. The poet's

---

23 Liam Inglis, 'M'atuirse traochta na fearachoin aosta', in Ó Foghludha (eag.), *Cois na Bríde*, p. 40. An anonymous poet referred to holy mass in the churches of Ireland 'aithfrionn naomhtha a g-ceallaibh na h-Éireann'; 'Ionurbadh Sheaghain Bhuidhe', in Hardiman (eag.), *Irish minstrelsy*, ii, p. 84. There are numerous other cryptic references to the Stuarts (pp 170-71). Seán Clárach reflected this 'secrecy' in a contemporary song to the tune of the 'White Cockade', the popular Jacobite anthem: I will not tell you who is my love; That story will soon be told 'Ní mhaoidhfad féin cé hé mo stór,/Tá insint scéil 'n-a dhéidh go leór;/'; Seán Clárach Mac Domhnaill, 'Bímse buan ar bhuairt gach ló'; in Ó Foghludha (eag.), *Seán Clárach*, p. 46; Piaras Mac Gearailt promised that a nameless hero will heal all our pain and suffering 'Is geallaim go réidhfidh laoch gan ainm gach péin agus ceasna orainn'; Piaras Mac Gearailt, 'An gheallamhain', in Ó Foghludha (eag.), *Amhráin Phiarais Mhic Gearailt*, pp 36. **24** Muiris Ó Gríobhtha, 'Trém Aisling do smúineas', in Ó Foghludha (eag.), *Cois na Bríde*, pp 41-3. **25** Mac Craith, 'Filíocht Sheacaibíteach', p. 65. Ó Buachalla also notes Seán Clárach and Seán na Ráithíneach's knowledge of international politics. Similarly, Tadhg Ó Neachtain's commonplace book shows that he read *Harding's Dublin Impartial Newsletter*, *Walsh's Weekly Newsletter*, *Faulkner's Newsletter* and *Faulkner's Dublin Journal*; Ó Buachalla, *Aisling Ghéar*, p. 373; idem, 'Seacaibíteachas', p. 34; Buttimer, 'An Irish text on the War of Jerkins's ear', pp 77-9. **26** Chapman, 'Jacobite political argument', pp 203-4.

popular performance is self-evident from the first line of his song ' – Éistighidh lem ghlórtha' (listen to 'my' voice), sung to the tune of 'An saighdiúir gasta' – in which he urged his audience to listen to my voice and to spread his story to the sages, lions and heroes in Ireland who are without land or property. He rejoiced that Philip V was triumphant by land and sea, continually torturing George II whose fleet is broken and helpless. Meanwhile, the powerful elector of Bavaria had unexpectedly gained crowns and status as emperor in Europe with his hordes on the outskirts of Vienna:

> Éistighidh le mo ghlórtha a mórshliocht Mhilésius
> Is daoibh-se is deónach mo sceólta scaipe
> bhur saoithe cé leóinte, bhur leóghain 's bhur laochra
> i gcrích Fódhla gan fód gan fearann.
>
> Tá an báire le Pilib ar muir is ar tír
> ...
> Ag síorghreadadh Sheóirse go treórach gan traochadh.
> Tá an fleet briste breóite 's níl fóirthin aca;
>
> ...
> Tá Babharia comhachtach i gcoróinn is i gcéimibh
> Ina impire 'san Eóraip-sin sceól nár measadh
> Tá suidhchan a shlóighte ag bórdaibh Bhiénna.[27]

The poet was delighted that the queen (of Hungary, later Empress Maria Theresa) had been reduced to tears by her pursuers and that Kelvenhuller (her general) was powerless after his defeat at Breslau. With Prussian and Polish forces on the ramparts of Silesia, he rejoiced that Leopold I's crowd had been left accursed:

> Tá an Ríoghan go deórach, 's a tóir dá tafann;
> Tá Céilbhinhuller gan chumas gan chrích
> ag Bréslau do chuireadh an brise ar a bhuidhin.
> Tá Prussia agus Poland i bpórtaibh Shilésia
> Sin choidhce sliocht Leopóld fé cheó na mallacht.[28]

---

27 Seán Clárach Mac Domhnaill, 'Éistighidh lem ghlórtha', in Ó Foghludha (eag.), *Seán Clárach*, p. 55; Dover (ed.), *Letters*, i, p. 287. News of Maria Theresa's flight also featured in contemporary pamphlets, *The memoirs of the queen of Hungary*. 28 Seán Clárach Mac Domhnaill, 'Éistighidh lem ghlórtha', in Ó Foghludha (eag.), *Seán Clárach*, p. 55; Dover (ed.), *Letters*, i, p. 276; Dover (ed.), *Letters*, i, pp 107, 116, 134-5, 146, 167, 211. Muiris Ua Gríobhtha poem referred to the plight of the woman (Maria Theresa) who came without protection into the company of heroes ''S an bhean 'sa d'umhluigh teacht gan cuinse i bpáirt na laoch;'; Muiris Ua Griobhtha, 'An Seabhac Siubhail', in Ní Ógáin (eag.), *Duanaire*, ii, no. 9. Aindrias Mac Craith's poetry contains another reference to the

He boasted that the lion-like Montemar (the Spanish general) was moving like lightning to capture Mantua and Milan. Tuscany would soon fall to Philip and Don Carlos (son of Philip V of Spain), the wise king of Naples who was busy in the field with his father:

> Tá Montemar módhmhrach go treórach ag téarnamh
> Go loingseach, go leóghanda, go lóghmhar, lasmhar
> Le teinte, le tóirneach, le tórmach, le tréine
> Le saoithibh le slóightibh le ceólta catha
> Mantua is Milan táid tuilte dá bhuidhin.
> Tá Tuscani ag tuitim chum Pilib gan mhoill,
> Don Charolus mear cródha, an Rí nósmhar-san Naples,
> Ba gníomhach i ngleó cnuic i gcomhair le n-athair.[29]

Meanwhile Louis XV laid siege with his army at the gates of Hanover and Bremen while the hemmed-in Dutch dared not move:

> Tá Laoiseach 'n-a lóchrann go leónbhuilleach léidmheach
> Go díoghaltasach dó-bhriste i ndóchas daingean
> A mhuintir le dóirsibh Hanóbher is Brémen
> Tá cuing ar an Holloint is ní leómhfaidh preabadh.[30]

Seán na Ráithíneach Ó Murchú's optimism in the early 1740s contrasted starkly with the pessimism he expressed in the late 1720s. It is particularly evident in 'Is áthasach chímse na tíortha' (January 1741-2), 'Is dóigh le daoine' (21 September 1742), and 'Tá an bhliain seo ag teacht' (1744).[31] In this last song, sung to the tune of 'Jack the drummer', he celebrated the unity within Europe and the preparation of a massive army in Rome to perform military feats. He assured his listeners that a strong fleet led by sagacious lions (Charles Edward/ Maréchal Saxe?) has been unleashed across the sea with hosts on land or sea which would bring swords and cuirasses:

---

empire's combatants in contemporary poetry; Aindrias Mac Craith, 'Tá Pruise agus Póland fós ar mearthall' (Prussia and Poland are still raging); in Ó Foghludha (eag), *Éigse na Maighe*, pp 203-4. Although James II, on his death bed, had forgiven Leopold I (the holy Roman emperor) for his betrayal of a fellow monarch in 1688, Aindrias Mac Craith was not so gracious. **29** Seán Clárach Mac Domhnaill, 'Éistighidh lem ghlórtha', in Ó Foghludha (eag.), *Seán Clárach*, p. 55; Dover (ed.), *Letters*, i, p. 197; ibid., p. 310. **30** Seán Clárach Mac Domhnaill, 'Éistighidh lem ghlórtha', in Ó Foghludha (eag.), *Seán Clárach*, p. 54; Walpole to Mann, 25 Apr. 1743, in Dover (ed.), *Letters*, i, pp 269-70, 146-7, 170. **31** Seán na Ráithíneach Ó Murchú, 'Is áthasach chímse na tíortha [Jan. 1742]', in Torna (eag.), *Seán na Ráithíneach*, pp 237-8; idem, 'Is dóigh le daoine [Sept. 1742]', in ibid., pp 246-7; idem., 'Tá an bhliadhain seo ag teacht', in ibid., pp 255-7. Ó Buachalla has cited a series of expectant Irish poetry and song from this period; Ó Buachalla, *Aisling Ghéar*, pp 400-1.

Tá an Eóraip uile d' aontaoibh
an méid díobh ón Róimh a ngoirtear,
i gcóir gach rutha réab sinn
do léir-scaoileadh ar lár;
leóghain chliste is tréan-flít,
is féinnidhigh ar fhód nó ar uisce,
is tógfaidh cuisne cléibh dhínn
is glaodhmaois hurrá.[32]

Seán Clárach Mac Domhnaill reacted quickly to the news that Charles Edward had finally landed in Scotland. In his song 'Seal do bhíos im mhaighdin shéimh' (to the tune 'Over the hills and far away') he earnestly wished that he might see the love of his heart crowned which would lift the terrible gloom from the Irish. He hoped that every king in the world, would bow to him [Charles Edward], the love of his heart, the prince and king, the star that has risen in the south whose voice was as sweet as the birds:

Go bhfeicead-sa coróinn ar stór mo chléibh
A thógfaidh ceó agus brón de Ghaedhil
Gach Rí atá sa domhan dá mhéad
Ag umhladh dó le cognamh Dé
...
Isé mo rogha é a thoghas dam féin
...

Grádh mo chroidh-se an prionnsa, an Réx
Isé siúd an réiltann d'éirigh théas
gur binne a ghlór 'ná ceól na n-éan
de bharr na gcnoc 's in imigéan.[33]

Seán Clárach's poem 'Gach Gaoidhal geal greanmhar' announced the arrival of the prince in Scotland. He lauded his early successes, the real hope of French assistance, and a landing by the Irish Brigades in Ireland. He rejoiced that the calm and powerful Louis was coming, fierce, angry, manly and in great strength

---

32 Seán na Ráithíneach Ó Murchú, 'Tá an bhliain seo ag teacht ', in Ó Donnchadha (eag.), *Seán na Ráithíneach*, pp 255-7. See McLynn, *France and the Jacobite rising of 1745*; Black, *Culloden and the '45*, chapter 4. 33 Seán Clárach Mac Domhnaill,, 'Seal do bhíos im mhaighdin shéimh', in Ó Foghludha (eag.), *Seán Clárach*, p. 56. Ó Donnchadha claimed that the poet had links with Cormac Spáinneach Mac Cárthaigh who may have been well informed regarding the activities of continental Jacobites; Ó Donnchadha (eag.), *Seán na Ráithíneach*, p. 464. Another poem composed in 1744 relayed the rumours of the prince's arrival in Scotland; Séamus de Barra, 'An lá chuladh Cormac do bheith ag teacht go hAlbain'; de Brún, *Clár na lámhscríbhinní Gaeilge i gColáiste Ollscoil Chorcaí*, (index, 'Séarlas Rí). See also Tadhg Gaelach Súilleabháin, 'An lá tháinig Séarlas Stubart go hAlbain sa mbliain 1745'; Ní Shéaghdha, *Cat. of Ir. mss. in the N.L.I*, iii, p. 42.

to root out the foreigners. He believed that a Stuart would have the crown. He rejoiced that the English game was nearly played out and that they said their psalms like they seldom did before. While the Irish Brigades made their way to Ireland, Charles mowed down the plunderers in Scotland. He promised that one thousand ships in full sail were speedily crossing the sea from the country which the brave youth left and that old George would shit his trousers:

Tá Laoiseach lasmhar go calma comhachtach
Fíochmhar, feargach, fearamhail, fórsach
Ag tigheacht go neartmhar chum Danar a leónadh
Is beidh Stíobhart measaimse i gceannas na corónach.

...

Atá báire Shasana i ngar a bheith traochta
Radh na salm do b'annamh dhá dhéanamh
Atáid na fir chalma ag tarraint go hÉire
Séarlas in Alba ag gearradh na méirleach.

Tá míle barc is a bhfeara go seólta
Le fíoch ag tarraint chum caladh tar bóchna
Don tír dá dtagadh an ghasra chródha
Ina bhríste do leathfadh an sean-duine Seóirse.[34]

In another song, he assured his audience that Caesar (Charles Edward) and his strong fleet are coming and that the Gaels will be freed from bondage ('Tá Caesar le tréantruip ag tíocht/Is saorfaidh ó dhaorbhroid na Gaedhil').[35] His contemporary Aindrias Mac Craith celebrated the arrival of the resolute brave man (Charles Edward) in the ports of Scotland, with enough of his friends (the Irish Brigades) in a troop ('is an calm-fhear chródha ar phórtaibh Alban/'S go leor dá charaidh 'na ghárda').[36]

---

34 Seán Clárach Mac Domhnaill,, 'Gach Gaoidhal geal greanmhar', in Ó Foghludha (eag.), *Seán Clárach*, p. 7. These sentiments are also reiterated in his 'Ag taisteal dom trí na críocha ar cuaird'; ibid., p. 75. A post-boy was pilloried for heralding the Pretender's coronation in Scotland in 1746; Crofton-Croker, *Researches*, p. 201. Jacobite scare-mongering in England claimed that 'the Young Man is coming with great aid from Lewis and our troops must be called home'; *The chronicle of Charles the young man*, no. 18, in *A full collection of all the proclamations and orders published by the authority of Charles, prince of Wales.* Walpole's correspondence bristled with news of 'the Young Pretender's' defeat of Cope, and rumours of 10,000 men and thirty transports and ten battleships off Dunkirk; Walpole to Mann, in Dover (ed.), *Letters*, ii, p. 66. 35 Seán Clárach Mac Domhnaill, 'A chéibhfhionn bheag bhéaltaine bhaoth' in Ó Foghludha (eag.), *Seán Clárach*, p. 74. 36 Aindrias Mac Craith, 'Tá Pruise agus Póland fós ar mearthall' (A.D. 1745); Ó Foghludha (eag.), *Éigse na Máighe*, p. 203. Ó Buachalla cites numerous other references to the Wild Geese returning in this period; Ó Buachalla, *Aisling Ghéar*, pp 411-3. This elation also dominated contemporary Scots-Gaelic poetry. Mac Mhaighstir Alasdair, cousin of the famous Flora McDonnell and a volunteer in the

Mac Craith, composing in 1746, believed that a Stuart would soon possess Ireland, that the bards would sing, the chapels would be in the possession of the true (Roman Catholic) church, and the Johns (English) would be banished. Many of his contemporaries on both sides of the English Channel shared his confidence in the ultimate triumph of the Stuart cause in the aftermath of Falkirk. Mac Craith gloated on the 1000s who died at Falkirk, the fact that the Campbells and Johnny Cope were undone and he expressed the hope that Ireland would soon be in the possession of the Gaels. Charles would then be king and the foreigners would be forever aimless:

> Beidh Banba, geallaim, ag Stíobhart
> beidh cantain, is laoithe ag lucht ceol,
> beidh a gcealla ag an eaglais fhíre
> 'S is fada uaidh síos bheidh na Seóin
>
> ...
>
> Ag Falkirk do cailleadh na mílte,
> Tá Campbells go claoidhte agus Cope
> beidh sealbh na Banba ag Gaoidhlaibh,
> 'S na Danair seo choidhche gan treóir,
> beidh Carolus feasta ina rígh againn
> is beidh an aindeis go cinnte ar na Seóin![37]

In a poem composed to commemorate Charles Edward's invasion of England, Éadbhard de Nógla asked his audience if they had heard the stories of the brave-hearted lion, whose health should be drunk, who had performed an intricate dance through the snow from Scotland to Carlisle, despite (George) Wade and (Johnny) Cope, who were smitten by the progeny of the brave lion:

> An gcualabhair sceólta leóghain an deagh-chroidhe
> …
> A shláinte dh'ól ba chóir a thaithighe

---

prince's army, lauded the prince's arrival in his eulogy 'Oran do'n Phrionnsa'; Alasdair Mac Mhaighstir Alasdair, 'Oran do'n Phrionnsa', in Campbell (eag.), *Songs of the '45*, p. 48. See also Nighean Aonghuis Óig, 'Oran air teachd Phríonnsa Tearlach', in ibid., p. 22; Iain Rua Stiubhart, 'Urnuigh Iain Ruaidh', ibid., p. 185. English verse also rejoiced at the arrival of the prince; 'Jacobite Songs'; U.L., Cambs., Ddd .25, 61, pp 15, 20, 22, 48, 54, 61; *A full collection of poems upon Charles, prince of Wales*, pp 11, 18.   **37** Aindrias Mac Craith, 'A dhálta nár dalladh le dlaoithe'; Ó Foghludha (eag.), *Éigse na Máighe*, pp 204-5. Jacobite sedition was not exclusively the confine of Irish poets. The papers of the Protestant Jacobite fifth earl of Orrery contain poems of a seditious nature relating to Charles Edward's exploits in Scotland; 'Satire on [the Whig general] Hawley'; 'The ode on the victory at Gladsmuir [Preston Pans]' and 'The verses spoken aloud by a young lady in her sleep'; 'Orrery papers; letters, essays poems and others performances' (Harvard, Ms Eng., 218.2, fols 304, 349, N.L.I., mf. p. 786).

Is fá n-a dheóin och! ólam cainnín
Rinnce nódh mhúin tré shneachtaíbh
Ó Albain mhóir go teóra Charlisle
Wade is Cope cé mór do meastaoi.
Le síol na leógan gcródha smachtuigheadh.[38]

Despite the manoeuvres of Viscount Clare, and the heroic attempts of Lally to get across to England or Ireland, Jacobite hopes proved unfounded. Instead the poets were left to ponder a missed opportunity.[39] Liam Dall Ó hIfearnáin laid the blame squarely at the feet of the Frenchman (Louis XV) who had betrayed Prince Charles: 'Ó d'imir an Francach cam ar Charolus'.[40] Eoghan an Mhéirín Mac Cárthaigh blamed the Scots. He lamented that it was not a duke or his retinue, who all stayed loyal and did not collapse in the heat of battle but the treachery of his own people who sold Caesar (Charles Edward) to them:

Ní diúic ná a bhuidhean do chlaoidh go léir
Mo dhíograis cléibh nár staon i ngléo
Acht trú bocht fill dá mhuinntir féin
Do dhíol go claon mo Chaesar leó.[41]

Seán Clárach knew of the tribulations of the prince in the heather after Culloden. His poem 'Is fada dham in uaigneas' inscribed: 'After the expulsion of the Pretender from Scotland' ('Tar éis an ruaig do chur ar an bPretender as Albain'), described his sojourn in sadness and the trouble in his mind since the hard trick (an allusion to the Irish card game 'twenty-five')[42] had been played on the true king's friends. He mourned that the prince had been insultingly expelled from the

38 Éadhbhárd de Nógla, 'An gcualabhair sceólta leóghain an deagh-chroidhe', in Ó Foghludha (eag.), *Mil na hÉigse*, p. 46.   39 A. N., Archives Anciennes, vol. 3152, fols 42, 65, 73, 100, 148-9, 150-1, 199, 223, 276, N.L.I., mf. p. 151; A. N., Archives Anciennes, vol. 3154 no. 39, N.L.I., mf. P. 153.   40 Liam Dall Ó hIfearnáin, 'Is atuirseach fann i dteannta ar caitheamh mé', in Ó Foghludha, (eag.), *Ar bhruach na Coille Muaire*, p. 52. The popular anthem 'Óró sé do bheatha abhaile' addressed Young Charles, son of James and expressed great sorrow at his coming to Ireland, without a thread of a sock but undone by the French 'A Shéarlais óig, a mhic rí Shéamais/'sé mo mhór chreach do thriall ar Éirinn/gan aon ruainne ort stocaí no léine/ach do choscairt leis na Franncaigh'; Anon., 'Óró sé do bheatha abhaile' in Ó Muirgheasa (eag.), *Céad de cheoltaibh Uladh*, p. 151. See also Ó Buachalla, 'Irish Jacobite poetry', p. 49. The Irish exiles held similar opinions of French treachery; R.A., Ms 276, fol. 27. Charles Wogan spoke of the 'ill will which blew from the French; R.A., Ms 276, fol. 110. Also see Fagan (ed.), *Stuart papers*, ii, p. 43.   41 Ó Foghludha (eag.), *Eoghan an Mheirín*, p. 43. Another poet censored those 'who sold him before the play', Ó Muirithe, 'Tho' not in full stile compleat', p. 96. Their Scottish counterpart Alasdair Mac Mhaighstir Alasdair censured the English. He lamented that the English had betrayed and foresook him ''S mur deanadh fir Shagsuinn do mhealladh 's do thréigsinn'; Alasdair Mac Mhaighstir Alasdair, 'Tearlach Mac Sheamuis', in Campbell (eag.), *Songs of the '45*, p. 54. The Scottish Gaels had been vanquished at Culloden, but like their Gaelic brethren in Ireland after Aughrim, they still looked to their exiled monarch for deliverance; Campbell (eag.), *Songs of the '45*, pp 97-105, 188; Cambeul and Collinson (eag.), *Seann Orain Innse Gall*, iii, p. 133.   42 There are numerous other references to 'twenty-five' (p. 171, fn.

crown to travel around the coasts where the poet does not know his whereabouts or whether he is still alive:

> [Tar éis an ruaig do chur ar an bPretender as Albain.]
> Is fada dham in uaigneas 's is buartha bhíos m'intinn
> ...
> Ó himreadh beart an chruaidh-chlis ar chullacht an Ríogh chirt
> 'S an prionnsa gur díbreadh le díomas ón gcoróinn;
> A thaisteal súd tar cuantaibh ná a thuairisc ní fríoth dam
> An fios fá'n domhan cá ngabhann sé nó an dóigh go maireann beo.[43]

Another of Seán Clárach poems, 'Is fada mé dubhach', captured the mood of Irish Gaeldom in the aftermath of Culloden. They were momentarily despondent but ultimately optimistic of deliverance from Philip V and Louis XV at the head of the brigades, and others would help Charles Stuart to gain the victory and the proper submission of Britain to him. This would enable Lord Clare to return to his own inheritance shortly:

> Pilib is Laoiseach cinn na sluagh
> Is tuille ná ríomhthar linn do luadh
> 'S do Charolus Stíobhart guidhfad buadh
> Is umhalfa Breatain dóibh
> ...
> Do nuig Tiarna an Chláir dá rádh leis casadh
> 'N-a dhútha ar ais go fóill.[44]

These allusions to Lord Clare are significant. He commanded the Irish Brigade at Fontenoy, later received the coveted maréchal of France's baton, and remained a Jacobite until his death in 1762.[45]

252; p. 261, fn. 92). **43** Seán Clárach Mac Domhnaill, 'Is fada dham in uaigneas', in Ó Foghludha (eag.), *Seán Clárach*, p.103. See also Seán Clárach Mac Domhnaill, 'Sin choidhche clár Luairc támhach gan treóir', in Ó Foghludha (eag.), *Seán Clárach*, p. 90. The cameo of hunted prince had already entered the Whig literary tradition; *An ode to be performed at the castle of Dublin on 30 October*, p. 5. **44** Seán Clárach Mac Domhnaill, 'Is fada mé dubhach', in Ó Foghludha (eag.), *Seán Clárach*, p. 113. **45** Maréchal Saxe had requested that Lord Clare be sent as part of the expedition against England in 1744; Beresford, 'Ireland', p. 165. See also Mac Donnell, 'Documents relating to the involvement of the Irish Brigades in the rebellion of 1745', pp 3-22; Crofton-Croker, *Researches*, p. 201. Contemporary Irish poetry contains many other references to Lord Clare's return; Ó Buachalla, *Aisling Ghéar*, pp 416, 591. See also Seán Clárach Mac Domhnaill, 'Bímse buan ar buairt gach ló, in Ó Foghludha (eag.), *Seán Clárach*, p. 113. For another poem on Charles's banishment from Scotland; Piaras Mac Gearailt, 'An tAodhaire Óg', in idem (eag.), *Amhráin Phiarais*, p. 93. Ó Foghludha later attributed this song to Liam Inglis; idem, (eag.), *Cois na Bríde*, p. 24. Liam Inglis promised that with liveliness the bright earl of Clare will come 'Le confadh triallfaidh Iarla an Chláir ghil', in Inglis; 'A Éadbháird Aoibhinn Uasail Áluinn' in idem (eag.), *Cois na Bríde*, p. 42. While Charles Edward made his way into Scotland, Éadbhard de Nógla expressed the hope

A similar optimism pervaded Liam Inglis's 'Ar maidin ag caoidh dham' where he met the faithful messenger of the white hawk (Charles Edward). She informs him that the leader would come with one thousand ships to banish the foreigners, while the brave hounds of Louis XV (the Irish Brigade) would relieve the Gaels. Retribution would quickly follow. The black-haired fanatics and the mean-hearted, disagreeable wretch (George II) would be cast on the dungheap:

> ...
>
> [Is mé] teachtaire díleas an tSeabhaic Bháin
>
> ...
>
> "Is dearbh a chaoin-fhir, 's a ghreann dáimh
> Go dtaistealfa an taoiseach go teann tráth
> Le seascadh ar míle
> de bharcaibh go buidheanmhar
> Chum Danair do dhíbirt don tseann-áit
>
> ...
>
> In 'fhochair do chífear go lonn-lán
> Gasra Gaoidhlach an antláis
> Calm-choin Laoisigh
> Is fearra sa choimheascar
> Is aicme le fíor-ghail on nglonn-Spáinn.
> Níl Fanatic cíor-dhubh is gann-cháil
> Cé ceannasach suidheann sin ag ceann cláir
> Ná smalaire an chroidhe bhoicht
> Is ceachardha i gcuibhreann
> Ná caithfeam 'san aoileach, dá bpleangcáil.[46]

In the song 'An tAodhaire óg' (composed to the tune of the 'Princess Royal') following Charles Edward's expulsion from Scotland in 1746, Inglis lamented the distressed condition of Ireland, the sweet wife of Art who was in captivity, imprisoned and crying out every day. While her heroes were weak and her clergy

---

that Lord Clare and the friend of the brave lion from the banks of the lovely Lee (Clancarthy) will come to his aid 'Tá dalta Bhriain Boirmhe ó bhord an Phairtín/Is cara na leógan gcródha ón nglan-Laoi so ó Mhadraoid'; in idem, 'Is cráidhte an scéal so léightear dúinn' (It is terrible this story which is read to us), in *Míl na hÉigse*, p. 48; During the Seven Years' War, Éadbard de Nógla promised that there is a threat from afar from the bright earl of Clare and it is proper to drink his health 'Tá bagairt le cian ar Thighearna an Chláir ghil.../'S is cuibhe trí dhíogras a shláinte d'ól'; in 'Éadbhard de Nógla, 'Is fada fé chiach mé gan riar ar dhántaibh', in idem (eag.), *Míl na hÉigse*, p. 51. See also Murphy, *Killaloe*, p. 209. According to the local Clare M.P. Francis Burton, part-owner of some of Clare's huge confiscated estate, who had met the expatriate lord in France. Lord Clare retained interest in the affairs of his vast Irish estate until the end of his martial career; Willes's Letters relating to Ireland *c.*1759 (B.L., Add. Ms 29, 352, fol. 47). These have been edited; Kelly (ed.), *Letters of Lord Chief Baron Willes 1757-1762*. Lord Clare's compatriot Robert MacCarthy, fifth earl of Clancarthy also remained preoccupied with his confiscated estate; Mac Allester, *A series of letters*, i, pp 124-5, 127-8, 132. **46** Liam Inglis, 'Ar maidin ag caoidh dham', in Ó Foghludha (eag.), *Cois na Bríde*, pp 22-3. See also ibid., pp 24-5.

without justice, the muse had foresaken her weeping poets. Harking back to the traditional function of the poet as the mediator between the king and his kingdom, like his English and Scottish Jacobite contemporaries, Inglis recapitulated the dreary decay which resulted from 'Éire's' (Ireland's) abandonment of the young shepherd (Charles Edward). The salmon had deserted the waterfall, the birds shunned their songs, while the oak (the symbol of the house of Stuart) commanded no respect; its branches were twisted and the mountains were shrouded in mist:

> Is darach an bheart do chéile ghil Airt
> bheith i ndaor-bhroid, i ngéibheann 's ag éigheamh gach ló;
> Is géar-ghuirt a scread ag reabadh a bas
> Is méala i in eagruith 's i néallaibh bróin;
> ...
> A laochra go lag, a cléirigh gan cheart,
> A héigeas gan dréacht, ag maothughadh a ndeór
> 'S na faol-choin gur scaip a tréada ar fad
> Ó b'éigean dó tréigean, – an tAodhaire Óg.
> Níl éigne ar eas, ná gaortha go glas,
> Acht éanlaith go héadmhar ag séanadh a gceóil
> Ar aon dair níl meas acht a ngéaga go cas
> 'S na sléibhthe in éinfeacht fé bhréidhibh ceóidh.[47]

Inglis followed the standard trope of the brazen harlot, a favourite among Irish literati from Séathrún Céitinn to Aogán Ó Rathaille, in his poem 'Póiní an leasa'. The grieving woman (Ireland) formerly wedded to Eoghan and his father was now the young harlot of British George. The poet mourned that the wife of the warlike lion (Charles Edward) has yielded to the advances of this greasy, smug stranger. He pointed out the error of her ways, the decay and depression on her churches and the sorrow and danger which affected her clergy. Her hour of deliverance approached, however, as the young Caesar in Rome (Charles Edward) of the race she had married before, was coming across the sea and that he was the legitimate spouse of Ireland:

> Is baoth mo ghlórtha, is dóigh nár mheathas
> Cé gur phósas Eoghan is a athair
> Is gléigeal snódh
> Mo ghéag ar ndóigh

---

47 Liam Inglis, 'An tAodhaire Óg', in Ó Foghludha (eag.), *Cois na Bríde*, p. 24. Piaras Mac Gearailt, in a note written on a version of this poem from 1766, asks that God might bestow some sense on the half-wit who recited this verse for it was Liam Inglis 'go dtuga Dia ciall don leath-éarla adubhairt an duanóg seo, ó 's é Liam Inglis é'; in ibid., p. 25. See also Cullen, *Hidden Ireland: a reassessment*, p. 10. However, MacGearailt's dismissal of Jacobitism, must be balanced against his earlier enthusiasm for the Jacobite cause (Introduction, p. 47); Above fns. 23, 45; pp 343-5, fns 74-76.

'S me im mhéirdrigh óig ag Seóirse Breatan.
Mo léan, mo bhrón, do ghlórtha mheabhail
A chéile chóir na leógan lannach
A ghné mar rós
Is baoth an gnó
Duit géill ná góbhail le stróinse smeartha.
Féach-sa, a óig-bhean mhódhmhrach mhaiseach
T'fhéinnidh feóidhthe is ceó ar do cheallaibh
An chléir go deórach
Baolgach brónach
Tréig-se Seóirse, is gheóbhair a mhalairt.
Tá Caesar óg sa Róimh 'n-a bheathaidh
Aon den phór úd phosais cheana
Ag gléasadh a shlóighthe
Ag teacht thar bóchna
Is é sin nóchar Phóiní an leasa.[48]

Seán Clárach's 'Bímse buan ar buairt gach ló, dedicated to Jenny Cameron of Glendessary, suggested that rumours of the prince's 'amour' had reached the ears of the poet. This is one of a series of Irish songs which pays tribute to the lesser known Scottish-Jacobite heroine. The poet promised that he would not reveal who was his love as it would soon become apparent. He would pray to the all-powerful son of God that his hero would return safe from all danger:

Ní mhaoidhfadh féin cé hé mo stór,
Tá innsint scéil 'n-a dheidh go leór;
Acht guidhim chum Aenmhic Dé na gcómhacht
go dtíghé mo laoch gan bhaoghal beó.[49]

Like many other Jacobite songs, it is composed to the tune of 'The White Cockade'.[50] Although the Irish poets continued to plead for the return of the

---

48 Liam Inglis, 'Póiní an leasa', in ibid., p. 25. The 'slut' also features in the Scottish Jacobite tradition; 'Jamie come kiss me now', in Hogg (ed.), *Jacobite Relics*, i, p. 144. **49** Seán Clárach Mac Domhnaill, 'Bímse buan ar buairt gach ló', in Ó Foghludha (eag.), *Seán Clárach*, pp 45-7. See also O'Daly (eag.), *Reliques of Irish Jacobite poetry*, p. 26. An tAthair Ó Briain composed a poem to the tune of Jenny Cameron, 'A chara is a bhráthair, fáilte óm chroí romhat', *Cat. of Ir. mss. in R.I.A.*, fasc. 16-20, p. 2071. According to de Blácam, words in one of Seán Clárach's songs purportedly came from the mouth of Flora McDonnell; de Blácam, *Gaelic literature surveyed*, p. 316. Diarmuid Ó Muirithe has edited English versions of Seán Clárach's songs, 'Tho' not in full stile compleat', pp 100-1. References to this alleged liaison between Charles Edward and Jenny Cameron occurred in other sources. The Scottish Episcopalian bishop Forbes recorded a slanderous verse on Jenny, Prince Charles's 'hussy'; Forbes (ed.), *Lyon in Mourning*, ii, p. 2. The Jacobite double-agent Oliver McAllester remarked on the widespread circulation of this 'ridiculous', 'false', and 'ill-founded' report of the liaison between Jenny Cameron and Charles Edward; McAllester, *A series of letters*, i, p. 32. Also see MacClean, *Bonnie Prince Charlie*, pp 49, 134. **50** O'Daly provides a background note on the 'White

prince, a new sense of urgency emerged in some of the verse after Culloden, as exemplified in the anonymous 'Súil cabhrach Éireann'. The anonymous poet lamented that they did not hear the host coming ashore nor the roar of the big guns in Howth and warned Charles Edward that if he did not come soon their enemies would be victorious and their sway too great in Ireland:

> Mar nach cluinim an uaill, ag tarraingt chum cuain
> Ná lámhach gunnaídhe-mór a mBínn Eadair;-
> Muna d-tagad síbh go luath, beidh ár namhuid-ne go buan,
> a ngradam ró mhór a n-Éirinn.[51]

Such desperation can be easily exaggerated, however, as the Munster literati continued to pin their hopes on Charles until at least the end of the 1750s.

Their Ulster colleagues were no less infatuated with the Stuarts. This runs contrary to the long-standing misconception that has surrounded late-seventeenth-century and eighteenth-century Ulster poetry which deems it to be unresponsive to the cult of the Stuarts. The Stuart cause remained a live issue all over Ireland during the first half of the eighteenth-century and no poet could afford to ignore it.[52] Séamas Dall MacCuarta keened both Somhairle Mac Domhnaill and the former Jacobite soldier Murcha Crúis in the late-seventeenth and early-eighteenth century. He also extolled the rapparees and Christopher Fleming, the exiled seventeenth baron of Slane.[53] Raghnall Dall Mac Domhnaill

Cockade' in the Irish literary tradition; O'Daly (eag.), *Poets and poetry*, p. 51; Seán Ó Tuama, 'An Cnóta Bán' (The White Cockade), in Flower *Cat. Ir. mss in B.L.*, ii, p. 186. Wauchope claims that the wearing of the White Cockade originated at the Boyne when Irish Jacobites put folded white paper in their hats to distinguish them from their Williamite adversaries who wore sprigs of oak, see Wauchope, *Sarsfield*, p. 112. **51** Anon, 'Súil cabhrach Éireann', in Hardiman (eag.), *Irish minstrelsy*, ii, p. 36. This theme dominated the poetry of contemporary Scotland. Alasdair Mac Mhaighisdir Alasdair warned Charles Edward that if he did not soon come and assist them with force, stores, weapons and swords, they would be ruined by the oppressive power of George 'Mur tig thu gu tràth 's gum fòirinn thú oirnn/Le neart, le stòras is le claidhean/Fannaichidh sinne le fòirneart cruaidh Dhéors'; Campbell (eag.), *Songs of the '45*, p. 124. Scots-Gaelic defiance is best exemplified by John McCodrum who promised that when the Gaels assembled for battle, armed with sharp Spanish lances and helmets that they (the Whigs) would dearly pay in blood and goods and not a groat would be left unpaid for Culloden 'Nuair chruinnicheas na Gàidheal, An làthair troda/Le 'n geur lannan Spàinneach/ 'S an dèarrsadh chlogad/Pàighidh iad gu daor/Ann am fuil 's an gaorr,/'S cha bhi bonn gun dìoladh, /De bhlàr Chúil-lodair'; Matheson (eag.), *Songs of John Mac Codrum*, p. 10. **52** Ó Fiaich, 'Filíocht Chúige Uladh', pp 81-2. Ó Buachalla makes a similar point: 'Is léir nach bhfuil an t-ionad ceannasach céanna ag an Stíobhartach i saothar fhilí aitheantúla Oirialla (Mac Cuarta, Mac a Liondáin, Ó Doirnín, Mac Cumhaigh) is atá i bhfilíocht na Mumhan ach fós is ó chúige Uladh a thagann cuid de na dánta Seacaibíteacha is suimiúla agus is neamhghnáthaí dá bhfuil ar marthain'; Ó Buachalla, *Aisling Ghéar*, p. 599. **53** Séamas Dall Mac Cuarta, 'Tuireamh Shomhairle Mhic Dhomhnaill', in Ó Gallchóir (eag.), *Séamas Dall*, p, 63. See also Séamas Dall Mac Cuarta, 'Tuireamh Mhurcha Crúis', in ibid., p. 32; Séamas Dall Mac Cuarta agus Aodh Mac Oireachtaigh,'S' is léir liom uaim' (B.L., Add. Ms 18, 749, fol. 133); Séamas Dall Mac Cuarta' Barún Shláine', in Ó Gallchóir (eag.), *Séamas Dall*, pp 70, 91-3. For the unease caused in Protestant Ireland by the reversal of

traced the impeccable genealogy of James III, and hoped that he would soon come to the rescue of the Gaels. His colleague Pádraig Mac a Liondain trusted James III, the French and the Ulster exile Brían Ó Ceallaigh.[54] In spite of these examples, Ulster poetry lacks the fervent enthusiasm for the Stuart cause evident in the poetry of Munster. Yet, on reflection, the paucity of evidence for a poetic cult of the Stuarts in Ulster is easily explained. Poets were far fewer on the ground in Ulster than in Munster. Just as Culloden can be viewed as the Aughrim of Scotland, so the battle of Scarriffhollis (1650) could be considered the Aughrim of Ulster. The outcome of this battle, compounded by the failure to reverse successive plantation settlements at the restoration of Charles II in 1660, decimated the Ulster Catholic aristocracy and gentry. Lacking their traditional patrons, the numbers of professional poets in Ulster dwindled and only Oirialla (modern south Armagh, south Monaghan, north Louth and north Meath) maintained a flourishing manuscript tradition. Moreover, there were less colonel-proprietors and senior officers in the Irish Brigades in the French and Spanish armies from this area; recruiting networks would therefore have been less sophisticated and effective, and soldiers would have been more difficult to recruit and transport.

Of all eighteenth-century Irish poets, Séamas na Sróine Fada and Peadar Ó Doirnín[55] exhibited the least concern (bordering at times on indifference and

---

Christopher Fleming, seventeenth baron Slane's outlawry (Williams (ed.), *Correspondence*, i, p. 130).
54 See p. 160, fn. 193. Mac a Liondain describes this youth (Ó Ceallaigh) as being manly, fleet and talented, jumping on a steed accompanying King James III in victory. He warned that all persons who do not yield that, the well seasoned mountain-boys would torture them soon and Brian would be coming lively and brisk with the French to strengthen the weak demoralised hordes and kill hundreds. 'Is fearúil tapaidh tréitheach an mac seo ar each ag léimneach,/ar gcasadh isteach don réacs, an treas Séamas le bua;/gach neach nach nglacann géilleadh, beidh dalta dleacht an tsléibhe/le cleasa brasa na mbéimeanna/á gcréachtadh go luath.../beidh Brían go tapaidh meanmnach/go dian ag teacht na bhFranncach/ ag riar an iomad fann lag/is ag marú na gcéadt'; Mac Uidhir (eag), *Pádraig Mac a Liondaín*, pp 9-10. Mag Uidhir also allows for the possibility that this poem may refer to a local poet and Jacobite supporter of that name, in which case the poem was a subtle satire on the Jacobite cause; quoted in Hughes, 'Gaelic poets and scribes' (forthcoming). I would like to thank Dr Hughes for making this unpublished paper available to me. Ó Buachalla suggests 1719 as a possible date for this poem; Ó Buachalla, *Aisling Ghéar*, p. 321. See also Ó Fiaich, 'Filíocht Chúige Uladh', pp 80-129.
55 Ó Doirnín's poetry must be treated with caution because of the tendency of Nioclás Ó Cearnaigh (Nicholas O'Kearney) and Matthew Moore Graham to attribute their own work to Ó Doirnín; Ó Buachalla (ed.), *Peadar Ó Doirnín*, pp 27, 29; De Rís, *Peadar Ó Doirnín*, p. xi. Neither Ó Buachalla or de Rís included any of these dubious compositions in their editions of the poet's poems and songs. In this study, no poem is used which is considered to be editorially contaminated. De Rís included one poem in his collection called 'Agallamh le héinín' which related to Charles Edward and the 'Forty-five' (de Rís, p. 10). In the notes to the poems at the end of the volume, he cast doubt over the authorship of some of the verses. I have not include it in my examination of his work. My caution has been recently justified by Ó Buachalla. He states at the outset that Ó Cearnaigh attributed the poem to Ó Doirnín. Nevertheless he (Ó Buachalla) used it to back up his claim that the poet may have harboured Jacobite sympathies; Ó Buachalla, *Aisling Ghéar*, p. 602. Art Hughes has recently shed further light on the activities of Graham and Ó Cearnaigh although neither he or any other serious scholar has questioned the editorial practices of de Rís and Ó Buachalla.

hostility) towards the house of Stuart.[56] Indeed many of Ó Doirnín's poems are peppered with anti-Stuart sentiment. In one poem 'Agallamh le cnoc na Teamhrach' Ó Doirnín lamented that it was James II who left him in great sorrow ('sé an dara Séamas do chloígh mo chéadfaí is d'fhág mé faoi bhrón'). He also bemoaned the fact that many good men of true Gaelic lineage suffered heart-ache at the Boyne ('Dob iomaí tréanfhear den fhíorfhuil Ghaelach fuair crá croí ag Bóinn').[57] In his exasperated rant 'Is fada ag éisteacht mé', he noted that because of the name James, many Irish went into desperate battle and were overthrown ('Den ainm chéanna [Séamas] fá ndeachaigh Gaela i gcathaibh géara mo bhrón dá gcloí').[58] Elsewhere he reiterated the words of the impoverished Jacobite soldier who lamented that last year he was uniformed and armed but this year he was begging for alms ('Do bhí mé anuraidh in airm is in éide/ach taím i mbliana ag iarraidh déirce').[59] Finally, in his satire on Fr Quinn of Creggan, County Armagh ('An Cléireach Bán'), Ó Doirnín listed the five woes which befell Ireland; the Vikings, the Anglo-Normans, Henry VIII, Elizabeth I, Cromwell and James II.[60]

Ó Doirnín's 'Tá Bearád i Londain' (There's a hat in London) has been constantly quoted as indicative of the poet's anti-Jacobitism. A casual perusal of the song affords little scope for contradiction. He mocked the hat (crown) in London and lamented that many strong men have died trying to win it. He joked that Sir Wully (the duke of Cumberland) thinks it belongs to his dad (George II) and the bonnet-wearers (the Jacobites) consider that it is the property of Charlie (Charles Edward). Continuing in this light satirical vein, the poet depicted the Englishmen vowing that they will never part with the hat as it is theirs by right while the plaid-wearers (the Jacobites) say they will sever bones and not stop their racket until it is placed on Charlie:

> Tá bearád i Londain 's is iomaí fear láidir
> a cailleadh ina thimpeall fán tulaigh a tharrtháil,
> measann Sir Wully gur cuibhe dá dháid é
> is creideann lucht boinéad gur cumadh do Chathal é,
> is iombó!
>
> Creideann fir Shacsan nach scaraid go bráth
> le seilbh an chaipín ós acu ba gnáth é,

---

56 Séamas na Sróine Fada, 'A Rígh Seóirse, mo dhianstór fein tú', *Cat. of Ir. mss. in R.I.A.*, fasc. 1-5, p. 308. See also 'Aig seo an t-excommunication do fúar Séamas no srón tré a mhíodhumhluigheacht don eaglais', ibid. An anti-Jacobite song in an Irish manuscript in the R.I.A. urged the claims of the Hanoverian George; *Cat. of Ir. mss. in the R.I.A*, iii, p. 413, no. 9. **57** Peadar Ó Doirnín, 'Agallamh le Cnoc na Teamhrach', in de Rís (eag.), *Ó Doirnín*, p. 7. **58** Peadar Ó Doirnín, 'Is fada ag éisteacht mé', in de Rís (eag.), *Ó Doirnín*, p. 8. **59** Peadar Ó Doirnín, 'Is fada ag éisteacht mé', in de Rís (eag.), *Ó Doirnín*, pp xxiii; Peadar Ó Doirnín, 'Tairngire dheárscnaí', in ibid., p. 40; Ó Muirgheasa (eag.), *Céad de cheoltaibh Uladh*, p. 6., 8 **60** Peadar Ó Doirnín, 'An Cléireach Bán', in Ó Buachalla (eag), *Ó Doirnín*, p. 44.

ach deirid lucht breacán go ngearrfaidh siad cnámha
is nach scoirid dá racán go gcuirid ar Chathal é,
is iombó![61]

Ó Doirnín's apparently jaundiced view displays something more than a
'scigaithris': he provided vivid detail of the prince's military exploits, his defeat
of Johnny Cope and his retreat at Manchester. The word 'espaidh' (scarcity) is
particularly significant as Charles Edward was unable to feed his starving
highlanders on the night before Culloden. Ó Doirnín pinpointed the inability
of Maréchal Saxe's invasion force to get out of Calais as crucial for the failure of
the 'Forty-five'.[62] In relation to the campaign itself, he noted that the plaid stood
bravely against the hosts between Lochaber, Berwick and Falkirk where Cope
and his party got a beating but on the border of Manchester, scarcity took its toll
on Charlie. He surmised that had Saxe (who was at the head of his friends in the
provinces far away) and his lads came, Ireland and Britain would be with the
youth and the hat would be speedily put on Charlie's head. Saxe's failure allowed
Sir Wully to gather his comrades from everywhere and he had three against one
on the field of battle. Although the bonnet stooped to change the tartan, Charlie
would not have been defeated there only for Lord George Murray; the Jacobite
commander:

> Is cróga do sheasaigh an breacán an báire
> ar na slóite ó Loch Abair go Barraic is go Falkirk,
> mar bhfuair Cope a thasáil is a raibh ina phártaí,
> ach ar theorainn Mhanchester bhain easpaidh de Chathal é,
> is iombó!

> Ach munab é Saxe a bhí i gceannas a chairde
> sna cóigibh bhí i bhfad uaidh, is a ghasra nach dtáinig,
> bheadh Fódla agus Breatain gan stad ag an bpáiste
> is chóireofaí a cháipín go tapaidh ar Chathal ann,
> is iombó!

> Chnuasaigh Sir Wully a bhunaidh as gach áit ann,
> bhí triúr in aghaidh an duine aige ar thulaigh na spairne,

---

61 Peadar Ó Doirnín, 'Tá Bearád i Londain', in de Rís (eag.), *Ó Doirnín*, p. 13. See also Ó Fiaich, 'Filíocht Chúige Uladh', pp 80-129. Éamonn Ó Tuathail and Nioclás Ó Cearnaigh noted the popularity of this song in the late nineteenth century; Ó Tuathail (eag.), *Trí rainn agus amhrán*, no. xviii, Ó Buachalla, *Aisling Ghéar*, p. 603. **62** Ó Buachalla also takes this view, suggesting that Mac Cumhaigh and Ó Doirnín had in-depth knowledge of, and great interest in, Charles Edward's activities; Ó Buachalla, *Aisling Ghéar*, p. 601. Cullen effectively dismissed this poem as 'a send up of the aisling'; Cullen, *The Hidden Ireland: a reassessment*, p. 10.

d'umhlaigh an boinéad an breacán a dh'áthrach
is murab é Mac Uí Mhuirí, ní bhrisfí ar Chathal ann,
is iombó![63]

Ó Doirnín's colleague Art Mac Cumhaigh also emphasised the significance of the U-turn at Manchester: from that day at Manchester he would have to flee as Charles and his people were left behind on the mountains without shelter ('Ón lá sin Manchester 'sé mheasaim go mbéad ar siúl, D'fhág Cathal is a bhunadh gan urraim fá na sléibhtibh cuíl').[64] In the last verse, Ó Doirnín lamented that Charles and Cumberland did not meet on a lonely plain armed with two good clubs; he would back Charles, beating Cumberland in the pit of his belly:

Mo léan nachar chas siad ar machaire fásaigh
le chéile, is gan neach acu a bhéarfadh dóibh tarrtháil,
is péire maith bataí, is fearr aige Cathal díobh,
is é ag réabfadh easnacha shacáin-a-mhála!
Is iombo![65]

The use Ó Doirnín's poetry, therefore, to demonstrate the absence of Jacobite sentiment in the Ulster literary tradition is far from persuasive. Love is its dominant theme (with a passing interest in anti-clericalism and Caiptín Fuiscí' i.e. whiskey).[66] The Jacobite element may also have been underplayed because of its compromising implications for his patron Sir Arthur Brownlow (the younger). Brownlow's father patronised Irish-language manuscript production and the apostasy of his mother led to accusations of his being a crypto-papist and a closet Jacobite.[67] These accusations might well explain why Ó Doirnín steered clear of overt support of the Stuart cause, and engaged instead in the type of political flippancy which pervaded 'The Independent Man', the only English poem with which he is credited.[68] Ó Doirnín and the rapparee Séamas Mac Mhurchaidh were allegedly involved in assembling a group on Sliabh gCuillinn (Slieve

---

63 Peadar Ó Doirnín, 'Tá Bearád i Londain', in de Rís (eag.), *Ó Doirnín,* p. 13. This censure of Murray is particularly striking as it is also evident in the poetry of his Scottish contemporary John Roy Stewart of Badenoch; Campbell (eag.), *Songs of the '45,* pp 173, 181. This dissatisfaction with Lord George reflected contemporary reality. Friction between Murray and the Irishmen of Moidart is well documented; MacClean, *Bonnie Prince Charlie,* p. 201. McLynn believed that Murray made 'disastrous blunders'; McLynn, *Bonnie Prince Charlie,* pp 183, 215. The Anglo-Scottish literary tradition surmised that 'he [Charles Edward] boldly did fight, but was falsely advised'; Crawford, 'Political and protest songs', p. 19. Two Irish historians have made robust defences of John O'Sullivan's sullied reputation; McCarthy, 'The Young Pretender's head-piece', pp 113-20; Eager, 'Colonel John O'Sullivan', pp 623-8. **64** Art Mac Cumhaigh, 'Agallamh le Caisleán na Glasdromainne', in Ó Fiaich (eag.), *Art Mac Cumhaigh,* p. 83. **65** Peadar Ó Doirnín,' Tá Bearád i Londain', in de Rís (eag.), *Ó Doirnín,* p. 14. **66** Ó Buachalla (eag.), *Ó Doirnín: Amhráin,* p. 36. **67** *Seasonable advice to the free-holders of Armagh,* pp 14-15; Ó Buachalla, 'Arthur Brownlow: a gentleman more curious than ordinary', pp 24-8. **68** Peadar Ó Doirnín, 'The Independent Man', in Ó Buachalla (eag.), *Ó Doirnín: Amhráin,* p. 12.

Gullion) in support of Bonnie Prince Charlie.[69] If so, his caution or disillusionment in the immediate aftermath of the Battle of Culloden is easy to understand.

Some Jacobite sympathies also appear in his other poems such as 'Suirí Mhuiris Uí Ghormáin', where Ó Doirnín alludes to King James's crown as opposed to King George's.[70] Despite his exasperation with stories from James II's war and the subsequent sufferings of the Gaels, he equated their restoration with the availability of freehold land to every prince of noble stock:

> Is fada ag éisteacht mé leis na scéal-sa
> ó chogadh Shéamais, an dóú rí
> den ainm chéanna, fá ndeachaigh Gaela
> i gcathaibh géara, mo bhrón, dá chloí
> go dtiocfadh éifeacht is fearann saor
> ag gach flaith ó fhréimh mar ba chóir sa chrích.[71]

This preoccupation with freehold land occurs elsewhere in the Irish literary tradition. One of his contemporaries. Aindrias Mac Craith, also hoped that the tyrants would be cleaned out as the boors did in Ireland and 'our' towns delivered from high rents ('do ghlanfadh as Éirinn mar a dhainfir na méirleach,/is ár mbailte do shaoradh ó ard-chíos').[72] Art Mac Cumhaigh surmised that if he obtained a lease and land he would be happily and merrily composing verse and would not have to leave the country ('Mar bhfuighinnse léagsa ar fhearann saor ann,/Ag cumadh vearsaí go ceolmhar caoin,/'S nárbh fhiú damh éalú i dtír ó chéile').[73] In a song composed to the tune 'An Chraoibhín Aoibhinn', Muiris Ó Gríobhtha looked forward to the alleviation of rents, oppressive payments and taxes ('gan cíos, íoc daoirse, cáin ná tóir!').[74] His Scottish contemporary Aonghas Mac Dhomhnuill in Scotland promised his audience that they would get plenty more land than their inheritance without tribute, tax or rents ('Gheibh sibh pailleas gach dùthcha, Cha n-è ur dùthchas as nì leibh, Agus ragha gach fearain Gun gearradh gun chìs air').[75]

---

69 de Rís (eag.), *Ó Doirnín*, pp xxiii-xxiv; Murray, 'A Creggan Outlaw', pp 96, 100; Ó Buachalla, *Aisling Ghéar*, p. 603. Ó Doirnín and Mac Mhurchaidh's endeavours might not be so implausible given that an emissary named Patrick Wall arrived in Scotland from Ireland with a message of support for Charles Edward; Beresford, 'Ireland', app. iv, A and C; see also Connolly, *Religion*, p. 246. Fr James Doyle said that he had been sent all around the province of Leinster by a priest to sound out the dispositions of the Catholic clergy; Fagan (ed.), *Stuart papers*, ii, pp 177-8. **70** Peadar Ó Doirnín 'Suirí Mhuiris Uí Ghormáin', in de Rís (eag.), *Ó Doirnín*, pp 28-9. **71** Peadar Ó Doirnín,' Is fada ag éisteacht mé', in de Rís (eag.), *Ó Doirnín*, p. 8. The Jacobite dimension with which the Houghers have been credited may not be altogether unfounded. Furthermore, the call for cheap land and lower taxes were central to the Whiteboy campaigns. **72** Aindrias Mac Craith, 'Séan Buidhe', in Hardiman (eag.), *Irish minstrelsy*, ii, pp 50-1. See also Cullen, *The Hidden Ireland: a reassessment*, pp 9-28-9'. **73** Art Mac Cumhaigh, 'Aisling Airt Mhic Chumhaigh', in Ó Fiaich (eag.), *Mac Cumhaigh*, p. 112. **74** 'Muiris Ó Gríobhtha', in Walsh (eag.), *Reliques*, p. 93. **75** Aonghas Mac Dhomhnuill, 'Oran brosnachaidh do na Gaidheil', in Campbell (eag.), *Songs of the '45*, p. 14. See also ibid., introd., xxiii.

In the last verse of the poem 'Is fada mé ag éisteacht', Ó Doirnín's submerged Jacobite sympathies surface. He alluded to the possible rehabilitation of the Catholic church in the event of a Stuart restoration. He claimed that if the story should be as he says, then his appearance would be attractive and he'd be young again and he would spend time listening to holy psalms in every church in Ireland and praising the king (presumably James III):

> Dá mbíodh na scéala mar a deir mo bhéal-sa
> ba dheas mo ghléas is bheinn óg arís,
> bheinn seal ag éisteacht le sailm naofa
> i ngach ceall in Éirinn ag mór-mholadh an rí.[76]

In Ulster poetry, historical developments meant that religious issues were relatively more important. The decimation and social dissolution of the Ulster aristocracy and gentry after 1607, 1609 and 1641 and the concentration of non-Catholics in the province had obvious implications for the poets's dependence on clerical rather than landed patronage. While quick to satirise the parsimony of particular clerics, the Ulster literati enjoyed the support of the Catholic clergy.[77] Ó Doirnín, not noted either for his piety or his Jacobitism, equated a Stuart restoration with a new era of religious tolerance in his poem 'Is fada ag éisteacht mé'.[78] Religious themes also figured in the poetry of his Munster contemporaries, including Diarmuid Ó Súilleabháin,[79] Liam Inglis,[80] and Seán Clárach.[81]

---

76 Peadar Ó Doirnín, 'Is fada ag éisteacht mé', in de Rís (eag.), *Ó Doirnín*, p. 9.   **77** Ó Doirnín, 'An Dá Sheáin', in Ó Buachalla (eag.), *Ó Doirnín: Amhráin*, p. 33; Art Mac Cumháigh, 'Máire Chaoch', in Ó Fiaich (eag.), *Art Mac Cumhaigh*, p. 110; Peadar Ó Doirnín, 'An Cléireach Bán', in Ó Buachalla (eag.), *Ó Doirnín: Amhráin*, p. 44.   **78** Ó Doirnín, 'Is fada ag éisteacht mé', in de Rís (eag.), *Ó Doirnín*, p. 8. Luther's family 'Clann Liútair' are the object of his scorn in his poem 'Agallamh le Cnoc na Teamhrach'; ibid., p. 7.   **79** He hopes that the church will forever be sweetly and melodiously singing its psalms and psalters 'Beidh eaglais gan dearmad go binn-ghlórach/A salmaibh a saltraibh go caoin ceólmhar'; Diarmuid Ó Súilleabháin, 'A Alba ó shealbhais an Rí cóir cirt', in Ó Foghludha (eag.), *Cois na Ruachtaighe*, p. 48.   **80** Liam Inglis, 'An sean-duine Seóirse', in O'Daly (eag.), *Poets and poetry*, p. 96. The anonymous author of Óró sé do bheatha abhaile' promised that on Charles's arrival they (Charles Edward and the French) will make the heretics dance 'Agus bainfidh siad [Séarlas agus na Francaigh] rinnc a's éir'cighibh'; 'Óró sé do bheatha abhaile', in Ó Muirgheasa (eag.), *Céad de cheoltaibh Uladh*, p. 151. Mac Cumhaigh's abused 'Clann Liútair', 'New Lights', 'Secéders', 'Old Presbyterians' and 'Quakers' in his poem 'Tagra an Dá Theampall'; Art Mac Cumhaigh 'Tagra an Dá Theampall', in Ó Fiaich (eag.), *Art Mac Cumhaigh*, p. 86. Seán Clárach attacked the followers of Luther and Calvin in the English versions of his verse; Ó Muirithe, 'Tho' not in full stile compleat', p. 99.   **81** The poet promised that all the clergy will have scope and authority, nobody will be able to go against them, rewards will be offered every day for poetry. 'Beidh scóip ag cléir na cruinne is reacht,/'S ní leómhfaidh aon' na gcoinne teacht,/beidh duais gach lae dá luadh don éigis/Acht duanta is dréachta sheinim seal./'; Seán Clárach Mac Domhnaill, 'A Ríoghan uasal shuairc, in Ó Foghludha (eag.), *Seán Clárach*, p. 47. See also his 'Freagra ar an mbean Albanaigh' [The answer to the Scottish woman], composed to the Jacobite tune of 'The White Cockade'. Eoghan Rua surmised that on Charles' return the learned clergy will not need disguise 'beidh cléir na g-ceacht gan púicín', Eoghan Rua O Súilleabháin, 'Filleadh Rígh Searluis', in Walsh (eag.), *Reliques*, p. 64.

II

The optimism of the Irish (and Scots-Gaelic) poets throughout this period was mirrored by that of the Irish exiles on whom they rested their greatest hopes. Count Daniel O'Sullivan of Berehaven contemplated the possibility of Irish *émigré* participation in a Spanish invasion of Ireland in 1740. He complained that he had been overlooked for a promotion in 'his most catholic majesty's army', an oversight 'which would disgust your loyal subjects of that kingdom' (Ireland).[82] Whatever his motives, his correspondence illustrates that some of the Wild Geese did intend to unsheath their swords in their native land, as foretold both by the Irish literati and the Whig press.

Sir Charles Wogan, one of the most active and flamboyant of all Irish Jacobite exiles, typified the optimism evident within their ranks.[83] While he and many of his *émigré* brethren prospered in the French and Spanish service, they retained a definite sense of loyalty to the deposed house of Stuart.[84] Their genuine Jacobitism underpinned a nostalgic preoccupation with their native land. Wogan's martial career bears comparison with Sarsfield's, Clare's, Dillon's or Lally's. He escaped from Newgate after the 'Fifteen', rescued the Princess Clementina from Innsbruck in 1719, and received a string of resulting honours, including a knighthood and membership of the Roman senate. He was eventually appointed governor of La Mancha, a city, in Wogan's own words, 'so celebrated for the life and labours of the famed Don Quixote'.[85] He deemed this an appropriate tribute to the most famous knight in Europe, but an honour that did not in any way eclipse his affection for Ireland. Indeed Wogan claimed that he 'should have a better estate at home than ever his [Don Quixote's] fathers enjoyed, and a tomb too where no man of honour may be ashamed to lie'.[86]

82 Count Daniel O'Sullivan of Berehaven to James III, Coruna, 15 June 1740 (R.A., Ms 223, fol. 143). There are numerous examples of this type of rhetoric in the Stuart papers; R.A., Ms 228, fol. 138; Ms 235, fol. 62; Ms 240, fol. 61; Ms 256, fol. 181. In spite of this, Edgar expressed doubt as to the loyalty of some of the Irish; R.A., Ms 245, fol. 109.   **83** Flood, *Wogan*.   **84** The sentiments in 'An Cruiscín lán', the Irish-Brigade drinking-song typified this *émigré mentalité*: 'We are tearful, gloomy and sad, for a long time travelling in loneliness across the sea, alongside optimistic, brave-hearted men. To stave off sadness and without declining we often taste the full jug, without declining the full jug, We will always drink the little jug, health to my love who is travelling across the sea from us goodbye. 'Is déarach dealbh dubhach sinn,/Tréimhse ag taisteal triúch bím/I gcéin tar lear i gcúigibh fáin;/Taobh le fearaibh úr-chroidheach/Ba mhéinn liom stad le dúil ghrinn/Gan claonadh ag blaiseadh an Chrúiscín lán, lán, lán,/Gan claonadh ag blaiseadh an Chrúiscín lán/Ólfaimid an crúiscín,/Sláinte gheal mo mhuirnín/A bhfuil a thaisteal chughainn tar taoide slán, slán, slán!'; Anon. An Chrúiscín lán', in Ó Foghludha (eag.), *Mil na hÉigse*, p. 59. John O'Daly believed that this was a drinking song of the Irish Brigades; Ní Ógáin (eag.), *Duanaire*, i, p. 110. The Irish language was purportedly in regular use among the Brigades; Cullen, 'The politics of Caoineadh Airt Uí Laoire', p. 18. See below, pp 307-8, fn. 152; p. 261, fns. 90-91.   **85** Wogan to James III, 8 Oct. 1744 (R.A., Ms 260, fol. 118). J. T. Gilbert edited a contemporary memoir; Gilbert (ed.), *Narrative of the detention of Maria, Clementine Stuart*. A film was also made about this rescue in the 1950s; Mullin, 'The ranks of death' (T.C.D., Ms 7180, p. 256).   **86** Wogan to James III, 8 Oct. 1744 (R.A., Ms 206, fol. 118);

Wogan's dreams of further chivalry in this period appeared at this time more realistic than those of Cervantes's deluded nobleman. The Irish Jacobite clergyman James McKenna, reporting from Thivelmont, informed James Edgar, James III's secretary, of the flurry of activity which took place there in late 1744. McKenna expressed great hopes for Maréchal Saxe's invasion of England with two hundred captured transports, an army of 'fifteen thousand horse and foot, besides a regiment of Irish'. His optimism at the possible involvement of the Irish Brigades justified the hostile opinions of Hoadly, Forman and D'Anvers regarding the unholy and temporary Franco-English *détente* and the political loyalties of the Brigades.[87]

McKenna appreciated the pivotal role of the Irish Catholic church in the cultivation and maintenance of the Jacobite ideology. Testimony to that role is provided by the close relationship between the clergy and the Jacobite literati. Reiterating his loyalty to James III, McKenna promised Edgar that he would:

> maintain and uphold his [James III's] undoubted and natural right with his royal honour and dignity amongst his subjects at home as I have hitherto done, and to the utmost of my power shall inspire those abroad as well as others with whom I happen to converse to do the same by retaining them in continual hopes of a happy restoration.[88]

From his self-imposed exile in Bagnères, France, the veteran Jacobite Bishop Sylvester Lloyd joined this expectant chorus, and regretted his inability to accompany Charles Edward to Scotland:

> God Almighty shower down his choicest blessings upon our dear king and his royal issue. God prosper them and crown all their undertakings with success and that I may see and hear it so before I die is my continual prayer. If I had not been so weak as I was I would have followed his royal highness wherever he went tho' it were only to hear from him every day for I scarce have a word of him in this place which breaks my heart.[89]

Flood, *Wogan*, p. 99; Hayes, *Irish swordmen*, p. 299.   **87** McKenna to Edgar, 11 Dec. 1744 (R.A., Ms 260, fol. 125). Fagan (ed) *Stuart papers*, ii, pp 16-17. See also *Fau. Dub. J.*, 26 Mar. 1745; Cunningham (ed.), *Letters of Horace Walpole*, i, p. 378. For a useful biographical profile of Maréchal Saxe; O'Carroll, 'Marshal Saxe', pp 249-53. Samuel Boyse, author of the contemporary *An impartial history of the late rebellion in 1745*, discussed 'the Irish regiments in the French and Spanish service' whom he deemed 'a constant and regular force always ready (by connivance or permission of these powers) to assist in the restoration of the person whom they regarded as their lawful sovereign; Boyse, *An impartial history*, p. 58.   **88** McKenna to Edgar, Elixim, near Bravant (Brabant), 22 Feb. 1745 (R.A., Ms 262, fol. 187). McKenna also corresponded with his cousin in the 'Irlanda' Regiment in Spain; R.A., Ms 270, fol. 110. A long list of the French army and the Irish Regiments was published in the press; *Fau. Dub. J.*, 26 Mar. 1745.   **89** Sylvester Lloyd to Edgar [James III?], 15 May 1745 (R.A., Ms 264, fol. 172).

The exiled Irish Jacobites were no less affected by news of the prince's arrival in Scotland than their contemporaries in Ireland. Some devoured the newsletters which circulated through the Irish continental community and clamoured for intelligence from such unlikely sources as English smugglers. Others endeavoured to take a more active role in the 'Forty-five'.[90] Sir Felix O'Neill of the Fews, instrumental in Bonnie Prince Charlie's flight to Skye, and immortalised in the poetry of Art Mac Cumhaigh, declared a willingness to sacrifice himself in imitation of his ancestors. He laid particular emphasis on his potential usefulness in Ireland.[91] Owen O'Sullivan, another of the Wild Geese, wished that he had wings to follow his prince.[92] Apart from the lack of wings, hard currency provided the main reason why many of the loyal Irish Jacobites in Spain failed to assemble under the unfurled Stuart standard at Glenfinnan:

> You remark very well the difficulty for many of them to quit at present the employments they are in, but the other reason you hint one still stronger, besides very few of them are in a condition to make that journey if the court of Spain does not order a supply for them at the same time if it grants leave for absenting themselves, and even then 'tis not everyone who would be willing to go should he be sent.[93]

The prince's exploits fascinated the Irish diaspora, strengthening opinion there that the European political situation augured well for his affairs.[94]

Having commended Charles Edward for his heroic endeavours to deliver 'his majesty's [James III's] subjects from tyranny and usurpation', an unnamed member of the O'Hanlon family alluded to the hidden agenda of the Irish Brigades. Attached to the French army 'whom we have followed in some expeditions', O'Hanlon informed Edgar that they were 'ever seeking a proper opportunity to push into Great Britain and join his majesty's forces'.[95] Dominic

---

90 Heguerty to James III, Paris, 15 Aug. 1745 (R.A., Ms 267, fol. 22); (R.A., Ms 267, fol. 58). **91** Felix O' Neill to Edgar, 26 Aug. 1745 (R.A., Ms 267, fol. 67). See also R.A., Ms 228, fol. 138; R.A., Ms 267, fol. 166; R.A., Ms 267, fol. 67; R.A., Ms 279, fol. 72; R.A., Ms 286, fol. 169. *Ascanius: the young adventurer*, a seditious account of the 'Forty-five', spoke of Charles Edward's regard for the 'humane' and 'compassionate' O'Neill; *Ascanius*, pp 106-16, 69. Art Mac Cumhaigh appreciated 'Féilimí's' importance to the Stuart cause; 'Agallamh le Caisleán na Glasdromainne', in Ó Fiaich (eag.), *Art Mac Cumhaigh*, p. 82, line 11. Ó Fiaich study of the O'Neills of the Fews contains a general profile on Sir Felix; Ó Fiaich, 'The O'Neills of the Fews', pp 308-15. See also Hayes, *Biographical dictionary*, p. 250. **92** Owen O'Sullivan to Edgar, 27 Aug. 1745 (R.A., Ms 267, fol. 69). **93** William Lacy to Edgar, 2 Sept. 1745 (R.A., Ms 267, fol. 111). **94** See McDonnell to Edgar, 30 Sept. 1745 (R.A., Ms 267, fols 101). See also R.A., 267, fols 150, 156; Ms 268, fol. 72. According to McLynn, only limited numbers of Irish soldiers from France were allowed to join the prince in Scotland; McLynn, *France and the Jacobite rising of 1745*, p. 81. **95** O'Hanlon to Edgar, 8 Sept. 1745 (R.A., Ms 267, fol. 157). Nevertheless, James III was unwilling to sanction a wholesale descent on Scotland by the Irish Brigades without the permission of the French king; R.A., Ms 267, fol. 183.

Heguerty, who acted as the eyes and ears of James III in Paris, also promoted a Spanish-sponsored invasion of Ireland. He conferred with senior members of the French ministry including le comte de Maurepas, le comte D'Argenson and Orry, who desired that 'he would give them thoughts on the manner of conveying three Brigades to England'. Heguerty assured James (reflecting the French ministry's opinion) 'that your majesty may depend on a considerable diversion in Ireland on the Spanish side'.[96]

The assiduous Charles Wogan spearheaded these attempts to induce the Spanish court to provide the necessary funds and arms to supply the beleaguered prince. He relayed a list of Irish officers in both Italy and Oran who were prepared to join the prince in Scotland and then re-iterated his hopes for a restoration of his king and a return to his native land. He also commented on his need to go in disguise on his arrival in England 'because I am attainted by an act of parliament in England for almost 30 years which renders me incapable, as yet of my inheritance at home [Ireland]'.[97] Revelling in the latest successes of his young master, he reminded his monarch of the prospect of a restoration to their respective birthrights' and 'the satisfaction of seeing each other at home after so tedious and irksome a banishment'.[98]

Wogan, however, experienced the agonised frustration of Irish Jacobites in both France and Spain, caused by the unwillingness of the Catholic princes to fully support the 'Forty-five'. His disdain for French duplicity echoed his criticisms of France in the 1730s:

> notwithstanding all the instances I made of the prince having landed or an account of the 'Elizabeth's' return with the arms she had on board and that his friends among whom he had landed, were useless, to him, since he did not have arms to put in their hands, and many other pathetic representations ... but they gave no credit to their own ministers at the Hague and Paris; all this delay, and the uncouth situation I knew the prince must be in, and some other disagreeable circumstances of letters writ to persons in this court blaming the prince's enterprise as 'rash and inconsiderate' not to say worse, fired my blood to that degree and filled my head with such dismal ideas of the prince being abandoned, even by the court where his address had been so kindly received, that I was seized with a violent fever.[99]

96 Heguerty to James III, 14 Sept. 1745 (R.A., Ms 268, fol. 17); McLynn, *France and Jacobite rising of 1745*, pp 55, 67, 76, 82, 176, 186-96, 214; idem, 'Ireland and the Jacobite rising', pp 345-7.   97 Wogan to James III, 5 July 1745 (R.A., Ms 269, fol. 49). See also R.A., Ms 389, fol. 68. Lord Boyle, Speaker of the House of Commons, received an unusual petition from David Fitzgerald regarding Colonel Baggot's endeavours to get him to raise a regiment in Ireland on the prince's landing that he 'might then hope to recover the lands forfeited by his grand-father in King James's cause'; Gordon-Seaton, *Prisoners of the '45*, i, p. 202.   98 Wogan to James III, 15 Dec. 1745 (R.A., Ms 271, fol. 100). 99 Wogan to James III, 5 Oct. 1745 (R.A., Ms 269, fol. 49).

Despite the failure of the 'Forty-five', many Irish exiles concluded, along with their Irish (and Scots-Gaelic) contemporaries, that the Jacobite cause was not dead. The fate of the fugitive prince momentarily preoccupied them in the immediate aftermath of Culloden, and his escape in some way compensated for the failure of the uprising.[100] The bitter pill of defeat was rendered more palatable by the prince's astounding progress in England and Scotland, against all the odds and in contradiction of the councils and efforts of the great powers. His miraculous escape from the clutches of the 'Cromwell'-like elector of Hanover also augured well for the eventual triumph of the Stuart cause. Wogan shared the irrepressible optimism of the literati in the ultimate triumph of the cause, an optimism shared by their Jacobite counterparts in England and Scotland.[101]

Monod argues that Charles Edward's expulsion from France under the terms of the Treaty of Aix-la-Chapelle in 1748, dispelled the myth that the Irish exiles served the Stuarts rather than the king of France. This did not seem so obvious to contemporaries. Le comte 'Argenson, the French war minister, feared that the prince's expulsion from France would lead to a total rift with the Stuarts, involving the withdrawal of the Irish regiments from France. Although these fears were not realised, the Seven Years War showed that many of the Irish Brigade officers and the rank and file retained their Jacobitism.[102]

III

Awareness of European political developments and the course of the 1745 rebellion was not confined to a mere handful of Irish Jacobite poets or well-placed *émigrés*. Other contemporary sources shed light on the effects of these events on the respective Jacobite and anti-Jacobite traditions. Irish Catholic attitudes are reflected in popular rioting as early as the outbreak of the War of Jenkins's Ear in 1739. The Quakers, whipping-boys of the Irish Catholic Jacobites since the death of James Cotter, bore the brunt of their wrath in the aftermath of the fifth of November celebrations. At Timahoe, County Kildare, a group of rioters set up the Pretender in effigy, burned the house of William Hall and attacked and destroyed the Quaker meeting house. The military arrested fifteen papists, leading to the raising of a local mob which issued threats against informers and promised speedy deliverance for their imprisoned confederates.[103] These attacks on the Timahoe Quakers were precipitated by the earlier burning

---

100 Wogan to James III, 23 Aug. 1746 (R.A., Ms 276, fol. 110). These sentiments were expressed by other exiles in the period; R.A., Ms 277, fol. 127; Ms 278, fol. 163. **101** Wogan to James III, 15 Dec. 1746 (R.A., Ms 279, fol. 186); McLynn, *Bonnie Prince Charlie*, p. 353. **102** Monod, *Jacobitism*, p. 109; McLynn, *Bonnie Prince Charlie*, pp 369-70. **103** Devonshire to the Secretary of State, 12 Jan. 1739 (P.R.O., S.P., 63/403/7); Information of William Arnett, Timahoe, Co. Kildare, 14 Jan. 1739 (P.R.O., S.P., 63/403/9). A proclamation was issued against those concerned in this burning; *Twenty-third report of the deputy-keeper*, p. 66.

of effigies of the Pretender and Blessed Virgin Mary. One of the alleged Quakers, claiming membership of the Church of Ireland, readily admitted burning the Pretender's image but strenuously denied insulting the Blessed Virgin.[104]

Writing from Kanturk, County Cork, in 1739, Richard Purcell noted the excitement among the 'common people' at the prospects of a Spanish invasion. He initially believed that their preoccupation with looming famine would 'dampen their enthusiasm 'and 'cool their courage', as no part of the country contained enough provisions to facilitate an invading force. However, in late summer, he was perturbed by the frantic military preparations in Cork, Kinsale and Limerick, and the attitude of the 'starving' papists.[105] In spite of the escalation of theft and robberies. He believed, however, that 'the loss of the potatoes' would be enough to 'prevent their entering into open action'.[106] He informed Percival of the preparations which were being made to resist invasion. These would not have passed unnoticed by his Catholic contemporaries:

> We in this kingdom apprehend a war with France is near at hand, and the papists (though nine in ten of them are reduced to the greatest want by the loss of the potatoes and the great price of corn) are generally elated thereof.[107]

Other Munster Protestants experienced similar fears. Richard Toler linked widespread smuggling in south Munster with rumours of war. These were promulgated by a ship-captain who 'spoke the sentiments of France' and pronounced that 'the French flag would in three months be hoisted in Ireland by only two thousand French being sent there'. However, these 'would be joined in a few days by 50,000 men here ready for that purpose'.[108]

The intercourse between Irish Jacobites and the continent reinforced local expectations and also underlined the dangers of clandestine correspondence. An intercepted letter from Bernard Ward (presumably Don Bernardo Ward, later foreign minister of Spain) in Madrid to Carrickmacross, County Monaghan in 1739 concurred with Purcell and Toler's reports. It promised war in Ireland and England within six months:

> I assure you that it will be very hard living in the country in a little time for the papists, as they term you, for nothing is surer than a bloody war will break out over Ireland and England in less than six months. Therefore a populous city is the best refuge for one of your sort in those times

---

104 *Pue's O.*, 12-15 Jan. 1740.   **105** R. Purcell to Perceval, Kanturk, 21 Mar. 1739 (B.L., Add. Ms 47,001A, fol. 53).   **106** Purcell to Perceval, Feb. 1740 (B.L., Add. Ms 47,001A, fols 41).   **107** Purcell to Perceval, 17 Oct. 1740 (B.L. Add. Ms 47, 001A, fol. 96). See also B.L. Add. Ms 47, 001A, fols 69, 73, 75; B. L., Add. Ms 24,138, fol. 11. See also pp 303, fn. 119; 304, fn. 127; 305, fn. 135.   **108** Richard Toler to Henry Hamilton, 25 Sept. 1739 (P.R.O., S.P., 63/402/16).

where the profession of people are not much regarded. Please make no declaration of this last piece of news to the rabble of the country nor any person whatsoever for particular reasons but I give you a caution to guard yourselves against the approaching storm.[109]

At this time, Catholics appeared more than ordinarily assertive in the vicinity of the predominantly Protestant town of Dundalk. Nonetheless the Protestant inhabitants of the Ulster towns of Newry (Down), Monaghan (Monaghan), Dromore (Tyrone) and Castleblaney (Monaghan) enthusiastically acclaimed the war against Spain in November 1739, amid toasts to 'the king, the prince and princess of Wales, England's wooden walls and a good barking to the Spaniards'. In Munster, where Protestants were heavily outnumbered, they were considerably less vocal. Their fears were exacerbated by the removal of troops from Ireland, recurring rumours of a French invasion and resulting Catholic haughtiness.[110] According to Lord Lieutenant Devonshire, the country appeared to be defenceless. Lacking a militia, Protestants felt powerless to deal with the twin threats of internal revolt and external invasion. Devonshire even suggested that 'the Irish papists of this country have (as I am well informed) flattered themselves with hopes of seeing an army of French landing at Cork'. He claimed that 'they have carried their insolence to that pitch as even to look out for an easterly wind to favour a descent on these kingdoms'.[111]

Four essays (originally in French) published in Dublin disputed this picture of Irish Catholic arrogance, claiming that Catholics in the city were more subdued and in 'sunken spirits'. No doubt, these 'sunken spirits' were affected by the smug self-confidence which often emanated from the predominantly Protestant citadel. They contrasted with the anxiety expressed by small, isolated Protestant communities in predominantly Catholic areas throughout the country. 'The better sort' were 'fond of news and well versed in public affairs' while the 'vulgar' (Protestants) were 'bigots to the house of Austria', ' impatient to fight and are even become petulant and suspicious of the cause of our [France's] inactivity

---

109 'Intercepted letter from Madrid from Bernard Ward', 29 Aug. 1739 (P.R.O., S.P., 63/402/13). Contemporary correspondents stressed the dangers of letters being intercepted or opened; Giblin (ed.), 'Catalogue' part 6, vols 133-5g, p. 84; R.A., Ms 225, fol. 155; Fagan (ed.), *Stuart papers*, i, pp 285, 291, 300, 302, ii, p. 15. P.R.O., S.P., 63/402/15; Harvard, Ms Eng., 218, vol. 4, fol. 65, N.L.I., mf. p. 787; Higgins, *Swift's politics*, p. 19; P.R.O., S.P., 63/402/81; R.A., Ms 201, fol. 120; Fenning, 'Michael MacDonogh', p. 151. For the high-political Jacobite context; McLynn, *Bonnie Prince Charlie*, pp 67-8. **110** *Fau. Dub. J.*, 6-10 Nov., 13-17 Nov., 27 Nov.-1 Dec. 1739. Similar gatherings took place in Munster; Buttimer (ed.), 'An Irish text on the War of Jenkins's Ear', p. 81. An Irish *émigré* expressed hopes of the possibility of French involvement; N.L.I., Ms 2478, fol. 73. See also P.R.O., S.P., 63/402/107. Newcastle related rumours of arms shipments, embarkation of troops and fears of an Ormondist invasion; P.R.O., S.P., 67/11/73; B.L., Add. Ms 24, 138, fol. 11; See also *Fau. Dub. J.*, 19 June 1739; For Franco-Jacobite intrigue and the possibility of an invasion of Scotland by the Irish Brigades on Scotland; Hayes, *Irish swordsmen*, p. 233. **111** Devonshire to Secretary of State, 17 Nov. 1739 (P.R.O., S.P., 63/402/107). Major General John Ligonier's 'Plan for the defence of Cork' (*c.*1740) show that these fears were taken seriously at a local level; [Ligonier], 'Plan for the defence of Cork', pp 708-11.

and moderation'.[112] Invasion fears and faint rumblings of the forthcoming war recalled the last Jacobite invasion to some Protestant minds. The Stuart claimant re-emerged as the inveterate enemy of the Protestant 'religion, property and liberties' in the company of 'a certain power [Spain or France], who has for some years taken upon him to dispose of kingdoms and principalities at will'.[113] These Protestant apprehensions, exacerbated by renewed instances of recruitment for French service, resulted in the disarming of the Catholics.[114] The arrival in Madrid of the veteran duke of Ormonde, and a possible liaison with Charles Edward, was also reported in high political circles.[115]

Historians have considered the optimism of the Irish literati as naive and unrealistic.[116] Nevertheless Newcastle's despair in response to the triumphs of Britain's enemies on the continent provides a counterpoint to the exhilaration of contemporary Jacobite literati and the general Catholic populace; 'the French armies in Germany carry all before them and either love or fear will soon make France quite masters over all that part of Europe'. Furthermore, he added that 'the election of the elector of Bavaria can no longer be in doubt and the letters from France and Holland talk pretty positively of a neutrality with France or his majesty's electoral dominions'.[117]

The immediate prospect of a Jacobite descent and its effects on local expectations permeated government reports and the letters of Whig commentators. Invasion rumours flourished in the early 1740s, inspired by the mobilisation of the French fleet at Brest, and by the movement of troops through Dublin for

---

112 *Four essays in French relating to the kingdom of Ireland,* pp 21-3.   **113** *The groans of Ireland in a letter to a member of parliament begun about Christmas 1739.*   **114** For the disarming of papists; *Pue's O.,* 20-4 Nov. 1739; *Fau. Dub. Jnr.,* 20-4 Nov. 1739. The Jacobite bishop Sylvester Lloyd described this disarming as 'a terrible stroke against us'; Fagan, *Divided loyalties,* p. 77 References to recruiting circulate in contemporary despatches; P.R.O., S.P., 63/402/170; P.R.O., S.P., 63/405/71. A severe pelting was given to one perjurer against recruiters; Brady (ed.), *Catholics,* p. 316; see also *Pue's O.,* 17-21 Mar. 1741. Two Irish Brigade officers were arrested at Harwich; *Fau. Dub. J.,* 20 Mar. 1743-44. A proclamation promised £1000 for anyone who would discover officers enlisting for the foreign service; N.L.W., Ms 3580C. Sylvester Lloyd sent a report of this recruitment bill to Daniel O'Brien in Rome; Fagan (ed.), *Stuart papers,* i, p. 276. A report in *Pue's Occurrence* in April 1746 referred to one Lawrence Ryan, a Romish priest, who was brought in under a strong guard and lodg'd in gaol, being charged with dispersing commissions from the Pretender and other treasonable practices'; *Pue's O.,* 19-22 Apr. 1746.   **115** W. Smith to Devonshire, 16 Feb. 1739/40 (P.R.O., S.P., 63/403/39). See also B.L., Add. Ms 24, 138, fol. 11; Giblin (ed.), 'Catalogue' part 6, vols 133-5g, p. 85. The prospect of a Spanish invasion also featured in a letter of Francis Burton of May 1740. While he remained unconvinced of the immediacy of the threat, he did not disparage its existence, referring to the 'great preparations which had been made', the 'thirty-four thousand men camped near Ferroll' and the Queen of Spain's determination to 'burn some of our towns'; N.A., Ievers Papers, Ms 5592. High political discourse resonates with reference to Ireland's strategic importance; *H.M.C., 14th report,* appendix, x, part- ix, pp 57-8; Doran, *Mann and manners of the court of Florence,* p. 34; Dover (ed.), *Letters,* i, pp 160, 174.   **116** Cullen, *The Hidden Ireland: a reassessment,* pp 11, 16-17, 48; Connolly, *Religion,* p. 248; Canny, review of Ó Buachalla, p. 28. Irwin, review of Fagan, p. 477.   **117** Newcastle to Devonshire, 17 Sept. 1741 (N.L.I., Special List 335 [1], Chatworth papers T.3.58.180). Michael Mc Donogh reported in April 1741 that common opinion held that there would be a general war and the French would be obliged to restore the king for their own sake; Fagan (ed.), *Stuart papers,* i, p. 324.

shipment to Flanders.[118] Richard Purcell commented on the attitudes of the 'vulgar papists' to these developments. He alluded to their positive reaction to the appearance of a comet, and to pompous accounts in 'their newspapers of congratulations to the Pretender in Rome on the arrival of his son in France'. The fact that Lord Lieutenant Devonshire recalled his baggage from a ship bound for England allegedly 'gave them great spirits and their priests and them talk foolishly and seditiously on the subject'.[119] Purcell further observed that 'we are in this part of the country greatly alarmed at the news of a design to invade England and we shall continue in the greatest uneasiness 'til we know the event. The papists are generally elated but I do not suspect they will become riotous 'till they can be certain of the assistance of foreign aid'.[120] Elsewhere he added that 'the papists are still quiet but have great expectations that the French will invade England, Scotland and this kingdom in favour of the Pretender's son and that they will have success. Their inclination to rebel is not to be doubted but they want arms'.[121]

Purcell was not a lone figure, crying wolf in the wilderness of south Munster. Walter Peard and Edmund Spenser spoke of the 'great alarm', 'dreadful apprehension' and 'great flurry' among the Protestants of Cork city at the possibility of an attack by the Brest squadron.[122] The unease within the ranks of Cork Corporation was such that they sent some of the army and eight of their cannon down river to prevent a French landing.[123] An Englishman in County Cork reported that the 'Irish grow insolent; one whom I discharged told my wife he hoped to see the day when he would not be obliged to slave for 5d'.[124] A memoir relating to the estates of Arthur Price, Church of Ireland archbishop of Cashel, from July 1744 complained that 'some of the papists, not only of the poorest but the middling sort, expect some strange revolution that makes them so unwilling to part with their money'. Elsewhere in County Cork there were complaints that 'the papists that owe money will pay none'.[125]

Perceval's attention was also called to the 'inconceivable damp upon the common people' caused by the arrest, and seizure of the papers, of the Irish Tory and Jacobite magnate James Barry, fourth earl of Barrymore. Although Barrymore's political activities were almost exclusively confined to England, the common Irish were well aware of his zeal for the Stuart cause. Purcell added

118 Stanwell Jones to [?], 27 Feb. 1743 (N.A., Ms 3036,125 [vol. 6], fol. 2, fol. 43). See also *Fau. Dub. J.*, 14 Feb. 1744; 26 Mar. 1744; 31 Mar. 1744. An embarkation of troops from Ireland was cancelled due to the danger of an invasion; N.L.I., Ms special list 335 [1] Chatworth papers; see also ibid., fols 285, 286, 290, 294, 307. 119 Purcell to Perceval, 24 Feb. 1743 (B.L., Add. Ms 47,001 B, fol. 48). Ó Buachalla notes Tadhg Ó Neachtain's response to the appearance of a comet in this period; Ó Buachalla, *Aisling Ghéar*, p. 399. 120 Purcell to Perceval, 2 Mar. 1743 (B.L., Add. Ms 47,001B, fol. 49). 121 Purcell to Perceval, 6 Mar. 1743 (B.L., 47, 001B, fol. 55). See also; B.L., Add. Ms 24,137, fol. 138, no. 224, 47; Walpole to Mann, in Dover (ed.), *Letters*, i, pp 345-7, 350-4. 122 Peard and Spenser to Price, Feb. 1744, 27 Oct. 1745 (N.L.W., Ms 3579D and 3580C). 123 Peard to Price, 2 Dec. 1744 (N.L.W., Ms 3579D). 124 Cited in Morley, *An crann os coill*, p. 134. 125 Quoted in Connolly, *Religion*, p. 246.

that Lord Barrymore might 'in ten days have 20,000 well-made strong young fellows at his heels'.[126] Another report from February 1744 suggested that ships on the south west coast caused 'great alarm' and claimed that 'nothing is talked of here but an immediate invasion'.[127]

These rumours were not confined to the Jacobite heartland of south Munster. From Killybegs, County Donegal, it was reported that 'our Irish are grown so superb on account of this war that they don't know what end of them is uppermost'. In contrast, the reaction of the local, minority Protestant populace sheds some light on their siege-mentality: 'we in these little villages are keeping what guard we can for we had an account privately they were to make a descent on us last night. The Catholics state 'publicly that Ireland is their property and will fight for it'.[128] In the midst of the 'Forty-five', he noted that 'the common people here are very uppish and would be fond of a change of government'.[129]

Continuing rumours of a French invasion of Ireland in 1743 and 1744 brought the wrath of the administration down upon the Catholics in the period immediately preceding the 'Forty-five'.[130] An attempt to seize Dr James O'Gallagher of Raphoe in 1743 resulted in the fatal shooting of Fr O'Heguerty, the aged parish priest of Killygarvan, County Donegal.[131] The grand jury of Kilkenny made a presentment in 1744 against Colman O'Shaughnessy, bishop of Ossory, on the grounds that he had been domestic chaplain to the Pretender.[132] Sylvester Lloyd was hounded out of Ireland and 'only escaped by a

126 Cooley to Perceval, 17 Mar. 1743 (B.L., Add. Ms 47, 004B, fol. 31). A memorial from George Keith, the Jacobite earl marischal of Scotland, of 20 August 1745, mentions Barrymore, Orrery and Clancarthy as being prepared to raise the standard of King James in their respective parts of the kingdom; Beresford; 'Ireland', p. 177. For Barrymore's Irish political patronage network, see; N.L.W., Ms 3579 D. Stephen Coppinger, one of the sons of Stephen Coppinger of Ballyvolane, County Cork, who accompanied Sarsfield to France after the war, returned from La Rochelle c.1716. Barrymore brought him to England in the 1730s to find a wife among the English Catholic Jacobite gentry; Copinger, *History of the Copingers or Coppingers*, p. 192. Coppinger's name was among persons who had a cipher accorded to them in Ireland in the 1720s; Fagan (ed.), *Stuart papers*, i, p. 64. Richard Barry, Barrymore's second son, served as secretary to his father in his negotiations with France. Barrymore sent him to join the abortive French invasion of England in 1744 where he formed a close friendship with Charles Edward and earned the praise of the French commander Maréchal Saxe. His father later sent him to Derby with promises of support for the prince. He continued to correspond with Charles Edward from Ireland after the battle of Culloden and he was probably in London for the prince's visit in 1750; Sedwick, *The Commons, 1715-54*, i, p. 442. 127 Quoted in Connolly, *Religion*, p. 257. 128 Henry McCullough to Murray of Broughton, 17 Mar. 1744, cited in Kirkham, 'Murray of Broughton estate', p. 370. 129 Thomas Addi to Murray of Broughton, Mar. 1746, quoted in [Addi], 'Letter to Murray of Broughton', pp 398-404. 130 Testa to Cardinal Valenti, Brussels, 10 Apr. 1744, in Giblin (ed.), 'Catalogue', part 6, vols 133-5g, pp 98-9. See also Fagan (ed.) *Stuart papers*, ii, p. 32. Kelly states that 'the last significant phase of repressive anti-Catholic legislation spanned the difficult years 1739-45', Kelly, 'The impact of the penal laws', p. 157. Fenning calls it 'a last and savage bout of persecution'; Fenning, *Irish Dominican province*, p. 93. Fagan states that in February 1744, with war between France and England threatening and the possibility of an invasion by a Jacobite force, the greatest persecution since the days of Queen Anne was initiated, Fagan, *Divided loyalties*, p. 77. 131 Moran, *Catholics under the penal laws*, p. 27. 132 Moran, *Catholics under the penal laws*, p. 33. O'Shaughnessy had left his post as lecturer in Philosophy in the University of Paris to accompany James III to Scotland in 1708; Fenning, *Irish Dominican province*, p. 111.

miracle'. Ambrose O'Callaghan, bishop of Ferns, another faithful Jacobite agent, died in August 1744, 'worn out by his efforts to avoid arrest'.[133] Writing in 1745, after he had been accused of treason, Michael MacDonogh, bishop of Kilmore, stated that 'the storms and tempests in which we have nearly been lost are only beginning to subside'. He had to change house twelve times in two months because of a charge of high treason sworn against him.[134]

The ruling oligarchy also ruthlessly suppressed occasional Jacobite displays. A man named Callaghan was pilloried for toasting the health of Lord Clare, held by many in Ireland to be the likely leader of an invasion force.[135] In Ulster, a Down farmer was arrested for drinking the Pretender's health and declaring 'that he would drink it over and over again in spite of all present, who might kiss his arse for that if he was hanged for it, five hundred of them should hang along with him'.[136] The trial of James Heggarty at Derry assizes in April 1744 for toasting James III's health provides a glimpse of the Jacobite drinking-culture which permeated the English, Scots Gaelic and Irish Jacobite tradition.[137] Having pilloried and pelted the unfortunate Heggarty, the crowd burned the Stuart king and his two sons in effigy amid toasts to King George, the success of his army, the glorious memory of William III and the queen of Hungary (Empress Maria Theresa) and her allies. There 'never appeared a greater spirit of zeal and loyalty ... or a stronger inclination to humble the French king and his allies'.[138]

The annual Protestant celebrations of the anniversary of the 1641 rebellion in Youghal, County Cork, indulged in a similar assault on Jacobite symbolism. The effigy of Charles Edward was dressed in the familiar trappings of Jacobitism – highland plaid, white cockade and blue bonnet. It also displayed the derogatory symbols of illegitimacy and popery – the warming-pan and the rosary beads.[139] It also mirrors the hostile world of Whig and anti Jacobite ritual, such as the customary burning of the Pretender in effigy in County Cork on the duke of Cumberland's birthday.[140]

---

133 Fagan, *Divided loyalties*, pp 62, 77. Thomas Burke also claimed that John Brett, appointed to Killala a year previously, had only narrowly escaped capture in 1744; Fenning, *Irish Dominican province*, pp 187-8.   **134** Fenning, 'Michael MacDonogh', p. 151; idem, *Irish Dominican province*, p. 188. See also Kelly, 'The Catholic Church in Ardagh', p. 75; Power, *Tipperary*, p. 239; Murphy, *Killaloe*, p. 82.   **135** Crofton-Croker, *Researches*, p. 201.   **136** Quoted in Connolly, *Religion*, pp 245-6. See also P.R.O.N.I., D2092/1/7, p. 40. Sergeant Matthew Gordon of Warburton's regiment of dragoons (based in Athlone) received 300 lashes of the cat o'nine tails for uttering disrespectful words about George II; McLynn, 'Good behaviour', p. 50.   **137** *Dub. J.*, 10-14 Apr. 1744. *Pue's Occurrences* of 25-9 March 1746 reported four instances of people being pilloried for treasonable words; *Pue's O.*, 25-9 Mar. 1746. See also *Pue's O.*, 1-5 Apr. 1746. **138** *Dub. J.*, 10-14 Apr. 1744. Walpole's correspondence to Horace Mann described the changing fortunes of the queen of Hungary and the king of France; Dover (ed.), *Letters*, i, pp 107, 116, 134-5, 146-7, 160, 167, 170-2, 174, 197, 211, 235, 269-70, 276, 287, 291, 310.   **139** *Fau. Dub. J.*, 29 Oct.-2 Nov. 1745. The Pretender's illegitimacy also featured in contemporary pamphlets; Fowke, *The duty of subjects to a good prince considered*, p. 22; Maclaine, *A sermon preached at Antrim, 18 December 1745*, p. 20. The doctrine of hereditary right was also attacked; Foulke, *The duty of subjects*, p. 22; Maclaine, *A sermon preached at Antrim, December 18 1745*, p. 20.   **140** *Pue's O.*, 19-22 Apr. 1746.

These demonstrative rituals had a twin purpose: reassuring Hanoverians while simultaneously intimidating Jacobites.[141] Such shows of popular Protestant defiance masked their real fears of invasion, and their unease at the possible intentions of Jacobite partisans in Ireland.[142]

Isolated incidences of treasonable utterances and muted support for the Jacobite cause illuminate a popular Jacobite underworld. For obvious linguistic, cultural and political reasons many of these popular Jacobite displays would mostly have taken place in a predominantly Irish-speaking milieu, away from the prying eyes and ears of Protestant Whig officials. Many of them have only survived in the context of the Irish literary tradition. Tadhg Gaelach Ó Súilleabháin dedicated a verse to Domhnall Ó Faoláin, who was imprisoned for toasting the Pretender's health.[143] Seán Clárach hoped that a plague would descend on the heads of those that would not drink the health of his 'black laddie' ('Is pláigh ar an gcóbach do leómhfadh bheith claoin/Ná hólfadh deaghshláinte ar mo mhacaomh').[144] His colleague Piaras Mac Gearailt promised that he would always toast the health of the strong brave lion ('Ólfam feasta a shláinte, Mo leóghan lannach láidir').[145] In a macaronic verse which he composed when working as a casual labourer in Newfoundland, Donnchadh Rua Mac Conmara called his listeners to 'Come drink a health boys to loyal George, Our chief commander-not ordained by Christ ('nár orduigh Críost').[146] James Clarence Mangan's translation of one of Mac Coitir's poem Welcome to the prince of Ossory concluded by promising to drink victory to Charles.[147] In 1746 Aindrias Mac Craith urged his listeners to call for a can of cider to drink Charles's health forever ('le gárdas glaoigh go heascadh ar channa saghdair/sláinte Shéarlais taoscann feasta timpeall').[148] Elsewhere he wished (in a song to the tune of 'Charlie over the water') that Charles Stuart would be happy and victorious and we will

---

141 While the Derry Protestants sought to humiliate the French king, the press attempted to sully him further in Catholic eyes. It provided another example of his ingratitude to the Irish Brigade 'who under Lord Clare behaved themselves with great bravery when the French were repulsed and retreated behind the Irish from the fire of their garrisons'. The same paper noted that the French king 'rewarded the troops of his own nation without taking the least notice of the Irish'; *Dub. J.*, 7-10 July 1744. 142 Between April 1744 and February 1745, local Protestant fears in County Cork again revolved around French preparations. They stressed the inevitability of Papist collusion and the buoyancy of the latter group at rumours of the resignation of the English ministry and their hopes of 'great matters' in favour of the Pretender; B.L., Add. Ms 47, 001B, fol. 61; see also ibid. fol. 94. Horace Walpole believed in both French invincibility and Irish Catholic unreliability, in Dover (ed.), *Letters*, i, pp 370; ibid., ii, 19, 51. 143 Ó Foghludha (eag.), *Tadhg Gaelach*, p. 111. In the State papers for 1743-5, Nicholas Rogers and Eveline Cruickshanks have noted that most seditious word cases in contemporary London involved Irishmen; Rogers, 'Popular disaffection', pp 70-100. Rogers, 'Popular protest', pp 5-27. 144 Seán Clárach Mac Domhnaill, 'Comhracann mo Mhacaomh', in Ó Foghludha (eag.), *Seán Clárach*, p. 60. 145 Piaras Mac Gearailt, 'A Mhalaí beag ó', in Ó Foghludha (eag.), *Amhráin Phiarais Mhic Gearailt*, p. 30. Piaras Mac Gearailt, re-writing in 1767, mocked the many idiots in a public-house who sang this song 'Is iomdha glór diomhaoin i gceann an tí a chom an t-amhrán so'; Ó Foghludha (eag.), *Amhráin Phiarais Mhic Gearailt*, p. 17. 146 Donnchadh Rua Mac Conmara, 'As I was walking one evening fair', in Ó Foghludha (eag.), *Donnchadh Ruadh*, p. 36. 147 James Clarence Mangan/Liam Dall Ó hIfearnáin, Welcome to the Prince of Ossory, in Ó Foghludha (eag.), *Ar bhruach na Coille Muaire*, p. 90. 148 Comer-Bruen, 'An Mangaire Súgach', p. 178.

pour out and drink his health ('Fá bhuaidh bheith a séanmhar ag Séarlas Mac Stíobhart/is taosgamaoid timchioll a shláinte').[149]

Faced with a Franco-Jacobite invasion and aware of this close association between Catholicism and Jacobitism, the government adopted a tough line towards the Catholic clergy. A royal proclamation, publicly displayed in each town, offered bounties of £30 for a priest, £50 for a bishop and £40 for a monk or Jesuit.[150] This persecution stemmed from French successes in Flanders, and particularly at Fontenoy.[151] A major turning point in the titanic struggle between Saxe and Cumberland, Fontenoy also provided one of the finest hours of the Irish Brigade in this campaign, and became the subject of numerous poems and pamphlets. A contemporary ode in the Stuart papers described the Irish forces:

> Hibernia's sons alas they number few
> But still their minds are brave and hearts are true.
> Expelled their seats, forced from their native land
> By tyrant lords around the world to roam.
> And full of generous love and freedom find
> That man to their true worth is not unkind.
> Let truth be once avowed where 'ere they go
> Nations conspire to stifle all their woe
> And kings with joy adopt them as their own
> How oft' the bulwark of a monarch's throne.[152]

---

149 Walsh (eag.), *Reliques of Irish Jacobite poetry*, pp 107-8. A manuscript in the Royal Irish Academy contained a poem where the months of the year drink the health of King James', *Cat. of Ir. mss. in the R. I. A.*, iii, p. 413. Seditious Jacobites toasts of their kind also survive in the Ulster folk tradition. One example would seem to refer to the 'Fifteen' or the 'Forty-five'. It wished a long life to the cocks who crow in Scotland that will raise all England ... and will make the Scottish (Presbyterians?) dance 'Fad saoghil do na coiligh a sgairteas i nAlbain a mhúsglas Sasain uilig, a thógás a' cában i nÉirinn, a bheireas ar na hAlbanaigh a dhul a damhsa', Ó Muirgheasa (eag.), *Seanfhocla Uladh* (B.Á.C., 1931), p. 96. See also ibid., p. 302. Alasdair Mhac Mhaighstir Alasdair called on his audience to fill a health to James and Charles, in Campbell (eag.), *Songs of the '45*, p. 72; see also Forbes (ed.), *The lyon in mourning*, i, p. 244. Ó Buachalla quotes a whole series of other seditious Jacobite toasts of this type; Ó Buachalla, *Aisling Ghéar*, pp 357-9, 655-6. **150** Manning, 'Dr Nicholas Madgett's Constitutio Ecclesiastico', p. 80. See also Brady (ed.), *Catholics*, p. 65. **151** Copie d'une lettre de mr le maréchal de Saxe, au camp d'Anthoin, 12 Mars 1745 (A.N., Dept. de la Guerre, vol. 3075, fol. 167, N.L.I., mf. p. 189). See also 'La relation de la Bataille', 11 Mai 1745 (A.N., Dept. de la Guerre, A.I. Ms 3090, fol. 160 N.L.I., mf. p. 150); Lettre de mai. de Saxe, 12 Mai 1745, (A.N., Ministère de la Guerre, A.I. 3084, fols 169-72 N.L.I., mf. p. 150); 'Copie d'une lettre de mr le comte de Lowendal à madame, la comtesse', 10 Mai 1745 (A.N., Dept. de la Guerre, A.I., 3090, fol. 146, N.L.I., mf. p. 150); 'Le maréchal de Saxe', 13 Mai 1745 (A.N., Dept. de la Guerre, A.I., 3090, fol. 154, N.L.I., mf. p. 150); (R.A., Ms 265, fol. 116; Ms 285, fol. 125). A French victory in this battle raised Irish Jacobite spirits, while at the same time it precipitated religious persecution; O'Brien (ed.), *Catholic Ireland*, p. 17. The battle of Fontenoy also featured in the contemporary press in this period; *Fontenoy: A new satyric ballad.* **152** 'Battle of Fontenoy' (R.A., Box 3/23, folder 2). The Irish exiles were elated in Paris on receipt of news of the victory; Walsh, 'Letters from Fontenoy', pp 237-48. In 1746 Lord Clare implored McDonagh not to forget 'the memorable day they had at Fontenoy, and the other glorious days in which they had a share', quoted in O'Conor, *Military memoirs of the Irish nation*, p. 366. Ignatius Murphy states that this letter was written to McDonagh while he was recruiting in County

Richard Edwards commented on the conflicting war news from Flanders presented in *Pue's Occurrences* and *Faulkner's Journal.* He showed 'how zealously our Roman Catholics are affected by the success of the French in Flanders'. Mocking Catholic and Protestant coffee-table jousting, he noted how the former 'read that the French have taken Ghent', while the latter 'falls on him with a detachment from Buthiane'. He joked that although the Frenchman again 'cut off our communications with Ostend, the patriot still elects the emperor' and when 'Catholics come to a march made by those of his belief in Flanders, the other table is informed of it and raises another twenty thousand [men] in Holland to restore us'.[153]

Contemporary correspondence and the popular press reported on the military exploits of the prince in Scotland, and the possibility of a timely Franco-Jacobite invasion. They focused in particular on the raising of the Stuart standard at Glenfinnan by Charles Edward, his defeat of Sir John Cope at Preston Pans, and the news that seven or eight thousand of the Irish Brigades were congregated in Dunkirk.[154] Cope's defeat at Preston Pans had 'shocked' the

Clare; Murphy, *Diocese of Killaloe*, p. 209; For a recent view of the Irish contribution to the French victory at Fontenoy, see Ó hAnnracháin, 'The Irish Brigade at Lafelt', p. 2. In his commemorative poem, Voltaire praised Lord Clare and the Irish for avenging their king (James III), their country and their temples 'Clare avec les Irlandois qu'anamie notre example/Vengé ses rois trahis, sa patrie et ses temples', quoted in Hume-Weygand, 'Epic of the Wild Geese', p. 29. In spite of this, the Louth-born John Drumgoole attacked Voltaire for failing to adequately acknowledge the Irish part in snatching victory from the jaws of defeat; Hayes, *Biographical dictionary*, p. 73; Hayes, 'John Drumgoole', p. 215. Hayes also referred to a poem in the British Library headed 'Uilleachan Dubh ó re MacGearuilt ba maior a n-arm na Fraingce' which possibly referred to James Fitzgerald, a major in the Irish Brigade, who fought at Bergen-op-Zoom and had a good knowledge of Irish; Hayes, *Biographical dictionary*, p. 92. Hayes also claimed that Irish was spoken in the regiments; ibid., pp 107-21; O'Callaghan, *Irish Brigades*, pp 345-67, 407; Cullen, 'The politics of Caoineadh Airt Uí Laoire', p. 18. The battle of Fontenoy was immortalised in the Young Irelander Thomas Davis's heroic poem 'Fontenoy'. It holds a unique place in the Irish nationalist tradition. For the text of Davis's, 'The Battle of Fontenoy' and its influence of the Irish nationalist and military traditions; Davis, *Essays and poems*, pp 217-19; Bryan, 'Thomas Davis as a military influence', pp 554, 556, 557; Gavan-Duffy, *Ballad poetry of Ireland; The Irish Brigade song-book*; Gwynn and Kettle, *Battle-songs of the Irish Brigades*; Lawless, *With the Wild Geese*, p. 30; Power, 'Bicentenary of Fontenoy', pp 175-82; Mullin, 'Ranks of death', pp 323-6, 365-6. An iconographical tradition of the Irish Brigade and the battle of Fontenoy also emerged in the nineteenth century; The *United Irish Newspaper* contained a colour print of the Irish Brigade, 'The Christmas after Fontenoy' (N.L.I., *United Irish Cartoons*). See also Murtagh, 'Irish soldiers abroad', p. 299. Even in the twentieth century the battle held a greater fascination for Irish army officers and military enthusiasts than Kilmichael, Crossbarry or any of the victories of the Irish Republican Army during the War of Independence. Numerous articles relating to 'Fontenoy' appeared in the pages of *An Cosantóir*, the Irish army's military journal. They examined the role of the Irish Brigades in the French victory, the tendency of English and French historians to underplay that contribution and the debate regarding their capture of flags from the Coldstream Guards; Fitzgerald, 'Fontenoy', 599-607, 666-71; Beglin, 'The Battle of Fontenoy', pp 499-505; Petrie, 'The Irish Brigade at Fontenoy', pp 161-2; Lynch, 'Fontenoy', pp 441-4. **153** Richard Edwards to Francis Price, 4 Aug. 1745 (*H.M.C.*, 15th *report, appendix*, vii, p. 333). See also *Seasonable advice to the Protestants*, p. 36. **154** Newcastle to Chesterfield, 5 Sept. 1745 (P.R.O., S.P., 63/408/68). On 27 Sept. 1745 a ship arrived in Dundalk and the news which the captain told so alarmed the authorities that he and his mate were brought before a magistrate and swore an affidavit concerning the rout of Johnny Cope; Rushe, *History of Monaghan*, p. 59. See also P.R.O., S.P., 63/408/72; *Dub. J.*, 14-17 Sept. 1745; 63/408/110-111;

Protestants and 'elated' the papists.[155] Richard Purcell also reported that Scottish rumours influenced Catholic elation and Protestant apprehensions. He alluded to 'the high spirits of the papists at rebel successes in this most rappish [rapparee] country'.[156] Reports from Crookhaven, in County Cork, linked the second son of James III (Henry Benedict, duke of York) to a Spanish ship which arrived in December 1745. It was laden with arms, and had among its crew a Dublin priest and a captain in the Spanish army. These should not be totally dismissed as unrealistic. Henry had joined Maréchal Saxe at Dunkirk with a view to crossing the Channel, the Spanish had sent arms and money to Scotland and Catholic clergy and officers could be justifiably associated with the 'Forty-five'.[157]

Anti-Jacobite fulminations resonated in the press from the Church of Ireland bishops of Dromore (George Marlay), Elphin (Edward Synge), Clonfert (John Whitcombe), Armagh (John Hoadly) and Tuam (Josiah Hort). They invoked anti-papist rhetoric against 'the pernicious tendency of popery', the numerical superiority of Irish papists and the potential threat from 'the long abjured Pretender' and his Roman, French and Spanish confederates'.[158] Although

---

H.M.C., *Various collections*, xiii, p. III; A.N., Archives Anciennes Ms 3152, no. 2-3; B.L., Add. Ms 47, 001B, fols 127, 129, 131, 134-5, 148. There is evidence of contact between Ireland and Jacobite Scotland; McLynn, 'Ireland and the Jacobite rising of 1745', p. 343; Petrie, 'Irishmen and the '45', p. 276. The survival of folk traditions relating to sightings of Bonnie Prince Charlie in Cork, Donegal and Galway attest to his popularity in the folk tradition; Ó Buachalla, *Aisling Ghéar*, p. 434; McKenna, 'Legends of Bonnie Prince Charlie's travels in Donegal', pp 48-61; Prebble, 'The Glencolmcille tradition of Prince Charles Edward', pp 196-205. A handkerchief which this stranger used on a nose bleed was used to cure the king's evil [scrofula] for generations; O'Boyle, 'A memoir of the Young Pretender', pp 112-14. The Jacobites sent out lookalikes of the prince throughout the highlands and one of these may have gone to Ireland. I would like to thank Professor Macinnes for bringing this to my attention, Lord Lieutenant Chesterfield believed that Jacobite leaders would flee to Ireland after the defeat of the prince's forces. **155** Russell to Perceval, 8 Oct. 1745 (B.L., Add. Ms 47,001B, fol. 148). Irish exiles acted imprudently in Whitehaven after Cope's defeat; Cullen, *The Hidden Ireland: a reassessment* p. 18; McLynn, *Ireland and the Jacobite rising of 1745*, p. 339. Catholics in Connaught wore tartan plaid in the aftermath of Preston Pans; Petrie, 'Ireland and the '45', p. 276. 'The common report from all parts is that he [Charles Edward] goes on very prosperously since even the women [possibly Jenny Cameron or Colonel Anne Mackintosh who raised a regiment for Charles Edward and took her own husband into custody] take up arms for him against their own husbands'; N.L.I., Ms 2478, fols 365, 373; Pittock, *Inventing and resisting*, p. 87. Later she reported that 'as to our prince we are assured from good friends he is safe but where no one can tell'; N.L.I., Ms 2478, fol. 373. **156** Purcell to Perceval, 6 Dec. 1745 (B.L., Add. Ms 47, 001B, fol. 169). See also *Original letters to an honest sailor*. **157** Thomas Thornton to Chesterfield, Crookhaven, 17 Dec. 1745 (P.R.O., S.P., 63/408/255). This was probably the same ship which was captured by Ephraim Cooke, commander of the privateer *Ambuscade*, and for which he was presented with the freedom of the city of Cork in a silver box; Franklin, 'Extracts', p. 53. See also B.L., Add. Ms 47, 001B, fol. 174. **158** Brady (ed.), *Catholics*, 8-15 Oct. 1745, pp 68-9; *Seasonable advice*, p. 36; *The Free Briton's advice to the Pretender's declaration*, p. 5; Barrington, *A sermon preached at St Andrew's*, p. II; *Monsieur Pretendant and Signioro Pretenderillo*; Henry, *A Phillippic oration against the Pretender's son*, p. 4; Maclaine, *A sermon preached at Antrim December 18 1745*, pp 20-2; Berkeley, *An impartial history of the life and death of James II*; *The question whether Great Britain and Ireland can be otherwise than miserable under a popish king*; *Loyalty to our king and the safety of our country*, pp 5, 18.

these sermons and pamphlets sought to gird the loins of the Irish Protestant nation, they also reflected on many aspects of Irish Jacobitism which featured in contemporary literature and clerical and *émigré* correspondence with the Stuart court.[159]

Chesterfield, lord lieutenant of Ireland (January 1745-August 1746), adopted a less belligerent attitude towards Irish Catholics than that expressed by the local Protestants. Utilising Swift's spirit to appeal to their reason and common sense, he reminded Catholics that they 'would not be one hair the better' if the Pretender should succeed. He implored them not to be seduced by the religious catch-cries of the contending Catholic and Protestant clergy, who were primarily interested in tithes, abbey-lands, money and power.[160] Chesterfield's *Queries humbly proposed to the consideration of the public* (inspired by Bishop Berkeley, the other great evangelist of Irish patriotism) pursued an identical line of reasoning. Opting for the less objectionable title of Roman Catholic as opposed to papist, Chesterfield stressed Irish Catholic passivity in recent Jacobite rebellions and underlined their deficiency in arms. Nonetheless, he advised the granting of rewards to discover concealed weapons, and advocated incarcerating the most considerable Catholic noblemen in Dublin for the duration of the rebellion. The northern counties would be capable of raising 40,000 men to assist their English brethren in the suppression of a popish rebellion or external invasion, and Chesterfield convinced himself that Protestants would diligently fight for their religion and liberties.[161] While he was willing to trust Catholics who professed their respect for the government, he would leave no methods untried to establish whether they had acted contrary to these professions.[162]

Chesterfield's capacity for reasonable government asserted itself in his refusal to over-react and in his prudent and restrained conduct during the crisis.[163] His attitude is typified by his witty retort to the zealous Church of Ireland bishop who rushed to his chamber in the early morning with news that the Jacobites were going to rise. Consulting his watch, he replied 'I fancy they are, my lord, for it is 9.00'.[164] At the same time, however, he warned a suspected Jacobite that 'if the Irish behaved liked faithful subjects, they would be treated as such. If they act in a different manner, I will be worse than Cromwell'.[165] Given that he also

---

159 The *Answer to the Pretender's declaration* supplemented these religious fears with the military, economic, strategic and economic impracticalities of a Stuart restoration; *An answer to the Pretender's declaration*; *The layman's sermon*, pp 3-4, 15; Fowke, *The duty of subjects to a good prince considered*, p. 22; Brooke, *The Farmer's six letters*, pp 2, 16. Another contemporary pamphlet put forward an opposite Jacobite view; *The miserable state of Scotland since the union briefly stated*, p. 49, in *A full collection of all the proclamations and orders published by the authority of Charles, prince of Wales*. **160** [Lord Chesterfield], *The Drapier's second letter*, pp 2, 3, 6; Dickson, *New foundations*, p. 94. **161** [Lord Chesterfield], *Queries humbly proposed to the consideration of the public*, pp 3, 5, 7, 8. **162** Layden, 'Chesterfield in Ireland', p. 11. **163** Layden, 'Chesterfield in Ireland', p. 1; Connolly, *Religion*, pp 244-6. In 1743/4 the lord lieutenant ordered the pursuit of clergy and the closure of mass houses to be suspended; Kelly, 'The impact of the penal laws', p. 158. **164** Quoted in Petrie, *The Jacobite movement, the first phase*, p. 62. **165** Maty (ed.), *Memoirs of Lord Chesterfield* (London, 1777), i, p. 156, quoted in

advocated starving the inhabitants of the Scottish highlands, there is little reason to doubt his sincerity.[166] His capable performance in Ireland earned him the ringing approval of King George and contributed to the absence of widespread unrest. While Chesterfield did little to provoke Catholics into armed revolt, he occasionally indulged in anti-Jacobite rhetoric, reassuring Protestants with his sabre-rattling against the Stuart claimant, 'the seat of superstition and tyranny' [Rome], 'the enemies of the liberties of Europe' [France and Spain] and the menace of popery in Ireland'. On a practical level, he extended the £50,000 bounty on the Stuart princes to Ireland, placed an embargo on corn exports to disaffected areas in Scotland and called for reinforcements of 30,000 muskets and 10,000 broadswords.[167]

Chesterfield received a constant stream of reports from Whitehall regarding the rebellion in Scotland. These included news of the retreat from Derby and the re-capture of Carlisle, which justified his restrained approach.[168] Newspapers were filled with intelligence regarding the rebellion in Scotland and the activities of the fugitive prince's confederates but they rejected the likelihood of an invasion of Ireland.[169] Chesterfield took nothing for granted. Dismissive of the possibility of internal disorder in Ireland and confident of Cumberland's eventual triumph over the rebels in Scotland, he nonetheless encamped ten existing companies of each regiment at Bennet's Bridge, County Kilkenny. He also retained sixteen new ones for garrison duties and ordered the dragoons to be ready to serve the foot. Proclamations offered generous rewards for the fugitive Scottish rebels, whom he believed would flock to Ireland in the aftermath of Cumberland's expected victory.[170]

Protestants greeted Cumberland's defeat of the Jacobites at Culloden on 16 April 1746 with universal acclamation: this Anti-Christ of Jacobitism became the dazzling icon of Irish popular Protestantism.[171] The post-war autopsies in the popular press contained lists of Irish prisoners taken on Culloden Moor, confirming the suspicions of those Protestants who railed against the Irish regiments in the 1730s. One report contained the last speech of an Irish deserter who, having made the ultimate sacrifice for his exiled king, expired with his

Shellabarger, *Lord Chesterfield*, p. 226. **166** Lenman, *The Jacobite risings in Britain*, p. 262. **167** Newcastle to Chesterfield. 9 Oct. 1745 (P.R.O., S.P., 63/408/142). See also P.R.O., S.P., 63/408/ 157, 159, 161, 165, 167, 196, 221. **168** Newcastle to Chesterfield, 6 Jan. 1746 (P.R.O., S.P., 63/409/1-3). **169** *Fau. Dub. J.,* 15-18 Mar. 1745-6; *Pue's O.,* 11-15 Mar. 1746; *Fau. Dub. J.,* 29 Mar.-1 Apr. 1745-6; *Pue's O.,* Apr. 19-22 1746. **170** Chesterfield to Newcastle, 1 Apr. 1746 (P.R.O., S.P., 63/409/124). See also P.R.O., S.P., 63/409/120. For the 1745 militia array, see O'Brien (ed.), *Parliament, politics and people,* pp 36-7; McLynn, 'Ireland and the Jacobite rising, pp 340-2. A member of the McGregor clan allegedly visited Cavan to recruit for Prince Charles; Rushe, *Monaghan for two hundred years,* p. 61. **171** *Nelson's Dub. Cour.,* 19 Dec. 1747. Purcell informed Perceval that 'there has been great rejoicing all over the kingdom for the victory over the rebels which we believe to have been so complete as to put it out of their power to be further troublesome'; B.L., Add. Ms 47, 002A, fol. 37. See also Spenser to Price, 15 May 1746 (N.L.W., Ms 3580C); Kelly, 'The glorious and immortal memory', p. 40.

cause on his lips.[172] Cork Protestants rejoiced at the news of the 'late happy success in Scotland', which mortified the papists of 'low and desperate fortunes', who 'now own that they never again expect such another good chance to put a popish king on the throne of England'.[173]

In his thanksgiving sermon for the suppression of rebellion, Moses Magill summarised Protestant attitudes in the aftermath of the 'Forty-five'. Restating orthodox arguments against popery, hereditary right, heresy, arbitrary power, Jacobite challenges to the British constitution and Protestant religion and liberty, Magill reminded his congregation of the dangers posed by this latest stirring of the seemingly dormant Jacobite snake. He reflected on Charles Edward's challenge to the Hanoverian dynasty by his capture of Scotland, the gravity of which has often been understated by those historians who discount Jacobitism after 1691 and emphasise the inevitable onward march of the Protestant nation in both Britain and Ireland.[174] Similarly, Magill's attempts to explain the 'remarkable silence' of the papists in this period should not be lost on those who have too quickly dismissed the survival of Jacobitism in Ireland. Such a view ignores the elaborate military operations undertaken to counteract any attempted rising, the relative size of the Irish military establishment, the indolent opportunism of the English and Scottish Jacobites and the political and military priorities of the Stuart court.[175] Magill's opinion regarding the impossibility of genuine Catholic deference towards the house of Hanover is reflected in Irish Jacobite poetry, and in the rhetoric used by the Catholic clergy and episcopal hopefuls when writing to their Stuart master:

> We must confess that the papists of this kingdom have been remarkable silent and peaceable in this critical juncture of affairs. But whether the prudent and wise administration of our excellent governor, their own policy and deep-concerted designs contributed more to this inoffensive behaviour, than true principle or persuasion, can no longer be a secret to any who look upon their past actions. For you might as well pretend to reason an Ethiopian out of his colour, or inspire the rapacious vulture with the gentleness of a dove, as to believe that they can be friends to a government, who are obliged by all ties of religion as well as inclination to favour every attempt to pervert it.[176]

---

172 Two Irishmen who had deserted to the Jacobites were executed at Tyburn; *Pue's O.,* 11-15 Nov. 1746. One of those executed stated that he died 'because his k[ing] was not on the t[hrone]'; *Pue's O.,* 15-18 Nov. 1746. *Pue's Occurrences* published a list of the Franco-Irish prisoners of war; *Pue's O.,* 29 Apr.-3 May 1746; *Pue's O.,* 3-6 May 1746. Mac Donnell, 'Some documents relating to the involvement of the Irish Brigade in the rebellion of 1745', pp 3-22.   **173** R. Purcell to Perceval, 20 May 1746 (B.L., Add. Ms 47, 002A, fol. 39).   **174** Connolly, *Religion;* Bartlett, *Fall and rise.* There are opposing views; Black, 'Could the Jacobites have won?', pp 24-9; Wagner, 'Scotland in the late eighteenth century', p. 148.   **175** Beresford, 'Ireland', p. 175; introduction, pp 29-30.   **176** Magill, *A sermon preached in the parish church of St Mary's Dublin,* p. 16. Henry Brooke attacked those who would insinuate that there was

IV

The tendency to view Irish Jacobite inactivity as conclusive testimony of Irish Catholic indifference towards the house of Stuart not only distorts the testimonies of the poets, *émigrés* and the greater Catholic populace, but also the evidence of Jacobite sympathy in the popular press. After the debacle of the 'Forty-five', writings in defence of Charles Edward surfaced in the press. The adventures of 'The Wanderer' achieved mythical status, not only in Ireland but in the English and Scottish press as well.[177]

There was good reason however for Jacobites to exercise circumspection in sympathising with Charles Edward in public. Catholic adherence to Jacobitism and the doctrine of passive obedience[178] are two explanations for their limited printed contributions to political debate in the first half of the eighteenth-century.[179] The striking exceptions were Cornelius Nary who considered the Jacobite cause worthy of respect, and Dr John Curry whose major work on the 1641 rebellion included in its index the Jacobite tract *Gallienus Redivivus* and Charles Leslie's account of William III's complicity the massacre of the Mac Donnells of Glencoe in 1692.[180]

The Wanderer, printed for William Brien and Richard James in Dublin in 1747, contributed to the mythologising of Charles Edward, already evident in the other kingdoms.[181] The author was at pains to stress his loyalty to the house of Hanover, a wise move in view of the prosecution of the author of the seditious Jacobite pamphlet *Ascanius* which appeared in the same year's and which the

no necessity for a general alarm; [Brooke], *The Farmer's six letters*, p. 16. This close relationship between Catholicism and Jacobitism remained a major theme of the popular Protestant tradition; *The axe laid to the root*, pp 4-5. The successive invasion scares of the Seven Year's War and the associations between Whiteboyism and Jacobitism prompted the witch-hunt against Fr Nicholas Sheehy in the 1760s, show that the author's opinions survived in the popular Protestant consciousness. See also *The chevalier's hopes*, pp 4-5, 17; Kelly, 'The glorious and immortal memory', pp 25-52.   **177** Pittock, *Poetry*, pp 162-78; Monod, *Jacobitism*, pp 81-8.   **178** Goldie, 'Political thought of the Anglican revolution', pp. 102-37.   **179** Leighton, *Catholicism*, p. 11. Leighton believed that Charles O'Conor, the leading Hanoverian conformist of the period, did not adopt his pro-Hanoverian stance until the 1750s. O'Conor's public utterances could be viewed in the context of his struggle to hold on to his lands; his 'pseudo-Whiggery' might have been a political device, as was his choosing to avoid the thorny question of Jacobitism until the 1760s; see ibid., pp 58, 101-4. Many historians, including Cullen, have seized on O'Conor's oft'-quoted 'as for the Pretender I neither like or detest his cause …' and his opinion 'that the affairs of this kingdom may be well enough administered with or without him [the Pretender]' to underline his diffidence towards the Stuarts, without giving due regard to his ongoing litigation; Cullen, *The Hidden Ireland: a reassessment*, p. 10. O'Conor's diary shows his opportunistic attitude towards the rebellion. He noted that the son of King James is in Scotland, troubling the three kingdoms and cautiously added that he did not know whether it is a good thing 'Mac Rígh Séamais anois in Albain ag buadhairt na dtrí ríoghacht. Níl a fhios agam nach amhlaidh is fearr'. The following April, having been informed that the civil war had gone completely against the Scots, he added, if it is true, it is for the best 'Más fíor so as amhlaidh is fearr é'; Beresford, 'Ireland', pp 176-7. Ó Buachalla does not doubt O'Conor's anti-Jacobitism but sees it as an exceptional revolutionary political ideology with a modern slant to it; Ó Buachalla, *Aisling Ghéar*, p. 422.   **180** Leighton, *Catholicism*, pp 58, 174.   **181** *The Wanderer*, p. 13. Charles Edward's manifesto to his rightful subjects was printed in Dublin in August 1745; Hayes, author of *The Wanderer* had clearly read.[182] His tract exhibited a Scott-like romantic attachment to Charles Edward, and an appreciation of the Stuart prince, thinly veiled by Hanoverian royalist rhetoric.[183] The author, using traditional Jacobite arguments, questioned the legitimacy of the Glorious Revolution and the attainder against the Stuart prince (the future James III) 'driven out [of the kingdom] long before he had the use of reasoning, while consequently he was incapable of doing good or harm'.[184] He refuted the smear of cowardice against Charles Edward by the ingenious reasoning that it detracted from the triumphs of Cumberland.[185] The writer dismissed allegations of rashness against 'The Wanderer' and the aspersions which had been cast upon the Scottish nation. He castigated the fickle English whose idle promises had induced the luckless prince to pursue his father's cause in the first instance.[186] He believed that the bravery of the 'Young Adventurer' should not be denied, and he was deemed worthy of employment in the armies of a foreign prince.[187] His reference to the design laid before the Stuart king for a conquest of Britain or Ireland reflected similar memoirs despatched by Irish *émigrés* in France and Spain. The author shared the Stuart king's opinion that the political spirit of the Irish nation had been broken, and that they no longer possessed the means or the inclination to engage in such a hopeless adventure. He reflected on the Stuart king's misgivings about the cultivation of internal rebellion in his usurped kingdoms, and portrayed the French king as the evil genius of the Stuarts.

The author of *The Wanderer* perceived that the Catholic populace had been leaderless, disarmed and unwilling to intensify their persecution by the English. This conforms with the claims of other memoirs from Irish Jacobites to the exiled court from the 1690s to the 1760s, and shows the impact of the penal laws on the contemporary political consciousness. His disdain at the English destruction of the ancient Irish reflected the attitude of Nicholas Plunkett:

> In Ireland the ancient families had been trampled underfoot by the English to whom they, especially those who had not politically conformed to the Protestant religion, were little (if at all) better than the slaves in America; that the Roman Catholics were a considerable body and he might expect a powerful assistance from men who hoped to recover not

Biographical dictionary, p. 323.   **182** *Ascanius.* Piaras Mac Gearailt was aware of this pseudonym for Charles Edward. In one poem he expressed the belief that the crown will be on Ascanius; 'Is beidh coróin ar Ascánius'; Piaras Mac Gearailt, 'A Mhalaí beag ó', in Ó Foghludha (eag.), *Amhráin Phiarais*, p. 30.   **183** *The Wanderer.* The label of 'Young Adventurer' featured in contemporary literature; [Brooke], *The Farmer's six letters*, p. 5. Histories of the 1745 rebellion circulated in contemporary Dublin; *Genuine memoirs of John Murray, late secretary to the young Pretender; A genuine and authentic history; A history of the rebellion raised against his majesty King George II;* Boyse, *Impartial history of the late rebellion.* **184** The author also dwelt on his father's (James III's) 'long and irksome wanderings'; *The Wanderer,* p. 6; *Ascanius,* pp 76-7.   **185** *The Wanderer,* pp 8-11. See also *Ascanius,* pp 12, 14, 21-2, 38, 43-5, 79, 87-88, 91.   **186** *The Wanderer,* pp 12, 13. See also *Ascanius,* pp 16-17, 24.   **187** *The Wanderer,* p. 15.

only their liberty but their estates and obtain a free exercise of their religion.[188]

The author believed that Jacobite impotency, French perfidy and British naval supremacy would cure the young Pretender of his wanderlust.[189] Britain's naval supremacy had rested heavily on dependable Protestant winds in the period 1744 to 1746 when it had frustrated successive invasion attempts by Maréchal Saxe, Lord Clare and Thomas Lally. It proved unable to inhibit the considerable volume of traffic between France and Scotland during the 'Forty-five'. It also did not prevent the eventual rescue of the fugitive prince, or stifle successive invasion scares which disturbed Ireland and Britain during the latter years of the Seven Years War.

The sentiments expressed in 'The Wanderer' also featured in contemporary Jacobite and Whig writings. Charles Wogan, Donnchadh Rua Mac Conmara, Eoghan an Mhéirín Mac Cárthaigh and the author of *The axe laid to the root* all condemned French duplicitous opportunism during and after the 'Forty-five'. *The Wanderer's* description of the adverse political and religious welfare of Irish Catholics also echoed Abbé Mac Geoghegan's *Histoire d'Irlande*, published in Paris between 1758 and 1762, and Bernard Rothe's description of post-'Forty-five' Catholicism.[190]

V

The survival of Jacobitism in this period is clearly demonstrated by the fact that Catholic clergymen retained an interest in Jacobite politics in spite of Charles Edward's failure to regain his father's crowns. This is borne out by the post-rebellion correspondence of the Irish Jesuit Fr Bernard Rothe to James III in 1748. A clandestine meeting of higher clergy and laity in London had orchestrated a campaign to persuade the imperial government to intercede on behalf of Irish Catholics at the peace conference at Breda, which preceded the Treaty of Aix-la-Chapelle (1748). Fundamental points regarding the tenuous position of Irish Catholicism can be gleaned from Rothe's letter. If this approach to the

---

188 *The Wanderer*, pp 18. See also *Ascanius*, p. iv; Geoghegan, 'A Jacobite history', p. 41. **189** *The Wanderer*, p. 71. See also *Ascanius*, p. 25. Such trust in the 'wooden walls' had been central to Archbishop King's sense of Hanoverian inviolability in the first decades of the century and featured in the writings of Sir Richard Cox; Cox, *A charge delivered to the Grand Jury at the general quarter-sessions of the peace held for the county of Cork at Bandon-Bridge, 12 July 1748*, p. 19. **190** See p. 238, fns 40-1. Mac Geoghegan's *History* stated that 'the manner in which the Irish have been treated is contrary to the principles of Magna Carta, that celebrated code in which the English nation glories, and of which they boast: the Irish are deprived of that liberty which, according even to their oppressors, should be the portion of all mankind. They are forced to submit to a hateful yoke; they have exerted themselves in favour of their lawful prince; their resistance to usurpation is considered as rebellion ...'; Geoghegan, 'A Jacobite history', p. 41.

emperor represented an attempt by Irish Catholics to 'shift for themselves' at Aix-la-Chapelle, then it was not taken without due recourse to the exiled king in Rome. This prince's father had effectively given them the same advice nearly sixty years earlier in the aftermath of the battle of the Boyne. Rothe felt obligated to sell this package to the Stuart king with the promise that it would prevent the total extinction of Irish Catholicism, and ensure the survival of Irish Catholic loyalty to his luckless cause. This underlined the pivotal position which James III retained in Irish Catholic affairs until his death in 1766:

> The Catholics of Ireland, whose continual persecution since the Revolution was much increased by the prince of Wales's glorious actions in Great Britain, thought the juncture of this peace [Treaty of Aix-la Chapelle] a favourable circumstance for obtaining some relaxation of the rigours of the laws, a making or appearing every day against them. A small number of them, privately commissioned by most of the gentry and prime persons of the Catholic clergy at home, met in London and debated the matter. By the general situation in Europe and by some hints they had by persons in prime business, they thought the most efficacious remedy would be to apply to the court of Vienna for a strong recommendation in favour of the Catholics of Ireland ... Far from being contrary to his majesty's interest, [it] might promote it by saving from a total extinction those principles which tie most strictly subjects to allegiance, and attaches particularly the greatest number of Irish to your majesty's person and cause.[191]

The Monaghan cleric, Dr James McKenna, who had kept in close contact with the Stuart court throughout the 'Forty-five', followed the adventures of the elusive prince. He relayed his information in cipher from Brussels, alluding to the triumphs of 'the Velvet Dresser of Eden' (Saxe) against 'Judith's flowers' (the allies) and, in particular, 'Mr Van Scheuter' (Cumberland). McKenna also included reports on the executed Jacobite lords Kilmarnock and Balmerino. He provided his contact in Rome with a prospective correspondent in Dublin, (J. White at Robert White's, a merchant in Thomas Street), from whom he might obtain intelligence.[192] He laid particular emphasis on 'Mr Traveller in Fl.' (Louis

191 Fr Bernard Rothe to James III, Paris. 23 Dec. 1748 (R.A., Ms 295, fol. 164), edited in Fagan (ed.), *Stuart papers*, ii, pp 99-100. Charles Wogan and Jacobite pamphleteers described the Irish as 'spartan helots' and criticised England's breaches of public faith; *The Thistle*, pp 12, 16 and 18; *The miserable state of Scotland since the union*, p. 47; *A full collection of all the proclamations and orders published by the authority of Charles, prince of Wales*; Flood, *Wogan*, pp 136, 146. 192 Fr James McKenna to Edgar, 13 October 1746 (R.A., Ms 278, fol. 70). See also R.A., Ms 277, fol. 70; R.A., Ms 277, fol. 137. The execution of Kilmarnock and Balmerino and other Jacobite trials absorbed the Dublin press; *Memoirs of the lives and families of the Lords Kilmarnock, Cromartie and Balmerino*; Foster, *Account of the behaviour of the late earl of Kilmarnock*; *A review of Mr James Foster's account*; *Memoirs of the life of Lord*

XV in Flanders), 'the miscarriages of Judith' (the allies) there, 'the factor's motions in Nongiva' (Avignon) and 'Aderb' (Breda), 'the death of G. Reinogil' (General [Francis] Ligonier), 'the Jobber's [Whig?] fear of Mr Traveller' (Louis XV) and his 'velvet dressers' (Irish Brigades?) and the ineffectuality of 'Mr Van Scheuter' (Cumberland).[193] His clerical colleague Luke Geoghegan also sent information from London regarding the need for '6,000 flasks of red or white foreign [soldiers]' which he believed would 'complete our happiness'.[194]

The preliminary peace articles from The Hague disgusted one Irish Protestant pamphleteer, particularly the Dutch proposal to grant a subsidy to the exiled Stuarts in return for a solemn commitment never again to disturb the tranquillity of Britain or Europe. He cast aspersions on the Dutch for exaggerating the disruptive potential of the Stuart claimant in European politics. However, this understatement of the Jacobite threat is at odds with the political history of Europe during the first half of the eighteenth-century. It ignores the extent to which France and Spain (and other European powers including Sweden, Russia and even Austria) continually manipulated the Stuart cause for their own short-term political expediency. This dismissive pamphlet, written less than four years after 40,000 French had mobilised in support of the Stuart cause at Dunkirk, also ignores the fact that Charles Edward had succeeded in temporarily capturing most of Scotland with minimal assistance from those powers who would have been expected to assist him. It also belied the consternation which he caused in Hanoverian Britain, and the extent to which he remained a trump-card in a possible French invasion of Britain until the end of the Seven Years War:

> The wise Dutchman has undoubtedly a great passion towards Europe and thinks it full time after such prodigious hard work in killing and being killed, that its wearied inhabitants should go to sleep quietly and not be disturbed by the barking of that dog the Pretender who will never let them rest in peace, but make them start in unstilled slumbers unless Britain will concur in coaxing him and then all Europe may sleep together...I never, till now, imagined the young Italian gentleman of such importance that all Europe might not sleep until he had his fee. [195]

Lovat; A free examination of the modern romance entitled the life of Lovat; Account of the behaviour of Lovat; Account of the pedigree and actions of Lovat; Memoirs of the life and character of Charles Radcliffe; Proceedings of the court of St. Margaret's Hill. **193** Fr McKenna to Edgar, 12 Mar. 1747 (R.A., Ms 282, fol. 44); Fagan (ed.), *Stuart papers*, ii, pp 57-8. McKenna later petitioned for the diocese of Clogher in May 1747 and provided other cryptic information regarding Charles Edward; R.A., Ms 284, fol. 11. He expressed optimism at the possibility of another French sponsored invasion at the end of 1747; R.A., Ms 288, fol. 62. See also R.A., Ms 292, fol. 166; R.A., Ms 289, fol. 137. **194** Geoghegan to Edgar, London, 29 Mar. 1749 (R.A., Ms 297, fol. 133). **195** *Remarks on the preliminary articles of peace*, p. 5.

He believed that the main drawback of this financial proposal to satisfy the Stuarts was that the French and the pope had already expended vast amounts in support of the Stuarts, and that Great Britain would undoubtedly end up footing the bill. Moreover, the payment of one single farthing to the Stuarts would be 'as much as an acknowledgment of his right to the throne of Great Britain'. The greatest authority behind the house of Hanover remained the voice of the people (a dubious claim when the entire population of the three kingdoms is taken into consideration). He also maintained that Charles Edward would discount any faith with heretics and use the money to attempt to regain his throne.[196]

The peace-talks also interested the Irish poet Éadbhárd de Nógla. He expressed dismay at the conclusion of the Treaty of Aix-la-Chapelle, (1748) ('Nuair a socruigheadh ar chonradh Aix-la Chapelle') in his poem 'Is craidhte an scéal seo léightear dúinn' (It is terrible this news which has been read to us). His verse sheds further light on the role of the poet in the diffusion and inter-pretation of English-language European war news. The subject-matter of this poem shows beyond any reasonable doubt that Irish-speakers had access to European military and diplomatic intelligence that was at least as accurate as the material available in contemporary pamphlets. The poet appraises the diplomatic and military welfare of the major European powers and dynasties at the conclusion of the war of the Austrian succession and contrasts them with the woeful state of the Stuart cause. The English hero (George II/Cumberland) were agreeable in the cause with the great prince of Paris (Louis XV). The states of Holland were powerful at the negotiations although bruised and crushed in battle. Spain and Don Carlos, king of Naples have been humbled. However, the poet has no concern for these but for his powerful young, unhappy man, the dark lamented youth (James III). Although Maria (Theresa, the holy Roman Empress) has been left withour succour and her husband stripped to no more status than a duke, the poet did not sympathise with her sorrow. Geneva was free without discontent/and the great man in Modena (the duke of Modena) was cheerful. Nobody was unhappy but the dark lamented youth.

> Tá ráib an Bhéarla réidh 'san chúis
> Le prionnsa Phárais mhóir
> 'S an Stát on Haolland tréan 'san chúirt
> fuair brughadh agus cárnadh i ngleó;

---

196 *Remarks on the preliminary articles of peace*, pp 6, 15, 18. However, this Dutch proposal served as a precursor to George III's granting of a pension to Henry, Cardinal York, after he had been deprived of his episcopal see of Frescati by soldiers of the French republic in the 1790s; MacClean, *Bonnie Prince Charlie*, pp 371-2. Although this claim that Charles Edward would discount any faith made with heretics reflected orthodox rhetoric, it certainly showed an appreciation of the Stuart prince's determination to regain the throne of his ancestors at any cost. This was justified by the ease with which he embraced Protestantism in the 1750s.

Tá an Spáinneach maol gan faobhar 'na lúib,
'S Don Carlos Réx ó Naples chughainn,
'S níl cás liom é acht mo thréin-fhear dubhach,
M'uíleaceán dubh óg.

Tá Máire, an chael-bhean mhaordha ar siubhal
Gan congnadh d'fhagháil chun bróg,
's gan d'fhagháil de réim dá céile acht Diúic,
's ní cumha liom fath a ndeór;
Ta stát Genébha saor gan smúit
'S an sáir-fhear séimh Modéna subhach
mo lá is mo léan gan éinne dubhach
Acht m'uileachán dubh óg.[197]

Support for the Stuarts involved more than the occasional cryptic correspondence or critical pamphlet. An attack on a Whig reveller in post-rebellion
Ireland suggests that not all Irish Jacobites were totally overawed in the aftermath
of the 'Forty-five'. One Irish gentleman, at least, was unwilling to follow Nary
or later O'Conor's lead in pandering to Protestant sensibilities with hollow praise
for the hero of popular Protestantism:

> Friday evening as a housekeeper in Drumcondra lane was celebrating
> King William's birthday by putting on a bonfire and firing his musket,
> a gentleman's coach came up to him and after treating him with very
> insolent language, kicked the fire about him and having wrenched the
> gun out of his hand struck him herewith so violently on the head and
> made off that his life is despaired of.[198]

Protestants, for their part, made few conciliatory gestures towards Catholics.
Celebrations on the anniversary of Aughrim took place with the usual demonstrations of joy and gratitude. They included the additional spectacle of a
reading from King's *State of the Protestants* by a person whose paternal grand-
father had refused to drink damnation to the prince of Orange in 1688, and
whose maternal grand-uncles fought at the Boyne with the Enniskilliners.[199] If
they chose to fête those heroes of the 1690s, they took a tough line against any

---

197 Éadbhard de Nógla, 'Is cráidhte an scéal seo léightear dúinn' Ó Foghludha (eag.), *Mil na hEigse*,
p. 48. For terms of Treaty of Aix-la-Chapelle, see Cannon, *Oxford companion to British history*, p. 14.
The poet's praise for the duke of Modena might have something to do with the fact he was related
to 'James III'. A poet called 'Tadhg an Tarta' noted that he got his news from the Friday paper 'i
nóchtain na hAoine'; Ó Buachalla, *Aisling Ghéar*, p. 372. Tadhg Ó Neachtain' was preoccupied with
the contemporary press; ibid., pp 372-84. See Introduction, p. 47; p. 277, fn. 25; pp 339-40, fns. 69-
70. **198** *Dub. Week. J.*, 12 Nov. 1748. **199** *Censor*, 8-15 July 1749 (P.R.O., S.P., 63/411/82). The
Culloden commemoration featured in the press; *Pue's O.*, 18-21 Apr. 1752. Bartlett has described this

who ventured to toast Charles Edward: John Costello of Ennis, County Clare, who had dared to drink his health, was pilloried and imprisoned:

> Saturday last the assizes ended in Ennis, John Costello was found guilty of drinking the Pretender's son's health by the name of Prince Charles Stuart and sentenced to be pilloried, imprisoned and to give security for his good behaviour. [200]

The most persuasive testimony to the relevance of Jacobitism in this period is provided by James III's continued role as nominator to Irish bishoprics.[201] One such instance is documented by the Jacobite agent, Fr James McKenna. He petitioned James III for the vacancy in the 'farm' (diocese) of Kilmore' caused by the recent death of the 'overseer' (bishop), Michael MacDonogh.[202] Daniel O'Reilly, one of his rivals, complained of the unseemly scramble in Rome for this latest post before the wishes of the Kilmore clergy were known. His letter reproached the Stuart king, attacking his partiality for the regular clergy and men of 'low' and 'mean' birth. This social bias remained a feature of ecclesiastical politics in the period of James III's suzerainty over the Irish episcopate. However, he did vouch for the loyalty and gentility of the major Catholic families of the diocese.[203] James regularly canvassed the clergy and laity at diocesan level, displaying his sensitivity to their wishes, as well as reminding them of his influence on their religious (and political) lives.

With the death of Bernard McMahon, 'prime overseer' (bishop) of Armagh in May 1747, James McKenna diverted his attention from the disputed Kilmore diocese. He sought the powerful patronage of Segnior Barisesu (James III) and referred to James and Cardinal Protector (Nereo) Corsini's earlier receipt of postulations on his behalf from the clergy and laity of that diocese, and his support from the Protestant and Catholic gentry. This particular diocese contained the baronies of Upper and Lower Truagh which comprised the lands of his ancestors forfeited at the rebellion (1641).[204] Despite failing to attain this episcopal nomination, this persistent cleric continued to ingratiate himself with the king and his faithful secretary, James Edgar. He sent them presents of linen in early 1750,

---

work as one of the three works in the Protestant triptych; Bartlett, *Fall and rise*, p. 7.   **200** *Pue's O.*, 3-7 Sept. 1751.   **201** Giblin, 'The Stuart nomination of bishops 1687-1765', pp 35-47.   **202** Fr McKenna to Edgar, 7 Feb. 1747 (R.A., Ms 281, fol. 65). The deceased MacDonogh had served as confessor to James III and Bonnie Prince Charlie before assuming the bishopric of Kilmore; Fenning, 'Michael MacDonogh', pp 139-40.   **203** O'Reilly to [Edgar?], Antwerp, 3 Feb. 1747 (R.A., Ms 281, fol. 51). See also R.A., Ms 279, fol. 72; R.A. Ms 282, fol. 82. The Protestant pamphlet tradition of the post-'Forty-five' period derided Catholics as 'the professed slaves of a foreign bishop and a Popish Pretender'; *Seasonable advice*, p. 9.   **204** Fr McKenna to Edgar, Dublin, 31 May 1747 (R.A., Ms 284, fol. 11). See also R.A., Ms 294, fol. 186; R.A., Ms 295, fol. 175. Ross McMahon's elevation to Armagh left Clogher vacant Petitions for the primacy were sent for Bishop Stuart from Randal O'Neill, the only surviving son of Sir Gordon O'Neill; R.A., Ms 296, fol. 48.

along with information on the strength of Jacobite feeling in Ireland during the Seven Years War, and reports on the internal wrangling amongst the Irish Catholic episcopate regarding the Stuart nomination of bishops. The indirect route chosen for his trans-shipment of the linen, through the Irish Jacobite *entrepôt* of Leghorn, and through the good offices of a Dublin merchant called Cosgrove, showed the continued interaction between Ireland and Europe necessitated circumvention and caution.[205] The vacant see of Cork attracted solicitations by prospective candidates (including William Carroll, Thomas Mahony and Dr John O'Brien) to the Stuart court in exile.[206] A postulation in favour of Dr O'Brien, signed by thirty-seven Irish Catholic notables, refuted aspersions cast on his gentility. The petition recounted the sufferings of his forebears for the Stuart cause, and pontificated against mechanical professions and trades.[207]

While the Irish clergy clamoured for episcopal benefices, Henry, duke of York, shared his father's despair and opted for a cardinal's hat.[208] His religious zeal did not meet with unequivocal approval from the Irish Jacobite exiles, including one who later clamoured for a position in the Irish mission. John O'Sullivan expressed disbelief but ultimate resignation to King James's pleasure. Myles McDonnell shared Charles Edward's despondency, fully aware of the extent to which the Stuart dynasty had been irreparably damaged by its latest association with the old bugbears of 'popery' and 'bigotry'.[209] His forthrightness did little to damage his episcopal career prospects, as Edgar later informed him that he should secure postulations from the clergy and gentry for the next diocese that fell vacant in Connaught.[210] McDonnell excused his inability to 'form a party in the usual way', but left Edgar in no doubt of his impeccable Jacobite genealogy and his inclination to return to his native province.[211]

VI

In view of the material surveyed in this chapter, the received wisdom concerning the failure of the 1745 rebellion to impact on Ireland should be re-considered. From the outbreak of the War of Jenkins's Ear to the end of the War of the

---

205 Fr McKenna to Edgar, Dublin, 13 Oct. 1750 (R.A., Ms 311, fol. 162).   **206** For examples of petitions in favour of W. Carroll's gentility and postulations in favour of Dr O'Brien; R.A., Ms 283, fol. 118; see also R.A., Ms 284, fol. 173; R.A., Ms 287, fols 14, 86; Ms 379, fol. 109; Ms 288, fol. 70. **207** Petition from the gentlemen of County Cork, 3 July 1747 (R.A., Ms 285, fol. 43). For similar disdain for vile mechanical professions; Fagan (ed.), *Stuart papers*, i, p. 173.   **208** McLynn, *Bonnie Prince Charlie*, pp 327-8.   **209** Sir J. O'Sullivan to Edgar, 14 July 1747 (R.A., Ms 285, fol. 125). See also R.A., Ms 285, fol. 142; Ms 286, fol. 59.   **210** Myles McDonnell to James III, 15 July 1747 (R.A., Ms 285, fol. 126). See also R.A., Ms 285, fol. 200; R.A., Ms 286, fol. 76; R.A., Ms 305, fol. 52.   **211** Myles McDonnell to Edgar, 1 Oct. 1747 (R.A., Ms 287, fol. 86). For Edgar's answer to Fr Nugent's appeal for a bishopric; R.A., Ms 299, fol. 33. Dr Mark Skerett later sent a coded message to the Stuart court regarding 'skilful farmers' and 'the landlords'; R.A., Ms 301, fol. 79; see also Fagan (ed), *Stuart papers*, ii, pp 4, 23, 116.

Austrian Succession, Irish poets and their audience had an acute awareness of European and domestic political and military affairs, and their possible consequences for the Stuart cause. Jacobitism also surfaced in seditious health-drinking and attacks on Hanoverian royalists. Irish Jacobites retained their clandestine links with continental Europe through intermittent recruitment and privateer activity. The Stuart king also maintained a hold on Irish Catholics through episcopal appointments. In the aftermath of the 'Forty-five', clerics continued to petition James III for episcopal and canonical preferments. Irish-based clergymen, such as the mobile and prolific James McKenna, supplied the court with analyses of Irish ecclesiastical and European political developments. Correspondence, nominations and postulations from, for and on behalf of Irish episcopal candidates deployed Jacobite rhetoric which reflected the sentiments of their exiled brethren, and stressed ecclesiastical and temporal loyalty to king and country. The survival of Jacobite zeal helps explain the struggle for the conscience of the Irish Catholics which would be waged in the late 1750s and 1760s, between Jacobite royalists and Hanoverian accomodationalists.

Although members of the Irish diaspora corresponded with their exiled king throughout this period and petitioned him for charity, relics, indulgences, medals and touch-pieces, a more active Jacobitism emerged among the *émigrés* with the outbreak of war with Spain in 1739. Influential Irish exiles (Charles Wogan, Abbé Tyrrell, John Burke of Clanricarde, Thomas Lally, Felix O'Neill, John Redmond and Patrick D'Arcy) viewed Ireland as a possible destination for a Jacobite invasion. All of these men (with the exception of Wogan who relied on first-hand evidence) visited their native land and provided the Stuart court with accurate intelligence. Others sought to join the impending invasion forces. With the failure of the 'Forty-five', their attention turned to the prince's providential rescue and the duplicity of France, before resuming their petitions for episcopal, canonical and military preferment.

Protestant opinion oscillated between complacency and fear. It observed Catholic exhilaration, expectation and arrogance at the developments in the European and later domestic theatres. It celebrated the declaration of war with Spain, victories at Dettingen and Culloden, and engaged in numerous effigy burnings, loyal toastings and the foundation of loyal societies in the aftermath of the 'Forty-five'. The real threat of a Franco-Spanish invasion persisted throughout the period, and the press reported battles fought between Saxe and Cumberland, and the conduct of the Irish Brigades in their engagements. Local political figures remained fully aware of the naval preparations for an amphibious onslaught against England or Ireland in 1743 and 1744. The haughtiness of the Catholics in rural areas, and the related activities of recruiters and privateers, compounded their apprehensions.

The Chesterfield's administration adopted a policy of conditional toleration during the 'Forty-five'. Nevertheless, his railings against 'the Pretender' and popery, his swift proclamation of the Stuart princes and his extensive military preparations, reassured Protestants. Moreover, the self-confidence which emanated from Dublin Castle and its confines should be contrasted with evidence from more vulnerable Protestant communities scattered through south Munster, Connaught and north-east Ulster. They often felt isolated amongst their majority Catholic neighbours or felt threatened by their close proximity to the Scottish theatre of war in 1745-6. Finally, the invasion threats which persisted during the Seven Years War provide a ringing refuttal of a casual dismissal of Catholic expectations or Protestant fears.

CHAPTER 7

''S gan oidhre Rí Séamas i mBreatain 'na dhéidh':[1] the Jacobite twilight, 1752-66

The era between the Seven Years War and the death of James III in 1766 constitutes the penultimate phase of the Jacobite era in Ireland. Although the Treaty of Aix-la-Chapelle (1748) concluded the War of the Austrian Succession, it provided only a brief respite in the unresolved conflict between Europe's greatest naval power (Britain) and land power (France) which was not to be decided until Waterloo. A subsidy treaty between Britain and Russia in 1755 compelled Frederick the Great of Prussia to seek an accommodation with Britain. This diplomatic initiative resulted in the Treaty of Westminster in January 1756, a mutual defensive pact to counter French aggression against Hanover and Austrian pretensions towards its lost province of Silesia. An isolated and embittered Austria turned to her old enemy France, signing the Treaty of Versailles in May 1758. These new alliances constituted a 'diplomatic revolution', radically transforming the old system (in which Britain, the Empire and Holland arrayed themselves against France (and later Bourbon Spain). The conflict itself began with Frederick the Great's pre-emptive strike on Saxony in August 1756. After suffering setbacks at Kölin (June 1757) and Hastenbeck (July 1757), the Prusso-British alliance scored stunning victories at Rossbach (1757), Minden (1758) and in the colonial territories of Louisbourg and India. French desperation forced Choiseul, the new French minister of war, to attempt to draw Charles Edward into a French-sponsored invasion of the three kingdoms.[2]

Choiseul threw all his energy and resources into the most ambitious and aggressive project against Britain and Ireland since 1688. It was intended that there would be three simultaneous expeditions against the three kingdoms. Charles Edward had arrived in Paris on 25 November 1756 and met with a number of prominent members of the French military, including the Irish Jacobite Thomas Lally, the duc de Richelieu and Choiseul himself. Admiral Conflan's Brest fleet, which was designated to transport Maréchal d'Aiguillon's

---

1 Art Mac Cumhaigh, 'Moladh Shéamais Pluincéad', in Ó Fiaich (eag.), *Art Mac Cumhaigh*, p. 129.   2 Szechi, *The Jacobites*, Duffy, *The Wild Goose and the Eagle*, Nordmann, 'Choiseul and the last Jacobite attempt of 1759', pp 204-7; McLynn, *The Jacobites*, pp 35-8; Black, *Culloden and the '45*, p. 201.

army from Quiberon Bay, was intercepted and destroyed by Admiral Hawke in the Royal Navy's most memorable action since La Hogue.

Irish Jacobitism retained the same characteristics and the same personnel in its twilight years. European diplomatic developments and military engagements engaged the attention of Irish Jacobites. The poets responded to invasion rumours with renewed entreaties to Charles Edward and the Wild Geese. They monitored political and military events from Moscow to the Mississippi, and balked at any accommodation with the Hanoverians. Irish clerics sent information regarding Irish secular and ecclesiastical politics to the Stuart king in Rome. The *émigrés* upon whom they depended for deliverance still proposed invasion schemes during the Seven Years War. The death of James III, and the waning of Irish political influence at the French and Spanish courts eroded the Jacobite interest in continental Europe. At the same time, a social and ideological rift emerged within the Irish Catholic polity. The Catholic aristocratic, gentry and mercantile interest advocated an accommodation with the Hanoverian *status quo*, while doctrinaire Jacobites mobilised the Stuart king's still formidable ideological arsenal to scuttle these conciliatory schemes. Catholic overtures to the Hanoverian regime became more frequent and successful in the late 1750s and 1760s.

I

Although Ireland had not been the target of the 1745 invasion, the French threat and related Irish Jacobite sedition still concerned Dublin Castle between the end of the War of the Austrian Succession (1748) and the conclusion of the Seven Years War (1763). William Stanhope, earl of Harrington, lord lieutenant of Ireland (November 1746-December 1750), saw the necessity of preparing the country's defences in case of an invasion. Accordingly, he proposed an imme-diate array of the militia, and called for an exact report on the state of the forts in the realm. He also urged the recruitment of additional forces in Great Britain, but warned against the admission of papists into the army.[3]

At a local level, Richard Purcell remained sceptical about the possibility of a French invasion. Hinting at the emerging split within Jacobitism, he claimed that if the French landed they were unlikely to be joined by any people of 'interest', 'power' or 'consequence'. He assumed that 'the papists, notwith-standing their disaffection, would not risk a rebellion after the destruction of the Scots'. Nevertheless, he noted the continuing contact between Ireland and Europe. Pointing to collusion between French privateers and Irish Catholics,

---

3 Harrington to Newcastle, 5 Oct. 1747 (P.R.O., S.P., 63/410/67). Horace Walpole informed Horace Mann of a Spanish plot and the fear of a rebellion and Jacobite invasion; Doran (ed.), *Mann and manners at the court of Florence*, i, p. 241. See also ibid., i, pp 260, 291.

he asserted that the punitive Robbery Act prevented the French from ravaging the Irish coast as their Catholic allies footed the bill for any depredations.[4]

The arrival of suspected French officers raised the old bugbears of treasonable correspondence and recruitment. Harrington petitioned for similar powers to open suspected correspondence as those granted to Chesterfield's government during the 'Forty-five'.[5] The discovery of a diversionary Irish invasion 'plot' might suggest that his caution was not unfounded. This 'plot' emanated from a Dubliner called Oliver Macallester, who later turned out to be a double agent. He had aided the 'Forty-five' prisoners in London and had gone to Paris to serve Eneas McDonnell, the Jacobite banker. In France he kept company with prominent Irish Jacobites such as Robert McCarthy, fifth earl of Clancarthy and the sixth viscount Clare. He subsequently presented a very long memoir to Louis XV in 1759 which advocated a landing in Ireland on behalf of the Stuarts.[6] This was not an isolated incident. Patrick D'Arcy, aide-de-camp to Maréchal Saxe and a veteran of Fontenoy and the 'Forty-five', travelled to Ireland after 1746 where he made a military examination of its coasts and harbours, probing the popular attitude to a French expedition.[7] During the Seven Years War, other Irish *émigré* correspondence to the French and Stuart courts advocated similar Jacobite expeditions, and stressed the prospect of participation by loyal Jacobites in Ireland.

The paucity of surviving secret correspondence might be explained by its attendant hazards. As late as 1751, Patrick Bradley, Catholic bishop of Derry, used this excuse to explain his failure to express his gratitude to his patron King James:

> I must confess I have been long silent: but it was with the deepest concern and merely for want of an opportunity of giving free vent to the overflowings of a grateful heart, thoroughly sensible of your majesty's transcending goodness towards me. But being now got into another country where I am not forced to act with that reserve and circumlocution which are absolutely necessary on the other side of the water, I seize the happy moment with transports of joy.[8]

---

4 Purcell to Perceval, 12 Nov. 1747 (B.L., Add. Ms 47, 002A, fol. 133).   **5** Harrington to Newcastle, 20 Oct. 1747 (P.R.O., S.P., 63/410/88). Harrington issued a proclamation against the exportation of corn and other provisions to France and Spain; P.R.O., S.P., 63/410/72, 166. For other clandestine links between Ireland and France; P.R.O., S.P., 67/ 11/313 [157]. According to one pamphlet, a French defeat of Holland and the capture of her naval ports and shipping would permit a subsequent invasion of Ireland which in turn would uncover the true sentiments of the papists; *The state of the nation for the year 1747*, p. 27.   **6** Dunne to James III, Paris, 6 Aug. 1747 (R.A., Ms 286, fol. 59). See also Hayes, *Biographical dictionary*, pp 161-2; Mac Allester, *A series of letters discovering an intended invasion*. Mac Allister may have turned informer as a result of being embroiled in this plot. For biographical notes on Lords Clancarthy and Clare; Hayes, *Biographical dictionary*, pp 29, 32.   **7** Hayes, *Biographical dictionary*, p. 52.   **8** Bradley to James III, Paris, 15 May 1751 (R.A., Ms 321, fol. 96). Bradley (Brullaghan, Brolacan) had served in the public chapel of the Sardinian embassy since 1737. He wrote from Paris on 15 May 1751 to thank James III for his nomination and then paid a brief visit to his diocese. Soon after his return to London he resigned his diocese; Fenning, *Irish Dominican province*, p. 230. Lady Westmeath, wife of John, fifth earl, claimed that Irish people 'dared not write since all the letters were opened'; Fagan (ed.), *Stuart Papers*, ii,

Such circumspection remained necessary during the 1750s. Writing to Rome on the representations of some Irish Catholics to the Hanoverian throne, and their attempts to repudiate the Stuart nomination of bishops, James McKenna noted the difficulties in using ciphers and the scarcity of reliable messengers.[9]

The earl of Dorset, lord lieutenant of Ireland (September 1751-April 1755), received reports of Catholic disaffection in 1751. These centred around the activities of two Jacobite agents named Foley and Colonel Mahony. Foley had allegedly carried correspondence between the Stuart court and its Irish sympathisers, while Colonel Mahony had recently 'gone into that kingdom' as a recruiter. At the same time, Nicholas Sweetman, Catholic bishop of Ferns, was brought to Dublin under strong guard from Wexford, and lodged in the Marshalsea for allegedly encouraging recruiting.[10] Dorset was advised to exercise the utmost caution 'in the use of letters of a very discreet nature'.[11] A letter from Jacobites in County Clare, along with a covering note written by Florence Henchy (Henessy), was intercepted and sent to the lord lieutenant. It related to the proceeding of Jacobites in Ennis, who were 'evidently engaged in treasonable correspondence'. Henchy was later sentenced to death for providing information about the British Fleet during the Seven Years War. His method was to send the information written in lemon juice between the lines of letters to his brother, who served as chaplain to the Spanish Ambassador in The Hague.[12]

The Jacobite spectre reappeared in the late summer of 1752, in the period immediately before the outbreak of the Seven Years War. Newcastle reported excitedly to Dorset that Charles Edward had arrived in Ireland as part of a grand agitation, which involved the Pretender's move to Avignon.[13] Although aware of the already legendary imagination of the British ambassador to Florence, Sir Horace Mann, the probable source of this information, he urged Dorset to carry out the necessary private enquiries, but cautioned against raising unnecessary alarm.[14] The need for such prudence appeared justified, given the association

p. 174. An intercepted letter survived written by Lawrence Donnellan to John Wodberry. Donnellan asked him to make use of his interest with the friends of the Pretender that he might be appointed successor to Killaloe; Lecky, *Irel.*, i, p. 416. **9** J. McKenna to O'Brien [Edgar], Dublin, Dec. 1759 (R.A., Ms 397, fol. 48). See also R.A., 352, fol. 169; R.A., Ms 361, fol. 60; Fagan (ed.), *Stuart papers*, ii, p. 238. **10** Holdernesse to the lord lieutenant, 10 Oct. 1751 (P.R.O., S.P., 67/12/10[5]). See also P.R.O., S.P., 63/414192. These were not isolated incidents. Three men (Dennis Dun, Thomas Derig and Dennis McCarthy) were executed in Cork between 1749-52 for recruiting; Hume-Weygand, 'Epic of the Wild Geese', p. 31. Thomas Herlihy, William Jones and Thomas Dove were hanged in Broad Lane in the same period for enlisting; O' Mahony, 'Morty Oge O' Sullivan', p. 120. Cullen maintains that recruitment was a 'live issue' in Cork between 1748-52; Cullen, 'The politics of Caoineadh Airt Uí Laoire', p. 17. See also Ó hAnnracháin, 'Irish Brigade at Lafelt', p. 3. The Irish diaspora appreciated the dangers of wholesale recruitment at the time; Fagan (ed.), *Stuart papers*, ii, pp 171-2. The press reported on Sweetman's arrest on the charge of being a Jacobite; Brady (ed.), *Catholics*, p. 80; Fagan (ed.), *Stuart papers*, ii, pp 178, 317; Grattan-Flood, *History of Ferns*, p. 211; Whelan, *Tree of liberty*, pp 17-18. **11** Holdernesse to Dorset, Whitehall, 4 Apr. 1752 (P.R.O., S.P., 67/12/38 [19]). See also P.R.O., S.P. 63/412/288. Fagan (ed), *Stuart papers*, ii, p. 162. **12** Murphy, *History of the diocese of Killaloe*, p. 56. **13** Newcastle to Dorset, Hanover, 12/28 Aug. 1752 (P.R.O., S.P., 63/412/337); Lang, *Pickle the spy*, p. 134. **14** P.R.O., S.P., 63/412/337; see also P.R.O., S.P., 63/412/341; 63/413/77.

between Jacobitism and the Whiteboys, an agrarian movement which had emerged in Munster and Leinster around this time. Two rioters who were arrested for levelling ditches in Celbridge, County Kildare, in 1753 had been heard drinking 'health and success to Prince Charles Stuart'. Their activities induced some to believe that 'there may be more to the bottom of this than breaking down a common'.[15] This opinion was prevalent on both sides of the Irish Sea. According to a report in *Felix Farley's Bristol Journal* for June 1753, rioters in Kilcock, County Kildare were accompanied by pipers and fiddlers who played 'disaffected' tunes, including the popular Jacobite anthem 'The king will enjoy his own again'.[16] A report from County Cork credited the Whiteboys with singing 'disaffected and treasonable songs', often to the tune of another Jacobite anthem 'The White Cockade'.[17] This association between Whiteboyism and Jacobitism retained its shock-value among Protestants until the mid-1760s.

News of the approaching war and the activities of returned *émigrés*, privateers and recruiters for foreign service revived popular Protestant fears of the Pretender.[18] Rumours of a French invasion, which Lord Inchiquin spread in Dublin in 1755, disquieted the Dublin populace.[19] The dangers of such a landing became apparent with reports of French preparations at Dunkirk, Brest and Toulon, the proposals for raising men as in 1708 and 1715, and unfavourable accounts from America.[20] Furthermore, the lord lieutenant received intelligence regarding two French engineers who had purportedly come to inspect fortifications in the kingdom. He continued surveillance of returned 'Wild Geese' and recruiters, including two unnamed Catholic priests in Waterford, who were perceived to be up to no good.[21] Contemporary unrest in Dublin also assumed a distinctively Jacobite flavour as the mob wore white cockades.[22]

---

15 Bartholemew Vigors to Eleanor Cliffe, 7 July 1753 (N.L.I., Vigors papers, Ainsworth reports, fol. 2548). **16** Burtchaell, 'Bristol news in the 1750s', p. 16; *Pue's O.*, 26-30 June 1753; Kelly, 'The Whiteboys in 1762', pp 19-26; Giblin (ed.), 'Catalogue', part 6, vols. 133-35g, pp 129-30; Donnelly, 'The Whiteboy movement', pp 22, 29. **17** Ó Buachalla, *Aisling Ghéar*, p. 632. It is probably no coincidence that the Whiteboy, ('An Buachaill Bán') emerged in contemporary Irish literature; ibid., pp 634, 637-8. **18** Dorset to Robinson, 5 May 1754 (P.R.O., S.P., 63/413/180); Lord Duncannon called for 'a sloop of 20 guns to be stationed near Cork and Kinsale which may be of service in keeping the French fishing-boats in order...It is very likely that they carry off men to recruit for the Irish regiments in the French service'; N.L.I., Special list 335[2], Chatsworth papers T. 3158/725. **19** Charles O'Hara to Lady Michael, 18 Apr. 1755 (Transcript of the O'Hara papers in P.R.O.N.I., T. 2812/10, N.L.I., Ms 16, 943, fol. 1). A report from Galway stated that 'the principal Roman Catholic gentlemen of Galway waited on the governor Stratford Eyre to assure him of their inviolable attachment and sincere affection to his majesty'; Brady (ed.), *Catholics*, p. 86. At this time, Harrington reported on the wretched state of the army; B.L., Egerton Ms 3435, fol. 86. Considerable anxiety was aroused in nearby Waterford at reported sightings of the French fleet off Dungarvan; Burtchaell, 'Bristol Irish news in the 1750s', p. 21. **20** Wilmot to Devonshire, St James's St, 24 Oct. 1755 (N.L.I., Special List 335[2], Chatsworth papers, T. 3158/950). See also ibid., T. 3158/807, 808B, 845, 993; Cunningham (ed.), *Letters of Sir Horace Walpole*, ii, p. 434; Dover (ed.), *Letters of Sir Horace Walpole*, iii, p. 114. **21** Robinson to the lord lieutenant of Ireland, 8 Aug. 1755 (P.R.O., S.P., 63/413/212). See also P.R.O., S.P., 63/413/229. These are probably the same priests who were under surveillance in County Waterford; P.R.O., S.P., 63/413/327. See also Beresford, 'Ireland, pp 199-200. **22** Harrington to the secretary of state, 25 Aug. 1755 (P.R.O., S.P., 63/413/287).

Further invasion rumours in early 1756 once again brought Jacobitism to the forefront of contemporary political discourse. Devonshire was told that a Prussian officer was recruiting for the French army.[23] A French general and an engineer had also allegedly visited Ireland to extract information about the strength of the garrisons there.[24] Horace Walpole, fourth earl of Orford, remained apprehensive and believed that the French designed to send a body of troops and thirty thousand arms into the kingdom. He supplied the lord lieutenant with news of the movements of the French army on the coast. As a consequence, Devonshire deployed a considerable quantity of artillery at the coastal forts of Charles Fort (near Kinsale, County Cork), Duncannon and Passage (near Waterford) and at Malin Island in County Galway.[25]

Other interested parties in Ireland also received 'invasion' news from abroad. A despatch from Paris in February 1756 detailed the movements of the Irish Brigades towards the coast. An intercepted letter from John Hetherington to (?) Dennis requested him to forward a letter to the writer's uncle asking him for sixty guineas for the purchase of a lieutenancy of horse (in the French service). Hetherington 'had been taken up in London, Canterbury and Dover for a French officer but a diploma Dr McCauley gave him saved him from hanging'. He concluded by saying that the Irish Regiments were marching near the coast.[26] The prospect of the Brigades's involvement in a possible French landing also dominated an affidavit sworn by Philip Dwyer, a mariner on board *The Penelope of London*. He had been captured by a French privateer called *Port Mahon* from St Malo on 5 September 1756, en route between Dublin and London. Nine days later he was brought before a judge in Morlaix who, on being told that the defendant was Irish, made detailed enquiries about the situation and forces based in Ireland. On being informed that 'there were forty thousand regular troops, horse and foot in the kingdom and that 'all the ports and garrisons were strongly defended', the judge 'made a more close inquiry about Cork, Kinsale and Waterford and what men of war were stationed there'. He also told the defendant that 'if he had a mind to entertain in any of the brigades in the French service, he would have a horse to carry him to any regiment he liked'. He concluded that 'he would soon be in his own country as it was expected that they would soon pay a visit there'. The defendant allegedly replied that 'his own king was able enough to release him and that if the French had a mind to pay a visit to Ireland they might be sure of a warm reception'.[27]

23 Fox to Devonshire, Jan. 1756 (P.R.O., S.P., 63/414/1-3). The Baker papers record the capture and incarceration of three French officers recruiting in Waterford; N.L.I., Baker papers, Ms 21000/2. 24 Anonymous letter to the lord lieutenant, 21 Jan. 1756 (N.L.I., Special List 335[2], Chatsworth papers T.3158/1084). 25 Walpole to Devonshire, 26 Feb. 1756 (N.L.I., Special List 335[2], Chatsworth papers T.3158/ 1151). See also N.L.I., Ms 9618, fol. 21; P.R.O., S.P., 63/414/67, 136, 138; Cunningham, *Letters*, ii, pp 507-8; McAnally, 'The militia array of 1756', pp 94-105; See Nordmann, 'Choiseul and the last Jacobite attempt of 1759', pp 201-7. 26 John Hetherington to Dennis [?], Paris, 7 Feb. 1756 (N.L.I., Ms 9618, fol. 21). James McKenna infomed Edgar that 'we are all on this side very apprehensive of an in[vasio]n or of some dozens coming upon us from Eden or Fr[ance]'; R.A., Ms 361, fol. 60. 27 John Hetherington to

The threat posed by French military preparations in 1759 were taken very seriously both in Whitehall and Dublin. William Pitt warned Bedford, on his embarkation for Ireland as lord lieutenant, of intelligence from France which suggested that the duc d'Aiguillon's eighteen thousand-strong force would land in Ireland.[28] Bedford expressed misgivings about putting the kingdom on full invasion alert, as such a move might panic the Protestant populace. He was worried at the continuing dilution of the Irish military establishment; 'further draughts of infantry can not be made without the utmost hazard of the peace in the present critical circumstances of affairs, especially if ever so small a descent of the enemy was made on any part of the extended coast of this island'.[29] Stressing the impossibility of a simultaneous gathering of the forces of the kingdom against a possible invasion, while still protecting the major centres of population, he questioned the potential loyalty of native Irish regiments which he suspected were filled with papists. He had 'no great dependence on their service against their own countrymen whether coming over from France in the French king's service or armed by him to rise in rebellion against their sovereign'. He reiterating widespread fears and expectations regarding the Irish Brigades in the French army and referred to 'sixteen thousand Irish papists' who had acquired knowledge of arms from service in the Irish Brigades.[30] Similar suspicions were aired in the popular press. The pamphlet *A candid inquiry why the natives of Ireland who are in London are more addicted to vice than the people of any other nation* outlined the continuing recruitment for the foreign service where 'great numbers of good subjects go by stealth at the risk of their lives'. The Irish 'make excellent soldiers and are justly esteemed the best soldiers in France'.[31]

Such rumours ran the risk of depressing Protestant spirits, while contemporary accounts confirmed that they enhanced the insolent optimism of at least some of their Catholic counterparts.[32] Robert Taylor of Plunkett Street, Dublin heard 'insinuations and reports tending to reflect on the times and that something extraordinary would happen'. James Killeen sang a seditious song which

Dennis [?], Paris, 7 Feb. 1756 (N.L.I., Ms 9618, fol. 21); Affidavit sworn by Phillip Dwyer, 19 Oct. 1756 (P.R.O., S.P., 63/414/304); see also Fagan (ed.), *Stuart papers*, ii pp 238-9. The actual size of the establishment is discussed in the Introduction, pp 29-30 **28** Pitt to Bedford, 19 Oct. 1759 (P.R.O., S.P. 63/416/75). See also B.L., Add. Ms 24, 137, fol. 155; B.L., Add. Ms 24, 138, fols 41-2; B.L., Add. Ms 29, 252, fol. 24; Dover (ed.), *Letters*, iii, pp 319, 323, 325, 327, 339, 347, 361; Cunningham (ed.), *Letters*, iii pp 237, 241-2, 248, 252; McAllester, *A series of letters*, ii, p. 15. **29** Bedford to Pitt, 3 Jan. 1758 (P.R.O., S.P., 63/415/170). See also B.L., Add. Ms 24, 137, fol. 28. **30** Bedford to Pitt, 3 Jan. 1758 (P.R.O., S.P., 63/415/170). Although these claims are obviously exaggerated it is important to note that Bedford eventually decided to leave garrisons inland that would have borne the brunt of a French invasion to prevent Catholic uprisings; Leighton, *Catholicism*, p. 168. Fears of a French invasion circulated in Dublin, Limerick, Kilkenny and Waterford in the early-1760s; *A letter to Daniel Toler,* in Griffith (ed.), *Miscellaneous tracts*, p. 241. **31** *A candid enquiry why the natives of Ireland who are in London are more addicted to vice than the people of any other nation*, p. 10. These figures are contradicted by Cullen and Ó hAnnracháin; Introduction, pp 32-3. Nevertheless, the possible effect of this type of alarmist literature on the respective political communities is more important than the actuality. **32** Bedford to Pitt, 19 Oct. 1759 (P.R.O., S.P., 63/416/101). See also P.R.O., S.P., 63/416/211, 234-7; N.L.I., 9618, fol. 40; S.P., 63/417/130.

contained the words 'when Charlie comes we will get plunder and careers'.[33] John Ryder, Church of Ireland archbishop of Tuam, stated that the government could not depend on the loyalty of the greater Catholic populace in the event of a French invasion. He also hinted at the fissure which had begun to develop in Irish Catholic opinion. The leading Catholic gentry, while 'insisting that there were no plans for a rising ... did not conceal from us their fears that the populace, of which 99% were Catholics, would not be restrained from violence at the landing of a foreign force'.[34]

Ryder's belief that Jacobitism survived at a local level is justified by a contemporary account from an Englishman, who wrote from among the 'lower sort of people' in the west of Ireland. Taking shelter from the rain in a small hut, his host turned out to be an inveterate Jacobite who 'loved King James in his heart'. This provides a cameo picture of what is seldom recorded in contemporary Ireland, a value-free interchange between an Englishman and a 'common' Irish Jacobite.[35] Rioting among Dublin's lower orders in late 1759 purportedly related to an address of loyalty to King George. This had been penned by Charles O'Conor of Belanagare on behalf of the Catholic merchants of Dublin, in response to a threatened French attack on northern Ireland.[36]

Despite the strategic realignment by an accomodationist Irish Catholic political interest (below p. 357), Jacobitism survived at a popular level. The re-emergence of Whiteboyism in Counties Limerick, Cork, Tipperary, Waterford and Kilkenny in the 1760s provided a new bugbear, at a time when Britain was quietly allowing Jacobitism to recede into the background.[37] Agrarian grievances provided the main motivation for Whiteboy activities but rumours of French

33 Bedford to Pitt, 29 Jan. 1760 (N.L.I., Ms. 9618, fol. 86). 34 Quoted in Connolly, *Religion*, p. 245. Bartlett notes that an address by four hundred Catholics to Lord Lieutenant Bedford on the occasion of a threatened French invasion had been opposed by most of the Catholic gentry and hierarchy; Bartlett, *Fall and rise*, pp 63. Sir James Caldwell reiterated this claim in *An Address to the House of Commons of Ireland in 1771*, 'In the first place the French are all apprized that the lower class of the Roman Catholics in Ireland, who outnumber the Protestants there at least three to one, would join and support them with the utmost alacrity and joy. At the same time they must with the greatest reasons be convinced, that the most sensible of the titular bishops and priests, as well as the Roman Catholics of landed interest and in trade, would be most averse to any attempt by the French to distress their native country'; quoted in Morley, 'Idé-eolaíocht an tSeacaibíteachais in Éirinn agus in Albain', p. 21. 35 Woods, 'Irish travel writings as source-material', p. 175. Charles Kelly's request for touch-pieces on behalf of his niece in Ireland show that she had faith in James's ability to cure the king's evil; Charles Kelly to Lumisden, 21 Nov. 1762 (R.A., Ms 414, fol. 89). 36 O'Conor to Dr Curry, 8 Dec. 1759, in Ward, Wrynn and Ward (ed.), *Letters*, p. 78. McLaughlin claims that 'Dublin Catholics were caught up in a much narrower argument on the principle of whether to make a declaration of loyalty to the king'. He also suggests that 'these divisions are all too clear in the Riot Act of 1759'; McLaughlin, 'Crisis for the Irish in Bourdeaux', p. 140. During a riot against a rumoured Act of Union in 1759, the mob insulted the earl of Inchiquin 'but hearing his name was O'Brien [of the race of 'Brían Bóraimhe' (Brian Boru), the powerful eleventh century 'Árd-Rí Éireann', their rage turned to acclamation'. They later stormed the House of Lords and put an old woman seated on the throne and sent out for pipes and tobacco for her, quoted in Gilbert, *Streets of Dublin*, pp 732-3. This act might be an allusion to 'Queen Sive', a popular icon among the Munster Whiteboys. 37 Leighton, *Catholicism*, pp 61-2.

and Spanish military involvement, the white shirts and cockades of the Whiteboys, as well as their 'seditious' and disaffected songs, had Jacobite connotations which unnerved Protestants in an era of renewed Catholic political activity.[38]

The association between Whiteboyism and fear of the Pretender surfaced in a series of depositions from County Tipperary in 1767-8. They claimed that the Whiteboys aimed to raise a spirit of sedition to support a foreign invasion in favour of prince Charles ('Charles III'). Fr Nicholas Sheehy was pinpointed as being heavily involved in their activities.[39] Sheehy's execution on a trumped-up charge of murder in 1766 was a witch-hunt of the type orchestrated against Sir James Cotter in the 1720s.[40] Sir Edward Newenham noted his (Sheehy's) public refusal to drink the duke of Cumberland's health on the anniversary of the battle of Culloden, or the 'glorious and immortal memory' of William III, whom Sheehy deemed 'the greatest plunderer and enemy his country ever had'.[41] Fr William Egan, the Catholic vicar-general of Sheehy's diocese (and later Dr Peter Creagh's successor as Roman Catholic archbishop of Tuam), refused to appear at Sheehy's trial to testify to his loyalty.[42] When Sheehy's body was carried past Egan's house, his blood was sprinkled on the door-post. The popular Irish tradition lambasted Egan and Creagh for their betrayal of Sheehy: Bagwell and Maude pierced you in the heart, Egan and Creagh sold you ('Bagwell agus Maude do chráidh an croidhe agat/Egan agus an Creach do dhíol tú').[43] His death occasioned great dissatisfaction and complaint among Catholics. They took their revenge in September 1770 when several hundred gathered and stoned to death the executioner who had hanged Sheehy.[44]

Some Protestants expressed fears of Jacobitism in the late 1760s and 1770s, while propertied Catholics sought to shake off the last embarrassing vestiges of their loyalty to the Stuarts. Newspaper reports from 1765, 1766 and 1767 attacked the proposal to impose a simple test oath on Catholics; 'while perjury remains a principle of the popish religion, it is surely ridiculous to establish such a test'.[45] Nicholas, sixth viscount Taaffe, a retired, high-ranking officer of Maria Theresa, was recruited by O'Conor to add his name to pamphlets in favour of

---

38 Donnelly, 'The Whiteboy movement 1761-5', pp 20-55; Bric, 'The Whiteboys in County Tipperary' pp 148–62; Kelly, 'The Whiteboys in 1762', pp 19-26. Franco-Irish officers were allegedly in Ireland and in contact with the Whiteboys; Redington (ed.), *Calendar of Home Office papers*, pp 84, 88; B.L., Eg. Ms 47, 014B, fol. 125; Giblin (ed.), 'Catalogue', part 7, vol. 135Hh-137, p. 56. There were rumours of a French invasion as late as 1768; B.L., Add. Ms 24, 137, fol. 123; Beresford, 'Ireland', pp 261-2. Bartlett records a retrospective view of a Jacobite dimension to Whiteboyism from the 1790s; Bartlett, 'An account of the Whiteboys from the 1790s', pp 141-9.   **39** Musgrave, *Memoirs of the Irish rebellion of 1798*, pp 595-603; O'Connell, 'The plot against Fr Nicholas Sheehy', pp 49-61. Power provides the best recent account of the trial and execution of Sheehy; Power, 'Fr Nicholas Sheehy', pp 62-78.   **40** Power, 'Fr Nicholas Sheehy', p. 62. Bartlett considered the lack of reference to the Sheehy and Cotter's executions in volume iv of the *N.H.I.* to be 'glaring omissions'; Bartlett, 'Review article', p. 216.   **41** Russell, *Observations by Sir Edward Newenham*, p. 4; Bartlett, *Fall and rise*, p. 69.   **42** Connolly, *Religion*, p. 228.   **43** Quoted in Burke, *Clonmel*, p. 390.   **44** Power, 'Fr Nicholas Sheehy', p. 75.   **45** Brady (ed.), *Catholics*, 14 Dec. 1765, p. 118.

the Roman Catholics of Ireland. A riposte against Taaffe and his campaign sought to remind readers 'that the Irish popish bishops are nominated by the Pretender, that neither clergy or laity amongst them have ever given, or offered to give, though pressed to it by some of their own church, any pledge of loyalty to the present government'.[46] Another correspondent recited a brief historical outline of Catholic and Protestant positions relative to the Hanoverian establishment. He reminded the authorities of Protestant resoluteness 'which will, if unchecked, deter all its enemies, popish or otherwise affected'. The loyal protestations of Taaffe and the Catholic Committee were dismissed; 'all the water in the Thames will not wash a papist clean or make him a trusty subject to a Protestant prince'.[47]

Residual references to Jacobitism cropped up in other contemporary sources. Two curious entries in the De Vesci and O'Malley papers from 1779 claimed that some Catholics still refused allegiance to the Hanoverians. Another more plausible possibility is that Protestant scare-mongers deployed the old Jacobite smear against their Catholic counterparts. The first note utilised Jacobite rhetoric in questioning the parentage of George I and the rights of the house of Hanover to rule the three kingdoms. The author attacked 'certain erastian heretics, vulgarly denominated Protestants' who have 'withheld the crowns, sovereignties, territories and dominions of Ireland and Great Britain during the term of ninety years from their lawful kings ... James II of blessed memory, James III and his present majesty Charles III' .... 'After the death of the princess regent Anne', they 'totally excluded the royal house of Stewart and did place on the throne George, duke of Hanover not only in the wrong of James III but also the duke of Savoy'. After George's death, 'they placed on the throne his wife's bastard George II and after his decease the son of the princess of Saxe-Gotha'. The note warned that any inhabitant of Maryborough (Portlaoise), County Laois who continued to hold office under the traitor George III would suffer death without benefit of clergy.[48]

The second entry, an anonymous proclamation directed to Dr Boyd and Mr Shee in Castlebar, County Mayo, followed the same theme. It warned all Protestants to recant and throw up offices and employment, or they would be massacred before 1 May; 'that the king on the throne was a usurper and Charles Stuart was the true one ...'. George O'Malley believed that 'some light-headed priest had a hand in it'. The fact that he related this threat to the repeal of the penal laws might suggest the real source of its conception: 'If this be the fruit of

46 Brady (ed.), *Catholics*, p. 123. See also Bartlett, *Fall and rise*, p. 54.   **47** Brady (ed.), *Catholics*, p. 126. Whelan notes Lord Shelburne's use of the Jacobite threat to facilitate the establishment of a garrison at Nedeen ('Neidín', anglicized Kenmare); Whelan, *Tree of liberty*, p. 35.   **48** To Mr Evans in Maryborough, [postmark Lisburn]', 26 Jan. 1779 (N.L.I., De Vesci papers, mf. p. 6798). These papers have recently been deposited in the N.L.I. Seditious letters of this nature also surfaced in contemporary England; see Monod, *Jacobitism*, pp 123-5.

the relaxation of the penal laws, it resembles rescinding the American stamp acts ... '.[49] Longfield's rueful letter to Lord Shannon may reveal the true motivation behind these anonymous letters. He bemoaned the demise of the Stuart threat which had (in his opinion) prevented the Hanoverians from selling out the Protestant interest in Ireland: 'We want an efficient Pretender to recall this king back to those principles which placed his family on the throne'.[50] The unwillingness of the Anglo-Irish ascendancy to make any political concessions ensured that a popular cult of loyalty to the house of Hanover failed to emerge among Catholics in this period. The seeds of French radicalism and republicanism would quickly germinate in the fertile soils of Catholic discontent.

In the 1770s, the lack of references to the Stuart claimant in the contemporary press and popular political discourse shows that he had slowly faded into political oblivion, or the realms of sentimental antiquarianism.[51] Indeed the Hanoverian Royalist priest Fr Arthur O'Leary even suggested that Charles Edward was dead, a rumour no doubt fuelled by his continual disappearances and his gross abuse of alcohol. It might also be see as a pre-emptive strike to counter any French attempts to manipulate the old magic which was still associated with the name of the 'Bonnie Prince':

> The most part of yourselves can remember that in the war of 1745, they [the French] prevailed upon the Pretender to invade Scotland. This adventurer, after suffering more hardships than any romantic hero we read of, no sooner returned to Paris, than, at the solicitation of the English ambassador, he was forced to leave the kingdom of France. He died about two months since, without issue, and by his death had rid the kingdom of all fears arising from the pretensions of that family, that commenced our destruction and completed our ruin. Of this I think fit to inform you, as in all likelihood, if the French landed here, some might give out that he is in their camp, in order to deceive you by an imposture, which would end in your destruction.[52]

On a visit to Rome on Christmas Day 1785, Henry George Quin, son of a wealthy Dublin doctor, came face to face with the ailing Charles Edward in attendance at the pope's celebration of high mass. This association between 'Pretender' and 'popery' had survived in the Protestant and Catholic psyche for a century, a relationship which Charles Edward had so desperately tried to repudiate. Quin's slightly patronising sympathy for the broken figure of the

49 O'Malley to O'Malley, 1 May 1779, in Ainsworth (ed.), 'Survey of documents in private keeping', p. 193; Whelan, *Tree of liberty*, pp 40, 42–5. 50 Longfield to Shannon, 16 July 1778, quoted in Whelan, *Tree of liberty*, p. 103. 51 McLynn, *Bonnie Prince Charlie*, pp 38–41. 52 *Finn's Leinster Journal*, 4 Sept. 1779. Bishop Hervey doubted that the French could be so hard driven as to consider employing such a 'sot' [Charles Edward]; Childe-Pemberton, *Earl Bishop*, i, p. 203.

Stuart claimant contrasts strongly with the spectre of 'the Pretender' that gripped many Protestants over the previous century:

> The Pretender was in a kind of lodge next to the singing men and after the mass was over I went to the door of the lodge to see him come out. He is so infirm as to be carried with his chair by his footmen. He is now old and pale ... His face is something like Lord Carhampton. He had the garter but the blue was not sufficiently dark. I could not help feeling for him as he passed by. His natural daughter, the countess of Albany, was in the same box as him.[53]

II

The survival of Jacobitism at a local level is exemplified by the Irish literati's continual preoccupation with the Stuarts. Indeed the Stuart cause and the fall-out from the Seven Years War dominated contemporary Irish political poetry. The poets joined the doctrinaire Jacobite clergy and the exiles in refusing to seek an accommodation with the Hanoverians. The Munster poets renewed their entreaties to Prince Charles and his partisans in the Irish Brigades. They commented on the ongoing European war and sang the praises of prominent executed recruits and rapparees. Seán Ua Cuinneagain's, 'Teacht na n-geuna fiadhain', composed to the tune 'Seán Buidhe' in 1754, reiterated his trust in the birds who were called geese who would help Prince Charles, the greatest warrior since Fionn Mac Cumhaill, to tear, destroy and scatter the rotten pigs (The English/Protestants):

> Casfaidh na h-éanluith dá n-gairmthear "Géana"
> An arm go gléasda gan spár puinn,
> Ag cabhair le Séarlas – an caithbhile is tréine,
> Dár sheasaimh ó d'eagadar cnámha Fhinn!
> Creachfaid 's céasfaid
> 'S sgaipfid na bréan-toirc.[54]

The poet Eoghan an Mhéirín Mac Cárthaigh trusted the brave dragon of the true blood of McCarthy (Charles Edward/fifth earl of Clancarthy?) ('A dhragain Chuthaigh de Chárrth-fhuil úir')[55] and those who did not abandon Spain and Louis ('Is an méid noch d'fhág an Spáinn is Laoiseach').[56] His colleague Muiris Ó Gríobhtha, in a song composed to the tune 'An Craoibhín Aoibhín' longed

---

53 Quoted in Fox. (ed.), *Treasures of the library of Trinity College Dublin*, p. 185. Ingamell's provides a useful note on Quin and his travels in Europe; Ingamells, *Dictionary*, p. 791. **54** Seán Ua Cuinneagáin, 'Teacht na ngeuna fiadhaine', in O'Daly (eag.), *Poets and the poetry of Munster* (Dublin, 1849), p. 170. **55** Ó Foghludha (eag.), *Eoghan an Mhéirín*, p. 23. **56** Ó Foghludha (eag.), *Eoghan an Mhéirín*, p. 31.

for the arrival of the illustrious Louis as a spearhead for the troops, with thousands of valiant heroes in accompaniment, leading warriors from Britain and Gaels coming gladly from Scotland:

> Tá Laoiseach lasmhar ina thaca ag am bhuidheansa
> ar san Chraoibhín Aoibhinn áluinn óg
> 'S na millte galach le gaisge dá choimhdeacht
> ag an Chraoibhín Aoibhinn áluinn óg
> Atá laochradh ceannais ó Bhreatainn go bríoghmhar
> Gaoidhil go greantadh a 's sliocht Alban aoirde.[57]

Tadhg Gaelach Ó Súilleabháin praised the battle-hardened, fiercely determined warriors of the Gael ('gasra ghéirchatha Ghaedhlach dheaghghníomhach').[58] Aindrias Mac Craith lauded Charles and his well-prepared armada ('Carolus lonn 's a chabhlach gléasta').[59] The veteran Seán Clárach Mac Domhnaill praised the gentle brave men of the noble race of Milesius ('na fir-chaoin chródha dhe chóir-sliochd Mhilésius')[60] and the reliable Scots who would come back across the sea without doubt with the true spouse of Gráinne Mhaol ('Fíor-Scoit na tíre do crádhadh le pléidh/Fillfidh gan mhoill chughainn tar sáil gan bhréig i gcoimhdeacht an ríogh chirt is Gráinne Mhaol').[61] A contemporary poem by the ailing Seán Clárach and Micheál Baclámhach's translation of Dónall Mac Cárthaigh 'na Buile's 'Is tuirseach lag bhímse sas nimhneach mo dhéara' also eulogised the Wild Geese and the Stuart cause.[62]

The laments composed by Proinnsias Ó Súilleabháin and Domhnall Ó Conaill on the death of Muircheartach Ó Súilleabháin Béarra (a Franco-Austrian recruiter, smuggler and proclaimed tory, who had been shot and impaled on 4 May 1754) underlined the continued association between recruitment, rappareeism and the Irish Brigades, even in the Jacobite twilight. Like the Stuart king and the Wild Geese, the outlaw had become a prominent figure in the popular literary tradition and had been continually associated with Jacobitism throughout this period. Ó Súilleabháin lamented the death of the hero of noble Gaelic lineage from Béarra at the hands of the treacherous churls.

---

57 Muiris Ó Gríobhtha, 'An Chraoibhín Aoibhín', in Walsh (eag.), *Reliques of Irish Jacobite poetry*, p. 93.
58 Tadhg Gaelach Ó Súilleabháin, 'Ar maidin indé dham', in Ó Foghludha (eag.), *Tadhg Gaelach*, p. 104.
59 Aindrias Mac Craith, 'Duain na Saoirse', in Comer-Bruen, 'Aindrias Mac Craith', p. 92.   60 'Síle Ní Ghadhra', in Hardiman (eag.), *Irish minstrelsy*, ii, p. 54.   61 A Shaoi ghlain de phríomh scoth', in Ó Foghludha (eag.), *Seán Clárach*, p. 85; Hardiman (eag.), *Irish minstrelsy*, ii, p. 54. Eoghan Rua Ó Súilleabháin hoped that valiant Charles and his hearty troop will attack us easily by sea 'Tá Séarlus mear' 'sa thrúip ghroidhe, D'ár n-íonsaidhe go h-éasga ar seól'; Filleadh Rí Séarluis', in Walsh (eag.), *Reliques of Irish Jacobite poetry*, p. 64. Tierney and Hayes provide useful surveys of Ireland and the Seven Years War; Tierney, 'Ireland in the Seven Years War', pp 175-85; Hayes, 'Irishmen in the Seven Years War', pp 413-18.   62 Ó Muirithe, 'Tho' not in full stile compleat', p. 98; Seán Clárach Mac Domhnaill, 'Seán Clárach ar leaba a bháis go Éamonn de bhFál', in Ó Foghludha (eag.), *Seán Clárach*, pp 32-3.

Muircheartach was the support of the country and the patron of the clergy who bestowed wine and money on the poets:

> Is doilg liom shaoithe de phrímh-shliocht Ghaoidhil Ghlais
> Ag bodaigh an fhill gach laoi dá dtraochadh
> Níor goineadh mo chróidhe tré oidhe na n-éarlamh
> Gur crochadh go fíor an laoích ó Bhéarra.

> Borb-fhear gróidhe agus taoiseach tréanmhar
> Do foilceadh go fíor den rí-fhuil Éibhir,
> Cabhair na dtíortha is díon na cléire
> Do bhronnadh an fíon is cíos don éigse.[63]

Ó Conaill's 'marbhnadh', which he purportedly composed the night before he himself was hanged (27 August 1754), provided further evidence for the politicisation of the smuggler and recruiter. He bemoaned the spiking and exhibiting of Muircheartach's fair head and recalled seeing him one day with his sword drawn for combat, and imagined the swathes he would have cut through the soldiers of King George. He alluded to the titles and commendations he received in Spain and France, particularly the lace uniform bestowed upon him by Lady Clare as a captain in the French guards. In Ireland, however, he had been forced to yield to the force of the foreigners:

> A Mhuirtí, a rí-mháighistir is truagh an cás tú bheith ró-lag –
> Do cheann geal ót chorp áluinn is é anáirde mar "seó" aca,
> Do chonnac-sa féin lá tú is do chlaidheamh sáithte chum chómhraic,
> Is go ndéanfá-sa beárna tré ghardaí Rí Seóirse!
>
> ...
>
> I bParais thugais bárr leat, sa Spáinn fuarais *title*
> Thug baintighearna an Chláir duit culaidh lása ar fheidhme;
> It chaptaein do thárlais ar ghárdaibh na Fraincge
> Acht go hÉirinn níorbh fholáir duit teacht spás chum ár gcaillte.[64]

---

63 Proinnsias Ó Súilleabháin, 'Ar bhás Mhuircheartaigh Óig Uí Shúilleabháin', in Ó Foghludha (eag.), *Cois na Ruachtaighe*, p. 79. See also Froude, *English in Ireland*, i, pp 450-55; Madden, *Reflections and resolutions*, p. 15; Lecky, *Ireland*, i, p. 274.   **64** Domhnall Ó Conaill, 'Marbhna Dhomhnaill Uí Chonaill', in Ó Foghludha (eag.), *Cois na Ruachtaighe*, p. 84. Muircheartach allegedly received a richly-mounted sword from the Empress Maria Theresa and he wore a gold-laced uniform for being the finest man in the French army; O' Mahony. 'Morty Oge O'Sullivan', p. 99. He was proclaimed on 14 Oct. 1732; *Dub. Gaz.*, 14 Oct. 1732. Sullivan and O'Connell, two companions of Muircheartach, were executed and had their heads spiked side by side with their confederate; O'Mahony, 'Morty Oge O' Sullivan', p. 120; Beresford, 'Ireland', p. 160; Tierney, 'Ireland in the Seven Years War', p. 178. Cullen provides the best recent examination of O'Sullivan's career; Cullen, *Emergence of modern Ireland*, pp 32-3.

The outlaw cult in contemporary Ulster also had a Jacobite dimension. Séamas Mac Mhurchaidh, 'An Beirneach Mór', (Seamus McMurphy), friend of the Ulster poet Ó Doirnín and victim of the infamous Johnston of the Fews, emerged as Ó Súilleabháin Béarra's counterpart in the eighteenth-century Ulster. Both Mac Mhurchaidh himself and Ó Doirnín have been credited with joint authorship of his 'marbhna'. The poet asked the victim why he never suspected that his own people would betray him and why he did not flee in the night before being sold below his price. Another verse provided a Jacobite context for Mac Mhurchaidh, lamenting that he had not been involved in the battle of Aughrim, in the throng of the war-camp at their head as leader:

A Shéamais Mhic Mhurchaidh, a rímharcaigh chlúitigh,
a phlanda den fhíorfhuil a shíolraigh ó uaisle,
cad chuige nár smaoinigh tú do dhaoine bheith dod ruagadh
nuair nár éalaigh tú san oíche sular díoladh faoi do luach thú?
…
An lá sin ag briseadh Eachdhroim is orainn bhí an buaireamh,
trua nach bhfaca mé mo chonairt is í cóirithe gléasta;
is trua nach é an cogadh é is na fir, gabháil i gcampa,
agus Séamas Mac Murchaidh i dtús ann mar cheannfort.[65]

The Irish poets primarily concerned themselves with the war in Europe in this period. Like many of his literary predecessors, the priest-poet Liam Inglis composed his verse from the war news in local newspapers and set it to popular Jacobite tunes for the benefit of an Irish-speaking public. He espoused the cause of the king of France, the empresses of Austria and Russia and the heroic deeds of their illustrious generals, including Ulysses Browne who took the field against Frederick the Great of Prussia. In his poem 'Leastar an Bhráthar' (1757), he supplies an allegorical account of the Seven Years War, based on information gleaned from the local *Cork Journal*. According to the poet, the king of Prussia

---

65 Peadar Ó Doirnín/Séamas Mac Mhurchaidh, 'Marbhna Shéamais Mhic Mhurchaidh', in de Rís (eag.), *Ó Doirnín*, pp 53-4. This song remained popular in the Ulster folk tradition; Murray, 'A South Armagh outlaw', p. 96. See p, 293, fn. 69. In a similar way, 'Pádraig Fléimionn (Patrick Fleming), a confederate of the arch-tory Redmond O' Hanlon, was killed in Inniskeen, County Monaghan, in 1680 on his way to a rendezvous with Archbishop Oliver Plunkett who had interceded with the government to secure his pardon. He later became the tragic hero of the popular 'Mairgneadh Phádraig Fléimionn'. An anti-Jacobite pamphlet from the early-eighteenth century which referred to 'St Redmond Hanlon' and 'St Patrick Fleming' suggests that Fleming and O'Hanlon had become associated with the popular Jacobite cult; Murray, 'The lament for Patrick Fleming', pp 75-92; *A sermon preached before the duke of Lorraine and the Pretender* (undated c. 1715-6). The cult of the outlaw emerged elsewhere in the Irish tradition. A 'caoineadh' attributed to the wife of the Waterford outlaw William Crotty, executed in 1743, was popular among the Irish speakers of the Comeragh Mountains; Cavenagh, 'William Crotty, outlaw and popular hero', p. 93; Butler, 'Crotty the robber' pp 12, 54, 88, 105. An Irish poem on the early eighteenth-century Cork rapparee 'Shawn Rua' survived among Irish speakers in County Cork up the great famine of 1845-7; [Anon], 'Shawn Rua: a tradition of Macroom', p. 79.

suddenly unsheathed his sword and waged war against the gentle, amiable
Empress Maria Theresa who sends Browne like Fionn (Mac Cumhaill, the mythical Irish hero of the Irish Fiannaíocht cycle) against him. Meanwhile, the empress
of Russia joined the fray as an important ally to her Austrian counterpart while the
ingenius French spread like a flood across the plains of Italy. The poet rejoiced
that with all Europe in the French king's pocket, the noise of the waves is annoying
(Admiral Edward) Hawke whose fleet has been trapped in the Bay of Biscay:

> Nochtann a cholg go hobann 'n-a láimh dheis
> Is cuireann cogadh go hullamh ar Mháire –
> An bhain-ímpre mhíonla, mhánla,
> Chuir sí an Brúnach mar Fhionn 'san áth roimhe
>
> ...
>
> Tá ag triall adtuaidh sluagh go táinteach
> Ó ríoghain Ruise ursa thábhachtach,
> Tá ag triall andeas go prap le dásacht
> Frangcaigh chliste mar thuile le fánadh;
> Tá anoir ag triall ó iaith Iodáile
> Curadha cathbhuadhach eachluath láidir;
> Tá an Eóraip uile 'n-a chuimhil-a-mhála
>
> ...
>
> Tá torann tonn ag bodhradh Hawke thoir
> Is é gan im, gan meidhg, gan bláthaigh
> Tá a chabhlach uile i Muir Bhioscáine.[66]

He continued his allegorical narrative of the Seven Years War in the woeful tale
of the theft of his shoes, 'Mo ghearán crua le hUaislibh Fódhla'. He satirically
emphasised the difficulties of the king of Prussia and William, son of (King)
George (Cumberland), under oppression in Hanover. The 'Butcher' was at that
time in the grip of the brave Frenchmen, unable to move by coach or swift
horse, and lying flat on his fat arse:

> Acht mac ár dtriath-na Uilliam mac Sheóirse
> Atá fá chiach i ndiaidh Hanóbhar!
> Atá sé i dteannta ag Frangcaigh chródha
> In amhgar, in antart, i bpóna;
> Ní tualaing é ar ghluaiseacht i gcóiste
> Nó ar luath-each fá mhuar-phlaic a thóna.[67]

66 Liam Inglis, 'Leastar an bhráthar', in Ó Foghludha (eag.), *Cois na Bríde*, p. 27. Éadbhárd de Nógla
replied to this poem in the same year, 'Mo chumha is mo dhanaid', in ibid., p. 28; See Buttimer, 'Gaelic
literature and contemporary Irish life', pp 589, 591, 594, 596. Ulysses Browne's campaigns against Frederick
the Great are discussed in his biography; Duffy, *The Wild Goose and the Eagle*.   **67** Liam Inglis, 'Mo
ghearán chruaidh le hUaislibh Fódhla', in Ó Foghludha (eag.), *Cois na Bríde*, p. 31.

Inglis also offered a glimpse of Catholic reaction to the fate of Admiral John Byng who was arrested, tried and executed for his failure to relieve Majorca. In a song addressed to Éadbhárd de Nógla (Edward Nagle, son of the Jacobite lawyer Patrick Nagle, a close friend of the executed Jacobite leader James Cotter, and sung to the popular Jacobite tune 'An Craoibhín Aoibhinn Álainn Óg'), Inglis engaged in some clever word play at Byng's expense: It is sweet for us to hear of Byng and his friends in sorrow (''S is binn linn Byng is a chairde i mbrón').[68] In his reply Éadbhárd de Nógla mocked that we no longer need Byng as he is in sorrow (''S ní díth linn Byng mar atá fá bhrón').[69]

The continued woes of the elector of Hanover provided the main themes of another Inglis poem 'An eól díbhse a dhaoine i bhFonn Fáil'. This provides a further example of the role of the poets in the diffusion of news to the Irish-speaking public. To his great joy, George was defeated and in such great distress that if he soiled his trousers the tide would not clean his arse. Prague would not fall and that the king (Fredrick the Great) would be scorched by Count Daun. Thunder (military might) was coming across the sea in the form of the French king and his hosts to exalt the Stuart. The bright, brave, true-blooded soldier (Charles Edward) would soon be surrounded by bishops and priests in abundance:

> An eól díbhse i a dhaoine i bhfonn Fáil
> Seóirse go claoidhte 's i lom-ghábha?
> Aiteas mo chroidhe istigh
> Mar theagmhuig a bhríste
> 'S is ná glanfadh an taoide a theampán!
> ...
> Geallaimse díbhse nár gabhadh Prág
> ...
> 'S do greadadh an Rí le Count Daun
> ...
> Tá tóirneach ar bóchna agus foghail ghnáth
> Agus gheóbhthar poll dóighte sa chómhlán
> Airgfidh Laoiseach
> A mbailte 's a dtíortha
> Is casfaidh an Stíobhart go ceann-árd:

---

68 Inglis, 'A Éadbháird aoibhinn uasail áluinn', in Ó Foghludha (eag.), *Cois na Bríde*, p. 43.   **69** Éadbhárd de Nógla, 'Is fada fé chiach mé gan riar ar dhántaibh', in Ó Foghludha (eag.), *Míl na hÉigse*, p. 51. There was a major political fallout from Byng's failure; Shannon papers (N.L.I., Special List 206[1]). Also Cunningham (ed.), *Letters*, iii, p. 19; Dover (ed.), *Letters*, iii, p. 149. Several pamphlets related to this were published in Dublin and circulated by street hawkers; *The trial of Admiral John Byng with appendix; Proceedings in parliament to release from the obligation of secrecy for the trial of Admiral Byng; Appeal to the people containing genuine letter of Admiral Byng to the admiralty*, [Ben Ader], *The chronicle of B[yn]g, the son of the great B[yn]g; Bungiana or an assemblance of what-d'-ye-call-'ems relative to the conduct of a certain naval commander; Conduct of the ministry in which among other things the arguments made use of in two pamphlets lately published entitled a letter and an appeal in defence of Admiral Byng*.

Faraire 'en fhíor-fhuil tá fionn breágh
Ba mhaise don ríoghacht é fé bheann cháidh;
Beidh easpuig 'n-a thimcheall
Is sagairt go líonmhar
'S a mbeatha aca dílis go seang sámh.[70]

His colleague Pádraig Ó hÉigceartaigh, commended him on his poem, its wealth of genuine truth, without exaggeration on the wars in which 'our' enemies have been laid low. These stirring compliments should be borne in mind by those who wish to evaluate the effects of the Seven Years War in Ireland and the political content of eighteenth-century poetry.

Is acfuinneach aoibhinn do rann bhreágh
'S is dearbhtha díleas gan antlás
Is tarraingthe líonmhar
Na cathanna coimheascair
'N-ar leagadh ár naímhde go fann tláth.[71]

In another of his poems, 'Atá an báire imeartha réidh', Inglis gloated on the strength of the (Austrian) warrior (General-Count) Daun who, with the strong Russians, would outmanoeuvre the Prussian king. The French general Contades would pursue the English and Brunswick (the British commander) was without direction. Not content solely with providing news of the European war, he turned to the Canadian and American theatres which had become the main area of British military activity in early-1758. In Canada, he noted the distress of (the British admiral, Edward) Boscawen in the straits of St Cassien. He rejoiced that in America the devil is on them altogether as they were left oppressed and afflicted after the battle at Ticonderoga where only one-third of them survived. Moreover, at Fort De Quesne they lay with their arses to the sun (stretched out dead) on the shattered timbers of their fallen flags:

...
Atá Daun an curadh go cumasach tréan
'S dár leat is dubhach atá a námhaid;

70 Liam Inglis, 'An eól díbhse a dhaoine i bhfonn Fáil', in Ó Foghludha (eag.), *Cois na Bríde*, p. 32. Walpole's correspondence provides a useful contemporary context; Dover (ed.), *Letters*, iii, pp 229-30. There are other examples of poems addressed to the poets and the people of Ireland 'A éigse shuairc', the sages of Ireland 'A shaoithibh Éireann' the good men of Ireland 'gach sáirfhear glé de shairshliocht Airt', the poor Gaels 'A Ghael bhoicht'; Ó Buachalla, *Aisling Ghéar*, p. 607. See also p. 277, fn 25-6.
71 Pádraig Ó hÉigcearthaigh, 'Is acfuinneach aoibhinn', in Ó Foghludha (eag.), *Cois na Bríde*, p. 33. In his poem 'An Fanuidhe', to the popular Jacobite tune 'Over the water to Charlie' Tadhg Gaelach Ó Súilleabháin promised that Maria (Theresa) would have her crowns and lands ('a coróin is a críocha ag Máire'), in Ó Foghludha (eag.), *Tadhg Gaelach*, pp 106-7.

Ní tláth na Ruisigh i siomsa na bpléar,
Ní táir an ursa iad ag druidim le baoghal
Is breágh do chluichfidh an Pruiseach is an scaoth
Is fágaimíd súd mar atá sé!

…

Contades glacfaidh an t-amas go cóir
Is cionnárd a leanfaidh na danair sa tóir;
Atá Brunswick i riocht puic gan treóir
Is fágaimíd súd mar atá sé!

…

Féach ar an amhgar, 'n-a bhfuil cabhlach Boscawen
Féach ar an dteannta n-a raibh ag St Cás.
Is fágaimís sud mar atá sé!

In Americe siar tá an diabhal ortha ar fad,
Do fágadh 'san ngliadh iad fá chiach is fá cheas,
Ní tháinig leath a dtrian as, acht iarmhar beag lag
An lá san do bhíodar ag Ticonderoga;

Ag Fort Dhu Quesne ní léire bhí a mbail
Do túrnadh gach n-aon ar an gcléir Senegal
Atá a dtóin leis an ngréin ag baoltaigh na mbrat
Is fágaimíd súd mar atá sé![72]

In his poem 'Do Mheidhbhín Ní Shúilleabháin', Inglis reported that war-like bands were coming across the sea in fast ships in black floods. On their arrival, the songs of the clergy would again be heard in the church of Christ with the sweet knell (of the bell) to summon all. The progeny of the Gaels will be in the fine houses and restored to their inheritance, while the group that it is now strong (the Protestants/English) will be reduced and the tables turned on the churls who extinguished poetry:

Tar bhóchna ghlais i luing chaoil
Go aoird gcrainn na ndubh-shruthain,
Tig slóighte cliste i bhfeidhm cloidhimh
Le cruinn-ghaoith go lúthmhar lán,

…

---

72 Liam Inglis, 'Atá an báire imeartha réidh; in Ó Foghludha (eag.), _Cois na Bríde_, p. 38. Ó Foghludha dated this poem to 1757 while Buttimer opted for 1758. Contemporary official correspondence provides a useful political context for this poetry; Walpole to Mann, 3 July 1757, in Power (ed.), _Letters of Horace Walpole_, iii, pp 229-30; Dover (ed.), _Letters_, iii, p. 241; Buttimer, 'Gaelic literature and contemporary Irish life', p. 594.

Beidh ceól na cléire i gcill Chríost
Agus creidhill bhinn dá mhúscailt tráth,
beidh pór na nGaedhal n' a ndeigh-thigheas
'S a n-oidhrí 'n-a ndúthchas gnáth,
An slógh atá tréan gan puinn bríghe–
Na claidhrí do mhuc an dáimh–
Le fóirneart géaga Raidhrí
Agus Meidhbhín Ní Shúilleabháin.[73]

Cumberland's defeat at Haslenbeck in 1757, and the loss of George II's electoral lands to France, prompted Inglis's biting satire on King George, 'Is ró-dhian a screadann'. Inglis mocked George II for losing Hanover, Hesse Cassel and his forefathers' ancestral lands. He rejoiced that the elector no longer had the shelter of Britain, nor the lands of Ireland, nor the fidelity of the Scots since he cut their throats. George's defeat would spell death for the clergy of Calvin while the learned clergy of (St) Peter (the Catholic clergy) would endure forever:

Is ró-dhian a screadann an sean-duine Seóirse
Ó, a Dhia, cá rachad? níl agam Hanóbhar,
Ná fós Hesse-Cassel, mo bháile beag cómhgair,
Ná fód mo shean-athrach, táid airgthe dóighte!

…

Ní díon dam Breatain ná fearanna Fódla,
Ní díleas dam Alba ó ghearras a scórnach,
Ní díreach dam Danair – ní cara dham cómhursa
Sínidh im beathaidh mé is caithidh fén bhfód mé!

Mo chiach! Mo lagar! Ní fheadar cá ngeobhaid sin –
Iarmhar Chailbhin do sheachain na cómhachta –
I mbliadhna béam bascaithe leagaithe leóinte
Is cliar chliste Pheadair 's a mbeatha go deó aca![74]

In his poem, 'Atá an fhuireann so thall gan amhras díleas', Inglis named the main benefactor of the elector's defeat, 'An Craoibhín Aoibhinn Álainn Óg' (Charles Edward). His arrival would ensure that the poets would no longer be

---

73 Liam Inglis, 'Do Mheidhbhín Ní Shúilleabháin', Ó Foghludha (eag.), *Cois na Bríde*, p. 40. **74** Inglis, 'Is ró-dhian a screadann', in Ó Foghludha (eag.), *Cois na Bríde*, p. 35. 'Seán Buidhe', a poem falsely credited to Seán Clárach (who died in 1754) also attacked the duke of Cumberland after his defeat in Hanover in 1757; B.L., Add. Ms 31,874, fol. 14. In a contemporary poem Piaras Mac Gearailt called Little Molly (Ireland) to his side to tell her with great joy that George is crying and roaring 'Siúd a stóir, láimh liom/Is inneósad duit le háthas/go bhfuil Seóirse ag gol is ag scairtigh'; Piaras Mac Gearailt, 'A Mhalaí beag ó', in Ó Foghludha (eag.), *Amhráin Phiarais Mhic Gearailt*, p. 30.

afraid to speak their treason; those who broke the Friday fast (Protestants) would be under pressure and fear; before three months, the Gaels would get freedom of speech and their Catholic clergy would receive funeral offerings:

> Dá dtigeadh an t-aon so ghlaodhaim le hintinn
> 'S a thaisteal thar tuinn do gheóbhainn cead spóirt,
> 'S nár bh'eagal don éigse a dtréason d'innsint
> Gur b'iad lucht briste na hAoine do thuill a ndóghadh;
>
> ...
>
> Sul a gcaithfeam trí mhí gheóbhaid Gaoidhil cead labhartha
> ...
> bheadh an t-airgead marbh ag ár sagairt mar shaoirse
> Leis an gCraoibhín aoibhinn áluinn óg.[75]

The continued reversals suffered by Britain and its allies in 1758 also gladdened his contemporary, Piaras Mac Gearailt. In 'Duan na Saoirse', he reported how the French had harried the weakened Ferdinand of Hesse Cassel, Henry (duke of York) was exhausted by (Count) Daun, Prussia was greatly weakened and distressed by the fight. The British army and navy fared little better in the period. (Admiral Charles) Saunders's fleet had been scattered, while (Admiral George) Rodney and his fleet was trapped without hope of relief. Black Cumberland lay tortured with the gout and Hawke was held fast like a thief:

> Tá Ferdinand go fann 's an Franncach taobh leis
> 'S Hannraoi traochta ag dáimh dár ndóigh;
> Tá scaipeadh ar na hamhais, cá ngeabhaid ní léir dham-
> Prussia tá tréith-lag is dáil do 'n ngleó;
> Sanders gan bail 's a chabhlach réabtha,
> Rodney i gcúl gan cognamh ó éin-fhear
> Cumberland dubhach 's an gúta 'á chéasadh
> Agus *Hold thief* déanta de Hawke ó ló.[76]

Mac Gearailt also celebrated the fact that George and his people were sick, Hanover would not provide shelter for him and the duke of York would be obliterated before winter, along with his fat-bellied consort:

---

[75] Liam Inglis, 'Atá an fhuireann seo thall gan amhras díleas', in Ó Foghludha (eag.), *Cois na Bríde*, p. 36. Another poet, Uilliam Mac Cairteáin an Dúna, urged his listeners not to mention that it is treason for a person to remark on the slavery of this world 'Ná tuigídh a cháirde a rá gur treason/do dhuine dá dtráchtadh ar dhála an tsaoighil seo'; 'Faisg Lámha', in O'Daly (ed.), *Poets and poetry*, p. 28. [76] Piaras Mac Gearailt, 'Duan na Saoirse', in Ó Foghludha (eag.), *Amhráin Phiarais*, pp 24-5. Máire Comer-Bruen and Ó Foghludha attributed this verse to Aindrias Mac Craith; Comer-Bruen, 'Aindrias Mac Craith', p. 92. See also Aindrias MacCraith, 'Is fada mé i gcumha gan tnúth le téarnamh', in Ó Foghludha (eag.), *Éigse na Máighe*, pp 211-12.

Tá Seóirse go breóite, 's a mhuinntir,
'S a choróin air ní mhaoidhfear 'ar ndóin;
Hanóbher ní dóigh liom gur díon dó
n-a cómhgar go suidhfeadh chum próinn.
Beidh an Diúc of York múchta fé 'n ngeimhreadh.
's a bhanntracht, an bhuidhean bholg-mhór.[77]

Inglis himself rejoiced that the sound of the waves was deafening Hawke ('Tá torann tonn ag bodhradh Hawke'),[78] while Tadhg Gaelach promised that the hosts of Silesia would be prepared and companion-like and that Maria Theresa would regain her lands and crown ('Beidh slóighte Shílisia go cóirithe cuibhrithe /A coróinn is a críocha ag Máire').[79]

Liam Dall Ó hIfearnáin's song 'A Phádraig na n-Árann' also reflected popular Jacobite sentiment at the arrival of Captain François Thurot in Carrickfergus in 1760. He lauded the landing of the great warrior Thurot in Ulster with abundant strength. He urged his listeners to jump to it, stand up, take heart and be lively and to encourage these hawks (soldiers) who were near for sport. He tried to coax them under the standards of the lions (the Irish Brigades) to free Ireland from the yoke of the tyrants. The poet related rumours of this tribe's strength, mocked the weakness of George and the feebleness of Cumberland as (William) Pitt (the elder) lay on his arse in parliament. Meanwhile, the plaided highlanders gathered together for battle inspired by their long war-pipes, welcoming Charlie home to his crown:[80]

77 Piaras Mac Gearailt, 'An Caol-Druimeann Óg', in Ó Foghludha (eag.), *Amhráin Phiarais*, p. 40.   78 Liam Inglis, 'Leastar an bhráthar, in Ó Foghludha (eag.), *Cois na Bríde*, p. 27. The poet Seán Ó Cuinneagáin expected that Fr Uilliam (Inglis) will be providing for brothers since Hawke lost the battle 'Biaidh an tAthair Uilliam ag riar ar bhráithribh/Ó cailleadh a ngliadh no bh-fiann an hácach';'An Chraoibhín Aoibhinn', in O'Daly (eag.), *Poets and poetry*, p. 70.   79 Tadhg Gaelach Ó Súilleabháin, 'An Fánuidhe', in Ó Foghludha (eag.), *Tadhg Gaelach*, pp 106-7. A useful comparative perspective is provided by examining the Jacobite *genre* as cultivated by the Scottish poets. Post-war unease in the Highlands, the proscription of the tartan and the disarming of the clans brought many waverers and Whigs into the Jacobite fold. This is reflected in the millennial tone of the verses of such Scots-Gaelic poets as Alasdair Mac Mhaighstir Alasdair, John McCodrum of North Uist, Rob Donn McKay of Sutherlandshire, Duncan Ban McIntyre of Argyllshire; McDonald (eag.), *Songs of Duncan Ban Mc Intyre*, p. 8; Matheson (eag.), *Songs of John McCodrum*, pp 6, 12; Campbell (eag.), *Songs of the '45*, pp 236, 242-3. A list sent to the exiled court in 1758 contained the names and numbers of clans and lowlanders still loyal to the Jacobite cause and indicates a state of affairs even more potentially challenging to the Hanoverian regime than the 1745 rebellion. In comparison with his Irish Jacobite contemporaries at home and abroad, the author believed that the success of an English invasion rested on a diversionary invasion of Scotland with the five Irish regiments, the Royal Scots and Ogilvy's Regiments; 'List of the loyal clans in Scotland and what number they would raise immediately in arms' *c.*1758 (R.A., Ms 389, fol. 93); See also 'Advantages de la France pour le rétablissement des Stuarts à le marquis de Latuornelle', *c.*1756 (R.A., Ms 363, fol. 28). The most recent view of post-rebellion Scotland is Macinnes, 'The aftermath of the '45', pp 103-13; Macinnes, *Clanship, commerce and the House of Stuart.* Jacobitism in Scotland between 1745-60 is the subject of Doron Zimmerman's doctoral thesis, Emmanuel College, Cambridge.   80 References to Scotland proliferate in the Irish literary tradition. Piaras Mac Gearailt hoped that the free Scottish clans and the poor Gaels will follow with eagerness, blood-lust and stealth

...

Ar chualais mar tháinig
Go Cúige Uladh an ghárda
Thúrot 'n-a shláinte le hiomarca scóip!
Preab! bí it sheasamh! Glac meanmna is bíoga
Gríosuigh na seabhaic tá it aice chun spóirt
Beidh píbí dá shéide,
Le claidheamh a mbeidh faobhar air
Is racham in éifeacht fé bhrataibh na leóghain.

Éisigh 'a Ghaedhla, 'atá cráidhte ag méirligh
Glacaidh bhur dtréan-airm gaisce 'n bhur ndóid;
bíodh hurrá go súgach
Anois ó tá an prionnsa
Is a ghárdaí go dúbalta ag tarraingt in bhur gcómhair
...

Tá an rúta so láidir má 's fíor gach a ráidhtar,
An crobhaire cionn-árd is a bhuime gan bhrón
Seóirse go lán-lag
Is Cumberland cráidhte
Pitt insa phárlimint caithte ar a thóin!
Na Hielans ag tarraint fé phlaidibh 'n-a dtrúpanna
Is a bpíobanna fada dá spreagadh chum ceóil
Ringce ar gach maol-chnoc
le háthas na scléipe
Ag cur fáilte roimh Shéarlas abhaile 'n-a choróinn.[81]

to send the rotten pigs far across the sea without clothes or a night's provisions 'Beidh saor-chlanna Scuit ,beidh Gaeidhil bhochta ar inneall/Go faobhrach, fuilteach, fír-ghlic,/Séidfear thar sruith na bréan-tuirc le bruid/Gan éadach ná cuid na hoidhche'; Piaras Mac Gearailt, 'Cé h-é sin amuigh?', in Ó Foghludha (eag.), *Amhráin Phiarais*, pp 103-4. Elsewhere he placed his hopes on Charles, Louis, King Philip and a lively troop from Scotland 'Séarlas, L[aoisea]ch Rí P[ili]b is buidhean mhear ó chrích Alba'; Piaras Mac Gearailt, 'Buaidh na nGaedheal', in idem (eag.), *Amhráin Phiarais*, pp 41-2. Donnchadh Rua Mac Conmara promised that we will take the warrior Charles home again and there will be help for him in Scotland and in Ireland 'Do thabharfimís abhaile arís an faraire Séarlus/'S bheadh cabhair dhó i nAlba nó mealladh mé, 's in Éire'; Donnchadha Rua, Eachtra ghiolla an amaráin', in Ó Foghludha (eag.), *Donnchadh Ruadh*, p. 28. Seán Ó Cuinneagáin stressed that Scotland's breast was rent with happiness 'Tá Alba stiallta g-cliabh le h-áthus'; Seán Ó Cuinneagáin, 'An Chraoibhín Aoibhinn', in O'Daly (ed.), *Poets and poetry*, p. 70. Muiris Ó Gríobhtha lauded the polished Gaels from the highland hosts 'Gaoidhil go greantadh as sliocht Alban aoirde'; in Ó Gríobhtha, in Walsh (ed.), *Reliques of Irish Jacobite poetry*, p. 93. Liam Dall Ó Ifearnáin promised that the dark-haired daughters of the highlands crown with wreaths for the monarch of three islands; translation by Mangan of a poem by Ó hIfearnáin, Welcome to the Prince of Ossory, in Ó Foghludha (eag.), *Ar Bhruach na Coille Muaire*, p. 89. **81** Liam Dall Ó Ifearnáin, 'A Phádraig na n-Árann', in ibid., p. 58. Thurot's action caused a certain amount of agitation in Ireland; Giblin (ed.), 'Catalogue', part 6, 133-5g, pp 120, 122; *Genuine and curious memoirs of the famous Captain*

Liam Dall's optimism cannot be dismissed as totally groundless. Thurot's action can be seen as a possible precipitant of subsequent disturbances in Munster. The landing showed what could have been achieved with the right degree of commitment from the French.[82]

The survival of such Jacobite sentiment in contemporary Irish poetry and the relationship between the Irish language, Catholicism and Jacobitism should be continually borne in mind. A memoir from 1764 concerning Fr William Egan, parish priest of Clonmel and a possible candidate for episcopal preferment, stressed the close links between the survival of Catholicism, and the hatred of all things English. Egan was beyond reproach in public, and preached well in English. His ignorance of Irish made him 'incapable of instructing the people in the country district who, fortunately, have no other language'. The Irish Catholics's 'dislike of the English language is one of the means used by providence for the preservation of the Catholic religion among them'.[83]

A residual loyalty to Charles Stuart survived in the Irish literary tradition into the 1770s and 1780s. This sentiment, and indeed the political awareness of contemporary Irish poetry, has been dismissed by Seán Connolly as meaningless, formulaic, literary convention. Commenting on Eoghan Rua Ó Súilleabháin's poem 'Tá an cruadhtan ar Sheóirse' which refers to Comte d'Estaing, a French naval commander in the American War of Independence, Connolly suggests that 'the poet's delight in the difficulties engulfing the Hanoverian dynasty was conveyed in a web of confused and inconsistent images in which the American colonists were not mentioned at all while the emperor was somehow imagined to be among Britain's enemies'. In fact, this poem focused on an obscure dynastic struggle between two minor scions of the Wittelsbach family, known as the War of the Bavarian Succession, which seemed likely to involve Hanover in conflict with Austria: it is no surprise therefore that the emperor was allotted a place among King George's enemies.[84]

Eoghan Rua's knowledge of European politics and the American Revolution was not exceptional. Poems composed by other poets showed an awareness of

---

Thurot. **82** Cullen, *Emergence of modern Ireland,* pp 13, 196, 197; McLynn, *Jacobites,* p. 38; Beresford, 'Thurot and the French attack on Carrickfergus', pp 55-70. **83** Memoir concerning Fr Egan, PP of Clonmel, *c.*1764, in Giblin (ed.), 'Catalogue', part 6, vols. 133-5g, p. 136. This Fr Egan later became hated for being seen to abandon Fr Nicholas Sheehy; Burke, *Clonmel,* pp 389-90. Proficiency in the Irish language was not only deemed useful but absolutely vital. In 1764 Dr Fitzsimons, Catholic archbishop of Dublin, stated that even in Dublin confessors could not discharge their duties unless they were proficient in Irish, Walsh, *Irish continental college movement,* p. 158. Similarly, one of the stipulations for setting up a new Catholic parish on the south-side of the Thames (London) in 1773 was that the priest would be skilled in the English and Irish tongues; Brady, 'The Irish language in London', pp 32-3. **84** Connolly, *Religion,* p. 248. For the text of this poem; Ó Foghludha (eag.), *Eoghan Rua Ó Súilleabháin,* pp 83-5. In a paper which locates this poem in its proper political context Morley has commented; 'Somewhat inconsistently, in view of his dismissal of the song's political relevance, Professor Connolly has more recently cited Ó Súilleabháin's song in support of the startling assertion that the 'central premise' of Irish Jacobitism was the 'continued incorporation' of the country in the 'British State'; Morley, 'Tá an cruatan ar Sheoirse' – folklore or politics?', pp 112-21. **85** The Cork poet Colmán Mac Cárthaigh reacted to the American revolution by

events across the Atlantic Ocean.[85] The Clare poet Tomás Ó Míocháin cele-
brated the British evacuation of Boston on St Patrick's Day 1776 during the
American War of Independence. In his song 'Ar dtréigean Bhoston d'arm
Shasana, 1776', composed to the tune 'Washington's frolic' or 'An fear buile gan
bhríste', he rejoiced at the eternal destruction and scattering of (Admiral William)
Howe and the English and praised the stalwart (George) Washington at the head
of his kingdom. It also had an unequivocal Jacobite bias. As a result of this 'game',
Ó Míocháin hoped that Ireland would soon have her lawful faithful spouse, the
serene Charles Stuart:

> Is fonn 's is aiteas liom Howe is na Sasanaigh
> Tabhartha, treascartha choíche,
> Is an crobhaire, Washington, cabharthach, calma,
> I gceann is i gceannas a ríochta; ...
> D'éis an chluiche seo Éire léigfear
> Dá céile dlitheach ceart díleas,
> An féine fuinneamhach faobhrach fulangach
> Séarlas soineanta Stíobhart.[86]

The links between Charles Edward and the American war may seem prepos-
terous; yet the possibility becomes more plausible when set in the context of the
work of Frank McLynn, the prince's most authoritative biographer. He claims
that an offer was made by the Bostonians in 1775 to Charles Edward that he
should be the figurehead of a provisional American government. McLynn also
underlines the prince's intense interest in the American War. The poetry of Art
Mac Cumhaigh also bears testament to residual Jacobitism in Ulster. Tomás Ó
Fiaich, has emphasised the poet's fixation on the O'Neills of the Fews, as opposed
to the Stuarts.[87] This concern to differentiate between their two causes seems

---

reviewing the progress of the war, extolling the exploits of the American generals Washington, Lee and
Jones and assessing the its European implications. He also predicted that Charles Edward would regain his
kingdoms, the Catholic religion would be restored and the indigenous Irish would regain their usurped
role at the head of society; Whelan, 'Bantry Bay', p. 98. Vincent Morley has examined 14 published and
unpublished Irish poems relating to the American Revolution as part of his forthcoming monograph.
86 Tomás Ó Míocháin, 'Ar dtréigean Bhoston d'arm Shasana, 1776', in Ó Muirithe (eag.), *Ó Míocháin:
Filíocht*, p. 84. There are numerous reference to the American Revolution in the Irish tradition; Buttimer,
'Cogadh Sagsana Nua Sonn', pp 63-103. Buttimer notes numerous references to Jacobitism in the *Freeman's
Journal*; Buttimer, 'Cogadh Sagsana Nua Sonn', p. 75. Charles Edward showed great interest in the
American War; McLynn, *Bonnie Prince Charlie*, p. 519. Monod suggests that after defeats in America,
Charles Edward's secretary John Baptist Caryll was approaching an unreceptive French government in
relation to another attempt on Scotland; Monod, *Jacobitism*, p. 219. McLynn also suggests that 'the
neurotic fusspot Sir Horace Mann feared that the serious disturbances in Ireland in 1782-3 presaged some
new Jacobite scheme'; McLynn, *Bonnie Prince Charlie*, p. 531. Sir Walter Scott claimed that he had seen the
proposal made by the colonists to 'Charles III' to set up his standard in 1778 among the Stuart papers.
Andrew Lang failed to locate this document; Petrie, *The Jacobite movement, the last phase*, pp 173-5.   **87**
Ó Fiaich (eag.), *Mac Cumhaigh*, p. 47. Nonetheless, Ó Fiaich stated that the part played by Felix O'Neill
of Creggan in the great adventure of 1745-6 may have given the prince an extra claim on his affections;

misplaced when one considers the careers of this family in the Spanish army and the Stuart prince's relationship with Felix O'Neill, a member of (the staunch Jacobite) Lally's regiment. Moreover, it ignores the Stuart theme in much of Mac Cumhaigh's other poetry. In his 'Agallamh le Caisleán na Glasdromainne', Mac Cumhaigh bore testimony to the large part which Captain Felix O'Neill of the darling progeny of O'Neill would play in arraying Prince Charles for battle despite the court wranglers ('Féilim an gleacaí de aicme Shíl Néill na rún,/A chuirfidh Séarlas i mbratach ar neamhchead do lucht pléid' i gcúirt').[88] In his 'Tagra an dá theampall', the Catholic church informed its Protestant counterpart that he was tired of George's rule and that it would not be long until King Charles (III) would make it sorry:

> Dá nochtadh dhuit féin, 'réir chothrom an scéil,
> Gurb atuirseach mé faoi Sheóirse,
> Is ar fheartaibh Mhic Dé, nár mhairidh tú i gcéim,
> Nó go gcuirfidh rí Séarlas brón ort.[89]

Even the optimistic Mac Cumhaigh finally conceded that the Stuart cause was hopeless, and that they no longer cured the sufferings of the Gaels. The loss of its leaders had left Ireland crestfallen and the progeny of James no longer ruled Britain:

> 'S nach léigheasann na Stíobhartaigh caoineadh na nGael
> ...
> Ó d'éag siad na taoisigh, d'fhág Éire go cloíte
> 'S gan oidhre Rí Séamas i mBreatain 'na dhéidh.[90]

III

The Irish *émigrés*, particularly the soldiers of the Irish Brigades, became associated with Whiteboy activity and recruitment in political discourse. However, from a slightly earlier period (immediately after the 1745 rebellion) their contact with the Jacobite court assumed its characteristic post-war passivity. The testimony of Richard O'Mulryan in 1740 contained all the usual tropes of the displaced Irish Jacobite, especially his acute sense of exile, and the *camraderie* within the close-knit ranks of the Irish *émigré* community. Appealing to James's 'paternal affections for his distressed, loyal and faithful Irishman' whose family

---

ibid., p. 236.   **88** Art Mac Cumhaigh, 'Agallamh le Caisleán na Glasdromainne', in Ó Fiaich (eag.), *Mac Cumhaigh*, p. 82.   **89** Art Mac Cumhaigh, 'Tagra an Dá Theampall', in Ó Fiaich (eag.), *Mac Cumhaigh*, p. 87.   **90** Art Mac Cumhaigh, 'Moladh Shéamais Pluincéad', in Ó Fiaich (eag.), *Mac Cumhaigh*, p. 129.

had been 'rent and torn apart by a usurping government', O'Mulryan requested a royal title so that he might be exempt from the payment of taxes. He engaged in the customary obsequious rhetoric for the restoration of his 'lawful and glorious prince' and re-echoed his sense of exile:

> I crave with all humanity at your majesty's hands with regards to a foreign nation which would perhaps not be refused me in my native country from which I shall ever willingly banish myself until it shall please God to restore your royal family to its hereditary dominions.[91]

In 1759 Richard Warren also requested a peerage from James III, in response to the English act recalling British subjects from the service of the Bourbon princes. This illustrates the difficulties which Stuart devotees encountered from the dictates of the Hanoverian government, familial pressures and the social constraints of *ancien régime* France. Warren resisted his brother's endeavours to persuade him to return to Ireland as heir to his sizeable estate of £1500 per annum, and forfeited an annual remittance from Ireland of £200. He pleaded with his king for a peerage so that he might avail of a lucrative marriage proposal.[92] The need to communicate with James on all matters pertaining to his Irish and Scottish subjects in the French army featured in Lord Thomond's letter of March 1751. James's patronage still remained extremely useful for any of his exiled subjects who sought promotion in the armies of France or Spain.[93]

Some native and *émigré* Irish trumpeted loyalist pedigrees, and appealed for titles and preferments; others petitioned the king directly for charity. These alms, however small, were usually given, and they reinforced the perception of James as a generous prince. Maurice Hearne, sent by the Catholic bishop of Waterford to Bordeaux to study for the Irish mission, was captured and imprisoned for three years in the English fleet. He subsequently petitioned his exiled king for financial assistance.[94] Gratitude to the monarch for past favours permeated Elizabeth O'Connor's presentation of 'a draught of my own making' ['poitín'?] to her king before Christmas.[95] In 1750 charitable petitions to the exiled Stuart monarch proliferated among those Irish who had come to Rome to gain indulgences. These solicitations were usually endorsed and ensured that the recipients returned to Ireland with tales of the king's generosity which guaranteed that he

91 R. O'Mulryan to James III, Paris, 7 Apr. 1747 (R.A., Ms 282, fol. 139).   **92** R. Warren to James III, Versailles, 30 June 1759 (R.A., Ms 394, fol. 55). Warren later participated in the abortive 1759 descent; R.A., Ms 397, fol. 146. For profiles; Tomasson, 'The lucky colonel', pp 15-19; Hayes, *Irish swordmen*, pp 108, 257-303; idem, *Biographical dictionary*, pp 312-14; Ruvigny, *Jacobite peerage*, p. 183; Little, 'Outline for the life of Warren of Corduff', pp 242-52, 296-303. The best recent case study of the exiled Irish community in this period is McLaughlin, 'A crisis for the Irish in Bordeaux', pp 127-47.   **93** Thomond to James III, 6 Mar. 1751 (R.A., Ms 319, fol. 21). See also R.A., Ms 319, fol. 44.   **94** R.A., Ms 28, fol. 128); R.A., Ms 283, fol. 124; Fagan (ed), *Stuart papers*, ii, pp 53, 118, 124 .

retained the affection of many of his subjects.[96] Mary Butler, last surviving daughter of Lord Galmoy and sister of the Lord Butler who had been killed at King James's side at Malplaquet (1708), also appealed to his generosity. She emphasised her distressed condition, her family's losses for the Stuarts and the king's great concern for his exiled subjects. However, she appreciated the financial burden which Charles Edward placed on the king. This displayed a more personal relationship between exiled king and *émigré* subject than is normally found in royal etiquette.[97] The sense of national *camaraderie* among the Irish community can also be demonstrated by the extent to which the Irish Colleges, acting as forerunners of Irish embassies, provided a port of call and a refuge for those who carried out the king's business.[98] This sustained the Jacobite ideology, and maintain links between Ireland and the exiles. For example, Augustine Cheevers, who had received the king's preferment for the diocese of Ardagh, resolved to remain in Cadiz to solicit alms among the Irish *émigrés* 'for the poor helpless children of Ireland'.[99]

Émigré attachment to their native land often meant more than the occasional charitable donation. James Rice, an Irish merchant at Rouen, provided Colonel Daniel O'Brien with an alternative (if somewhat outlandish) plan for meddling in contemporary Irish politics. Expressing a 'true and natural zeal for his native country', Rice advocated the exploitation of the rift which had recently arisen in Irish political life between Lord Lieutenant Dorset, George Stone, Church of Ireland archbishop of Armagh and his cabal, and James, earl of Kildare, 'chief nobleman of the kingdom'. Kildare had presented a remonstrance of the grievances of that 'unhappy kingdom' to King George. Rice advocated sending Robert Fitzmaurice, a captain in Rothe's Regiment, and a relation of many of the chief Irish noble families, to persuade Kildare to embrace the Stuart cause and set himself up as lord lieutenant at the head of an Irish Jacobite administration. Rice then returned to the subject of his present prosperity and his native birthright. He was willing 'to sacrifice my life and fortune for his majesty, his royal family and my unhappy native country when his majesty thinks proper to command'.[100] Other exiles persisted in their correspondence with the Stuart court. They pleaded with their king to use his influence for episcopal and political preferments and reiterated their loyalty to the cause and their hopes for his restoration.[101]

95 O'Connor to James III, 11 Dec. 1748 (R.A., Ms 295, fol. 120). See also R.A., Ms 309, fol. 58; R.A., Ms 334, fol. 89. **96** R.A., Ms 303, fol. 45. See also R.A., Ms 304, fols 17, 66; R.A., Ms 306, fols 11, 15-17, 74, 109; R.A., Ms 343, fol. 51; R.A., Ms 345, fol. 38; R.A., Ms 379, fol. 57; R.A., Ms 380, fol. 127; Fagan (ed.), *Stuart papers*, ii, pp 53, 106, 123-4, 127, 128-9, 197, 246, 251-3, 260. **97** Butler to James III, 22 June 1750 (R.A., Ms 308, fol. 40). There are other examples. Indeed Ó Buachalla states that these petitions were still being sent to 'Charles III' in the 1770s; Ó Buachalla, *Aisling Ghéar*, pp 429-31. **98** Bourk to Edgar, 26 Jan. 1751 (R.A., Ms 317, fol. 143); See also Griffin, *The Irish on the continent in the eighteenth century*, pp 460-3. **99** Cheevers to James, 15 Mar. 1752 (R.A., Ms 330, fol. 70). Cheevers to the king, Cadiz, 6 Sept. 1751 (R.A., Ms 324, fol. 125). **100** Rice to [O'Brien], Rouen 24 Dec. 1753 (R.A., Ms 345, fol. 118). **101** R.A., Ms 346, fol. 50; R.A., Ms 352, fol. 176; R.A., Ms 353, fol. 126; R.A., Ms 354, fol. 43; R.A., Ms 355, fol. 9.

Rice's belief in the existence of a Jacobite interest at the heart of the Irish administration probably stemmed from the tendency of his Irish Protestant counterparts to use Jacobitism as a stick to beat political opponents. Jacobitism remained sufficiently potent to be used as a means of discomforting rivals. In the fanciful *Letter from his g*[race], *the l*[ord] *p*[rimate] *of all I*[reland] *to the chevalier de St George*, the archbishop of Armagh (George Stone) was tainted as a Jacobite activist and sympathiser. He purportedly prophesised the end of heresy by which 'your majesty's [James III] great and religious brother of France [Louis XV] is the mighty instrument of its demolition as I, and my co-adjutors, shall be, under his majesty's direction, in this'.[102] However, in this case, the Protestants feared the king of France and the Pretender represented nothing more than a harmless by-stander. In *The haberdasher's sermon preached in Taylor's Hall on 21 December 1754*, patriot sentiment became equated with Jacobitism. The author, John Gast, sought to show that 'the red-list people and their adherents were enemies to their country', and secondly that they were Jacobites who fomented divisions 'in order to bring in the Pretender'.[103]

Émigré correspondence with the Stuart courts and the French king testifies to the centrality of Jacobitism as a feature of their contemporary political culture. Its habitual optimism was sometimes tempered following the estrangement of the French king from his would-be confederate Charles Edward. The exiles's disquiet with Charles Edward's intransigence did not, however, signify a terminal cooling of Irish *émigré* Jacobite zeal. Rather, it ultimately mirrored James III's disquiet at Charles Edward's continual snubs to the French king, and the over-riding political reality that Charles Edward needed Louis XV more than Louis XV needed him.[104]

One commentator, Dominic Heguerty (whose father Daniel had left Brookhall, County Donegal, after his attainder in 1691) reaffirmed his Jacobite principles, and described the woes which had befallen Britain under the forty year-old Hanoverian yoke. The standard Jacobite arguments of spiralling indebt-edness, and the usurping house's territorial commitments on the continent, were used to justify his call for an amalgamation of the powers of Europe against Britain's martial tyranny. A French-sponsored invasion of England must be

---

102 *A letter from his g*[race], *the l*[ord] *p*[rimate] *of all I*[reland] *to the chevalier de St George*.   **103** [Gast], *The haberdasher's sermon*, p. 8. See also *Queries to the Querist*. Sir Arthur Brownlow was accused of Jacobitism because of the apostasy of his mother; *Seasonable advice to the freeholders of Armagh*, p. 14. In his *Faction overthrown*, Gast again used Jacobitism as a weapon against the 'patriots'. He assured his listeners that only 'France and the Pretender' threatened their liberties and that those who denied this 'talked treason, downright treason against his majesty and the Hanoverian succession' and that 'only a Jacobite would say such things'; Gast, *Faction overthrown*, pp 7, 11. These attacks might help explain the earl of Kildare's vigorous reaction to the serious charge that he neglected the glorious memory; Kelly, 'The glorious and immortal memory', p. 40.   **104** Heguerty to Edgar, Paris, 10 Nov. 1755 (R.A., Ms 359, fol. 152). See also R.A., Ms 360, fol. 47. Beresford provides a detailed discussion of Heguerty's relationship with Charles Edward between the 'Forty-five' and the Seven Years War. He also notes his continual emphasis on a Franco-Jacobite invasion of Ireland; Beresford, 'Ireland', pp 169-73, 195, 208-20.

'headed by the only man who would make them welcome there' (Charles Edward).[105] He discussed the possibility of a Stuart-led French invasion of either Scotland or Ireland as a prerequisite to the proclamation of Charles Edward as king. Although the proposal to acquire the crowns of Scotland and Ireland for Charles Edward typified French opportunism and infuriated the Stuart prince, it cannot be interpreted solely as the termination of Heguerty's Jacobite loyalty. Like Charles Edward (and unlike the French government), he would have viewed such a move as a stepping-stone to the subjugation of all three kingdoms.[106]

On the more positive side, influential French-based Irish Jacobites, such as Myles MacDonnell and the illustrious veteran of the Irish Brigades, General Charles Edward Rothe, were confident of an improvement in Jacobite fortunes.[107] Similarly, Thomas Lally, governor of Bologna, whose military prowess had been proven on the fields of Dettingen (1743) and Fontenoy (1745) and at the walls of Bergen-op-Zoom (1746), remained convinced that the prince was still France's most powerful trump card. He advocated sending a diversionary force of 8–10,000 men to Ireland or Scotland. He also shared the prince's opinion that the ailing condition of George II and the weakness of the prince of Wales (Frederick) augured well for the Jacobite cause. Lally believed that the prospect of a Stuart restoration never appeared brighter:

> We have actually seven thousand men upon the coast of Brittany, Normandy and Flanders, sixty thousand foot and ten thousand horse; all said troops will be encamped the first of July. We have also an immense number of all warlike stores such as cannons, mortars, guns and about five or six hundred boats or transports in Dunkerque, Calais, Boulogne, Dieppe, Le Havre and St Malo, Granville and Brest which keep England in constant ferment ... I find they would not be averse to the venturing of eight or ten thousand men in either Scotland or Ireland. I prevailed with them so far as to oblige them to provide six thousand sabres and as many coats which will be ready on some part of our coasts before the first of September. They are sensible of the impossibility of landing a body of thirty or forty thousand men in any part of England unless there was a private intelligence in the country or with the English fleet which is a thing that cannot be expected ... All sensible men are convinced that the government will be overturned and that if the elector

---

105 O'Heguerty to Charles, 25 Jan. 1756 (R.A., Ms 363, fol. 65). See also R.A., Ms 362, fol. 167; R.A., Ms 363, fol. 26; R.A. 363, fol. 147; R.A., Ms 365, fol. 58;. R.A., Ms 364, fol. 65. The Abbess of Yprès had earlier talked of the elector of Hanover 'feathering his nest in Hanover', in Fagan (ed.), *Stuart papers*, i, p. 295.   106 Heguerty to Charles 21 July 1756 (R.A., Ms 363, fol. 147). There is a note on Heguerty in Hayes, *Biographical dictionary*, p. 116.   107 Myles McDonnell to [Edgar], Corunna, 27 Dec. 1755 (R.A., Ms 360, fol. 100). See also R.A., Ms 360, fol. 162. Beresford suggests that 'Irish integration in French society was far from complete on the outbreak of the Seven Years War'; Beresford, 'Ireland', p. 197.

was 30 years he would have a chance to be as absolute as Harry the Eight but God be thanked he is 73 and his son [Frederick] is weak so I never had better hopes.[108]

His colleague, the Kilkenny-born Jesuit Fr Bernard Rothe, proposed that a concrete agreement be made between James III and Louis XV, in relation to a French landing in England. All matters pertaining to the choice of troops, generals and equipment should be left to 'his most christian majesty'. His call for caution and discretion recognised the fraught relationship between the French King and Charles Edward, whom he urged not to come into French territory until called for.[109] His hopes for a favourable turn in the Stuart king's affairs appeared more realistic following French successes in Bohemia, and Frederick the Great of Prussia's flight from the besieged city of Prague. The rupture between the Empress Maria Theresa and the elector of Hanover and the increasing dissent in England also raised Jacobite expectations. He stated that Catholics enjoyed the greatest tranquillity since 1688 due to the level of Protestant trepidation in Ireland. Rothe's belief that this new-found freedom remained subject to Protestant perceptions, revealed the continuing psychological burden of the penal laws on Irish Catholics in the period.[110]

Rothe's optimism was not totally unfounded. A 'tableau politique et militaire pour la campagne de la présente anneé 1757' proposed availing of England's present political difficulties, to effect an invasion of England with 30,000 soldiers and 4,000 cavalry, backed up by a battalion of artillery. A diversion to Ireland by the Irish Brigades remained a mandatory requirement for the success of such a venture.[111]

The cryptic correspondence of Fr McKenna mirrored the hopes of Jacobites resident in Ireland. If 'the Factor' mentioned in this letter is Charles Edward and if one can believe McKenna's claim that he knew the whereabouts of the elusive prince he was one of a few Jacobites at this time who actually did. This might suggest that he (McKenna) was also in contact with the Irish Jacobite cabal which centred around George Kelly and Thomas Lally who were close confidants of the prince in this period.

I had an account from the L. N. the Linen Hall [Ireland] yesterday telling that the *customers* cry out they wish even for your factor [Charles

108 Lally to Charles, 18 May 1756 (R.A 362, fol. 146); Beresford, 'Ireland', p. 192. For notes on Lally, see Hayes, *Irish swordmen in France*, pp 223-47; Ruvigny, *Jacobite peerage*, pp 119-20.   109 Fr Rothe to James III, Paris, 10 Jan. 1757 (R.A., Ms 368, fol. 27). Although by June of that year Rothe had suspected that the Franco-Jacobite invasion was nothing more than a ploy to keep the English land forces at home, his pessimism was short-lived; Fr Rothe to James III, 13 June 1757 (R.A., Ms 372, fol. 55).   110 Fr Rothe to James III, 4 July 1757 (R.A., Ms 373, fol. 26). For examples of this 'persecution complex' among the Irish disapora; McLoughlin, 'A crisis for the Irish in Bordeaux in 1756' pp 135-8, 140-1; Hayes, *Irish Swordsmen*, p. 11.   111 'Tableau politique et militaire pour la campagne de la présente anneé 1757' (R.A., Ms 378, fol. 53).

Edward] with his friendly F.R. [France] to come now to their relief. God grant them their desires and soon, as they really expect, either this season or at farthest the next. Be well assured that your factor's place of abode is not yet discovered, but I do everywhere assure his friends that you and he are living and, by God's blessing, well. Our youngster [lord lieutenant] is now every day expected here from East or Eutropia. I suppose you know him the *Hunter* of drofdeb [Bedford], and we begin to be very apprehensive of the same against you, and us, as were endeavoured in our last Change [parliament] as the same spirits do still predominantly in each party of the *Dealers* [patriot party], *Jobbers* [court party] amongst us. The *Jobbers* and *Citizens* with their adherents look very demure especially since the late almost total *paid* or payment [defeat] of the Velvet Dresser of P.R.[Prussia] and of Mr Van Scheuter [Cumberland], which you all well know of by this time. Who if he returns to the East as he desires, we are thinking of his fate somewhat like to that of Gnib [Byng] or worse.[112]

Richard Burke was optimistic that the war in Europe would continue 'until the saddle [crown] is set upon the right horse [Charles Edward]'.[113] He wrote in the context of widespread rumours of a French invasion. This situation also occasioned Dominic Heguerty's reproachful letter to Charles Edward, protesting against the latter's refusal to contemplate a French-sponsored invasion of Ireland. Heguerty appreciated that the prince's hopes were bound hand and foot with the military plans of the French king:

> My heart is broken with grief to see you reject an invitation calculated to put a crown on your head which you throw under your feet; you disoblige a king who never forgets and seldom forgives. If you can do without his majesty, in the name of God go on but if to the contrary what do you expect must be the consequence of your refusing this invitation?[114]

Heguerty's last correspondence to the prince has been interpreted as a stinging rebuke of Charles Edward's francophobia, and as a disavowal of Jacobitism. The letter may also have been a despairing last-ditch attempt to entice Charles

---

112 Fr James McKenna to James, Dublin, 23 Aug. 1757 (R.A., Ms 374, fol. 49), edited in Fagan (ed.), *Stuart papers*, ii, pp 213-14. Mc Lynn, *Bonnie Prince Charlie*, p. 348. McKenna's optimism contrasted with the nervous opinions of the fifth earl of Cork who bauked at France's military might; 'Answer to a letter, the earl of Cork', 12 June 1756, in 'Letters to and from the earl of Cork' (Harvard Eng. Ms 218, 2f, vol. 6, N.L.I., mf. p. 787). 113 Burke to Edgar, Naples, December 1758 (R.A., Ms 387, fol. 145). See also R.A., Ms 388, fol. 146. 114 Heguerty to the prince, 17 Nov. 1758 (R.A., Ms 387, fol.[2]). See also R.A., Ms 387, fol. 17; R.A., Ms 388 fol. 134. For Heguerty's earlier Irish invasion plans during the '45; McLynn, *France and the Jacobite rising of 1745*, p. 82.

Edward into the latest French invasion scheme. In doing so, he accurately presented the stark reality of Charles Edward's hopeless political situation. However, he also reminded him of the impossibility of the Irish straying from their loyalty to his blood.[115]

While Heguerty may have wavered in his loyalty to Charles Edward, le Chevalier Redmond, maréchal de camp to the duc d'Aguillon, advocated the separation of Ireland from England. Redmond was well aware of the frosty relationship between Louis XV, the French ministry and Charles Edward. He accepted that his proposed separation of the two kingdoms would not have been acceptable to all his compatriots in France. He therefore chose to peripheralise Charles Edward in this latest venture, not by virtue of his relationship with the French king but in terms of his abjuration of the Roman Catholic faith.[116]

Redmond's next invasion proposal to Louis Charles Auguste Fouquet, Maréchal Belle-Isle, stressed that the advantages from the subjugation of Ireland far outweighed the risks. The richest and most advantageous ports of Cork, Waterford, Wexford and Dublin were in the south of the country, and easily accessible to Maréchal Conflans from his base in Brest. After their contemptuous treatment at the hands of the Hanoverians, the Irish people would eagerly embrace the French invasion force. He believed that the 'common Irish' wanted nothing more than a Catholic army in their country to deliver them from oppression, and allow them the free exercise of their religion. Redmond's suggestion that the French issue a declaration against the Pretender to the United Provinces clearly illustrates his diffidence towards the Stuarts. It could, however, also have been a shrewd political ploy to neutralise a potentially hostile neighbour. He finally emphasised that Irish hopes rested on the French and the great number of their compatriots in that service.[117] Although both Heguerty and Redmond were obliged to underplay or totally repudiate the Stuart cause, contrasting sentiments from the Irish *émigrés* in this period reveal the ideological struggle between Jacobite sentimentality and French *realpolitik*.[118]

---

115 Heguerty to Charles Edward, 10 June 1759 (R.A., Ms 390, fol. 34). Beresford provides a detailed insight of Heguerty's activities in this period; Beresford, 'Ireland', pp 208-20.   **116** 'Le Chevalier Redmond à Mr le duc d'Harcourt', 2 July 1758, in 'Recueil des lettres officelles de Mr le duc d'Harcourt, duc de Loiges et autres concernant la marine, la guerre en Europe pendant le mois de Juillet' (A.N., Ministère de la Guerre, vol. 3534, vol. 2, fol. 4, N.L.I., mf. p. 154). For a discussion, see Beresford, 'Ireland', p. 231. Charles Edward's 'apostasy' refers to the open secret that he had visited England in 1750 where he met the Oxford divine William King, prior of St Mary's, and formally disavowed Catholicism; Mc Lynn, *Charles Edward Stuart*, p. 399.   **117** Le Chevalier Redmond à maréchal de Belle-Isle, 13 July 1759 (A.N. Ministère de la Guerre, vol. 3534, fol. 102, N.L.I., mf. p. 154); Beresford, 'Ireland', p. 321. Patrick Murphy's 'Essai historique et politique sur l'Irlande' also states that a French invasion force would receive the support of all sections of the Catholic population, quoted in Beresford, 'Ireland', p. 245. Walpole's correspondence suggests the possibility of an Anglo-Dutch war in this period and English disdain for greedy Dutch merchants; Cunningham (ed.), *Letters*, iii, p. 194.   **118** Beresford, 'Ireland', pp 139, 197. See also Clancarthy to the prince, 1 July 1759 (R.A., Ms 394, fol. 66). Patrick D'Arcy's letter to Lord

The failure of this last realistic possibility of a Jacobite invasion produced a further shift in the tone of *émigré* correspondence with the Stuart court. They returned to the familiar platitudes: new year's greetings, pleas for patronage and seeking to exploit James's standing at the French court.[119] By this time, however, the political influence of the Irish diaspora had begun to disintegrate. The decline of Jacobitism contributed to this decay. Writing from France in 1756, Daniel O'Conor (brother of Charles O'Conor of Belanagare) lamented that in the Irish Brigades he 'saw himself as in a society of foreigners'. He continued that 'perhaps there is not one-tenth part of us Irish, our national enthusiasm is no more'. Three years later, he stated that the rank and file of the brigade was largely recruited from 'robbers and criminals from all parts of the world' and that he wished to return home to Ireland despite his native country's 'enslaved' condition.[120]

In his *Series of letters discovering the scheme projected by France in 1759*, however, the double-agent Oliver McAllester provided a different view of the racial and ideological make-up of the officer-corps of one Irish regiment (Lally's), 'which had been reduced to a handful of skeletons in India'.[121] Having been 'recruited', 'made complete' and 'well-officered' after the disastrous French campaign in India, he believed that no 'regiment in France made a more brilliant or martial appearance with respect to uniforms, drums, muffs and officers'. Many of these comprised 'old veterans who had made their retreats after serving many campaigns but were now entered in the service again with hearts full of joy in hopes of seeing once more their native soil and leaving their old maligned carcases at home'.[122] As late as 1768, a similar idea was trumpeted by the author of *Considerations upon the augmentation of the army*.

Clancarthy gives an insight into the delicate position of Irish Jacobites in the French service; R.A., Ms 396, fol. 118. See also R.A., Ms 414, fol. 11; R.A., Ms 403, fol. 201; McLoughlin, 'A crisis for the Irish in Bordeaux', pp 127-47. **119** Mary Francis Fermor to James III, 31 Dec. 1760 (R.A., Ms 404, fol. 185). See also R.A., Ms 408, fol. 199; R.A., Ms 401, fol. 140. **120** Hayes, *Irish swordmen*, pp 10-11. In 1762 Lord Trimbleston informed Halifax that 'the officers of the Irish Brigades were so disgusted with the service in which they were engaged that if a door was opened to them by his majesty [George III] they would crowd into it', quoted in Redington (ed.), *Calendar of Home office papers*, p. 154. There is corroborative contemporary evidence of *émigré* terror at the penal laws and their belief that Ireland was a place of imprisonment; McLaughlin, 'A crisis for the Irish in Bordeaux', pp 135-8, 140-1; Macnamara, 'Letters of an Irish exile', p. 242. A contributory factor to this decline was the acrimonious confrontation between the Thomond and Lismore O'Briens. Lord Clancarthy believed that this had detrimental implications for Jacobitism among the Irish exiles; R.A. 411, fol. 158; Hayes, *Biographical dictionary*, p. 215. McAllester claimed that Clancarthy criticised Charles Edward for his indulgence of beggarly Scotsmen; McAllester, *A series of letters*, i, pp 123-7. Daniel O'Connell's letter to his brother in Kerry from the French service in 1774 grieved that 'our unfortunate nation is fallen into utter contempt among the French since the death of Lord Clare whose favour with the king and the recent memories of Fontenoy and Lauffelt still supported us', quoted in Murphy, *Killaloe*, p. 222. O'Callaghan notes the example of an Irish Brigade officer who left the French king's service because of Lally's execution; O'Callaghan, *Irish brigades*, p. 578. Murtagh claims that Lally's death was deeply resented by the Irish Brigades. He also states that the decline of Jacobitism contributed to the lessening of the ideological motivation within the Brigades; Murtagh, 'Irish soldiers abroad', pp 300, 314. **121** O'Callaghan, *Irish brigades*, pp 505-79. **122** McAllester, *A series of letters*, ii, p. 186; see also Fagan (ed.), *Stuart papers*, ii, p. 258.

Men born and educated in every province, in every town, in every corner and spot of this island, are to be found in the dominions and under the allegiance of France and Spain ... Ireland they still consider as their natural inheritance, and the claim of original possession is transmitted amongst them from generation to generation. To revisit the land of their forefathers, and to enjoy again the property they have forfeited, is a favourite topic of their discourses, and the object ever present to their hopes .... Innovators and robbers are the characters we are described under; and, as such, should the fateful opportunity happen, we must expect to be treated.[123]

IV

Although Jacobitism survived in clerical, literary and popular circles, as well as among the exiles in the aftermath of the 'Forty-five', the failure of the rebellion precipitated a rift in Irish Catholic political opinion between Hanoverian conformists and die-hard Jacobite royalists.[124] On the one hand, a conformist Catholic aristocratic and mercantile element sought an accommodation with the existing regime; a Jacobite restoration receded as the main thrust of their strategy for the redress of Catholic grievances. On the other hand, a doctrinaire Jacobite element, especially in Irish clerical circles, continually reiterated their loyalty to the exiled king, and attempted to frustrate any approaches to the Hanoverians. An exclusive emphasis on conformist initiatives ignores the fact that Jacobitism retained much influence until well into the second half of the eighteenth century.[125] The intermittent struggle of the following decade and the difficulties in formulating a compromise on the question of a Hanoverian oath, demonstrated that James III retained many friends in Catholic circles until his death in 1766. To over-emphasise the early history of the Catholic Committee in the historiography of the late 1750s and early 1760s is to misunderstand and

---

123 *Considerations upon the augmentation of the army*, quoted in Morley, 'Idé-eolaíocht an tSeacaibíteachais in Éirinn agus in Albain', p. 19. The exact numbers of Irish soldiers in the Irish Brigades in this period awaits further investigation. General-Count Alexander O'Reilly was a son of John O'Reilly of Kilbride, County Cavan, who had raised a regiment for James II and fought at the Boyne. Alexander joined the Austrian Army in the 1750s and served there until he entered the Spanish service in 1762 where he received the rank of lieutenant-general and was later appointed Generalissmo of the Spanish army. He once told an Irish priest that it was his ambition to lead a Spanish army into Ireland, to expel the English and end the tyrannical system under which the people suffered. When he heard that the Baltrasna O'Reillys had conformed to the Established Church he promised that the first thing he would do was burn to the ground their ancestral house, polluted by conforming kinsmen whom he would put to the sword; quoted in O'Connell, *Schools and scholars of Breiffni*, pp 645-7. **124** Fagan charts the earlier attempts to arrive at an accomodation with the existing regime, and the attendant difficulties; Fagan, *Divided loyalties*, pp 12, 15, 36, 62-7. **125** See Leighton, *Catholicism*, pp 10, 11, 16 and 19, 91, 93, 109; Fenning, *Undoing of the friars*, p. 168.

misrepresent what was esentially a rearguard action against the forces of doctrinaire Jacobitism and anti-Jacobite reaction.

James Hamilton (Viscount Limerick, and later earl of Clanbrassill) was the prime mover behind a scheme in the mid-1750s whereby some Catholic priests would be registered under certain conditions, while the rest (mainly the regulars) would be forced to leave the country. He was supported by prominent Church of Ireland clergymen, including Richard Chenevix (Killaloe), Edward Synge (Elphin) and Robert Clayton (Clogher). On the Catholic side, the most prominent advocates of compromise and accomodation were Charles O'Conor, the leading intellectual within the Catholic Committee[126] and a lineal descendant of the O'Connor kings of Connaught, and Robert Barnewall, Baron Trimbleston, who succeeded to the title in 1746 and played a prominent role in Irish Catholic affairs until his death in 1779. They endeavours received some support from Michael Reilly, Roman Catholic archbishop of Armagh, and three senior clergy from the archdiocese of Dublin; Patrick Fitzsimons (vicar-general and future archbishop of Dublin), John Clinch (parish-priest of St Francis St, vicar-general) and Richard Lincoln, archdeacon of Glendalough, coadjutor of Dublin, and Fitzsimons's predecessor as archbishop.

Reaction to this controversy showed that James III still had the resources in Ireland to counter the intrigues of those Catholics who proposed any accommodation with the house of Hanover. The 'treasonable' machinations of Patrick Fitzsimons and his confederates Joseph Clinch, John Murphy and Richard Lincoln, outraged one anonymous Jacobite. He accused these clerics of undermining James III's authority by marginalising his role in episcopal nomination, and by urging prospective candidates to make their representations directly to the pope or Cardinal Corsini, cardinal-protector of Ireland. The anonymous author disparaged the lowly origins of Fitzsimons's group and stressed that ancient Catholic families preferred to bring their petitions to their own king instead of an Italian, even if he was the cardinal-protector of the Irish Catholic church.[127]

This affront to the exiled king's dignity showed that his prestige had begun to wane although he still remained a considerable force in Irish ecclesiastical politics. Representations in favour of the respective candidates for the vacant diocese of Killaloe and Meath reveal that some Catholics appreciated James's primary role in episcopal nomination.[128] Similarly, Anthony Blake, newly appointed bishop of Ardagh, assured James III in June 1756, that the Stuart king

---

126 For Catholic Committee, see Bartlett, *Fall and rise*, p. 60. **127** Anonymous to his majesty King James III, 16 Apr. 1753 (R.A., Ms 340, fol. 138). Fenning has shown that some voices of dissension were raised against the Stuart right of nomination; Fenning, *Undoing of the friars*, pp 52, 76, 158, 172. 179. For an examination of this controversy; idem, *Irish Dominican province*, p. 221. **128** Petition regarding the diocese of Killaloe, inscribed McMahon, Comte d'Eguilly, 28 June 1756 (B.L., Add. Ms 20, 662, fol. 168); Felix O'Doherty to [Edgar], Pascara, 9 July 1756 (R.A., Ms 363, fol. 111); Wall, 'Catholic loyalty to pope and king', pp 18, 21.

retained the unflinching devotion of the Irish Catholic episcopate. Paying tribute to the many favours which had been showered on his family by the Stuarts, in particular from James III's 'worthy father', Blake thanked him for this latest episcopal honour. He emphasised the close links between his pastoral duties and the complementary secular duty of promoting the king's cause.[129]

Despite Blake's assurances to James III, there were ominous straws in the wind. In a speech to the House of Commons of 2 January 1756, Hamilton highlighted the unhappy condition of the Protestant interest in Ireland. He identified two major evils – Jacobitism and the popish clergy – 'all under the strongest oaths of allegience to the Pretender'. All Irishmen who entered the French service must be prevented from returning to Ireland and he advocated driving 'a wedge between popery and Jacobitism' and 'untwisting the cord of popery and Jacobitism'.[130] He proposed the legal recognition and registration of the parochial clergy, on the condition that the registered priests would swear allegiance to George II. They would become good subjects, ready to inform against the itinerant friars, 'those restless emissaries of France and Rome'.[131]

Despite the genuine quest for compromise, divisions opened in the ranks of the Catholic laity and gentry. As the nominee of the exiled Stuart king, Archbishop Lincoln could not readily repudiate his loyalty, while at the same time he did not wish to antagonise the government on the outbreak of war with France. His *laissez-faire* policy increasingly exasperated aristocratic and mercantile interest within the Catholic Committee. Charles O'Conor readily admitted in private that Jacobitism created the main difficulty in Catholic acceptance of the act. These representations were being made only ten years after the 'Forty-five' and at a time when the outbreak of war resuscitated Jacobite hopes in some circles.[132] Hamilton's bill also foundered on the suspicions of the Protestant hierarchy. Archbishop Stone resented any implication that the Protestant clergy were in any way answerable for the strength of popery. He also questioned the timing of an oath of loyalty for Catholics and believed that it would be better to aid and encourage the Protestant religion instead of giving legal recognition to Catholicism. On 29 January 1756 a proposal in the House of Lords to give the bill a third reading in three months passed by eighteen votes to sixteen. As this date was after the proroguing of parliament, however, the vote was considered a defeat.

---

129 Anthony Blake to James III, Galway, 20 Oct. 1756 (R.A., Ms 366, fol. 25).   130 Fenning, *Irish Dominican province*, p. 268; Fagan, *Divided loyalties*, p. 94.   131 There have been a number of recent accounts of this controversy; Fenning, *Irish Dominican province*, pp 267-70; Bartlett, *Fall and rise*, pp 56-62; Fagan, *Divided loyalties*, pp 87-111. For O'Conor's political activities; Ward and Ward, 'The ordeal of O'Conor of Belanagare', pp 6-15. Fagan claims that Lincoln was involved in 'tight-rope diplomacy' in this period; Fagan, *Divided loyalties*, p. 89. Bartlett states that Lincoln was not a supporter of Hamilton's efforts; Bartlett, *Fall and rise*, p. 56.   132 Leighton, *Catholicism*, p. 57. O'Conor stated his own opposition on religious grounds; O'Conor to Dr Curry, 18 Nov. 1757, in Ward, Wrynn and Ward (ed.), *Letters of Charles O'Conor of Belanagare*, p. 45. For O'Conor's criticism of 'The Hyper-Doctor' (Lincoln), see Bartlett, *Fall and rise*, p. 62.

James McKenna kept the Stuart court abreast with developments. In a letter from of 5 February 1756, he informed Edgar 'that there were eighteen of the buyers [privy council members] in the change for us and sixteen against us'. Ironically McKenna viewed the overseer of Elphin (Edward Synge) as the villian of the piece while 'the good Inglese overseer of Armagh [Primate Stone] stood strenuously for us', thereby thwarting any accommodation between the Catholic Church and the government which might erode the influence of the Stuart king.[133]

In spite of this setback, Hamilton proved resilient in his quest for an accommodation with the Catholic Church, even as he attempted to impose the laws against them. The arrest in April 1756 of Primate O'Reilly and a motley collection of his clergy and laity who had assembled in Dundalk for the distribution of holy oils showed that the old associations between Catholicism and Jacobitism had died hard among some Protestants. O'Reilly and his clergy were accused of gathering money for the Pretender, a treasonable offence and a very serious accusation in view of the looming war between Britain and France. Although this incident can be attributed to groundless Protestant scare-mongering, it must also be viewed in relation to continued Catholic unwillingness to abjure the Stuart king, the covert activities of Jacobite agents such as James McKenna and Anthony Blake and the fierce anti-government sentiment in contemporary poetry.[134] O'Reilly's appearance before Hamilton in the latter's capacity as a local magistrate laid the ground for renewed efforts to seek an accommodation. These were continued under the new lord lieutenant, the duke of Bedford, who took up office in September 1757. These efforts culminated in a modified bill which was also thrown out by the Irish privy council on 21 January 1758.

The so-called 'Trimbleston pastoral', signed in the castle of Lord Trimbleston, self-appointed leader of the Catholic cause, was another probable consequence of Hamilton's circumstantial 'meeting' with the archbishop after his arrest.   It caused considerable division among the Catholic hierarchy and laity. Trimbleston's influence over O'Reilly ensured that his pastoral letter of support for the government had the backing of the bishops of the Armagh province. It sought to counter what they considered to be unjustified Protestant prejudices against Catholic principles and to pave the way for the next bill which the signatories expected to be presented before parliament. Instead of an oath of loyalty, all it required of the Catholic populace was that they prayed for George II. Although it was only a draft, it became the subject of heated discussion and

---

133 James McKenna to Edgar, Dublin. 5 Feb. 1756 (R.A., Ms 361, fol. 60).   **134** Fenning, *Irish Dominican province*, p. 270. It was not an isolated incident in the 1750s. James Dunne, bishop of Ossory, alleged that he was forced to abandon his ministry after being accused by his Protestant counterpart of being an emissary for the chevalier de St George, in Fagan (ed.), *Stuart papers*, ii, p. 176. See also ibid., ii, p. 178. An anonymous letter in 1755 preserved in the Melville papers warned that Catholic bishops were urging their flocks to stand by France and the Pretender; quoted in Bartlett, *Fall and rise*, pp 55-6.

heart-searching in higher ecclesiastical circles. Its greatest antagonist, the Dominican Thomas Burke stressed that the pastoral was direct contravention of the third canon of the Fourth Lateran Council which asserted the papal power to depose kings. He also informed Archbishop Lincoln that any priest who read the text from the altar or prayed for George II would take his life in his hands. Burke added that he himself as a schoolboy would have stoned such a priest off the altar and he maintained that this feeling remained strong among the people.[135] Augustine Cheevers, whom Thomas Burke dubbed the 'Judas among the regulars' (for supporting the pastoral), attempted to justify his stance in a letter to Charles O'Kelly. He received a stinging reply in which O'Kelly described the pain it had given James III to whom Cheevers owed more than any other bishop in the country.[136]

The Irish Jacobite poet Liam Dall Ó hIfearnáin also dealt with the issue of an oath of loyalty and prayers to the Hanoverian monarch. He was disgusted when George II ordered a public fast for the success of his arms on the outbreak of the Seven Years War. Liam Dall expressed surprise that a leader or powerful bishop should give him a Friday with fasting that a Stuart might take the crown. He assured his audience that he had no intention of praying for George's dynasty and did not doubt that he was without sin by disobeying this injunction to pray on a Friday for them. On the contrary, he maintained that Louis XV and his warmongering allies could stretch his neck with a thick rope if he ever prayed in any way for that crowd:

> [Nuair a d'órduigh Rí Shasana troscadh chum buadh catha]
> Car bh' íongnadh taoiseach nó easpog cómhachtach
> Do thabhairt saoirse Dia hAoine agus troscadh damh-sa
> Le díograis chum Stíobhairt do ghlacadh coróinneach
> Is gan smaoineadh go nguidhfinn le sleachta Sheóirse
>
> ...
>
> Ní shílim im smaointe gur peaca dhamh-sa
> Gan guidhchan Dia hAoine le haicme den tsórt san
>
> ...
>
> Bíd sin ag Laoiseach dá ngreadadh i gcómhrac
> Is ríghthe gach críche ag teacht i gcómhar leis.
> Mo phíopa do shíneadh le reamhar-chórda
> Dá nguidhinn-se i slíghe ar bith ar mhaitheas leó san.[137]

135 Fenning, *Irish Dominican province*, p. 271. Papal deposing and dispensing powers were enshrined in the third canon of the Fourth Lateran Council, convoked in 1215, which brought the church to the height of its power in medieval Europe; Fagan, *Divided loyalties*, pp 113-15. 136 Fenning, *Irish Dominican province*, pp 273-4. 137 Liam Dall Ó hIfearnáin, 'Car bh' íongnadh taoiseach nó easpog cómhachtach', in Ó Foghludha (eag.), *Ar bhruach na Coille Muaire*, p. 51. Prút and Ó Buachalla dated Ó hIfearnáin's

Although the tide had turned against the supporters of James III by 1759, Jacobitism's continuing vigour is shown by Fr McKenna's efforts on behalf of the Stuart king. Having succeeded in weaning some of 'the better sort' of Catholics away from an accommodation with the Elector, McKenna ridiculed the lowly origins of those 'upstart moneyed rascals' who subscribed to the Hanoverian oath:

> I have indeed on my part and in my way dissuaded numbers and espe-
> cially of our better sort from it and have succeeded so that a sad parcel
> of upstart moneyed rascals must not dismay us now no more than
> hitherto. You'll please to remark that not one of my name, though
> numerous they be here, has meddled therein nor never may.[138]

Fr Bernard Rothe called these reports of Catholic bishops praying for the Hanoverians 'treason and madness'[139] and castigated Lord Trimblestown as having 'the wrongest head I ever have known or heard of'.[140] Although powerless to prevent such representations, the exiled king could stifle the ambitions of those accommodationalists who sought episcopal appointments. In a letter to the Stuart court of 23 April 1758, Bishop John O'Brien of Cloyne rejoiced that 'the subscribers of the infamous pastoral are now in great confusion'. He added, 'the confusion of some of them proceeds only from a just apprehension that the work [the Trimbleston pastoral] will exclude them from a certain succession lately opened by the death of their chief [Primate O'Reilly, d. 4 February 1758]'. The nomination of Anthony Blake as his successor justified O'Brien's confidence and showed that James III still had it in his power to thwart the episcopal ambitions of those who attempted to interfere with his prerogative. Thomas Burke, another staunch Jacobite loyalist, whom Lincoln claimed was 'panting for a mitre', also reaped the rewards of his espousal of the Stuart cause by his elevation to the see of Ossory.[141]

In spite of these set-backs, O'Conor and the Catholic Committee still sought to integrate themselves into the Hanoverian regime by divesting themselves of the Jacobite stigma. In doing so, they regularly praised the Protestant hero William of Orange, The contemporary Irish Catholic pamphlet tradition reinterpretated William III as a champion of civil and religious liberties, Catholic as well as Protestant. The author of *The Catholic's letter to the Roman Catholics of Ireland* sought by a clever juxtaposition to disassociate William from

poem to a proclamation of fasts and prayers in the reign of George III in 1760; Prút, 'Liam Dall Ó hIfearnáin', p. 203; Ó Buachalla, *Aisling Ghéar*, pp 644-5. **138** Fr James McKenna to Edgar, Dublin, Dec. 1759 (R.A., Ms 397, fol. 48). **139** Fr Bernard Rothe to Edgar, 25 Feb. 1760 (R.A., Ms 399, fol. 55). **140** Rothe to Edgar, 3 Mar. 1760 (R.A., Ms 399, fol. 104). **141** John O'Brien, bishop of Cloyne, to Colonel Daniel O Brien, earl of Lismore, 23 Apr. 1758 (R.A. Ms. 380, fol. 164), quoted in Fagan (ed.) *Stuart papers*, ii, p. 222. See also ibid., ii, p. 226; Fagan, *Divided loyalties*, p. 119.

the excesses of Anne's (a Stuart) reign. He vilified the Stuart dynasty, understated Irish Catholic Jacobitism and praised Irish passivity since the end of the Jacobite war. The author's own political motives and his protracted litigation to retain his ancestral lands magnifies the danger of taking his opinions as representative of popular Catholic opinion.[142] *The Catholic's letter to the Roman Catholics of Ireland on the late French invasion* conceded that there were still Catholics who wished success to the enemy. The author wondered at 'the attachment some among us have for the Stewart family'. He attacked James I and his successors (Charles I and II) for upholding laws initiated against Catholics under Elizabeth I. James II 'who lived and died a good Catholic had hurt the church more than all the foregoing'. By supporting the Stuarts, Irish Catholics lost 'the flower of our nobility and are now subject to many penal laws'. He deemed Queen Anne to be the worst of all monarchs as 'our chapels and churches were often shut up and the clergy more oppressed than they have been since'. Given Irish sufferings under the Stuarts, the author described as 'ridiculous and absurd' the encouragement given by some of 'our' weak people to the 'Young Adventurer' (Charles Edward) in 1745. Despite Charles Edward's recent apostasy, Catholics still adhered to him 'on a presumption of his being of the family of Stewart', 'the very presumption which would have drawn my affection entirely from him, as we have suffered too much from that family'.[143] In *The case of the Roman Catholics of Ireland* (1755), O'Conor emphasised the political passivity within the Irish Catholic community.[144] The Irish had grown 'listless' and 'indifferent' with regards to 'pain' or 'liberty'. 'Like men long confined', they soothe themselves into 'unmanly stupefaction', growing 'regardless of all events' and think of nothing above or beyond the present condition. O'Conor refers to the total lack of Catholic participation in the political life of the first half of the eighteenth century as the 'silence of grievance'. It should not be solely attributed to the apathy suggested by O'Conor, however, but also to their adherence to Jacobitism, an attachment which he now sought to underplay.

O'Conor's *astutia politica* praise of William III, and his continued attacks on the Stuarts, in particular Queen Anne, did not impress one of his contemporaries, the historian Dr Ferdinando Warner.[145] He reproached O'Conor for his failure to adequately address the 'principal objection' to Catholics, namely

---

142 P. 313, fn. 179.　**143** Anon, [C. O'Conor?], *The Catholic's letter to the Roman Catholics of Ireland.* O'Conor continued to praise King William III and attack Queen Anne; O'Conor; *Case of the Roman Catholics of Ireland,* pp 43-5. Charles Edward's apostasy prompted Patrick Murphy, a Spanish-based Irish exile, to propose setting a Spanish prince on the Irish throne from whom the Irish would enjoy the privileges of professing their religion, the return of their arms and estates, as well as an end to the tyranny which has reigned for seventy years; 'Essai historique et politique d'Irlande' 10 Feb. 1760 (B.N., Affaires Étrangères (Espagne) Ms 527, fols. 178-98, N.L.I., mf. p. 2878); See also Beresford, 'Ireland', pp 245-50. **144** Connolly, *Religion,* p. 3. **145** [C. O'Conor], *Case of the Roman Catholics of Ireland,* pp 37-38, 43, 45. There are other instances in his correspondence where O'Conor played politics with the cult of King William, in Ward and Ward (ed.), *Letters,* i, p. 29; [O'Conor and Curry], *Observations on the popery laws,* p. 18.

their 'known', 'necessary' and 'unavoidable' attachment to 'the Pretender'. Responding to Warner, O'Conor drew on Sir William Temple's account of Dutch Catholics in the aftermath of the Great Revolution in the Low Countries, to question the 'fatal' or 'unavoidable' attachment of Irish Catholics for over seventy years to a much less formidable Pretender than Philip II of Spain. His aphorism on Irish Jacobitism accurately summarises the relationship between Ireland and the exiled Stuarts, and their second-class citizenship within the Hanoverian state: 'Such a *fatal attachment* has no precedent in the history of any other country on earth'.[146] Shortly afterwards, however, O'Conor privately conceded that the Stuarts remained an issue which Catholics should avoid at all costs, unless publicly challenged by Protestants:

> Our masters are silent about him [the Pretender] and to them let us leave his political resurrection ... We need not expose ourselves to fastening any such knot on ourselves by reviving any popular topics at present about the person to be abjured, at least I think so. When the Pretender is publicly objected to us, it will then be time to speak out on that subject.[147]

This Gordian knot of Jacobitism was finally loosed by the death of James III in January 1766. After he had been laid to rest in St Peter's with all the splendour due to a king, the Vatican took the opportunity to rid itself of the diplomatic millstone of Jacobitism by refusing to recognise the dissolute Charles Edward, prince of Wales, as 'Charles III'. Some Jacobite clerics refused to follow the pope's lead. The heads of the English and Scots Colleges, and the Franciscan and Dominican houses, defied papal dictates by having the Te Deum sung in Charles's honour on his arrival in Rome. All these, including Patrick Kirwan, prior of St Sixtus and Clement, received Charles Edward at their respective establishments and afforded him full kingly honours. Their open flaunting of papal authority resulted in immediate banishment from the Papal States. John Thomas Troy, who would emerge in later eighteenth century as the most influential Irish prelates since the Reformation, spoke of this 'extraordinary and unexpected event which will be forever remembered by the members of this house', which had prevented him (Troy) 'from waiting on his majesty'.[148]

It was only in 1774 that the question of an oath for Catholics was finally settled: an act of that year permitted 'his majesty's [George III] subjects of whatever persuasion to testify their allegiance to him'. Leighton has remarked that 'those who opposed the oath in 1774 had good reasons unconnected with Jacobite sentiment for adopting the course they did. Yet in some cases such as

146 O'Conor to Dr Curry, 10 Nov. 1761, in Ward, Wrynn and Ward (ed.), *Letters*, i, pp 114-15. **147** Ward, Wrynn and Ward (ed.), *Letters*, i, p. 117. It was only in 1771 that O'Conor could say with any confidence that 'we have no Pretender to the throne at present'; [O'Conor and Curry], *Observations on the popery laws*, p. 19. **148** Fenning, *Irish Dominican province*, pp 357-8.

the Bishop of Ferns (Nicholas Sweetman), we may be fairly certain that it was loyalty to Charles III which prevented subscription'.[149]

V

The fortunes of Irish Jacobitism subsided between the end of the War of the Austrian Succession and the death of James III in 1766. The poets still clung to their affection for the Stuarts. They longed for the arrival of Charles Edward and the Irish Brigades to dismantle the penal code, restore the fortunes of the Catholic Church, re-establish the dispossessed aristocracy and gentry and banish the Protestants. Jacobite sentiment also survived through the fitful correspondence which flowed between Ireland and the Stuart court in this period, mainly through the clergy. A residual Jacobite interest also persisted at the local level, which manifested itself through seditious health-drinking and residual recruiting for foreign servicere. The cosmetic Jacobitism of the Dublin mob in the late 1750s and the Whiteboys's utilisation of Jacobite imagery shows that Jacobitism survived at a popular level. At the very least, it indicated that these embryonic political interests were grafted onto an older Jacobite stalk.

The exiles continued their petitions for charity, preferments and certificates of *noblesse*, and constantly reiterated their good wishes, loyalty and devotion to the Jacobite cause in the aftermath of the 1745 rebellion. Their 'native land' and the 'persecution' caused by the penal code remained their concern. With the outbreak of the Seven Years War, prominent exiles were confident of the success of a French landing in Britain and again advocated a diversionary landing in Ireland. The decline of the Irish interest in French military and political life, following the death of influential Jacobites such as Thomas Lally and Lord Clare, severed the links between the Stuart king and the Irish Brigades. The decline of James III, and the subsequent descent of his son into alcoholism, scandal and 'apostasy', further weakened the links between Ireland and the Stuart court.[150] Although Irish Protestants still feared France in the 1760s and 1770s, Arthur Dillon's hopes of unsheathing his sword for his native land in the 1790s belonged to a period when republicanism had superseded both the Jacobite and Bourbon threats.[151]

---

149 Leighton, *Catholicism*, p. 57. Fenning called Thomas Burke of Ossory, who opposed the test oath in the 1770s, 'the last of the Jacobites'; Fenning, *Irish Dominican province*, p. 373. See also Childe Pemberton, *Earl bishop*, i, p. 207.There are a number of recent examination of this controversy which highlight the difficulties involved'; Bartlett, *Fall and rise*, pp 78-81; Kelly, 'A wild Capuchin in Cork', pp 39-62. 150 Griffin stated that refusal of the frustrated and dissolute prince to extend the patronage his father had granted to the exiles, the execution of Lally and the rank and file becoming increasingly foreigners dissolved the political influence of the Brigades; Griffin, *Irish on the continent in the eighteenth century*, p. 465. 151 Bartlett and Jeffreys (ed.), *A military history of Ireland*, p. 308. In her work on the descendants of the Wild Geese in France, Renagh Holohan has remarked that 'many of them are as out of step with

A struggle for the conscience of the Irish Catholic community took place between Jacobite royalists and those that advocated a settlement with the house of Hanover. Catholic magnates and gentlemen, such as Lord Trimbleston, Charles O'Conor and the members of the Catholic Committee, spearheaded these attempts to break the 'fatal attachment' of the Irish to the house of Stuart. The lukewarm reaction of many Catholic clergymen and the endeavours of doctrinaire Jacobite royalists initially stifled these plans. James III retained the loyalty of many Irish Catholics until his death in 1766. Although some sections of the Catholic hierarchy and laity divested themselves of Jacobitism, their Protestant political adversaries taunted them with the continuing association between Catholicism and Jacobitism. By the end of the 1770s, some Protestants even mourned the political demise of Jacobitism, which they believed caused the Hanoverians to prematurely repeal the penal laws, and to betray the foundational principles that had put them on the thrones of England, Scotland and Ireland.

modern France as they are with modern Ireland. They are almost to a man staunchly royalist and universally refer to the Old Pretender as Jacques Trois and in many cases call their sons Charles Edouard'; Holohan, *The Irish chateaux*, p. 5.

Conclusion

Irish political leaders, from Burke to Tone, generally disavowed Jacobitism in the period between the death of Charles Edward in 1788 and the end of the eighteenth century. While most Protestants accepted Tone's assurance that Irish Catholics were no longer Jacobites, the very fact that he needed to address the issue testifies to the longevity of the Irish Jacobite tradition.[1] In his *Letter to Sir Hercules Langrishe*, Edmund Burke mocked the continuing Protestant preoccupation with their three greatest bugaboos, the Stuart Pretender, the pope and the king of France, who had all been cut down to size (as he believed) in the course of the eighteenth century. He dismissed as ludicrous the possibility of the pope absolving King George's subjects from their allegiance and sending Henry, Cardinal York ('Henry IX') to rule them as his viceroy:

> As little shall I detain you with matters that can as little obtain admission into a mind like yours; such as the fear, or pretence of fear, that, in spite of your own power, and the trifling power of Great Britain, you may be conquered by the pope; or that this commodious bugbear (who is of infinitely more use to those who pretend to fear, than to those who love him) will absolve his majestie's subjects from their allegiance, and send over the Cardinal of York to rule them as his viceroy; or that, by the plenitude of his power, he will take that fierce tyrant, the king of the French, out of his jail and arm that nation (which on all occasions treats his holiness so very politely) with his bulls and pardons, to invade poor old Ireland, to reduce you to popery and slavery, into the wooden shoes of that arbitrary monarch.[2]

Burke's confidence notwithstanding, the Jacobite shadow lingered on the popular political horizon. The work of Jim Smyth and Kevin Whelan shows the Janus-headed nature of Defenderism in the 1780s and 1790s. Having utilised Jacobitism to impede the repeal of the penal laws, some Protestants now believed that the Defenders and United Irishmen aimed to overturn the Glor-

---

1 Leighton, *Catholicism*, p. 143; Whelan, *Tree of liberty*, p. 47.   2 Burke, *Letter to Sir Hercules Langrishe*, p. 50.

ious Revolution. The raid for arms on the house of one O'Flynn in County Meath in 1797 uncovered ancient title deeds to lands which had been forfeited in 1641. A political tract entitled *The poor man's catechism* advocated 'dividing the ancient estates among the descendants of those who were pillaged by English invaders'.[3] The Defenders signalled the democratisation of the political culture of Catholics, the transition from Jacobite to Jacobin.[4] In relation to General Jean Joseph Humbert's Irish campaign in 1798, Connolly remarks that he was received not as the bearer of liberty, equality and brotherhood but in the name of the confessional and dynastic loyalties of the *ancien régime*, a cast of 'ghosts that had been born in the Ireland of Anne and George I coming back to haunt the age of Pitt and Napoleon' for a brief period.[5] A perusal of Irish and continental sources would suggest that many of Connolly's ghosts had not gone away but had haunted the Irish polity throughout the century.

Residual Jacobitism, and the transition from Jacobitism through Jacobinism to O'Connellite Catholic nationalism, is evident in the poetry of Mícheál Óg Ó Longáin, the principal guardians of the Irish literary tradition in Munster in the late eighteenth and early-nineteenth centuries.[6] In his poem 'Seal im Aonar Cois Leasa', Ó Longáin utilised the Jacobite literary device of the 'aisling'. One day, while contemplating the decay and demise of the Irish aristocracy and gentry, the poet is accosted by a beautiful woman. When questioned as to her identity, she replied that she was a worried woman astray among Englishmen. The poet assured her that a star in the high heavens would come soon on a punitive expedition to rouse the Irish and release them from captivity and hardship:

Seal is mé im aonar cois leasa in uaigneas,
go cathach faon léanmhar tré mheath dár n-uaislibh,
tig ainnir tséimh mhaorga 'na seasamh suas liom
ler caitheadh mé in éagruith gan acmhainn luaile

...

D'fheagair bé mhaorga na ndearg ngrua mé
Go blasta béilbhéasach san teangain uasail

---

3 Smyth, *Men of no property*, passim; Whelan, *Tree of liberty*, pp 42-5. **4** Whelan, *Tree of liberty*, pp 33, 35, 40, 47, 48-9; Bartlett, *Fall and rise*, pp 5, 11. The spate of Catholic families seeking the reversal of outlawries and the recognition of Jacobite titles in the aftermath of the relief of the 1780s caused considerable anxiety among Protestants; Whelan, 'Underground gentry', p. 151. The hanging and shooting of the effigies of James II and Mary of Modena as late as October 1800 may have resulted from the association between Defenderism, the United Irishmen and Jacobitism; quoted in Kelly, 'Glorious and immortal memory', p. 50. Clark has noted the continuity between Jacobitism and Jacobinism in late eighteenth-century English radicalism; Clarke, *English Society*, pp 307-8, 318-19, 374. Pittock identifies an emerging 'Jacobitism of the left' in the work of the Scottish poets Robert 'Robbie' Burns and Joseph Ritson, where the 'Tree of Liberty' replaced 'The Royal Oak'; Pittock, *Poetry*, chapters 6 and 7. See also Monod, *Jacobitism*, pp 41-3; Donaldson, *Jacobite song, political myth and national identity*, passim. The most recent examination of Defenderism is Smyth, *Men of no property*, passim. **5** Connolly, *Religion*, p. 249.

> ní neach den tréad réilteann sin chanais thuas mé,
> ach bean ar strae méise idir Ghallaibh buartha
>
> Aitchim féin réilteann na bhflaitheas uachtrach
> le peannaid ghéar d'aontaigh teacht seal dár bhfuascladh,
> go scaipidh daorghéibhinn is ceasna chruatain
> do mhaicne Gael éachtach i bhfearann Tuathail.[7]

In another poem, 'Maidean im Aonarán', he encountered the same woman. This time he is informed that she is Éire, the wife a succession of the mythical kings of Ireland. That James III ('Séamas Óg') had joined this illustrious group showed the extent to which he had been relegated to the realms of myth.[8] In his poem, 'I dTairngreacht Naomh', Ó Longáin employed the prophetic message, a favoured Jacobite literary device, to herald the rescue of the long suffering Gaels who would rise up in arms against the rotten Calvinists. In this case, however, the United Irishman Arthur O'Connor replaced 'James III' and 'Bonnie Prince Charlie' as the poet's hero and bright Caesar:

> I dtarngaireacht naomh is léir go bhfaca
> scéal beag deas le lua,
> ar leathain tsliocht Éabha a théacht go tapa
> tréan i dtreasaibh tua;...
> A Chlanna bocht' Gael tá i bpéin le fada
> éiridh feasta suas,
> go nglanaid sin Éire mhaorga bhuach
> ó scamallaibh daora an chlaontruip chruaidh
> go mbeidh mar a chéile i gcéim 's i gcruas
> gan tnúth gan teacs go deo
> is gabhaidh go géar ag gléas bhur n-arm
> is déanaidh treas gan trua;
>
> ...
>
> is dearbh go ndéanfaidh claonshliocht Chailbhin
> bhréin do leagadh anuas;
>
> ...
>
> mo chara 's mo lao-se an Caesar suairc,
> an faraire séimh gan chlaon gan chruas,

6 Louis Cullen has rather unfairly dismissed Ó Longáin as a commissioned transcriber; Cullen, *The Hidden Ireland: a reassessment*, p. 49. Evidence also exists of surviving Jacobitism in the English language tradition; 'An old Jacobite ballad found in an alehouse at Old Laughlin along with the United Irishman's Oath' [no date] (N.A., Rebellion papers 620/52/37). **7** Mícheál Ó Longáin, 'Seal im Aonar cois leasa', in Ó Donnchadha (eag.), *Ó Longáin*, pp 70-1. **8** Mícheál Ó Longáin, 'Maidean im Aonarán', in Ó Donnchadha (eag.), *Ó Longáin*, pp 78-9.

gurab fada bhiaidh sé 's ghaolta suas
's gach trúp do ghabhann leo.[9]

In 'Scéal do réab mo chroí ionam', the poet bemoaned the apathy and loss of direction of the Gaels with Lord Edward Fitzgerald in prison and the noble Arthur O'Connor across the sea:

A chlanna Gael sin réidh sibh choíche,
d'imigh bhur dtreoir, níl spéis ná brí ionaibh:
sin é an Gearaltach ceangailte i ngeimhleach
is Artúr uasal uaibh tar taoide.[10]

Returning to the 'aisling' in his poem 'Ag Taisteal le sleasaibh na Laoi', he put forward another contender for Éire's affections. In this case, he chose his own first cousin Tomás Ó Longáin, alias 'Captain Stíl' (Captain Steele), whose transportation to Botany Bay had caused Éire such heartbreak. She asserted that her sadness would not dissolve until the enemies of her love were weakened, reduced, dead and trembling:

Ar cheard na bhflaitheas naofa 's an Mac a fuair péin 'nár dtaoibh
go raibh námhaid mo charad chléibhse lag marbh traochta tinn,
is mac Seáin mhic Pheadair ghléghil, 'sé an fear dá nglaotar Stíl,
do theacht slán tar ais go hÉirinn gan bhascadh béim ná díth.[11]

His poem 'Déinidh go Subhach a Ghaela', written to commemorate the return of Napoleon Bonaparte from Egypt in 1799, and the possibility of an imminent invasion of Britain, presented a far more formidable candidate for the favour of 'Éire' and the reduction of the troops of rotten Orangemen ('Brúigidh, bascaidh, réabaidh, leagaidh, séididh síos/trúip na nOrange mbréana').[12] Although some of Ó Longáin's Catholic contemporaries would have questioned Napoleon's suitability as the successor to the Stuart princes and the worthy recipient of Éire's affections and the loyalty of her children, Ó Longáin's next candidate received the ringing endorsement of all sections of the Catholic community from the

---

9 Mícheál Ó Longáin, 'I dtarngaireacht naomh', in Ó Donnchadha (eag.), *Ó Longáin*, pp 80-1, 147.
10 Mícheál Ó Longáin, 'Scéal do réab mo chroí ionam', in Ó Donnchadha (eag.), *Ó Longáin*, p. 88. For a profile of Arthur O'Connor, see McDermott, 'Arthur O'Connor', pp 48-70. 11 Mícheál Ó Longáin, 'Ag taisteal le sleasaibh na Laoi', in Ó Donnchadha (eag.), *Ó Longáin*, p. 97. 12 Mícheál Ó Longáin, 'Deinidh go subhrach a Gheala', in Ó Donnchadha (eag.), *Ó Longáin*, p. 101. Other citations to Bonaparte exist in the Irish tradition; Micheál Ó Cearbhalláin, 'Bónaigh ón Fhrainc [1809]', in Laoide (eag.), *Duanaire na Midhe*, p. 11; Ó Muirgheasa (eag.), *Dhá chéad de cheoltaibh Uladh*, p. 24; Anon., 'Preacháin Chill Chainnigh' agus Anon, 'Bualadh Ros Mhic Thriúin', in Ó hÓgáin (eag.), *Duanaire Osraíoch*, pp 38-9. The Madden Collection in Cambridge U.L. contains many popular Napoleonic ballads in English; U.L., Cambs. Madden 24 , fols 217, 375, 591 and Madden 25 fols 274, 300, 333, 335-6.

higher clergy to the forty shilling freeholder. The gay hawk who was never oppressive or hard on the ordinary people, the prince of the royal blood of the family of Milesius and the hero of Ó Longáin's poem 'Gurab fada suas bhias Dónall' was Daniel O'Connell:

Gurab fada suas bhias Dónall
i ngradam bhuan 's i gcomhachtaibh,
an seabhac suairc nár chleacht bheith gruama,
cas ná cruaidh lem shórtsa;
gas de mhuartsliocht Eoghain
aibidh uasal eolach,

...

flaith de rífhuil Chlann Mhíligh
dalta díleas d'Éirinn.[13]

In the nineteenth century, O'Connell emerged as the undisputed hero of the Irish literary tradition. Gearóid Ó Tuathaigh believes that he was 'the unrivalled hero of the hour for Irish-speaking writers'. Indeed, Ó Buachalla states that 'The Liberator' was the final heir of the messianic mantle which had passed from Hugh O'Neill to Ball Dearg Ó Dónaill and had remained in the possession of the Stuarts for nearly two centuries.

II

Although Jacobitism has re-emerged as a major topic in English and Scottish historiography over the last decade, Irish support for the deposed house of Stuart has been largely ignored. This is itself indicative of the general neglect of the history of the period between the Battle of the Boyne in 1691 and the emergence of secret societies in the latter part of the eighteenth century. Disproportionate attention has been given to the Protestant Ascendancy and the origin, outbreak

---

13 Mícheál Ó Longáin, 'Gur fada suas bhias Dónall', in Ó Donnchadha (eag.), *Ó Longáin*, p. 133; Ó Tuathaigh, 'Gaelic Ireland, popular politics and Daniel O'Connell', pp 26, 27, 29; Ó Buachalla, 'Irish Jacobite poetry', pp 115-6. The priest-poet James Vale's poem 'Síle Ní Ghadhra' also eulogised Daniel O'Connell as the son of Síle Ní Ghadhra (Ireland) 'mac Shíghle Ní Ghadhra', quoted in Morley, 'Idé-eolaíocht an tSeacaibíteachais in Éirinn agus in Albain', p. 23: The anonymous poets of Ossory also lavished praise on O'Connell; Anon, 'Carraig Seac' agus Anon, 'Oíche na dtinte cnámh', in Ó hÓgáin (eag.), *Duanaire Osraíoch*, pp 42, 44. J.C. O'Callaghan, the historian of the Irish Brigades, symbolically crowned O'Connell as 'high king' of Ireland at a monster meeting on the Hill of Tara; Boylan (ed.), *Dictionary of Irish Biography*, p. 303. O'Connell also featured prominently in the English-language ballad tradition in Ireland; U.L., Cambs. Madden 24 fols 242-3, 260-61, 369, 326, 359, 365, 386, 432, 465-6, 500, 502, 516, 531, 534, 544, 561, 563, 567-72, 585, 608, 648; ibid., fols 25, 50, 58, 61, 62, 63, 66, 81, 94, 403, 483, 531). According to Leerssen, broadsheet ballads of the period mix old-fashioned aisling-style messianism with the names of Bonaparte and O'Connell, and the end of Protestantism was foretold by the prophecies of Pastorini; Leerssen, *Remembrance and imagination*, p. 88.

and nature of the 1798 rebellion. Recent surveys of eighteenth-century Ireland have failed to address the age-old bias towards the last thirty years of the century. Their failure to utilise Irish-language and continental source-material has supported an anglocentric view of eighteenth-century Ireland. The poetry in particular has been dismissed as lacking substantive political content, representing nothing more than the stylised output of a learned literary caste. More careful study suggests that it did not flourish in a political vacuum. Compared thematically with contemporary Scots-Gaelic and English Jacobite writings, and with Whig, anti-Jacobite rhetoric, Irish Jacobite poetry shows an acute awareness of the workings of local, British and European politics and its ramifications for the Stuart cause. Irish literature provides the single most important source for Irish Jacobitism and the poets served an absolutely vital function in the diffusion of English-language war-news to an Irish-speaking public.

Irish Jacobitism (like its English and Scottish counterparts) involved far more than a blind loyalty to the Stuarts. Many Irishmen looked to the exiled house to restore their confiscated lands, to reverse the political dominance of the Protestant Ascendancy, and to rehabilitate the Roman Catholic church and the Irish language. Irish poets tailored Jacobitism to suit their community's particular needs: the Stuart cause was evoked to demand the right to bear arms, to drive out Protestants, to inherit land, to take out leases, to vote in elections and to promote Irish language and literature. Irish Jacobitism in the eighteenth-century constituted more than a folkloric residue surviving from the political shipwreck of the cause itself at the end of the seventeenth century. Seventeenth-century confiscations ensured that the Irish Jacobite tradition was not totally characterised by an aristocracy and gentry-led and clan-inspired movement, in the manner of its English and Scottish counterparts. Nevertheless, it was associated with members of the Catholic aristocracy at home and abroad and 'underground gentry', the Wild Geese ('na géannna fiáine') and the Irish Brigades ('na leoin tar toinn') and was promoted by the Catholic hierarchy and clergy. These interests often communicated with the Stuart court, patronised poets and were associated with recruitment. They enabled Jacobitism to survive as a vibrant political ideology until at least the 1760s.

The most striking characteristeric of the Irish Catholic Jacobite community in the 1680s and 1690s was its ideological cohesion. The clergy and Catholic aristocracy and gentry's mobilisation of the populace in defence of the Stuart cause during the Jacobite war had vital consequences for the nature of Irish Jacobitism in the late seventeenth and early eighteenth century. Rappareeism was the most potent manifestation of popular Jacobitism in this period. Pikemen and rapparees had an unequivocal political dimension, as was recognised by James II's royal proclamation legitimising their actions. Jacobite soldiers were also drawn into the ranks of the rapparees by the inability of their leadership to provide for their material welfare. This connection was cemented during the war and in the later 1690s by the Williamite government's readiness to target the Catholic clergy and their congregations as rapparee sympathisers. This further broadened the base of Irish Jacobitism and ensured that the rapparee played a leading role in the Irish Jacobite 'theatre of death', along with the privateer and recruit.

From the early eighteenth century, Irish Catholic Jacobitism interacted with Europe through Catholic clergymen, merchants, privateers and recruiting officers. Irish Jacobites also carefully monitored the shifting fortunes of the major European dynasties. The more forthright public expressions of Jacobite solidarity – attacks on Whigs and riots on the Stuart king's birthday – should be set in this context. Their recurrence show that Irish Jacobitism survived the lean years between 1719 and 1739. Other features of this Jacobite tradition emerged later in the century against the background of clandestine continental Catholic links. These include popular riot, crime and recruitment, seditious health-drinking, attacks on Hanoverian royalists, and above all a vibrant literary tradition. The controversy regarding episcopal nominations by James III energised the struggle for the Irish Catholic conscience in the late 1750s and 1760s, between Jacobite royalists and Hanoverian conformists. Despite the latter's ultimate triumph by the early 1770s, a residual Jacobitism was evident in Defenderism and even among the United Irishmen. Contemporary Irish poetry indicates that Jacobitism survived as a popular political ideology until the transition from Jacobite to Jacobin, and O'Connell's emergence as heir to the Stuart mantle. Irish Catholics undoubtedly displayed a fatal attachment to Jacobitism. Thousands died at Aughrim, and on the battlefields of Europe, while many more were killed as rapparees and recruits. On a more general level, the Jacobite threat ensured the continual implementation of the penal laws which affected all Catholics. In spite of this, many Irish Catholics grimly clung to the Stuart cause.

Anti-Jacobitism played a pivotal role in the formation of the political ethos of the Irish Whigs. Catholic hopes and Protestant fears mirrored each other throughout the eighteenth century. Denunciations of 'the Pretender' rained down from pulpit and political platform, while the press focused on the Pretender's intrigues on the continent. To dismiss these fears of the Jacobite threat as delusions is to accuse Irish Protestants of collective paranoia for most of the eighteenth century. They considered neither the Pretender's permanent exclusion or the Hanoverian succession as inevitabilities in the early eighteenth century. This oscillation continued during the War of the Spanish Succession with demonstrations of communal delight at allied victories and unease at military preparations and Jacobite invasion scares. The press remained fixated on the Pretender's movements in France and his eventual defeat did not totally exorcise the Jacobite spectre.

Although the 1719 invasion did not directly involve Ireland, Irish Protestants remained aware of the Stuart king and his Irish army-in-waiting. With the failure of Ormonde's invasion, however, they developed a more detached fascination with the Pretender and his European confederates. The South Sea Bubble, the Atterbury and Layer Plots and the Wood's half-pence controversy reverberated in Ireland and served to re-direct their attention towards the Pretender. Some commentators believed that Wood's half-pence created the possibility of a novel alliance between Whigs and Jacobites. A revived Spanish-Jacobite intrigue, and the short-lived Austro-Spanish alliance, heightened Protestant fears during the 1720s and the activities of major continental-based Jacobite figures dominated the press. The failure of a realistic Jacobite challenge to the Hanoverian regime to emerge at this time transformed the Pretender from the bugbear of the Irish Protestant nation to a rather pathetic figure. The Irish Protestant backlash against French recruiting in Ireland in 1730, however, and the eventual breakdown of the Anglo-French *détente* justified warnings against premature dismissals of Jacobitism.

During the 1745 rebellion, Protestant disquiet was masked and assuaged by the fervent celebration of British victories, Jacobite effigy burnings, Hanoverian toastings and the foundation of loyal societies. The press and local political figures remained fully aware of French invasion preparations in 1743 and 1744. The self-confidence that emanated from Dublin Castle during the Chesterfield administration should be contrasted with the vulnerability felt by Protestants in rural, predominantly Catholic areas. Despite the failure of the 'Forty-five' and French invasion plans during the Seven Years War, conservative Protestants still feared Jacobitism into the late 1760s and 1770s. It is ironic that at the same time Catholics were beginning to shed any remaining vestiges of Stuart loyalty the fatal attachment of many Irish Protestants to 'the Pretender' was a decisive factor in preventing the emergence of a popular Catholic cult of loyalty to the house of Hanover in the 1770s and 1780s. This absence would prove a major factor in the decline of the Protestant Ascendancy, the emergence of the Act of Union, the securing of Catholic Emancipation and the reversal of the revolutionary settlement.

Recruitment for foreign service provided another visible manifestation of Jacobitism throughout the first fifty years of the eighteenth century. The numbers recruited, their motivation and their ultimate destination awaits further research in foreign archives. Contemporary evidence referred to them as prospective Stuart allies; these witness accounts often display a considerable grasp of Jacobite high-politics. Recruiters emphasised the authenticity of their commissions from the Stuart claimant and the possibility of an imminent return through a Jacobite invasion. James III's service and that of the king of Spain provided an outlet for militant Irish Jacobitism in the immediate aftermath of the Hanoverian Succession. George II's granting of permission to the French king to recruit for the Irish Brigade in the late 1720s provoked a Protestant backlash in Ireland and a pamphlet controversy, which portrayed the brigade as a Jacobite army-in-waiting. Apart from the involvement of the usual clerical, mercantile and *émigré* interests in recruiting, depositions from the 1720s implicated the surviving Catholic aristocracy and gentry, as well as leading converts in south Munster. This image of the Irish Brigade as the personal army of the Stuart king survived in Jacobite high-politics and in Irish political culture until the 1750s. Although the Whig political interest was accused of exploiting recruitment as an excuse for the judicial murder of Jacobites, the Irish Jacobite 'theatre of death' constituted a fatal attachment for those who were hanged, drawn and quartered in the first half of the eighteenth century.

A further neglected aspect of eighteenth-century Irish history is the disproportionately large influence exerted on Irish politics (both Whig and Jacobite) by the Irish exiles in France and Spain. In conjunction with their service to temporal and spiritual masters, many of them retained their old allegiance to the exiled Stuarts. The Irish diaspora left an indelible mark on the history of Jacobite Ireland. Their presence as an expectant aristocracy, gentry and Jacobite army-in-exile can no longer be considered a creation of the excited pens of later nationalists such as Davis, Lawless, O'Conor and O'Callaghan. The Irish diaspora was crucial to the European dimension of Irish Jacobitism. The links between Ireland and her exiles influenced the elaboration, maintenance and survival of Jacobite ideology until the end of the 1750s. In periods of political inactivity, the exiles commented on European politics, and sought patronage, pensions, preferments, titles and memorabilia from James III. The Stuart papers demonstrate constant contact between Ireland and the exiles and highlight popular Jacobite activities such as toasting, duelling and singing.

The Stuart king reciprocated this contact with the *émigrés* by repeatedly turning to Irish generals and colonel-proprietors to obtain preferments for his loyal subjects. *Émigré* rhetoric bristled with Irish Jacobite self-righteousness and their persecution mentality. They boasted their willingness to serve the cause and return to their native lands and possessions. These declarations cannot be lightly dismissed as hollow rhetoric purely because these men were earning their bread in the armies of France and Spain. Many of the most influential Irish exiles were kept informed regarding the strength of the Whig garrison. They forcefully advocated an invasion of Ireland during the first half of the eighteenth century.

Their hopes rested on support for the Stuarts from the major European powers particularly France and Spain, but occasionally Sweden, Austria and Russia. Illicit correspondence between Ireland and the continent also sustained Irish Jacobitism. The Catholic clergy were crucial in this regard. The activities of prominent Irish Jacobites (Patrick Sarsfield, Justin McCarthy, Gordon O'Neill, Randall MacDonnell, George Kelly, Ormonde, James Francis Edward Sarsfield, Lord Dillon, Daniel O'Brien, Charles Wogan, Francis Glascock and Lord Orrery) demonstrate official and unofficial contact between Ireland and the continent. Further links were provided by French and Spanish privateers and gun-runners, visitors to Rome, the numerous postulations for episcopal preferments, and the interchange between Ireland and its emigrant colonies in

Spain, France and Italy. These reinforced the Irish Jacobite ideology in an era of relative political quiescence and created conditions in which Jacobite ritual could flourish.

A more active brand of Jacobitism re-emerged with the outbreak of the War of Jenkins's Ear in 1739 and the eruption of the War of the Austrian Succession. Exiles reiterated their willingness to serve the Stuarts, their religion and 'oppressed country'. Pivotal Irish *émigrés* (Wogan, Lally, Clancarthy, Clare, Patrick D'Arcy, Sir Daniel O'Carroll and Felix and Henry O'Neill) justified Catholic optimism by seeking to join in the 'Forty-five' and relieve 'their poor countrymen'. A conflict of interest between Stuart loyalty and French *realpolitik* infected *émigré* ranks in the late 1750s. Heavy casualties, the decline of recruitment, the death of James III and the demise of a number of prominent Irish officers in the French service eroded the Irish interest within the rank and file of the Irish Brigades.

The Tory political supremacy in the early-eighteenth century helped to nourish a small Irish Protestant Jacobite interest. It expressed itself in Jacobite rhetoric and an influx of seditious pamphlet literature from England. A Protestant Jacobite interest also survived in Dublin and among some rural-based Protestant clergy. Jacobite sedition in Antrim can possibly be attributed to the earl of Antrim's patronage of non-juring clergy and his ties with Scotland. Dissension in Derry and Kilkenny was linked to the political and religious leanings of their bishops, and in the latter case to the second duke of Ormonde's influential patronage. Between 1713 and 1716, there was an upsurge of Protestant Jacobite activity in Trinity College, in particularly toasting and pamphleteering, which sometimes spilled out onto the streets and galvanised a Jacobite 'mob'.

The succession of George I precipitated a sharp decline in Protestant Jacobitism. Although it occasionally re-surfaced in seditious toasts for Ormonde and the High-Church, it increasingly became the preserve of English-based Anglo-Irish magnates and a narrow literary circle which included individuals such as Thomas Sheridan, Lord Barrymore and Lord Orrery. Individual Protestants, particularly converts such as Knightley Chetwood, Charles McCarthy (Cormac Spáinneach) and Lord Kingston, remained associated with the phenomenon in the minds of Whigs and Jacobites alike. This small Irish Protestant Jacobite interest provided some notable victims of the 'fatal attachment' to the Stuarts. Charles Leslie languished in Europe while his inheritance was whittled away through legal wrangles, before he returned and died a broken man in 1721. William Sheridan, Church of Ireland bishop of Kilmore, was deprived of his diocese for refusing to abjure James II and died in penjury in London. His namesake Thomas Sheridan lost his benefice because of an attack from the pulpit on George II. Walter Crosby escaped conviction and execution for treason in the 1690s, only to die in a duel in France in 1698 at the hands of another Jacobite. Edmund Bingley suffered the lash, disendowment and exile. George Kelly was expelled from Trinity College, and incarcerated in the Tower of London for ten years for his part in the Atterbury Plot. Some of the country's greatest landowners, including Lords Orrery, Barrymore and Granard, suffered harassment, imprisonment or exile because of the Jacobite cause. Ormonde, one of the most influential and respected of all the Jacobites, paid dearly in land and titles for his loyalty to the Stuarts.

The strength of this Irish Jacobite community at home and abroad and the fear of Jacobitism, which survived among Irish Protestants, means that Ireland's failure to mount a serious challenge to the Hanoverian regime should no longer be used to dismiss the central importance of the Jacobite ideology to Irish political life for most of the eighteenth century. Despite a ruinous war, the exile of the Jacobite army, aristocracy and gentry (Ireland's peripheralisation in Jacobite politics and the widespread belief that she served as the arsenal of Hanoverian Britain) Irish Jacobitism survived the 'shipwreck' of Aughrim. The Stuart king and his allies missed many opportunities to utilise the Irish theatre as Louis XIV had done in 1689 and 1691. In retrospect, we can only speculate on Ireland's capacity, with foreign assistance, to mount a realistic challenge to the Hanoverian regime. With the landing of a sizeable and well-armed contingent of the Irish Brigade, Irish Jacobites would almost certainly have provided a more formidable threat than their Scottish and English contemporaries.

Bibliography

GENERAL REFERENCE

Bibliography of British history, Stuart period 1603–1714, second ed. (Oxford, 1970).
Boylan, H. (ed.), *A dictionary of Irish biography* (Dublin, 1998).
Brady, A. and Cleeve, B., *A dictionary of Irish writers* (Gigginstown, 1985).
Cannon, J. (ed.) *Oxford companion to British history* (Oxford, 1997).
The concise dictionary of national biography (Oxford, 1985).
Collins, P., *County Monaghan sources in the Public Record Office of Northern Ireland* (Belfast, 1998).
Connolly, S., (ed.), *The Oxford companion to Irish history* (Oxford, 1998).
Dictionnaire de Biographie Française, i-xcii (Paris, 1933–).
Dictionary of National Biography. From the earliest times to 1900. Edited by Stephen, L. and Lee, S. 22 vols (1921–22). Continued by *Dictionary of National Biography, supplement* (London, 1901/11–).
Dinneen, P. [Ua Duinnín], *Foclóir Gaeilge-Béarla* (Dublin, 1927).
Fryde, E., Greenway, D. and Roy, I. (ed.), *Handbook of British chronology*, third ed. (Cambridge, 1986).
Hayes, R., *Biographical dictionary of Irishmen in France* (Dublin, 1949).
——, *Manuscript sources for the history of Irish civilisation*, 11 vols (Boston, 1965).
——, *Manuscript sources for the history of Irish civilisation*, first supplement, 3 vols (Boston, 1979).
——, *Sources for the history of Irish civilisation.* Articles in Irish periodicals, 9 vols (Boston, 1970).
Ingamells, J., *A dictionary of British and Irish travellers in Italy 1701–1800* (Yale, 1997).
Munter, R., *A dictionary of the print trade in Ireland 1550–1775* (New York, 1988).
Sweeny, T., *Ireland and the printed word 1475–1700* (Dublin, 1997).
Welch, R. (ed.), *The Oxford companion to Irish literature* (Oxford, 1996).

GUIDES

Abbott, T., *Catalogue of the manuscripts in the library of Trinity College Dublin* (Dublin, 1921).
A catalogue of the books and pamphlets in the Bradshaw collection, 3 vols (Cambridge, 1916).

de Brún, P., *Clár na lámhscríbhinní Gaeilge, Cóláiste Ollscoile Chorcaí:* 'Cnuasach Thorna' (B.Á.C., 1967).

List and index society, vols 119, 188, 205, State Papers foreign, France S.P. 78, 1723–38 (London, 1975–82).

Ní Shéaghdha, N., *Catalogue of Irish manuscripts in the National Library,* 11 fasc. (Dublin, 1961–90).

Ó Conchúir, B., *Clár na lámhscríbhinní Gaeilge, Ollscoil Chorcaí:* 'Cnuasach Uí Mhurchú' (B.Á.C., 1991).

O' Grady, S. and Flower, R., *Catalogue of the Irish manuscripts in the British Museum* [Library], 2 vols (London, 1926, 1953).

O'Rahilly, T., *Catalogue of Irish manuscripts in the Royal Irish Academy,* 28 fascs. Two index vols, edited by Mulcrone, K. (Dublin, 1926–70).

Russell, C. and Prendergast, J., *An account of the Carte papers in the Bodleian Library Oxford* (London, 1871).

The twenty-third report of the deputy-keeper of the Public Records in Ireland (Dublin, 1891).

Wood, H., *A guide to the records deposited in the Public Record Office of Ireland* (Dublin, 1919).

MANUSCRIPT SOURCES

Archives du Ministère des Affaires Étrangères, Paris
Affaires Étrangères, correspondence politique [Espagne] vol. 527.

Archives Nationales, Paris
Archives Anciennes, correspondance, vols. 3152, 3154, 3534–5.

Archives de la Guerre, Vincennes
Ministère de la Guerre, series guerre, vols 3059, 3184.

Bibliothèque Nationàle
Fonds Français Ms. 12, 161: 'Lettre d'un officier Irlandais à son fils' *c.*18th cent.
Fonds Français Ms. 7487–8: Extraits des lettres, Dec. 1692–Jan. 1693 and various memoirs on Ireland in the eighteenth century.
Fonds Guerre Ms. A1 vol. 3075, 3084, 3090.

Bodleian Library Oxford
Carte 40   Correspondence of the first duke of Ormond (1680s).
Carte 170   Copies and letters of the lords justice 1691–3.
Carte 208–9   Nairne papers (*c.*1690–1715).
Carte 210–11   Papers of the exiled Stuarts, re. Irish history 1689–1729.
Carte 227   Correspondence of T. Carte with G. Clarke 1731–5.
Carte 216–17   Correspondence and papers of the dukes of Ormond 1680s.
Carte 229   Nine treatises on Irish subjects by [N.] Plunkett (*c.*1700–15).
Eng. Hist. b. 125 Letters of the lord lieutenant and lords justice 1711–13.
Eng. Hist. *c.*41–2 Official letters of the second duke of Ormonde 1710–13.
Rawlinson d. 921B Proclamation issued at Cork by the rapparees, Dec. 1694.

British Library

Additional Manuscripts

9709	Letters of Sir R. Southwell, secretary of state, June-Dec. 1690.
9716–7	Despatches of the lords justice to Ormonde 1692–1706.
9750	Miscellaneous letters and papers relating to Ireland 1636–1711.
9762	Papers of William Blathwayt relating to the army 1686–1705.
15,892–4	Letters of the duke of Ormond to the earl of Rochester 1684–5.
15,893–4	Letters from the earl of Clarendon 1686–7.
15,892–5	Correspondence of the earl of Rochester 1701–3.
18,749	Poetry by Ó Doirnín, MacCubhthaigh and others.
20,311	Miscellaneous papers relating to England 1701–3.
20,662	Letters addressed to Luigi Gualterio, archbishop of Myra.
20,720	Petition of the corporation of Limerick to the lords justice, Oct. 1710.
21,122–3	Letters of Marmaduke Coghill to Edward Southwell 1722–1734.
21,128	Political tracts by Sir William Petty (1680s).
21,136–8	Miscellaneous documents relative to the history of Ireland from the Southwell papers, ii, 1691–1701; iii, 1702–5; vol. iv, 1706–1761.
21,896	Letters relating to the family of James Stuart, 'the Old Pretender' 1726–45.
23,904	Poems, political and humorous with a few prose pieces, chiefly from the reign of Queen Anne.
24,137–8	Abstract of letters and papers relating to the kingdom of Ireland 1724–83.
27,946	Irish poems, scribe E. O'Cavanagh 1825–9.
28,724	Measures for securing the government of Ireland and lessening the number of papists (1690s).
28,880	Ellis Papers, vol. vi, 1696.
28,887–8	Correspondence of John Ellis, Apr.-Dec. 1701, Jan.–June 1702.
28,938–9	Ellis papers vol., ii, 1680–90, vol. iii, 1691–95.
29,352	Letters of Chief Baron Willes relating to Ireland.
29,981	Jacobite songs and ballads.
31,874	Collection of songs by the poets of Munster.
31,877	Miscellaneous poems in Irish, chiefly collected by T. Danaher.
32,095	Malet Ms, vol., State papers and historical documents 1677–95.
33,567	Collection of historical and other poems in Irish.
33,950	Letter-books of the duke of Ormonde relating to Jacobite schemes 1718–19.
34,126	Miscellaneous music, vocal and instrumental, including a large number of Scottish, Irish and other airs *c.*1788.
34,195	Original warrants and papers 1576–1763.
34,773	Southwell papers; relating to Irish affairs 1686–1741.
36,137–9	Hardwicke papers, vol. iv, 1728–Sept. 1729; vol. v, Sept. 1729–Dec. 1730; vol. vi, 1731–33.

36,296	'A journal of my travels since the Revolution' by John Stevens'.
37,531	Register of letters of the lords justice of Ireland, Apr.–Aug. 1702.
38,145	Letter book of the earl of Tyrconnell, Oct. 1689–Jun. 1690, captured after the battle of the Boyne.
38,153–7	Letters from Richard Cox to Robert and Edward Southwell 1687–1727.
38,713	War-office and other correspondence 1690–1759.
39,923	Letters and papers chiefly relating to the Jacobites 1668–1790.
40,766	Poems, eulogistic and erotic.
40,773–5	Vernon papers, vol. iii, Dec. 1698–May 1699; vol. v, July 1701–Feb. 1702.
47,001–29	Egmont papers.

Egerton Manuscripts

133	Religious: Ossianic and other poetry; scribe; Diarmuid Ó Conchubhair 1711–20.
139	Poems, Leinster/Ulster district, 17th and 18th cents.
150	A miscellany in prose and verse in Irish 1773–4.
165	'Jacobides and Carina' by Séan Ó Neachtain.
197	Miscellaneous papers from the Southwell collection.

Lansdowne Manuscripts

352	Extracts from letters written to Archbishop William Wake 1714–18.
1236	Letters of royal, noble and eminent persons of Great Britain.

Sloane Manuscripts

3323	Miscellaneous papers.

Stowe Manuscripts

228–232	Hanover papers, vol. ii, Jan. 171–July 1717; vol. iii, July 1716⁄7, vol. ix, 1717–19.
247	Craggs papers, vol. ii, 1719–20, regarding the Spanish expedition to Ireland 1719.
250	Transcripts of intercepted Jacobite correspondence, Apr.–Aug. 1722.
750	Letters from lawyers, scholars and others to Thomas Parker, lord chief justice.

Cambridge University Library

Strype Collection	Letters to Rev John Strype from members of the Bonnell family c.1659–1711.

Harvard, Houghton Library

Eng. His.	Letters, essays and poems of the fourth and fifth earls of Orrery.

Lambeth Palace Library, Westminster

Gibson Papers,	vol. 7.

Marsh's Library Dublin

Marsh Z.3.1.1 [xii]   Deposition of Rev John Smith of Balentoy in County Antrim, 28 Feb. 1716.

Marsh Z.3.1.1.[xxiv] Proclamation by the lords justice and council (*c.*1719).

Marsh Z.3.1.1 [cxii] Examination of Rev William Harris of Fishamble Street taken before the Hon. William Caulfield on his majesty's kings bench, 30 Oct. 1717.

National Archives of Ireland, Dublin

2446–7   Irish correspondence and King's letters 1697–1798.

3036   Calendar and index to Southwell papers destroyed in 1922.

5992   Ievers papers, 1669–1870.

620   Rebellion papers.

Wyche Papers   Papers of Cyril Wyche, lord justice 1674–94.

National Library of Ireland

476–477   Tracts and pamphlets by [Nicholas] Plunkett *c.*1690–1715.

942–6, 1539–42   Philip Crossle's extracts from various newspapers.

999   A collection of several manuscripts 1704.

1793   200 printed proclamations 1673–1716.

2055–6   Letter-books of Archbishop William King 1716–28.

2411, 32, 41, 78   Ormonde papers.

2532   Ancient inheritance of the Waddings of Ballycogley, 1733.

4245   Letter-book of Richard Cox 1711–12.

5367   Regiment de Dillon, 1691–1738 [typed manuscript].

9609–12,9016–8   P.R.O.N.I. typescript calendar of the State Papers 1717–29, 1745–65.

11, 472   Flowers papers 1682–95.

11, 481   Letters to Lord Castledurrow 1715–47.

11, 949   County Louth Grand Jury presentment books.

21, 000/2   Baker papers.

22, 321–3   Dillon letters 1733–39.

Molesworth Papers   Letters of Robert Molesworth to his wife, 1689–1719 (N.L.I., mf p. 3753–4).

De Vesci Papers   Jacobite manifesto addressed to the corporation of Maryborough, January 1779.

G. 697 f. 3   Irish verse, eighteenth century.

G. 92 f. 300   Tales and verse 1816–17.

Special lists and reports on private collections in the N.L.I.

Special List 335   Chatsworth papers.

Special List 329   De Ros papers.

Report 126   De Ros papers.

Private Coll., no. 6 Fingall papers.

Interim report   Inchiquin papers

Special List 337   O'Hara papers.
Special List 319   Rosse papers.
Special List 298   Rossmore papers.
Report 309   Sarsfield papers.
Special List 206[i] Shannon papers, Boyles of Castlemartyr.
Special List 393   Shannon papers.

National Library of Scotland
Add. Ms. 14, 266   David Nairne's diary *c.*1690–1710.

National Library of Wales
3579D, 3580C   Puleston letters.

Public Record Office, London
S.P., 34/12; 35/1, 49; 63/336, 355, 356, 357, 358, 359, 361, 363, 364, 365, 366, 367, 369,
    370, 372, 373, 374, 376, 377, 378, 380, 382, 383, 384, 385, 386, 387, 388, 391, 392,
    393, 395, 396, 401, 402, 403, 405, 406, 408, 409, 410, 411, 412, 413, 418, 419.
S.P. 67/1–12.

Royal Archive, Windsor
2499, Pamphlets by Sir Thomas Sheridan 1702, 1709.
Stuart papers *c.*1717–1760 vols: 41, 49, 50, 51, 52, 54, 56, 58, 59, 61, 64, 66, 68, 69, 70,
    71, 72, 79, 80, 81, 82, 83, 86, 90, 92, 94, 96, 99, 102, 106, 107, 108, 110, 111, 112, 113,
    114, 116, 118, 119, 122, 124, 126, 127, 128, 130, 136, 140, 141, 146, 147, 152, 157, 160,
    161, 162, 163, 166, 167, 168, 169, 170, 172, 174, 176, 177, 178, 179, 180, 182, 183, 184,
    185, 186, 188, 190, 191, 192, 194, 195, 197, 198, 200, 201, 202, 205, 206, 209, 212, 213,
    215, 216, 222, 223, 226, 228, 230, 232, 235, 240, 241, 242, 243, 244, 245, 247, 249,
    256, 260, 262, 264, 267, 268, 269, 270, 272, 273, 274, 276, 277, 278, 279, 281, 282,
    283, 284, 285, 286, 287, 288, 294, 295, 296, 297, 299, 301, 303, 304, 305, 306, 308,
    309, 311, 319, 321, 324, 330, 334, 340, 343, 345, 361, 363, 366, 367, 369, 372, 379,
    380, 388, 394, 395, 397, 398, 399, 401, 403, 404, 408, 411, 414, Box. 3/23 folder 2.

Royal Irish Academy
23. O. 35   Miscellaneous eighteenth-century.
23. A. 45   Miscellaneous eighteenth-century.
A. IV. 2   Miscellaneous seventeenth-century.
23. D. 6m   'An Iomarbháigh', eighteenth-century.
23. D. 9   Eighteenth-century.
23. A. 40   Eighteenth-century. Genealogical.
23. C.21   Verses, letters, history, genealogical, nineteenth-century.
23. L.5   Nineteenth-century, modern and Ossianic verse.
23. G. 8   Eighteenth-century verse.

Trinity College Dublin
750/ 1–11   Correspondence of William King, bishop of Derry and
                   archbishop of Dublin, 1699–1723.

749 (i), (ii)	Correspondence of George Clarke, secretary of state for war, June- Oct. 1690.
883 (i–ii)	Memoirs and notes relating to natural history, antiquity and statistics of Ireland, including a tour made in 1709.
884 (a)	A Journey to Connaught 1709 by Sir Samuel Molyneux.
1178	A collection of letters and other documents relating to Irish matters in the seventeenth and eighteenth centuries.
1179–81	Papers relating to affairs of state of Ireland, formerly belonging to Robert Southwell.
2011	Deeds, letters and other papers concerning affairs in Cork,
2022–3	Two letter-books of the duke of Shrewsbury 1713–14.
2532–37	Transcripts by Edward Phelps of the damaged letter-books of Archbishop King 1708–18.
1995–2008	Lyons-King papers.
7180	Thomas Mullin, 'The ranks of death'; the life and times of the Irish Brigades'.

*Note: All sources referred to in this text in the French archives, the Public Records Office London, and Harvard University Library have been consulted on microfilm in the National Library of Ireland. I also used microfilm copies of the Stuart papers in Cambridge University Library.

NEWSPAPERS AND PRINTED PRIMARY SOURCES

Historical Manuscripts Commissions
*Bath, vols i-*iv (London, 1904–68).
The manuscripts and correspondence of the duke of Buccleuch and Queensbury, vol. i, *15th report,* part viii (London, 1897), vol. ii (London, 1903), vol. i (London, 1899), vol. ii^1 *(*London, 1903), vol. ii^2 (London, 1902), vol. iii (London, 1926).
The manuscripts and correspondence of James, first earl of Charlemont, vol. i (London, 1891).
Downshire Manuscripts, vols i-iv: *Papers of Sir William Trumbull* (London, 1924–40).
Papers of the earl of Egmont, 2 vols (London, 1909).
Report on the manuscripts of Allen George Finch esq. of Burley-on-the-Hill, Rutland, 4 vols (London, 1913–47).
Le Fleming manuscripts (London, 1890).
Leyborne-Popham manuscripts (London, 1899).
Hastings manuscript, 4 vols (London, 1928–47).
Manuscripts of the marquis of Ormonde O.S., 3 vols (London, 1899–1909); N.S., 8 vols (London, 1902–20).
Manuscripts of Lord Polwarth, 4 vols (London, 1911–61).
Manuscripts of the duke of Portland, 8 vols (London, 1891–9).
Puleston Mss (London, 1898).
Manuscripts of the duke of Somerset, marquis of Ailesbury and the Rev Sir T.H.G. Puleston Bart, 15th report (London, 1898).

Calendar of the Stuart papers belonging to his majesty the king preserved in Windsor Castle, 9 vols (London, 1902–23).
Various collections, 3 vols (London, 1901–13).
First to Fifteenth report (London, 1870–97).

Newspapers

Dalton's Dublin Impartial Newsletter.
Dickson's Postman.
Dublin Evening Post.
Dublin Impartial Newsletter.
Dublin Postman.
Faulkner's Dublin Journal.
Flying Post.
Harding's Dublin Impartial Newsletter.
Hume's Courant.
Nelson's Dublin Courant.
Lloyd's Newsletter.
Reilly's Dublin Newsletter.
Walsh's Mercury.
Walsh's Dublin Postboy.
Weekly Post.

Dickson's Intelligencer.
Dublin Courant.
Dublin Gazette.
Dublin Newsletter.
Dublin Weekly Journal
Finn's Leinster Journal.
The Freeholder.
Harding's Weekly Impartial Newsletter.
Impartial Intelligencer.
Needham's Postman.
Pue's Occurrences.
St. James' Evening Post.
Walsh's Castle Courant.
Walsh's Dublin Weekly Impartial Newsletter.
Whalley's Newsletter.

The newspapers listed in this work have been largely consulted from the microfilm collection of eighteenth-century Irish newspapers held in the National Library of Ireland, Trinity College Dublin, the Royal Irish Academy, and Dublin City Library. This was published by University Microfilms Limited. For dates of the available editions, the newspapers listed in the book and the best guide to their location, see J. O'Toole, *Newsplan: Report of the Newsplan project in Ireland* (Dublin and London, 1991), revised edition by Sara Smith, London, 1998.

Printed Primary Sources

The twenty-third report of the deputy-keeper of the Public Records Office, app. ii (Dublin, 1891).
[Addi, T.], 'Letter to Murray of Broughton' in *Donegal Annual*, xii (1979), no. 3, pp 398–404.
Ainsworth, J. (ed.), 'Survey of documents in private keeping' in *Anal. Hib.*, xxv (1967), pp 1–253.
Barry, J. (ed.) ,'The groans of Ireland' in *Ir. Sword*, ii (1956–7), pp 130–6.
Berkeley, G., *The works of George Berkeley, late bishop of Cloyne in Ireland, to which is added an account of his life and several of his letters* (Dublin, 1784).
Berwick, E. (ed.), *The Rawdon papers* (London, 1819).
Blake, M. (ed.), *Blake family records 1600–1700*, 2nd series (London, 1905).
Boulter, H. *Letters written by his excellency Hugh Boulter, lord primate of Ireland to several ministers of state in England and some others containing an account of the most interesting transactions which passed in Ireland*, 2 vols (Dublin, 1770).
Brady, J. (ed.), *Catholics and catholicism in the eighteenth-century press* (Maynooth, 1965).

Buttimer, C. (ed.), 'An Irish text on the War of Jenkins's Ear' in de Brún, P. and Ó Murchú, M. (ed.), *Celtica: essays in honour of Brían Ó Cuív* (Dublin, 1990), pp 75–98.

[Byrne, M.] *Memoirs of Miles Byrne*, repr. (Shannon, 1972).

Calendar of the State Papers, domestic, 1547–1695, 81 vols (London, 1867–77).

Calendar of the State Papers, domestic [James II], 3 vols (London, 1960–72).

Campbell, J. (eag.), *Highland songs of the '45*, repr. (Edinburgh, 1984).

—, (eag.), 'The lost songs of the '45' in *Scottish Gaelic Studies*, iv (1935), pp 24–30.

Cambeul, I. and Collinson, I. (eag.), *Seann Orain Innse Gall*, 3 vols (Oxford, 1981).

State letters of Henry, earl of Clarendon, lord lieutenant of Ireland and his lordship's diary for the years 1687, 1688, 1689 and 1690, 2 vols (Oxford, 1765).

'The Chetwood letters' in *Kildare Arch. Soc. Jnr.*, ix (1918–21), pp 381–6, 410–15; x (1922–8), pp 100–6.

Clarke, J. (ed.), *Life of James II*, 2 vols (London, 1816).

Comer-Bruen, M. and Ó hÓgáin, D., (eag.), *An Mangaire Súgach. Beatha agus saothar* (B.Á.C., 1996).

Comyn, D. and Dinneen, P. (ed.), *Foras Feasa ar Éirinn*, 4 vols, repr. (Dublin, 1987).

Conan-Doyle, A., 'Cremona' in *An Cosantóir*, i, no. 10 (1941), pp 302–3.

Crawford, T. (ed.), 'Political and protest songs' in *Scottish Studies*, xiv (1970), pp 1–35.

Crofton-Croker, T. (ed.), *The historical songs of Ireland illustrative of the struggle between James II and William III* (London, 1841).

Cunningham, P. (ed.), *The letters of Horace Walpole, fourth earl of Orford*, 9 vols (London, 1891).

Danaher, K. and Simms, J. (ed.), *The Danish forces in Ireland 1689–91* (Dublin, 1962).

[Davis, T.], *Essays and poems with a centenary memoir* (Dublin, 1945).

de Breffny, B. (ed.), 'Letters from Connaught to a Wild Goose' in *Irish Ancestor*, x (1978), pp 81–99.

de Brún, P. (ed.), 'Two Bréifne manuscripts' in *Bréifne*, iv (1972), pp 426–37.

de Rís, S. (eag.), *Peadar Ó Doirnín* (B.Á.C., 1969).

Dickson, W., *The Jacobite attempt of 1719* (Edinburgh, 1895).

Dover, Lord (ed.), *Letters of Horace Walpole, earl of Orford*, 3 vols (London, 1833).

(Drake, P.), *Amiable renegade. The memoirs of Captain Peter Drake 1671–1753* (California, 1960).

Dunton, J., *Teague Land or a merry ramble to the Wild Irish. Letters from Ireland, 1698*, repr. (Dublin, 1982).

Fagan, P. (ed.), *Ireland in the Stuart papers: Correspondence and documents of Irish interest from the Stuart papers in the Royal Archive in Windsor Castle*, 2 vols (Dublin, 1996).

Faulkner, A. (ed.), 'An Irish diary of the war in Ireland' in *Coll. Hib.*, xx (1979), pp 21–30.

Fenning, H. (ed.), *The Fottrell papers. An edition of the papers found on the person of Fr John Fottrell, provincial of the Dominicians in Ireland at his arrest in 1739* (Belfast, 1980).

Forbes, R. (ed.), *The lyon in mourning: or a collection of the speeches, letters, journals etc. relative to the affairs of Prince Charles Edward*, 3 vols repr. (Edinburgh, 1975).

Franciscan Fathers (ed.), *Luke Wadding* (Dublin, 1957).

[Freke, E.], 'Mrs Elizabeth Freke, her diary, 1671–1714' in *J.C.H.A.S.*, xvii (1911), pp 45–58.

Giblin, C. (ed.), 'Catalogue of material of Irish interest in the Nunziatura di Fiandra', part 1, vols 1–50, in *Coll. Hib.*, i (1958), pp 7–26; part 2, vols 51–80, in ibid., ii (1960), pp 7–137; part 3, vols 81–101, in ibid., iv (1961), pp 7–131; part 4, vols 102–122, in ibid., v (1962), pp 7–126; part 5, vols 122–132, in ibid., ix (1966), pp 7–71; part 6, vols 133–135g, in ibid., x (1967), pp 7–139; part 7, vols 135–137, in ibid., xi (1968), pp 53–90.

Franklin, D., 'Extracts from the letterbook of Denham Ffrancklyn' in *J.C.H.A.S*, 2nd series, i (1895), pp 49–61.

Gilbert, J. (ed.), *A Jacobite narrative of the war in Ireland 1689–91*, repr. (Shannon, 1971).

—, (ed.), *Narrative of the detention, liberation and marriage of Maria Clementine Stuart*, repr. (Dublin, 1984).

Gordon-Seaton, B. (ed.), *Prisoners of the '45*, 3 vols (Edinburgh, 1929).

Hardiman, J. (eag.), *Irish minstrelsy*, 2 vols, repr. (Shannon, 1972).

Hayes, R. (ed.), 'An unpublished eighteenth-century Franco-Irish manuscript' in *Studies*, xxviii (1939), pp 475–84.

Hayes, R. (ed.), 'Reflections of an Irish Brigade officer' in *Ir. Sword*, i (1949–53), pp 68–75.

Hayton, D. (ed.), 'An Irish parliamentary diary from the reign of Queen Anne' in *Anal. Hib.*, xxx (1982), pp 99–149.

Hickson, M. (ed.), *Selections from old Kerry records*, 2 vols (London, 1872).

Hogan, E. (ed.), *The Jacobite war in Ireland 1688–91* (Dublin, 1894).

Hogan, F. (ed.), *Négociations de monsieur le compte d'Avaux 1689–1691* (Dublin, 1934–56).

Hogan, W. and Ó Buachalla, L. (ed.), 'The letters and papers of James Cotter Jnr. 1689–1720' in *J.C.H.A.S.*, cxvii (Jan.–Dec. 1963), pp 66–96.

Hogg, J. (ed.), *The Jacobite relics of Scotland*, 2 vols (Paisley, 1874).

Hyde, D. (ed.), 'Eagles in exile', in *Ir. Sword*, viii (1967–8), p. 47.

—, (eag.), *Songs attributed to Raftery*, repr. (Shannon, 1973).

The Irish Brigade song-book (London, 1869).

Jacobite songs (London, 1755).

Journals of the House of Commons, ii, *1692–1713* (Dublin, 1796).

Kelly, J. (ed.), *The letters of Lord Chief Baron Willes 1757–1762* (Aberystwyth, 1990).

—, (ed.), 'The Whiteboys in 1762: A contemporary account' in *J.C.H.A.S.*, xciv, (1989), pp 19–26.

Kelly, P. (ed.), 'The improvement of Ireland' in *Anal. Hib.*, xxxv (1992), pp 45–86.

Killeen, J. (eag.), 'The address to Sir Richard Cox' in *Éigse*, xix (1983), pp 276–81.

Knott, E. (ed.), *The poems of Tadhg Dall Ó hUiginn*, 2 vols (London, 1922–26).

Laoide, S. (eag.), *Duanaire na Midhe* (B.Á.C., 1914).

Larkin, P., (ed.), 'Popish riot in south County Derry, 1725' in *S.A.*, viii (1976), pp 97–110.

Larrauri, G., *Historia del consulado de Bilbao*, 2 vols (Bilbao, 1913–14).

(Ligonier, J.), 'A plan for the defence of Cork, 1740' in *An Cosantóir*, i, no. 23 (1941), pp 708–11.

Lord, G. de F. (ed.), *Poems on the affairs of state 1660–1714*, 7 vols (London, 1963–75).

(Loveday, J.), *A diary of a tour in 1732* (Edinburgh, 1890).

Mac Donald, A. (eag.), *Songs of Duncan Bán Mc Intyre* (Edinburgh, 1952).

Mac Donald, A. and Mac Donald, A. (eag.), *The McDonald collection of Gaelic poetry* (Inverness, 1911).

MacErlean, J. (eag.), *Duanaire Dháibhidh Uí Bhruadair*, 3 vols (London, 1917).

Mackenzie, A. (eag.), *Orain Iain Luim* (Edinburgh, 1964).

Macnamara, G. (ed.), 'Letters of an Irish exile' in *Journal of the Limerick Field-club*, iii (1905–8), pp 238–47.

Macpherson, J. (ed.), *Original papers; containing the secret history of Great Britain from the Restoration to the accession of the house of Hanover*, 2 vols (London, 1775).

Mac Quoid, G. (eag.), *Jacobite songs and ballads* (London, 1888).

Mag Uidhir, S. (eag.), *Pádraig Mac a Liondáin: dánta* (B.Á.C., 1977).

Manning, M., 'Dr Nicholas Madgett's Constitutio Ecclesiastico' in *J.K.A.H.S.*, ix (1976), pp 68–91.

Matheson, W. (eag.), *An Clarsair Dall. Orain Ruaidhri Mhic Mhuirich agus a chuid ciuil* (Edinburgh, 1970).

Matheson, W. (eag.), *The songs of John MacCodrum* (Edinburgh, 1938).

Maty, M. (ed.), *Memoirs of Lord Chesterfield*, 3 vols (Dublin, 1777).

McLysaght, E. (ed.), *The Kenmare papers* (Dublin, 1970).

Melvin, P. (ed.), 'Sir Paul Rycaut's memoranda' in *Anal. Hib.*, xxvii (1972), pp 125–83.

—, (ed.), 'Letters of Lord Longford and others on Irish affairs' in *Anal. Hib.*, xxxii (1985), pp 35–121.

Meyers, J. (ed.), *Elizabethan Ireland: a selection from Elizabethan writers* (Connecticut, 1983).

Mhág Craith, C. (eag.), *Dáin na mbráthar mionúr* (B. Á. C., 1967).

Moody, T.W; Mc Dowell, R.B and Woods C.J. (ed.), *The writings of Theobald Wolfe Tone*, 3 vols, (Oxford, 2001).

Moran, P. (ed.), *Spicilegium Ossoriense*, 3 vols (Dublin, 1878).

Mulloy, S. (ed.), *Franco-Irish correspondence, December 1689–February 1690*, 3 vols (Dublin, 1984).

Murray, R., (ed.), *The journal of John Stevens 1689–91* (Oxford, 1912).

Ní Chinnéide, S. (eag.), 'Dialann Í Chonchúir' in *Galvia*, iv (1957), pp 4–18.

Ní Fhaircheallaigh, Ú. (eag.), *Filidheacht Sheagháin Uí Neachtain* (B.Á.C., 1911).

Ní Ógáin, R. (eag.), *Duanaire Gaedhilge*, 3 vols (B.Á.C., 1921).

Ó Baoill, C. (eag.), *Eachann bacach agus baird eile de Chloinn Ghill Eathain* (Edinburgh, 1979).

—, (eag.), *Bàrdachad Shìlis Na Ceapaich* (Edinburgh, 1972).

Ó Buachalla, B. (eag.), *Nua-Dhuanaire*, ii (B. Á. C., 1976).

—, (eag.), 'Briseadh na Bóinne' in *Éigse*, xxiii (1989), pp 83–107.

—, (eag.), *Peadar Ó Doirnín: amhráin* (B.Á.C., 1970).

—, (eag.), *Cathal Buí: amhráin* (B.Á.C., 1975).

(ed.), 'Irish Jacobitism in official documents' in *E. C. I.*, viii (1993), pp 128–38.

O'Callaghan, J. (ed.), *Macariae Excidium: the destruction of Cyprus* (Dublin, 1850).

Ó Coigligh, C. (eag.), *Raiftearaí: amhráin agus dánta* (B.Á.C., 1987).

Ó Conaire, B. (eag.), *Éigse: duanaire nua na hArdteistiméireachta* (B.Á.C., 1974).

Ó Concheanainn, T. (eag.), *Nua-dhuanaire,* iii (B. Á. C., 1978).

(Ó Cróinín, S.), *Seanchas Ó Chairbre* (eag. Ó Cróinín, D.), (B.Á.C., 1985).

Ó Cuív, B. (eag.) *Párliament na mBan* (B.Á.C., 1952).

O'Daly, J. (eag.), *The poets and poetry of Munster* (Dublin, 1848).

—, (eag.), *The poets and poetry of Munster, with metrical translations by Éirionnach,* 2nd series (Dublin, 1860).

Ó Donnchadha, R. (eag.), *Mícheál Óg Ó Longáin* (B.Á.C., 1994).

Ó Donnchadha, T. (eag.), *Seán na Ráithíneach* (B.Á.C., 1954).

—, (eag.), *Amhráin Dhiarmada Mac Seáin Bhuidhe Mac Cárrthaigh* (B.Á.C., 1916).

O'Donovan, J. (eag.), *The tribes of Ireland* (Dublin, 1852).

Ó Fiaich, T. (eag.), *Art Mac Cumhaigh: dánta* (B.Á.C., 1973).

O'Flaherty, R., *Ogygia, or a chronological account of Irish events* [ed., Hely, J.], (Dublin, 1793).

Ó Foghludha, R. (eag.), *Amhráin Phiarais Mhic Gearailt 1700–1788* (B.Á.C., 1905).

—, (eag.), *Ar bhruach na coille muaire. Liam Dall Ó hIfearnáin* (B.Á.C., 1939).

—, (eag.), *Carn Tighearnaigh. An tAthair Conchubhar Ó Briain 1650–1720* (B.Á.C., 1938).

—, (eag.), *Cois na Bríde. An tAthair Liam Inglis 1709–88* (B.Á.C., 1938).

—, (eag.), *Cois na Cora. Liam Ruadh Mac Coitir 1690–1738* (B.Á.C., 1937).

—, (eag.), *Cois na Ruachtaighe. Clann tSúilleabháin Chaoil* (B.Á.C., 1938).

—, (eag.), *Donnchadh Ruadh Mac Conmara 1715–1810* (B.Á.C., 1933).

—, (eag.), *Éigse na Máighe* (B.Á.C., 1932).

—, (eag.), *Eoghan An Mhéirín Mac Cárrthaigh 1691–1756* (B.Á.C., 1938).

—, (eag), *Eoghan Ruadh Ó Súilleabháin 1748–1784* (B.Á.C., 1937).

—, (eag.), *Mil na hÉigse: Duanaire i gcomhair an árd-teastais* (B.Á.C., 1945).

—, (eag.), *Seán Clárach Mac Domhnaill 1691–1754* (B.Á.C., 1932).

—, (eag.), *Tadhg Gaelach Ó Súilleabháin 1715–1795* (B.Á.C., 1929).

Ó Gallchóir, S. (eag.), *Séamas Dall Mac Cuarta: dánta* (B.Á.C., 1971).

Ó hAnluain, E. (eag.), *Seon Ó hUaithnín* (B.Á.C., 1973).

Ó hÓgáin, D. (eag.), *Duanaire Osraíoch* (B. Á. C., 1980).

O'Malley, O. (ed.), 'O' Malleys between 1651–1715' in *Galway. His. Arch. Soc. Jnr.,* xxv (1952) pp 32–46.

Ó Muirgheasa, É. (eag.), *Céad de cheoltaibh Uladh* (B.Á.C., 1915).

—, (eag.), *Dhá chéad de cheoltaibh Uladh,* 3rd ed., (B.A.C., 1974).

—, (eag.), *Amhráin Airt Mhic Chobhthaigh* (Dún Dealgan, 1926).

—, (eag.), *Seanfhocla Uladh* (B.Á.C., 1931).

Ó Muirithe, D. (ed.), 'Tho' not in full style compleat: Jacobite songs from Gaelic manuscript sources', in *E.C.I.,* vi (1991), pp 93–103.

—, (eag.), *Tomás Ó Míocháin* (B.Á.C., 1988).

O'Rahilly, C. (eag.), *Five seventeenth-century political poems* (Dublin, 1952).

O'Rahilly, T.F. (eag.), 'Deasgan Tuanach: Selections from modern Clare poets' in *Irish Monthly,* lii-liii (1924–5), pp 655–7.

Ó Tuama, S. and Kinsella, T. (ed.), *An Duanaire 1600–1900. Poems of the dispossessed* (B.Á.C., 1981).

Ó Tuathail, É. (eag.), *Rainn agus amhráin. Cnuasacht rann agus amhrán ó chonndae na Mí, ó chonndae Lughmhaidh agus ó chonndae Ard Mhacha* (B.Á.C., 1923).

Petrie, C. (ed.), *The duke of Berwick and his son. Some unpublished letters and papers* (London, 1951).

Power, P. (ed.), *A bishop of the penal times: letters and reports of John Brenan, bishop of Waterford 1671–1693 and archbishop of Cashel 1677–1693* (Cork, 1932).

Redington, J. (ed.), *Calendar of the Home Office Papers 1760–65* (London, 1878).

Swords, L. (ed.), 'Calendar of Irish material in the files of Jean Fromant, notary at Paris, May 1701–Jan 1730' in *Coll. Hib.* xxxiv–xxxv (1992–3), pp 77–116; xxxv–vi (1994–5), pp 85–140.

Teeling, C. H., *History of the rebellion of 1798*, repr. (Shannon, 1972).

Transactions of the Iberno-Celtic Society, i (Dublin, 1820).

Ua Duinnín, P. (eag.), *Dánta Aodhagáin Uí Rathaille* (London, 1900).

—, (eag.), *Eoghan Ruadh Ó Suilleabháin* (B.Á.C., 1923).

—, (eag.), *Seafraidh Ó Donnchadha an Ghleanna* (B.Á.C., 1902).

—, and Ó Donnchadha, T., (eag), *Dánta Aodhagáin Uí Rathaille* (London, 1911).

Ua Muireadhaigh, L. (eag.), *Ceolta Óméith* (Dún Dealgan, 1920).

[Vernon, E.], *Original letters to an honest sailor* (London, 1746).

Vigours, P.D., 'An account of the reception of a new charter from King James II to the town of New Ross, March 1687' in *Royal Historical and Archeological Association of Ireland*, ix, 4th series (1889), pp 133–6.

Walsh, E. (eag.), *Reliques of Irish Jacobite poetry*, 2nd ed. (Dublin, 1866).

Walsh, P. (ed.), *A poet's manuscript* (Drogheda, 1927).

Ward, R. and Ward, C. (ed.), *The letters of Charles O' Conor of Belanagare* (Ann Arbor, 1980).

Ward, R., Ward, C. and Wrynn, J. (ed.), *The letters of Charles O' Conor of Belanagare* (Washington, 1988).

Williams, H. (ed.), *Correspondence of Jonathan Swift*, 5 vols (Oxford, 1963).

Zimmerman, G. (ed.), *Songs of Irish Rebellion. Political street-ballads and rebel songs* (Zürich, 1967).

PAMPHLETS AND BOOKS

An account of the behaviour of Lord Lovat from the time his death sentence was delivered to the day of execution (Dublin, 1747).

An account of the discovery of a notorious design to disturb the government (Dublin, 1710).

An account of the pedigree and actions of Simon Fraser, lord Lovat (Dublin, 1746).

An account of the present state of Ireland giving a full relation of the new establishment made by the late King James (London, 1689).

An account of the present state of Ireland giving a full relation of the new establishment made to the right honourable the earl of Shrewsbury, 8 June 1689 (London, 1689).

An account of the present state of Ireland under King James and the deplorable condition of Protestants (London, 1690).

An address given to the late King James by the titular Archbishop of Dublin (London, 1690).

(Ben Ader, I), *The chronicle of B[yn]g the son of the great B[yn]g that lived in the reign of Queen Felicia* (Dublin, 1756).

Advice to Protestants being a prefatory address to all her majesties Protestant subjects of all persuasions (Dublin, 1714).

Advice from the stars in a letter to the pretended Doctor Whalley (Dublin, 1714).

Alls out at last or see who has been taken in the wrong (Dublin, 1714).

An answer to all that has ever been said or insinuated in favour of a popish Pretender, exhibited in an abstract of the state of the Protestants (London, 1713).

An apology for the Protestants of Ireland in a brief narrative of the late revolution in that kingdom (London, 1689).

An appeal to the people containing the genuine and entire letter of Admiral Byng to the secretary of the admiralty (Dublin, 1757).

Appendixes referred to in the report from the committee appointed by the House of Commons to examine Christopher Layer and others (London, 1722).

Articles of impeachment of high treason against James, earl of Derwentwater (Dublin, 1716).

Ascanius or the Young Adventurer. A true story (London, 1747).

Asgill, J., *The Pretender's Declaration english'd by Mr Asgill with a postscript before it in relation to Dr Lesley's letters sent after it* (London, 1715).

Ashe, St George, *A sermon preached at Christschurch in Dublin, 30 January 1716 to their excellencies the lords justice* (Dublin, 1716).

(Atterbury, F.), *English advice to the freeholders of England* (London, 1715).

The axe laid to the root: offered for putting the popish clergy of Ireland under some better regulations (Dublin, 1749).

(T.B.), *Memoirs of the life and character of the late duke of Ormonde, dedicated to the Rt. Hon. Charles Butler* (Dublin, 1730).

Baker, M., *A sermon preached on 23 October 1715* (Dublin, 1715).

Barrington, B., *A sermon preached at St Andrew's before the honourable House of Commons* (Dublin, 1745).

Bell, R., *Description of the condition and manners of the Irish peasants between 1780–1790* (London, 1804).

Berkeley, G., *An impartial history of the life and death of James* II (Dublin, 1745).

Beware of the Pretender: a great hurricane at court for they are all fallen out at last (Dublin, 1712).

Blair, J., *Two sermons preached in Londonderry, 8 December 1714, a day of thanksgiving by the Presbyterians for the accession of George I* (Belfast, 1715).

The Bog Trotter's March (London, n.d.).

Boyse, S., *An impartial history of the late rebellion in 1745 from authentic memoirs, particularly the journal of a general officer and other original papers, yet unpublished, with the character of persons principally concerned to which is prefixed by way of introduction a compendium account of the royal house of Stuart* (Dublin, 1746?).

(Brewester, F.), *Discourse concerning Ireland and the different interests thereof in answer to the Exon and Burnstaple petition* (London, 1697).

Browne, P., *Of drinking the memory of the dead, being the substance of a discourse delivered to the clergy of the diocese of Cork on the fourth of November 1713* (Dublin, 1713).

—, *A second part of drinking in remembrance of the dead* (Dublin, 1714).

(Brooke, H.), *The Farmer's six letters to the Protestants of Ireland* (Dublin, 1746).

(Buckley, R.), *Animadversions on the proposals for sending back the nobility and gentry of Ireland* (London, 1690).

Bungiana or an assemblage of what-d'-ye-call-'ems in prose and verse that have occasionally appeared relative to the conduct of a certain naval commander (Dublin, 1757).

Burke, E., *A letter to Sir Hercules Langrishe* (Dublin, 1792).

(Burnet, G.), *Bishop Burnet's history of the birth of the Pretender* (Dublin, 1723).

Burscough, W., *A sermon preached in Christ's Church on Wed 9 January being the day appointed for a general fast to implore the blessing of Almighty God on his majestie's arms in the present war against Spain* (Dublin, 1739).

Campbell, T., *A philosophical survey of the south of Ireland* (London, 1777).

A candid enquiry why the natives of Ireland who are in London are more addicted to vice than the people of any other nation (London, 1754).

A catalogue of the titles of the acts that passed both Houses of Parliament begun at Dublin, 7 May 1689 (Dublin, 1748).

Cato's letter to the bishop of Rochester ([Dublin?], 1723).

Cato's vision (Dublin, 1723).

A caveat against the Pretender, being a short but impartial history of some of the assassinations, murders and inhumane slaughters committed by papists against Protestants (London, 1723).

(Chesterfield, Lord), *The Drapier's second letter to the people of Ireland* (Dublin 1745).

—, *Queries humbly proposed to the consideration of the public* (Dublin, 1745–6).

The Chevalier's hopes (Dublin, 1745).

The church and monarchy secured by the return of his grace the duke of Ormond and the change of the late ministry (Dublin, 1710).

The civil and military articles of Limerick exactly printed from letters patent (London, 1692).

A collection of three letters which arrived here from Edinburgh ... with other news from Great Britain (Dublin, 1715–6).

The complaint of a family who being rich turned away a good steward and afterwards became miserable (London, 1715).

A complete and authentick history of the rise, progress and extinction of the late rebellion and of the proceedings against the principal persons concerned therein (Dublin, 1747).

Conduct of the ministry impartially explained in a letter to the merchants of London in which among other things the arguments made use of in two pamphlets lately published intitled A letter and an appeal to the people in defence of Admiral Byng *are answered* (Dublin, 1756).

A conference between an Enniskilliner of the duke of Schomberg's Army and an Irish trooper near the duke of Berwick's camp ([Dublin?], 1689).

A conference between a Papist and a Protestant concerning the present fears of Londonderry and Ireland (London, 1689).

A continuation of some pretended reasons for his majesty [William III] *issuing a general pardon to the rebels of Ireland* (Dublin, 1689).

A copy of a letter from a person of distinction at the Hague to the Abbé de la Ville on the order against publishing newspapers in Paris in which is contained a multitude of particulars relating to the battle of Fontenoy that have not hitherto been made publick (London, 1745).

Count O' Hanlon's downfall. A true and exact account of the killing of the arch-tory and traitor Redmond O' Hanlon, 25 April 1681 (Dublin, 1681).

Cox, M., *A sermon preached in Christ's Church Dublin, 20 March 1747 before the Incorporated Society for promoting English Protestant Schools in Ireland* (Dublin, 1748).

—, *A charge delivered to the grand jury at the general quarter sessions of the peace held for the County of Cork, 12 July 1748* (Dublin, 1748).

Curry, J., *Historical and critical review of the civil wars in Ireland*, 2 vols (Dublin, 1786).

The danger of Europe from the growing power of France with some free thoughts on remedies by the author of The duke of Anjou's succession considered (Dublin, 1702).

D'Anvergne, E., *The history of the campaign in the Spanish Netherlands, Ann. Dom. 1694* (London, 1694).

D'Anvers, C., *The craftsman's first letter of advice to the people of Great Britain and Ireland with respect to some French officers being arrived in Ireland in order to raise recruits for His Gallick Majesty* (London, 1730).

—, *Craftsman's Extraordinary in a letter of advice to the people of Great Britain and Ireland with respect to some French officers being arrived in the kingdom in order to raise recruits for his Gallick Majesty* (London, 1730).

D'Assigny, S., *A short relation of the brave exploits of the Vaudois, into which is added some few cautions to the Protestants of Ireland written for our encouragement against popery* (Dublin, 1699).

D'Urvey, T., *The triennial mayor, or the new rapparees* (London, 1691).

The dauphine of France's speech to the pretended prince of Wales on his departure from the court of St Germain to Dunkirk (Dublin, [1708?]).

Davies, R., *Loyalty to King George, in a sermon preached in Cork on 23 October 1715* (Dublin, 1715).

The declaration of William and Mary, King and Queen of England, France and Ireland to their loving subjects in the Kingdom of Ireland, 22 February 1689 (Dublin, 1689).

Defoe, D., *Bold advice or proposals for the entire rooting out of Jacobitism in Great Britain* (London, 1715).

[Defoe, D.] *Hanover or Rome, showing the absolute necessity of assisting his majesty with such a sufficient force as may totally extinguish the forces of the Pretender's open and secret abettors* (Dublin, 1715).

[Defoe, D.] *A trumpet blown in the north and sounded in the ear of John Erskine, called by men of the world, duke of Mar by a ministering friend of the people called Quakers* (Dublin, 1715).

A dialogue between the late King James and the prince of Conty (London, 1697).

A dialogue between Dr Lesly and the Pretender upon the occasion of the death of the late Queen Mary [of Modena] (Dublin, 1718).

A diary of the several reports as well true as false daily spread throughout the nation for 24 September 1688 to the coronation of King William in April 1689, to which is added a post-script (London, 1704).

A diary of the siege of Limerick with the articles at large both civil and military (London, 1692).

A discovery against the Pretender's adherents and others of this kingdom from Cork (Dublin, 1714).

[Dromgold, J.] Reflexions sur un imprimé intitulé La bataille de Fontenoy: pöeme (Paris, 1745).

The duke of Anjou's succession considered (Dublin, 1701).

The duke of Anjou's succession further considered (Dublin, 1701).

(Dulany, E.), *A sermon preached before the King in Christ's Church on Ash Wednesday by Father Edmund Dulany, Franciscan Fryer* (Dublin, 1689).

Dunton, J., *The Dublin scuffle* (Dublin, 1699); new edition Dublin, 2000.

An elegy on the death of Frances, countess of Tyrconnell who departed this life at her lodgings on Ormond Key Dublin, aged 102, 7 March 1730 (Dublin, 1730).

An elegy on the death of his grace, James, duke of Ormonde who departed this life, 12 November 1730 (Dublin, 1730).

An elegy on the deplorable death of Mr Thomas Sheridan, author of Alexander's overthrow or the downfall of Babylon, *who departed this mortal life on 8 March 1722* (Dublin, 1722).

The episcopal clergy of Aberdeen's address to the Pretender, 29 December 1715 (Dublin, 1716).

An epistle from a lady in England to a gentleman at Avignon (Dublin, 1717).

An essay upon the interest of England in the present circumstance of affairs (Dublin, 1701).

An exact relation of the present posture of affairs in Ireland (London, 1693).

An exact survey of the duke of Ormonde's campaign in Spain with reflections on all his marchings and camps, with a post-script with remarks on a late published list of Irish papists now in the French king's service (London, 1703).

An excellent new song called Too good to be true (Dublin, 1724).

An express from Ballentoy, near Londonderry, 26 May 1708 (Dublin, 1708).

An express from the earl of Galway with the particulars of the late bloody battle fought with the duke of Berwick in Spain, 29 May 1707 (Dublin, 1707).

An express from Holland with an account of the duke of Berwick being dead of his wounds, 14 May 1706 (Dublin, 1706).

An express from Ross giving an account of a French privateer that landed 80 men which stripped the inhabitants and plundered the town of Fethard, 5 May 1707 (Dublin, 1707).

A faithful history of the northern affairs from the accession of the late King James to the crown to the siege of Londonderry (London, 1690).

(Forrel, J.), *The Irish Hudibras or Fingallian prince, taken from the sixth book of Virgil's Aeneid* (London, 1689).

Finnmore, W., *The Pretender's foot-exercise by the author of* Dragoon's exercise *and* Answer to Polyphemus (Dublin, 1720).

—, *The Pretender's exercise to his Irish dragoons and his Wild Geese* [Dublin?, 1720?].

Fontenoy. A new satyric ballad (Dublin, 1745).

A form of prayer for a general fast and humiliation, Wednesday, 21 November 1741 (Dublin, 1741).

Forman, C., *A letter to Rt. Hon. Sir R. Sutton for disbanding the Irish regiments in the service of France and Spain* (Dublin, 1728).

—, *A defence of the courage, honour and loyalty of the Irish nation in answer to the scandalous reflections of the Free Briton and others* (London, 1731); (Dublin, 1736).

Foster, J., *An account of the behaviour of the late earl of Kilmarnock after his sentence and on the day before his execution* (Dublin, 1746).

Forster, N., *A sermon preached before the lords justice of Ireland at Christ's Church on 1 March 1715* (Dublin, 1715).

Forster, N., *Unanimity in the present time of danger in a sermon preached before the lords justice, 5 February 1716* (Dublin, 1716).

Four essays in French relating to the kingdom of Ireland (Dublin, 1739).

Fowke, J., *The duty of a subject to a good prince considered, 20 October 1745* (Dublin, 1745).

Foy, N., *A sermon preached in Christ's Church on 23 October 1698 being an anniversary for putting an end to the Irish rebellion which broke out on that day 1641* (Dublin, 1698).

The Free Briton's answer to the Pretender's declaration supposed to have been written by his grace the archbishop of York (Dublin, 1745).

A free examination of the modern romance intitled Memoirs of the life of Lord Lovat (Dublin, 1746).

French, N., *The unkinde deserter of loyal men and true friends* (Brussels, 1676).

—, *A narrative of the settlement and sale of Ireland* (Louvain, 1668).

The French king's speech of condolence to the pretended prince of Wales at the death of late King James (Dublin, 1701).

The fulfilling of prophecies or the prophecies and predictions of the late learned and Rev James Ussher (London, 1689).

A full collection of all the poems upon Charles, prince of Wales (London, 1745).

A full collection of all the proclamations and orders published by the authority of Charles, prince of Wales, regent of Scotland, England, France and Ireland (London, 1745).

A full and impartial account of the tryal of Fr Higgins, prebendary of Christ's Church (London, 1712).

A full and impartial account of the secret consults, negotiations, strategems and intrigues of the Romish party in Ireland from 1660–1689 (London, 1689).

A full and true account of the besieging and taking of Carrickfergus, 31 August 1689 (London, 1689).

A full and true account of the surprising and apprehending of Captain Fitzgerald and four of his rapparees (Dublin, 1717).

A full and true account of the late brave actions performed by the Inniskilling men and some English and Dutch forces under Colonel Wolsley against a great body of Irish troops under the command of the duke of Berwick at the town of Cavan (London, 1690).

Gast, J., *Faction overthrown, or a more fair warning and good advice to the nobility, gentry and commonality of Ireland* (Dublin, 1755).

(Gast, J.), *The Haberdashers sermon preached in Taylor's Hall, 21 December 1754* (Dublin, 1754).

Genuine and curious memoirs of the famous Captain Thurot (Dublin, 1760).

Genuine and impartial memoir of the life and character of Charles Radcliffe (Dublin, 1746).

Genuine memoirs of John Murray, late secretary to the Young Pretender (Dublin, 1747).

Good news for England or a speedy, safe and easy way how Ireland may be reduced to the obedience of the crown of England in 6 months time (London, 1689).

Grand jury presentment, 25 May 1705 (Dublin, 1705).

Great news from Dublin in a letter from an Irish gentleman to his friend in London, 29 January 1690 (London, 1690).

Great news from Ireland giving an account of what has passed in Ireland since the landing of the Danes (London, 1690).

Griffith, A. (ed.), *Miscellaneous tracts* (Dublin, 1788).

[Griffyth, W.], *Villare Hibernicum, being an exact account of the provinces, castles, counties, bishopricks, fortifications, cities, towns, garrisons ... which have been reduced by his majesties army since landing in Ireland, with an impartial account of the siege of Limerick* (London, 1690).

The groans of Ireland in a letter to a member of parliament (Dublin, 1741).

[Guerin,?] *La victoire de Fontenoy: pöeme au roy* (Paris, 1745).

[Hamilton, A.], *A true relation of the actions of the Inniskillen men* (London, 1690).

Henry, W., *A philippic oration against the Pretender's son and his adherents addressed to the protestants of the north of Ireland* ([Dublin?], 1745).

Her majesties prerogative in Ireland, the authority of the government and privy council there and the rights and liberties of the city of Dublin asserted and maintained (London, 1712).

Her majesty's most gracious speech to both houses of parliament on Friday, 7 December 1711 (Dublin, 1711).

Higgins, F., *A sermon preached before their excellencies the lords justice at Christs' Church, Dublin; on Tuesday 28 August being the day appointed for a solemn thanks-giving to Almighty God for the late glorious success on forcing enemy lines in the Spanish Netherlands by the arms of her majesty and her allies under the command of the duke of Marborough* (London, 1707).

His grace the duke of Schomberg's character according to the ignorant notions the Irish papists have formed of him from some old prophecies ([London?], [1688/9?]).

An historical essay upon the loyalty of the Presbyterians of Great Britain and Ireland from the reformation to this present year (Belfast, 1712).

A history of the rebellion raised against his majesty King George II (Dublin, 1746).

The history of the wars in Ireland between their majesties army and the forces of the late King James ... by an officer of the royal army (London, 1690).

Hoadly, B., *The present delusion of many Protestants considered in a sermon preached 5 November 1715* (Dublin, 1715).

—, *An enquiry into the reasons of the conduct of Great Britain with relation to the present state of affairs* (Dublin, 1727).

Hooke, N., *The secret history of Colonel Hooke's negotiations in Scotland in favour of the Pretender* (Dublin, 1760).

How stands your succession now? You have made a fine kettle of fish out of it (Dublin, 1714).

Howard, R., *A sermon preached in Christ's Church before their excellencies, the lords justices 23 October 1722* (Dublin, 1722).

Humble address to the right hon. lords spiritual and temporal (Dublin, 1726).

(Hutchinson, F.), *Advice concerning the manner of receiving popish converts and encourag-ing both priests and others to live in amity with the Church of Ireland* (Dublin, 1730).

Impartial enquiry into the causes of the present fears and dangers of the government, being a discourse between the lord lieutenant and one of his deputies (London, 1692).

The indictment and arraignment of John Price Esquire, late receiver-general in Ireland (London, 1689).

[Ingoldsby, R.], *Remarks of the honourable Brigadier-General Ingoldsby in relation to the late action at Fontenoy. In a letter from a gentleman to his friend in the country* (London, 1745).

The Irish rendezvous or a description of Tyrconnell's army of tories (London, 1689).

Irish willingness to throw off the English yoke/revenge: An answer to the late King James declaration to his pretended subjects in the kingdom of England (Dublin, 1689).

James II. *The Jacobite Hudibras* (London, 1692).

The journal of the battle of Fontenoy: as it was drawn up, and published by order of his most christian majesty. Translated from the French (London, 1745).

A journal of what has happened in the north of Ireland since the landing of the duke of Schomberg to the surrender of Carrickfergus August 1689 (Belfast, 1689).

A just and modest vindication of the Protestants of Ireland (London, 1689).

Justice done to the late ministry on the charge of their design to make the Pretender king of Great Britain proved from their conduct to be groundless (Dublin, 1715).

Kennedy, M., *A chronological, genealogical and historical dissertation of the royal family of the Stuarts beginning with Milesius of the stock of those they call the Milesian Irish and ending with his present majesty James III of England and Ireland, and of Scotland the eight* (Paris, 1705).

Keogh, J., *A vindication of the antiquity of Ireland* (Dublin, 1748).

(Ketch, J.), *John Ketch, his letter to the director of the South Sea* (Dublin, 1721).

King, W., *The state of the Protestants in Ireland under the late King James's government* (London, 1692).

—, *An impartial account of King James's behaviour to his Protestant subjects of Ireland* (Cambridge, 1746).

—, *An answer to all that has ever been said or insinuated in favour of the popish Pretender exhibited in an abstract of the state of the Protestants* (London, 1713).

King William's statue or the 1st of July (Dublin, [post-1698?]).

Kirkpatrick, J., *A thanksgiving sermon preached in Belfast being the happy day of the coronation* (Belfast, 1714).

Labour lost or a new ballad of the three blunderbuss aldermen and a scurvy recorder together with their wives who are gone to the baths to improve their tails while their husbands are gone to London to improve their understandings (Dublin, 1710).

Lambert, R., *A sermon preached to the Protestants now residing in London, 23 October 1708* (London, 1708).

The last speech and dying words of Charles Calaher, alias Cullmore, 17 February 1719 (Dublin, 1719).

The last speech and dying words of Patrick Calaher, nephew to the great Cullmore and two Arthur Quinns, 21 February 1719 (Dublin, 1719).

The last speech and dying words of Captain McDermott who was formerly concerned in listing men for the Pretender and was hanged and quartered at Cavan, 30 March 1723 for most barbarously murdering one John Dalley on the high road (Dublin, 1725).

The last speech and dying words of Daniel O'Neill, 4 June 1718 (Dublin, 1718).

The last speech and dying words of Moses Nowland who is to be hanged at St Stephen's Green, 6 July 1726 (Dublin, 1726).

The last will and testament of the late King James with his advice to the pretended prince of Wales (Dublin, 1725).

The late King James's second manifesto answered paragraph by paragraph (Dublin, 1697).

The late King of Spain's will and the treaty of partition of the kingdom of Spain (Dublin, 1700).

The layman's sermon occasioned by the present rebellion which was (or ought to have been) preached at St Paul's Cross, 1 October 1745 (Dublin and Belfast, 1745).

Leslie, C., *An Answer to the book entitled* The state of the Protestants in Ireland under the late King James's government (London, 1692).

—, *A postscript to Mr Higgins's sermon, very necessary for the better understanding of it* (Dublin, 1707).

A letter from on board Major-General Kirke giving a full account of the posture of affairs of Londonderry 27 July, 1689 (London, 1689).

A letter to the clergy of the Church of England on the occasion of the commitment of the Rt Rev lord bishop of Rochester to the Tower of London (Cork, 1715).

A letter from the Count Sinzendorf, chancellor of the court, to his imperial majesty sent to Monsieur De Palm 20 February 1727 (Dublin, 1727).

A letter to Daniel Toler esq. relative to the death of the Rev Nicholas Sheehy, in Griffith, A., (ed.), *Miscellaneous tracts* (Dublin, 1788).

A letter from the duke of Schomberg's camp giving an account of the English and Irish armies (London, 1689).

A letter from a friend concerning a French invasion to restore the late King James to his throne (Dublin, 1692).

A letter from a gentleman in Armagh to his friend in Dublin giving an account of the rapparees that killed Captain Groves and robbed several other persons with the beheading of the chief of them, 17 July 1697 ([Dublin?], 1697).

A letter from a gentleman in Cork to his friend in Dublin giving a full and true account of the whole tryal and condemnation of Fr Martin, a popish abbot, at the assizes held there, 31 March 1709 (Dublin, 1709).

A letter from a gentleman in Ireland to his friend in London on the occasion of a pamphlet entitled A vindication of the present government of Ireland under his excellency Richard, earl of Tyrconnell (Dublin, 1688).

A letter of his g[race] the l[ord] p[rimate] of all I[reland] to the chevalier de St George (London, 1754).

A letter from the lord W[har]ton to the earl of Cad[o]gan wherein is a particular account of the late conference and the cause of the unhappy difference of the chevalier de St .George and his holiness the pope, concerning his now educating his son a Protestant (Dublin, n.d.).

A letter from Paris giving an account of the death of the late queen-dowager and her disowning the Pretender (Dublin, 1718)

A letter to the Protestant dissenters of Ireland (Dublin, 1745).

Life and character of James Butler (Dublin, 1730).

The life of James Coigly (London, 1798).

A list of King James II's Irish and popish forces in France (London, 1697).

Lock, R., *Letter to a friend about the presentment* (Dublin, 1706).

Loyalty to our king and the safety of our country against all popish emissaries and pretenders as to his sacred majesty King George II (Dublin, 1745).

MacAllester, O., *A series of letters discovering the scheme projected by France in MDCCLIX for an intended invasion upon England with flat-bottomed boats*, 2 vols (London, 1762).

Maclaine, A., *A sermon preached at Antrim being the national fast, 18 December 1745* (Dublin, 1746).

(Mac O'Lero, pseud.), *The rapparee saint* (London, 1691).

Madden, S., *Reflections and resolutions proper for the gentlemen of Ireland*, (Dublin, 1738).

—, *Memoirs of the twentieth century, being original letters of state under George II, relating to the most important events in Great Britain and Europe, received and revealed in 1728 and now published for the first time* (London, 1733).

Magill, M., *A sermon preached in the parish church of St Mary's Dublin in general thanksgiving for the suppression of the late rebellion* (Dublin, 1746).

The mantle thrown off or the Irishman dissected, in a letter from a gentleman to his friend in London, 23 August 1689 (London, 1689).

Maule, H., *God's goodness visible in our deliverance from popery* (Dublin, 1757).

Memoirs concerning the campaign of the three kings William, Lewis and James in the year 1692 with reflections on the general endeavours of Lewis the 14th to effect his designs of James II to remount the throne (London, 1693).

Memoirs of the chevalier de Saint George (London, 1712).

Memoirs of the life and character of Charles Radcliffe (Dublin, 1746).

Memoirs of the life of the late duke of Ormonde written by himself (London, 1741).

Memoirs of the lives and families of the Lords Kilmarnock, Cromartie and Balmerino (Dublin, 1746)

Memoirs of the life of Lord Lovat (Dublin, 1746).

Memoirs of the marshal duke of Berwick written by himself with a summary continuation from the year 1716 to his death in 1734, to which work is prefixed a sketch of an historical panegyric of the Marshal by the president Montesquieu (London, 1774).

Memoirs of the queen of Hungary written by herself and found in Vienna after she retired from that city (Dublin, 1742).

A memorial from his most christian majesty presented by the count de Briond, ambassador to the United Provinces, containing reasons for accepting the late king of Spain's will (Dublin, 1700).

The miserable state of Scotland since the union briefly stated (Edinburgh, 1745).

Mephibosheth and Ziba or an appeal of the Protestants of Ireland to the king (London, 1689).

Moffet, W., *The Irish Hudibras. Hesperi-Neso Graphia or a description of the Western Isle, in 8 cantos* (Dublin, 1724; London, 1755).

Molyneux, S., *A Journal of the three months royal campaign of his majesty in Ireland, together with a true and perfect diary of the siege of Limerick* (Dublin, 1690).

Monsieur Pretendent and Signoro Pretenderillo, a poem (Dublin, 1745).

Musgrave, R., *Memoirs of the Irish Rebellion of 1798*, fourth ed. (Enniscorthy, 1995).

A new poem in commemoration of the 10 June being the birthday of the chevalier de St George (Dublin, n.d.).

A new song called the sorrowful lamentation for Anthony Bulger, James Costolow, Edward Quin, John Allen, Christopher Farrel, Edward Higgins, John Weasly, Peter Duff, William Lyons, John Gaffany, Patrick Barnewall, Owen Connelly, James Barry, James Matthews, Thomas Mullen, Patrick Murphy, James Shelvy, 19 January 1722, taken on board a sloop at the bar of Dublin who were supposed to be listed for the Pretender (Dublin, 1721/2).

A new year's gift for the late rapparees: a satyr (London, 1691)

A new year's gift for the tories, alias the rapparees (London, 1691).

(Newenham, E.), *Observations by Sir Edward Newenham on some late publications with the remarks on the epithets of invader and plunderer on the Orange societies and fraternities of United Irishmen* (Dublin, 1804).

(Oates, T.), *Picture of the late King James* (London, 1696).

Observations on the report of the committee of secrecy (Dublin, 1715).

O'Conor, C. and Curry, J., *Observations on the popery laws*, 2nd ed. (Dublin, 1771).

—, *The case of the Roman Catholics of Ireland wherein the principles and conduct of that party are fully explained and vindicated* (Dublin, 1755).

—, *A vindication of a pamphlet lately published entitled* The case of the Roman Catholics of Ireland (Dublin, 1755).

—, *A cottager's remark on the Farmer's* Spirit of party (Dublin, 1754).

[O'Conor, C.?], *The Catholic's letter to the Roman Catholics of Ireland on the late French invasion* (Dublin, 1760).

An ode to be performed at the castle of Dublin on 30 October, being the birthday of his most excellent and sacred majesty George II (Dublin, 1745).

Ode on the present war with Spain (Dublin, 1740).

[Panckoucke, A.J.], *Recueil de pieces choisies de Fontenoy a louange de sa majesté* (Lille, 1745?).

A part and full account of several great matters relating to Ireland, of burning and destroying of several places by the romish army 24 August 1689 (London, 1689).

Philips, G., *The interest of England in the preservation of Ireland* (London, 1689).

A pill to purge state melancholy or a collection of excellent new songs, 1 March 1715 (Dublin, 1715).

A poem on the occasion of the funeral of John, duke of Marlborough (Dublin, 1723).

A poem upon the arrival of his most serene majesty King George (Dublin, 1714).

A poem on the arrival of his royal highness Prince Frederick (Dublin, 1722).

The pope's speech to the college of cardinals, 19 November 1701 (Dublin, 1701).

The popish champion or a compleat history of the life and military actions of Tyrconnell (London, 1689).

The practice of the Pretender and his agents in Paris and Rome (Dublin, n.d.).

The Presbyterian Jacobites, being a full and true relation of a late meeting of 3,000 Jacobites under the command of a Presbyterian minister and his deputy who administered to them the solemn league and covenant (Dublin, 1712).

The present condition of Londonderry with a particular relation of the cruelties acted by the Irish and French papists on the Protestants of Ireland ([London/Dublin?], 1689).

Present dangerous condition of the Protestants in Ireland with a new order of Tyrconils, 19 February 1689 (London, 1689).

The present state of Europe or the Historical Mercury, September 1690 (London, 1690).

Proceedings of the court of St Margaret's Hill on the trials of Francis Townley, George Fletcher, Thomas Chadwick, William Bretah, Thomas Deacon, John Barnwick, James Dawson, Christopher Taylor, Andrew Blood, John Sanderson, Thomas Syddall, James Willday, and Charles Deacon, officers in the same regiment, and David Morgan esq, counsellor-at-law (Dublin, 1746).

The proceedings of the right honourable the lords spiritual and temporal in parliament assembled upon the bill intituled an act to release from the obligation of the oath of secrecy the members of the court-martial appointed for the trial of Admiral Byng (Dublin, 1757).

The profit and loss of Great Britain in the present war with Spain July 1739–July 1741 (Dublin, 1741).

Queries to the Querist or a series of 141 queries, to which is added six humorous toasts by Moll Waller (Dublin, 1754).

The question whether Great Britain and Ireland can be otherwise than miserable under a popish king (Dublin, 1745).

A reason for his majesty issuing a general pardon to the rebels of Ireland that will submit without exception of the considerable and influencing men amongst them, 30 August 1689 (London, 1689).

Reasons for a war from the imminent danger with which Europe is threatened by the exorbitant power of the house of Bourbon (Dublin, 1734).

Reasons of the utmost importance to Great Britain and Ireland against receiving the Pretender and restoring the popish line (Dublin, 1727).

Reilly, H., *Ireland's case briefly stated* (Paris/Louvain, 1695).

—, *An impartial history of Ireland: to which is annexed* A Remonstrance of the nobility and gentry to Charles II, The last speech and dying words of Oliver Plunkett and the case of the Roman Catholics of Ireland humbly represented to both houses of parliament by the Rev. Dr. Nary, repr. (London, 1744).

A relation of what most remarkably happened during the last campaign in Ireland betwixt his majesties royal army and the forces of the prince of Orange (Dublin, 1689).

The religious turncoat or the trimming observation (Dublin, 1711).

Remarks on the preliminary articles of peace as they were lately transmitted to us from The Hague wherein the articles relating to the granting of a subsidy to the Pretender by the house of Hanover, for securing their hereditary succession on the crown of Great Britain, is proved to be the highest insult on the present (Dublin, 1748).

Remarks on the affairs and trade of England and Ireland (London, 1691).

Remarks on the case of the honourable Brigadier-General Ingoldsby in relation to the late action at Fontenoy (London, 1745).

A report from the committee appointed by order of the House of Commons to examine Christopher Layer and others (Dublin, 1722).

Report from the committee appointed to inspect the several reports of the late judges and other proceedings in relation to the election of magistrates for the city of Dublin 6 June 1716 (Dublin, 1716).

Report from the committee of secrecy appointed by order of the House of Commons to examine several books and papers laid before the house relating to the late negotiations of peace (Dublin, 1715).

The report of the judges of the assizes of north-east circuit of Ulster upon a memorial given to the lords justice of Ireland by his grace the lord primate and the lord bishop of Down and Connor (Dublin, 1714).

Resolution of the high and mighty lords of the states general of the United Netherlands for supporting the succession to the crown of Great Britain to the illustrious house of Hanover, 15 August 1714 (Dublin, 1714).

A review of Mr Foster's account of the behaviour of the late earl of Kilmarnock (Dublin, 1746).

A review of Dr. Sherlock's Case of allegiance *with an answer to his vindication* (London, 1691).

The royal flight or the conquest of Ireland, a new farce (London, 1690).

The royal voyage or an Irish expedition (London, 1690).

Rundle, T., *A sermon preached in Christ's Church, 23 October 1735 before his grace, Lionel duke of Dorset* (Dublin, 1735).

The sad and lamentable state of the Protestants in Ireland, being an account of the barbarous proceedings of the natives against the English (London, 1689).

(Sanders, R.), *The argument of one of the Queen's Council against Mr Dudley Moore, in the Queen's Bench* (Dublin, 1713).

(Sargeant, J.), *An historical romance of the wars between the mighty giant Gallieno and the great knight Nasonius* ([Dublin?], 1694).

Seasonable advice to the freeholders of Armagh by a brother freeholder, second ed. (Dublin, 1752).

Seasonable advice to Protestants, containing some means of reviving and strengthening the Protestant interest (Cork, 1745).

The second part of Lilili Bulero bullen a la. The second part was added after the landing of King William (n.p., n.d.).

Secret memoirs of the new treaty of alliance with France (Dublin, 1716).

A sermon preached before the duke of Lorraine and the Pretender at Lorraine upon the arrival of the Irish recruits in general, by 'Bishop Mac Gwyre' of Killarney [n.p, n d].

A sermon preached by a new father in the Jesuit chapel at the Kings Inns Dublin on St Patrick's Day, 1688 (London, 1688).

A sermon preached to the Protestants of Ireland in London, 23 October 1713 (Dublin, 1713).

A sermon of thanksgiving for the happy success of his majesties arms against the rebels in July 1685, preached in Kilkenny on 23 August 1685, to his excellency Richard, earl of Tyrconnell (Dublin, 1685).

Sherlock, W., *The case of the allegiance due to sovereign powers stated and resolved according to scripture and reason* (London, 1691).

A short account of the late proceedings of the University of Dublin against Forbes with a full and satisfactory answer to all objections made against his degradation ([Dublin?], 1708).

Some queries for the better understanding of a list of James II's Irish and popish forces in France (London, 1697).

Some reflections on a pamphlet entituled A faithful history of the northern affairs of Ireland from the late King James his accession to the crown to the siege of Londonderry (Dublin, 1691).

The speech of Captain Fitzgerald, C Burn, F. Burn ... etc. to be executed at Blessington on 27 December 1717 (Dublin, 1717).

The speech of the late King James II at the opening of the session of parliament held in Dublin (Dublin, 1748).

The spirit of Jacobitism, or a dialogue between King William and Benting (London, 1695).

The Squire and the Cardinal (?, 1740?).

The state of the nation from the year 1747 and respecting 1748 inscribed to a member of the present parliament (Dublin, 1748).

Story, G., *A true and impartial account of the most material occurrences in the kingdom of Ireland in the last two years* (London, 1691).

—, *An impartial history of the wars of Ireland with a continuation thereof, in two parts from the time that the duke of Schomberg landed with an army in that kingdom to 23 March 1691/2* (London, 1693).

Story, W., *A sermon preached before the House of Commons, 5 November 1737* (Dublin, 1737).

—, *A sermon preached before his excellency the lord lieutenant and a numerous assembly of the Protestant gentlemen of Ireland* (London, 1714).

The succession of Spain discussed (Dublin, 1701).

The Swan-Tripe Club in Dublin: a Satyr (Dublin, 1706)

Swift, J., *A modest proposal for preventing the children of poor people in Ireland from being a burden to their parents or country, and for making them beneficial to the public* (Dublin, 1729).

——., *On poetry. A rhapsody* (Dublin, 1728, 1734).

Synge, E., *A sermon preached in St Andrew's on the anniversary of the Irish rebellion, 23 October 1725* (Dublin, 1725).

Taaffe, N., *Observations on the affairs of Ireland from the settlement of 1691 to the present time* (Dublin, 1766).

Tennison, R., *A sermon preached to the Protestants of Ireland in the city of London at St Helen's, 23 October 1690* (Dublin, 1691).

This day arrived from Cork the copy of a letter from James Butler, late duke of Ormonde, 4 November 1727 (Dublin, 1727).

The thistle: a dispassionate examination of the prejudice of Englishmen in general to the Scottish nation (Edinburgh, 1746).

To his grace the duke of Ormonde upon his second accession to the government of Ireland (Dublin, 1710).

To Lieutenant-General Ginkle, commander-in-chief of all their majesties forces in Ireland ([?], 1691).

To the Queen's most excellent majesty, the humble address of the knights, citizens and burgesses in the parliament assembled, 21 December 1713 (Dublin, 1713).

(Travers, J.), *His defence of King William of glorious memory published on occasion of abusing the statue in College Green* (Dublin, 1700).

Travers, J., *A sermon preached in St Andrew's Church before the hon House of Commons, 8 October 1695* (Dublin, 1695).

—, *A sermon preached in St Andrew's church of Dublin before the honourable House of Commons, 23 October 1698, being the anniversary thanksgiving from the deliverance from the Irish Rebellion of 1641* (Dublin, 1698).

Trenchard, J., *An answer to the late King James declaration at St Germain, 17 April 1693* (London, 1693).

Trenchard, J., *A list of King James's Irish and popish forces in France ready when called for in answer to an argument against a land force* (London, 1697).

[Tressan, Louis Elizabeth de la Vergne, Comte de] *Reponse a Mr de Voltaire sur son pöeme sur la bataille de Fontenoy* (Paris, 1745).

The trial of Admiral John Byng at a court-martial as taken by Mr Charles Fearre plus an appendix containing all the orders, letters of intelligence, papers etc. read in the court (Dublin, 1757).

The trial and examination of Capt. Cullmore, a proclaimed tory and was noted for being guilty of bloody murthers, rapes and robberies in the county of Armagh, 21 February 1719 (Dublin, 1719).

The trials of Mr Standish Barry esq, Mr James Butler, Mr Edward Barry, clerk, Mr Patrick Stack, Mr Charles Doran and several other persons concerned in sending or listing men for the Pretender, some cleared, some others condemned to be hanged and quartered, 20 May 1722 (Dublin, 1722).

A true account of the present state of Ireland and a full relation of the establishment made by King James by a person who with great difficulty left Dublin 8 June 1689. (London, 1689).

A true and faithful account of the present state and condition of the kingdom of Ireland (London, 1690).

A true and faithful narrative of the Protestant successes against the late King James's army and the French in Ireland (London, 1689).

A true and impartial history of the wars of Ireland, Flanders, on the Rhine and in Savoy etc., in two parts (London, 1695).

Tyrconnell's proceedings in Ireland and motion in council as to the burning of Dublin (London, 1688).

Undeniable reasons for suspending the habeas corpus act for securing traitors (Cork, 1722).

Upon the fringes, so commonly called by the vulgar, 16 July 1722 ([Dublin?], 1722).

A view of the court of St Germain from the years 1690–1698 with an account of the entertainment Protestants met with there directed to the malcontents in England (London, 1695).

A vindication of the present ministry from the clamours raised against them upon occasion of the new preliminaries (London, 1711).

A vindication of the Rev Henry Sacherevell from the false, scandalous and malicious aspersions cast upon him in the late infamous pamphlet entitled The Modern Fanatick (Dublin, 1712).

The wanderer or surprizing escape, a narrative founded on true facts (Dublin, 1747).

Wellwood, J., *An answer to the late King James's declaration to all his Protestant subjects in the kingdom of England, Dublin Castle, 5 May 1689* (London, 1689).

[Wellwood, J.], *An answer to the Pretender's declaration or a calm address to all parties in religion, whether Protestant or Catholic on the score of the present rebellion* (Dublin, 1745).

Wettenall, E., *Hexapla Jacobaea. A specimen of loyalty towards his present majesty James II in six pieces by an Irish Protestant bishop* (Dublin, 1686).

—, *A sermon preached on 23 October 1692 before his excellency the lord lieutenant and the lords spiritual and temporal and divers of the Commons in Christ's Church Cathedral Dublin* (Dublin, 1692).

Whalley, J., *A decree of the stars for Cornelius Carter* (Dublin, 1710).

Whittingham, C., *A sermon preached at St Peter's Dublin, 4 November 1733* (Dublin, 1733).

The whole tryal of Captain Moses Nowland who was try'd and condemned at the king's bench for listing men for the Pretender 28 June 1726 (Dublin, 1726).

The whole account of the arraignment and confinement of Thomas Grace, Coll. Luttrell's cousin, who is now fast and double boulted in Newgate for perjury (Dublin, 1718).

The whole tryal and examination of Thomas Caddy and Richard Wilson, who were try'd at the King's Bench the 4th of this instant February for the murder of Henry Luttrel (Dublin, 1718).

Wilson, J., *A sermon preached at Christ's Church before their excellencies the lords justice on 29 May 1713 being the anniversary of the happy restoration* (Dublin, 1713).

*Note: All pamphlets cited in this book have been consulted in the Bradshaw Collection (Cambridge U.L.), the Thorpe Collection, July Collection (N.L.I.), the Haliday Collection (R.I.A.), the Gilbert Collection (Dublin Corporation Library, Pearse St.) and miscellaneous collections in Trinity College Library, The British Library, the Bodleian Library Oxford, Mac Bean Collection, University of Aberdeen, Univ. of Texas at Austin, University of Minnesota Minneapolis and via the O.C.L.C. and English Short Title catalogues.

SECONDARY SOURCES

[Anon], 'Shawn Rua, the rapparee: a tradition of Macroom' in *J.C.H.A.S.*, xi (1905), pp 67–79.

Asch, R. (ed.) *Three nations. A common history of England, Scotland and Ireland 1600–1920* (Bochum, 1993).

Barnard, T., 'Farewell to Old Ireland' in *Hist. Jn*, xxxiv, no. 4 (1993), pp 309–28.

—, 'Landlords and urban life: Youghal and the Boyles 1641-1740', in *Irish Historic Settlement*, v (1995), pp 1–5.

—, and Fenlon, J., (ed.), *The dukes of Ormond, 1610-1745* (London, 2000).

—, review of S. Connolly, *Religion, law and power* in *I.H.S.*, xxviii (1993), pp 320–23.

Bartlett, T., 'An account of the Whiteboys from the 1790s' in *Tipp. Hist. Jn.* (1991), pp 141–9.

—., 'Army and society in eighteenth-century Ireland' in Maguire, W. (ed.), *Kings in conflict*, pp 173–82.

—, *The fall and rise of the Irish nation. The Catholic question 1690–1830* (London, 1992).

—, review of *A New History of Ireland* in *Past and Present*, cxvi (1987), pp 206–19.

—, and Hayton, D. (ed.), *Penal era and golden age: essays in Irish history 1690–1800* (Belfast, 1979).

—, and Jeffreys, K. (ed.), *A military history of Ireland* (Cambridge, 1996).

Baynes, J., *The Jacobite rising of 1715* (London, 1970).

Beckett, J., *The cavalier duke* (Belfast, 1990).

—, *The making of modern Ireland* (London, 1981).

Beddard, R. (ed.) *The revolutions of 1688* (Oxford, 1991).

Begley, J., *The diocese of Limerick from 1691 to the present time* (Dublin, 1938).

Beglin, D., 'The battle of Fontenoy' in *An Cosantóir*, xx, no. 10 (1960), pp 499–505.

Beresford, M., 'Francois Thurot and the French attack at Carrickfergus' in *Ir. Sword*, x (1972), pp 255–70.

Berresford-Ellis, P., *The Boyne water. The battle of the Boyne, 1690* (London, 1976).

Bigger, F.J., 'A Huguenot hero of 1704' in *C. H. A. S. J.*, *2nd series*, iv (1898), pp 287–307.

Black, J., *British foreign policy in the age of Walpole* (Edinburgh, 1985).

—, *Britain in the age of Walpole* (London, 1984).

—, *Culloden and the '45* (Gloucestershire, 1993).

—, 'Could the Jacobites have won?' in *History Today*, xl (1995), pp 24–30.

—, 'The end of a tradition: a survey of eighteenth-century literature' in *Stud. Hib.*, i (1961), pp 128–51.

Blüche, F., *Louis XIV* (London, 1990).

Bolster, E., *A history of the diocese of Cork* (Cork, 1989).

Boyce, G., *Nationalism in Ireland* (London, 1982).

—, Eccleshall, R. and Geoghegan, V. (ed.), *Political thought in Ireland since the seventeenth century* (London, 1993).

Boyce, G and O'Day, A (ed.), The making of modern Irish history (London, 1996).

Boyle, P., 'The Irish College in Paris 1578–1901' in *I.E.R.*, xi (1901), pp. 193–210.

—, *The Irish College in Rome 1578–1901* (Dublin, 1901).

Bracken, D., 'Piracy and poverty: aspects of the Irish Jacobite experience in France 1691-1720', in O'Conor, *Irish in Europe*, p. 127-43.

Brady, C. (ed.), *Interpreting Irish history: the debate on historical revisionism* (Dublin, 1994).

—, (ed.), *Worsted in the game. Losers in Irish history* (Dublin, 1989). (This is *also* Ciarán Brady)

Brady, J., 'The church in Ireland under the penal code' in Corish, (ed.), *A history of Irish Catholicism.*

—, 'The Irish language in London', in *Ir. Monthly*, xxxi (1949), pp 32–3.

Breathnach, C., 'Archbishop J. Brenan, his life and work 1625–1693' in *Tipp. Hist. Jn.* (1993), pp 148–56.

Breathnach, P., 'Oral and written transmission of poetry in the eighteenth century' in *E.C.I.*, ii (1987), pp 57–67.

Breathnach, R., 'The end of a tradition. A survey of eighteenth-century Gaelic literature, in *Stud. Hib.*, i (1960), pp 128-50.

—, 'The lady and the King: a theme in Irish literature' in *Studies*, xlii (1953), pp 321–36.

Bric, M., 'The Whiteboys in County Tipperary', in Nolan (ed.), *Tipperary*, pp 148–68.

Burke, O.J., *The history of the Catholic archbishops of Tuam* (Dublin, 1882).

Burke, W., *The Irish priest in penal times 1660–1760*, repr. (Shannon, 1969).

—, *The church in Ireland under the penal code* (Dublin, 1921).

—, *History of Clonmel*, repr. (Kilkenny, 1983).

Bruns, J., 'Some details on the Sheridans (1646-1746)' in *Ir. Sword*, ii (1954–6), pp 65–6.

—, 'The early years of Sir Thomas Sheridan (1684–1746)' in *Ir. Sword*, ii (1954–6), pp 256–9.

—, 'Sheridan letters' in *Ir. Sword*, ii (1954–6), p. 375.

Burtchaell, J., 'Bristol Irish news in the 1750s' in *Decies: Journal of the Waterford Archaeological and Historical Society*, lii (1996), pp 13–38.

Butler, M., 'Crotty the robber' in *Waterford and South-East of Ireland Archaeological Journal*, xii, no. 1 (Jan.-Mar. 1909), pp 12, 54, 88, 105.

Buttimer, C., 'Cogadh Sagsana Nua Sonn: reporting the American Revolution' in *Studia Hib.*, xxviii (1994), pp 63–103.

—, 'Gaelic literature and contemporary Irish life' in Buttimer, C., and O' Flanagan, P. (ed.), *Cork*, pp 585–653.

—, and O' Flanagan, P. (ed.), *Cork: history and society* (Dublin, 1993).

Caball, M., 'Providence and exile in seventeenth-century Ireland' in *I.H.S.*, xxix (1994), pp 174–88.

Campbell, J., 'The tour of Edward Lhuyd in Ireland 1699–1700' in *Celtica*, v (1960), pp 218–28.

Campbell-Ross, I., review of *A new history of Ireland*, iv' in *E.C.I.*, i (1986), pp 208–11.

Canny, N., (ed.) *Europeans on the move. Studies on European migration* (Oxford, 1994).

—, 'The formation of the Gaelic mind: religion, politics and Gaelic Irish literature', in *Past and Present*, xcv (1982), pp 91–116.

—, 'Irish resistance to Empire 1641, 1690 and 1798' in Stone (ed.), *An imperial state at war*, pp 288–321.

—, review of B. Ó Buachalla, 'Na Stíobhartaigh agus an t-aos léinn, Cing Séamus' in *I.H.S.*, xxiv (1984), pp 278–81.

[Caulfield, J.], 'Records of the Sarsfield family of County Cork' in *J.C.H.A.S*, xxi (1915), pp 82–91, 131–6.

Cavanagh, M., 'William Crotty, outlaw and popular hero' in *Waterford and South-East of Ireland Archaeological Journal*, xii (1909), p. 90.

Chaloner-Smith, J., *British mezzotinto portraits*, 4 vols., (London, 1878-83).

Charnock, J., *Biographia Navalis*, 6 vols (London, 1794–8).

Childs, J., *The army, James II and the Glorious revolution* (Manchester, 1980).

—, 'The Williamite war 1689–91' in Bartlett and Jeffreys (ed.), *Military history of Ireland*, pp 188–211.

Clark, J., *English Society 1688–1832* (London, 1991).

Colley, L., *Britons: forging the nation 1707–1837* (London, 1992).

Comerford, R., Cullen, M., Hill, J. and Lennon, C. (ed.), *Religion, conflict and co-existence in Ireland: essays presented to Monsignor Corish* (Dublin, 1990).

Connolly, J., *Labour in Irish history* (Dublin, 1910).

Connolly, S., 'Approaches to Irish popular culture' in *Bullán*, ii (1996), pp 83–101.

—, 'The defence of Protestant Ireland' in Bartlett and Jeffreys (ed.), *Military history of Ireland*, pp 231–47.

—, 'Eighteenth-century Ireland' in Boyce, and O'Day, (ed.), *The making of modern Irish history*, pp 15–34.

—, 'The Houghers: agrarian protest in early-eighteenth century Ireland' in Philbin, (ed.), *Nationalism and popular protest in Ireland*, pp 139–62.

—, (ed.), *Kingdoms united: Great Britain and Ireland since 1500* (Dublin, 1998).

—, 'Law, order, and popular unrest in Iar-Connaught in the eighteenth century: the case of the Houghers' in Corish, (ed.), *Radicals, rebels and establishments*, pp 51–69.

—, *Priests and people in pre-Famine Ireland* (Dublin, 1982).

—, 'Religion and history: Review article' in *Ir. Ec. and soc. hist.* x (1983), pp 66–86.

—, *Religion, law and power: the making of Protestant Ireland 1660–1760* (Oxford, 1992).

—, 'Violence and order in eighteenth-century Ireland' in O'Flanagan, P., Ferguson, P. and Whelan, K. (ed.), *Rural Ireland 1600–1900*, pp. 42–61.

Copinger, W.H., *History of the Copingers or Coppingers* (Manchester, 1884).

Corish, P., *The Catholic community in the seventeenth and eighteenth centuries* (Dublin, 1981).

—, *History of Irish Catholicism* (Dublin, 1992)

Corish, P. (ed.) *Radicals, reblels and establishments* (Belfast, 1985)

Corkery, D., *The Hidden Ireland*, repr. (Dublin, 1975).

Corp, E., 'James Fitzjames, 1st duke of Berwick. A new identification for a portrait by Hyacinthe Rigaud', in *Apollo* June 1995, pp 53–61.

Cosgrave, A., and Mc Cartney, D. (ed.), *Studies in Irish history presented to Robin Dudley-Edwards* (Dublin, 1979).

Crawford, T., 'Political and protest songs in eighteenth-century Scotland' in *Scottish Studies*, xiv (1970), pp 1–35.

Creighton, S., 'The penal laws in Ireland and documents in the archive of Propaganda Fide 1691–1731' in *Proc. Ir. Cat. Hist. Comm.* (1961), pp. 5–9.

Crofton-Croker, T., *Researches in the south of Ireland illustrative of the scenery, architectural remains and the manners and superstitions of the peasantry, with an appendix containing a private narrative of 1798* (London, 1824).

Cruickshanks, E. (ed.), *Ideology and conspiracy: aspects of Jacobitism 1689–1759* (Edinburgh, 1982).

—, *Political untouchables: the Tories and the '45* (London, 1979).

—, 'Lord North, Christopher Layer and the Atterbury Plot 1720–23' in Cruickshanks, Cruickshanks, E. and Black, J. (ed.) *The Jacobite challenge* (Edinburgh, 1988) pp 92–106.

—, and Corp, E.(ed), *The Stuart court in exile and the Jacobites* (London, 1995).

—, and Erskine-Hill, H., *The Atterbury plot* (forthcoming).

—, and Erskine-Hill, H., 'The Waltham Black-Act and Jacobitism' in *Journal of British Studies*, xxiv (1985), pp 358–65.

Cullen, L., *The emergence of modern Ireland* (London, 1981).

—, *An economic history of Ireland since 1660* (London, 1972).

—, 'Catholic social classes under the penal laws' in Power and Whelan (ed.), *Endurance and Emergence*, pp 57–85.

—, 'The Hidden Ireland: the re-assessment of a concept' in *Stud. Hib.*, ix (1969), pp 7–48.

—, The *Hidden Ireland: the re-assessment of a concept*, repr. (Gigginstown, 1988).

—, 'Catholics under the penal laws' in *E.C.I*, i (1986), pp 23–37.

—, 'The contemporary and later politics of Caoineadh Airt Uí Laoire' in *E.C.I.*, viii (1993), pp 7–39.

—, 'The Irish diaspora of the seventeenth and eighteenth centuries' in Canny, N. (ed.), *Europeans on the move.*

—, 'The Galway smuggling trade in the 1730s' in *Galway Hist. and Arch. Soc. Jnr.*, xxx (1962), pp 7–40.

—, 'The overseas trade of Waterford as seen from the ledger of Courtenay and Ridgeway' in *R.S.A.I. Jn.*, lxxxviii (1958), pp 165–78.

—, 'Patrons, teachers and literacy in Irish 1700–1880' in Daly and Dickson (ed.), *Origins of popular literacy* , pp 15–45.

—, 'The smuggling trade of Ireland in the eighteenth century' in *R.I.A. Proc.*, lxvii (1969), C, pp 149–75.

—, et Furet, F. (ed.), *Irlande et France, xviie-xxe siècles. Pour une histoire rurale comparée* (Paris, 1980).

D'Alton, J., *Illustrations historical and genealogical of King James's Irish army list*, 2 vols (Dublin, 1860).

Daly, M. and Dickson, D. (ed.), *Origins of popular literacy in Ireland* (Dublin, 1990).

D'Arcy, F., 'Exiles and strangers: the case of the Wogans' in O'Brien (ed.), *Parliament, politics and people*, pp 171–85.

Davitt, M., *The fall of feudalism in Ireland* (Dublin, 1904).

de Blácam, A., *Gaelic literature surveyed*, repr. (Dublin, 1973).

de Brún, P., Ó Coileáin, S. and Ó Riain, P., (eag.), *Folia Gadelica* (Cork, 1983).

Dickson, D., *Arctic Ireland: The extraordinary story of the great frost and the forgotten famine of 1740–41* (Belfast, 1997).

—, *New Foundations: Ireland 1600–1800*, 2nd ed. (Dublin, 2000).

Doherty, R. *The Williamite war in Ireland* (Dublin, 1998).

Donaldson, W., *Jacobite song, political myth and national identity* (Aberdeen, 1988).

Donnelly, J., Miller, K. (ed.), *Irish popular culture 1650–1850* (Dublin, 1998).

—, 'The Whiteboy movement' in *I.H.S.*, xxi (1978–79), pp 20–54.

Donnelly, P., *A history of the parish of Ardstraw and Castlederg* (Strabane, 1978).

Doran, J.(ed.), *Mann and manners at the court of Florence 1740–1786*, 2 vols (London, 1876).

Dowling, P., *The hedge schools of Ireland* (Dublin, 1935).

Dudley-Edwards, O., 'Who was Mac An Cheannuidhe? A mystery of the birth of the Aisling' in *North Munster Antiq. Jn.*, xxxiii (1991), pp 55–78.

Dudley-Edwards, R., 'An agenda for Irish history 1978–2018' in Brady (ed.), *Interpreting Irish history*, pp 54–71.

Duffy, C., *The wild goose and the eagle: a life of Marshal Brown 1705-57* (London, 1964).

Duffy, S., *Ireland in the middle ages* (Dublin, 1997).

—, 'Interview with James Lydon' in *History Ireland*, iii, no. 1, (1995), pp 11–14.

Dunlop, R., 'Ireland in the eighteenth century' in *Cambridge Modern History*, vi (1909), pp 479–84.

Dunne, T., 'Gaelic responses to conquest and colonisation: the evidence of poetry' in *Stud. Hib.*, xx (1980), pp 7–31.

Eager, R., 'Colonel John O'Sullivan', in *An Cosantóir*, xix, no. 12 (1949), pp 623–8.

Elliot, J., *Imperial Spain 1496-1716* (Middlesex, 1978).

Elliott, M., 'Irishry right down to the roots' in *The Guardian*, 24 July 1993.

Erlanger, P., *Louis XIV* (London, 1970).

Erskine-Hill, H., 'Literature and the Jacobite cause: Was there a rhetoric of Jacobitism?' in Cruickshanks, (ed.), *Ideology and conspiracy*, pp 49–70.

—, *Poetry of opposition and revolution: Dryden to Wordsworth* (Oxford, 1996).

Fagan, P., *Divided loyalties: the question of an oath for Irish Catholics* (Dublin, 1997).

—, *Dublin's turbulent priest: Cornelius Nary 1658-1738* (Dublin, 1991).

—, 'The Dublin Catholic mob 1700–50' in *E.C.I.*, iv (1989), pp 133–42.

—, *The second city: a portrait of Dublin* (Dublin, 1986).

—, *An Irish bishop in penal times. The chequered career of Sylvester Lloyd 1680–1747* (Dublin, 1993).

Fenning, H., 'A guide to eighteenth-century reports of Irish dioceses in the Archives of Propaganda Fide' in *Collect. Hib.*, xi (1968), pp 19–36.

—, *The Irish Dominican province 1698-1797* (Dublin, 1990).

—, 'Michael MacDonogh O.P., Bishop of Kilmore 1728–1746' in *I.E.R.*, cvi, no. 2 (1966), pp 138–53.

—, *Publications of Irish Catholic interest 1700–1800. An experimental check-list* (Rome, 1973).

—, 'Some broadsheets, chiefly from Cork, 1709–1821' in *Coll. Hib.*, xxxviii (1996), pp 118–41.

—, *The undoing of the friars* (Louvain, 1972).

Ferguson, K., 'The organisation of King William's army in Ireland 1689–92' in *Ir. Sword*, xviii (1990), pp 62–80.

Fitzgerald, F., 'Fontenoy' in *An Cosantóir*, v, no. 11 (1945), pp 599–607; v, no. 12 (1945), pp 666–71.

Fitzgerald, G., 'The decline of the Irish language in Ireland 1771-1871' in Daly and Dickson (ed.), *Origins of popular literacy*, pp 59–73.

—, 'Estimates for baronies of minimal level of Irish speaking amongst successive decennial cohorts 1771–81 to 1861–71'; in *R.I.A., Proc.*, (1984), C, pp. 117–55.

Flanagan, P., 'The diocese of Clogher in 1714' in *Clogher Record*, i, no. 2 (1954), pp 39–42; ii (1955), pp 125–31.

Flood, J., *The life of the chevalier Wogan* (Dublin, 1922).

Flood, W., *A history of Irish music*, repr. (Shannon, 1970).

Fox, P. (ed.), *The treasures of the library: Trinity College Dublin* (Dublin, 1986).

Froude, J.A., The *English in Ireland in the eighteenth century*, 3 vols (London, 1872–4).

Garnham, N., *The courts, crime and criminal law in Ireland 1692-1760* (Dublin, 1996).

Gavan-Duffy, C. (ed.), *The ballad poetry of Ireland* (Dublin, 1845).

Geoghegan, V., 'A Jacobite history. The Abbé Macgeoghegan's *History of Ireland* in *E.C.I.*, vi (1991), pp 37–55.

Giblin, C., 'Roger O'Connor, an Irishman in the French and papal service' in *Ir. Sword*, ii (1954–56), pp 309–14.

—, 'The Stuart nomination of bishops 1687–1765' in *Proc. Ir. Cat. Hist. Comm.* (1955–57), pp 35–47.

—, 'Material relating to Ireland in the Albani collection of manuscripts in the Vatican Archives' in *Proc. Ir. Cat. Hist. Comm.* (Dublin, 1965), pp 10–17.

Gibson, J., *Playing the Scottish card. The Franco-Jacobite invasion of 1708* (Edinburgh, 1995).

Gilbert, J., *The streets of Dublin* (Dublin, 1852). [I have used the copy in the reading room of the R.I.A. which is irregularly paginated and contains pasted cuttings from the *Irish Quarterly Review*, Call no. R.R. 55/c/46].

Gillespie, R., 'The Irish Protestants and James II' in I.*H.S.*, *xxviii* (1992), pp 124–34.

—, and Moran, G. (ed.), *Longford: essays in county history* (Dublin, 1991).

—, and O'Sullivan, H. (ed.), *The Borderlands: essays in the study of the Ulster-Leinster border* (Belfast, 1989).

Gleeson, J., *History of the Ely O'Carroll territory of ancient Ormond*, repr. (Kilkenny, 1982).

Gooch, G., *Louis XV* (London, 1956).

Goldie, M., 'The political thought of the Anglican revolution', in Beddard (ed.) *Revolutions of 1688*, pp 102-37.

Grattan-Flood, W., *History of the diocese of Ferns* (Waterford, 1916).

Griffin. W., *The Irish on the continent in the eighteenth century* (Wisconsin, 1979).

Grosjean, A., 'Scottish-Scandanavian seventeenth-century links: a case study of the SSNE database' in *Northern Studies*, *xxxii* (1997), pp 105–21.

Guy, A., 'The Irish military establishment 1660–1776' in Bartlett and Jeffreys (ed.), *Military history of Ireland*, pp 211–31.

Gwynn, S. and Kettle, T., *Battle songs of the Irish Brigades* (Dublin and London, 1915).

Harden, T., *Bandit country: the I.R.A. and South Armagh* (London, 1999).

Harris, W., *The whole works of Sir James Ware concerning Ireland revised and improved*, 2 vols (Dublin, 1764).

Harrison, A., *Ag cruinniú meala. Anthony Raymond 1675–1726: Ministéir Phrotas-túnach agus léinn na Gaeilge i mBaile Átha Cliath* (B.Á.C., 1988).

Hastings, A., *The construction of nationhood: ethnicity, religion and nationalism* (Cambridge, 1997).

Hay, D. et al. (ed.) *Albion's fatal tree: crime and society in eighteenth-century England* (New York, 1975).

Hayden, M., 'Prince Charles Edward and his Irish friends' in *Studies*, xxiii (1934), pp 95–109.

Hayes, R., 'A famous Irish war correspondent' in *Studies*, xxxvi *(Mar.* 1947*)*, pp 40–48.

—, 'Ireland and Jacobitism' in *Studies*, xxxviii (1949), pp 101–6.

—, 'Irish casualties in the French military service' in *Ir. Sword*, i (1949–53), pp 198–201.

—, *Irish swordsmen of France* (Dublin, 1934).

—, 'Irishmen in the Seven Years's War' in *Studies*, xxxii (1943) pp 413–18.

—, 'John Drumgoole of Walshestowne' in *L.A.J.*, x (1941–4), p. 215.

—, *Old Irish links with France: some echoes of exiled Ireland* (Dublin, 1940).

—, 'Sir Edward Scott' in *Ir. Sword*, i (1949–53), p.156.

—, 'An unpublished eighteenth-century Franco-Irish manuscript' in *Studies*, xxviii (1939), pp 475–84.

Hayes-McCoy, G., 'Irish soldiers and the '45' in Rynne (ed.), *North Munster studies*, pp 315–32.

—, 'The Wild Geese', in *An Cosantóir*, xiii, no. 7 (1953), pp 335–46.

Hayton, D., 'The crisis in Ireland and the disintegration of Queen Anne's last ministry' in *I.H.S.*, xxii (1981), pp 193–215.

—, review of Whelan and Power (ed.), *Endurance and emergence* in *I.H.S.*, xxviii, no. 112 (1993), pp 488–52.

Hempton, D., *Religion and political culture in Britain and Ireland* (Cambridge, 1996).

Henry, G., *The Irish military community in Spanish Flanders 1586–1621* (Cork, 1992).

Heussaf, A., *Filí agus cléir san ochtú haois déag* (B.Á.C., 1993).

Higgins, B., 'Ireland from the going of Sarsfield to the coming of Tone' in *Wolfe Tone annual* (1943), pp 13–120.

Hobsbawm, E., *Primitive rebels* (Manchester, 1959).

—, *Bandits* (London, 1972).

Higgins, I., *Swift's politics. A study in disaffection* (Cambridge, 1994).

Holohan, R., *The Irish chateaux. In search of descendants of the Wild Geese* (Dublin, 1989).

Hume-Weygand, J., 'Epic of the wild geese' in *University Review*, iii, no. 2 (1962), pp 25–35.

Irwin, L., 'Sarsfield: the man and myth' in Whelan (ed.), *The last of the great wars*, pp 108–26.

—, review of Fagan (ed.), *Ireland and the Stuart papers* in *I.H.S.*, xxx, no. 119 (1997), pp 477–9.

James, F., *Ireland in the Empire: a history of Ireland from the Williamite wars to the eve of the American Revolution* (Cambridge, Mass., 1973).

Johnston, S., 'The Irish establishment' in *Ir. Sword*, i (1949–53), pp 33–6.

Joseph, G., 'On the trail of Latin-American bandits: A re-examination of peasant resistance' in Rodríguez (ed.), *Patterns of contention in Mexican history*, pp 293–336.

Kelly, J., 'The abduction of women of fortune in eighteenth-century Ireland' in *E.C.I.*, ix (1994), pp 7–43.

—, 'The Catholic church in the diocese of Ardagh 1650–1870' in Gillespie and Moran (ed.), *Longford*, pp 63–91.

—, *That damned thing called honour. The duel in Irish history* (Dublin, 1995).

—, 'The glorious and immortal memory: commemoration and Protestant identity in Ireland, 1660–1800' in *R.I.A. Proc.* 94 C (1994), pp 25–52.

Kelly, J. and Keogh, D. (ed) *History of the diocese of Dublin* (Dublin, 2000).

—, 'The impact of the penal laws', in Kelly, and Keogh, (ed.), *History of the diocese of Dublin*, pp 144–75.

—, review of Fagan, *An Irish bishop* in *E.C.I.*, ix (1994), pp 151–2.

—, review of Fagan, (ed.), *Ireland in the Stuart papers* in *E.C.I.* xi (1996), pp 167–8.

—, 'A wild Capuchin of Cork: Arthur O'Leary' in Moran, (ed.), *Radical Irish priests*, pp 39–62.

Kelly, P., 'A light to the blind: the voice of the dispossessed elite in the generation after the defeat at Limerick' in *I.H.S.*, xxiv (1985), pp 431–62.

—, review of Fagan, P. (ed), *Ireland in the Stuart papers* , in *Parliamentary history*, xvi, pt. 2 (1996), pp 249–51.

Kenyon, J., *The Popish plot* (London, 1972).

Keogh, D., Review of Fenning, *Irish Dominican province* in *E.C.I.*, ix (1994), pp 153–4.

Kinane, V., Review of McDonnell and Healy, *Gold-tooled bookbindings* in *E.C.I.*, iii (1988), pp 157–58.

Kirkham, G., 'No more to be got from the cat but the skin': management, land-holding and economic change on the Murray of Broughton estate 1670–1755' in Nolan, Ronayne and Dunleavy (ed.), *Donegal*, pp 357–81.

Lang, A., *Pickle the spy* (London, 1897).

Lawless, E., *With the wild geese* (London, 1902).

Lecky, W., *A history of Ireland in the eighteenth century*, 5 vols (London, 1892).

Leerssen, J., *Mere Irish and Fíor-Ghael* repr. (Cork, 1996).

—, *Remembrance and imagination: Patterns in the historical and literary representation of Ireland in the eighteenth and nineteenth centuries* (Cork, 1996).

Leighton, C., *Catholicism in a Protestant kingdom* (Dublin, 1994).

Lenman, B., *The Jacobite risings in Britain 1689–1746* (London, 1980).

Le Roy, A., *Louis XV* (London, 1939).

Linebaugh, P., *The London hanged. Crime and civil society in eighteenth-century London* (London, 1991).

Linehan, D., 'Index to the manuscripts of military interest in the N.L.I.' in *Ir. Sword*, ii (1954–56), pp 33–9.

Little, G., 'Outline for the life of Warren of Corduff' in *D.H.R.*, xxii (1968), pp 242–52, 296–303.

Litton, F., 'Daniel Huony, Admiral of the royal navy in Spain 1683–1771' in *Dál gCáis*, v (1979), pp 51–9.

Livingstone, P., *The Fermanagh story. A documentary history of County Fermanagh from earliest times to the present day* (Enniskillen, 1969).

Lydon, J., *The making of Ireland* (London, 1998).

Lynch, P., 'Fontenoy', in *An Cosantóir*, i, no. 14 (1941), pp 441–4.

Lyne, G., 'Dr Dermot Lyne: An Irish Catholic landowner in Cork and Kerry under the penal laws' in *J.K.A.H.S.*, viii (1975), pp 45–72.

Lyons, F.S.L., 'The burden of our history' in Brady (ed.), *Interpreting Irish history*, pp 87–105.

MacCairteáin, C., 'Preface to Agallamh na bhFíoraon' in *Irisleabhar Muighe Nuadhad* (1913), pp 34–6.

Macaulay, T., *The history of England from the accession of James* II, [ed. Firth, C.], 6 vols (London, 1913–15).

Macinnes, A., 'The aftermath of the '45' in Woosnam-Savage, (ed.), *1745*, pp 103–13.

—, *Clanship, commerce and the house of Stuart 1603–1788* (East Lothian, 1996).

Maclean, F., *Bonnie Prince Charlie* (London, 1988).

MacCraith, M., 'Filíocht Sheacaibíteach na Gaeilge: ionar gan uaim?' in *E.C.I.*, ix (1994), pp 57–75.

—, 'review of Ó Buachalla, *Aisling Ghéar* in *E.C.I.* xiii (1998), pp 166–71.

MacDonnell, H., *The Wild Geese of the Antrim MacDonnells* (Dublin, 1996).

—, 'Jacobitism and the third and fourth earls of Antrim' in *The Glynns*, xiii (1985), pp 50–5.

—, (ed.), 'Some documents relating to the involvement of the Irish Brigades in the rebellion of 1745' in *Ir. Sword,* xvi (1980–1), pp 3–22.

MacQuoid, G., *Jacobite songs and ballads* (London, 1888).

MacSwiney, M., 'Two distinguished Irishmen in the Spanish service' in *Studies, xxviii* (1939), pp 63–84.

Maguire, W. (ed.), *Kings in conflict: the revolutionary war in Ireland 1688–91* (Belfast, 1990).

Maxwell, C., *Country and town under the Georges* (Dundalk, 1949).

McAnally, H., 'The militia array in Ireland in 1756' in *Ir. Sword,* i (1949–53), pp 94–105.

McAskill, A., 'Life in the highlands as seen through the eyes of the poets of that period, seventeenth and eighteenth centuries' in *Trans. Gaelic Soc. Inverness,* xli (1950–51), pp 157–77.

McCarthy, D., *Collections on Irish church history from manuscripts of the late Rev. L.F. Renahan* (Dublin, 1861).

McCarthy, S., 'The Young Pretender's Kerry head-piece' in *C.H.A.S.J.,* xvi (1910), pp 113–20.

McCaughey, T., review of Cruickshanks (ed.), *Ideology and conspiracy* in *I.H.S.,* xxiv (1984), pp 113–5.

McDermott, F., 'Arthur O' Connor' in *I.H.S.,* xv (1966), pp 48–70.

MacDonagh, O., *Daniel O'Connell* (London, 1991).

McGuire, J., 'The Church of Ireland in the Glorious Revolution of 1688' in Cosgrove, and McCartney, (ed.), *Studies in Irish history,* pp 137–49.

—, 'Richard Butler, earl of Tyrconnell', in Brady (ed.), *Worsted in the game,* pp 73–85.

—, 'The Treaty of Limerick' in Whelan (ed.), *The last of the great wars,* pp 127–39.

McGurk, J., "Wild Geese". The Irish in European armies (sixteenth to eighteenth centuries) in O'Sullivan, P. (ed), *The Irish worldwide,* pp 36–62.

McKenna, R., 'Legends of Bonnie Prince Charlie's travels in Donegal in 1746' in *Éire-Ireland* vol. x (1975), pp 48–61.

McLaughlin, M. and Warner, C., *The Wild Geese. The Irish Brigades of France and Spain* (London 1980).

McLaughlin, T., 'A crisis for the Irish in Bordeaux, 1756' in O'Dea and Whelan (ed.), *Nations and Nationalisms,* pp 127–47.

McLynn, F., "Good behaviour" Irish Catholics and the Jacobite rising of 1745 ', in *Éire-Ireland,* xvi (1981), pp 43-58.

—, 'Ireland and the Jacobite Rising of 1745' in *Ir. Sword,* xiii (1977–79), pp 339–53.

—, *The Jacobites* (London, 1985).

—, *France and the Jacobite risings of 1745* (Edinburgh, 1981).

—, *Charles Edward Stuart: Bonnie Prince Charlie. A tragedy in many acts* repr. (Oxford, 1991).

McLysaght, E., *Irish life in the seventeenth century,* repr. (Dublin, 1979).

McRory, M., 'Life and times of Doctor Patrick Donnelly 1649–1716' in *S.A.,* v (1969–70), pp 3–33.

McSweeny, M., 'Two distinguished Irishmen in the Spanish service' in *Studies,* xxviii, no. 109 (1939), pp 63–84.

Meagher, J., 'Glimpses of eighteenth-century priests' in *Rep. Novum*, ii, no. 7 (1957–8), pp 129–47.

Melvin, P., 'Irish soldiers and plotters in Williamite England' (part 1) in *Ir. Sword*, viii, 52 (1979), pp 256–67; (part 2); xiii, 53 (1979), pp 353–68; (part 3); xiv (1981), pp 271–86.

Miller, J., 'The earl of Tyrconnell and James II's Irish policy', in *Hist. Jn.*, xx (1977), pp 802–23.

—, *James* II: *a study in kingship* (London, 1989).

Miller, P., *James* III (London, 1971).

[Mitchel, J.] *The history of Ireland ancient and modern taken from the most authentic accounts and dedicated to the Irish Brigade by the Abbé Mac Geoghegan with a continuation from the treaty of Limerick to the present time* (New York, 1884).

Mitchison, R. (ed.), *The roots of nationalism: studies in North Europe* (Edinburgh, 1980).

Molloy, D., 'In search of wild geese' in *Éire-Ireland*, v (1970), pp 3–14.

Monod, P., *Jacobitism and the English people* 1688–1788, repr. (Cambridge 1993).

Moody, T. and Vaughan, W. (ed.), *A new history of Ireland*, iv (Oxford, 1986).

Moran, G. (ed.), *Radical Irish priests 1660–1970* (Dublin, 1998).

Moran, P., *The Catholics of Ireland under the penal laws in the eighteenth century* (London, 1899).

Morley, V., *An crann os coill. Aodh Buí Mac Cruitín c. 1680–1755* (B.Á.C., 1995).

—, 'Idé-eolaíocht an tSeacaibíteachais in Éirinn agus in Albain' in *Oghma*, ix (1997), pp 14–24.

—, '"Tá an cruatan ar Sheoirse" – folklore or politics?', in *E.C.I.*, xiii (Dublin, 1998), pp 112–22.

Munter, R., *The history of the Irish newspaper 1685–1760* (Cambridge, 1967).

Murdoch, S., 'The database in early-modern Scottish history: Scandanavia and Northern Europe 1580–1707' in *Northern Studies*, xxxii (1997), pp 83–103.

Murphy, G., 'Notes on aisling poetry', in *Éigse*, i (1939), pp 40–50.

—, 'Royalist Ireland' in *Studies*, xxiv (1935), pp 589–604.

Murphy, I., *The diocese of Killaloe in the eighteenth century* (Dublin, 1991).

Murphy, J.A. (ed.), *The French are in the bay. The expedition to Bantry Bay 1796* (Dublin, 1997).

Murphy, S., 'Irish Jacobitism and Freemasonry' in *E.C.I.*, ix (1994), pp 75–83.

Murray, L., *The history of the parish of Creggan in the seventeenth and eighteenth centuries* (Dublin, 1940).

—, 'The lament for Patrick Fleming' in *L.A.J.*, viii (1933), pp 75–92.

—, 'A South Armagh outlaw' in *L.A.J.*, ix (1937–40), pp 96–114.

Murray, R., *Revolutionary Ireland and its settlement* (London, 1911).

Murtagh, D. and Murtagh, H., 'The Irish Jacobite army 1689–91' in *Ir. Sword*, xviii (1990), pp 30–48.

Murtagh, H., 'The War in Ireland' in Maguire (ed.), *Kings in conflict*, pp 61–92.

—, 'Irish soldiers abroad 1600–1800' in Bartlett and Jeffreys (ed.), *A military history of Ireland*, pp 294–315.

Neely, W., *Kilkenny. An urban history* (Belfast, 1989).

Ní Fhlathartaigh, R., *Clár amhrán Bhaile na hInse* (B.Á.C. 1976).

Nolan, W., Ronayne, L. and Dunleavy, M., (ed.), *Donegal: history and society* (Dublin, 1995).

—, (ed.), *Tipperary: history and society* (Dublin, 1985).

Nokes, D., *Jonathan Swift: A hypocrite reversed* (Oxford, 1985).

Nordmann, C., 'Choiseul and the last Jacobite attempt of 1759' in Cruickshanks and Black (ed.), *Ideology and conspiracy,* pp 201–17.

O'Boyle, E., 'A memoir of the Young Pretender' in *Journal of the Donegal Society* [later *Donegal Annual*], ii (1948), pp 112–14.

O'Brien, G., *Parliament, politics and people: essays in eighteenth-century Irish history* (London, 1989).

Ó Buachalla, B., 'Arthur Brownlow: a gentleman more curious than ordinary', *in Ulster local studies* vii, no. 2 (1982), pp 24–8.

—, *Aisling Ghéar: na Stíobhartaigh agus an t-aos léinn 1601–1788* (B.Á.C., 1996).

—, 'Irish Jacobite poetry' in *Irish Review,* xii (1992), pp 40–50.

—, 'Irish Jacobitism and Irish nationalism: the literary evidence', in O'Dea and Whelan (ed.), *Nations and Nationalisms,* pp 103–19.

—, 'James our true king: the ideology of Irish royalism' in Boyce, Eccleshall, and Geoghegan (ed.), *Political thought in Ireland,* pp 7–35.

—, Lillibulero agus eile', in *Comhar.* Márta-Iúil 1987.

—, 'The making of a Cork Jacobite' in Buttimer and O'Flanagan (ed.), *Cork,* pp 469–98.

—, 'An mheisiasacht agus an aisling' in de Brún et al. (ed.), *Folia Goidelica,* pp 72–87.

—, 'Na Stíobhartaigh agus an t-aos léinn: Cing Séamas' in *R.I.A., Proc.,* lxxxiii (1983), C, pp 82–134.

—, 'Ó Corcora agus an *Hidden Ireland*' in *Scríobh,* iv (1979), pp 109–38.

—, review of Cruickshanks and Black (ed.), *The Jacobite challenge* in *E.C.I.,* iv (1989), pp 186–90.

—, review of O'Riordan, *The Gaelic mind* in *E.C.I.,* vii (1992), pp 149–75.

—, 'Seacaibíteachas Thaidhg Uí Neachtain' in *Stud. Hib.,* xxvi (1990–91), pp 31–64.

O'Callaghan, J. C., *History of the Irish brigades in the service of France,* repr. (Shannon, 1969).

O'Carroll, D., 'Marshal Saxe' in *Ir. Sword,* xix (1995), pp 249–53.

O'Ceallaigh, D., (ed.) *Reconsiderations of Irish history and culture. Selected papers from the Desmond Greaves Summer School 1989-93* (Dublin, 1994)

Ó Ciardha, É., 'Buachaillí an tsléibhe agus bodaigh gan chéill': Toraíochas agus Rapairíochas i gCúige Uladh agus i dtuaisceart Chonnacht sa seachtú agus san ochtú haois déag' in *Stud. Hib.,* xxix (1995–7), pp 59–85.

—, review of Fagan (ed.), *Ireland in the Stuart papers* in *Hist. Irel.,* iv, no. 2 (1996), pp 53–55.

—, review of Ó Saothraí, *An Ministir Gaelach* in *I.H.S.,* xxx (1997), pp 481–3.

—, 'Tory' and 'Rapparee', in Welch (ed.), *Oxford companion to Irish literature* (Oxford, 1996), pp 490, 566.

—, 'The Stuarts and deliverance in Irish and Scots-Gaelic poetry 1690-1760' in Connolly (ed.), *Kingdoms united,* pp 78–94.

—, 'The unkinde deserter and the bright duke: the dukes of Ormond in the Irish royalist tradition' in Barnard and Fenlon (ed.), *The dukes of Ormond,* pp 177–93.

—, 'A voice from the Jacobite underground: Liam Inglis, in Moran, (ed.), *Radical Irish priests*, pp 16–39.

Ó Cléirigh, G., 'Cérbh é Mac an cheannaí?' in *Irisleabhar Mhá Nuad* (1993), pp 7–34.

Ó Conchúir, B., *Scríobhaithe Chorcaí 1700–1800* (Dún Dealgan, 1982).

O'Connell, M., *The last colonel of the Irish Brigades*, 2 vols (London, 1892).

O'Connell, P., 'The plot against Fr Nicholas Sheehy' in *Proc. Ir. Cath. Hist. Comm* (1965–7), pp 49–61.

—, *Schools and scholars of Breiffne* (Dublin, 1942).

O'Conor, C., 'Charles O'Conor of Belanagare' in *Studies*, xxiii (1934), pp 124–43.

O'Conor, M., *Military history of the Irish nation* (Dublin, 1845).

—, *The Irish Brigades or memoirs of the most eminent Irish military commanders* (Dublin, 1855).

—, *A history of Irish Catholics from the settlement in 1691* (Dublin, 1813).

—, O'Conor, T. (ed.), *The Irish in Europe 1580-1815* (Dublin, 2001).

Ó Cuív, B., 'The Irish language in the early modern period' in *N.H.I.*, iii, pp 509–45.

—, (ed.), *A view of the Irish language* (Dublin, 1966).

O'Dea M. and Whelan, K. (ed.), *Nations and Nationalisms: France, Britain, Ireland and the eighteenth-century context* (Oxford, 1995).

O'Donovan, T., 'The Irish Brigade in the service of France' in *An Cosantóir*, xix, no. 3 (1959), pp 147–52.

Ó Fiaich, T., 'Art McCooey and his times' in *S.A.*, vi (1972), pp 217–51.

—, 'Filíocht Uladh mar fhoinse staire san ochtú haois déag' in *Stud. Hib.*, xi (1971), pp 80–129.

—, 'Political and social background of the Ulster poets' in *Léachtaí Cholmcille*, i (1970), pp 23–34.

—, 'Irish poetry and the clergy' in *Léachtaí Cholmcille*, iv (1975), pp 30–56.

—, 'The O'Neills of the Fews' in *S.A.*, vii (1973), pp 1–65; vii (1974), pp 263–315; viii (1977), pp 386–413.

Ó Fiannachta P., *Léas ar ár litríocht* (B.Á.C., 1974).

O'Flanagan, P., Ferguson, P. and Whelan, K. (ed.), *Rural Ireland 1600–1800: Modernisation and change* (Cork, 1987).

Ó Grada, C., 'The saga of the Great Famine' in Brady (ed.), *Interpreting Irish history*, pp 269–285.

Ó Héalaí, P., 'Seán Clárach', in *Léachtaí Cholm Cillle*, iv (1975), pp 88–100.

O'Hanlon, T., *The highwayman in Irish history* (Dublin, 1932).

Ó hAnnracháin, E., 'An analysis of the Fitzjames cavalry regiment, 1737' in *Ir. Sword*, xix (1995), pp 253–76.

—, 'The Irish Brigade at Lafelt: phyrric victory and aftermath' in *J.C.H.A.S.*, cii (1997), pp 1–22.

—, 'Irish veterans in the Invalides: the Tipperary contingent' in *Tipp. Jn.* (1998), pp 158–90.

Ó hÓgáin, D., 'An stair agus an litríocht béil' in *Léachtaí Cholmcille*, xiv (1983) pp 173–96.

—, 'Folklore and literature 1700-1850' in Daly and Dickson (ed.), *Origins of popular literacy*, pp 1–15.

Ó Madagáin, B., *An Ghaeilge i Luimneach 1700–1900* (B.Á.C., 1974).

O' Mahony, J., 'Morty Oge O' Sullivan, captain of the wild geese', in *C.H.A.S.J.*, i (1892), pp 95–99, 120.

Ó Murchú, L., review of Ó hAnluain (eag.), *Seon Ó hUaithnín*, in *Stud. Hib.*, xv (1975), pp 199–202.

Ó Murchadha, C., 'The Moughra affair and the bizarre career of Patrick Hurley' in *The Other Clare*, xvii (1993), pp 48–56.

O'Reilly, A. *The Irish at home, at court and in the camp, with souvenirs of the 'Brigade'. Reminiscences of an emigrant Milesian* (New York, 1856).

O'Riordan, M., *The Gaelic mind and the collapse of the Gaelic world* (Cork, 1990).

—, 'Historical perspectives on the Hidden Ireland' in *Irish Review*, iv (1988), pp 73–82.

O'Rorke, T., *The history of Sligo: town and country*, 2 vols (Dublin, 1890).

Ó Saothraí S *An Ministir Gaelach Uilliam Mac Néill agus an oidhreacht a d'fhág againn* (Beál Feirste, 1992).

O'Sullivan, P. (ed.) *The Irish worldwide heritage, identity patterns of emigration* (London, 1992).

Ó Tuama, S., *Filí faoi sceimhle: Seán Ó Riordáin agus Aogán Ó Rathaille* (B.Á.C., 1978).

—, *Cúirt, tuath agus bruachbhaile* (B.Á.C., 1990).

Ó Tuathaigh, G., 'Irish historiographical revisionism' in Brady (ed.), *Interpreting Irish history*, pp 306–27.

—, 'Gaelic Ireland, popular politics and Daniel O'Connell' in *Galway. His. Arc. Soc. Jn.*, xxxiv (1974–5), pp 21–34

Paterson, T., 'Ragnall Dall Mac Domhnaill' in *L.A.J.*, x (1941–4), pp 42–50.

Petrie, C., 'The Battle of Almanza' in *Ir. Sword*, ii (1954–6), pp 6–11.

—, 'A French project for the invasion of Ireland at the beginning of the eighteenth century' in *Ir. Sword*, i (1949–53), pp 10–13.

—, *The marshal duke of Berwick* (London, 1953).

—, 'Ireland in the '45' in *Ir. Sword*, ii (1954–6), pp 275–82.

—, 'Ireland in French and Spanish strategy 1588–1815' in *Ir. Sword,* vi (1963–4), pp 154–65.

—, 'The Irish Brigade at Fontenoy' in *An Cosantóir*, viii, no. 3 (1948), pp 161–2.

—, *The Jacobite movement* (London, 1959).

—, *The Jacobite movement. The last phase 1716–1807* (London, 1950).

Philbin, C. (ed) *Nationalism and popular protest in Ireland* (Cambridge, 1987).

Phillips, J.W., *Printing and book-selling in Dublin 1670–1800* (Dublin, 1998).

Pillogret, R., 'Louis XIV and Ireland' in Whelan (ed.), *The last of the great wars*, pp 1–17.

Pittock, M., *Poetry and Jacobite politics in eighteenth-century Britain and Ireland* (Cambridge, 1994).

—, *Inventing and resisting: Britain* (London, 1997).

Power, P., 'Bicentenary of Fontenoy' in *Studies,* xxxiv (1945), pp 175–82.

—, *Waterford and Lismore. A compendious history of the united dioceses* (Dublin, 1937).

Power, T., *Land and politics in eighteenth-century Tipperary* (Oxford, 1993).

—, 'Converts' in Power and Whelan (ed.), *Endurance and Emergence*, pp 101–28.

—, 'Fr Nicholas Sheehy ' in Moran, (ed.), *Radical Irish priests*, pp 62–79.

—, and Whelan, K. (ed.), *Endurance and Emergence: Catholics in Ireland in the eighteenth century* (Dublin, 1990).

Prebble, J., 'The Glencolmcille tradition of Prince Charles Edward' in *Ir. Sword*, vii (1955–6), pp 196–205.

Prendergast, J., *Ireland from Restoration to Revolution* (London, 1887).

Prút, L., 'Aon-fhile an leanúnachais: Liam Dall Ó hIfearnáin' in Nolan (ed.), *Tipperary*, pp 185–214.

Quinn, D., *The Elizabethans and the Irish* (New York, 1969).

Raymond-Redmond, J., 'Military and political memoirs of the Redmond family', in *C.H.A.S.J.*, xxvii (1921), pp 22–35; 73–8.

Risk, M., 'Seán Ó Neachtain: an eighteenth-century writer' in *Stud. Hib.*, xv (1975), pp 47–61.

Rodríguez, J., *Patterns of contention in Mexican history* (Wilmington, Del., 1992).

Rogers, N., 'Popular disaffection in London during the '45' in *London Journal*, i (1975), pp 5–27.

—, 'Popular protest in early-Hanoverian London', *Past and Present*, cxxviii (1978), pp 70–100.

Rushe, D., *History of Monaghan for 200 years*, repr. (Monaghan, 1996).

—, *Monaghan in the eighteenth century* (Dundalk, 1916).

Ruvigny, Marquis de, *Jacobite peerage* (Edinburgh, 1904).

Rynne, E. (ed.), *North Munster studies. Essays in commemoration of Monsignor Michael Moloney* (Limerick, 1967).

Sedwick, R. (ed.), *The Commons 1715–54*, 2 vols (London, 1970).

Sergeant, P., *Little Jennings and fighting Dick Talbot. A life of the duke and duchess of Tyrconnell*, 2 vols (London, 1913).

Sharp, R. *The engraved record of the Jacobite movement* (Aldershot, 1996)

Shellabarger, S., *Lord Chesterfield* (London, 1953).

Sherry, T., 'The present horrid conspiracy: Dublin press coverage of two political trials in the 1720s' in *E.C.I.*, iv (1989), pp 143–57.

Shield, A and Lang, A., *The king over the water* (London, 1907).

Shirley, E., *The history of the County Monaghan* (London, 1879).

Simms, J., 'Catholics and the franchise 1692–1728' in *I.H.S.*, xii (1960), pp 28–37.

—, 'Connaught in the eighteenth century' in *I.H.S.*, xi (1958–59), pp 116–33.

—, 'Dean Swift and County Armagh' in *S.A.*, vi (1972), pp 131–41.

—, *Jacobite Ireland* (London, 1969; repr. Dublin, 2000).

—, 'The making of a penal law (2 Anne c.6., 1703–4)', in *I.H.S.*, xii (1960), pp 105–18.

—, 'Remembering 1690' in *Studies*, lxiii (1974), pp 231–42.

—, 'The surrender of Limerick 1691' in *Ir. Sword*, ii (1954–6), pp 225–28.

—, *War and politics in Ireland 1649–1730* Ed. Hayton, D. and O'Brien, G. (Dublin, 1986).

—, 'The war of the two kings' in *N.H.I.*, iii (Oxford, 1976), pp 478–508.

Steele, R., 'Fitzjames's regiment of horse of the Irish Brigade in the French service' in *Ir. Sword*, ii (1954–6), pp 188–94.

Smyth, J., *Men of no property. Irish radicals and popular politics in the late eighteenth century* (Dublin, 1993).

St. Leger, A., review of Ressinger, *Memoirs of Reverend Jaques Fontaine* in *J.C.H.A.S.* ic (1994), p. 159.

Stone, L. (ed.), *An imperial state at war 1689–1815* (London, 1994).

Stradling, R., *The Spanish monarchy and the Irish mercenaries. The Wild Geese in Spain 1618–1668* (Cork, 1994).

Stewart, E.M., *All for Prince Charlie or the Irish Cavalier* (Dublin, [n.d.]).

Swords, L. (ed.), *The Irish-French connection 1578–1978* (Paris, 1978).

—, 'Patrick Donnelly 1649–1719' in *S. A.*, xv (1992), pp 84–98.

Szechi, D., 'Constructing a Jacobite: The social and intellectual origins of George Lockhart of Carnwath' in *Hist. Jn.*, xl, no. 4 (1997), pp 977–96.

—, *The Jacobites: Britain and Europe* (Manchester, 1994).

—, The Jacobite theatre of death', in Cruickshanks and Black (ed.), *Jacobite challenge*, pp 57–73.

Thomas, P., 'Jacobitism in Wales' in *Welsh History Review*, i (1962), pp 279–300.

Thomson, D., *An introduction to Gaelic poetry* (Edinburgh, 1989).

—, *Gaelic poetry in the eighteenth century* (Aberdeen, 1993).

Thompson, E.P. *The making of the English working class* (London, 1968).

—, *Whigs and hunters: the origins of the Black Acts* (London, 1990).

Tierney, M., 'Ireland in the Seven Years's War' in *Studies, xxxiii* (1943), pp 175–85.

Tomasson, K., 'The lucky colonel' [Colonel Richard Warren] in *Ir. Sword*, vii (1965–6), pp 15–19.

Ua Casaide, S., 'The birth-place of Tadhg Gaelach' in *Journal of the Waterford and South-East Archaeological Society*, xviii, no. 1, (1915), pp 27–31.

Wagner, M., 'Scotland in the late eighteenth century' in Asch (ed.) *Three nations*, pp 147–59.

M. Wall, *Catholic Ireland in the eighteenth century* ed. G. O'Brien (Dublin, 1989).

—, 'Catholic loyalty to king and pope in eighteenth-century Ireland' in *Proc. of Ir. Cat. His. Comm* (1960), pp 17–25.

—, *The penal laws 1691–1760. Church and state from the treaty of Limerick to the accession of George* III (Dundalk, 1961).

Walsh, M., 'Letters from Fontenoy' in *Ir. Sword*, xix (1995), pp 237–48.

—, 'Sir Toby Bourke: politician and diplomat' in Cruickshanks and Corp (ed.), *Stuart court in exile*, pp 143–55.

Walsh, R., 'Glimpses of Irish Catholicism in penal times 1697–1725' in *I.E.R.*, xx (1906–11), pp 259–72.

Walsh, T., *The Irish continental college movement* (Cork, 1973).

Ward C. and Ward, R., 'The ordeal of O'Conor of Belanagare' in *Éire-Ireland* (1979), pp 6–15.

Watson, S., 'Coimhlint an dá chultúr. Gaeil agus Gaill i bhfilíocht chúige Uladh san ochtú haois déag' in *E.C.I.*, iii (1989), pp 85–105.

Wauchope, P., *Patrick Sarsfield and the Williamite war* (Dublin, 1992).

Whelan, B. (ed.), *The last of the great wars: essays on the war of the three kings in Ireland 1688–91* (Limerick, 1995).

Whelan, K., 'Bantry Bay: the wider context' in Murphy, J. A. (ed.), *The French are in the bay*, pp 95–120.

—, 'The recent writing of Irish history' in *U.C.D. History Review*, i (1991), pp 27–35.

—, 'Interview with Louis Cullen' in *Hist. Ire.*, ii (1994), pp 10–13.

—, *Tree of liberty: Radicalism, Catholicism and the construction of Irish identity 1760-1830* (Cork, 1996).

—, 'An underground gentry? Catholic middlemen in eighteenth century Ireland', in Donnelly and Miller (ed) *Irish popular culture*, pp 118–73.

Whyte, I. and White, K., *On the trail of the Jacobites* (London, 1990).

Wilson, D., *The history of the future* (Toronto, 2000).

Winslow, C., 'Sussex smugglers' in Hay et al. (ed.) *Albion's fatal tree*, pp 119–67.

Woods, C., 'Irish travel writings as source-material' in I.*H.S.*, *xxviii* (1992), pp 171–84.

Woosnam-Savage, R. (ed.), *1745: Charles Edward Stuart and the Jacobites* (Glasgow, 1995).

Unpublished theses

Beresford, M. de la Poer, 'Ireland in the French Strategy 1691–1789' (M. Litt., T.C.D. 1975).

Caball, M., 'A study of intellectual reaction and continuity in Irish bardic poetry composed during the reigns of Elizabeth I and James I' (D.Phil., Oxford, 1991).

Chapman, P., Jacobite political argument in England 1714–1766' (Ph.D., Cambridge, 1983).

Comer-Bruen, M., 'Aindrias Mac Craith, An Mangaire Súgach. Tráchtas ar a shaol agus a shaothar' (M. Litt., T.C.D., 1967).

De Valera, A., 'Antiquarian and historical investigations in Ireland in the eighteenth century' (M.A., U.C.D., 1978).

Doyle, T., 'The politics of the Protestant Ascendancy: Politics, religion and society in Protestant Ireland 1700–1710' (Ph.D., U.C.D., 1996).

Ferguson, K., 'The army in Ireland from the Restoration until the Act of Union 1660–1800' (Ph.D., T.C.D., 1982).

Genet-Rouffiac, N., 'La première génération de l'exil Jacobite à Paris et Saint Germain-en-laye 1688–1715' (Thèse de Doctorat, École practique des hautes études scientifiques, historiques et philologiques, 1995).

Goldie, M., 'Tory political thought 1689–1714' (Ph.D., Cambridge, 1977).

Hayton, D., 'Ireland and the English ministers 1706–16: A study in the formulation and working of government policy in the early eighteenth century' (D. Phil., Oxford, 1975).

Hopkins, P., 'Aspects of Jacobite conspiracy in the reign of William III' (Ph.D., Cambridge, 1981).

Layden, T., 'Chesterfield in Ireland 1745–6' (VIIIB, undergraduate thesis, U.C.D., 1982).

McCoy, J., 'Local political culture in the Hanoverian Empire', (D.Phil. thesis, Oxford, 1994).

McGrath, C., 'Securing the Protestant interest 1692–5: policy, politics and parliament in Ireland in the aftermath of the Glorious Revolution' (M.A., U.C.D., 1991).

Morley, V., 'Hugh MacCurtin: eighteenth-century poet and antiquarian' (M. Phil., U.C.D., 1992).

Ó Ciardha, É., '"Buachaillí an tSléibhe agus Bodaigh gan Chéill": Woodkerne, tories and rapparees in Ulster and north Connaught in the seventeenth century' (M.A., U.C.D., 1991).

O'Donoghue, J., 'Ireland and the Jacobite threat 1700–1727' (M.A., U.C.C., 1992).

Risk, M., The Poems of Seán Ó Neachtain (Ph.D., T.C.D., 1951).

Rouffiac, N., 'Un épisode de la présence Britannique en France: Les Jacobites à Paris et Saint Germain-en-Laye 1688–1715' (École Nationale des Chartes, 1991).

Smyth, J., 'Popular politicisation in Ireland in the 1790s' (Ph.D., Cambridge, 1989).

Zimmermann, D., 'The Jacobite movement in Scotland and in exile 1746–59' (Ph.D., Cambridge, 1999).

Conference papers and forthcoming papers

Donaldson, W. 'Jacobite song, political myth and national identity', paper delivered at the quincentennial conference on Jacobitism, Scotland and the Enlightenment, University of Aberdeen, 29 July-3 Aug. 1995.

Hughes, A., 'Gaelic poets and scribes of the south Armagh hinterland in the eighteenth and nineteenth centuries', in Hughes, A., McCorry, F. and Weatherup, R. (ed.), *Armagh: history and society* (forthcoming).

Morley, V., 'Differing perspectives: the expression of Jacobitism in the Gaelic literatures of Ireland and Scotland', paper delivered to the tenth biennial conference of Irish historians in Britain, 12–14 Apr. 1996.

Ó Tuathaigh, G., 'The Hidden Ireland: Interpreting Irish history' paper delivered at E.S.B. Lecture series, 29 Fitzwilliam St., 12 Nov.1994.

Chronology of Events

	Ireland	England/Scotland	Europe/World
1685	Feb 6: James, duke of York, becomes kin.g James II of England, Scotland and Ireland on the death of his brother Charles II June 20: Richard Talbot, Irish Catholic champion is created earl of Tyrconnell July: Rebellions of Monmouth and Argyll are crushed		
1686	Jan: Henry Hyde, second earl of Clarendon, is sworn in as lord lieutenant June 5: Tyrconnell is appointed to command the Irish army		July: League of Augsburg (Holy Roman Empire, The Netherlands, Sweden and various German states) is formed to resist Louis XIV
1687	Feb 12: Tyrconnell is sworn in as lord deputy		
1688	Dec 7: Apprentice boys shut the gates of Derry against the earl of Antrim's regiment	June 10: Mary of Modena gives birth to James Francis Edward, prince of Wales June 30: The 'Seven Bishops' arrested by James for refusing to promulgate Declaration of Indulgence Nov 5: William of Orange lands at Torbay Dec 10: Mary of Modena escapes to France with the prince of Wales Dec 23: James II escapes to France on the second attempt	Sept: Pope Innocent XI refuses to appoint French candidate to the archbishopric of Cologne; Louis XIV invades the Rhineland Nov 16: Louis XIV declares war on the Dutch Republic
1689	Mar 12: James lands in Kinsale Apr 18: James is refused entry into the city of Derry May 1: Inconclusive battle between English and French fleets off Bantry Bay	Feb 13: William and Mary accept the Bill of Rights and are declared joint sovereigns of England, Scotland and Ireland Mar 25: Scottish parliament declares throne 'forfaulted'	

	Ireland	England/Scotland	Europe/World
		Apr: William and Mary proclaimed joint monarchs of Scotland	
	June 18: James issues a proclamation providing for circulation of 'brass money'	May 7: England declares war on France	
	June 22: Irish parliament repeals the 'Act of Settlement'	May 18: 'Bonnie Dundee', the Jacobite commander, musters the clans at Lochaber	
	July 31: Jacobite army under Viscount Mountcashel is defeated by the Enniskilliners at Newtownbutler	July 27: Dundee defeats Hugh MacKay of Scourie on the Braes of Killliecrankie, but is mortally wounded	
	July 31: Williamite army under the duke of Schomberg lands in Bangor, County Down	Aug 21: Cannon's Scots Jacobite army is repulsed by the Cameronians at Dunkeld	
1690	Mar 13: Danish mercenary army under duke of Würtemberg arrives in Belfast Lough	Feb 1: Over 400 Anglican clergy and five bishops are deprived of their sees and livings for refusing the oaths to William and Mary	
	Apr 18: Irish regiments under Lord Mountcashel leave Cork for France	May 1: Buchan's Scots Jacobite army routed on the Haughs of Cromdale, beginning of guerilla war in the highlands	
	May 14: Jacobite garrison under Sir Teague O'Regan surrenders Charlemont Fort to Schomberg	Jun 7: Presbyterianism officially re-established in Scotland	
	June 14: William lands at Carrickfergus	June 30: Anglo-Dutch fleet defeated at Beachy Head	
	July 1: William's army defeats James at the Boyne		
	July 4: James sails from Kinsale for France		
	July 6 William enters Dublin		
	July 17-24: William fails to take Athlone		
	Aug 9-30: William fails to take Limerick during its first siege		
	Sept 5: William leaves for England		
	Sept 28: Cork surrenders to the duke of Marlborough		
1691	Jan 14: Tyrconnell arrives back in Ireland from St Germain	June 30: Earl of Bredalbane negotiates truce in the Highland War while the Jacobite clans seek James's permission to negotiate surrender	
	May 9: Marquis de St Ruth arrives in Ireland to take command of the Jacobite army	Dec 2: James gives permission to the clans to surrender and take the oath of allegiance	
	June 21-30: Ginkel, the Williamite commander, besieges and takes Athlone		
	July 12: Ginkel slaughters Irish Jacobite army at Aughrim		
	July 21: Galway surrenders to Ginkel		
	Aug 25: Second siege of Limerick begins		
	Sept 14: Sligo surrenders to		

Ireland	England/Scotland	Europe/World
Williamites Oct 3: Treaty of Limerick brings the sige of Limerick and the war to an end Dec 22: Sarsfield sails for France with 12,000 Irish Jacobites, 'The flight of the Wild Geese'		
1692 April 6: Irish privy council begins hearing claims under the treaty of Limerick	Jan: Jacobite clans surrender to the government Feb 13: Massacre of the MacDonalds of Glencoe on pretext that the have not taken oath of allegiance	May 19-24/Aug 3: Irish Jacobite army take part in a French defeat of William at Steenkirk May 19: James arrives at La Hogue to join invasion force May 19-20: Anglo-Dutch fleet scatter French at Barfluer May 24: French invasion fleet defeated off La Hogue June 18: Birth of Lousia Maria Theresa ('La Consolatrix') to Mary of Modena and James at St Germain
1693		July 19/29: Patrick Sarsfield is mortally wounded at Landen (Neerwinden)
1694	Dec 28: Queen Mary II dies	
1695 Sept 7: Irish parliament passes acts disarming Catholics and forbidding them sending their children abroad for education		Oct: Preparations for a co-ordinated French invasion and Jacobite rising ('Fenwick Plot')
1696	Feb: Berwick dispatched to England to evaluate strength of Jacobite forces Feb 15: Jacobite plot to assassinate William is foiled in London Feb 22: Mass arrest of Jacobite conspirators Mar-Apr: Seven Jacobite conspirators tried and executed, 5 more condemned to life imprisonment without trial by act of parliament *c.*Jun: Onset of four years of famine in Scotland ('King William's ill years')	May 1: French invasion plan abandoned

Ireland	*England/Scotland*	*Europe/World*
	Dec 23: Fenwick condemned to death by act of attainder	
1697 Sept 25: Banishment Act (9 Will III, c 1) requires Catholic bishops, vicars-general deans and regular clergy to leave Ireland by May 1 1698		Sept 10: Peace of Ryswick between France and the allies (England, Holland and Spain) brings the Nine Years War to an end. Louis XIV recognizes William III as *de facto* king of England Oct 20: Emperor Leopold I makes peace with Louis XIV
1699 Jan 26: Irish parliament passes 'An act to prevent papists being solicitors'	Feb 1: English Act (10 Will III, c. 1) directs that foreign troops in Ireland should be disbanded and limits the royal army to 12, 000	
1700	Apr 11: Act of Resumption in England cancels William's grants of forfeited land and appoints trustees to sell estates	
1701	Apr 24: Act of Succession designating house of Hanover as William III and Princess Anne's heirs	Aug 27/Sept 7: Grand Alliance (England, Dutch Republic and the Habsburg emperor is formed against France following the death of Charles II of Spain and Louis XI V's acceptance of the throne for his grandson Phillippe, duc d'Anjou Sept 6/17: James II dies at St Germain, Louis XIV recognizes his son as 'James III'
1702 Feb 27: English Act (I Anne, stat 2, c. 17) requires office-holders, lawyers and school-masters in Ireland to take the oath of Abjuration (declaring Anne to be rightful queen and disclaiming 'The Pretender')	Mar 7: Abjuration Act requiring formal renunciation of allegiance to 'prince of Wales' Mar 8: William III dies and is succeeded by Queen Anne	Jan 20-21/Jan 31-Feb 1: Irish Jacobite soldiers under Daniel O'Mahony take part in French defence of Cremona against Prince Eugene of Savoy May 4: Outbreak of the War of the Spanish

	Ireland	England/Scotland	Europe/World
1703		May-Oct: Simon Fraser, Lord Lovat concocts fake ('Scotch') plot in the highlands	Succession
1704	Mar 4: Irish parliament passes 'Act to prevent the further growth of popery' Registration Act (2 Anne, c.7), requires Catholic clergy to register with clerks of the peace at next quarter sessions		Aug 2/13: Duke of Marlborough and Prince Eugene of Savoy defeats a Franco-Bavarian Army at Blenheim
1705		Aug-Sept: Nathaniel Hooke reconnoitres Scotland to assess seriousness of Jacobite pledge of support for a French invasion	
1706		Oct-Dec: Passage of the Act of Union between Scotland and England	May 12/23: Marlborough defeats the French at Ramillies
1707		Apr-Sept: Hooke returns to Scotland to plan rebellion with the Jacobite leaders	Apr 14/25 Duke of Berwick, in command of Irish and French troops, defeats the earl of Galway at Almanza
1708		Mar 12 French arrive at Forth of Firth but miss Jacobite signals. The French admiral Forbain refuses Stuart claimants pleas to land him on Scottish soil	Feb 27: 'James III' arrives in Dunkirk but is struck down with measles. Royal Navy squadron arrives off Dunkirk the same day Mar 6: French expedition under Forbain evades Royal Navy and sails for Scotland
1709	Dec: 'Hougher' disturbances begin in Connaught		Aug 31/Sept 11: Marlborough defeats French at Malplaquet
1711	Jan 22: Sir Constantine Phipps appointed lord chancellor July 3: James Butler, second duke of Ormonde, sworn in as lord lieutenant	Sept 27: Preliminary articles for a separate peace made public by Robert Harley, earl of Oxford	
1712		Jan 1: Ormonde is appointed commander of the British armies in Europe in place of the duke of Marlborough	

	Ireland	*England/Scotland*	*Europe/World*
1713			Feb 18: 'James III' leaves France for Lorraine Mar 31/Apr 11: Treaty of Utrecht ends the war of the Spanish Succession
1714		Aug 1: Queen Anne dies, succeeded by George Guelph, elector of Hanover 'George I'	Aug 10: 'James III' arrives in France seeking French help, Louis XIV sends him back to Lorraine
1715	Nov 12: Opening of George I's Irish parliament. William Connolly elected speaker	Jan: Whigs win crushing election victory Mar 26: Bolingbroke flees to France June-Aug: Intensive wave of pro-Jacobite riots sweeps midlands and north of England Aug 8: Ormonde flees to Paris Sept 6: Earl of Mar raises the Jacobite standard at Braemar, Aberdeenshire Sept 14: Lord Hay captures Perth for the Jacobites Oct 28: Ormond abandons attempt to land in the west country and returns to France Nov 13: Indecisive Battle of Sheriffmuir between Jacobites under Mar and Hanoverian loyalists under Argyll Nov 14: Jacobite army forced to capitulate at Preston Dec 22: 'James III' lands at Peterhead, near Aberdeen, in Scotland	July 27/Aug 7: Ormonde arrives in Paris to join the Jacobites and lead a Jacobite assault on the south of England 21 Aug/Sept 1: Louis XIV dies and is succeeded by his great-grandson Louis XV, control of France passes to his nephew Philippe duc d'Orléans
1716	June 20: Act (2 Geo I, c. 8) confiscates Ormonde's estate and abolishes Tipperary palatinate	Jan 23: Stuart claimant crowned 'James VIII' in Perth Feb 4: 'James III' and Mar leave Scotland	Mar 23: Jacobite court moves to the papal state of Avignon Nov 17/28: Anti-Spanish Dual Alliance between Great Britain and France (becomes Triple Alliance by accession of Dutch Republic, Dec 24 1716/Jan 4 1717) and the Quadruple Alliance (1718) with the addition of the empire

	Ireland	England/Scotland	Europe/World
1717		Jan 29: Swedish ambassador arrested in London; 'Swedish Plot' aborted	Jan 25: Jacobite court departs Lorraine for Avignon Feb: Jacobite court settles in Urbino
1718			Jun-Mar 1718: Ormond in negotiations with Peter the great of Russia Dec 17: Great Britain declares war on Spain Apr 28: Death of Mary of Modena Aug 11: Anglo-Dutch fleet decisively defeat Spanish off Cape Passaro Oct: Preparations for a Spanish-Jacobite invasion of England Dec: Death of Charles XII of Sweden
1719	Aug 10: House of Commons approves heads of anti-popery bill, invalidating reversionary leases by Catholics and providing that unregistered priests found in Ireland after May 1 1720 will be branded on the cheek Aug 25: Lord lieutenant transmits anti-popery bill as amended by privy council to change penalty from branding to castration (The amendment is rejected by English privy council)	Apr 9: Earl Marschal lands with two ships on the isle of Lewis Apr 13: Jacobites set up headquarters at Eilean Donan Castle Jun 5: Marschal and a small group of Spanish soldiers and Scots Jacobites defeated at battle of Glensheil	Feb 24: Main Spanish invasion force (destined for England) sails from Cadiz Feb 25: Secondary Spanish invasion force (destined for Scotland) sails from Los Pasejes Mar: Ormonde appointed captain-general of Spain for projected invasion of England Mar 7: James arrives in Spain and is proclaimed king in Madrid Mar 18: Main Spanish expedition dispersed by storm Apr 16/27: Charles Wogan rescues Princess Clementina Sobieska from Imperial custody in Innsbruck Aug 22: Marriage of James and Clementina celebrated by the pope in Rome
1720	Apr 7: Declaratory Act (6 Geo I, c. 5 [G.B.]) asserts British parliament's right to legislate for Ireland Apr 7: Execution of Sir James	Sept 26-8: Widespread panic caused by the 'South Sea Bubble'	Dec 22: Birth of Charles Edward Stuart

	Ireland	England/Scotland	Europe/World
1721	Cotter	Apr 4: Robert Walpole becomes first lord of the treasury	
1722	July 12: Letters patent granting William Wood of Wolverhampton exclusive rights of coining half-pence and farthings for circulation in Ireland	May-Sept: Ministry arrests most of the 'Atterbury' Plotters, including the 4th earl of Orrery and George Kelly Nov 27: Charles Layer convicted of treason	
1723		May 17: Layer executed	Oct: Renewed negotiations between Peter the great and the Jacobites Nov 21; Death of Philippe duc d'Orélans, regent of France
1724	Feb/Mar: First of Swift's Drapier's Letters, *A letter to the shopkeepers and common people of Ireland, concerning the brass half-pence coined by Mr Woods* Aug 6: Swift's second Drapier's letter Aug 31: Hugh Boulter, bishop of Bristol, appointed archbishop of Armagh Sept 5: Swift's third Drapier's Letter Oct 22 Lord Carteret sworn in as lord lieutenant Oct 22: Swift's fourth Drapier's letter Oct 27: Cornelius Nary's *Case of the Roman Catholics of Ireland* published in Dublin		
1725			Jan 28: Death of Peter the Great, end of negotiations with the Russians Feb 22: John Hay appointed Jacobite secretary of state and enobled as earl of Inverness Feb 23: Birth of Henry Benedict, duke of York Apr 29; Alliance of Vienna between Austria and Spain
1726		Swift's *Gulliver's Travels* is published in London	Sept: Stuart Court withdraws to Bologna

	Ireland	England/Scotland	Europe/World
1727	Nov 28: opening of George II's Irish parliament	June 11: George I dies, succeeded by George II	Mid Jun: James returns to Lorraine (incognito) July 31: James forced to return to Avignon
1728	May 6: Catholics deprived of parliamentary franchise (1 Geo. II, c. 9, s. 7)		
1729	Oct: Swifts, *Modest Proposal* published anonymously		Apr: Jacobite court arrives in Rome
1731			May 5/16: Treaty of Vienna, between Great Britain and Austria, marks the end of the Franco-British détente
1734	Apr 29: Act (7 Geo II, c. 6) prohibits converts to the established church who have Catholic wives from educating their children as Catholics or from acting as justices of the peace Nov: George Faulkiner, 'prince of Dublin printers', publishes first three volumes of the collected works of Jonathan Swift		
1735			Sept 30: Outbreak of the War of the Polish succession, diplomatic isolation of Britain
1738	Mar 23: Act (11 George II, c.7) for preventing enlistment for the foreign service Dec. 27: Severe frost sets in (continuing until mid-Feb 1740), causing distress, famine and mortality		
1739		Oct 8/19: Great Britiain declares war on Spain, 'War of Jenkin's ear'	
1740	Mar 31 Act (13 Geo II, c. 6) reinforces prohibitions on Catholics keeping arms		May: Lord Barrymore visits Paris on behalf of Jacobite Tory ministry to urge France to invade in the cause of 'James III' May 20/31: Frederick II ('the great') becomes king of Prussia

Ireland	England/Scotland	Europe/World
		Oct 9/20: Emperor Charles VI dies, succeded under terms of 'Pragmatic sanction' by Maria Theresa Dec 5/16: Prussia Invades Silesia, beginning the War of the Austrian Succession
1741 'Bliadhain an áir' [year of the slaughter], mortality from famine estimated to be as high as 400,000		
1742	Feb 11: Walpole resigns as lord treasurer	
1743	Aug-Oct: James Butler sounds out English Jacobite support for a French invasion	Jan 18: Death of Cardinal Fleury Dec 30: Charles Edward leaves Rome for Paris
1744	Feb 14: British government discovers plot, mass arrests	Feb 24: French invasion plans wrecked by storm Feb 28: French shelve invasion plans Mar 4/15: France declares war on Great Britain Aug: Charles Edward begins preparations for a descent on Scotland
1745 Aug 31: Earl of Chesterfield is sworn in as lord lieutenant Oct 9: Chesterfield's extends bounty of 50,000 sterling on the heads of the Stuart princes to Ireland	July 23: Charles Edward lands at Eriskay Aug 19: Jacobite standard raised at Glenfinnan Sept 21: Jacobites defeats Hanoverian Army under John Cope at Preston Pans Nov. French begin invasion preparations Nov 8: Jacobite army crosses into England Nov 10-15: Siege of Carlisle Nov 17: Charles Edward enters Carlisle Dec 6 'Black Friday', panic in London, run on the Bank of England. Charles Edward's army retreats from Derby Dec 5: Jacobite army over-rule Charles Edward and return to Scotland Dec 20: Jacobite army re-enters Scotland	May 11: Battle of Fontenoy, Maréchal Saxe defeats British and Dutch forces under the duke of Cumberland, Irish Brigades distinguish themselves in the battle July 5: Charles Edward sets sail from Nantes for Scotland on board *Du Teillay*. It is attacked by H.M.S. *Lion* Dec 23-5: Henry Benedict arrives in Boulogne, French expedition bottled up in Dunkirk and Calais by the Royal Navy

	Ireland	England/Scotland	Europe/World
1746		Jan 17: Jacobite army under Lord George Murray defeats Hawley at Falkirk Apr 16: Jacobite army defeated at Culloden April 17-20: Jacobite army rallies at Ruthven but is dispersed by Charles Edward Apr-Sept: Cumberland wrecks havoc in the Highlands, Charles Edward 'in the heather' June 28-29: Flora McDonnell accompanies Charles Edward 'over the sea to Skye'	Sept 30: Charles Edward arrives back in France on board *L'heureux*, captained by Richard Warren
1747			Jan-Feb: Charles Edward solicits support in Spain Jun 22: Henry Benedict enters Catholic church and is raised to cardinalate
1748			Oct 18: Peace of Aix-La Chapelle brings the war of the Austrian Succession to an end Nov 30: Charles Edward is arrested on Louis XV's order and incarcerated in Vincennes Dec 3: Charles Edward released and forced to leave France Dec 16: Charles Edward arrives in Avignon
1750		5-12 Sept: Charles Edward visits London, consults with Jacobite leaders and converts to Anglicanism	
1752		Sept 2: Julian Calendar (old style) ceases to have effect in British dominions, following day officially becoming Sept. 14 under Gregorian Calendar (new style)	
1755	June: Publication of Charles O'Conor's *Case of the Roman Catholics of Ireland*		
1756	Oct 12: Earl of Clanbrassil	Britain declares war on France, 'Seven Years War' begins	

	Ireland	*England/Scotland*	*Europe/World*
	(formerly Lord Limerick) introduces a bill into the House of Commons for controlling Catholic priests and bishops (rejected by British Privy Council)		
1759	Dec 3: Riots in Dublin on rumours of legislative union with Britain		Feb 5: Charles Edward meets Choiseul to discuss Jacobite invasion of England Nov 20: Battle of Quiberon Bay. Heavy losses inflicted on French Atlantic Navy by Royal Navy under Admiral Hawke, thereby thwarting an amphibious assault on England and Ireland by an army under Maréchal Thomond
1760	Feb 21: Thurot lands French force in Belfast Lough, capturing Carrickfergus *c.*Mar 31: Meeting of Catholics at Elephant Tavern, Essex Street, Dublin, giving rise to 'Catholic Committee'	Oct 25: George II dies, succeeded by his grandson George III Jan 4: Britain declares war on Spain	
1761	*c.* Oct.-Dec: Beginnings of 'Whiteboy' agitation in Munster		July 9: Peter III, tsar of Russia, is deposed and succeeded by his wife Catherine ('the great')
1762	*c.* Feb 1: Catholic nobility and gentry sign address offering services to King George III Feb 23: Secretary of State conveys king's appreciation of Catholics's offer Apr 12: House of Commons rejects motion for address to the lord lieutenant asking whether there is any intention of sending Catholics to be employed in Portuguese service		
1763			Feb 10: Peace of Paris brings Seven Years War to a close
1765			Mar 22: Stamp Act (5 Geo III, c. 12 [G.B.]) imposes stamp duties on American colonists
1766	Mar 15: Rev. Nicholas Sheehy,		

Ireland	England/Scotland	Europe/World
Catholic priest, is executed at Clonmel folowing his conviction for instigating 'Whiteboys' to commit murder June 7 Tumultuous Rising Act (5 Geo III, c. 8) directed against the 'Whiteboys' *c.* Aug: Viscount Taaffe's *Observations on the affairs of Ireland*		Jan 1: 'James III' dies in Rome Jan 14: Pope Clement XIII refuses to acknowledge Charles Edward as 'Charles III'
1775		
1776		Apr 19: Skirmish at Lexington, Massachusetts, between British troops and local militia, American War of Independence begins June 17: Battle of Bunker Hill, near Boston, victory for the British
1777		July 4: Declaration of American Independence Oct 17: British forces under General Burgoyne surrender at Saratoga, New York
1778	Jan 25: Earl of Buckinghamshire sworn in as lord lieutenant	
1781		Feb 6: Treaty of allegiance between France and the American colonists leading to war between France and Britain
1785		Oct 19: Earl Cornwallis surrenders at Yorktown, virtual end of the American War
1788		Dec: Jacobite court returns to Rome
1789		Jan 30: Death of Charles Edward Stuart
		July 14: Fall of the Bastille

Index of first lines

Note: This index of first lines is based on collections of poetry edited between the eighteenth and twentieth centuries. It should be cross-referenced with the footnotes and with the indexes of first lines in the various repositories of Irish manuscripts listed in the bibliography. The best standardized index of first lines for Jacobitism and Irish poetry in this period is Breandán Ó Buachalla's, *Aisling Ghéar*.

Index